Jump Over the Moon: Selected Professional Readings

Pamela Petrick Barron
Jennifer Q. Burley

Jump Over the Moon

Selected Professional Readings

Holt, Rinehart and Winston
New York Chicago San Francisco Philadelphia
Montreal Toronto London Sydney
Tokyo Mexico City Rio de Janeiro Madrid

The *Jump Over the Moon* telecourse is a co-production of the University of South Carolina and the South Carolina Educational Television Network. Information about the course and related materials may be obtained from Susan Bridwell, Director, Telecommunications Instruction, University of South Carolina, 915 Gregg Street, Columbia, SC 29208.

Library of Congress Cataloging in Publication Data

Barron, Pamela Petrick.
Jump over the moon.

1. Children—Books and reading—Addresses, essays, lectures. 2. Children's literature—History and criticism—Addresses, essays, lectures. 3. Illustrated books, Children's—Addresses, essays, lectures. 4. Picture-books for children—Addresses, essays, lectures. 5. Reading (Elementary)—Addresses, essays, lectures. I. Burley, Jennifer Q. II. Title.
Z1037.A1B26 1984 808.06'8 84-10796

ISBN 0-03-063383-4

Address correspondence to:
383 Madison Avenue
New York, N.Y. 10017

Printed in the United States of America
Published simultaneously in Canada
6 7 090 9 8 7 6 5 4 3 2

CBS COLLEGE PUBLISHING
Holt, Rinehart and Winston
The Dryden Press
Saunders College Publishing

Preface

Incredible as it seems, we learn at least half of everything we will ever know before we reach the age of four. An additional 30 percent of our knowledge is accumulated by eight years of age. Researchers tell us that children who are introduced to books at an early age and who are read to on a regular basis become better readers themselves. Because of these findings, it is no wonder that there is so much emphasis on bringing children and books together in early childhood education. We have spent three years developing and producing a college-level telecourse designed to assist both professionals and nonprofessionals concerned with selecting books for young children.

The telecourse *Jump Over the Moon: Sharing Literature with Young Children* was created to introduce viewers to the world of picture books for children from birth through age nine. While researching the topics for this series, we became even more aware of the beauty and diversity of picture books. We also made a startling discovery. Nowhere could we locate a textbook that dealt solely with picture books; most devoted only one or two chapters to this topic at best. When writing an in-depth treatment of topics such as the alphabet, counting, and concept books, we found it necessary to do a great deal of research in the professional literature. While we discovered numerous articles concerned with picture books, we also found that the articles had not been collected in one source. Thus the need for this anthology became apparent.

Although initially designed for use with the telecourse, this anthology can be used independently of the telecourse. The collection systematically pulls together and makes accessible articles dealing with the more basic concerns of the literature for early childhood. The readings included were selected with specific learning purposes in mind. The first was introduce, reinforce, or expand the concepts. Because the reading of these articles is designed as a developmental process, comprehensive articles on the various topics are included. Some present conflicting points of view, and they do not necessarily represent the opinion of the editors. The learning strategy is to expose readers to various viewpoints in order to sharpen their own critical thinking skills.

The second purpose was to include many articles that offer suggestions for introducing children to the joys of books. These suggestions will aid practitioners in developing their own creative methods for sharing books with young children. Finally, the anthology provides a collection of readings devoted primarily to picture books especially appropriate for both professionals and nonprofessionals concerned with children's literature.

The book's arrangement is based on the developmental needs of children that books can satisfy. The introductory section includes two articles that present conflicting definitions of picture books. Also included are articles that address the complexity and diversity of picture books by pointing out that many are appropriate for intermediate-age children. The remaining articles are concerned with how children learn and the importance of reading to children.

Mother Goose books are the first type of picture book introduced. Mother Goose seemed a logical place to begin because rhymes are generally a child's first introduction to literature. That Mother Goose rhymes are an important part of a child's literary heritage, and not intended for very young children only, is evidenced by the many references to such rhymes in adult conversation and literature. This point is emphasized, and many suggestions for sharing the rhymes are offered in this section.

Poetry followed naturally as the second type of book presented because Mother Goose rhymes are often used to introduce children to poetry. Since poetry is sometimes a neglected area of children's literature, many of these articles contain useful suggestions for incorporating poetry into children's lives.

Articles on alphabet and counting books are included next since these two types of book are basic building blocks for reading and math education. As young children become more aware of the world around them, they can be introduced to wordless picture books in which the child's own powers of observation tell the story. The articles in this section present ways these books may be used to develop reading readiness and teach visual literacy.

Articles on illustrations explain how children learn to discriminate between various styles and media and how they begin to express personal preferences for illustrations in the books they select.

The natural curiosity of children leads them to informational books as they seek to learn more about their environment. Books of contemporary realism are useful in helping children to understand that problems and situations they encounter are common to everyone.

As young children's imaginations develop, they can be introduced to folktales, which require that they be able to distinguish between fact and fantasy. Many of these traditional tales provide the material for storytelling, the subject of the next section of articles.

The section on sharing picture books is a potpourri of ideas for adults and children who will be reading together. The final section is devoted to controlled vocabulary books, which are designed to launch children into the world of independent reading.

Working on a project of this magnitude has been both a rewarding and a frustrating experience. At times we wondered if there would be "life" after *Jump Over the Moon,* especially since we have watched our children grow from infants to toddlers to preschoolers while the project consumed many of our waking hours. An added bonus was being able to share the many beautiful books we discovered with them.

P.P.B.
J.Q.B.

Contents

Part 1 Introduction

E Is for Easy. E Is for Enormously Difficult 3
Johanna Hurwitz

Readability and Children's Picture Books 7
Adrianne P. Hunt and Janet R. Reuter

In Search of the Perfect Picture Book Definition 12
Zena Sutherland and Betsy Hearne

Johnny Still Can't Read 14
Daniel Melcher

Reading with an Infant 32
Linda Leonard Lamme

The Young Child and You—Learning Together 41
Alice S. Honig

Part 2 Mother Goose

From the Cradle to the Classroom 55
Jacqueline L. Chaparro

Mother Goose's Garnishings 62
Maurice Sendak

Mother Goose—Elucidated 69
Margaret Chisholm

Part 3 Poetry

Making the Poetry Connection 77
Barbara Holland Baskin, Karen H. Harris, and Coleen C. Salley

The Pied Pipers of Poetry 87
Verna Hildebrand and Rebecca Peña Hines

The Changing Picture of Poetry Books for Children 96
Nancy Larrick

Poetry in the Story Hour 102
Nancy Larrick

Part 4 Alphabet and Counting Books

Alphabet Books: A Neglected Genre 115
John Warren Stewig

Using Children's Literature to Teach Mathematics 121
Muriel Rogie Radebaugh

Part 5 Wordless Picture Books

Wordless Picture Books and the Young Language-Disabled Child 133
Karen D'Angelo

Use Wordless Picture Books to Teach Reading, Visual Literacy and to Study Literature 139
Patricia Jean Cianciolo

Children's Literature Versus Wordless "Books" 145
Patrick Groff

Part 6 Illustrations

The Visual Language of the Picture Book 157
Olga Richard

Picture Play in Children's Books: A Celebration of Visual Awareness 167
Peggy Whalen-Levitt

Illustrators, Books, and Children: An Illustrator's Viewpoint 175
Celia Berridge

Picture Books for Children Who Are Masters of Few Words 183
Barbara Lucas

Remediation and Reinforcement: Books for Children with Visual Perception Impairments 186
Mary M. Banbury

Part 7 Informational Books

The Art of Nonfiction 195
Betty Bacon

Writing the Literature of Fact 204
Jo Carr

Characteristics of Good Science Materials for Young Readers 214
Illa Podendorf

An Evaluation of Biography 220
Denise M. Wilms

What Do We Do about Bad Biographies? 226
Jo Carr

Part 8 Contemporary Realistic Fiction

Toward Pluralism: Resources for Avoiding Stereotypes and Bias in Children's Literature 239
Arthur N. Applebee

The Aged in Young Children's Literature 245
Phyliss Winet Barnum

Guidelines for Equal Treatment of the Sexes 249
McGraw-Hill Book Company

Little Girls and Picture Books: Problem and Solution 261
Kathy Byrne de Filippo

Children's Perceptions of Death: A Look at the Appropriateness of Selected Picture Books 267
Robert G. Delisle and Abigail S. Woods McNamee

Children's Literature and Early Childhood Separation Experiences 277
Joan Fassler

Part 9 Folktales

Folktales for Children 291
Gertrude B. Herman

Comparison of Folk Tale Variants 300
Elinor P. Ross

What Ever Happened to Little Red Riding Hood? A Study of a Nursery Tale 305
Nancy A. Mavrogenes and Joan S. Cummins

The Uses of Bettelheim's *The Uses of Enchantment* 310
Anthony Arthur

The Brothers Grimm: Folktale Style and Romantic Theories 316
Christa Kamenetsky

Part 10 Storytelling

Storytelling: Preparation and Presentation 325
Augusta Baker and Ellin Greene

Storytellers in the Classroom 332
Stewart Marsden

Pictures Used with Storytelling 337
Anne Pellowski

Part 11 Sharing Picture Books

Do Swans Really Eat Fudgesicles? The Picture Book and Child Drama 348
Robert Barton and David Booth

Twenty-Four Things to Do with a Book 358
Geoff Fox

Presenting Literature to Children 361
Terry D. Johnson

Books . . . Love 'Em and Use 'Em 369
Carol Hurst

Selecting Picture Storybooks for Young Children with Learning Disabilities 404
Jed P. Luchow

Should Picture Books and Young Children Be Matched? 410
Patrick Groff

Word Meaning and the Literary Experience in Early Childhood 418
Dorothy H. Cohen

The Effect of Literature on Vocabulary and Reading Achievement 434
Dorothy H. Cohen

Reading, Imagination, and Television 441
Dorothy G. Singer

Encouraging Children's Creative Oral Responses through Nonnarrative Films 448
Jill P. May

The Picture Book Projected 456
Morton Schindel

Walt Disney's Interpretation of Children's Literature 461
Jill P. May

Film Productions of Children's Books: Weston Woods Studios and Disney 472
Jill P. May

Creating Preschool Resource Centers 480
Eileen M. Earhart

Beyond Illustration: Information about Art in Children's Picture Books 487
Ruth Straus Gainer

Part 12 Controlled Vocabulary Books

What the Cat in the Hat Begat 495
David C. Davis

What the Cat in the Hat Begat, Begat 499
Robert E. Newman

I Can Read! Predictable Books as Resources for Reading and Writing Instruction 502
Lynn K. Rhodes

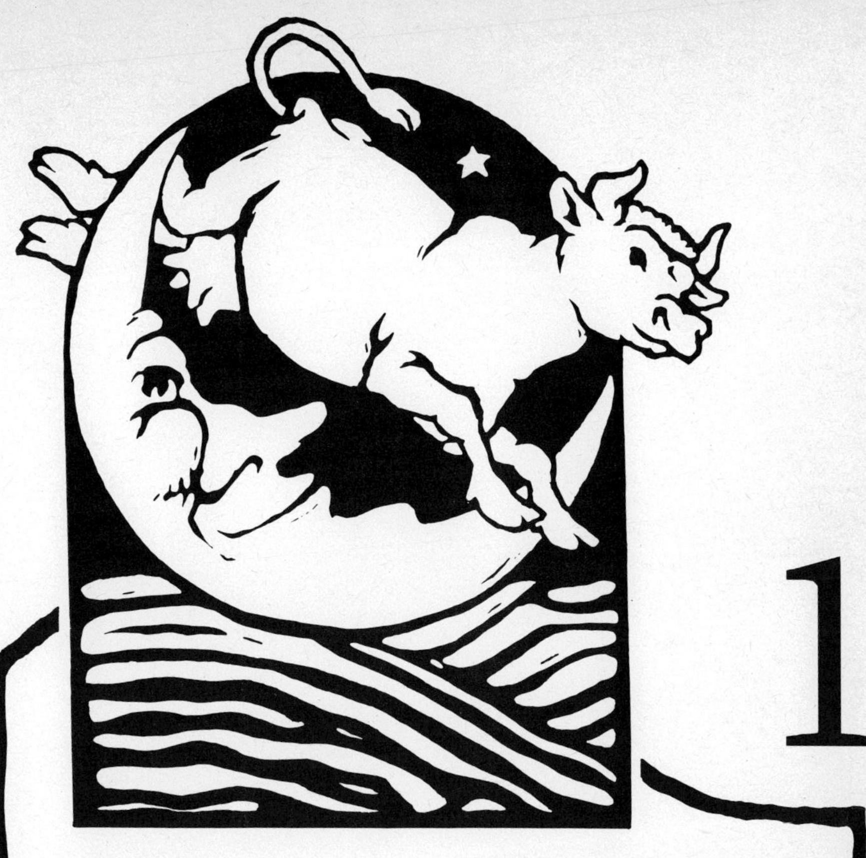

1

Introduction

E Is for Easy: E Is for Enormously Difficult

Johanna Hurwitz

Walk into almost any children's library and you will see the same thing: row after row of beautiful, slim volumes filled with brief stories and marvelous illustrations. The corner where these books are arranged is generally labeled "Picture Books" or "Easy Books" and every teacher, librarian, parent and child will quickly tell you, if you don't already know it, that these are the books for little children.

On the spine of each book there is usually painted "*E*" for easy. It is there to remind the student aides, or whoever it is that replaces books upon the library shelves, where to put the books. But the letter is unnecessary because the very format of the book—few words, and pictures on every page—identifies it immediately. By the time a child has comfortably mastered the art of reading, these *E* books are usually rejected. They are the baby books, to be looked at before one can read alone. Occasionally a child will pick up one of these and say nostalgically, "I read this when I was little." If the urge is strong to borrow and reread the book again, these *old* children of eight and nine will say, "I will take this home to show my little brother or sister." The sibling is sometimes invented on the spot as a cover for a desire that may be laughed at by others. After all, the book is labeled *E* and "E is for easy."

Working among children's books, I have discovered that *easy* is a misnomer. These *E* books may be elegant, entertaining, educational, emotionally supportive, exciting, eventful and evocative. Only a small group can genuinely be recognized as easy. Many, many more are enormously difficult. It is a waste not to use these books with older children, so I have begun to include them regularly in the curriculum of the upper grades. I am also trying to revise the views of both teachers and students toward such books.

Do you know how a czar eats potatoes? Not one sixth grader did, nor did many of them even know the word *czar*. So I showed them Anne Rose's deceptively simple book *How Does a Czar Eat Potatoes?* (1973). There she contrasts the wealth of the Russian ruler with her humble peasant father. There is exaggeration, but there is also truth and pathos. Her imaginary czar

SOURCE: *Language Arts*, April 1978, pp. 511–512.

drinks tea from a cup made of sugar, while her father can only drink tea and dream of sugar. In the end, it is evident who has the most zest for life and receives the most joy.

At first, the sixth graders protested, "Why are you showing us that baby book?" However, after a spirited discussion about values and what constitutes happiness, they were willing to concede my point. This *E* book was not easy, or at least if the words were easy, the concepts were not.

Since these simple picture books were meant to be read aloud to children by adults, they often contain a richer use of language than those books aimed at third, fourth, fifth and even sixth grade reading levels. Children have larger hearing than reading vocabularies, and reading aloud from these books helps this aural vocabulary to keep expanding.

The Bad Island by William Steig (1969) is filled with brilliantly colored pictures and wonderful language. The monsters that this author-artist has created make children of all ages laugh. Yet only fourth graders or children still older will be able to recognize that behind these zany creatures and their bizarre world is an allegory about good and evil.

Bang Bang You're Dead by Louise Fitzhugh (1969) has a similar message. It is not set in a fantasy world, but in the everyday surroundings of the child. It shows children playing at fighting and then really having a fight. Real fighting hurts, says this book. Nobody wins because even the victor may get a bloody nose or a loose tooth. It is a message about war that can be discussed at length with older children who bring more to the story than kindergarteners and first graders do.

Not all books need the heavy messages hidden in the text to make them too difficult to be understood. Sometimes the humor is too sophisticated to be caught. For example, *How Tom Beat Captain Najork and His Hired Sportsmen* by Russell Hoban (1974) is filled with invented terms and Britishisms. "What is a *bloater*?" a younger child will ask. A fourth or fifth grader does not need to know. They can guess that eating "greasy bloaters" must be horrid.

The picture books by Tomi Ungerer have several levels of humor. They are filled with tiny details that the eye picks out only after several exposures to the book. The texts are full of puns and word plays. Only the sophistication of an older student will be able to detect the humor in the menu that the young girl prepares for her giant master in *Zeralda's Ogre* (1967), or in the names and events in *I Am Papa Snap and These Are My Favorite No Such Stories* (1971).

A classic among picture books is *Many Moons* by James Thurber (1943). This book won the Caldecott Award from the American Library Association in 1944 for being the most distinguished picture book of the year. Although this is a prize for the art work, the text is of prime importance in quality picture books. Thurber tells the simple story of a little princess who asks for the moon and how her wish is granted. There is humor in the words of the Royal Mathematician, the Lord Chamberlain and the Royal Wizard which only older children will be able to discover. I like to astound older elementary students with the fact that every one of them knows more about the moon than the wisest astronomer of twenty-five years ago. If they insist that this isn't so, I tell them to read the article about the moon in the simplest encyclopedia in the school library and then they will know more. This book is a good introduction to a science unit about the solar system.

I do not know how you can teach social studies without using the picture editions of folk tales from all over the world. Sometimes these books are shelved with the *E* books because of their picture format, and sometimes they are classified as 398 and shelved with the folklore collection. Wherever they are, they generally remain overlooked by upper grade teachers who are afraid of showing "baby" books to their students. How much richer is the experience of those exposed to *The Terrible Troll Bird* by the D'Aulaires (1976), a tale from Norway; *My Mother Is the Most Beautiful Woman in the World* by Becky Rehyer (1945), a tale from Russia; *Three Gold Pieces* by Aliki (1967), a tale from Greece; *Simon Boom Gives a Wedding* by Yuri Suhl (1972), a Yiddish folk tale; *Usha the Mouse-maiden* by Gobhai (1969), a tale from India; *Rooster Brother* by Nonny Hogrogian (1974), a tale from Armenia, and *Why Mosquitoes Buzz in People's Ears* by Velma Aardema (1975), a tale from Africa. This list should be as long as the holdings in your school or local public library. Each picture folk tale helps to give the class a better sense of the spirit of the country which they are studying.

Easy books can stimulate creative writing in the classroom. A group of sixth graders that I worked with was motivated to write by the simple picture book *Fortunately* by Remy Charlip (1964). In this book the author alternates good news with bad: "fortunately"—"unfortunately". There is only one sentence per page. We compared this simple technique to sophisticated adventure novels, spell-binding movies and television episodes, where one is gripped with suspense, then relief, then suspense once again. Within minutes the entire class caught the mood and began writing.

> Fortunately, I found a bag of money.
> Unfortunately, it was counterfeit.

Another easy book which has successfully stimulated creative writing is *I Can't Said the Ant* by Polly Cameron (1961). It is a book of simple, yet clever rhymes.

> What's all the clatter about the platter
> Teapot fell said the dinner bell
> Teapot broke said the artichoke
> She went kerplop said the mop . . .

The entire story is a rhyme, using items to be found in a kitchen. A second and similar book by the same author is *The Green Machine* (1969). The action here has moved to the garden where all the hoes and rakes and plants hold a rhymed conversation. First and second graders laugh with delight. Fifth and sixth graders want to try this word game themselves. They look about the library and begin

> What's all the noise asked the boys
> Do your work said the clerk . . .

In a period when school budgets are being cut throughout the country, it is important to use every resource available to us as educators. The easy books on library shelves, which are the products of some of the best authors and artists, are too often neglected.

Instead of assuming that *E* stands for "easy," look again. Reevaluate these books and use them. *E* is not always for easy. *E* is also for enormously difficult. *P* is not merely a picture book. Look again. It may be profound.

References

Aardema, Velma. *Why Mosquitoes Buzz in People's Ears*. New York: The Dial Press, 1975.

Aliki. *Three Gold Pieces*. New York: Pantheon, 1967.

Cameron, Polly. *The Green Machine*. New York: Coward, McCann & Geoghegan, Inc., 1969.

———. *I Can't Said the Ant*. New York: Coward, McCann & Geoghegan, Inc., 1961.

Charlip, Remy. *Fortunately*. New York: Parents' Magazine Press, 1964.

D'Aulaire, Ingri and Edgar Parin. *The Terrible Troll Bird*. New York: Doubleday & Co., 1976.

Fitzhugh, Louise. *Bang Bang You're Dead*. New York: Harper & Row, 1969.

Gobhai, Mehlli. *Usha the Mouse-maiden*. New York: Hawthorne Books, Inc., 1969.

Hoban, Russell. *How Tom Beat Captain Najork and His Hired Sportsmen*. New York: Atheneum, 1974.

Hogrogian, Nonny. *Rooster Brother*. New York: Macmillan Co., 1974.

Reyher, Becky. *My Mother Is the Most Beautiful Woman in the World*. New York: Lothrop, Lee & Shepard, 1945.

Rose, Anne. *How Does a Czar Eat Potatoes?* New York: Lothrop, Lee & Shepard, 1973.

Steig, William. *The Bad Island*. New York: Simon & Schuster, 1969.

Suhl, Yuri. *Simon Boom Gives a Wedding*. New York: Four Winds Press, 1972.

Thurber, James. *Many Moons*. New York: Harcourt Brace Jovanovich, Inc., 1943.

Ungerer, Tomi. *I Am Papa Snap and These Are My Favorite No Such Stories*. New York: Harper & Row, 1971.

———. *Zeralda's Ogre*. New York: Harper & Row, 1967.

Readability and Children's Picture Books

Adrianne P. Hunt
Janet R. Reuter

A children's room of a public library contains numerous appealing, beautifully illustrated picture books, conveniently displayed on child-size shelves and tables. The children for whom these books are intended, preschoolers and primary grade youngsters, browse and choose those they will take home, with parents helping in the selection or urging their children to hurry. The scene is repeated in elementary school libraries and classrooms.

What becomes of the books, once checked out and in the hands of these youngsters? Will the children be left to explore the illustrations and imaginative language alone, or will parents and teachers share the stories with them? Do the adults concerned assume that the children will be able to read and enjoy the books independently, simply because they *are* children's books, or do they understand that picture books are meant to be read to children by adults?

Observation has led the writers to conclude that in far too many cases it is the former situation that occurs. Well-meaning parents and teachers supply guidance and encouragement in the selection process, may provide follow-up discussion and activities after the books have been read, but too rarely provide the all important sharing aloud of the illustrations and text.

Observation of this misuse of picture books led to the idea that a study of the readability levels of a sample of picture books would be helpful to the parents and teachers of the very young. Huck (1976, p. 109) notes, "Most picture storybooks require a reading ability level of at least third grade and are generally read *to* children. They are written for the young child's interest and appreciation level, not his reading ability level."

A review of the literature revealed no definitive support for Huck's statement and in fact indicated a scarcity of any recent research at all in the area of the children's picture books. The purpose of this study was, then, to calculate the readability level of a typical sample of picture books available to children.

SOURCE: *Reading Teacher*, October 1978, pp. 23–27. Reprinted with permission of the authors and the International Reading Association.

Examining the Books

Huck (pp. 107–8) defines picture books as "that group of books in which pictures and text are considered to be of equal importance." Fusion of pictures and text is essential to unity of presentation in such books; a child, having heard the text and seen the pictures once, should be able to retell the story from the pictures.

A related category of books are those designated as easy-to-read. Also intended for the youngest readers, they are written with a controlled vocabulary and are designed to be read independently. Although these books do not usually fulfill the aesthetic and language goals of literature, Shepherd (1976, p. 2) affirms that they do provide the "necessary bridge between being a listener and being a reader."

Books to be included in this study were defined as all those books children might choose from the picture book section of a library, and thus both picture books and easy-to-read books were part of the sample. The sample was chosen from the Children's Room of the Akron (Ohio) Public Library. Random sampling from the approximately 3400 picture books and easy-to-read books available produced a list of 52 picture books and easy readers. The sample had no duplication of authors, contained a balance of literary types, and appeared to be representative of the selection available to children. Of these books, 4 were published in the 1940s, 4 in the 1950s, 14 in the 1960s and 30 in the 1970s.

Books in the sample were then analyzed for readability level with Fry's readability graph (Fry 1968) based on sentence and word length (no account taken of frequency of vocabulary used). Grade level indexes are indicated with the list of books examined.

Readability levels of the 52 books ranged from grades one through seven, with the largest number of books (15) written at the first grade level, and the numbers of books per grade level decreasing, predictably, as grade level increased. The median, 26 books, fell between second and third grade level, indicating that half of the sample was indexed at third grade level or above. It is interesting to note that, while most of the easy-to-read books were indexed appropriately at first, second, and third grade levels, one of them had a grade six level of readability!

The reader should note that the sample was defined so as to approximate the effect of a child's random selection of books from the shelves. No attempt was made to include the most widely circulated books.

Implications for Parents, Teachers

Realizing the limitations of readability formulas, the writers suggest that many of the books in the sample cannot and should not be used independently by the children for whom they are intended. Individual examination of the books yielded several instances of long and involved complex sentences. Frequent subtleties of plot and illustration called for amplification and discussion between adult reader and child listener. Phrases such as "dollop of dirt," "dragonfly rattles low, "exquisite flakes," "boondoggle team," "reinforced air holes," "trailing mossy camouflage," "aeronautical engineer," and "meadow rue" were encountered. The fun of word plays, the cadence of language, and the literary effects of many of the books would be lost to a child busily involved in the mechanics of decoding.

Popp and Porter (1975, pp. 92 and 94), in describing their work with readability and children's trade books, note that the "qualities to which human beings are more sensitive will likely always fall outside the range of a practical formula." They further caution that books vary in difficulty from one part to another and that "average" grade level assignments do not insure that a child will be able to read an entire book equally well. Similarly, Moe (1974, p. 4) states, "Most authors of children's trade books—even those intended for the very young child—have never admitted to writing their books with a predetermined vocabulary . . . . Indeed, some authors of children's trade books seem to strive for diversity and complexity." Griffin (1970) reminds us that informed common sense and thoughtful judgment are the most effective standards for use in evaluating children's books.

The writers do not suggest that readability formulas be used to match books and children, but rather that adults consider carefully what is lost when children are asked to read a book alone. The values of reading aloud to children are many. Shepherd (1976, pp. 7–8) notes that sharing books aids in conceptual development and vocabulary expansion, produces awareness of a variety of syntactical patterns, and alerts the listener to the symbolic function of language and its flexibility. Griffin (1970, p. 25) agrees, stating that the skillful use of books with young children can increase their word banks, widen their background of experiences, extend their listening and comprehending ability, and expand their capacity to relate to the environment.

Furth (1970) pessimistically describes American elementary schools as places in which early reading experiences fail to challenge, and discourage, rather than encourage, thinking. This need not be so. When shared by eager children and enthusiastic adults, picture books can be the medium through which younsters are introduced to the world of quality literature and to the love of books.

References

Fry, Edward. "A Readability Formula that Saves Time." *Journal of Reading*, vol. 11, no. 7 (April 1968), pp. 513–16.

Furth, Hans G. *Piaget for Teachers*. Englewood Cliffs, N.J.: Prentice-Hall, Inc., 1970.

Griffin, Louise. *Books in Preschool: A Guide to Selecting, Purchasing, and Using Children's Books*. ED 038 178. Urbana, Ill.: ERIC Clearinghouse on Early Childhood Education, 1970.

Huck, Charlotte S. *Children's Literature in the Elementary School,* 3rd ed. New York, N.Y.; Holt, Rinehart & Winston, 1978.

Moe, Alden J. A Comparative Study of Vocabulary Diversity: The Speaking Vocabularies of First-Grade Children. The Vocabularies of Selected First-Grade Primers, and The Vocabularies of Selected First-Grade Trade Books. Paper presented at the annual meeting of the American Educational Research Association, Chicago, Ill., April 1974. ED 090 520. Arlington, Va.: ERIC Document Reproduction Service.

Popp, Helen M. and Douglas Porter. Measuring the Readability of Children's Trade Books. Unpublished study, Harvard Graduate School of Education. July 1975, ED 113 684. Arlington, Va.: ERIC Document Reproduction Service.

Shepherd, Richard C. The Use of "Trade Books" in a Reading Program. Paper presented at the Annual Convention of the International Reading Association, Anaheim, California. May 1976. ED 123 594. Arlington, Va.: ERIC Document Reproduction Service.

Readability Levels of Books Examined in the Study

Book	*Grade Level**
Adshead, Gladys L. *Brownies, They're Moving!*** H. Z. Walck, 1970.	4
Anglund, Joan Walsh. *A Friend is Someone Who Likes You*.** Harcourt Brace Jovanovich, 1958.	3
Bannon, Laura. *Red Mittens*.** Houghton Mifflin, 1946.	2
Becker, John Leonard. *Seven Little Rabbits*. Walker, 1973.	6
Bernstein, Margery. *Earth Namer: A California Indian Myth*. Scribner's, 1974.	1
Bond, Michael and Fred Banbery. *Paddington at the Circus*.** Random House, 1974.	3
Brenner, Barbara. *Baltimore Orioles*. Harper & Row, 1974.	1
Brown, Margaret Wise. *Country Noisy Book*. Harper & Row, 1940.	2
Burchard, Marshall. *I Know a Baseball Player*. Putnam, 1975.	2
Carrick, Carol. *The Pond*. Macmillan, 1970.	4
Charushin, Evgenii Ivanovich. *The Little Gray Wolf*.** Macmillan, 1983.	5
Conover, Chris. *Six Little Ducks*. Crowell, 1976.	5
Delton, Judy. *Two Good Friends*. Crown, 1974.	2
Disney Productions. *Walt Disney's Brer Rabbit and His Friends*.** Random House, 1973.	1
Early, Margaret. *Sun Up*.** Harcourt Brace Jovanovich, 1974.	1
Farber, Norma. *Where's Gomer?* Dutton, 1974.	2
Fox, Paula. *Good Ethan*.** Bradbury, 1973.	3
Friskey, Margaret. *Indian Two Feet and His Horse*.** Childrens Press, 1959.	1
Gates, Arthur Irving. Tommy Little.** Macmillan, 1951.	1
Gilbreath, Alice Thompson. *Beginning-to-Read Riddles and Jokes*.** Follett, 1967.	1
Greenburg, Polly. *Oh Lord, I Wish I Was a Buzzard*. Macmillan, 1968.	4
Harrison, David Lee. *Little Turtle's Big Adventure*. Random House, 1969.	2
Hirawa, Yasuko. *Song of the Sour Plum*. Walker, 1968.	2
Hood, Flora Mae. *One Luminaria for Antonio*.** Putnam, 1968.	6
Ipcar, Dahlov. *The Cat Came Back*. Knopf, 1971.	4

Readability Levels of Books Examined in the Study

Book	*Grade Level**
Keats, Ezra Jack. *Apt. 3*. Macmillan, 1971.	3
Kitt, Tamra. *Jake*. London: Abelard-Schuman, 1969.	1
Kraus, Robert. *Whose Mouse Are You?* Macmillan, 1970.	1
Leaf, Munro. *Boo, Who Used to Be Scared of the Dark*. Random House, 1948.	5
Lexau, Joan. *Olaf Reads*.** Dial Press, 1961.	1
Lobel, Anita. *King Rooster, Queen Hen*.** Greenwillow, 1975.	3
MacDonald, Golden. *Red Light, Green Light*. Doubleday, 1944.	1
Marshall, James. *Willis*. Houghton Mifflin, 1974.	3
Miles, Miska. *Apricot ABC*. Little, Brown, 1969.	6
Morris, Robert A. *Seahorse*.** Harper & Row, 1972.	2
Murdocca, Salvatore. *Tuttle's Shell*.** Lothrop, Lee and Shepard, 1976.	2
Palmer, Helen Marion. *A Fish Out of Water*. Beginner Books, 1961.	1
Pinkwater, Manus. *Three Big Hogs*. Seabury Press, 1975.	4
Rand, Ann. *Did a Bear Just Walk There?* Harcourt Brace Jovanovich, 1968.	6
Rinkoff, Barbara. *The Case of the Stolen Code Book*. Crown, 1971.	1
Sachs, Marilyn. *Matt's Mitt*. Doubleday, 1975.	4
Schlein, Miriam. *The Girl Who Would Rather Climb Trees*. Harcourt Brace Jovanovich, 1975.	3
Sendak, Maurice. *Some Swell Pup: or Are You Sure You Want a Dog?* Farrar, Straus and Giroux, 1976.	1
Shaw, Richard. *Who Are You Today?* Warne, 1970.	7
Skorpen, Liesel Moak. *Outside My Window*. Harper & Row, 1968.	2
Stiles, Martha Bennett. *Dougal Looks for Birds*. Four Winds Press, 1972.	3
Thurman, Judith. *I'd Like to Try a Monster's Eye*. Atheneum, 1977.	1
Ungerer, Tomi. *The Mellops Go Diving for Treasure*. Harper, 1957.	5
Waber, Bernard. *Lyle and the Birthday Party*. Houghton Mifflin, 1966.	5
Welch, Martha McKeen. *Saucy*. Coward, McCann & Geoghegan, 1968.	3
Winn, Marie. *The Man Who Made Fine Tops*.** Simon and Schuster, 1970.	3
Zaffo, George J. *The Giant Book of Things in Space*. Doubleday, 1969.	2

*Determined by the Fry formula, 1968

**Easy-to-read

In Search of the Perfect Picture Book Definition

Zena Sutherland
Betsy Hearne

Well, of *course* you know what a picture book is. A book for a small child. No, it's a book that has more pictures than text. No? There don't have to be more pictures, they just have to be more important? But that's true of many books for older children! Clearly, this calls for a definition. The term "picture book" has been rattling around for a long time (and will probably go on doing so), but it might be useful to pin down exactly what we mean by it.

We feel a picture book is one in which the pictures either dominate the text or are as important. In other words we'd give it some latitude. The clearest examples of one group where illustrations are of paramount importance are ABC books, books about shapes, counting books, and wordless books. Although some alphabet books have rhyming texts, for example Wanda Gág's *ABC Bunny* and Fritz Eichenberg's *Ape in a Cape,* the pages are dominated by the illustrations and the letters of the alphabet. *Bruno Munari's ABC* associates each letter with words beginning with that letter, but it is the color, design, and humor of the pictures that hold the attention.

In *Brian Wildsmith's ABC* the words—with their initial letters—serve simply as captions for the 26 vivid paintings. John Reiss, in *Numbers and Shapes,* focuses solely on visual aspects: in Mitsumasa Anno's *Anno's Counting Book,* there are no words and only one numeral on each double-page spread; yet through the pictures the artist introduces not only numbers but the concepts of time, seasons, and sets. And in such books as John Goodall's *Paddy Pork* stories or Mercer Mayer's *A Boy, a Dog, a Frog, and a Friend,* there are no words at all; the story is told through the pictures.

A second group of books is that in which the text and the pictures are of equal importance, in which neither would be as effective alone. They range from those for very young children, like Dorothy Corey's *You Go Away* or the Provensens' *Our Animal Friends at Maple Hill Farm,* to books for older readers, like David Macaulay's *Castle* or Tunis's *Colonial Living,* both books in which the reader moves continuously back and forth between text and

SOURCE: *Wilson Library Bulletin,* October, 1977, pp. 158–160. Reprinted with permission of the publisher.

pictures. Margaret Musgrove's *Ashanti to Zulu* falls into this category; the pictures by Leo and Diane Dillon need the text to effect their full message as much as the text needs the illustrations.

The picture story is the largest category in the picture book genre; most of the Caldecott award books are in this group. While it is possible for a story for young children to be sparsely illustrated or to have illustrations that neither extend nor complement the text, it is the exception. In most picture story books, the balance between print and illustrations is maintained so that neither is as effective without the other, although they may not be *necessary* for each other, as in the second category. In William Steig's *The Amazing Bone,* for example, the pictures give only part of the story's details, while the text would be the poorer without such visual additions as a ghostly representation of the noises made by the bone.

Mary Raynor, in *Mr. and Mrs. Pig's Evening Out,* lets the reader anticipate the text by showing in her pictures that the babysitter is a wolf several pages before the deceptively sedate sitter gives her name. The last picture shows, more eloquently than words could, the peaceful relaxation of the porcine parents after the piglets have disposed of Mrs. Wolf. In *Make Way for Ducklings,* Robert McCloskey tells a perennially engaging story, but it is the picture of the ducklings crossing a busy street while a policeman holds up traffic that most children remember. Again, the story and the pictures are almost inseparable.

Books designed for beginning readers are usually put in the picture book category, but their inclusion seems dubious. They may perhaps be better designated as early-reading illustrated books. If one examines Joan Lexau's *The Homework Caper*—illustrated by Syd Hoff—and Arnold Lobel's *Frog and Toad Are Friends* (which are fiction), or Paul Showers's *Look at Your Eyes* and Eleanor Lapp's *The Mice Came in Early This Year* (which are nonfiction), it seems clear that the text is most important and can indeed stand alone, while the illustrations, engaging or informative as they may be, function more as extensions or corroborating devices than as entities.

One cannot, of course, generalize about this group. Some books for beginning readers (Anne Rockwell's *The Toolbox,* for example) have pictures that are as important as, or more important than, the text and are obviously more suitable for the second picture book category. Some concept books, like books about shapes, are picture books, whereas others introduce abstract ideas that require explanations more intricate than illustrations can provide.

Some adaptations of folktales or fairy tales in single-tale editions may have few illustrations, or pictures so placed that they are not an integral part of the reading experience, while others are heavily illustrated by pictures that participate in the narrative flow. Some nursery rhyme books are profusely illustrated, like *The Mother Goose Treasury* by Raymond Briggs; the color, vigor, and humor indicate that the pictures are meant for children's enjoyment as much as the rhymes. Yet in *The Oxford Nursery Rhyme Book,* compiled by Iona and Peter Opie, the small black-and-white pictures (most of which are reproductions of early engravings) indicate—along with the small print and print-filled pages—that this is a source book for adults even if the rhymes and ballads can be read aloud to children. It is certainly not a picture book.

So we go back to our definition of picture books as those in which the illustrations dominate a text that may range from nonexistent to complementary; equal but not separate. It is impossible to define without drawing parameters and therefore assuming an arbitrary stance. Recognizing that there are exceptions and borderline books, we would hope only to clarify the definition of a picture book to include the broadest possibilities of the genre.

Johnny Still Can't Read

Daniel Melcher

Once upon a time, the slow readers in our schools just dropped out. Nowadays they aren't allowed to, and there isn't a school that isn't acutely embarrassed by the number of its reading failures, rarely below 20 percent of the pupils. According to the U.S. Office of Education, some seven million elementary and secondary school pupils have reading problems severe enough to make them potentially unable to compete in society. This is not to say that the children whom the schools count as "reading failures" couldn't pass a literacy test. Our nation is, according to the census figures, almost 100 percent "literate." Just about everyone can do more than just read and write his name. Far too many, however, do not read for pleasure and do not look upon print as a practical means of self-enlightenment. Print is nearly as impenetrable to them as musical notation is to most of the rest of us. Call them slow readers, call them nonreaders, call them dyslexics—whatever word you use,

SOURCE: *School Library Journal,* October 15, 1973, pp. 79–87.

for them reading is a skill they never quite master. For them speech is speech, but reading is deciphering a code.

Early reading is sometimes discussed as if the issue was whether to let a pushy mother gain an unfair advantage for the child. The question is asked whether early reading *should* be encouraged, unless a way can be found to make it effectively available to all children, not just some.

Instinctively, many educators respond to this problem by proposing to lower the age for starting school. California school officials are currently seeking to lower it to age four; New York State school officials are thinking of recommending that children begin school at age three. The assumption is that only in this way can children from deprived homes be prevented from falling behind children from more privileged homes; that the child in the classroom must inevitably be learning more than the child in the home—at least the average home.

Unless and until all or most children routinely learn to read early, the schools will have the thankless task of trying to start the nonreaders on material geared to their reading level, such as, "Look, Jane, see the dog." Out on the playground the same youngsters have been debating about space satellites and using a speaking vocabulary in excess of 5000 words, yet they are expected to go back into the classroom and get interested in word-counted "baby stuff" geared to an assumed *reading vocabulary* of 50 words.

Assumptions about Nonreaders

Many of us clung briefly to the hope that Rudolf Flesch had the answer (phonics) to this reading problem in his best-selling book *Why Johnny Can't Read and What You Can Do About It* (Harper, 1955). Unfortunately, those schools that had been using phonics right along sadly admitted that even with a strong phonics program, an unacceptably high percentage of children had to be counted as reading failures.

The temptation has been to assume that it is children who come from deprived home environments who become the nonreaders. Perhaps *more* nonreaders come from the less privileged homes, but highly privileged homes also produce their share of nonreaders, and not infrequently a nonreader will have brothers and sisters who read very well indeed.

At first glance, that seems to leave "intelligence" as the significant variable, a theory supported by examination scores *unless* the exams are oral so that the student's ability to answer the question isn't limited by his ability to read it. On oral exams, many nonreaders do quite well.

Though the incidence of nonreaders, even in privileged school populations, rarely goes *below* 20 to 25 percent, there is reason to suspect that the incidence of true nonreaders may not go much *higher* either, even among children from grossly underprivileged homes, once you allow for those whose "nonreading" is more a protest against assignments they can't relate to than a true disability. In his *Hooked on Books* (Berkeley, 1968), Daniel Fader tells of a reform school in which some of the nonreaders of *Dick and Jane* suddenly became avid readers when allowed to read books such as *Black Like Me* or *The Autobiography of Malcolm X*.

Among themselves, educators tend to blame themselves (i.e., their methods) for their reading failures and have been desperately seeking better methods. They have tried phonics and they have tried the "look and say" method. They have tried reading aloud and reading silently. They have tried beginning reading and instruction earlier, in kindergarten, and starting it later, in second grade. They have tried placing the slow starters in special classes, so they can be given extra drill.

There is really only one thing they haven't explored—the possibility that the age for starting school is far *too late* to start learning to read, just as it would be far too late to begin learning to talk. They haven't really explored the possibilities of encouraging youngsters to learn to read at home, as early as they learn to talk, and by the same unstructured methods. This is hardly surprising. After all, teachers don't get a child until he is of "school age." What happens between a mother and a two year old is not only outside their experience, it is presumed to be outside their assignment and beyond their reach.

Reading Readiness

Famous early readers include John Stuart Mill, George Bernard Shaw, and Norbert Wiener. It was easy to assume, however, that such early readers as these either had exceptional intelligence or had exceptional help from exceptional parents—or most likely both. It was easy to assume that early reading could not, in any case, provide a solution to the schools' problems, since few children could be expected to have the gift, and even fewer could be expected to have parents with the necessary time, dedication, or skill to teach them to read. Once this basic assumption had been made—namely that it was superior intelligence that led to early reading, rather than early reading that might have helped release the superior intelligence—many a study was made that seemed to buttress the assumption.

For example, the concept of "reading readiness" was developed, and tests for measuring reading readiness were devised. It was observed that the child who can already read his name before he starts school generally makes quicker progress with the school's reading lessons; accordingly, such a child was assumed to have reached a state of "reading readiness" by age five or six and was placed in a "fast class." Other children who brought no such "pre-reading" skills from home were assumed to need more time for reading development and were often put in a "slow class." (If, however, a mother proposed to help develop earlier reading readiness in her preschooler, she would be warned against it. If she asked what harm it could do, she was frequently offered the improbably unscientific observation that caveats developed out of experiments in toilet training could be assumed to apply to the teaching of reading as well.)

Physiological Development and Reading

Careful studies were made as to the age at which the average child walks, talks, and reads—from which the inference was drawn that since the average child *did* wait until age six to begin reading, then this must be the age at which he *should* begin reading. (The very same "logic" applied in Great Britain, where reading instruction starts in kindergarten, would, of course, "prove" that reading instruction, should start at age five.)

One investigator thought that reading readiness might hinge to some extent on the simple development of the capacity to see fine detail, and demonstrated that at age five only one child in ten could distinguish a *b* from a *d*. (Of course, it could equally well have been that only children who could already read would see any *reason* to distinguish a *b* from a *d*.)

Another investigator, noting that the average child's brain is not even fully developed until age seven or eight, theorized that the cells involved in reading might not be fully developed by the time a child reaches the age for entering school. (Of course, in this case, it could also be that brain development, like muscle development, is a *result*, not a *prerequisite*, of brain use.)

Many investigators are now beginning to suspect that *any* child can learn to read as early as he learns to talk, and will do so far more easily at that age than at a later age, just as he can learn a second language far more easily at the age when he is just starting to talk. They are beginning to believe that reading is in *no way* a higher skill than speech, and can in fact be learned along with speech by employing much the same informal and unstructured methods. John Holt has said, "If we taught them to talk the way we teach them to read—they'd never learn," and Professor Dolores Durkin, in her book *Teaching Them to Read* (Allyn & Bacon, 1970), says, "So far as is now known, nothing about six-year-old children makes this age level the very best time for beginning reading."

When some of these assumptions were questioned—as in books such as Glenn Doman's *How to Teach Your Baby to Read* (Random, 1964), Siegfried and Therese Engelmann's *Give Your Child a Superior Mind* (S & S, 1966), David Engler's *How to Raise Your Child's IQ* (Criterion, 1958), and Joan Beck's *How to Raise a Brighter Child* (Trident, 1967)—the reaction from many educators was that mothers (often described as "too emotionally involved") should keep hands off, should not "push" the child, should not "spoil his precious childhood," and should not risk teaching him reading habits that he would only have to unlearn later. Nothing would be gained from early reading it was said, since any seeming initial advantage would even itself out by the sixth grade in any case.

Happily, evidence is piling up that these assumptions aren't valid and never were. (I say "happily" because the research that was being done within the context of these rather negative assumptions had pretty much come to a dead end. Some new breakthrough was badly needed.)

The Work of Doman, Delacato, and Fay

Some of the most impressive evidence that a child (any child) can learn to read as early as he learns to talk is to be found in the work being done by Glenn Doman and Carl Delacato at the Institutes for the Achievement of Human Potential in Philadelphia. They got into reading almost by accident. Their primary work is with children who often cannot walk or talk, let alone read, the kind of children who sometimes have to be taught to breathe, and who might have to be institutionalized if they cannot be successfully treated. Their goal is to develop normal functions in children with mental or motor handicaps originating from brain injury, children diagnosed as cerebral palsied, autistic, athetoid, spastic, epileptic, hyperactive, mentally retarded, or emotionally disturbed.

Thus the children they see would not by the wildest stretch of the imagination be expected to assay very high in "reading readiness." (Doman's own story of this work will be published by Doubleday in the spring of 1974 under the title *The Brain Injured Child.*) Nevertheless, these children are routinely learning to read within eight months after joining the program, often before they learn to talk. In fact, out of 399 children under age four, sequentially accepted for treatment, some 385 learned to read before their fifth birthday. Furthermore, they learned at home, since the treatments were all carried out at home, and it was Mother who did it, usually with a few minutes of instruction each day. (The child of two who learns even one word a day will have learned 365 words before he's three!)

One might suppose that such consistent success would have to be based on some broad-scale breakthrough in teaching methods. Dorman's view, however, is that there are really only two "secrets." First, you should start by age two if you can. Later is harder. Second, for at least the first few words, it pays to use VERY LARGE TYPE. Beyond that, almost any method works, provided you make a game out of it and stop before the child wants to stop.

Doman and Delacato's techniques for helping the brain-injured vary greatly with the diagnosis (age, symptoms, probable nature, and location of the brain injury), but one overriding policy is to try to compensate for any reduced capacity to see, hear, or feel by radically increasing *opportunities* for the child to see, hear, or feel. In fact, a double increase is indicated—first just to get through to the child, then to help him catch up. It isn't easy, however, to think up ways to keep a handicapped child interested and active throughout every waking hour, seeing, hearing, feeling, moving, experimenting, correlating. You have to use every resource you can find. *Reading has proved to be one of the most valuable resources.*

In the beginning, simply learning to read was a better game than pattycake, and as soon as the children got the general idea—namely that printed words have spoken equivalents—they'd start on their own to decipher package labels, newspaper headlines, advertisements, and books. These were not, remember, children who had been selected for their promise. In fact, to begin with, Dorman's typical four-year-old brain-injured patient might be performing at no higher a level than that of a normal two year old.

Nevertheless, these hurt children almost invariably learned to read and had fun doing it. Take, for example, two-year-old Mary R. Her mother, who had been instructed not to "push"—not to teach her more than one word a day—reported that Mary had taken to the game so enthusiastically that the first thing she would say when taken from her crib in the morning was, "Let's get the new word!"

Or take bilingual two-and-one-half-year-old Susan, who, on the fourth day of the word game, was holding the card for her fourth word, *table,* and just beginning to sense the potentials of reading. In great excitement, she held up the card for the Puerto Rican maid to see and said in Spanish, "Look, look, I can read it, it says *mesa.*"

In point of fact, the home may be a far better place than the classroom for doing a number of things. (It is often charged that mothers are "too emotionally involved," but "emotionally involved" is nearly synonymous with "highly motivated," and, besides, this tiresome label seems generally to come from educators themselves who regard mothers with all the emotional detachment with which a trade unionist regards a scab.)

Glenn Doman faced a "moment of truth" early in his career that resulted in his acquiring a deep and abiding respect for mothers. He was then a young man working with Temple Fay, the famous neurosurgeon. Comparing brain-injured children treated in a hospital with those left untreated at home, Fay and Doman had to face an uncomfortable moment of truth: the children remaining at home, with nothing but their mother's care, were not only doing as well as the ones being brought to the hospital for professional care—they were doing unmistakably better! In that instance, taking children out of the home turned out to be a very poor alternative to leaving them in the home, *even in underprivileged homes.*

In fact, the Doman case histories, indicate that again and again massive "enrichment of the environment" of severely retarded children has increased not only their skills, *but their head size*! With these children, brain capacity seems to increase in proportion to the demands made upon it, not in anticipation of them.

If you examine Doman's evidence, based on thousands of case histories, you have to believe that neither high IQ nor special aptitude is needed to enable children to learn to read as early as they learn to talk. Reading readiness may come with reading, not with age.

The Home Environment and Reading

The home is, after all, the place where children learn their native language—and learn it far, far better than any school will ever teach them a language.

If the best and most efficient learning we ever did was when we learned our own language—*before* we got to school—the methods we used warrant study. Perhaps it isn't the untrained mother who uses the wrong methods—perhaps it is the trained teacher who uses the wrong methods, misguidedly trying to improve on the methods that mothers (and Mother Nature) have been instinctively applying and perfecting for a million years.

Take the spoken word *milk*. In the classroom, the teacher would say something like, "Now children, what do we call this white liquid I have in this glass?" And every child would shrivel in his seat and pray, "I hope she doesn't call on me, I hope she doesn't call on me." Mother, on the other hand, just says "Drink your milk."

Or take the printed word *milk*. A teacher would spell it out on the blackboard, m-i-l-k, and then verbalize the letters. Mother would just let the carton sit on the kitchen table day after day, quietly proclaiming its contents. The child might easily get to the point where he could, without even thinking about it, "read" well enough to distinguish between cartons of whole milk, skimmed milk, buttermilk, or chocolate milk in the same unconscious way he could distinguish his Aunt Mary from his Aunt Margaret. If, however, you took note of this reading and set out to "help" him by saying, "Well, if you want to read, let me explain about the alphabet," the child might well back off, thinking, "I *thought* I was reading, but if it is that complicated, forget it."

Perhaps three questions need to be answered. First, *can* two year olds learn to read? Second, *if they can,* should they? Third, *if they can and should,* how can this privilege be made available to all two year olds, not just those whose parents have the time and inclination to encourage early reading and can be told how to go about it?

Reading and Motivation

It may well be that not more than ten percent of five year olds can perceive the difference between a *b* and a *d*. Considering that some 96 percent of Doman's brain-injured children under five could, nevertheless, read words, this may be like observing that very few children (or adults, for that matter) can tell the difference between a bee and a wasp unless at some point they have had some reason to take note of the distinction. It is not a matter of visual acuity; in fact, babies very early learn to tell Mommy from Auntie even though any two human faces differ far more subtly than a *b* and a *d*. This may explain, however, Doman's observation that if you want a child to take note of the difference between the words *mummy* and *daddy*, you would do well to start with lettering four or five inches high. The same would probably apply if your goal was to help an adult take notice of the differences between two Japanese characters. The problem is not whether the child *can* see detail. The problem is whether he takes notice of it.

A while ago, my then 15-month-old son Fred gave me a dramatic demonstration that the ability to see is primarily the ability to recognize and that seeing is not just an optical function, it is also a brain function.

We were leafing through *Life* magazine and had come to a full-page advertisement for golf clubs. Fred said excitedly, "Airplane, airplane."

I said, "I don't see any airplane. I see a golfer. He has a golf club. He's about to swing at the ball."

"No, no," Fred insisted, pointing, "airplane, airplane."

"Fred," I said, mystified, "that's not an airplane, that's a golfball."

"No! *Airplane*!" Fred persisted. Then I saw it. On one of the dimples of the golfball was the manufacturer's trademark, not more than 1/16 of an inch across, in the shape of an airplane. I don't know if Fred had ever seen a *golfball*, but he had long been greatly interested in airplanes.

Fred gave me another demonstration that indicated motivation may have more to do with reading ability than does visual acuity. Just after this second birthday, a dozen relatives and friends were gathered for a Christmas Eve party. Presents for everyone were stacked under the tree, and we decided to let them be opened in random sequence by having Fred bring them to his mother, one at a time, so that she could read the card and pass the package to the intended recipient. To our growing astonishment, the first 20 presents selected by Fred were all for him! At age two, he could infallibly recognize his own name, in any handwriting, large or small, whether spelled Fred, Red, or Frederic. I am only sorry we did not draw the obvious conclusion and provide incentives for extending his reading skills.

Even granting that children *can* learn to read as early as they learn to talk, however, the question remains: "Would this be wise?" Early reading could be both possible and safe without necessarily being significant. Considering, however, that the common condition of most children, most of the time, is *boredom* ("Do stop bothering Mother and go play with your toys or look at television!"), the resource of early reading cannot help but seem a potentially important means of enriching a child's environment. If a two year old seems to enjoy the process of learning to read (and at that age it is pretty hard to make him do anything he doesn't want to do) and if he enjoys reading itself, it seems too bad not to let him have that added resource.

Effects of Early Reading

You can say, "All right, suppose kids *can* learn to read as early as they learn to talk, but *should* they? Why take the risk of making them into misfits at school?" Fortunately, this fear has been laid to rest in a study of Professor Dolores Durkin entitled *Children Who Read Early* (Teachers' College Pr., Columbia Univ., 1966). Professor Durkin identified those children who could already read when they first entered the Oakland, California schools, and she noted their progress through six years. Her findings were unequivocal. Early readers were not harmed—they got on well both scholastically and socially. Furthermore (contrary to widely held assumptions), the early readers were by no means those with well-educated or pushy mothers; many seemed to have taught themselves to read. Nor did early reading necessarily correlate with other measures of high IQ.

When Professor Durkin began her study, only about one child in a hundred could read upon first entering school. Six years later the ratio was one in thirty. Resourceful first grade teachers would let such children read on their own or coach other children. The incidence of early readers could mount, however, from three percent to ten percent or even 20 percent without solving the schools' problems with the nonreaders.

Some reading specialists concede that early reading may do no harm but insist that it is not important either because by grade six everything will have evened out anyway. Not so, says Professor Durkin. Early reading is not only without adverse side effects, it also conveys positive and lasting benefits. She says, "The average achievement of early readers was significantly higher than that of comparably bright non-early readers, and this lead was maintained." She adds, "The value of an early start might be especially great for children with the lower IQ's.

Early Reading and Brain Patterning

Granted that universal early reading *may* be unattainable. On the other hand, given a high enough priority, maybe it isn't. And consider the advantages!

For instance, imagine the relief to a first grade teacher if she could start the children on books keyed to their interests instead of their reading limitations! Imagine the child's relief! Imagine the extra ground that could be covered if the time now spent on the teaching of reading could be allocated to other subjects! What a happy solution to the current problem of whether to place an early reader with his academic peers in the third grade, or with his chronological peers in the first grade!

And let's consider the possibilities that early reading might solve the problem of late reading and that those 20 percent who are reading failures might not be so if the schools got them earlier. For this 20 percent, perhaps the very delay between learning to talk at age two and learning to read at age six provides an opportunity for the brain to delay in organizing its language centers. No one has yet claimed to know for sure just how the mental processes of a good reader differ from those of a poor reader. It could, however (to borrow the terminology of the computer sciences), be far more a matter of *programming* than of *hardware*. It could be that we are all born with a brain (the hardware) fully adequate to handle both speech and print. It could be that our slow readers somehow got started on the wrong foot in their *method of use* of their mental equipment. Not even the best computer can perform properly if poorly programmed.

In most people, surely, the brain not only sets up a two-way filing system to equate the sound of a word with its meaning, but goes on to make this a three-way filing system that equates sound, sight, and meaning. Consider, however, the possibility that in the slow reader this efficient three-way system never got set up. Consider the possibility that the slow reader is slow precisely because he somehow got started storing his reading vocabulary separate from his speaking vocabulary.

Perhaps slow readers are a bit like hunt-and-peck typists. Their efficiency is low, but it would be even lower during any changeover, and the longer they stay with the wrong system, the harder any changeover becomes. If this is in fact what happens, it explains a lot. It explains, for example, why the slow reader often wants to sound out a word. He is, in effect, converting the print into speech, as a means of letting his reading centers ask his speech centers whether that word is in his speaking vocabulary.

This may also explain why some children tend to write some words backwards, *was* for *saw*, for example. Let's suppose that in a normal person the information on spelling is in the dominant hemisphere, as is also the control of the hand that does the writing. In an individual with mixed dominance, however, *print* (i.e., spelling) might have to be drawn from the subdominant hemisphere and then be reflected through the dominant hemisphere, mirrorlike, on its way to the writing hand. There have been numerous cases where reading and writing and spelling difficulties have cleared up after a change was made from writing right-handed to writing left-handed, and one thing that slow readers do tend to have in common is a tendency towards so-called mixed dominance. (One of the simple tests for mixed dominance is to hand the subject a rolled tube of paper and ask him to look through it. If, for example, he takes it with his right hand but puts it to his left eye, the examiner begins to suspect the existence of mixed dominance.)

As I mentioned this possibility one day, a friend broke in and said, "Listen, an experience my sister had in first grade may just support your theory. She was left-handed, but they insisted that she use her right hand for writing. One day she wrote a paper in which the first, third, and fifth lines went from left to right in the ordinary way, but the lines in between went from right to left. She herself saw nothing odd about it, but the rest of us could not decipher the second, fourth, and sixth lines without holding them up to a mirror. She had written the first line with her right hand, the second with her left hand, and so forth."

Something prompted me to go to the *Librarian's Glossary of Terms Used in Librarianship and the Book Crafts* and open to the word *boustrophedon.* Sure enough, this was defined as a style of writing practiced in ancient Greece for several centuries in which the odd-numbered lines were written from left to right and the even-numbered lines were written from right to left. In the latter, each letter and word were reversed, mirrorlike.

On impulse, I looked up the Greek alphabet, and, sure enough, no letter in it could be mistaken for any other merely by mirror reversal. In fact, further research revealed that the Greek scribes, like the Phoenician scribes before them, thought nothing of making mirror reversals of their letters. To them an E was an Ǝ, just as a → was a ←, and a ⊍ was a ⊍. Further research revealed that equivocal letter forms like our presentday *b*, *d*, *p*, and *q* did not come into use in any alphabet or language until more than a thousand years later.

Is this significant in the context of an article on dyslexia? I think it is. Man was a speaking animal for a million years before he was a writing animal. During all that time, and even longer, there must have been great survival value in being able to imagine how a thing would look if, the next time you saw it, it was facing the other way or you were looking at it from the other side. *Of course,* ⚲ would be seen as identical as ⚲. How else? So why wouldn't E be seen as identical to Ǝ?

I was startled to get what seemed like a confirmation of this during a holiday in the Galapagos Islands. As I walked among the sea lions sunning on the beach, one would occasionally open a sleepy eye and look me over. Usually he'd just shut it again—human visitors are neither a threat nor a novelty to these sea lions—but sometimes he would rear up and really inspect me. When this happened, he would not only do what we call a double take, cocking his head right, then left, but he would end by revolving that rubber neck of his to the point where he could look at me *upside down.* And this wasn't just happenstance, this seemed to be policy. Sea lion after sea lion really seemed to want to know what I'd look like if seen upside down.

Once I got into the water with the sea lions, I thought I saw the rationale for this. Under water, sea lions spend a great deal of their time upside down, corkscrewing or barrel rolling through the water. Functionally, I daresay it broadens their field of view. But it also means that a good part of the time they are seeing their world upside down. In all probability the ability to recognize things whether seen right side up or upside down—food, foe, or refuge—has unmistakable survival value.

Land-based humans don't have the same need to record an upside-down impression of things normally seen right side up, but have you noticed how often very young children *do* experiment with looking at their world upside down?

A sea lion would have no problem recognizing that a *b* was a *p* upside down and a *q* was a *d* upside down, just as an untutored preschooler would have no trouble recognizing that a *p* was just a *q* seen from behind and a *b* was a *d* seen from behind.

In the whole evolutionary history of the animal kingdom, even including man's first million years on earth, there was every reason to see a *b* as identical with a *d*, and no reason not to. Even after picture writing was invented, there was no reason to see a as different from a .

For a long, long time after the invention of the alphabet, the letters could go either way also. However, *words* couldn't go either way. The word *was*, seen from behind, becomes the word *saw*. As man became a reading animal and then graduated from pictographs to the use of an alphabet, suddenly, for the first time in the history of life on earth, it became *counterproductive* to take note of how something would look if seen from the other side.

I realize I am presenting not one but two hypotheses, which may or may not be related. Let me try to recap them.

1) Perhaps the slow reader has set up two sets of two-way files (sound/meaning and sight/meaning), whereas the fast reader has developed an integrated three-way file relating meaning, sound, *and* sight.

2) Where word reversals are part of the reading difficulties, perhaps print/meaning data are not being restricted to the hemisphere that controls the writing hand.

Let me leap, then, to another intriguing hypothesis. Doesn't it sound plausible that good readers have learned to *suppress* their brain's capacity to equate a word to its mirrored equivalent, whereas poor readers (at least those who tend to reversals like *was* for *saw* and *nip* for *pin*) have somehow *not* stumbled upon the value (for this sole purpose) of suppressing this otherwise useful and highly sophisticated brain capacity?

A high correlation between reading difficulty and mixed dominance has been fairly well established. This leaves unsettled, however, the question as to whether it was some inborn tendency toward mixed dominance that led to the failure to read properly, or perhaps the failure to read properly that left the brain without any pressing reason to resolve the mixed dominance. (Forms of life other than man are not known to show dominance or "handedness.")

A good, sobering question to ask of anyone who is letting himself get too absorbed in this kind of speculation is, "So what?" What if it could be shown that poor reading originates from inefficient neural organization of the reading function? Is that any different from saying that poor reading originates from poor reading habits, known all along?

Well, by this time, it won't surprise you to know that I think a way *exists* to forestall later reading difficulties. It is to get the brain off on the right foot by starting it on three-way correlations (meaning, sound, *and* sight) early enough to prevent it from inadvertently getting too far committed to two-way correlations of just meaning and sound. In point of fact, a very good start has been made with such educational television shows as *Sesame Street* and, especially, *Electric Company*. (The planned target of the latter was the second grader who was having reading difficulties, but preschoolers form its most enthusiastic audience.)

TV's commercials have also (accidentally) given preschoolers some pretty good opportunities to take in meaning/sound/sight correlations in the form of brand names and trademarks, opportunities often supplemented by visits to the supermarket, exposure to signs, etc. Given just this essentially accidental exposure to opportunities for meaning/sound/sight correlations, many preschoolers are figuring out reading for themselves, or, if you like, expediting their own "reading readiness."

If children are getting this far on their own without any planned help from us, think how much further and faster they might go if we gave them just a bit of conscious help! I *don't* suggest putting them in any classroom. I *don't* propose to "spoil their precious childhood" by drills or testing. I just propose we move more consciously and deliberately to enlarge their opportunities for subconscious absorption of sound/sight/meaning correlations.

The Montclair Reading Project

The town of Montclair, New Jersey has a voluntary project going whose goal is to have at least half of the town's children reading on their own by the time they enter first grade in the fall of 1976. The program was started in the spring of 1973. Within about four months, close to 400 mothers of two year olds had been contacted, and more than half of them had obtained the special materials provided and were swapping progress reports through a project newsletter.

The schools are not directly involved, but they will, of course, be judge and jury of the results when these children enter first grade. The superintendent of schools has said that the schools *must* know how to take full advantage of the results if the project succeeds.

There have, of course, been doubters. One man, a candidate for a degree in education at Montclair State College, wrote a letter to the *Montclair Times* charging that early reading might overstrain immature eyes. But a local eye doctor, responding, saw no danger whatever for the child with normal vision, and an actual advantage to the child with subnormal vision, insofar as this might be noticed earlier and thus get attention sooner.

Even if a dedicated group of volunteers can get half of Montclair's children reading before they enter kindergarten or first grade, the big question is, What good will it do? The schools would, presumably, still have to deal with the other children—and for all that can be argued to the contrary, it is certainly possible that the first grade of 1976 (estimated at 500 children) will contain the same 20 percent of dyslexics as would have been there without the program.

Suppose, however, the Montclair program succeeds. What have we learned? Well, if we get five out of ten of Montclair's two year olds reading before they get to school, this certainly will lay to rest the theory that only one child in ten is up to early reading.

Perhaps we shall also have demonstrated that what is called "reading readiness" is no more and no less than evidence that the child has started reading, i.e., that "reading readiness' comes *with reading*.

What I hope we shall also demonstrate is that none of the early readers develop reading problems, and that only the usual percentage of the other children do so. Should this be the case, it would seem safe to argue that early reading might well be *the* way to prevent late reading.

Suppose Montclair gets half its preschoolers reading through a volunteer effort of the mothers. What next? Won't this just create new problems, such as a gap between the readers (privileged) and the nonreaders (underprivileged)?

Preschoolers Are Ready to Read!

First, let it be said that other mothers than just those in Montclair are encouraging their preschoolers to read early, thus putting them in line for the consequent advantages over their fellows noted by Professor Durkin. Hundreds of thousands of mothers have purchased Doman's book *How to Teach Your Baby to Read*, and over 50,000 wrote in to the *Ladies Home Journal* for a special Early Reading Kit. (This was back in 1965. When these mothers were queried eight years later as to how they made out, half of those responding had successfully taught their preschoolers to read and were glad they had, about 40 percent had been talked out of trying it, and about ten percent had tried and failed or had not followed through.)

If early readers start ahead and stay ahead, as Professor Durkin tells us, the answer to any ensuing inequality of opportunity may not lie in discouraging early reading, but in extending it to all children either by means that don't depend entirely on Mother, or by means closer to those so demonstrably effective in teaching the child to talk.

Preschoolers *are* learning to read despite our assumption that they are not ready for it. If you doubt it, test any two year old on words like *stop, ice cream, milk,* and, of course, his own name. Some will continue on their own toward reading at a far more sophisticated level.

After one skeptical mother had surprised and convinced herself by this simple test that her boy of two and a half was actually reading, she began to realize that this had been going on for some time, quite without her notice. For example, she remembered how he had puzzled her by asking at the ice cream parlor, "Mother, what's Italian ice?" No one had spoken those words. She now realized that he had simply been reading them from a sign.

In another home, a three year old asked to have Campbell's chicken noodle soup for lunch, then brought the correct can from the shelf. Considering that there is *no way* to tell one kind of Campbell's soup from another except by words printed on the label and considering that the pantry shelf had contained other kinds, this mother was stunned to realize that her daughter was probably able to read the words *chicken noodle,* which proved to be true.

This kind of evidence that very young children are reading is sometimes dismissed on the ground that what they are doing isn't really reading, it is just pattern recognition. The premise seems to be that you aren't really reading it unless and until you can spell it. Isn't this pretty much like contending that no child is really speaking unless and until he can dissect his sentences into subject, verb, and predicate? The fact is, the only language we ever learn really fluently is the one we learn to speak long before knowing anything about its "rules" of grammar.

Phonics may be a far more useful tool than grammar (and Rudolf Flesch makes a strong case for giving every first grader a solid grounding in this technique for sounding out unfamiliar words), but first grade phonics does not preclude a *preschool* whole-word approach. In fact, the only weakness in the arguments of the "look-and-say" people may lie in their timing. Perhaps the "look-and-say" (impressionistic) approach is "right" for ages two, three, and four, whereas the phonics (analytical) approach should come along about the time the child is beginning to observe on his own that the construction of words seems to have a sometimes predictable logic.

During the teaching of reading in school, we concede, early on, that one must get past the stage of reading letter by letter and read word by word, if not phrase by phrase, but we continue to suppose that we simplify things by starting with the letters. Do we?

In this connection, let me report on some work being done in Japan. There, in the factory day care centers of the Sony Corporation, two year olds are routinely learning to read. Japan, however, has two ways of writing, the scholarly one using the ancient Chinese characters, of which there are thousands, one character to a word, and the "simplified" one in which an unlimited number of words can be built from a limited number of letters, somewhat as in English. It was assumed, of course, that two year olds would best begin with the simplified approach used in elementary and high school. To the great surprise of the investigators, two year olds seemed able to read in the scholarly mode as easily as in the simplified mode. They could tell two Chinese characters apart as easily as two human faces.

Incidentally, in these day care centers, operated under the supervision of the Early Development Association of Japan, two year olds are not only learning to read Japanese, but even learning to speak and read English, to play the violin, to do mathematics, and much more. A book about this work, entitled *Kindergarten Is Too Late*, has been a recent best seller in Japan. It was written by Masaru Ibuka, board chairman of Sony, who became acquainted with the Doman work on early reading when he was seeking help for his own brain-injured child.

The Role of Librarians and Publishers

Well, to keep this close to home, let's consider how public libraries could help. Let's say a mother comes in ready and anxious to surround her preschooler with materials to increase his opportunities to discover meaning/sound/sight correlations. She wants, basically, pictures of familiar things, each with the name underneath in large type.

If you will take a serious look at what you have to offer, seen in this perspective, you will be shocked to realize how little you have to offer.

One possibility is the *Pyramid Pocket Dictionary. No. 1* (75¢ in paperback, Pyramid, 1971). Although the type size is smaller than Doman would recommend and the type is seldom *under* the object described, as I personally feel it should be, at least you find 171 pictures of familiar things, each with its identifying word, and, what's more, the word-picture relationship is usually fairly unequivocal.

Another possibility is Richard Scarry's *Best Word Book Ever* (Golden Pr., 1963), with 1400 objects illustrated. However, once again the type is disappointingly small.

It seemed such a modest request—pictures of familiar things, each with its name beneath it, in large type, but try to find these. You will probably find your self proffering either things that don't meet the specifications at all (like alphabet books or read-aloud books with type *much* smaller than you remembered), or else you might dig up a disposable copy of an old Sears, Roebuck catalog and suggest that mother and child cut it up to make their own words-under-picture book.

I am, however, no little intrigued by the fact that children seem to be learning to read *from TV commercials*. Perhaps I will lay myself open to having my life time ALA membership recinded if I suggest that some of those children who became our very good readers may have gotten their very first meaning/sound/sight correlations from words like Exxon, A&P, Sugar Krispies, and the like. In the last analysis, reading is reading, and I guess I believe that any reading is better than no reading. I have no fear that the child who can read easily and well will spend his entire time reading junk. I have great and well-justified fear that the child who cannot read may have to spend all his school years on junk—the junk in the remedial readers.

We must all be concerned that at present each intensification of the schools' efforts to reach the reluctant reader seems to build reading resistance faster than reading competence. Too often the most conspicuous consequence of trying to "help" the slow reader by giving him extra drill is to make him hate books.

Before I close, let me return to the problem of finding books appropriate for use with two and three year olds who are beginning to read on their own. Libraries have no dearth of good books for Mother to read to them, and no dearth of materials to offer them once they are really reading, but, as mentioned before, practically nothing really suitable for helping them *graduate from listeners to readers.* (This is hardly surprising, inasmuch as we have been assuming they would not make that transition until age six.)

In all our picture books, the type is clearly for *Mother*. In our preschool story hours we read the type and show the pictures, under circumstances where even the readers can seldom read the small print. I hope that publishers will think about this and move to fill the gap. Let's have new editions of transitional books in which the type is handled *as if* it might be of as much interest to the child as the pictures. It will be.

I can hear someone saying, 'But surely we do now have plenty of lovely books in which the type is handled as if it might be of as much interest to the child as the pictures. They are called alphabet books." I would agree up to a point. Some alphabet books contain lovely pictures and large type, but, unhappily, they are by their very nature *phonics* oriented. If, as I am certainly persuaded, it is counterproductive to start telling two and three year olds about the *alphabet* before they have even fully grasped that there is such a thing as *print*, then true alphabet books would be most appropriately prepared for older children, or else divested of their pseudophonics content and offered just as word-and-picture books.

I say their "pseudophonics" content because some of them are very strange indeed if taken seriously. For example, let's say a mother comes in and asks for an alphabet book. Let's assume her child can read his name, he can read the names of everything advertised on TV, he has been watching *Electric Company, and he is beginning to ask about the letters*. Shall we give her perhaps Elizabeth MacKinstry's ABC book? If we do, her child is going to learn that G is for Gnomes!

Imagine the confusion of a child who is just on the verge of one of the greatest discoveries he will ever make, namely that there is a logic to the way words are constructed out of letters. He may not be very sure of himself yet, he may be just testing a hypothesis, he may be thinking that *if* A is for Acorn, and B is for Bee, and I is for Ice cream, then maybe G is for, well, maybe Gee whiz? But no. The book Mama is reading says that G is for Gnome, and that other ABC book by Bruno Munari says that K is for Knife or Knothole. Wouldn't you have thought that N would be for Gnome, or Knothole, or Knife? Well, you can just hear the child saying to himself, "Another good theory shot down."

I submit that this is serious. We can say if we like that an alphabet book is not a textbook, was never so intended, and is just a book to enjoy for its rhymes and pictures, and we can say if we like that it would be a shame to inhibit the author and illustrator with a lot of strictures about logic in spelling. But what if the mother is saying to us in effect, "Please give me an alphabet book *because my child is getting interested in the sounds of the letters*"?

At this point many of us, taking our cue from the reading experts, have 9just begged off, saying, "How old is he? Oh, well, he isn't ready for reading yet. Time enough for that when he gets to school. But if you want an alphabet book, we have some lovely ones." But have we? We have the Petersham's ABC, but in it K is for Knickerbocker, and T hasn't the T sound at all, it is for Thanksgiving. In Munari again, E is for Eye—and isn't *that* confusing!

Suppose Munari's editor had said, "Please, not E for Eye, perhaps E for Ear, or Eagle, or Evening?" Would such a stricture have reduced a work of the imagination to a pale imitation of a textbook?

Librarians and others working with preschoolers have thus far seldom been urged to encourage early reading and have often been advised to "leave it to the schools." The schools, however, have been failing that assignment. The schools' only chance for success may lie in new kinds of help from those people currently working in, or preparing to specialize in, the preschool area.

Reading with an Infant

Linda Leonard Lamme

A recent survey undertaken by two graduate students at the University of Florida revealed that very few parents of kindergartners had read to their children when they were infants (Browder & Skelton, 1977). Yet a number of writers and researchers have recommended to new parents that they share literature with their infants. Larrick (1975) states, "The time to begin is with the first feeding, pampering, and bathing, when the parent's singing or chanting and gentle conversation begin to set the stage for the infant's participation only a few months later." "It is important to start reading to the preschooler before the child is a year old," declares another source (Willems & Willems, 1975).

Several parents have written books about their families' reading experiences (Becker, 1936; Duff, 1944; Fenner, 1959; Berg, 1976). In each case family members read aloud with infants and included infants in the family's literature experiences. According to Becker, an infant "has not had all of his rights if he has not floated into consciousness to the sound of his mother's voice, singing" (p. 2). In the Duff home, books were pleasant necessities, "along with food, sleep, music and all out-of-doors" (p. 17).

The benefits derived from reading and singing to infants are many. Lind and Hardgrove report that, in the maternity wards of hospitals in Sweden, musicians teach parents of newborns lullabies, which serve an important function in the parent-infant bonding process. "Singing, rocking, and playing with a baby increase the parent's pleasure in that baby . . . causing the parent to observe the baby more closely" (Lind & Hardgrove, 1978, p. 9). Infants enjoy being cuddled and rocked, and it is helpful if they associate reading books with this warm physical encounter.

Infants acquire language at an astounding rate. Lind and Hardgrove found that "The singing of the mother elicits cooing and answering sounds from the infant," even in the first day of life. Irwin (1960) found that older infants (13 to 30 months) who were systematically read to by their parents

SOURCE: *Childhood Education*, April/May, 1980, pp. 285–90. Reprinted by permission of the author and the Association for Childhood Education International, 3615 Wisconsin Avenue, N.W., Washington D.C.

were able to produce more language sounds than a control group at 17 to 30 months. The Harvard Preschool Project (White & Watts, 1973) discovered that by age 2 differences in children's language ability were at least partially attributable to amount of interaction between mothers and children and to amount of time spent in activities designated as highly intellectual (e.g., reading a book). Reading provides variety to the language the baby hears, since adults tend to greatly simplify their language when talking directly to infants.

Reading can become a habitual activity. Infants thrive on routine. If reading becomes part of their regular, daily routine, books become an accepted part of their world and reading time is anticipated with joy. A foundation has been laid for routine reading during the toddler years, when the child makes more of his/her own decisions about what to do.

Many basic skills necessary for reading can be learned before the age of 1. Through much interaction with books, infants become aware that pictures have meaning. They begin to use their eyes to discriminate between different objects in a picture, as someone points them out and names them. They develop listening skills and the ability to differentiate among sounds. They also learn to turn the book's pages and become aware that books have a right side up. Each of these skills will help establish a solid foundation upon which future learning can build.

Types of Books for Infants

Infants enjoy a variety of literature. With a newborn, the sound of language becomes the most important element in book reading. Since the newborn is not focusing on pages, parents and other caregivers can read aloud some of their own adult literature to the newborn. Let the infant hear Mommy's and Daddy's voices as they read something they genuinely enjoy. The warmth of being held and the melodic sound of the voice may put the infant to sleep. Many infants have enjoyed such adult literature as the Bible, books of poetry, novels, the newspaper, and home and sports magazines.

Literature for infants can be classified into five categories: musical literature, point-and-say books, touch and smell books, cardboard books, cloth and plastic books, and early stories (Lamme, 1980).

Musical Literature

The earliest literature for infants is the musical literature of lullabies, songs and nursery rhymes. Parents and other caregivers can sing, chant or read as they rock the newborn child. Many nursery rhymes and songs are perfect accompaniment for daily routines, such as waking up, bathing and getting dressed; e.g., "Good Morning to You," "Hickory Dickory Dock," "Rub-a-Dub-Dub," "Row, Row, Row Your Boat" and "Diddle, Diddle Dumpling." A good Mother Goose collection is an invaluable source for this sort of natural chanting and singing. Although this singing and chanting is not reading, it won't be long before the baby can be propped up on a lap with a book as these familiar rhymes and songs are read. What fun parents will have when they see that their baby actually recognizes these rhymes!

Many Mother Goose and song collections are available. Parents and other caregivers will want a comprehensive collection for their own reference. Some include music and motions for finger plays as well. A suggested list follows:

Glazer, T. *Eye Winker, Tom Tinker, Chin Chopper: A Collection of Musical Finger Plays*. Doubleday, 1972.

Opie, Iona & Peter. *The Oxford Dictionary of Nursery Rhymes*. Oxford University Press, 1951.

Petersham, M. & M. *The Rooster Crows*. Macmillan, 1945.

Porter, Elizabeth. *Baby's Song Book*. Crowell, 1972.

Rosetti, C. *Sing Song: A Nursery Rhyme Book*. Macmillan, 1968.

Collections that infants enjoy when they can see pictures include:

Battaglia, Aurelius, *Mother Goose*. Random House Picturebook, 1973.

Fujikawa, G. *Mother Goose*. Grosset & Dunlap, 1975.

Rojankovsky, F. *The Tall Book of Mother Goose*. Harper & Row, 1942.

Tudor, T. *Mother Goose*. Henry Z. Walck, 1944/1976.

Wright, B. F. *The Real Mother Goose*. Rand McNally, 1978.

Point-and-Say Books

As infants begin focusing on pictures (2-4 months), they respond to books with colorful, clear, realistic, uncluttered illustrations, especially those that match their present and past life experiences: books about animals, toys, family members, pets, foods, cars, trucks, etc. Books with photographic illustrations are especially good.

When "reading" this type of literature to an infant, the adult points to each item in the picture while naming it clearly and then talks about it. "See the ball? That looks like Laurel's ball." After much adult pointing and naming, the infant will learn to point to pictures in response to, "Where's the puppy dog? Can you point to the puppy dog?" Turn pages very slowly for young infants, since page turning distracts them. Several series of "point-and-say" books follow:

Bruna, Dick. *A Story to Tell, The Fish, Miffy at the Zoo, I Can Dress Myself,* and others. Methuen.

First Step Series (Bedtime, Mealtime, Playtime, etc.). Brimax Books, 1973.

Teddy-Board Books (*Baby's First Book, Baby's First Toys,* etc.). Platt & Munk.

The Lady Bird Series (The Ladybird ABC). London: Lady Bird Books, Ltd.

ABC and counting books, as well as word books, are good for "point-and-say" reading.

Broomfield, R. *The Baby Animal ABC*. Puffin Books, 1976.

Cellini, *ABC*. Grosset & Dunlap, 1975.

Curry, N. *An Apple Is Red*. Bowmar, 1977.

Dunn, P. & T. *Things*. Doubleday, 1968.

Matthiesen, T. *ABC—An Alphabet Book*. Platt & Munk, 1968.

Pfloog, J. *Animals on the Farm*. Golden Press, 1977.

Rojankovsky, F. *Animals in the Zoo*. Alfred A. Knopf, 1962.

Scarry, R. *Early Words*. Random House, 1976.

Weisgard, L. *My First Picture Book*. Grosset & Dunlap, 1977.

Brimax Books. *Look at Us*. 1975.

Gyo Fujikawa's A to Z Picture Book. Grosset & Dunlap, 1974.

Touch and Smell Books

Infants use all of their senses to explore their environment. A number of books have capitalized on babies' desires to touch and smell things. Textured pages invite infants to touch, pull, sniff, play peek-a-boo, etc. Some, especially the "Sniffy" books, are more toys than books.

Golden Scratch and Sniff Books.

Golden Press/Western series, including *Pat the Bunny, The Touch Me Book, The Telephone Book, Who Lives Here? The Look, Look Book, What's in Mommy's Pocketbook?* and several other titles.

Golden Press, Richard Scarry Books, including *Egg in the Hole Book* and *Is This the House of Mistress Mouse?*

Random House, Sniffy Books, including *Papa's Pizza, Supermarket Magic, The Sniff and Tell Riddle Book,* and *Lowly Worm Sniffy Book*.

Cardboard Books

Books with sturdy pages are ideal for reading with infants and for leaving in playpens and cribs for infants to look at independently. When an adult is reading, the infant can be encouraged to turn pages. Even wet infant hands reaching out to pictures will not damage cardboard pages. As infants get older, they can be encouraged to handle books more and to play games, such as finding the page with the ________ on it. Cardboard editions make excellent involvement books for infants:

Fujikawa, G. *Surprise, Surprise, Our Best Friends, Sleepytime,* and many others. Grosset & Dunlap.

McNaught, H. *Baby Animals*. Random House.

Pfloog, J. *Kittens*. Random House.

Schlesinger, A. *Baby's Mother Goose*. Grosset & Dunlap, 1975.

Wilde, *Farm Animals*. Grosset & Dunlap, 1975.

Brimax Books. *Look at Us* (photographs). 1975.

Brimax Books. Counting Series—*Ten Little Ponies, One to Ten.*

Golden Sturdy Books—*I Am a Bunny, I Am a Puppy, I Am a Kitten, What Animals Do, I Am a Mouse, Book of Counting*.

Wild Animal Friends. Renewal Products.

Cloth Books and Plastic Books

Cloth books and plastic books that squeak and make other noises are more properly classified as toys. Infants have difficulty handling cloth books and may be tempted to treat paper books in the same rough way cloth books may be handled. Generally cloth books are not as useful for infants as sturdier books. If they are used at all, cloth books are best left in playpen or crib for baby to play with as a toy. Several publishers have widely available cloth book series. Only one, *My Zoo Book,* by Platt & Munk, contains realistic photographic illustrations.

Dean's Rag Book Co. *Dean's Washable Cloth Books*.

Golden Press. *Baby's First Golden Cloth Books*.

Grosset & Dunlap. *Puppet Cloth Books*.

Platt & Munk. *Perma-Life Books*.

Rand McNally. *Cloth Books*.

Early Stories

As infants become able to sit up in a lap and look at pictures, simple stories can be read to them. Stories can be read to infants if they have a central character who appears on each page, if they have few words per page, and if they are repetitious.

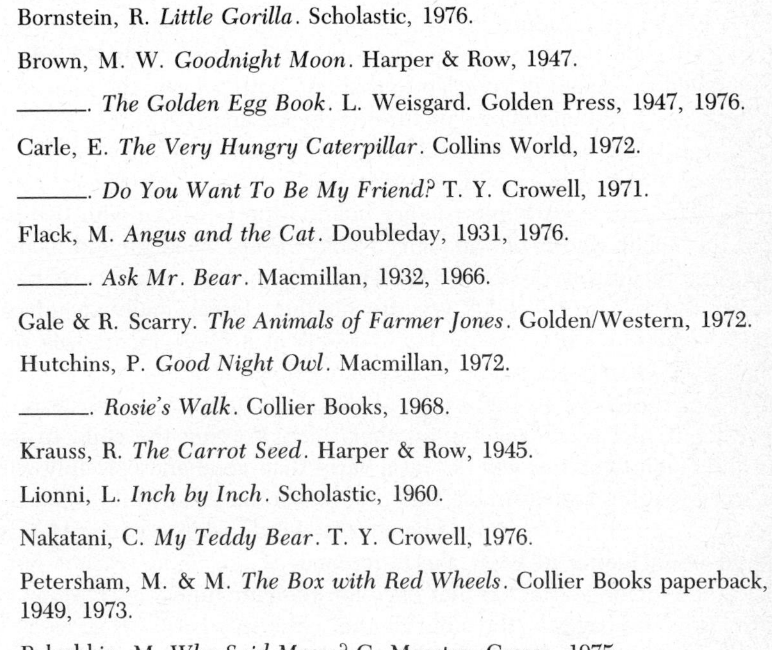

Bornstein, R. *Little Gorilla*. Scholastic, 1976.

Brown, M. W. *Goodnight Moon*. Harper & Row, 1947.

______. *The Golden Egg Book*. L. Weisgard. Golden Press, 1947, 1976.

Carle, E. *The Very Hungry Caterpillar*. Collins World, 1972.

______. *Do You Want To Be My Friend?* T. Y. Crowell, 1971.

Flack, M. *Angus and the Cat*. Doubleday, 1931, 1976.

______. *Ask Mr. Bear*. Macmillan, 1932, 1966.

Gale & R. Scarry. *The Animals of Farmer Jones*. Golden/Western, 1972.

Hutchins, P. *Good Night Owl*. Macmillan, 1972.

______. *Rosie's Walk*. Collier Books, 1968.

Krauss, R. *The Carrot Seed*. Harper & Row, 1945.

Lionni, L. *Inch by Inch*. Scholastic, 1960.

Nakatani, C. *My Teddy Bear*. T. Y. Crowell, 1976.

Petersham, M. & M. *The Box with Red Wheels*. Collier Books paperback, 1949, 1973.

Polushkin, M. *Who Said Meow?* G. Maestro, Crown, 1975.

Guidelines for Reading with an Infant

It has been mentioned previously that each type of book is read differently. There are a number of overall guidelines that may help an adult develop successful infant book reading sessions. Though no research has been conducted on the impact of story reading per se on infants less than 1 year old, research with older children and their parents has logical implications for infants. Research on parent-infant interaction can be carried over into the book reading situation as a specific application of a more general finding. Further, theoretical positions support recommendations to parents and other caregivers:

☐ Read when you are in a positive mood, when you feel like relaxing and would enjoy the experience.

☐ Select something *you* would like to read.

☐ Read when the infant is likely to want to sit still for a story. Just after a nap and before bed seem to be good times, for the child is just winding up to or winding down from a more active period; but the best times vary for each child. Read at some routine times and at some special times.

☐ Settle the child down for reading, perhaps by turning on the light and saying "light." The child will begin looking at the light and getting settled in and ready for the reading.

☐ Talk about what you are going to read before you begin (Flood, 1977).

☐ Hold the infant in your lap so that you both can see the pictures; that is, if the infant is old enough for pictures (Schickedanz, 1978). For a newborn, you can read while feeding the child or just rocking the child. You can make a simple bookrack from hooks screwed into a 12″ × 18″ piece of 1/4″ plywood, to hold your book while you are holding the newborn with two hands. But for the infant who is old enough to hold his/her head up and focus on a picture, lap reading is the most fun. The baby sits in your lap facing away from you and toward the book you are holding. Occasionally an infant will like to lie face down across your lap and look at a book on the sofa next to your lap (the infant is above the book looking down at it).

☐ Be responsive to the infant. If the child fusses or looks away, drop the book and go back to reading another time. Forcing the child to look at books and listen to stories will do more harm than good and certainly will not make story-reading a pleasurable time for you both. If the child is starting to get restless, speed up the story, change the words, skip a page. At this age the child is not going to know the difference. If the child reaches out, encourage the reaching—stay on that page for a longer time.

☐ Turn the pages so the child can help (Schickedanz, 1978). Keep all of the pages except the next one to be turned in your right hand. Then when the child starts to turn the pages, only one will turn and the child can turn pages as you read.

☐ Point to things in pictures as you are reading. When the infant starts reaching out, he/she will naturally point, too. You can then encourage pointing by responding to the items being pointed out. Naming things is likely to enhance the child's vocabulary (Nelson, 1973).

☐ Positively reinforce all attempts by the infant to point to things, to verbalize, to turn pages, etc. (Flood, 1977).

☐ Go over the book a second time—not reading it but just stopping at favorite pictures and talking with the infant after you are finished with the story.

☐ Use your voice effectively and make your reading interesting (White & Watts, 1973). Basically use a quiet, hushed, soft voice that will calm the infant and sound pleasing to the ear. Occasionally be expressive and dramatic; change your tone of voice for different characters; use sound effects that will encourage the child's participation, but not provoke fear. Read as though you are having fun and enjoying it; chances are you will be. Put variety into your voice, but remember you don't need to shout—the infant's ear is right next to your mouth.

☐ When the child is teething and everything goes into the mouth, you might try giving him/her something to chew on while you are reading. This avoids destroying books by using the pages as teething rings. On the other hand, don't jerk the book away from the infant as he/she is chewing on it. Replace the page with something that is chewable and gently remove the pages from the infant's mouth.

☐ When the child is grabbing (and tearing paper), give the child something soft to hold while story-reading, such as a stuffed animal. He/she will more likely pull at the stuffed animal than the book.

☐ In your story-reading, stay with a few familiar books that you repeat over and over again, while at the same time introducing new stories (Schickedanz, 1978). Read several books at one sitting if the infant is enjoying the experience. Start with something old, read something new, then end with something familiar.

☐ End gently—talk about the book and then gradually move on to something new (Flood, 1977). Store the books on a shelf where the child can see them and not with the other toys. Books are not toys and should not be handled like toys.

☐ Last, make reading a comfortable experience. Be sure the baby is warm enough, but not too warm. Sitting on your lap, he/she will be warmer than when playing independently. Be sure you are comfortable. Some families have a story reading chair near a lamp. The child gets used to reading a story when sitting in that special chair.

There are several things you should *not* do:

☐ Don't read when *you* don't feel like it.

☐ Don't read a story you don't enjoy.

☐ Don't let the child tear the pages of books. Keep books out of the infant's reach without supervision.

☐ Don't put books in the playpen where they are likely to be kicked, torn and chewed.

Conclusion

Reading with an infant is an area that has been largely ignored in both research literature and the practical publications for parents. If, as White concluded (1975, p. 4), "To begin to look at a child's educational development when he is 2 years of age is already much too late," more attention needs to be focused on parent-infant interaction.

There are hints from research conducted with older children that adults can enhance children's development by reading books with them and that the way in which they read may be important to children's acquisition of reading and language skills and enjoyment of literature. Studies of infants consistently show that the amount and variety of parent-infant interaction are related to children's language acquisition. Yet the part that book-reading might contribute to this interaction has not been rigorously investigated. The frequency of book-reading, the quality of the reading and the variety of literature read with an infant appear to influence the child's acquisition of language and reading skills.

Clearly, the origins of reading begin in the infant years. Vigorous scrutiny of these origins is needed to help caregivers fulfill their educational role with more certainty.

References

Becker, May L. *First Adventures in Reading: Introducing Children to Books*. New York: F. A. Stokes, 1936.

Berg, L. *Reading and Loving*. London: Heineman, 1976.

Browder, Jill, & Helen Skelton. "A Survey of the Home Reading Experiences of Kindergarten Children," unpublished manuscript, University of Florida, 1977.

Duff, Annis. *"Bequest of Wings": A Family's Pleasure with Books*. New York: Viking, 19–41.

Fenner, Phyllis. *Something Shared: Children and Books*. New York: John Day, 1959.

Flood, James. "Parental Styles in Reading Episodes with Young Children." *The Reading Teacher 35 (May 1977):864–67.*

Irwin, Orvis C. "Infant Speech: Effect of Systematic Reading of Stories." Journal of Speech and Hearing Research 3 (June 1960): 187–90.

Lamme, Linda L. et al. *Raising Readers*. New York: Walker & Co., 1980

Latrick, Nancy. "Home Influences on Early Reading." *Today's Education* 64 (Nov.–Dec., 1975): 77–79.

Lind, John, and Carol Hardgrove. "Lullabies." *Children Today* 7 (July–Aug. 1978): 7–16 and 36.

Nelson, Katherine. "Structure and Strategy in Learning to Talk." *Monographs of the Society for Research in Child Development*. Vol. 38 (1973). (1–2 Serial No. 149).

Schickedanz, Judith A. "Please Read That Story Again." Exploring Relationships Between Story Reading and Learning to Read." *Young Children* 33 (July 1978): 48–55.

White, B. L. *The First Three Years of Life*. Englewood Cliffs, NJ: Prentice-Hall, 1975.

White, B. L. and J. C. Watts. *Experience and Environment: Major Influences in the Development of the Young Child. Vol. 1*. Englewood Cliffs, NJ.: Prentice-Hall, 1973.

Willems, Arnold L., and Wanda I. Willems. "Please Read Me a Book!" *Language Arts* 52 (Sept. 1975): 831–35.

The Young Child and You—Learning Together

Alice S. Honig

What can adults learn from working with children, and what can children learn from interacting with adults? The special relationship of teacher, caregiver, or parent with a young child helps the adult develop as much as it helps the child grow. Adults and children benefit from seeing the world and themselves from the other's perspective.

What Adults Learn

How Children Think

We learn about how children think from children, particularly if we look and listen with open eyes and ears. How does the child perceive and understand the world? As Piaget has shown, young children have contradictory views of how the physical world works.

Today Robbie is sure that his toy will sink if dropped in a pail of water. Tomorrow he may confidently guess that the same toy will float. Amanda may judge that you and she have the same amount of orange juice if both of your tall glasses are full. As you carefully pour your juice into several shorter, skinnier glasses, the child may decide that you have more to drink than she does.

Young children can usually handle a change in one perceptual aspect of a situation, but they may be confused as they try to judge and balance a variety of factors (such as height and width) which need to be considered simultaneously. Think of the four-year-old eating at the kitchen table. His mother rushes in too late to stop a pot of food from burning on the stove. "Why didn't you call me?" she asks in exasperation. "But Mommy, you told me not to say another word until I finished everything on my plate!" protests

SOURCE: Reprinted by permission from *Young Children* 35 (May 1980): 2–10.

the child. It is hard for the young child to hold two concepts in mind simultaneously and evaluate the importance of each.

Children spend years actively exploring materials to learn about the properties of substances. For example, children gradually realize the total mass or weight of solids and liquids does not change despite changes in container shape or distribution of materials. Kamii and DeVries (1978) and Kamii and Lee-Katz (1979) have provided a variety of planned science experiences that can help young children understand levers or the properties of round versus square-sided objects.

An observant adult watching a child's behavior during many similar well-planned experiences can perceptively find out *how* a child thinks and reasons. Drisana pours a coffee pot full of water into a small cup. She watches intently as the water overflows and spills all over her hand. Mischief—or discovery of the relationship between container size and liquid quantity?

After Leticia has carried her load of large building blocks to the far end of the room, she may firmly announce that the blocks are much heavier in this corner than they were at the other end of the room. Young children often confuse their subjective internal feelings with the actual physical characteristics of toys or materials. Toys, just as groceries, feel heavier after they have been carried around for a while.

Adults can begin to learn *how* a young child thinks and reasons by *watching* each child's response to physical changes, such as breaking up a ball of clay into many pieces and judging the amount of clay present when compared to an unbroken ball. Most adults grin when a small child prefers to have a large copper penny rather than a skinny tiny dime. "More" may mean "bigger" at this stage rather than "more monetary value."

Five-year-old Erik, helping his mother dust and polish furniture, carefully poured a small amount of polish out on his dusting cloth. When mother turned around, the furniture polish bottle was lying on its side, and a puddle oozed onto the sofa. That viscous substances need to be stored upright or they will flow out is a lession in the physics of liquids.

Adults need to learn about children's concepts of number, space, quantity, time, and length, in addition to being aware of their knowledge of physical properties. Jovan easily counts by rote from 1 to 10 (1 2 3 4 5 6 7 8 9 10—maybe even " 'leven "). Yet if Jovan counts the number of bottles on his toy milk truck (which has five bottles), he may confidently start out "1,2,3,4,5" and continue on "6,7,8,9,10," counting some bottles more than once. The idea that the concept of number relates to the final count of single objects, each counted once, is difficult for young children to understand.

Have you ever watched the intense surprise on a child's face when a teacher counts snap-apart beads laid out first in a straight line and then in a circle? Even if the adult helps the child count beads in each position, the child may still refuse to believe that the circle and the straight line have the same quantity of beads. The child reasons that a straight line looks much longer, and therefore, should have more beads.

Children's sense of time also differs from adults'. After his parents have promised a holiday family visit, Kenny decisively and proudly announces, "I'm visiting my Grandpa tomorrow." Several months of waiting time, combined with the child's wishes, become "tomorrow."

Children's thoughts are often influenced by how things seem to them. Treating a young child to a Magic Show may disappoint a caregiver who expects her to be amazed. There may be nothing unreasonable to a four-year-old who delightedly watches a magician pull a rabbit out of a hat.

A strong relationship exists between a child's level of thinking and the ability to decide "moral" issues. Adults who are concerned about the moral development of small children can learn by child watching that a child's behavior, seemingly identical to that of an adult, may have a different meaning compared to the same action carried out by an adult. A teacher was driving a mother and toddler to a play group program. The young toddler reached out to touch the teacher's pocketbook lying on the car seat. The purse was invitingly stuffed with papers, keys and other mysterious shapes. As the baby slid her hand into the alluring "toy," the mother exclaimed sharply, "You little thief! What are you trying to steal now?" The toddler cried as the mother snatched baby's hand away from that interesting, leathery-slithery feeling bag bulging with treasures to handle, squeeze, and play with.

Adults need to learn to look at a child's behavior from the child's viewpoint. Otherwise, a child's curious explorations may be labeled deliberately as "naughty" by an adult who thinks about the meaning of the act from an adult perspective. Children can be helped to behave in appropriately polite ways without an adult's shaming them or expecting them to reason at an advanced level.

Teachers need to make sure that children understand their expectations for a class activity. Otherwise, teachers might inappropriately label a child as "disobedient." One nursery school teacher gave out collage materials to each child: a large sheet of construction paper; an assortment of feathers, buttons, glitter, and paper scraps; plus paste and a pair of scissors. Joey picked up his pair of scissors and vigorously and cheerfully cut up the large sheet of construction paper. "Oh no, Joey,' his teacher called out, "You're spoiling the collage paper." Joey looked up at her in bewildered surprise. Explanations are needed to help children understand the adult expectations for games and activities. We must be sensitive to the fact that children's initiative and creativity may be more important than our limited expectations and demonstrations.

Diane was happily coloring the inside of a paper plate. "No, Diane, color the outside," called out the teacher. Diane continued to adorn the center of her plate. "Diane, you'll need the inside to paste a picture on later," remarked a classroom aide passing by. The child tuned out the adult. "Oh, honey, you're supposed to color only the outside," reminded another teacher five minutes later. Diane looked up, thoroughly annoyed with the pestering adults. She turned her paper plate entirely over to the back side and retorted, "Outside! Why should I color the outside!" Be sure a child's understandings and values are considered before chastising.

How Children Feel

Children's emotional patterns, as well as their perceptions of the world, differ from adults. The young baby may be uncertain when Daddy or Mommy goes out that the parent will ever return again. Emotionally trivial events for adults may seem distressfully overwhelming to a young child who is just beginning to understand the social world as well as the physical world. Three-year-old Daryl and his mother were ready for a trip. Their plane was delayed, and hours dragged on as maintenance crews replaced some equipment. Suddenly Daryl sobbed aloud, "I'll never see Daddy again!" He felt genuinely terrified. Exaggeration? Not to a three-year-old who believed in this terrible possibility.

Five-year-old Daren cried as his father took a large pair of pruning shears and clipped the hedges hanging out over the driveway. A parent may be amused at such "babyishness," but to a child, the bushes were alive and should not be cut and hurt. Adults need to understand the stages of emotional development of children and their relationship to intellectual understanding.

Social understandings develop as young children interact with adults and other children. We need to notice how children play together. How do they solve their arguments? Does every quarrel end in fighting or a whining retreat to an adult? Does a child seem to need or demand adult attention quite frequently? Many emotional tensions of children are evidenced in actions such as sudden toy throwing, trouble falling asleep at naptime, hair or finger chewing, teeth grinding, irritability, and frustration at mild provocations such as another child's brushing past or having to wait for a turn at the new tricycle.

Do we learn when tiredness triggers troubles? Do we recognize when a child needs to wind down peacefully as a quiet time approaches? Transition times can be particularly difficult for toddlers in day care.

It is not enough for us to become perceptive observers of signals of social or emotional distress. We also need to develop strategies for helping children cope with their problems. A variety of skills may be needed. For example, an adult may calm a tense child by rubbing her back and crooning softly. Sometimes eye contact, a firm voice, and a light touch on impulsive hands will help a child to wait before grabbing a toy. Many adults are adept at forestalling problems before they begin. Mr. Richmond noticed that Arby had a short supply of patience. When an activity was planned which required each of four children to take a turn feeling under a cloth to find a toy that matched one of those items visible on the table, Mr. Richmond made sure that Arby was not the last child in the group to get a turn.

Adults can use many good discipline techniques (Hipple 1978) to help children who have emotional difficulties. Adults who resort to "Stop being a crybaby" or "Don't be so rough with Maria" are using techniques about as efficacious as snake oil remedy for ailments! A good YOU message (Gordon 1974) can help a child become able to express feelings and needs and helps reduce anger and tensions. "It looks like you are having troubles." "You seem to be really struggling with that puzzle." "It looks like you are feeling very mad right now." YOU statements can help children become aware of their feelings instead of just acting out.

Jason pouted and glared. He had just walked over to his favorite teacher to ask her to read a story to him. She was busy tying one child's shoelace and getting ready to toilet another child. Ms. Perez looked quietly at Jason. "Jason, are you feeling angry at me?" she asked gently. "Were you coming over to have a story time—and here I am, busy helping Lisa and Jackie?" Jason's eyes widened. How could his teacher understand all that? He stood stiffly and silently. "Jason, I promise you that I will come back and read with you right after I finish helping these children." She smiled at him. Jason's shoulder relaxed. Some of the stormy look cleared from his face. Adult promises, made perceptively and honestly, help ease emotional upsets for some children. Adult modeling of patience, consideration, tolerance, and generosity assists children in the long process of learning prosocial skills that will help them get along more easily with others.

We need to listen to and observe ourselves as we interact with young children. How many times do our voices get edgy or express our irritation? Would I want to hear my own voice tones if I were the child? Many young children have learned that if teachers or parents raise their voices three more times, then the children will really have to obey. Children learn from experience that an adult doesn't mean the prohibition until the adult voice takes on a certain edge or lowers to a special warning tone. We need to listen to ourselves as well as children to help them develop emotionally.

How can we help children learn more peaceful ways of playing and learn to share, empathize, and cooperate with each other? Caldwell (1977) has suggested that teachers need to use clear rules to help minimize crowd frictions. When children crowd up in a school corridor for a drink or when children are playing exuberantly outdoors, vigorous jostling can turn suddenly into aggression. Helping children find solutions to their interpersonal quarrels is a challenge. If both children want to carry a bucket of water to the wading pool outside at the same time, can they both find a way to resolve that conflict to the satisfaction of each? Sometimes an adult finds it hard to deal with aggravating situations between children. It seems easier to scold or disapprove or order a ready-made solution for the difficulties than to help children find their own solution.

Shure and Spivack (1978) have developed a program for parents and teachers to promote the use of problem-solving strategies in child conflict situations. They suggest four important aspects in helping young children learn to consider ways of solving their own conflicts in a play situation with peers:

a. Help a child *state the problem.*
b. Help children *become aware of their own and of other's feelings.*
c. Help a child *figure out the consequences* of her or his actions. (If Jack hits Joan to make her give him the red truck, then she is well likely to hit him back and hold on tight to the toy.)
d. Help children *think of alternative solutions* which they can accept in order to solve their difficulties.

Space, Materials, and Timing Promote Development

Planning is important in child care. Have you ever watched the chaos that can occur if nine children are permitted to play at a rectangular water table? In contrast, have you noted how peacefully and with what absorbed concentration four children can participate at each side of that same water table? If enough attractive activities are set out for children when they arrive at a child care facility, they will be able to make choices and busy themselves with a variety of materials.

Rules are important, although they need to be few and clear. Keeping promises to children and restating rules firmly and quietly often increases the children's sense of comfort about the child care environment. Intellectually, rules help a child focus on relevant details. Caregivers who can be relied on to keep rules and promises reinforce a child's faith and trust in adults. Tina and Lonnie were seated at a small table with a great hunk of red playdough available for both. Assorted cookie cutters and props were also available. Little by little the playdough to be drawn closer and closer toward Lonnie's end of the table. Tina pulled at the mass. Lonnie ignored her glares. She sang out loudly "Mrs. Kay, Lonnie's not *sharing*!" Mrs. Kay walked over to the table and quietly restated the sharing rule to both children. She explained briefly why the hunk of playdough needed to sit in the middle of the small work table. Both children continued creating playdough shapes together.

Children need time to make choices and change from one activity to another. Adults need to think carefully about how activities are sequenced. Are there enough alternations of quiet times with more active times? Do children get an opportunity to simmer down after vigorous outdoor play before being expected to come back inside and sit quietly for circle story time? Some teachers and parents use signals, such as a special chant or song or the dimming of lights, to indicate when children need to start getting ready to change activities.

Good room arrangements can facilitate good play experiences (Honig 1979) and vice versa. In one center, teachers strongly disapproved of children inundating their clay with water and then smearing the mushy clay. Yet the clay table was temptingly positioned adjacent to the sink. The five-year-olds at the clay table waited for the teacher to turn his back before they poured even more water onto their squishy clay wads. We can improve the quality of children's learning and living experiences as we increase environmental planning for young children.

How Children Develop Physically

Many children feel joyous and free using their limbs vigorously to run, jump, climb, roll, tumble, slither, skip, and hop. Others need adult encouragement to learn to climb on a jungle gym or to walk on a walkboard suspended a few inches up from the floor. Observation skills are necessary to evaluate each child. Program planning helps facilitate the growth of grace, agility, and facility both in dextrous small muscle activities, in sports and large muscle games, and in movement-to-music experiences (Honig 1979).

We must balance our fears for safety against the need of a child to explore, to test her limits, to try to throw a ball further, to climb higher, to add another block to that precariously balanced block tower. When we arrange for a baby to pick up cereal from a high chair tray or we set up a basketall hoop outdoors, we facilitate children's coordination and motor development. Adult warnings such as "Be careful, you will spill it all over you," often guarantee the occurrence of just such a mishap.

Motor skill building is important for handicapped children as well. A young college graduate, born without arms or legs, writes eloquently of his parents who constantly challenged him to try: "The basic thing my parents did was just to let me experiment and to encourage me to go and be Terry Haffner. I was never smothered or kept away from the action. I got snow inside my special boots and mud and dirt and stones inside my artificial arms" (Haffner 1976, p. 15).

Mears (1978) researched motor play in very young monkeys. She stressed the importance of self-reinforcing, self-motion play in presenting natural opportunities for encouraging and positively reinforcing pleasure in achievement: "Those individuals, both monkey and human, who gain self-confidence in the physical environment have made vital progress toward social role readiness (p. 378)." Learning skills in one area frequently increases confidence and competence in other areas of functioning.

How to Encourage Language Competence

Children naturally talk when they play together. Adults can help children gain power and mastery over their ability to understand others and to communicate their own needs and ideas about the world with these techniques:

Listen actively when children talk.
Give children chances to talk about their experiences.

Respond positively to children's talking.

Use music, chant, rhymes, and rhythms to enhance children's ease and delight in words.

Label experiences: "We are stroking the gerbil's *soft* fur." "Jimmy is brushing his teeth so *carefully*." "We are *almost* ready to bake our muffins." "The ball rolled *under* the table."

Read lots and lovingly and ask relevant questions to find out if the child is understanding what is happening (Blank 1973).

How to Be Better Matchmakers

We are not just Ms. or Mr. X, teaching the four- or five- or two-year-olds. We are Beth's teacher or Jose's teacher. How small are the steps we need to move to help a particular child learn a new skill or idea? Each of our children has special talents, special needs for support and encouragement, a special tempo, an individual response to frustration or overstimulation. The creative genius of a teacher lies in the ability to find ways to interact with each child according to that child's needs, to stretch an attention span, motivate a child to persist at a task, or provide opportunities to experiment with materials actively and autonomously.

What Children Learn

Children are learning about their environment and people in every situation. What do they learn when they are in a good child care center?

I Know What Is Expected Here

Children learn the routines, rules, and rhythms of their days. As they play, they learn about what activities occur regularly and which routines increase their sense of assurance. They notice how adults pace activities. Perhaps they also notice when they feel rushed or comfortable, restless and bored, or involved and energized.

A sense of order helps children develop a logical way of thinking about the world. There are places and spaces for different toys and activities. We wash before meals. When we want to join a jump rope game, we ask, "Can I play too?" We don't yank the rope away from the child holding it. A differentiated, well-arranged environment helps a young child know what activities happen in what spaces. Orderliness does not mean inflexible schedules for special trips and opportunities.

Children learn daily what they *can* do. They can slide, play with shaving cream, feed fish, play house, try new foods. They learn how to use materials. Sand is for sifting and pouring, but not for throwing. Books are for reading, not for tearing up or using as weapons.

Some rules can be made with the help of young children. For example, what are their ideas about what to do if they are mad at a friend? One child in a day care center was stopped by the secretary as she saw him walking determinedly out of the building. He explained to the surprised staff member, "I gotta get out of this place. I am feeling so mad at Tommy."

What happens to the child's expectations and understandings of adults when there are different rules for home and for center? Behaviors such as punching with fists, saying scatological words to others, and using sleeves rather than napkins may be sanctioned in one place but not another. Teachers can explain calmly, "We have our rules here. In your home, there may be another rule. Sometimes we have to learn different ways to be in different places." There should be rapport and congruence between home expectancies and rules and those in the child care setting. Whenever possible, build comfortable bridges so that ways familiar at home, such as the serving of ethnic foods and the use of culturally special songs, will be promoted in both environments.

I Can Choose

Children need to learn to be responsible for their own actions through taking the initiative. A child also needs to feel comfortable making incorrect guesses. Family-style meals allow children to take as many spoonfuls of a food as needed. Children can dish out a second portion without adult help if bowls of food are available at the table.

Adults can give children choices within the boundaries of the rules for the center. "What area do you want to play in *first* this morning?" "Would you like two carrot sticks or four?" Helping children make responsible choices does not mean that an adult abdicates a guidance role. Responsible functioning means that children will learn how to serve and help at mealtimes and how to sort and put away toys in appropriate spaces at cleanup time.

I Am Lovable

Children can feel free to learn and try different activities if they feel loved or cared for by adults. Bronfenbrenner remarked that every child needs "someone to be crazy about him or her (1977)." As adults show their pleasure and pride in the small daily accomplishments of young children, they build a secure trusting foundation for children to want to try to learn. Building a loving relationship is easier if the adult is readily available for cuddling, listening, and sharing when the child feels the need.

I Can Do It

From earliest toddlerhood, children express their need to do things for themselves and by themselves. Children often grow in self-satisfaction as they try to accomplish new developmental tasks. If a caregiver has learned to match needs with abilities, children will have more experience with success than failure as learning progresses. "I can figure out how to fix it." "I can read that book." "I can swim."

Young children are so anxious to prove their competence that sometimes they inaccurately gauge their skill levels. Children will increase in competence as we arrange their learning activities, as we interact with them in growth-enhancing ways, and as we encourage their trying hard at slightly difficult tasks. Carew (1976) described in detail ways in which fathers and mothers encourage and validate the competence of their small children. Teachers can learn much from these observational records.

I Can Use Language to Express Myself

The gift of language is a great power for young children. Language enables children to ask for what they need rather than fight or whine for it. Language also permits sociability between children and between adults and children. Preschool language communication may still be at a level where each child in a dialogue is unaware of the intent of the other, yet the conversation is eminently satisfying to each.

Children also play with language. Sometimes young children use language in picturesque ways used by adult poets. "They highered the price and they smallered the candy bar," exclaimed a child on receiving candy from an airport machine dispenser. Another toddler, whose father was taking her to the pediatrician for a checkup of an oral infection was told that the doctor would have her open her mouth wide. She asked whether the doctor was a dentist. When told no, the child thought awhile and asked, "Is he a doctor *pretending* to be a dentist?" Helping children develop their language skills entails priceless rewards for caregiving adults as well as pleasure and skill for children.

Adults Can Be Trusted

We have all seen older children who distrust adults. There are children in high schools who would never go to a teacher and ask for special tutoring. Other children grow up learning to avoid adults and adult responsibilities in their lives. They do not see adults as caring and cared for resource people.

Children need to learn that adults can be teaching, loving, and helping people. Teachers show children this through daily actions, courtesies, and gestures that do not detract from the child's feelings of competence. Such actions by adults will help children want to grow up like the caring adults around them.

References

Blank, M. *Teaching Learning in the Preschool. A Dialogue Approach*. Columbus, Ohio: Charles E. Merrill, 1973.

Bronfenbrenner, U. "Who Cares for America's Children?" Keynote address presented at the annual conference of the Association for Children's Services, Syracuse, New York, April 4, 1977.

Caldwell, B. M. "Aggression and Hostility in Young Children." *Young Children* 32, no. 2 (January 1977): 5–14.

Carew, J. V.; Chan, I.; and Halfer, C. *Observing Intelligence in Young Children*. Englewood Cliffs, N.J.: Prentice-Hall, 1976.

Gordon, T. *Parent Effectiveness Training*. New York: Wyden, 1974.

Haffner, T. "The Cap and Gown Feeling." *The Exceptional Parent* 6, no. 1 (1976): 13–17.

Hipple, M. L. "Classroom Discipline Problems? Fifteen Humane Solutions." *Childhood Education* 54 (1978): 183–187.

Honig, A. S. "Comparison of Child-Rearing Practices in Japan and in the People's Republic of China: A Personal View." *International Journal of Group Tensions* 8, nos. 1 and 2 (1978): 6–32.

Honig, A. S. "What You Need to Know to Select and Train Your Daycare Staff." *Child Care Quarterly* 8, no. 1 (1979): 19–35.

Kamii, C. and DeVries, R. *Physical Knowledge in Preschool Education*. Englewood Cliffs, N.J.: Prentice-Hall, 1978.

Kamii, C. and Lee-Katz, L. "Physics in Preschool Education: A Piagetian Approach." *Young Children* 34, no. 4 (May 1979): 4–9.

Mears, C. F. "Play and Development of Cosmic Confidence." *Developmental Psychology* 14, no. 4 (1978): 371–378.

Shure, M. B. and Spivack, G. *Problem-Solving Techniques in Childrearing*. San Francisco: Jossey-Bass, 1978.

2

Mother Goose

From the Cradle to the Classroom

Jacqueline L. Chaparro

As a child, remember how the old nursery rhymes provided the music as you skipped down the sidewalk, jumped rope, or played a clapping game? There was something magical about chanting "Rain, rain, go away" on a dreary rainy day, as if one could wish the rain away. I recall singing "London Bridge Is Falling Down" when the lines "Build it up with silver and gold" made it seem as though that magnificent glittering bridge really did crash into the river and was rebuilt with incredible speed. What fun it was to chant "This little pig went to market" after taking off our shoes and socks when getting ready for bed. Counting the little pigs was a nightly ritual in our home that came just before "Now I lay me down to sleep."

Often the images created by the rhymes were private and personal. Few of us knew or cared what Miss Muffet's tuffet or curds and whey were. But the words "sounded" right and were fun to play with. And there was a spider who "sat down beside her" and who increased in size to monstrous proportions. Or image the cow jumping over the moon in "Hey, Diddle, Diddle." Even now, after man's actual landing on that mysterious sphere, the rhyme is powerful and evocative.

Our own recollections of our childhood experiences with nursery rhymes tell us something about their importance for all children. Nursery rhymes and jingles are found in the oral tradition of cultures throughout the world. In our culture the Mother Goose rhymes are the literature of the cradle. They provide us with a link between the generations and, thus, are a significant part of our literary tradition. However, the nursery rhymes are not the sole province of early childhood. Older students who have not heard of the misadventures of "Humpty Dumpty" and "Jack and Jill" or the ingenuity displayed by "Peter, Peter, Pumpkin Eater" and the "Old Woman in the Shoe" in keeping track of their kinfolk are at a disadvantage. The kings, merchants, bakers, queens, little old men and women, mischievous boys and contrary maidens who provide the characters for the nursery rhymes need to be familiar to all students as these characters are alluded to over and over again in adult literature and conversation.

Where to Begin

How does one bring nursery rhymes into the elementary classroom? First, we must reacquaint ourselves with these old friends of our early childhood. Some we remember well because of the memories they conjure up for us. For me the rhyme "London Bridge Is Falling Down" will never be forgotten. Even when I hear or chant it today I am transported back to late December 1940. In those days we little girls were thoroughly immersed in the world of make-believe, complete with royalty, riches, and the absolute nature of good and evil as portrayed on our favorite radio program, "Let's Pretend." I can remember my sixth birthday and the wonderful party my parents planned for me. My best friend and I wore matching frilly pink and white cotton dresses with black velvet sashes which my mother had made especially for the occasion. All my friends came, my parents were together, and I had a brand new baby brother and our country seemed at peace. That afternoon we played "London Bridge Is Falling Down," chanting the rhyme as we acted it out. A short time later our country was at war, my family was separated and "Let's Pretend" left the air. Perhaps you too have experienced as a child nursery rhymes which are so much a part of your whole being that they will always be with you.

Other rhymes may have faded in your memory over the years but will come back to you once you have been reintroduced to them. And, of course, there are some rhymes which many of us did not become acquainted with during our childhood, so that reminiscing with a book of Mother Goose rhymes becomes a necessary, pleasurable and nostalgic task.

Initially, the rhymes are best shared with students without any visual stimuli, either print or pictures. It is primarily the sounds, rhymes, and personal images created by the rhymes that we want to share with our children. I like to think of the nursery rhymes as providing one vehicle for "playing with our language." We can create our interpretations of the sense and nonsense of the rhymes through the images we produce while listening and chanting. This means we need to know many rhymes "by heart" ourselves, and then pass this oral tradition on to our students so that they can play with the rhymes themselves.

Begin with your favorite rhymes. Those you know best and can share with the most enthusiasm and joy. These particular rhymes may not, and indeed, need not be the favorite of your students. Again, our links with our own childhood are very personal and the meaning or events symbolized by the rhymes may not occupy the same place in another's inner world. After reacquainting yourselves and acquainting your students with this rich storehouse of language models what might you do in the classroom to help students expand their language storehouse through experiencing nursery rhymes?

Aural-to-Oral Experiences

As a starter you might plan creative dramatic activities depicting the characters and actions of the rhymes. This is the simplest kind of activity to implement as it is appropriate for all age levels and requires no print materials or props of any kind. You and your students need only to know some nursery rhymes. Now you are all set to have fun with the many dramatic opportunities the nursery rhymes invite.

I have seen both teachers and students have a delightful experience taking parts for "The Three Little Kittens" and putting on an impromptu stage production in the classroom. The following format illustrates how the parts might be assigned. Note, there is a narrator who takes care of setting the stage and describing the action.

Narrator:	The three little kittens have lost their mittens And they began to cry
3 kittens (together):	Oh, mother dear, We greatly fear, Our mittens we have lost.
Mother:	What! Lost your mittens? You naughty kittens Then you shall have no pie.
Narrator:	The three little kittens, they found their mittens And they began to cry
3 kittens (together):	Oh, mother dear See here, See here Our mittens we have found.
Mother:	What, found your mittens. You good little kittens Now you shall have some pie.
3 kittens (together):	Meow, Meow, Meow.
Mother:	Yes, You shall have some pie.

Oh, the pathos created by the woeful kittens and the displeasure exhibited by Mother when she learns the mittens are missing. Take time to contrast the kittens' first and second set of "meows," and the change in Mother's tone of voice after the mittens are found. A simple activity? Yes, but full of meaningful language discoveries including the importance of pitch and juncture in expressing emotion using the same words.

Another nursery rhyme that lends itself well to this kind of oral interpretation is "Simple Simon." Again a narrator is needed to set the stage and describe the action. In this verse two narrators are used, the second one reciting the dialogue markers:

Narrator I:	Simple Simon met a pieman going to the fair.
Narrator II:	Said Simple Simon to the pieman
Simple Simon:	Let me taste your ware.
Narrator II:	Says the pieman to Simple Simon
Pieman:	Show me first your penny
Narrator II:	Says Simple Simon to the pieman
Simple Simon:	Indeed I have not any

A less familiar Mother Goose rhyme that lends itself to dramatization, which you may want to share with your students, is "Six Little Mice."

Narrator:	Six little mice sat down to spin. Pussy passed by and she peeped in.
Pussy:	What are you doing my little men?
Six mice (together):	Weaving coats for gentlemen.
Pussy:	Shall I come in and cut off your threads?
Six mice (together):	No, no, Mistress Pussy, you'd bite off our heads.
Pussy:	Oh, no, I'll not; I'll help you to spin.
Six mice (together):	That may be so, but you don't come it.

What fun you and your class can have with this rhyme. Is Pussy sincere, or trying to trick the mice? Are the mice fearful, or sure of themselves? This rhyme provides opportunities for students to create distinctly different kinds of characterizations while using the same dialogue.

The rhymes above are illustrations of the creative dramatic possibilities in nursery rhymes. "Pussy Cat, Pussy" and "Baa Baa Black Sheep" are additional examples of rhymes appropriate for this activity, which can be a precursor to "Readers Theater," in which the individual parts are read instead of recited from memory.

Other nursery rhymes are better suited for dramatization with the characters pantomiming the action while a student or group of students recite the rhyme. Some examples might include "Little Jack Horner," "Little Miss Muffet," "Peter, Peter, Pumpkin Eater" and all those rhymes that depict action but contain no dialogue.

A third group of rhymes that lend themselves to dramatic possibilities are those that have traditionally been used to accompany games, specific body movements, finger plays, counting, and jumping rope. "Ring Around the Rosie," "London Bridge Is Falling Down," and "The Farmer in the Dell" are still favorites at birthday parties. "Pat-A-Cake, Pat-A-Cake" and "Pease Porridge Hot" can still be heard on the playground when two little children get together to clap the rhyme. "One, Two, Buckle My Shoe" and "1,2,3,4,5, I Caught a Hare Alive" have enjoyed such popularity as counting rhymes in the nursery down through the generations that Bill Martin, Jr. has included both of them in his *Sounds I Remember* reader for young children (1972). His rationale is that these rhymes are familiar to most children in our culture and, therefore, children will experience success in beginning reading by seeing in print that which they already know through their ears. He suggests using these rhymes as a springboard for creating new lines through simple sentence transformations. In "1,2,3,4,5, I Caught a Hare Alive" the children can substitute other animals for the hare. In "One, Two, Buckle My Shoe" both the nouns and verbs can be substituted. "One, two, buckle my shoe" might be rewritten to read: "One, two, tie my shoe" or "one, two, buckle my belt."

Jump rope jingles abound in our culture, the origins of most being obscure. In some instances nursery rhymes have been adapted for jumping rope. Here a jump rope jingle adapted from an old Mother Goose rhyme that you may have missed in your childhood. Try sharing it with your students.

> Intery, mintery, cutery, corn,
> Apple seed and Briar thorn.
> Wire, briar, limberlock,
> Five geese in a flock.
> Site and sing by a spring,
> O-U-T and in again.

All of the above activities are appropriate for young children and require no prior experience with print. The dramatizations in which individual parts are assigned can be equally effective with older students and even adults.

A language extending activity that provides for a personal interpretation of the nursery rhymes is to have your students pretend they are a character or an object included in a nursery rhyme and respond to each of the lines in the rhyme from that character or object's point of view. The students' responses may be dictated or written by the students depending on their ages, backgrounds and abilities. The following dialogues were created by students using "Jack and Jill" as the original content. The reciter is the student(s) chanting the rhyme, one line at a time. The responder is a second student or group of students who are role playing a character or object and who respond to the line recited. In the first example the responder has assumed the role of the pail.

Reciter:	Jack and Jill went up the hill
Responder:	I wish they would walk together. I'm being pulled in two directions.
Reciter:	to fetch a pail of water
Responder:	I hope the water's not too cold today; I had frost on my sides yesterday.
Reciter:	Jack fell down
Responder:	Hey, something's going wrong
Reciter:	And broke his crown
Responder:	Clumsy kid
Reciter:	And Jill came tumbling after
Responder:	Oh, I'm falling . . . Ouch. I rolled over a rock . . .

Another student responded to the same rhyme assuming the role of Jill, creating a very different product.

Reciter:	Jack and Jill went up the hill
Responder:	I don't know why Mother made me come—it's his turn.
Reciter:	to fetch a pail of water
Responder:	And I got the water all by myself yesterday!
Reciter:	Jack fell down
Responder:	Isn't that just like him—the stumble bum
Reciter:	And broke his crown
Responder:	Oh, dear, I'll probably have to do all of his chores for the rest of the week.
Reciter:	And Jill came tumbling after
Responder:	Oh, Oh! Now who'll get the water.

Students of all ages can have fun with "poetic interface" activities with older students creating responses for each other's original rhymes.

Extending into Creative Writing Experiences

All of the activities suggested up to this point have only one basic requirement in the way of materials; you and your students will need to have a rich array of these rhymes stored in your repertoire of language experiences. Extending the language experiences to include other forms of expression through the use of print and media comes after the students have made friends with many of the Mother Goose characters in the oral tradition. Then puppets, the flannelboard, films, videotapes, slides, and the tape recorder may be effectively used in dramatizing the nursery rhymes. In addition, students can illustrate their favorite rhyme and ask classmates to identify the rhyme from their drawing. Older students can write "Who Am I" riddles for the various characters for their friends to guess. Posters, collages, dioramas, and a wide variety of art activities can be incorporated using the nursery rhymes as the theme.

Creative writing experiences might include creating headlines, want ads, and newspaper/television/radio accounts for various rhymes. Can you figure out who these well-known Mother Goose characters are?

Farmer's Kid Found Asleep on the Job
Husband and Wife Solve Mealtime Dilemma
Strong Wind Injures Baby
Local Swain Woos Curly Haired Lass

If you are not certain which rhymes these headlines refer to, in order they are: *Little Boy Blue, Jack Sprat, Rock-A-Bye-Baby,* and *Curly Locks.*

Children can make up their own headlines and ask each other to guess what rhyme is being described.

Lee Bennett Hopkins (1972) has suggested a variety of other classroom activities for using the Mother Goose rhymes with elementary students. He draws attention to the abundance of lost characters and objects described in rhymes. The students can create lost and found ads and share them with one another. A newspaper format can be developed with each student's ad listed in an appropriate category. Categories might include:

Animals
Bo Peep's Sheep

Food
Queen of Hearts Tarts

Belongings
Lucy Locket's Pocket

Newspaper stories can also be written about the travelers encountered in the rhymes or oral and/or written interviews with an array of these traveling characters might be set up as a radio or television program with the classroom. Imagine interviewing the "Fine Lady Upon a White Horse" on her way to Banbury Cross, "The Crooked Man" as he walked his crooked mile, "Pussy Cat" after his return from London where he visited the Queen, or the "King of Spain's Daughter" who traveled afar just to see this little nut tree that bore a silver nutmeg and a golden pear.

Enriching the Reading Program

An interest group in reading can be set up in the upper grades in which students compare the various collections of Mother Goose rhymes and how different illustrators have interpreted the rhymes. Variations in the written forms might also be studied. As these rhymes originated in the oral tradition, there is considerable variation in the written form of many of the rhymes.

For other students, there are numerous opportunities for studying word meanings in the rhymes, and the phenomenon of language evolution over the centuries. Words like *tuffet, dame, knave, squire, counting-house, parlour,* and *crown* either are not in our children's speaking vocabulary today or, as in the case of *crown* and *dame,* have taken on new meanings. An even more challenging activity for older students might be to study the origins of the rhymes themselves. The young child doesn't care that many of the rhymes had politically inspired origins or that they sometimes represented rather grizzly historical events. They simply delight in the lyrical and rhythmical flow of the rhymes and the magic they impart through the interactions of the sounds of the language and the child's imagination. However, older students might find it interesting to delve into the historical significance of some of the rhymes. Both *The Oxford Dictionary of Nursery Rhymes* (1962) and *The Annotated Mother Goose* (1962) are excellent references for this kind of activity.

The comments and suggestions shared here are meant to renew your acquaintance with the Mother Goose rhymes. Take time to reflect upon your childhood encounters with Mother Goose and then see that some of your past joys are passed on to your students.

References

Baring-Gould, William S. and Baring-Gould, Cecil, eds. *The Annotated Mother Goose*. New York: Bramhall House, 1962.

Hopkins, Lee Bennett. *Pass the Poetry Please*. New York: Citation Press, 1972.

Martin, Jr., Bill. *Sounds I Remember, Teachers Edition*. New York: Holt, Rinehart and Winston, Inc., 1972.

Opie, Iona and Opie, Peter, eds. *The Oxford Dictionary of Nursery Rhymes*. Oxford: Clarendon Press, 1962.

Mother Goose's Garnishings

Maurice Sendak

Only Mother Goose, that doughty old wonder bird, could have survived the assiduous attention of generations of champions and detractors, illustrators and anthologists. More than merely survive, she has positively flourished—younger, fresher, and more superbly beautiful than ever: witness the publication of Mother Goose books of every shape and size that has continued for generations, including the dozens now on the market in America. Among the

SOURCE: © *Book Week*, Fall Children's Issue, *Chicago Sun-Times*, October 31, 1965, pp. 5, 38–40. Reprinted with permission.

most popular of this latter group is *The Real Mother Goose,* being issued this fall in a 50th anniversary edition by Rand McNally and bearing on its cover a commemorative gold seal. The name and the seal raise a basic and puzzling question: Is there a *real* Mother Goose? The answers lies in an exploration of the origins of Mother Goose and perhaps some assessment of the art that has illustrated them from their earliest editions.

It is fairly well agreed that the earliest use of the name Mother Goose in the English language dates from a translation of the Perrault fairy tales, *Contes de Ma Mere L'oye,* published in England in 1729. But the man who first took the name and gave it to a collection of traditional verses was John Newbery, who published his *Mother Goose Melodies* in 1791. After that the name was retained only in America; the English usually refer to the works of Mother Goose simply as nursery rhymes, songs, jingles or melodies. So any collection of Mother Goose rhymes confronting the bewildered purchaser is, strictly speaking, just as "real" as the Rand McNally edition, perhaps even more real, depending on the particular selection of rhymes and the perception of the illustrator.

Transmitted almost entirely by word of mouth, Mother Goose rhymes span an immense stretch of time, from the lovely "White Bird Featherless," which appears in Latin in the 10th century, up to "Horsey, Keep Your Tail Up," a popular commercial song of the 1920s. The origin of this potpourri of anonymous rhymes is described by Iona and Peter Opie, authors of the most authoritative collections of Mother Goose ever published, *The Oxford Nursery Rhyme Book* and the comprehensive *Oxford Dictionary of Nursery Rhymes,* from which I have borrowed much of my historical data. The *Dictionary,* a work of remarkable scholarship, is filled with wealth of lore and generously sprinkled with some of the best examples of art illustrating Mother Goose.

The Opies note that the overwhelming majority of nursery rhymes were not originally composed for children, and that many would be *verboten* to children in the original wording. (The only "true" nursery rhymes, those specifically composed *for* children, are the rhyming alphabets, the lullabies and the infant amusements or poems accompanying a game created before 1800). This genesis explains the earthy, ambiguous, double-entendre quality of so many of the verses—that lusty dimension too often missing in modern editions. The boring custom of passing over a witty, rambunctious, sometimes little-known verse ("I had a little husband, No bigger than my thumb," for example) in favor of a saccharine and pallid one such as "Mary Had a Little Lamb," adulterates the rich flavor of Mother Goose and undermines the value of any given collection.

Even before John Newbery officially credited them to Mother Goose, the rhymes had their detractors. Negative criticism began as early as 1641 and has continued every since. William and Ceil Baring-Gould, in the introductory chapter to their informative and lively *Annotated Mother Goose* (Clarkson N. Potter), quote a Mr. Geoffrey Handley Taylor of Manchester,

England, who condemns at least 100 of the rhymes for their unsavory elements. In 1952, Taylor listed a series of—in his estimation—ghastlinesses that occur in the typical collection: 1 case of death by shriveling, 1 case of body snatching, 1 allusion to marriage as a form of death, 9 allusions to poverty and want, and so inanely on. No comment from Mother Goose. That indefatigable lady has been too preoccupied in promulgating her poetry, busily adding to and enlarging her conglomerate collection with snatches of ballads, bits of political satire, snips of plays, folk songs, street cries, proverbs, and all manner of lampooneries.

The poets have repeatedly testified to the greatness of Mother Goose. Walter de la Mare wrote that many of the verses are "tiny masterpieces of word craftsmanship. Her rhymes free the fancy, charm the tongue and ear, delight the inward eye." Robert Graves claims the best of the older ones are nearer to poetry than the greater part of *The Oxford Book of English Verse*. G. K. Chesterton observed that so simple a line as "Over the hills and far away" is one of the most beautiful in all English poetry.

The powerful rhythms of the verses combined with their great strength and resonance account largely for their appeal to the child's inborn musical fancy. But there is more to the rhymes than music. Andrew Lang called them "smooth stones from the brook of time, worn round by constant friction of tongues long silent"—an image that suggests the subtle presence of elusive, mythic, and mysterious elements transcending the nonsense.

This elusive quality of the verses—that something more than meets the eye—partially explains the unique difficulty of illustrating Mother Goose. While it is true that the great children's literature is always underlaid with deeper shades of meanings which the perceptive illustrators must interpret, the Mother Goose rhymes stubbornly offer still further resistance. For a start, they have about them a certain baldness that betrays the unwary artist into banalities; the deceptively simple verse seems to slip just out of reach, leaving the illustrator with egg on his face. Another difficulty is related to that quality of the verses de la Mare described as "delighting the inward eye." Characteristic of the best imaginative writing, they evoke their own images, thus placing the artist in the embarrassing position of having to contend with Mother Goose the illustrator as well as the poet.

To make things more difficult, there is no room here for a mere show of sensibility, as some artists might get away with, for example, when illustrating the poetry of Robert Louis Stevenson or even the fairy tales of Andersen and Grimm. If the true measure of the rhymes isn't taken in the pictures, then the artist has failed Mother Goose. And her revenge is swift, for no other writing I know of so ruthlessly exposes the illustrators' strengths and inadequacies.

So it is with trepidation that the artist must approach this formidable muse. These are basically two approaches: First, the direct, no-nonsense approach that puts the facts of the case into simple, down-to-earth images. Miss Muffet, her tuffet, curds, whey and spider, all clearly delineated so as to erase all possible confusions in the child's mind. This kind of illustrating does not pretend to any profound leaps of the imagination or depths of interpretation. It simply translates the literal truth into literal images. It is respectful, honest, often beautiful and, I imagine, for the literal-minded child, the best possible accompaniment to the rhymes.

Blanche Fisher Wright's illustrations for *The Real Mother Goose* accomplish all this and a bit more. Despite a somewhat heavy-handed, humorless touch, they have great charm and vigor; best of all they manage to achieve that air of coziness and warmth so essential to the baby book. The sentimentalized art-nouveau style (the pictures date from 1916) helps to enhance the snug effect by ringing the pictures round the verses and locking them safely in. If these illustrations do not catch the spirited quality of the verses or perform in an imaginative counterpoint to them, if they obstinately face away from the dark side of the matter and maintain a too sunny disposition, they still have the virtue of simple, honest homeliness. This book is an excellent introduction to the rhymes (there are some 300 included).

For a more perceptive interpretation of Mother Goose one must look elsewhere. Not, I hope, at *The Little Mother Goose*. Jessie Willcox Smith's illustrations, which were done around 1912, are hopelessly alien to the spirit of the rhymes. Pudgy, prissy pictures, some in clotted colors that dissolve into soggy sentiment, make for a volume that sweetens rather than interprets the verses.

In the 1870s Walter Crane and the superb English color printer Edmund Evans (whose pioneer work also made possible many of the Caldecott and Greenaway books) collaborated on *The Baby's Opera*, an illustrated edition of nursery rhymes set to traditional music. Crane was a tireless, ingenious designer.

In Crane's hands a child's picture book became a matter of art. Everything is beautifully balanced in *The Baby's Opera*, from the busybody activities of the tiny drawings decoratively arranged around the music to the cleverly spaced full-page pictures. There are devilish bits of action going on in corners, an abundance of detail and subtle color throughout. But there is a flaw in this little book and it lies, ironically enough, deep within its superstructure of design. It is a breath too designed, thus fatally imprisoning the life within its pages.

Along about 1877 Randolph Caldecott began his illustrations for some of the nursery rhymes, and no artist since has matched his accomplishments. Caldecott breathed life into the picture book. The design of his books, so deceptively simple, allowed him the greatest possible freedom in interpreting the verses. I spoke earlier of two basic approaches to illustrating the rhymes, the first being the more literal, direct approach; the second is the way Caldecott chose. As in a song, where every shade and nuance of the poem is illuminated and given greater meaning by the music, so Caldecott's pictures illuminate the rhymes. This is the *real* Mother Goose—marvelously imagined improvisations that playfully and rhythmically bounce off and around the verses without ever incongruously straying. If any name deserves to be permanently joined with that of Mother Goose, it is Randolph Caldecott. His picture books, published by Frederick Warne, should be among the first volumes given to every child.

Kate Greenaway, born the same month and year as Caldecott, was yet another contender for the honor of illustrating the real Mother Goose. Though probably more popular than Caldecott in her own time and certainly in our own, she can't hold a candle to him. When Caldecott's *Hey, Diddle Diddle* was about to be published, Miss Greenaway had an opportunity to see some of the originals, and in a letter to a friend she wrote: "They are so uncommonly clever. The dish running away with the spoon—you can't think how much he has made of it. I wish I had such a mind." Alas, she didn't and knew it. Her *Mother Goose or Old Nursery Rhymes* is, after Caldecott, an awful letdown. It is the great ancestor of the sentimental Mother Goose books, and it is hard not to blame Kate Greenaway for founding the line. For all its delicacy of design and exquisite color, for all its refinement of taste, there is little of the real Mother Goose in this lovely but antiseptic affair. The rhymes have been flounced out in a wardrobe of quaint Greenaway frocks, and they look stiff and inanimate; Greenaway's surface charm does not mitigate the atmosphere of chilly Victorianism at the heart of her prim interpretation. See, for example, the two disdainful young ladies who seem to rush off in shocked distaste at the amusing verse they supposedly illustrate. All they lack are scented hankies to disguise the bad odor of Goosey, Goosey, Gander.

If Greenaway fails, perhaps it is due most to her error in tangling with Mother Goose, a doomed relationship that glaringly exposed her shortcomings. When Greenaway illustrates Greenaway, as in her perfect, tiny almanacs, she ranks with the best.

A spiritual descendant of Caldecott is L. Leslie Brooke (1862–1940), who illustrated, besides his more famous Johnny Crow books, a number of Mother Goose collections. The best of the lot is *Ring O' Roses*. Brooke's unabashed admiration for Caldecott is obvious in every aspect of this book, from the clever juxtaposition of black-and-white drawings and color pictures to the characteristically Caldecottian manner of animating the verses with a sequence of pictures that both amplify and enrich them. The Brooke illustrations convey a tremendous robustness and are very funny in the real old Mother Goose way. And *Ring O' Roses* is no mere pastiche Caldecott. The pictures are pure Leslie Brooke in flavor, the warm, homely, ample flavor that can only be English.

Brooke's nursery rhyme books are a wonderful swing up and away from the sentimental morass Mother Goose found herself wading in through the first quarter of the 20th century. Though the Blanche Fisher Wright pictures for *The Real Mother Goose* are far superior to most nursery rhyme illustrations of that time, their literalness and sentimentality are typical of the period. Mother Goose had to wait for a later generation to again take up her cause with genuine imagination. In the meanwhile, the rhymes suffered the abuses of oversentimentality, which, with virus-like tenacity, has nearly choked the life out of them. And the malady lingers on. Exponents in our own time are Marguerite de Angeli, Tasha Tudor and Joan Walsh Anglund. Miss de Angeli's *Book of Nursery and Mother Goose Rhymes,* a large, spacious book, chock full of rhymes and cheerfully illustrated, is by far the best of the three. The stifling, sweet atmosphere is at least partially relieved by the artist's quick appreciation of Mother Goose's go power. The pictures move, and thanks to the generously designed space, they have ample room to bounce about. The vision, however, of Mother Goose as baby-cute is a distortion that badly weakens the fiber of the verses.

Tasha Tudor deserves praise for including among the 77 verses in her *Mother Goose* some little known and extremely beautiful rhymes. Unfortunately, her illustrations convey nothing of the magic inherent in the verses. She manages warm, touching bits of observation throughout the book, but they barely survive the oppressive flood of sentimentality. Poorly designed pages and soupy, garish full-color pictures combine to deliver the rhymes a graceless *coup de grace*. Not as graceless, however, as the one accomplished by Joan Walsh Anglund's *In A Pumpkin Shell*. Mother Goose has more than met her match in Miss Anglund, who is famous for larding her works with pious sentimentalities. With the best intentions she decided to stand poor Mother Goose on her head, no easy trick, and the fact of her having achieved this astounding maneuver with far greater success than any other artist places Miss Anglund in a formidable light. One cannot help doubting the authenticity of some of the rhymes selected for this "Mother Goose ABC" (L for love and T for thank, naturally), they are so Anglundian in attitude and the banal illustrations adhere to the spirit of the book. Simply, Miss Anglund has managed the impossible—a saintly Mother Goose.

Philip Reed, Brian Wildsmith and Barbara Cooney have recently illustrated nursery rhyme books, each of them interestingly. Within the limits of its modest conception, Miss Cooney's version of *The Courtship, Merry Marriage and Feast of Cock Robin and Jenny Wren, To Which is Added the Doleful Death of Cock Robin* is a genuine *tour de force*. These animated and charmingly imagined pictures focus to marvelous effect on the minute details of the action. There is an amusingly jaded *joie de vivre* combined with a nice subtlety of discrimination in the characterization of Cock Robin and his seedy crew. Jenny Wren is the perfect portrait of the well-rounded, "getting on" type, who thought she'd never be asked; her simultaneous wedding and widowhood is all the more affecting for her air of I-knew-it-couldn't-be-true. Though artful, prankish and contemporary in mood and manner, these pictures never stray beyond the poetic logic of the verse.

This is not the case with Brian Wildsmith's *Mother Goose*. His full-blown, decorator-color images grossly underestimate the poetry by grossly overshooting the mark; such irreverent treatment of Mother Goose as a mere excuse for noisy posturing is irritating. On most pages the verses are scrunched down at the bottom, denoting only too clearly their unimportance in relation to the pictures. Mother Goose looks positively intimidated as in the rhyme, "Hickety, Pickety, My Black Hen," where she is literally sat upon. This pretentious book is Cinemascope Mother Goose, Mother Goose gone Wildsmith, and she has lost her identity in the process.

It is kept intact in Philip Reed's *Mother Goose*, which has been deservedly praised for its graphic excellence, for the setting of repose and naturalness it provides for the verses. His wood engravings, printed in six colors, bear comparison with the 18th-century woodcuts that first graced the nursery rhyme page. Sadly, everything is here but the vivacity of those olden-day pictures; the repose is too reposeful, the quiet too quiet. The illustrations convey none of the nervy, nonsensical goings-on that beat through the verses. Reed's is an ambitious book that goes far, but I wish it had gone much further.

Joseph Low's *Mother Goose Riddle Rhymes* is a marvelously fresh, brilliantly colored, rebus Mother Goose which successfully captures the flavor of the racy old woodcuts. When executed with Mr. Low's wit, rhymes-into-picture-riddles is a happy device that neatly mirrors the quality of those verses devoted to puzzling or playing at games with the reader.

In Raymond Briggs' illustrations for three nursery rhyme collections *(The White Land, Fee Fi Fo Fum* and *Ring-a-Ring O'Roses),* a somewhat fussy technique does not detract from a genuinely funny, tongue-in-cheek literalness of interpretation. Charley Barley, after selling his poor dumbfounded wife for three duck eggs, really and truly does fly away, sanguine and blimplike, with arms outstretched into a yellow green sky. All the Briggs books achieve, with varying degrees of success, a fresh, windy, out-o'-doors Mother Goose.

I am ignoring here masses of tasteless Mother Goose books—shiny, screeching banalities that culminate in *Walt Disney's Mother Goose* (Golden Press), where, as in some ghastly nightmare, Jack Sprat, Cross Patch, Jumping Joan and all our Mother Goose friends are rubbed out, and Mickey and Minne Mouse and all those other egomaniacal Disney stars take over the nursery world (Donald Duck actually fills in for Humpty Dumpty and Minnie Mouse for Miss Muffet). The sorry rape of Mother Goose.

The Mother Goose book I like best, after the Caldecott books, is *The Only True Mother Goose Melodies*, a reproduction (published by Lothrop, Lee and Shepard in 1905) of an edition published in Boston in 1833 by Monroe and Francis, which, in turn was possibly a pirated edition of the John Newbery *Mother Goose Melodies* of 1791. The anonymous pictures are superb. Though badly reproduced, they are the very essence of Mother Goose—intensely alive, exceedingly droll ("to bed to bed says sleepy head," depicts a perfect moron type dropping turtles into a cooking pot). I agree with the Reverend Edward Everett Hale, who wrote in the introduction to this book that the artist who depicted the Man in the Moon (possibly Abel Bowen) ranks among "the original artists of the world." This picture graphically conceptualizes two aspects of nursery rhymes that, together, reveal a partial portrait of Mother Goose. A brick wall divides the picture through the center; on the right we see, vigorously drawn, a typical earthy Mother Goose buffoon slopping cold plum porridge over his head, while to the left—gracefully poised in mid-air, with one arm arched over the crescent moon and half his figure in mist—floats the ambiguous man in the moon, secret, magical and poetic. This is my favorite Mother Goose illustration.

What does Mother Goose have to say about her illustrators? Happily, nothing. But in the introduction to the 1833 edition of *The Only True Mother Goose Melodies*, she does have a bit to say about herself:

> "Fudge! I tell you that all their [critics of her rhymes] batterings can't deface my beauties, nor their wise pratings equal my wiser prattlings; and all imitators of my refreshing songs might as well write a new Billy Shakespeare as another Mother Goose—we two great poets were born together, and we shall go out of the world together.
>
> No, no, my melodies will never die,
> While nurses sing, or babies cry.

Modesty never did become her.

Mother Goose—Elucidated

Margaret Chisholm

For years students of children's literature have been intrigued with the "historical facts," stories, myths, and legends which purport to explain the origin of nursery rhymes or Mother Goose rhymes. Personally, I have pored over numerous histories of children's literature, the *Oxford Dictionary of Nursery Rhymes*, and *The Annotated Mother Goose* in the attempt to amalgamate all

SOURCE: *Elementary English* (December, 1972), pp. 1141–1144.

theories. I finally dismissed all these proposed origins of the rhymes as conjecture. Now I have changed my mind—I have found THE TRUTH. On a trip through Ireland, Scotland, Wales, and England I had the good fortune to travel with a lady who had been born in London and had devoted a lifetime to studying the history and literature of the British Isles. She first studied the literature and then traveled to the geographical location and checked with local historians to trace each clue and fragment of information.

She was particularly interested in Mother Goose rhymes and from all of the alternative explanations she had chosen those which she identified as historically acceptable and which had circumstantial evidence to support the historical explanation. We visited many of the settings and saw the evidence, which certainly seemed impressive.

Because of her sincere interest in literature and history, I am now convinced that her conclusions are the acceptable explanations. Here are the stories, so you may decide for yourself:

Mary, Mary quite contrary
How does your garden grow?
With silver bells and cockle shells
And pretty maids all in a row.

Mary in this nursery rhyme refers to Mary Queen of Scots, who went to France when she was a young girl to obtain her education. While she was in France, the religion of England changed to Protestant. When Mary returned to England after marrying the French Dauphin, of course, her Catholic religion was contrary to the rest of the country. The reference to bells referred to the call to mass and cockle shells were the symbols worn by those on pilgrimages. The pretty maids all in a row were these "Four Marys," the maids who were faithful to her until her execution.

Jack and Jill went up the hill
To fet a pail of water,
Jack fell down and broke his crown
And Jill came tumbling after.

Jack and Jill were originally Hjuki and Bil, the children of the moon of Norse mythology. The beginning letters of these names evolved from their original pronunciation to be identical so they would sound more euphonious. As children of the moon they controlled the ebb and flow of the tide. When the rhyme says they went up the hill this indicated the flow of the tide. When Jack fell down and broke his crown, this indicated the breaking waves of the tide turning. The ebb of the tide was described by the phrase "Jill came tumbling after."

Baa Baa black sheep
Have you any wool?
Yes, sir, Yes, sir,
Three bags full.

One for the master
And one for the dame
And one for the little boy
Who lives down the lane.

This rhyme stems from the time that the weaving of wool was a cottage industry. England wouldn't permit the export of wool from the country as raw wool, but insisted on selling it only as piece goods. As the people in the cottages wove the wool they tried to save as much of the wool for themselves as they possibly could by stretching the material and providing a certain length without using all of the raw wool. The one bag for the master was actually that woven into material, and the one bag for the dame was the amount they saved by fraudulent means. In 1275 an export tax was imposed on wool, so the one bag for the little boy who lives down the lane was the amount needed to pay the tax collector.

At that time black sheep were much sought after, as it was possible to make black stockings without dying the yarn. So the masters were accused of trying to keep all the black wool for themselves.

Little Jack Horner
Sat in the corner
Eating a Christmas pie.
He put in his thumb
And pulled out a plum
And said, "What a good boy am I!"

West of Torquay, in Southern England one can see the Glastonbury Tor, which is a granite outcropping at the tip of a high hill. Near this hill the ruins of the magnificent Glastonbury Abbey still stand.

Archeology and history substantiate that this site has been used as a place of worship since pre-historic times. On the wall of the abbey one can see the historical record of the names of the abbots of Glastonbury Abbey dating back to 601. The last name listed on the record is that of Richard Whyting in 1525. At the time when Henry VIII had ordered the dissolution of the monasteries, he first sent commissions out to assess all the wealth of the abbeys. The abbot, Richard Whyting, thought this problem would blow over, so he hid the wealth of the abbey. At that time, Glastonbury Abbey was known as the second richest in the country, second only to Westminster. When the commission discovered his deceit, the abbot and two monks were hanged on Glastonbury Tor on November 15th. Jack Horner was one of the persons who then helped to destroy the abbey. After the destruction he set out for London to report to the king. The timing would be plausible, as he would have left Glastonbury soon after November 15th and would have arrived in London around Christmas time, to tell the king "What a good boy am I," for helping to destroy the abbey and hang the deceitful abbot. As a reward he got a fat slice of the monastery land, which was the "plum." The

Horner family still live on lands near Glastonbury Abbey, but they now claim they paid an adequate amount of money for the land.

Ring-a-ring o'roses
A pocket full of posies.
A-tishoo! A-tishoo!
We all fall down.

This rhyme is said to go back to the time of the Great Plague. The first symptom a victim of the plague was supposed to develop was the red marks on his cheeks, which in the rhyme are referred to as "roses." The pocket full of posies were the herbs carried to ward off the plague. "A-Tishoo, A-Tishoo" indicated the next symptom, which was sneezing. Then the tragedy of death by the plague was described as "we all fall down."

Goosey, goosey gander
Whither shall I wander?
Upstairs and downstairs
And in my lady's chamber.
There I met an old man
Who would not say his prayers.
I took him by the left leg
And threw him down the stairs.

There seems to be no trace of how the first four lines of the verse originated, but the verse was revived in the 18th century to describe a Vice Chancellor at the University of Oxford whose name was Gandy. Even though he was considerably advanced in age he persisted in chasing the ladies. At that time the slang expression "gander" was used to describe a man who pursued the ladies. So this rhyme seemed to be both descriptive and appropriate. In his old age he was expected to be properly saying his prayers rather than chasing after the ladies.

Ride a cock-horse to Banbury Cross
To see a fine lady upon a white horse.
Rings on her fingers, and bells on her toes,
And she shall have music wherever she goes.

There is historical record of the "goodly Crosse" at Banbury being destroyed by the Puritans. In January, 1601, a Jesuit priest wrote "The inhabitants of Banbury being far gone in Puritanism, in a furious zeal tumultuously assailed the Cross that stood in the market place, and so defaced it that they scarcely left one stone upon another." Apparently no one recorded what was depicted on this cross to make them want to destroy it. It could have been the Virgin Mary, but she wouldn't have had rings on her fingers and bells on her toes. A more realistic possibility is that it could have been a representation of Lady Godiva as she had a house in that vicinity and her ride took place in Coventry, which is not far away. At first she was greatly idolized because her ride persuaded her husband to lower the taxes, but her unclothed state might have been what incensed the Puritans. The "cock-horse" was a term used to describe spirited horses, which were ridden by the Puritans in their zeal.

Humpty Dumpty sat on a wall;
Humpty Dumpty had a great fall.
All the king's horses,
And all the king's men,
Couldn't put Humpty together again.

The origin of this verse must have been a riddle to describe an egg. It became included in the literature, however, as "Humpty Dumpty," the name of a game. The game was played by girls who pulled their skirts over their ankles. At a signal they tipped backwards and had to regain their balance without taking their hands from their ankles. Often in the process they "had a great fall."

London Bridge is falling down,
Falling down, falling down;
London Bridge is falling down,
My fair lady.

This verse became popular in the time of Henry II, who had a wife named Eleanor. He gave London Bridge to her but she spent all of the income from the bridge on herself, so when it broke down it couldn't be repaired. It may seem strange to give someone a bridge, but in 1176 a toll tax was passed which charged ha'penny for a horse and a penny for a cart. In early times there was much legend and mystery connected with bridges and a bridge also controlled much of the economy, so many persons willed property to a bridge. Because of these various sources of income The Bridge Trust was established and one time the London Bridge had holdings worth 8½ million pounds. There are many verses to this rhyme, as each of the following lines form a verse:

Build it up with wood and clay,
Wood and clay will wash away.

Build it up with brick and mortar,
Brick and mortar will not stay.

Build it up with iron and steel,
Iron and steel will bend and bow.

Build it up with silver and gold,
Silver and gold will be stolen away.

Then we'll set a man to watch.

This last line refers to the ancient custom of walling up a man alive in the bridge. If a bridge could not stand, it was thought that a human sacrifice would appease the supernatural forces and then the bridge would be strong.

Some legends tell of children being buried in a bridge holding a candle and a loaf of bread, so that the food and light would keep this guardian of the bridge awake and watchful. Even in the pre-historic ruins of Maiden castle, in the area of Stonehenge, a skeleton was found at the foot of a bridge.

The last verses ask:

Suppose the man should fall asleep?
Give him a pipe to smoke all night.

To give the man a pipe is supposed to be the up-dated version of the legend of the candle and bread being used for maintaining vigilance. In any case London Bridge has a very tainted early reputation.

In the introduction to the *Oxford Dictionary of Nursery Rhymes*, Iona and Peter Opie state that nursery rhymes have been vested with mystic symbolism linked with social and political events, and attempts have been made to identify characters in the rhymes with real persons. The Opies state that the theories are so numerous they tend to cancel each other out.

The Opies are truly experts in the field and their statements are to be highly respected but I now have visited these locales and heard the true explanation from "my expert." My expert commented, "After you have explored all the possible theories and legends, you come up with the acceptable explanation that fits the geography, the history and the circumstantial evidence. Once you have done that you decide on your story and you had better jolly well stick with it." And with that, I pass these stories on to you, for I will stick with them.

Bibliography

Opie, Peter and Iona Archibald Opie. *The Oxford Dictionary of Nursery Rhymes*. Oxford at the Clarendon Press, 1951.

Baring-Gould, William S. and Ceil Baring-Gould. *The Annotated Mother Goose*. New York: Clarkson N. Potter, Inc., 1962.

3

Poetry

Making the Poetry Connection

Barbara Holland Baskin
Karen H. Harris
Coleen C. Salley

With only minor variations, activities in the early grades are similar in terms of intellectual performance. Imitating, practicing, matching, discriminating, proving, and comparing are all common scholastic behaviors. Students who master these skills in one setting are apt to apply them equally well to other academic tasks. They learn to excel, enjoying the security of single answer closure and their teacher's approbation for stellar performances. However, one unfortunate side effect of these early experiences is that they lay the groundwork for thinking in absolutes and certainties.

But children must soon learn that not all questions have a single right response. Poetry is one of the few countervailing influences to deliver this message in the lower grades. It encourages subjective response, rewards diversity, and widens the participatory base, making room for more kids in the winner's circle.

Poetry, therefore, should be one of the most widely enjoyed experiences in the elementary school. However, our college students assured us that that had not been their own experience nor did they see it during their observations of current school practice.

We raised this issue because, in teaching about children's literature, we had noted the enthusiastic reaction of our education students to picture books, folktales, myths, and other genres, but the initiation of a poetry unit evoked a palpable decline in this enthusiasm. In an effort to discover the sources of their antipathy, we questioned education students about their early experiences with poetry.

Generally, their earliest encounters—nursery rhymes, nonsense poetry, jumping and counting rhymes—were recalled with pleasure. Soon the nature of the experience changed: what had been free, spontaneous and optional became obligatory, structured and subject to criticism. "Good" poetry was introduced formally into the curriculum, and students were told what was

SOURCE: *Reading Teacher,* December 1976, pp. 259–265. Reprinted by permission of the authors and the International Reading Association.

acceptable and what was not, using standards that appeared unclear or arbitrary. It was obvious to them that their role was not to question or disagree; to do so was to court ridicule or censure.

These observations tended to have a chilling effect on the students' trust in their own judgment, and the whole topic became an academic bog where students were unwilling to venture without the comforting assurance of a clearly defined road map. The perils of an undissembling response to poetry left too much to chance. Students' anxiety was apparently carried over into college life and was reflected in an avoidance of any poetry which was not specifically assigned.

Although there may be some agreed upon classics, we ought to promote the concept that children are free to like them or not, and to have a different interpretation of the poet's vision than that of the teacher, the anthologist, or even the editor of the basal reader. To do otherwise is to risk the perpetuation of widespread hostility to poetry.

Our visits to elementary schools confirmed our students' observations that no revolution had taken place in the teaching of poetry. Although we viewed some exciting poetry sessions, many of the assignments and activities tended to be unimaginative, repetitive, burdensome, and joyless. The major faults clustered into three groups: (1) Poetry was used as a device to achieve unrelated academic purposes, such as handwriting practice, or as a "creative" experience celebrating such national or local events as Fire Prevention Week. (2) Children were overloaded with certain types of poetry activities. We silently commiserated with the many victims of Haiku overkill. (3) The most deplorable use of poetry, and one we mistakenly thought extinct, was the assignment of the memorization of a specified number of lines as punishment for misbehavior.

We were as disheartened as our students by what we saw, and determined to intervene. We explored with them means by which remediation of at least some of the problems might be attempted. Our intervention took the form of developing models which our students could take into the elementary grades, tailoring them to their youngsters' particular needs. Elements and aspects of successful lessons were teased out in debriefing discussions and our students were instructed to use those factors in constructing new assignments. Once they understood the components of a good assignment, they would not be locked into one or two surefire gimmicks, but could generate endless variations.

Our models had the following characteristics:

1. They were instantly appealing. The child would perceive them as enjoyable and not as academic chores.
2. Knowledge about the developmental patterns and interests of children would be exploited in choosing the content of individual lessons.
3. Poems that were available for use in the assignments would have a wide range of difficulty so that all reading levels could be accommodated.

4. Successful participation would require active, overt involvement with the poems and necessitate selective, evaluative or judgmental behaviors.

Using these criteria, we designed two prototype lessons which were field tested by our students in second and third grade classrooms.

The first assignment concerned weather. We had noticed an interest, almost an obsession, in studying weather in the lower elementary grades. Every second and third grade teacher seemed to have charts and symbols, calendars and displays about this topic. Since many of the classes featured daily weather reports, why not have poetic as well as meteorological reports?

The poetry reporter was required to describe the facet of the weather which was of interest or importance and select a poem which best expressed it. If it were foggy, sunny, or windy, an appropriate poem would be chosen to reflect this. This was not as simple as it first appeared. If it were raining, was the pensive mood of Elizabeth Coatsworth's "Rain Poem" (de Regniers, 1969, p. 24) just right?

> The rain was like a little mouse,
> quiet, small and gray.

Possibly the hard driving rain of Laura E. Richards' "The Umbrella Brigade" (Richards, 1955, p. 68) better suited the weather conditions:

> "Pitter, patter!" falls the rain
> On the school-room window-pane.
> Such a plashing! Such a dashing!
> Will it e'er be dry again?

Maybe Langston Hughes' "April Rain Song" (Hopkins, 1969, p. 8) best described the mood of this particular day:

> Let the rain kiss you.
> Let the rain beat upon your head with
>   silent liquid drops.
> The rain plays a little sleep-song on our
>   roof at night
> And I love the rain.

The assignment was successful for several important reasons. Variety was added to what had become essentially a routine classroom activity—affixing a paper umbrella, sun, or cloud on the current date of the calendar. The phenomenon of weather had an objective reality to which the children had been responding; now they were asked to react on an interpretive, feeling level as well. To do this they were required to read four or five poems in order to make their decision.

Additionally, the most significantly, the children were forced to think about the differences between the poems. The choice of a poem describing a light spring shower when a hurricane raged outside was clearly inappropriate.

In other words, children had to consider what kind of rain the poem was talking about. They had to attend to the poet's words or they were going to make a poor decision. Comprehension on a literal level was assured.

A third grade class, after pursuing the project seriously for a few days, capitulated to wishful thinking. One boy, tired of the gray wetness of a Louisiana winter, found Marie Louise Allen's "First Snow" (Arbuthnot, 1961, p. 179) and insisted on reading it:

> Snow makes whiteness where it falls,
> The bushes look like popcorn balls.

As he explained to the class: "We never have real snow, and it isn't fair." His unconventional attitude was contagious and the other children, to our delight, reshaped the assignment and created a new set of rules. The frivolity of Lewis Carroll's nonsense was now more appropriate (Peterson, 1954, p. 103):

> The sun was shining on the sea,
> Shining with all his might:
> And this was odd, because it was
> The middle of the night.

And Richard LeGalliene's "I Meant To Do My Work To-Day" (Larrick, 1965, p. 6) also helped to break the monotony of unrelieved dampness:

> I meant to do my work to-day—
> But a brown bird sang in the
> apple-tree
> And a butterfly flitted across the field,
> And a rainbow held out its shining
> hand—
> So what would I do but laugh and go?

The second assignment grew out of a class field trip. The children were taken to the zoo and photographed with the birds, fish, and animals there. These pictures formed the inspiration for the usual experience stories and language development activities, but they also suggested to us some literary possibilities. The children were asked to think about all the animals they had seen, select their favorite, and choose a poem they thought that animal would like to hear.

That a giraffe or hippopotamus might like to hear a poem was not considered the least outlandish by these second graders. Wording the task in this way rather than simply asking for a poem about a favorite animal, multiplied the response possibilities. While some children recognized the narcissistic traits of animals, they also thought that seals might like a poem about water, such as Rose Fyleman's "Very Lovely" (Arbuthnot, 1961, p. 158):

> Wouldn't it be lovely if the rain came
> down

Till the water was quite high over all
the town?
Wouldn't it be glorious? Wouldn't it
be fun?

They supposed that James Stephens' "White Fields" (Gross, 1968, p. 64) could make a likely playground for a polar bear:

In the winter time we go
Walking in the fields of snow.
Every fence and every tree,
Is as white as white can be.

They understood the sadness and longing of Carson McCullers' "Giraffe" (Hopkins, 1970, p. 24):

At the zoo I saw: a long-necked,
velvety giraffe
Was she dreaming of African jungles
and African plains
That she would never see again?

Again our requirements for a poetry assignment were met. The children, far from thinking this silly, considered it a real problem, the solution of which was intensely interesting and even important. That they identify strongly with animals was evidenced by one child's selection of Gwendolyn Brooks' "Pete at the Zoo" (Hopkins, 1971):

I wonder if the elephant
Is lonely in his stall
When all the boys and girls are gone
And there's no shout at all.

There was a definite excitement generated by hearing which animal was chosen and which poem it would presumably like. Justification of one's preferences was not required, but when explanations were volunteered, some unorthodox manifestations of the child's thinking were often revealed. Hearing a poem from peers, rather than only from teachers or books, increased attention level and provided extra exposure.

With these experiences as background, our college students were eager to develop and try out their own assignments. Some of the best were:

1. "Select a poem about something your mother would definitely not let you keep in your room!" This was an absolutely delicious idea and poems about snakes and lizards were much favored. Theodore Roethke's "The Bat" (Roethke, 1973, p. 37) was popular:

By day the bat is cousin to the mouse.
He likes the attic of an aging house.
He loops in crazy figures half the
night.
Among the trees that face the corner
light.

And it was generally agreed that most mothers were not as tolerant as Siddie Joe Johnson's mother was alleged to be in "Goat" (Gross, 1968, p. 6):

And though our mother was not able
To like goats dancing on her table
She never shut a door set wide
To let a little goat inside.

2. "Imagine you have been selected for the next space flight. Choose a poem about something you would certainly want to leave behind." Carl Sandburg's "Arithmetic" (Dunning, 1966, p. 58) and poems about schools and teachers were big winners in this category:

Arithmetic is numbers you squeeze
  from your head
to your hand to your pencil to your
  paper
till you get the right answer.

Lilian Moore's "Construction" (Moore, 1969) was also left on the launching pad by a girl worried about concrete encroachments:

The giant mouth
chews
rocks
spews them
and is back for
more.

3. "You are a famous movie producer. Your past hits include 'Lassie,' 'Gentle Ben' and 'Flipper.' Choose a poem about your next great star." This idea clearly had a glamorous component to it that added to its appeal and was readily accepted by the older students. Kornei Chukovsky's "Crocodile" (Gross, 1968, p. 33) seemed a natural choice for stardom since he was already endowed with so much talent:

Once there was a crocodile
A crocodile of taste and style
He strolled down Piccadilly
Singing carols in Swahili.

One young would-be producer opted for Palmer Brown's "The Spangled Pandemonium" (Arbuthnot, 1961, p. 123):

The Spangled Pandemonium
Is missing from the Zoo
He bent the bars the barest bit,
And slithered glibly through.

4. "Choose a poem about some person or creature you definitely don't want to invite to your next birthday party." Walter de la Mare's "Tired Tim"

(Livingston, 1972a, p. 49) was a definite candidate for rejection, as was Kaye Starbird's "Ann" (Hopkins, 1972, p. 22):

Poor Tired Tim! It's sad for him
He lags the long bright morning
  through,
Ever so tired of nothing to do.

Ann wears dresses with ruffles
If you please.
She has neat, curly hair
and a real gold ring:
—and she can't play anything.

5. "Choose a poem about the 'secret you' your teacher would never guess." Rachel Field's "My Inside-Self" (Field, 1957, p. 41) was a perfect choice:

My Inside-Self and my Outside Self
  Are Different as can be.
My Outside-Self wears gingham
    smocks,
  And very round is she.
But, oh my little Inside-Self—
  She dances lighter than a leaf.

"Rebellion in September" (Field, 1957, p. 10) expressed their restlessness:

Five and twelve make? Oh, dear me,
How the red leaves shine on the maple
  tree.
Eleven times three and thirty-three—
Why wasn't I born a bird or a tree?

6. "Tell me a really important question you never got asked." Marion Edey and Dorothy Grider pose a question in "The Little Fox" (Arbuthnot, 1961, p. 60), which one child liked:

Who came in the quiet night,
Trotting so lightly?
It was the russet fox who came
And with his shadow played a game.

Mary O'Neill's "What is Black?" (O'Neill, 1961, p. 19) was also chosen:

Black is the night
When there isn't a star
And you can't tell by looking
Where you are.
Think of what starlight
And lamplight would lack
If they couldn't lean against black . . .

7. "I'm tired of riding on the school bus. Tomorrow I'll. . . ." This assignment seemed to zero in on a universal sentiment and although most children agreed that any alternative was preferable, traveling on the backs of cheetahs, yaks or horses was especially popular. Other children preferred flying or skating, and Marchette Chute's "Skiing" (Chute, 1967, p. 69) appealed to several:

I'm very good at skiing
  I have a kind of knack
For I can do it frontways
  And also on my back.

Marci Ridlon's "Safari" (Hopkins, 1970a, p. 41) piqued one child's imagination:

I'm going on a safari
Maybe I'll take you
We'll cross the alley river and
Track a cat or two.

One girl saw herself accompanying a "Moose on the Loose" (Merriam, 1962, p. 11) by Eve Merriam:

I saw a moose out driving,
Speeding fast and far
I asked, "Why are you driving
In a dashing motor car?"

8. "Choose a poem for a friend who can't help thinking about lunch when it's only 9:05!" A feast of poems was served up for this theme. "A Taste of Purple" (Jacobs, 1967, p. 12) by Leland Jacobs was favored by some:

Grapes hang purple
In their bunches
Ready for September lunches

Another's taunting choice was Lucia and James Hymes' "Beans, Beans, Beans" (Hymes and Hymes, 1960, p. 34):

Baked beans,
Butter beans,
Big fat lima beans. . . .

During the development of these assignments, two factors quickly became apparent to our students. Experiences suitable for the lower grades were inappropriate for the upper ones. To ask a third grade child to find a poem a baboon would like was challenging; to ask this of a fifth grader was insulting. However, suggesting that fifth graders picture themselves as famous movie producers was intriguing. Second graders had no idea what a movie producer was and found the whole concept excessively abstract.

Further, the students discovered that a considerable amount of preparation was required for the successful completion of these tasks, particularly in getting ready for the younger child's participation. Poems had to be located on the child's reading level, typed out in primary face type on index cards, and arranged in some logical categories. The children, especially at first, needed guidance in selecting a category and browsing and choosing poems found there. For the older children, a careful assortment of anthologies containing poems which could potentially satisfy the stipulated requirements was a critical factor in the success of the lesson.

Many of the youngsters basked in their new perception that they could exercise control over the outcome of a lesson and that their decision could be based largely on their own ideas and feelings. With this new perspective, and buoyed up by the obviously happy experiences of the children, our college students were able to think about poetry as something pleasurable and to inch toward the concept that

> without poetry our world would be
> Locked within itself—no longer
>   enchanted by the poet's
> Spell.
>
> (Lewis, 1966, p. 15)

References

Adams, Adrienne. *Poetry of the Earth*. New York, N.Y.: Charles Scribner's Sons, 1972.

Aiken, Conrad. *Cats and Bats and Things with Wings*. New York, N.Y.: Atheneum Publishers, 1965.

Arbuthnot, May Hill. *Time for Poetry*. Rev. ed. Glenview, Ill.: Scott, Foresman and Company, 1961.

Baron, Virginia, Ed. *Here I Am!* New York, N.Y.: E.P. Dutton & Co., 1969.

Cassedy, Sylvia, Ed. *Birds, Frogs and Moonlight*. New York, N.Y.: Doubleday & Company, 1967.

Caudill, Rebecca. *Come Along!* New York, N.Y.: Holt, Rinehart and Winston, 1969.

Chute, Marchette. *Around and About*. New York, N.Y.: E.P. Dutton & Co., 1967.

Chute, Marchette. *Rhymes About Us*. New York, N.Y.: E.P. Dutton & Co., 1974.

Coatsworth, Elizabeth. *The Sparrow Bush*. New York, N.Y.: W.W. Norton & Company, 1966.

Cole, William. *Oh, How Silly*. New York, N.Y.: The Viking Press, 1970.

Cole, William. *Oh, What Nonsense*. New York, N.Y. The Viking Press, 1965.

Cullen, Countee. *The Last Zoo*. Chicago, Ill.: Follett Corporation, 1969.

de Regniers, Beatrice Shenk, Eva Moore and Mary Michaels White. *Poems Children Will Sit Still For*. New York, N.Y.: Scholastic Book Services, 1969.

Dunning, Stephen, Edward Lueders and Hugh Smith. *Reflections on a Gift of Watermelon Pickle*. Glenview, Ill.: Scott, Foresman and Company, 1966.

Field, Rachet. *Poems*. New York, N.Y.: Macmillan, 1957.

Fisher, Aileen. *Feathered Ones and Furry*. New York, N.Y.: Thomas Y. Crowell Company, 1971.

Fisher, Aileen. *In One Door and Out the Other*. New York, N.Y.: Thomas Y. Crowell Company, 1969.
Froman, Robert. *Street Poems*. New York, N.Y.: McCall, 1971.
Fujikawa, Gyo, Ed. *A Child's Book of Poems*. New York, N.Y.: Grosset & Dunlap, 1969.
Gross, Sarah Chokla. *Every Child's Book of Verse*. New York, N.Y.: Franklin Watts, 1968.
Hopkins, Lee Bennett. *The City Spreads Its Wings*. New York, N.Y.: Franklin Watts, 1970a.
Hopkins, Lee Bennett. *Girls Can Too*. New York, N.Y.: Franklin Watts, 1972.
Hopkins, Lee Bennett. *I Think I Saw a Snail*. New York, N.Y.: Crown Publishers, 1969.
Hopkins, Lee Bennett. *Zoo! A Book of Poems*. New York, N.Y. Crown Publishers, 1971.
Hopkins, Lee Bennett. *This Street's for Me!* New York, N.Y.: Crown Publishers, 1970b.
Hughes, Langston. *Don't You Turn Back*. New York, N.Y.: Alfred A. Knopf, 1969.
Hymes, Lucia and James L. Hymes Jr. *Hooray for Chocolate*. New York, N.Y.: William R. Scott, 1960.
Itse, Elizabeth, Ed. *Hey, Bug! And Other Poems about Little Things*. New York, N.Y.: American Heritage Publishing Co., 1972.
Jacobs, Leland B. *Is Somewhere Always Far Away?* New York, N.Y.: Holt, Rinehart and Winston, 1967.
Katz, Bobbi. *Upside Down and Inside Out*. New York, N.Y.: Franklin Watts, 1973.
Larnck, Nancy. *Piper, Pipe That Song Again*. New York, N.Y.: Random House, 1965.
Lewis, Richard, Ed. *In a Spring Garden*. New York, N.Y.: The Dial Press, 1965.
Lewis, Richard. *Miracles*. New York, N.Y.: Simon & Schuster, 1966.
Livingston, Myra Cohn. *Listen Children, Listen*. New York, N.Y.: Harcourt Brace Jovanovich, 1972a.
Livingston, Myra Cohn. *The Malibu and Other Poems*. New York, N.Y.: Antheneum Publishers, 1972b.
Livingston, Myra Cohn. *What a Wonderful Bird the Frog Are*. New York, N.Y.: Harcourt Brace Jovanovich, 1973.
Merriam, Eve. *There Is No Rhyme for Silver*. New York, N.Y.: Atheneum Publishers, 1962.
Moore, John Travers. *There's Motion Everywhere*. New York, N.Y.: Houghton Mifflin Company, 1970.
Moore, Lilian. *I Thought I Heard the City*. New York, N.Y.: Atheneum Publishers, 1969.
Morton, Miriam, Ed. *The Moon Is Like a Silver Sickle*. New York, N.Y.: Simon & Schuster, 1972.
O'Neill, Mary. *Fingers Are Always Bringing Me News*. New York, N.Y.: Doubleday & Company, 1969.
O'Neill, Mary. *Hailstones and Halibut Bones*. New York, N.Y.: Doubleday & Company, 1961.
O'Neill, Mary. *What Is That Sound?* New York, N.Y.: Atheneum Publishers, 1966.
Peterson, Isabel J. *The First Book of Poetry*. New York, N.Y.: Franklin Watts, 1954.
Prelutsky, Jack. *The Pack Rat's Day*. New York, N.Y.: Macmillan, 1974.
Prelutsky, Jack. *Toucans Two*. New York, N.Y.: Macmillan, 1970.

Richards, Laura. *Tirra Lirra*. Boston, Mass.: Little, Brown and Company, 1955.
Roethke, Theodore. *Dirty Dinky and Other Creatures*. New York, N.Y.: Doubleday & Company, 1973.
Soilka, Arnold. *And the Frog Went "Blah!"* New York, N.Y.: Charles Scribner's Sons, 1972.
Starbird, Kaye. *A Snail's a Failure Socially*. Philadelphia, Penna.: B. Lippincott Company, 1966.
Zolotow, Charlotte. *All That Sunlight*. New York, N.Y.: Harper & Row, 1967.

The Pied Pipers of Poetry

Verna Hildebrand
Rebecca Peña Hines

"I'm hiding. I'm hiding, and no one knows where," began Caroline, the nursery school teacher in a quiet secretive voice. She continues reciting Dorothy Aldis' "Hiding" (in *All Together*, 1952, p. 71) to the lively group of children. Because Caroline's voice is low, the children immediately stop chatting. Caroline's eyes meet those of the children as they listen attentively to learn what is happening in the poem.

Caroline uses poetry like the Pied Piper of Hamelin used music to encourage children to come "Tripping and skipping, [running] merrily after / The wonderful music with shouting and laughter" (in *The Complete Poetic and Dramatic Works of Robert Browning*, Browning, 1895, p. 268). A poet creatively puts together "those certain words in a certain cadence that makes poetry different from other literature forms" (Jacobsen, 1975, p. 19). Children seem attracted to poetry that captures how it is to see, smell, taste, hear, and touch when one is young.

Not everyone enjoys reading the same books or listening to the same music. Nor does everyone wish to explore the same type of poetry. However, you can probably remember many poems that could be shared with young children. If you choose poems that are personally enjoyable, then the enthusiasm will be apparent and contagious to children. Naturally every poem will not have equal appeal for every child, so one should make selections from a wide range of verse. Eventually, children may ask for certain poems by name or they may memorize favorites, and create their own poems.

Poetry offers children an opportunity to learn about and experience a variety of moods and feelings. Through choice of words the poet conveys mental images of objects and emotions in a few short lines. Read aloud some of the following poems to young children and observe the impact the verse has on them.

Benefits of Introducing Poetry to Young Children

Poetry can make significant contributions to programs for young children.

Enjoyment

The primary reason for introducing poetry to young children is because they have a natural affinity for it. They like playing with words, hearing unusual sounds, and identifying repetitions and rhymes. The lyrics of songs are a form of poetry that may be sung as well as spoken. Sometimes poetry is chanted. To keep enjoyment in poetry sessions, use appropriate facial expressions and voice changes depending on the tone of the poem. When working with young children, never isolate individual lines of a poem to analyze it as older students are sometimes required to do. Choose subjects familiar to children such as this perennial favorite.

Galoshes

Susie's galoshes
Make splishes and sploshes
And slooshes and sloshes
As Susie steps slowly
Along in the slush.
They stamp and they tramp
On the ice and concrete,
They get stuck in the muck and
  the mud;

But Susie likes much best to hear
The slippery slush
As it slooshes and sloshes
And splishes and sploshes,
All around her galoshes.

(Rhoda W. Bacmeister, in *My Poetry Book,* ed. J. Pierce, 1954, p. 6)

Substituting the names of children in the class can make a poem even more relevant.

Capturing Attention

A perfect poem for capturing attention is "Hiding." It is an excellent way to initiate a hiding game with young children.

"This Little Boy" is useful when it is important for children in a group to pay attention. Read it softly so they have to come close and remain quiet to hear the poem.

This Little Boy

This little boy is ready for bed
Low on his pillow he lays his head
Pulls up the covers so warm and tight
And there he sleeps all through the
night.

Morning comes! His eyes open wide!
Quickly he throws the covers aside!
Jumps out of bed, puts on his clothes,
And off to nursery school he goes!

(Author unknown)

Sharpening Listening Skills

In order to derive meaning from spoken communication, children must listen to what has been said and then convert it into something they understand. Poetry is especially valuable for helping sharpen children's listening skills. Children can also gain the experience of being listened to when they recite a poem to a parent, friend, or teacher.

A. A. Milne, a favorite poet of both adults and children, wrote *Winnie the Pooh* and many other works. His poem "Missing" (in *When We Were*

Very Young 1924, p. 54) always captures a child's interest. The poem starts with the provocative question, "Has anybody seen my mouse?" Children will also want to listen attentively to find out what happens in this popular wintertime verse.

Once There Was a Snowman

Once there was a snowman
Stood outside the door
Thought he'd like to come inside
And dance around the floor;
Thought he'd like to warm himself
By the firelight red;
Thought he'd like to climb
Upon the big white bed.

So he called the North Wind,
"Help me now I pray.
I'm completely frozen,
Standing here all day."

So the North Wind came along
And blew him in the door,
And now there's nothing left of him
But a puddle on the floor.

(Author unknown, in *The Golden Flute*, eds. A. Hubbard and A. Babbitt, 1932)

Creative Language Expression

Poets are masters of creative language. With a few words they can allow their readers to recall memories and mutual reactions. Making children aware of creative language is another contribution of poetry.

Most adults have probably read Robert Louis Stevenson's poem "The Swing" (in *A Child's Garden of Verses* 1885) that begins, "How do you like to go up in a swing,/Up in the air so blue?" and so wonderfully captures the feel of swinging. Children can easily imagine the feel of wind blowing their hair as the poem is being read.

Polly Chase Boyden captures another familiar childhood experience in her poem "Mud" (in *My Poetry Book*, ed. J. Pierce, 1954, p. 6).

Mud

Mud is very nice to feel

All squishy squashy between the toes!
I'd rather wade in wiggly mud
Than smell a yellow rose.

Nobody else but the rosebush knows
How nice mud feels
Between the toes.

"Mud" is an example of the poet sensitively observing a common subject, creating vivid images in a few words.

Children can also create vivid, original, and spontaneous expressions that are poetic. While playing on the swings, one boy said,

"I can push myself so high.
I can just fly into the sky."

Four- and five-year-old children often create simple rhymes. Try to record the rhymes promptly, so they will not be forgotten. This four-year-old child's verses were responded to by a friend.

"My name is Michael
I love to recycle."

"My name is Sandy
I love candy."

Another time this four-year-old, while swinging in the blooming mimosa tree and watching the bees flitting among the flowers, chanted

"I love to sing, sing, sing.
A bee likes to sting, sting, sting.
Ping-a-ty Ping!"

Special recognition can be given to a child's original poem by recording it for the child and perhaps typing a copy for a bulletin board. The poem could be accompanied by a drawing or picture. Poems by children can be collected and assembled into a booklet for the class. Children's self-concepts are enhanced, and their knowledge of language and its many forms expanded when they see their words are important enough to be written down. Of course, such recognition should be made in a noncompetitive way.

Teachers and parents can also be creative poets. Most children would be delighted to hear a poem composed in honor of a birthday, a class activity, or a favorite pet. Many of the poems that children enjoy today probably were written for a special child or two at home or at school. Certainly one can make creative adaptations of poems, ensuring a particularly effective presentation through the use of visual aids.

Guidance

Poems can occasionally be used to guide children into desired behavior. "See, I Can Do It All Myself with My Own Little Brush" (in *All Together*, Aldis,

1952, p. 25) encourages children's interest in brushing their teeth. The familiar finger play "Grandma's Spectacles" (Author unknown, in *Let's Do Fingerplays,* ed. M. Grayson, 1962) is a favorite for helping children relax before listening to a story. A poem such as this one by Mary Louise Allen (in *A Pocket Full of Poems,* 1957) can help children put on their mittens.

The Mitten Song

"Thumbs in the thumb-place
Fingers all together!"
This is the song
We sing in mitten-weather.
When it is cold,
It doesn't matter whether
Mittens are wool,
Or made of finest leather.
This is the song
We sing in mitten-weather.
"Thumbs in the thumb-place,
Fingers all together!"

Concept Development

Poetry can be used along with various real-life experiences to introduce, explain, and expand children's concepts. After watching squirrels in the park, children may enjoy this poem.

The Squirrel

Whiskey, frisky,
Hippity, hop,
Up he goes
To the tree top.

Whirly, twirly
Round and round,
Down he scampers
To the ground.

Furly, curly
What a tail;
Tall as a feather
Broad as a sail!

Where's his supper?
In the shell,
Snappity, crackity,
Out it fell.

(Author unknown)

Concepts of cultural heritage can also be expressed in poetry that focuses on customs, holidays, homes, family members, and values. Hanukkah, Christmas, piñatas, and birthdays are favorite topics.

Poems and finger plays that help locate and label the various parts of the body particularly appeal to three-year-old children. Milne's "Sneezles" (in *Now We Are Six*, 1927, p. 12) helps children look at the common cold with a sense of humor. Numerous poems and finger plays contain number concepts—an interesting way for children to remember the words for numbers and their sequences. By using finger motions along with numbers, the child learns to associate the numerals to a corresponding number of items.

Five Little Rabbits

Five little rabbits under a log
One said, "Hark! I hear a dog."
One said, "Look! I see a man."
One said, "Run! As fast as you can."
One said, "Pooh, I'm not afraid."
One said, "Shh, keep in the shade."

So they all lay still under the log
And the man passed by
And so did the dog.

(Author unknown)

Environmental awareness is creatively brought to children's attention by authors such as Aileen Fisher. She has several poetry books containing exquisite illustrations such as *Cricket in a Thicket* (1963), *Feathered Ones and Furry* (1971), and *Listen Rabbit* (1964).

Another concept children grasp well from poetry is the concept of rhyming. One can introduce this characteristic of some poetry by saying, "I know a poem," or "I know a rhyme." Of course, children also need to know that poems do not necessarily rhyme. In fact, those poems which have forced rhyming or a sing-song rhythm may be neither pleasing nor of great artistic merit.

Vocabulary Building

Vocabulary building is closely related to concept development. Newly learned concepts require new words. Poetry helps children recognize and understand these words. When young children are shown pussy willows in the spring, they are usually new to them—or they do not remember them from last spring.

Catkin

I have a little pussy
Her coat is warm and grey
She lives out in the meadow
Not very far away.

Now she's a little pussy
She'll never be a cat
For she's a pussy willow
Now what do you think of that?
Meow, meow, meow, meow,
SCAT!

(Author unknown, in *Time for Poetry*, ed. M. H. Arbuthnot, 1959)

Chanting the poem by going up the scale, then chanting back down the scale on the meows is a fun activity. Margaret Mead spoke of walking with her granddaughter past a floral shop displaying pussy willows. Looking in the window, the little girl observed, "They'll never be a cat." Sharing the poem "Catkin" had given them a sense of community. Teachers can broaden the sense of community by sharing with parents the poems their children are learning.

Children do not have to be familiar with every word in a poem to find it enjoyable. However, the concepts should be understandable to children. Introducing poetry with new words gives the teacher or parent an opportunity to talk about, demonstrate, or otherwise relate the new words to the child's experience.

Reading

Poetry makes many contributions to children as they begin to learn to read. Practice with rhyming is a good phonics exercise. Try Maurice Sendak's "Chicken Soup with Rice" (in *Chicken Soup with Rice,* 1962).

The desire to learn to read is fostered as children are exposed to a love of literature from teachers and parents who share poetry with them. Firsthand knowledge of many concepts helps children understand books and stories they read. A broad vocabulary and an appreciation for books contribute positively to children's interest in reading. More importantly, sharing, experiencing, listening, and contributing all lead to a love of poetry and literature that will enhance a child's motivation to learn to read.

Memory

Memory is stimulated by poetry. Short poems and songs are fun to remember and children will take pride in doing so. One clue to a child's developmental progress is through the ability to remember poems.

Humor

Humor, wit, and fantasy are part of many poems and are especially appropriate for kindergarteners. Usually younger children interpret poems with straightforward facts. Poems with nonsense and plays on words are for older children. For example, try singing Rose Bonne and Allan Mills' "I Know an Old Lady" (in *I Know an Old Lady,* 1961) to a class of kindergarteners. Some children find this story immensely humorous. Another truly funny poem for five-year-old children is Laura E. Richards' "Eletelephony" (in *Poems Children Will Sit Still For,* 1969, p. 92).

One's memory, the library, and friends are all excellent sources of poems for young children. Begin today to share poetry with children. Join the growing band of Pied Pipers of poetry.

References

Aldis, D. "Hiding" and "See, I Can Do It All Myself with My Own Little Brush." In *All Together*. New York: Putnam, 1952.

Allen, M. L. "The Mitten Song." In *A Pocket Full of Poems*. New York: Harper & Row, 1957.

Bacmeister, R. "Galoshes." In *My Poetry Book,* ed. J. Pierce. New York: Grosset & Dunlap, 1954.

Bonne, R., and Mills, A. "I Know an Old Lady." In *I Know an Old Lady*. New York: Rand McNally, 1961.

Boyden, P. C. "Mud." In *My Poetry Book,* ed. J. Pierce. New York: Grosset & Dunlap, 1954.

Browning, R. "The Pied Piper of Hamelin." In *The Complete Poetic and Dramatic Works of Robert Browning,* ed. H. E. Scudder. Boston: Houghton Mifflin, 1895.

"Catkin." In *Time for Poetry,* ed. M. H. Arbuthnot. Chicago: Scott, Foresman, 1959.

Fisher, A. *Cricket in a Thicket*. New York: Scribner, 1963.

Fisher, A. *Feathered Ones and Furry*. New York: Crowell, 1971.

Fisher, A. *Listen Rabbit*. New York: Crowell, 1964.

"Grandma's Spectacles." In *Let's Do Fingerplays,* ed. M. Grayson. Washington, D.C.: R. Luce, 1962.

Jacobsen, J. "The Instant of Knowing." *The Writer* (October 1975): 18–20.

Milne, A. A. "Sneezles." In *Now We Are Six*. New York: Dutton, 1924.
Milne, A. A. "Missing." In *When We Were Very Young*. New York: Dutton, 1924.
Richards, L. "Eletelphony." In *Poems Children Will Sit Still For,* eds. B.S. de Regniers, E. Moore, and M. M. White. New York: Scholastic, 1969.
Sendak, M. "Chicken Soup with Rice." In *Chicken Soup with Rice*. New York: Harper & Row, 1962.
Stevenson, R. L. "The Swing." In *A Child's Garden of Verses*. New York: Scribner, 1885.

The Changing Picture of Poetry Books for Children

Nancy Larrick

In the early 1800s, most poetry books for children were chapbooks sold by street vendors for a few pennies. They were tiny booklets, some as small as two by three inches, and crudely printed on poor paper. Sometimes the cover was of the same flimsy stock in a faded color, or a self-cover was used.

Chapbook verses and titles were didactic and condescending. The woodcuts used for illustration were usually stiff and formal, with no touch of gaiety or humor. It is easy to conclude that many were leftovers on the printer's shelf, for they often bore little resemblance to the accompanying text. The only color was added by hand, and often it was a heavy, careless hand. In some cases, as many as three colors were brushed on.

Apparently these poetry chapbooks for children were contrived to preach, to teach, and to make a profit from "little children" and "infant minds." They made their place in the world through quantity, not quality.

SOURCE: *Wilson Library Bulletin*, October 1980, pp. 113–117. Reprinted with permission of the publisher.

Two Shining Exceptions

Fortunately these first mass-market paperbacks were not the only poetry books for children. At least two shining exceptions pointed the way to better design and illustration.

The first was *Songs of Innocence* (1789), which was written, designed, illustrated, engraved, hand-colored, and bound by poet William Blake and his wife. In contrast to his earlier poems, which assumed children to be born in sin, Blake sang his "songs." Among the poems that remain popular today is "Piping down the valleys wild," a lilting and joyous poem.

Blake hand-lettered the words of each poem on a small copper plate, added beautifully drawn figures, then embellished the whole with garlands and scrolls. Pages were printed in brown, yellow, or blue for the ground color and red for the letters. Each copy was colored by hand to match the original drawing by Blake, and the poet ground and mixed his own colors.

These exquisite books, created with loving care, reached only a small audience in Blake's lifetime and created no great interest during a time when chapbooks were pouring from the presses.

A second exception to the dreary chapbook world of poetry for children appeared in book form in 1807: *The Butterfly's Ball,* written by William Roscoe and illustrated by William Mulready. The rather halting verse tells of a fairy picnic and makes no attempt to do anything other than entertain. The hand-colored drawings are joyous, mischievous, and fanciful.

Within a year 20,000 copies of this little book had been sold—each hand-colored. Clearly there was a market for the imaginative, the beautiful, and the colorful.

The Beginning of Color Printing

By 1865, the English printer Edmund Evans was pioneering in color printing. As an artist in his own right, Evans deplored "the raw colors and vulgar designs" in books for children. He was convinced that it was economically feasible to publish paperback books for children that were beautiful in color and design, if they were printed in sufficient quantity.

To put his plan into action, Evans recruited three artists who became pivotal figures in children's book illustration: Walter Crane, Kate Greenaway, and Randolph Caldecott. Each developed a distinctive style and used color with the utmost skill on beautifully designed pages.

Crane's illustrations were like minutely designed tapestries. Caldecott's reflected his infatuation with rural England—its humorous village people, cavorting sheep, prancing horses, and horn-blowing huntsmen.

Kate Greenaway was the only one of the three to illustrate her own poetry: *Under the Window* (1879) and *Marigold Garden* (1885). Although Greenaway's verses are slight, they tell of real children in everyday play and are often marked by sly humor. Her illustrations show children skipping, dancing, flying kites, rolling hoops, and picking flowers. All wear the dress of an earlier, quainter period. Every detail was prettiness personified. One of Kate Greenaway's friendly critics begged her to draw "flowers that won't look as if their leaves had been in curl papers all night." She never did, but her popularity soared in England, on the continent, and in America. It is estimated that in the twenty years after *Under the Window* was published, nearly one million copies of her books were printed and sold by Evans.

Humor Comes Into Its Own

The earliest poetry for children was almost totally lacking in humor. The accompanying illustrations were wooden, lifeless, and unsmiling.

One of the first to shatter the gloom was Edward Lear, whose *Book of Nonsense* was published in 1846 and *Nonsense Songs and Stories* in 1871. And nonsense they were—limericks, songs, and narrative poems—all ridiculous to an extreme with Lear's own black-and-white sketches making them doubly hiliarious. He used a heavy cartoon line and reveled in exaggeration.

Alice's Adventures in Wonderland by Lewis Carroll, with illustrations by Sir John Tenniel, a cartoonist for *Punch*, appeared in 1865. This is a fabulous fantasy which May Hill Arbuthnot called "several degrees wilder than Lear's books at their wildest." It included many nonsense poems and ditties, even one gibberish poem, "Jabberwocky."

Tenniel and Lewis Carroll became close collaborators. Each criticized the work of the other, down to the last whisker of the White Knight, and each heeded the criticism received. Tenniel's illustrations were faithful to the text and yet expressed the individuality of the artist. Tenniel's humor is gentle and ingenious, marked (as Arbuthnot puts it) by "poker-faced drollery."

Gradual Change

Despite Edmund Evan's dramatic success with large colorful books of poetry for children, designers, artists, and publishers were slow to follow his lead. For several decades, the graphic pattern for the new poetry books for children was a conservative one. Page size was seldom larger than six by eight inches, and illustrations were black-and-white line drawings.

For example, *A Child's Garden of Verses* by Robert Louis Stevenson, published in 1885 under the title *Penny Whistles,* was pictorially dull and colorless. The poems, however, showed remarkable understanding of children and remain popular to this day.

The poetry books of A. A. Milne—*When We Were Very Young* and *Now We Are Six*—came out in the 1920s with small pages, no color, and many tiny pen-and-ink drawings by Ernest P. Shepard. The illustrations are a delightful complement to the poems, catching the mood, the personality of children and even their toys to a remarkable degree. The poems became tremendously popular, but the book is quiet and understated in appearance.

The 1940s and '50s saw dramatic change in children's book illustration, due in part to improvements in color lithography and the mass-market success of books created by Artists and Writers Guild, Inc. The Little Golden Books led to the Giant Golden Books, and there were poetry books among them.

A striking example is *A Child's Garden of Verses,* illustrated for Golden Press by Alice and Martin Provensen, published in 1951 in full-color lithography. Several of the Provensen illustrations sweep across facing pages in spectacular display.

The Ambitious Decade

The idea of large, dramatically illustrated poetry picture books caught on among U.S. publishers during the 1960s. Taking a tip, perhaps, from numerous color success stories, several publishers eyed their own colorless poetry books and yearned for their paint pots.

In 1961, Random House brought out a choice poetry collection, *Poems to Read to the Very Young,* selected by Josette Frank and illustrated by Dagmar Wilson. This 32-page book was printed in full color.

In 1967, E. P. Dutton brought out *The Christopher Robin Book of Verse,* consisting of selections from the first two A. A. Milne poetry books with full-color illustrations by E. H. Shepard on alternate pages. The new color illustrations are so similar to the original black-and-white drawings in style and detail that it is easy to assume the Shepard merely added color to the originals: A closer look shows that these are fresh new paintings with all the charming detail and whimsy of the originals. Both illustrations and type are larger than in the original books.

Little, Brown assembled a collection of "the youngest verses" from three earlier poetry books by David McCord and published it under the title *Every Time I Climb a Tree* in 1967. Larger size and full-color illustrations by Marc Simont make this a vibrant picture book with humor, verve, and a decidedly modern flavor not found in the original black-and-white drawings by Henry B. Kane. A second McCord-Simont collaboration is *The Star in the Pail* (1975), also made up of "the youngest verses" from McCord's earlier collections.

Thomas Y. Crowell brought out a series of exquisite picture books, each consisting of one long poem by Aileen Fisher, with illustrations by such distinguished artists as Adrienne Adams, Symeon Shimin, and Janina Domanska. Both the verse and pictures have a freshness and spontaneity unknown in early books of poetry for children. Favorites in the Aileen Fisher group are *Going Barefoot, I Like Weather, In the Middle of the Night*, and *Listen, Rabbit*.

More Illustrations—Less Poetry

Reviewing the illustrated poetry books written in the late 1960s and early '70s, it is easy to wonder whether these are genuine poetry books for children, or picture books with a few poems thrown in.

For example, *No End of Nonsense*, verses translated from the German by Jack Prelutsky and illustrated by Wilfried Blecher, is a jumbo book with large, ultra-modern three-color illustrations that dominate facing pages—it contains only eleven poems. *It's Raining Said John Twaining*, a book of Danish nursery rhymes translated and illustrated by N. M. Bodecker, contains fresh, delightful rhymes—sometimes only a few lines to a page—under illustrations that fill most of the page. (These are, however, done in a very subtle kind of full color that never seems to intrude on the whole.) *Mother Goose Lost*, nursery rhymes collected by Nicholas Tucker with pictures by Trevor Stubley, has bold, full-color illustrations with large figures that seem to overwhelm the page, in marked contrast to the gentler colors and smaller, more restrained figures by Bodecker.

The Photographic Poetry Book

Perhaps the larger space devoted to illustration in books of poetry for children suggested using photographs, which can be blown up to sweep across a double-page spread or can be cropped to bleed for a more generous effect.

One of the first and most effective of the photographic poetry books was *Reflections on a Gift of Watermelon Pickle and Other Modern Poems* (1966) compiled by Stephen Dunning and others. The book was initiated as a paperback original by Scholastic Books. A paperback of modern poems for kids?

And with photographs at that? It become one of the most popular poetry books for young readers.

On City Streets (1968), *I Heard a Scream in the Street* (1970), *My Name is Black: An Anthology of Black Poets* (1974), and *Hosannah the Home Run!: Poems of Sports* (1972) were among the new anthologies using black-and-white photographs with striking effect. *Haiku: The Mood of Earth* (1971), written by Ann Atwood, was illustrated with her own full-color photographs.

Whether a black-and-white of littered streets, as in *On City Streets*, or a full-color close-up of an exquisite leaf, as in *Haiku: The Mood of Earth*, the photograph seemed to lend an authenticity that appealed to a generation clamoring for "relevance." As one young teenager put it, "It's real," which seemed to be what she needed at the time.

Poets Experiment

Some publishers felt they were going all out when they used lavish color on a large picture-book page of poetry. Others risked using photographs and were pleased to find them so popular. That was only the start. Soon the poets were out-experimenting the experimenters with "concrete poetry," "poems to see," and occasionally what seemed to be "poems to try to figure out."

For example, consider Robert Fromm's poem "Hot Enough to See," in *Seeing Things* (1970). It expects the reader to begin at the bottom of the page and read up to follow a road shimmering with heat. "The Stuck Horn" by Eve Merriam is a typographic pattern of letters—U, O, and W—stretching across the page to suggest the sound effects of the horn. In "Hark, Hark, the Dogs Do Bark," Eve Merriam uses type to add shock effect to her words. The poem of only sixty-six words fills two pages, beginning with billboard type one and three-quarter inches high, and dropping down to the final line in eight-point type: "Only the Roaches quietly crawl."

It's been a long journey from chapbooks to the more innovative of the modern poetry books for children. In the intervening years, new printing processes have been developed, new colors and new typefaces have been created, and a whole new concept of children's needs, interests, and capacities has emerged.

Poetry in the Story Hour

Nancy Larrick

A few years ago *Family Circle* carried an article by Marshall McLuhan which gave what I have come to think of as the key to a successful poetry hour for children—or for adults. The article, entitled "What TV Is Really Doing to Your Children," explains that the television instrument offers a continuous stream of some three million dots per second. The viewer must select the dots from which he creates his image. Thus he becomes a maker and participant—a process completely different from viewing movies or the printed page. "The movie viewer remains detached and is engaged in looking *at* the screen," McLuhan explains. "The TV viewer *is* the screen." This sense of involvement is what enthralls children, according to Dr. McLuhan.[1]

Through our experimentation in the Poetry Workshop at Lehigh University, we have become convinced that a child's appreciation of poetry depends upon his involvement—immediate involvement.

As Eve Merriam puts it in "How to Eat a Poem":[2] Don't be polite. Bite in. Pick it up and eat the juice that may run down your chin. It is ready and ripe now whenever you are. You do not need a knife or fork or spoon or plate or napkin or tablecloth For there is no core or stem or rind or pit or seed or skin to throw away.*

So with poetry we bite in and soon are licking up the juice with delight. No verbal preliminaries or motivation lest they become the knives and forks and spoons which get between us and the poem.

We find that involvement in poetry springs more easily among children and adults when we sit close together—preferably on the floor. When you are sitting, shoulder to shoulder in a close circle, the emotional involvement in a poem seems to come quickly and easily.

I like to begin with poems or songs which have a great deal of repetition so that children can quickly and easily chime in on repeated lines and phrases. They love this kind of impromptu choral reading. One favorite is so old that it is part of our oral folk literature. It begins:

SOURCE: Reprinted by permission of the American Library Association and the author from *Top of the News* 32 (January 1976): 151–161.

If all the seas were one sea
What a great sea that would be!

and then it goes on in the same pattern—so quickly identified that even first graders can pick it up and join in:

If all the trees were one tree
What a great tree that would be!
If all the axes were one axe
What a great axe that would be!

Then comes the narrator's section with a final line for all to come in on:

And if the great man took the great axe
and cut down the great tree
And let it fall into the great sea
What a great SPLASH that would be!

On the first try, we are feeling our way through words and lines that some may be unsure of. But when we try it again, we get more excitement—more drama—into it. And children love it.

Many modern poems have equally intriguing rhythm and repetition which invite group participation. Try David McCord's "The Pickety Fence," for example.[3]

The pickety fence
The pickety fence
Give it a lick it's
The pickety fence
Give it a lick it's
A clickety fence
Give it a lick it's
A lickety fence
Give it a lick
Give it a lick
Give it a lick
With a rickety stick
Pickety
Pickety
Pickety
Pick.*

You can have solo parts in reading that poem, with a chorus coming in on "Give it a lick/ Give it a lick/ Give it a lick." Or the children may suggest that the final "Pickety/ Pickety/ Pickety/ Pick" fade away as though a child and his clicking stick are fading into the distance. And, of course, children

*"The Pickety Fence" from *Every Time I Climb a Tree* by David McCord, Copyright © 1952 by David McCord. Reprinted by permission of Little.

love to do the background accompaniment with pencils and rulers going "pickety, pickety, lickety, clickety, rickety" while others chant the words. By the third or fourth go-round, you have quite a production, a tremendous involvement of the children.

Another favorite for this kind of impromptu choral reading is Aileen Fisher's poem "Weather is Full of the Nicest Sounds,"[4] which sparkles with wonderul sound words children love to imitate. Often we divide the poem up so that each child says one line. As you listen you will realize that each line is a choice example of onomatopoeia in the weatherman's vocabulary: *sings, hums, splashes, bangs, rumbles,* and many more.

Not only do children enjoy what they sometimes call "doing a poem," but they quickly build a repertoire of poems they know by ear because they have become involved from the very beginning.

Favorite songs with lots of repetition give opportunity for involvement too: "The Wheels of the Bus Go Round and Round," for example, or "The Bear Went Over the Mountain," "On Top of Old Smoky," and "Aikendrum."

By this time, many of these old folksongs have been used as the basis for picture books: "Mommy, Buy Me a China Doll,"[5] "Over in the Meadow,"[6] and "Frog Went a-Courtin'."[7] for example.

Children soon begin suggesting ways to divide up the song for different kinds of involvement—a solo with chorus, or a trio singing the question and the rest of the children replying, as in "Mommy, Buy Me a China Doll."

Improvisation follows easily with children suggesting new lines on the old pattern. "Aikendrum" is a favorite vehicle for improvisation.

Instead of a hat made of "good cream cheese," I'm never surprised to have someone sing out "His hat was made of bubble gum, of bubble gum, of bubble gum." And "His coat was made of pizza pie, of pizza pie, of pizza pie." In one sixth grade group, "She'll Be Comin' Round the Mountain" was completely modernized to the great delight of everyone. The kids abandoned the six white horses and sang,

"She'll be ridin' on a Honda when she comes,"

And then:

"She'll be wearin' a red bikini when she comes . . . Yippee!"

Music and Poetry

I am sure that I have always known that poetry is meant to be heard and that poetry and music go hand in hand. But it is only through the Poetry Workshop that I have learned that music and poetry are inseparable. It has a magnetic effect on the children of television who have learned to expect it continuously.

Sometimes we begin with Ella Jenkins' "You Sing a Song and I'll Sing a Song . . . And We'll All Sing a Song Together," and thus draw the little circle closer together as one group sings and then another.

Or we will begin with the old spiritual "Kum ba ya":

Someone's singing, Lord, kum-ba-ya

Then:

Someone's laughing, Lord, kum-ba-ya

Children soon learn that the rhythm changes with the meanings so they sing lightly and gayly "Someone's laughing, Lord"—even "Someone's giggling, Lord." Then they become very solemn as they sing "Someone's lonely, Lord," or "Someone's suffering, Lord."

Then we suggest they hum the melody softly as background to the reading of such poems as Langston Hughes' "The Dream Keeper"[8] or "April Rain Song."[9] Easily they change the tempo of their humming to fit the mood of the poem. And soon they learn that as the reading of the poem ends, the humming chorus can break into the words of the song in a lovely finale.

One of the most stirring segments of a poetry hour I ever saw was when a black teacher from New York taught a group of teachers at the NCTE in Atlanta to sing the fivefold Amen, pronounced *A-MIN* she told us. Then, she suggested we hum it while she read "Mother to Son"[10] by Langston Hughes. "At the end," she said, "Sing out with the words *Amin Amin Amin Amin Amin*." Without further rehearsal, we were totally swept into the emotional impact of the poem and music.

With this kind of involvement, children soon think up songs that set the tone for certain poems: "Take Me Out to the Ball Game," for example, for the narrative poem "Casey at the Bat." This is a good time to introduce the baseball poems in Alice Fleming's anthology *Hosannah the Home Run!* (Little, 1972). There's "The Base Stealer" by Robert Francis, "Dream of a Baseball Star" by Gregory Corso, and "Hits and Runs" by Carl Sandburg, among others. It can become a little production, weaving poetry and music and baseball into a memorable few minutes of the poetry hour. It is one that children ask for again and again.

The old spiritual "One Wide River" makes beautiful background music for *Prayers from the Ark* by Carmen Bernos de Gasztold. A rather stately tempo seems right for "Noah's Prayer,"[11] with which the book opens:

Lord
what a menagerie!
Between Your downpour and these animal cries
one cannot hear oneself think!
The days are long,
Lord.*

*From *Prayers from the Ark* by Carmen Benos de Gasztold, translated by Rumer Godden. Copyright © 1962 by Rumer Godden. Reprinted by permission of The Viking Press, Inc.

For "The Prayer of the Butterfly,"[12] the tempo of the lines changes and therefore the music must change:

Lord!
Where was I?
Oh yes! This flower, this sun,
thank You! Your world is beautiful!
This scent of roses . . .
Where was I?
A drop of dew
rolls to sparkle in a lily's heart.
I have to go . . .
Where I do not know!†

Frequently children write their own prayers from the ark and will read those in the poetry hour while their friends hum a melody for the background. Let me present two such poems from fourth graders.

"The Prayer of the Skunk"

Dear Lord
Why did you make me smell so bad?
Nobody likes me
except you.
My aroma does protect me
Help me to use it wisely
and sparingly.

—ANDY FREEH

"The Prayer of the Rabbit"

Oh, Lord,
Why did you make me so tasty?
Hunters like to
shoot and skin
and eat me.
But there's one thing
I'm thankful for—
little children
always love me.

—BOBBY GLICK

Often it is very effective to use a recording as background music for reading of a poem. You will find that children of all ages are full of ideas for such combinations. Let me give you some of these pairings of poem and recorded song:

†From *Prayers from the Ark* by Carmen Bernos de Gasztold, translated by Rumer Godden. Copyright © 1962 by Rumer Godden. Reprinted by permission of The Viking Press, Inc.

Karla Kuskin's "The Balloon"[13] read with Herb Alpert's recording of "Winds of Barcelona."

Whitman's "I Hear America Singing"[14] with Simon and Garfunkle's "America" as recorded by the Book Ends.

If you can play an autoharp or guitar, bring it into the poetry hour. Or invite the kids to bring their musical instruments. Just a little strumming—even an occasional chord—will add magic to the reading of poetry.

Much as I love that tight little circle on the floor, I know it has to break up sometime. For involvement in poetry suggests movement, body movement, not just musical accompaniment and sound effects.

Movement and Poetry

My students are doing more and more with movement as a means of involvement in poetry. I don't just mean finger play of the "Inky dinky spider" variety, which presupposes sitting still and moving only a few fingers according to a predetermined pattern. I mean body movement—sometimes wild, abandoned body movement, as interpretive of the mood and message of the poem.

A second grade teacher who had studied under a member of the Martha Graham troupe was the one who first made me realize the significance of body movement with poetry. For her term project in the Poetry Workshop, she asked to make a report on body movement and poetry. For her demonstration she wore a black leotard and gave us an exquisite interpretive dance as another student read four poems written by city kids about the city. She chose the poems from *I Heard a Scream in the Street* (Evans, 1970; Dell, 1972).

As she was about to start, several children happened to wander into our workshop, so on the spur of the moment she asked them if they would like to help. She posted them at various spots in the open floor area and told them to make the notions of walking without leaving the same spot. She would dance among them, she told them, as though going down the street where people were walking along. Wide-eyed, they agreed to help, and she gave her dance as these poems were read. It was an experience I shall never forget.

In another class—this time fourth grade—the teacher played part of Dvorak's "New World Symphony" as she read Aileen Fisher's *In the Middle of the Night*.[15] Then she repeated the music and asked the children to pretend they were taking a walk in the middle of the night as she read the poem against the musical background. Someone suggested it would be better if the room were darkened, so they drew the blinds and turned off the lights to create the mood for their interpretation of poem and music.

I wish you could have visited our Poetry Workshop at Lehigh two years ago when, for the first time, we were all part of a demonstration of body movement as a way to involvement in poetry for children. Two young teachers were in charge. The rest of us sat on the bare floor—all in a totally relaxed position—legs outstretched, arms hanging limp, heads dropping, and eyes closed.

As a poem was read, we were to express with our bodies how the poem made us feel—rising to a kneeling position, standing, swaying, leaping—whatever the poem seemed to call for. The reader began with "Noah's Prayer" from *Prayers from the Ark*. As I heard the words, I felt a strange involvement in the poem, for with eyes closed, I was detached from others in the group and felt free to lift my hands in supplication and then rise to my knees in prayer as Noah might have done. As other poems were read from the same book—"The Prayer of the Cat" and "The Prayer of the Old Horse," for example—I felt the same involvement, and I moved as the spirit of the poem seemed to guide me.

"The Prayer of the Ox"[16]—heavy, cumbersome, plodding—impelled me to do the same thing:

> Dear God, give me time
> Men are always so driven!
> Make them understand that I can never hurry.
> Give me time to eat
> Give me time to plod
> Give me time to sleep
> Give me time to think.*

Several days later, our two leaders showed a movie they had made of our spontaneous body movement to the reading of the poems. At first we giggled like children and cried, "Look at Liza!" . . . "Oh did I do that?" and so on. But, like children, we wanted to see it again, and on the second showing, and on the third, we could see pattern to the movement of all of us—slow and plodding for "The Prayer of the Ox," light and flitting for "The Prayer of the Butterfly." We saw that even our faces changed, from the almost tragic supplication of Noah to the carefree gaiety of the butterfly. To me it was a totally new way of approaching poetry—one I shall always remember.

I tell you this because I think an adult must experience this sort of involvement in order to recognize its significance and to be ready to lead children into similar partnership with the poet. Often we find that in a classroom it is better to have one of the children read the poems so that the adult—whether teacher or librarian—can be on the floor with other members of the class, participating on the same level and with the same abandonment of self.

Through body movement and interpretive dance we are getting into the

*From *Prayers of the Ark* by Carmen Bernos De Gasztold, translated by Rumer Godden.

performing arts as they bring involvement in poetry. And here, of course, we must include dramatization, pantomime, and puppets—all ideal for poetry.

Probably the simplest to bring about is impromptu dramatization or pantomime, with one or more children acting out the poem while it is being read aloud. Try Eve Merriam's "Bam, Bam, Bam"[17] or Vachel Lindsay's "The Mysterious Cat,"[18] with all the sound effects they suggest.

Or try the old ballad "Get Up and Bar the Door,"[19] with the story-line done by the reader and the Goodman and Goodwife each saying his or her own lines, while intruders gobble up the pudding and threaten to take off the old man's beard and kiss the Goodwife. Its earthy humor every child seems to love.

One group of eighth graders chose Shel Silverstein's poem "Beware, My Child,"[20] which they read with appropriate hissing and threatening tones:

Beware, my child,
Of the snaggle-toothed beast
He sleeps till noon,
and then makes his feast
on Hershey bars
and cakes of yeast
and anyone around—o.
So when you see him,
sneeze three times
and say three loud
and senseless rhymes
and give him all your
saved-up dimes
or else you'll ne'er be found—o.

For the Poetry Hour

With a little guidance, children begin to search out poems on the same theme and weave them into a sequence to present to the story hour. It may be a combination of poems by one poet—and John Ciardi and Eve Merriam are always favorites in something of this sort—or perhaps a group of poems by black poets or poems about the city. One group of fourth graders planned a poetry hour about the theme "Who Am I?" using Felice Holman's poem of that title[21] as a starter. They went on to include David McCord's "This is My Rock"[22] and Emily Dickinson's "I'm nobody. Who are you?"[23] They used background music and some chanting of lines and repeated phrases. It was a very moving little poetry series—perhaps more serious than most adults would have considered for this age level. But it was the children's own and deeply moving to them.

Another possibility is to combine folktales and poetry in a single story hour. Last fall one of my students—a fourth grade teacher—put on a fascinating program of Eskimo tales and poems. She used several stories from *The Day Tuk Became a Hunter and Other Eskimo Stories* by Ronald Melzack (Dodd, 1968), one from *The Blind Boy and the Loon and Other Eskimo Myths* by Ramona Maher (John Day, 1969), and poems taken from Richard Lewis' *I Breathe a New Song: Poems of the Eskimo* (Simon & Schuster), and *Beyond the High Hills*, poems collected by Knud Rasmussen (World, 1961).

Folktales, poems, and folk music from Africa can be woven into a beautiful program, perhaps with a recording of African drums in the background. At Christmas, select some of the Eleanor Farjean poems to be read over the humming of Christmas carols, the Russian folktale of *Baboushka and the Three Kings* (Parnassus, 1960), and then the old folksong "The Twelve Days of Christmas." You have the makings of a program in which everyone can have a part and which can be handled spontaneously and beautifully.

So far I have used the term poetry hour or poetry program to designate the presentation of poetry through oral reading and one or more of the performing arts. In almost every session of our Poetry Workshop—and almost every week of their classroom teaching—our students put on a poetry program of some sort. They soon report that the most effective programs are those the children have a large part in or which they present on their own.

Toward the end of a semester, I find these little poetry programs are growing into multimedia productions. For reasons I cannot quite explain, we have come to call them "poetry happenings." They serve as a sort of culminating production in a particular area. In addition to reading poetry aloud, chanting repeated lines, and even singing parts, children arrange background music, taped so that perfect sequence is assured. Added to that there may be pantomime and dance, plus colored slides to give the right mood or visual background. Often such a program includes poems written by the students, read along with those of published authors, and color slides made with an Ectographic Visual Master from the children's own paintings.

In all of the poetry workshops at Lehigh, we give our graduate students the chance to stage a poetry happening if they are so inclined. We find that when these adults—teachers, reading specialists, and librarians—have themselves planned a poetry happening and then take part, they bring out far more interest and enthusiasm from their own pupils.

Two years ago in the Library School of the University of Arizona such a poetry happening suddenly began to flower on the next to last day of the one-week workshop. We had heard the recording of Marian Seldes reading *Prayers from the Ark* (Folkways Record FL 9727) and talked about the possibility of using this with children, even as a means of stimulating their own poetry writing.

Someone suggested that in Arizona they might write *Prayers from the Desert* as more appropriate—which they did—one writing the prayer of the barrel cactus, another the prayer of the tumbleweed, another the prayer of the hog-nosed skunk, and so on. The results were fantastic—too good to keep to the silent pages on which they were written. This was Thursday afternoon, and Friday was the last day of the workshop. Half of the group of sixty-five adults agreed to present their poems through the visual arts—making a great mural on which they lettered their poems and decorated them with a collage of natural materials—a branch of cactus, a piece of tumbleweed, and so on.

The other half put on one of the most stirring poetry happenings I have ever seen—using color slides, recorded music, modern dance, some very simple properties (a scarf around someone's waist, a great golden disc to represent the sun god of the desert)—all to illustrate and dramatize their own poems, *The Prayers of the Desert*.

Thus have we been bringing poetry into the story hour. The possibilities are endless. Like the poem which Eve Merriam describes in "How to Eat a Poem," the children of television are "ready and ripe now whenever you are."

References

1. Marshall McLuhan, "What TV Is Really Doing to Your Children," *Family Circle*, March 1967.
2. From Eve Merriam, *It Doesn't Always Have to Rhyme* (Atheneum, 1964).
3. From David McCord, *Every Time I Climb a Tree* (Little, 1967).
4. From Aileen Fisher, *I Like Weather* (Crowell, 1963).
5. Harve Zemach, *Mommy, Buy Me a China Doll;* il. by Margot Zemach (Follett, 1966), OP.
6. John Langstaff, *Over in the Meadow;* il. by Feodor Rojankovsky (Harcourt, 1967); *Over in the Meadow;* il. by Ezra Jack Keats (Four Winds and Scholastic, 1972).
7. John Langstaff, *Frog Went a-Courtin';* il. by Feodor Rojankovsky (Harcourt, 1955).
8. From *Don't You Turn Back: Poems by Langston Hughes;* selected by Lee Bennett Hopkins (Knopf, 1969).
9. Ibid.
10. Ibid.
11. From Carmen Bernos de Gasztold, *Prayers from the Ark;* tr. by Rumer Godden (Viking, 1962).
12. Ibid.
13. From Karla Kuskin, *In the Middle of the Trees* (Harper, 1958).
14. From *Poems of Walt Whitman: Leaves of Grass;* selected by Lawrence Clark Powell (Crowell, 1964).
15. Aileen Fisher, *In the Middle of the Night* (Crowell, 1965).
16. From de Gasztold, *Prayers from the Ark*.
17. From Eve Merriam, *Catch a Little Rhyme* (Atheneum, 1966).
18. From Vachel Lindsay, *Johnny Appleseed and Other Poems* (Macmillan, 1930).
19. From *Piping Down the Valleys Wild;* ed. by Nancy Larrick (Delacorte, 1968; Dell, 1970).
20. Ibid.
21. From Felice Holman. *At the Top of My Voice and Other Poems* (Norton, 1970).
22. From David McCord. *Far and Few: Rhymes of the Never Was and Always Is* (Little, 1952; Dell, 1971).
23. From *Poems of Emily Dickinson;* selected by Helen Plotz (Crowell, 1964).

4

Counting Books

Alphabet Books: A Neglected Genre

John Warren Stewig

The ubiquitous alphabet book ranges from black-and-white photographs to highly saturated full color, from simplicity personified to densly packed overabundance. Such books are a common element in preschools, kindergartens, and first grades, but curiously disappear from children's environments shortly thereafter. Having been used to teach letter form, sequence, and in incidental fashion some vocabulary, they are abandoned by teachers and children alike.

Yet in so doing, a valuable opportunity is lost—the opportunity of developing children's ability to see and speak with clarity. The alphabet book is a useful tool for developing children's *visual literacy*, the ability to look clearly and analytically at a visual stimulus and interpret it. *Verbal literacy*, the ability to talk clearly and concisely about one's observations, comparisons, and reactions, can also be developed. Why are such tasks important?

About eighty percent of our information comes to us visually (Debes and Willians 1974). Our bombardment by visual stimuli is so universal that it hardly evokes comment. Yet where in the curriculum do we teach children to "read" such visual input—to examine it carefully part by part, extracting meaning and interacting with what is extracted? Such processes are central to the reading program, but few children learn to read pictures effectively, despite the value in visual literacy.

Another important goal is developing verbal literacy: the ability to put coherent thoughts into words, words into sentences, and sentences into larger units. Most of us spend more time communicating orally than either reading or writing. Yet where in elementary schools do we help children learn to express in words what they have taken in through their senses? Specifically, where do we help children learn to talk cogently and literately about what they see in pictures, and other visual stimuli they view?

Because instruction in visual and verbal literacy seems minimal, I would like to describe some approaches to developing these important skills. Such approaches are as yet a mosaic of interesting ideas, rather than a coherent philosophy or a unified approach to educating young children. One pair of authors, in describing a program of visual literacy, has commented: "Especially after the early grades, there is a tendency to minimize the visual aspects of communication and children are, in a sense, 'weaned away' from pictures and illustrations. . ." (Fransecky and Debes 1972, p. 23).

Instead of leading children away from pictures and toward the printed word, we can consider using visual materials to develop their ability to see, and to talk with greater fluency. One kind of material we can use is the alphabet book.

Children are seldom encouraged to study book illustrations and they are even less often asked to translate what they have learned in this visual mode into the verbal mode. Putting thoughts about what was learned visually into spoken words is an important thought challenge all children should experience.

Visual-Verbal Skills

In developing visual-verbal literacy, there are three sub-skills to be considered. These are sequential, from simple to more complex, and children should have opportunities to develop one skill before moving on to the next one.

The first of these skills is to *describe* objectively—clearly, concisely, concretely—what the child sees. What we are asking children to do is to study an object providing visual input, and then translate this input into words.

The second of these skills is an extension of the first—to *compare* two different objects, using common descriptors. Given two objects, can the child accurately describe the two, including the differences which exist? In looking at two pictures, can the child see what is similar about them, and what sets them apart from each other? If we have two alphabet books, can children describe how the illustrations are the same or different?

The third, more sophisticated, and most important of these visual-verbal skills is the ability to *value* one of the objects. We want children to develop the ability to say which picture they prefer, and why. This verbal ability is important because few are capable of more than an impoverished description of their evaluations. Listen to adults tell you what they like. Inchoate thoughts too often come out as insistent reiterations of what a person "likes." Indeed it is a rare individual who can give a convincing reason for a visual preference. Many adults insist, "I don't really know anything about art, but I know what I like." Such a statement not only tells the listener about an impoverished background, but also a muddled thought process and a paucity of verbal expression. Since this three-part ability is crucial for adults, and possible for children, what kinds of experiences should classroom teachers plan to develop children's visual-verbal literacy?

Materials to Use

Some writers describing visual literacy recommend film study. This is indeed an exciting possibility after preparatory experiences. For young children, such visual images on film move too quickly, and are not conducive to the study and reflection I am recommending. Additional drawbacks are the cost and relative inconvenience of film.

Rather, a plentiful, convenient, and relatively inexpensive source of material exists: illustrations in children's books. Much of what we do with developing visual and verbal skills can be done through books. Countless artists work in the field as picture and illustrated books proliferate rapidly. The teacher is at no loss, therefore, to find materials to help children develop these skills. Any type of picture or illustrated book can be used for this purpose, though in this instance we shall consider using alphabet books. It is a simple task to locate several alphabet books as a basis for practicing each of the three skills.

Variety in Style

In using illustrations from alphabet books as stimulus material, the teacher helps children study the illustrations for their own sake—not for the letter form or sequence possibilities, nor for the concept and vocabulary development possible. These are valid, albeit traditional uses for such books. Rather, we are examining illustration as an independent visual artifact, which has meaning of its own. With preschool children, we begin very simply, using one illustration and asking children to tell us what they see, to detail what they take in visually. What they see varies greatly, as alphabet books provide a wealth of artistic styles, expressed through a rich variety of artistic media.

It makes little difference whether you begin with the black ink fantasy drawings of Warburg (1968), the romanticism in subdued color of Tudor (1954), or the sharply delineated photography of Miller (1971). Such books naturally arouse the interest of the young. Instead of using the books only to encourage thinking about shapes of letters and their sequence, the teacher uses the books to increase visual and verbal fluency. Who can resist talking about Lionni's (1968) fuzzy mauve caterpillar, searching for words in a lush stencilled design of leaves? Or about Ipcar's (1964) toothy carpenter, only one in a varied menagerie?

All young children need is some planned encouragement from the teacher to start them on the road to increased oral fluency, through the delightful vehicle of pictures.

The teacher chooses one book, beginning with a visually simple one.

For example, one by Rey (1963) features bold black lines enclosing vibrant primary colors, a suitable background for Curious George, whom children delight in describing. Asking children "What do you see?" will elicit a simple enumeration of items. This is the first step, basic describing.

The teacher may structure the response quite specifically, giving an example first. "I see a giraffe eating grapes. What do you see?" The giraffe is only one of many creatures juxtaposed to unusual effect by Beni Montressor (1969). After simple identification of what is present, the teacher has children describe more specifically the nature of the object—"I see a brown bird with a long tail feather." The meticulous detailing of the quetzal is characteristic of Rojankovsky's (1962) animals. In contrast, viewing Piatti's (1966) illustration, one child said: "I see an orange monkey with a funny white face hanging in a tree." Piatti's black line boldly carves out a succession of strong geometric shapes from a stark background, quite unlike Rojankovsky's approach.

In the next stage, *comparing*, choose two books quite different in style, so the contrast is apparent. The fantasy of Chardiet (1971) is very unlike the evocative realism of Gordon's (1961) photographs. Later, as children develop describing skills, the teacher can use books done in similar styles. For example, during the first stages of comparing, try using Amelia Gibbon's (Howard 1967) book with thin black line showing precisely another time and place. This can be contrasted with the simplified geometry of Burningham (1964), whose solid queen could never confront Gibbon's nobleman. Similarly, Greenaway's (n.d.) delicately drawn pastel renditions of children contrast dramatically with the children in Steiner's (1965) book. I would not use Brown's (1959) book with Knight's (1961) book, because it is difficult for young children to discern differences. The use of color and line is similar, and greater contrast is needed when beginning this process with children. I would save Wildsmith's (1962) book and Munari's (1960) for later in the sequence, when children have developed skills of seeing and comparing. The subtle differences between the two provide a challenge to children with some experience in this process.

When developing the third skill, *valuing*, the teacher is careful to respect the child's reason for choosing the illustration preferred, even if it doesn't seem like a good reason. While we rule out such unfocussed responses as, "I like this one *because* . . ." we must respect children's reasons when they give them, even if they are not our own. When using the book by Williams (1957), a child said: "I like this one because the fish has a silly smile." This may not seem like a "good" reason to us. Nevertheless, the child understood the process of verbalizing the reason for his choice. When this occurs, we must be content with the reason until we can help the child develop more sophisticated visual judgements. One older child said of an illustration by Gag (1933), "I like the rabbit because he looks happy dancing with his feet off the ground." This comment is closer to our goal, a fluent oral response. The same is true of the valuing by a sixth grade child who said: "I like the lion because the way the *l's* overlap makes a nice repeat." Barry's (1961) use of stencil and stamping techniques with ink lines caught the child's attention. Then she went on to say, "I like it better than the jaguar because you can imagine more with the lion." We may not agree with her lack of appreciation of Fall's (1923) illustration, yet we must respect her judgement. More exposure to the singularly powerful renditions by that master of woodcut may result in a different evaluation at another time.

As you move from the simple monochrome illustrations in *Crictor* (Ungerer 1958) to the intricacies of *Mary Poppins from A to Z* (Travers 1962), children sharpen their visual judgements and their ability to describe.

Children's Response to Materials

Once teachers have selected the alphabet books to use with children, they are ready to begin. Ways to use materials and ways children may respond have been sketched briefly. Specific methods of presentation, types of questions asked to encourage observation and discussion, number of illustrations used, and session duration must depend on the group. The teacher will vary these factors to offer children opportunities for developing visual and verbal skills of describing.

While using the materials with children, I discovered that kindergarten children without previous experience in structural oral discussion delighted in describing what they saw in the book by Fujikawa (1974). They were developing the first skill—that of describing or enumerating. Since it was an initial experience, we began simply with one illustration and a few questions:

1. What do you see in the picture?
2. What colors has the artist used?
3. Where is this happening? How can you tell?

Older children, with a variety of previous oral experiences, were able to do quite well in *valuing,* as a result of close observation and practice in describing. A classroom teacher used three books (Brown, 1974; Miles 1969; Sendak 1962) in doing a three section unit on describing. The books were available in the room for a few days so children could observe them. It was challenging to the children to see how clearly they could observe what was there. Increasing observational skills is always a concomitant of this type of experience. One oral discussion session centered on describing what was included in each illustration. A second session centered on comparing two illustrations. During the third session children explained to their classmates their reason for preferring, or valuing, one of the three illustrations. There was little verbal impoverishment apparent as these children discussed articulately the reasons for their choice.

Visual and verbal skills, so crucial because they are most frequently used by adults, are paradoxically among those least often developed systematically in the elementary school. One reason for this is that component subskills are infrequently identified. Describing is an oral skill we use everyday. Three component sub-skills of describing have been identified. Because these sub-skills are crucial, children must be provided opportunities to detail, compare, and value orally. One effective way of encouraging children to do this is to use illustrations in alphabet books as motivation. The approach offers many advantages: The books are easy to locate, plentiful, and of much interest to children. The teacher using this approach will find children respond eagerly and in the pleasant process develop increased visual and verbal fluency.

References

Barry, Katharine. *A Is for Anything*. New York: Harcourt, Brace & World, Inc., 1961.

Brown, Marcia. *All Butterflies*. New York: Charles Scribner's Sons, 1974.

______. *Peter Piper's Alphabet*. New York: Charles Scribner's Sons, 1959.

Burningham, John. *ABCDEFGHIJKLMNOPQRSTUVWXYZ*. New York: Bobbs-Merrill Co., 1964.

Chardiet, Bernice. *C Is for Circus*. New York: Walker & Co., 1971.

Debes, John L. and Williams, Clarence M. "The Power of Visuals." *Instructor* 84 (December 1974):32–39.

Falls, C. B. *ABC*. New York: Doubleday & Co., Inc., 1923.

Fransecky, Robert G. and Debes, John L. *Visual Literacy: A Way to Learn—A Way to Teach*. Washington: Association for Educational Communication and Technology, 1972.

Fujikawa, Gyo. *A to Z Picture Book*. New York: Grosset & Dunlap, 1974.

Gag, Wanda. *The ABC Bunny*. New York: Coward McCann, Co., Inc., 1933.

Gordon, Isabel. *The ABC Hunt*. New York: Viking, 1961.

Greenaway, Kate. *A Apple Pie*. London: Fredrick Warne & Co., Ltd., n.d.

Howard, Frances. *An Illustrated Comic Alphabet*. New York: Henry L. Walck, 1967.

Ipcar, Dahlov. *I Love My Anteater with an A*. New York: Alfred A. Knopf, 1964.

Knight, Hilary. *Hilary Knight's ABC*. New York: Golden Press, 1961.

Lionni, Leo. *The Alphabet Tree*. Pantheon, 1968.

Miles, Miskà. *Apricot ABC*. Boston: Little, Brown & Co., 1969.

Miller, Barry. *Alphabet World*. New York: Macmillan, 1971.

Montressor, Beni. *A for Angel*. New York: Alfred A. Knopf, 1969.

Munari, Bruno. *ABC*. Cleveland: The World Pub. Co., 1960.

Piatti, Celestino. *Animal ABC*. Atheneum, 1966.

Rey, H. A. *Curious George Learns the Alphabet*. Boston: Houghton-Mifflin, 1963.

Rojankovsky, Feodor. *Animals in the Zoo*. New York: Alfred A. Knopf, 1962.

Sendak, Maurice. *Alligators All Around*. New York: Harper & Row, 1962.
Steiner, Charlotte. *Annie's ABC Kitten*. New York: Alfred A. Knopf, 1965.
Travers, P. L. *Mary Poppins from A to Z*. New York: Harcourt Brace & World, Inc., 1962.
Tudor, Tasha. *A Is for Anna Belle*. New York: Henry Z. Walck, Inc., 1954.
Ungerer, Tomi. *Crictor*. New York: Harper & Row, 1958.
Warboug, Sandol. *From Ambledee to Zumbledee*. Boston: Houghton-Mifflin, 1968.
Wildsmith, Brian. *ABC*. New York: Franklin Watts, Inc., 1962.
Williams, Garth. *The Big Golden Animal ABC*. New York: Simon & Schuster, 1957.

Using Children's Literature to Teach Mathematics

Muriel Rogie Radebaugh

In teaching mathematics to young children, we must look at the world through children's eyes (Baratta-Lorton, 1976). Young children learn concepts and relationships through direct, concrete experiences rather than through the mental manipulation of abstract ideas (Copeland, 1978; Furth, 1970).

Initially, learning math concepts depends on direct physical contact with objects. The pictorial stage (one step more abstract than concrete experience) may also begin at an early age. Large clear drawings which represent the distinctive features of common objects help children focus on the objects' abstract features (Gibson, 1975).

This article identifies children's books that may be used to supplement concrete experiences in math. Many of the books do not deal directly with mathematics topics but do lend themselves to reinforcing these concepts. This list is not exhaustive; it provides only a sample. Many others could be added by teachers and parents of young children.

SOURCE: *Reading Teacher*, May 1981, pp. 902–906. Reprinted with permission of the author and the International Reading Association.

Geometric Shapes

Children observe common geometric shapes in many objects they use every day. Wheels are circular, blocks may have square or rectangular sides. Parents and teachers can help children identify common two-dimensional geometric shapes and provide a basis for learning geometric concepts and spatial relations.

Bright, colorful illustrations in children's books may be used to help distinguish geometric shapes in familiar objects. After distinguishing among triangles, circles, and squares, children could design animals, people or objects with these geometric shapes. They could identify the shapes of three-dimensional objects in their homes or classroom: the square tiles of the ceiling, the triangular beak of a bird or the circular wheels of a doll carriage. A parent or teacher might place mystery items in a box and ask children first to feel them, without looking; to guess what they might be; and then to describe their geometric shape.

Useful books for these activities include:

Carle, Eric. *My Very First Book of Shapes*. Crowell, 1974.
Illustrations of common objects are matched with geometric shapes.

Curry, Nancy. *An Apple is Red*. Bowmar, 1967.
Photographs of fruit can lead to a discussion of geometric figures.

Emberley, Ed. *The Wing on a Flea*. Little, Brown, 1961.
Delightful text and illustrations point out triangles, rectangles, and circles in the world around us.

Feltser, Eleanor B. *The Sesame Street Book of Shapes*. Little, Brown, 1970.
Squares, circles, rectangles and triangles are shown with photographs of people and buildings illustrating real-life shapes.

Mayer, Mercer. *Bubble, Bubble*. Parents' Magazine Press, 1973.
The bubbles blown in this wordless book take on fantastic shapes.

Radlauer, Edward. *Motorcycle Mania*. Childrens Press, 1973.
Photographs of motorcyles provide examples of many geometric shapes.

Wildsmith, Brian. *Brian Wildsmith's One, Two, Three*. Watts, 1965.
This number book is colorfully illustrated with geometric shapes showing the numbers 1 through 10.

Comparison—Relative Size

Children are small, kittens and puppies are small, we now drive a small car, and one should put only a small amount of salt on the potatoes. How can all of these things be small when none are the same size?

Six and seven year olds, who, according to Piaget, are beginning to outgrow the egocentric thinking of early childhood, can begin to understand the concept of relative size. The following books may help children learn this abstract concept. For discussion after reading the teacher might ask questions such as "How big do you feel when you stand beside a grownup? How big would you feel if you were standing beside Thumbelina? Why are you sometimes large and sometimes small?"

Andersen, Hans Christian. *Thumbelina*. Scribner, 1961.
An old couple who long for a child find a tiny daughter no larger than a thimble.

Asbjornsen, P. C., and J. E. Moe. *The Three Billy Goats Gruff*. Harcourt, Brace and World, 1957.
This traditional tale describes characters of different sizes.

Brown, Margaret Wise. *Young Kangaroo*. William R. Scott, 1955.
As the young kangaroo grows, he learns more about the world around him.

Crume, Marion W. *Listen!* Bowmar, 1968.
Large, clear photographs by Cliff Roe depict adults and children observing sounds in the city.

Diot, Alain. *Better, Best, Bestest*. Harlan Quist, 1977.
Children boast that their father's car is bigger and better than anything in the world. The storyteller asks his father what he has that is bigger and better than anything in the world. The answer, a surprise to the child, introduces a variant meaning of the concept "bigger."

Froman, Robert. *Bigger and Smaller*. Crowell, 1971.
Large and small are determined by comparing one object with another; yet, an object may be large when compared to one object and small when compared to another.

Peet, Bill. *Huge Harold*. Houghton-Mifflin, 1961.
Harold was no ordinary rabbit. He was huge! After looking in vain for a home, he finds his niche in life.

Wolcott, Patty. *Tunafish Sandwiches*. Addisonian Press, 1975.
Beginning with little animals, the food chain is traced to tunafish sandwiches and you.

Ordinal Numbers

"I want to be first! Second!" Children learn quickly what ordinal position means. Ordinal numbers are often used by adults in giving directions, too.

Children are instructed to "Look in the second drawer" or to report a series of events in the correct order.

Remembering the sequence of a story lends itself well to activities using ordinals. What happened first in the story? What happened second? Which animal tried to help third? Pictures of the story could be ordered and matched with the words first, second, and third. Children could create masks for characters in animal stories and dramatize their appearance in the correct order.

The following books are simple stories with a definitive sequence of events. They help children become familiar with the process of reporting events in the order they took place.

Beim, Jerrold. *The Lost and Found Ball*. Webster, 1961.
Andy loses his new red ball in the tall grass and later finds it again.

Bishop, Claire Huchet, and Kurt Weise. *The Five Chinese Brothers*. Coward, McCann and Geoghegan, 1938.
Five Chinese brothers had special powers to use when the first Chinese brother was put into prison and doomed to be executed.

Clifton, Lucille. *My Brother Fine with Me*. Holt, Rinehart and Winston, 1975.
When her five-year-old brother decides to run away from home, Johnny is glad—at first.

Coombs, Patricia. *Dorrie and the Witch Doctor*. Lothrop, Lee and Shepard, 1967.
Aunt Agra comes to visit and things begin to go wrong, even though Dorrie tries her best to be good.

Daugherty, James. *The Picnic*. Viking, 1958.
Aesop's lion and mouse fable has a new dress.

Davis, Alice Vaught. *Timothy Turtle*. Harcourt, Brace and World, 1940.
Timothy Turtle landed on his back while sliding down the bank and was unable to turn over again. His friends tried to help him with no success, until Frog had a great idea.

Emberley, Barbara. *Drummer Hoff*. Prentice-Hall, 1967.
Many other people contributed to the firing of the cannon, but "Drummer Hoff fired it off."

Potter, Beatrix. *The Tale of Squirrel Nutkin*. Warne, 1903.
Squirrel Nutkin, rude and impertinent, is taught a lesson by Old Brown, the owl.

Tresselt, Alvin. *The Mitten*. Lothrop, Lee and Shepard, 1964.
A small boy drops a mitten in the snow while looking for firewood. When too many animals decide it would make a warm home, they leave it in tatters.

Number Concepts and Counting

Early in a young child's life, parents and older siblings point out number as an important attribute of sets of objects. "Look, Susie, two rabbits!" The rabbits could also be described as white, furry, small or squirming, and all of these attributes are more concrete and more readily perceived by the senses than the concept "two," but number concepts are important in our world and most children learn them early.

An adequate understanding of number concepts is the basis of all subsequent mathematical learning. The concept of a one-to-one correspondence between number names and objects or that three kittens are numerically equivalent to three cookies or three giants, is developed slowly over several years. Counting objects in books like *Tia Maria's Garden* or *Brian Wildsmith's One, Two, Threes* or noting that there are *two* wheels on a motorcycle aids in establishing the invariance of number in the child's mind. Picture books can serve as aids for identifying the simpler number concepts and later provide nonmanipulative objects for counting and mental calculations.

Number Concepts

Adler, Irving and Ruth. *Sets and Numbers for the Very Young*. John Day, 1969.
Simple examples of the numbers 1 through 10, the concept of sets, and counting.

Cole, William. *What's Good for a Four-Year-Old?* Holt, Rinehart and Winston, 1967.

Cole, William. *What's Good for a Three-Year-Old?* Holt, Rinehart and Winston, 1974.
There are many things that are good for three and four year olds, three or four on each page.

Radlauer, Edward. *Motorcycle Mania*. Childrens Press, 1973.
Photographs of motorcycles provide examples of geometric shapes and opportunities for counting.

Tudor, Tasha. *1 is One*. Walck, 1956.
Delicate illustrations accompany counting rhymes for the numbers 1 through 20.

Wildsmith, Brian. *Brian Wildsmith's One, Two, Threes*. Watts, 1965.
This number book is colorfully illustrated with geometric shapes illustrating the numbers 1 through 10.

Counting

Bishop, Claire Huchet. *Twenty-Two Bears*. Viking Press, 1964.
22 bears who live in the wild woods of Wyoming meet the child's bear and have a picnic.

Clark, Ann Nolan. *Tia Maria's Garden*. Viking Press, 1963.
The desert is Tia Maria's garden. She and the child walk in the morning, looking at the animals and the cacti.

Dalgliesh, Alice. *The Little Wooden Farmer*. Macmillan, 1968.
A ship captain collects animals for a farm couple.

Ehrlich, Amy. *The Everyday Train*. Dial Press, 1977.
Jane watches the train go by her house, noting the many kinds of freight cars it pulls.

Eichenberg, Fritz. *Dancing in the Moon*. Harcourt, Brace and World, 1955.
Counting rhymes for the numbers 1 through 20.

Ets, Marie Hall. *In the Forest*. Viking Press, 1945.
A child goes for a walk in the forest and all the animals join him for a picnic. They play games until his father wakes him so they can go home.

Feelings, Muriel. *Moja Means One: The Swahili Counting Book*. Dial Press, 1971.
This book presents the numbers 1 through 10 in Swahili. All illustrations are of East African scenes.

Fischer, Hans. *Pitschi*. Harcourt, Brace and World, 1953.
After trying to be many different animals, Pitschi, a small kitten decides it's best to be a kitten.

Risom, Ole. *I Am a Mouse*. Golden Press, 1964.
A happy mouse tells about himself and his way of life, providing comparisons of large/small, more/less.

Wohl, John and Stacey. *I Can Count the Petals of a Flower*. National Council of Teachers of Mathematics, 1975.
Beautiful photographs of flowers illustrate the numbers 1 through 16.

Wong, Herbert H., and Matthew F. Vessel. *My Ladybug*. Addison-Wesley, 1969.
A ladybug has fascinating mathematical properties—four wings, six legs, and so forth.

Addition

Adding is a logical extension of counting. It is more efficient than counting and requires a more abstract level of thinking. We want children to *think* mathematics, to manipulate numbers (not numerals) mentally and to understand the relationships involved in mathematical operations. Rather than counting the animals in *The Little Wooden Farmer* or *In the Forest,* children might add the number of animals who appear as the story progresses. They could add the number of cars Jane sees as the train goes by in *The Everyday Train*. Asking children to perform the calculations mentally gives teachers and parents a glimpse of the strategies employed in children's mathematical thinking.

For addition, use these books listed under "counting": Dalgliesh's *The Little Wooden Farmer,* Ehrlich's *The Everyday Train,* Ets' *In the Forest,* and Fischer's *Pitschi.*

History of Our Number System

While, technically, they might not be classified as children's literature, the following books can be used to teach the historical foundation of the Hindu-Arabic number system. To explore the history of numbers, children might perform the experiment described in Simon and Benedick's *The Day the Numbers Disappeared.* By inventing their own number system, children would understand more clearly the historical progression of our number system.

Asimov, Isaac. *How Did We Find Out about Numbers?* Walker and Co., 1973.
Traces the history of the Hindu-Arabic number system from finger counting and one-to-one correspondence through Sumerian, Egyptian, Chinese, and Roman systems.

St. John, Glory. *How to Count Like a Martian*. Walch, 1975.
A discussion of Egyptian, Babylonian, Mayan, Greek, Chinese, and Hindu counting systems, plus instructions for using binary systems and "Martian" counting in base 3.

Simon, Leonard, and Jeanne Benedick. *The Day the Numbers Disappeared*. Whittlesey, 1963.
When his class complained about arithmetic, Mr. Dibbs agreed to outlaw numbers, but life was complicated without them.

Other Mathematics Concepts

Money

Asch, Frank. *Good Lemonade*. Nelson, 1976.
All of Hank's advertising gimmicks couldn't sell his lemonade after the word got around that it tasted awful!

Credle, Ellis. *Little Pest Pico*. Nelson, 1969.
Chico earns four pesos to get a parrot, Pico, who can bray like a donkey and whistle the Mexican national anthem.

Attributes

DuBois, William Pene. *Lion*. Viking, 1955.
An artist, with some help from friends, creates a new animal to be sent to the planet Earth.

O'Leary, Alice. *Trolls and Witches of Norway*. O'Leary's of Olympia, 1964.
The witches and trolls of Norway are described by size, color and personality.

Large Numbers

Gag, Wanda. *Millions of Cats*. Coward-McCann, 1928.
An old man tries to choose a cat for his wife from among billions and trillions of cats.

Multiplication

Emberley, Barbara. *One Wide River to Cross*. Prentice-Hall, 1966.
An old folk song is adapted to telling of Noah's ark and the animals that entered one by one, two by two, three by three.

Fractions

Dennis, J. Richard. *Fractions Are Parts of Things*. Crowell, 1971.
Colorful illustrations show that objects can be divided into parts called fractions.

Nursery Rhymes and Fairy Tales

Nursery rhymes and fairy tales also provide material for teaching beginning math concepts to young children. "Baa, Baa, Black Sheep," for example, provides an instance of one-to-one correspondence. "The Kilkenney Cats" and "Two Birds," who disappear, give practice in beginning subtraction concepts and the idea that zero means "not any." Counting rhymes like "One, Two, Buckle My Shoe" provide repetition for learning number names.

Fairy tales such as "The Three Little Pigs" and "The Three Billy Goats Gruff" can teach number concepts to very young children. Number is emphasized throughout the stories, providing many opportunities for understanding its meaning.

Using children's literature as a springboard for mathematical experiences allows language and mathematics learning to grow together naturally and imaginatively.

References

Baratta-Lorton, Mary. *Math Their Way*. Menlo Park, Calif.: Addison-Wesley, 1976.

Copeland, Richard W. *How Children Learn Mathematics*. 3rd ed. New York, N.Y.: Macmillan, 1978.

Furth, Hans G. *Piaget for Teachers*. Englewood Cliffs, N.J.: Prentice-Hall, 1970.

Gibson, Eleanor J., and Harry Levin. *The Psychology of Reading*. Cambridge, Mass.: MIT Press, 1975.

5

Wordless Picture Books

Wordless Picture Books and the Young Language-Disabled Child

Karen D'Angelo

Language-disabled children or youth often have difficulty in communicating for one or a number of reasons. These children may exhibit oral language disabilities in the areas of articulation, voice, and/or communication (McCartan, 1977). Children with articulation and voice disorders exhibit speech problems such as omissions, substitutions, distortions, repetitions, prolongations, and problems with phonation and resonance. Children with communication disorders exhibit (a) an inability to use or understand a wide variety of words, (b) omissions or incorrect use of syntax, and (c) an inability to respond appropriately to questions.

According to McCartan (1977), communication disorders among language-disabled children are characterized by certain behaviors. These children generally demonstrate a knowledge of word meaning and usage that is below what can be expected for their chronological age. They often misuse pronouns, verb tenses, plurals, prepositions, adverbs, and conjunctions. They may fail to respond to a question, respond by repeating part of the question, or respond with an inappropriate answer. Language-disabled children exhibiting these communication disorders need numerous opportunities to develop satisfactory oral language skills which form the basis for learning to read.

Success in reading for language-disabled children or youth can begin in school or at home with wordless books. Picture books that tell stories but have no text are valuable for the language-disabled child who does not use or understand a wide variety of words and who does not use, or has not yet acquired, appropriate rules of syntax. Wordless books can promote those oral language and reading readiness skills necessary to becoming a successful reader (Degler, 1979; Larrick, 1976).

Wordless books are being published in increasing numbers today and can be found on most library shelves. They vary in artistic style and story content from simple to complex and share one valuable distinction—they contain pictures but no words. For each picture in a wordless book, a child can supply as little or as much oral language as ability allows. With these books,

SOURCE: *Teaching Exceptional Children*, September 1981, pp. 34–37.

a child is not hindered by or restricted to the print that normally occurs in books.

Ability to analyze and interpret pictures, which precedes reading words, is a natural step in the process of language development (Burns & Roe, 1976). A child who is able to interpret pictures possesses many of the basic vocabulary and oral skills necessary to read and understand print. Hillerich (1977) stated that "The child who cannot function satisfactorily at the oral level is not likely to be able to function in beginning reading" (p. 41).

Burns and Roe (1976) indicated that picture interpretation develops in stages from naming or enumerating objects to inventing dialog, making comparisons, describing and interpreting actions and events, and finally predicting and evaluating outcomes (p. 86). As a child's vocabulary and syntax develop, oral language can be expanded from production of a single word or phrase, to producing several phrases, followed by a complete sentence, two or more complete sentences, and finally production of a number of thoughts or sentences in logical order about the same topic.

Conversation between the child and teacher or parent about pictures in a wordless book can be structured to promote the development of these oral skills. Four simple starter questions which parallel both the natural growth of oral language and Burns and Roe's stages of picture interpretation can be used to initiate these conversations with a child:

What things do you see in the picture?
What is happening in the picture?
What do you think will happen next?
Why?

Following are suggestions for developing oral language and short summaries of various wordless picture books which seem most useful for this purpose.

Building Vocabulary

New words can be added to the child's vocabulary as pictures are examined and colors, shapes, objects, animals, and people are named or enumerated. "What things do you see in the picture?" can be asked to initiate this activity. If the child does not respond, the parent or teacher can provide appropriate nouns, verbs, or adjectives for the child to imitate. All wordless books offer opportunities to develop vocabulary, but a few books serve this purpose especially well because of their content. The following books provide relatively simple pictures containing few objects and little irrelevant detail:

Anno's Alphabet by Mitsumasa Anno (New York: Crowell, 1975). Contains pictures of wood block letters and drawings of objects to go with each letter.

Noah's Ark by Peter Spier (New York: Doubleday, 1977). Tells the Biblical story of Noah who loads the ark with all kinds of animals.

Count and See by Tana Hoban (New York: Macmillan, 1972). Contains photographs with counting from 1 to 15, by tens to 50 and ends with 100 peas in their pods.

Big Ones, Little Ones by Tana Hoban (New York: Greenwillow, 1976). Contains color photographs of adult animals with their young.

Do You Want to Be My Friend? by Eric Carle (New York: Crowell, 1971). Shows a mouse following one animal's tail after another in pursuit of a friend.

Elephant Buttons by Noriko Ueno (New York: Harper, 1973). Shows an elephant's buttons popping open to reveal a lion, whose buttons pop to reveal a horse . . . down to a mouse.

Producing Phrases and Sentences

Phrases and sentences that describe actions and events in pictures can be elicited from the child by asking "What is happening in the picture?" If the child does not respond appropriately, the parent or teacher might model desired sentence structure (e.g., combining noun and verb, adjective and noun, or adverb and verb). There are many wordless books that clearly show actions that can be explained and described in just a few words or phrases. As a child acquires vocabulary and syntax skills, dialog can be invented to accompany pictures, comparisons can be made, and actions can be interpreted in complete thoughts or sentences. Books that clearly portray actions and events include:

The Great Cat Chase by John Goodall (New York: Harcourt, Brace, Jovanovich, 1968). Tells the story of a cat who is dressed in doll clothes by children, jumps out of a carriage, and is pursued by them through a series of mishaps.

Changes, Changes by Pat Hutchins (New York: Collier, 1971). Shows two dolls who arrange and rearrange blocks to deal with problems brought on by a fire and a flood.

Journey to the Moon by Erich Fuchs (New York: Delacorte, 1969). Tells the story of the Apollo II Mission in photographs.

Out! Out! Out! by Martha Alexander (New York: Dial, 1968). Shows the chaos which develops when a bird enters the home of a little boy and adults try to capture it.

The Wrong Side of the Bed by Edward Ardizonne (Garden City, NY: Doubleday, 1970). Realistically shows several incidents in the day of a little boy who gets out of bed cross and scowling.

Frog Where Are You? and *Frog Goes to Dinner* by Mercer Mayer (New York: Dial, 1969; 1974). Contain three main characters: boy, dog and frog. In these humorous tales a fun-loving frog gets into all sorts of mischief.

Developing Sequence and Prediction Skills

Looking at pictures that tell a story from beginning to end offers the child an opportunity to produce statements in sequential order and to interpret and predict actions, events, and feelings. Asking questions such as, "What do you think will happen next?" and "Why?" can help develop these skills. Again, the parent or teacher might model a desired response for the child. If the child does not respond, prompting with another question such as, "Do you think the pony will . . . next"?, which requires only "yes" or "no," may elicit a response.

Many wordless books depict logical sequences of events that can be narrated and that lend themselves to judgment and evaluation of outcomes. Books that are particularly adaptable to developing oral skills in sequencing, prediction, and evaluation include:

Family by Ellie Simmons (New York: McKay, 1970). Tells the story of how a small girl deals with the arrival of a new baby.

The Apple and the Moth by Iela and Enzo Mari (New York: Pantheon, 1970). Contains illustrations that follow a moth through egg, caterpillar, cocoon, and adult stages.

The Chicken and the Egg by Iela and Enzo Mari (New York: Pantheon, 1969). Shows the process of an egg hatching.

Apples by Nonny Hogrogian (New York: Macmillan, 1971). Shows a parade of animals and people who carelessly toss apple cores away as an apple orchard appears.

The Self-Made Snowman by Fernando Krahn (Philadelphia: Lippincott, 1974). Shows the progression of events that begin with snow rolling down a mountain and end with creation of a snowman in the center of a town.

The Silver Poney by Lynd Ward (Boston: Houghton-Mifflin, 1973). Appropriate for an older child because of its length (83 pages). It tells the story of a lonely farm boy who takes imaginary trips all over the world on a winged horse.

Creating Positive Attitudes

As well as developing reading readiness and oral language skills, wordless picture books can be valuable for creating positive attitudes. When analyzing and interpreting pictures to tell a story, the child can supply as much or as little oral language as ability allows without a concern for correctly reading print. A child can successfully complete a picture reading task from which the possibility of failure has been removed. Good feelings about books, reading, and oneself can thus be created.

Interpreting pictures in wordless books can provide opportunities for developing the child's vocabulary and syntax by naming objects, inventing dialog, making comparisons, describing and interpreting actions, and predicting and evaluating outcomes. Oral language skills can be expanded from production of a single word or phrase to production of a number of complete thoughts or sentences. Both teachers and parents can explore these books with young language disabled children and youth either in school or at home. Wordless books can provide these children with opportunities for becoming successful readers.

References

Burns, P. C., & Roe, B. D. *Teaching Reading in Today's Elementary Schools*. Chicago: Rand McNally, 1976.

Degler, S. K. Putting Words into Wordless Books. *Reading Teacher,* 1979, 32(4), 399–402.

Hillerich, R. L. *Reading Fundamentals for Preschool and Primary Children*. Columbus, OH: Charles E. Merrill, 1977.

Larrick, N. *Wordless Picture Books and the Teaching of Reading*. *Reading Teacher,* 1976, 29(8), 743–746.

McCartan, K. *The Communicatively Disordered Child: Management Procedures for the Classroom*. Boston: Teaching Resources Corp., 1977.

Use Wordless Picture Books to Teach Reading, Visual Literacy and to Study Literature

Patricia Jean Cianciolo

There is an interesting development taking place in the juvenile trade book publishing arena. It is the appearance of story books which consist only of pictures and have no written text. This innovation permits the book artist to function at a very high level; he can use a graphic form to tell his story to the extent that his knowledge, imagination, and talents permit.

I discovered the wordless picture book about four years ago when I read *The Magic Stick* created by Kjell Ringi. The illustrations in *The Magic Stick*, as in the other wordless picture books I have discovered to date, carry the completed load in the way of literary connotation. The sequence of the illustrations tells a story without the use of the written word yet the story is told rapidly, accurately, and as convincingly as the reader is able to interpret or speak the language of these visuals. At the time I first saw Ringi's wordless picture book, I thought it a superb example of the fact that pictures do speak a language. A *universal* language, if you will. But one must be visually literate in order to speak (or read!) that universal language. In other words, one must be able to bring meaning and significance to the shapes, positions, and movements that are depicted by the book artist as he tells his stories in pictures.

New as the books without words may be to the field of children's literature, there are many of them readily available in school and public libraries. They vary considerably in quality of artistic accomplishment. Happily, there is a respectable dissimilarity in format, content, and style of art from book to book. Some are addressed to the very young child; others are far more appropriate for the sophisticated and mature youth or adult.

The creative teacher can use the wordless picture books in any number of learning experiences. Implementing some of the techniques peculiar to the language experience approach, they may be used to teach reading to those beginning to read, to illiterate adults, and to children in need of remedial reading instruction. They may be used to teach such visual literacy skills as literal translation of objects or situations presented in a visual or a sequence of illustrations arranged to transmit a fictional narrative and interpretation of figurative expressions presented visually. They may be used to help students

SOURCE: Reprinted by permission of the American Library Association and the author from *Top of the News* 29 (April 1973): 226–234.

of literature recognize and evaluate the author/artist's ability to develop in his fiction-in-pictures such basic components as plot development, characterization, theme, setting, and style.

Reading Instruction

In the language experience approach the child's real or vicarious experiences are used, and the child's dictated stories or those he has written himself reflect these experiences. The compositions serve as a basis for his reading materials. The written compositions and recorded oral compositions constitute the learner's reading vocabulary and it is the words used in these compositions that are used to teach phonetic and structural analysis skills, or any other reading skills, when the learner evidences a need for instruction or practice in them. When the wordless picture books are used to provide the experience (vicarious) upon which the compositions are based, the compositions may be created by an individual or by groups of students. The experience upon which the composition is based is that which is offered by the sequence and details presented in the wordless picture books. The younger the child the more closely allied to the child's here-and-now world must be the content and experience presented in the wordless picture book. As the learner becomes more mature and acquires a broader background of experience the content and experience depicted in the illustrations may be more removed from his here-and-now world; they may be more sophisticated in theme and fanciful in nature. The kindergarten-primary school child would appreciate the fun-filled adventure depicted in the little books by Mercer Mayer; *Boy, a Dog, and a Frog* and its sequel *Frog, Where Are You?* The child in the third grade and beyond would find *Journey to the Moon* by Erich Fuchs much more to his liking, for this picture book without words follows the day by day progress of the Apollo II mission, the launching, the flight, the landing, and the return to earth of the three astronauts. This narrative is presented in twelve stunning double-spread paintings and if the reader wants to verify his "reading" of these illustrations he may refer to the explanatory captions provided by the author; they are located on two pages preceding the paintings.

Visual Literacy

Growth in visual literacy depends upon exposure to visual literacy experiences and an awareness that visuals speak a language. It has been hypothesized that there is a hierarchy of visual skills. A visually literate person would be able to (a) read visuals with skill; (b) write with visuals expressing himself effectively; (c) know the grammar and syntaxes of visual language and be able to apply them; (d) be familiar with the tools of visual literacy and their use; (e) appreciate the masterworks of visual literacy, and (f) translate from visual language and vice versa.

Literal Interpretation

The ability to read on the literal level the sequence of visuals arranged to identify assorted objects or transmit a fictional narrative is one of the first skills one must have if he is visually literate. One example of a book which could be used to help nursery-kindergarten aged children recognize and name the illustrations is *Shapes and Things* by Tana Hoban. In it everyday objects such as tooth-brushes, a comb, toys, buttons, safety and stick pins, and eyeglasses are shown against black and white and children are introduced to the beauty of form. The visuals are done with photograms—photographs taken without the camera.

Not a wordless picture book in the strictest sense of the word, for there is a slight amount of verbal text, *Nothing Ever Happens on My Block* is one that might be used to teach visual literacy skills to the kindergarten or early primary grade child. Ellen Raskin has included so much action in the illustrations that a rather involved plot has been developed for this narrative fiction. Carefully close scrutiny of the little pictures is necessary if one is to appreciate the full impact of all that is taking place in this ironic story. While Chester sits on the curb stone in front of his staid Victorian house and complains that his life is dull, a series of numerous amusing and dramatic events are going on around him—a criminal is arrested, a house burns and is restored, children play tricks on an elderly lady, an armored truck is involved in an accident and $50 bills fly in all directions. Comparable to *Nothing Ever Happens on My Block,* but for older visual readers, are the books by Frank Asch. *George's Store, Linda,* and *Yellow, Yellow* have very brief texts, are action-filled, and detailed illustrations superabound. The plots in each of these books are simple enough but each is filled with surprises and zany fun. They constitute the efforts of a talented and sophisticated graphic artist. A capable and experienced visual literate would enjoy them.

Kjell Ringi uses color to lead the reader of *The Magic Stick* to the world of imagination. The real world in which the main book character lives is portrayed in black and white; the boy's make-believe world is portrayed through brilliantly colored pictures. The little boy imagines he can become a pirate with a telescope, a weight lifter, a general leading a parade, and so on. Six- and seven-year-olds would in all probability be able to interpret and respond to this use of color and black and white. They would respond with the same feelings and emotions as did the boy in the story—that of delight in finding and using the stick to bring about magic and then the obvious unhappiness when his friends approach him and cause him to toss away the stick and leave his world of make-believe.

Figurative Expressions

There are some wordless picture books that aptly present what John Debes called "visual puns" and "visual metaphors." *One, Two, Where's My Shoe* and *Snail Where Are You?* by Tomi Ungerer and *Topsy Turvies: Picture Books that Stretch the Imagination* by Mitsumasa Anno are examples of the "visual pun." Both of the Ungerer books are done in simple cartoon-type drawings. *One, Two, Where's My Shoe* is a playful pictorial search for a shoe. Likewise, in *Snail, Where Are You?* the reader searches for the snail. In each case the shoe and snail are found in the most unlikely places. The bodies of the birds in flight are shoes, as are the dog's snout, the man's torso, the ship's hull, the alligator's body, the Egyptian's mustache, the fish's mouth, the cannon's barrel, and so on. The snail shape is repeated in pictures of the waves, a violin, and a birthday party "blower." The pictures in *Topsy Turvies: Picture Books That Stretch the Imagination* are deceptively simple. Mitsumasa Anno presents optical illusions which form structures in which people can go upstairs to get a lower place, hang pictures on the ceiling, and walk walls. This book exemplifies a series of "visual puns" for children in the upper primary or middle grades.

An extended visual metaphor is evident in George Mendoza's *And I Must Hurry for the Sea Is Coming In*. The ironic ending of this book about a ghetto boy whose toy boat becomes a ship that rides the waves will surprise the children. Once they come to that point in the story they will be able to realize full well why the boy fantasized the events and circumstances that he did. The colored photographs were done by Wayne Dalrymple and tell this author's story superbly well. Older children and even adults will understand and react to (but not necessarily agree with perhaps) the theme of *And I Must Hurry for the Sea Is Coming In,* which is that there exists an "urgency in providing lives of dignity and strength for all children—'for the sea is coming in' and we had all better hurry." This book is a good example of a "multi-level" book. The young reader can enjoy on the literal level the visual metaphor that is presented via the photographs. The more mature, knowledgeable person who is aware of the realities of life, one who is an experienced and thoughtful reader of visuals, will grasp the powerful message expressed in the theme and will respect the skill with which the visual metaphor is expressed.

Literary Devices

There is much that the reader of literature would benefit from if he were able to recognize the devices that an author/artist makes use of to develop a plot. Knowledge of this nature would help the reader to become more sensitive to the elements of good writing and book illustrating; thus, he could appreciate more fully future reading. It would help him to see the work from the standpoint of the author and think as an author thinks when he creates his own stories. Some literary devices that might be identified in the wordless picture books and also commonly used by authors of verbal fictional narratives include devices used to develop the plot (backflashing and foreshadowing); the point of view from which the story is told (first person, second person, third person, and omniscient point of view); the mood of the story (fanciful, realistic, satirical, ironical, serious, or humorous); and the style in which the story is told.

In order to read the pantomime story that is told in *Bobo's Dream* by Martha Alexander, the child must first recognize that the actions portrayed in the balloon pictures represent dreams. It would appear that the reader of this story about a grateful dachshund's dream of returning his master's kindness would need to have at his command a rather advanced visual literacy skill; this manner of telling the story by depicting the dog's dreams in balloons, would probably be comparable to the device of telling a story from the omniscient point of view. This same point of view is used by the creator of *The Inspector*. Only the reader of this exciting but macabre picture book is fully aware of the inspector's plight, the hound's delight when consuming the monstrous creatures and its gradual but certain growth from a small apparently harmless dog to a huge, destructive, and hideous monster himself. Neither the hound nor the inspector is fully knowledgeable about his own or the other's state, but the reader is.

An example of a story that seems to exemplify the first person point of view is present in *Vicki* by Renate Meyer. In unusual full color paintings the reader is told by the little girl in the story how it feels to experience a spell of friendlessness. Her resolution to her problem, by the way, may surprise the readers but they probably would not debate the fact that it is a realistic and logical answer for her, yet not the one that they would resort to were they to suddenly find themselves alone and in need of a friend.

The Study of Literature

Elementary school children can be taught to distinguish between good and inferior stories. However, in order to make these distinctions they must have some understanding of the basic components of literature, namely, setting, theme, characterization, plot, and style. One may make use of the wordless picture books to gain understandings of these components of fiction.

Literary Style

Style as a component of fiction is a rather nebulous element to deal with in the study of literature. Yet, the style of art used by the book artist, his use of color and space, are among the basic factors that one must note and make some judgment about if one were to appraise the "literary style" of a wordless picture book.

Consider not only the manner or extent to which his style affects the unfolding or the development of the plot but how it creates a mood, portrays characters, and presents details about the setting of the story that is told in the picture book. For example, the line drawings done by Peter Parnall to tell the story of *The Inspector* are as macabre as the story and are very detailed. Only the visually literate person would benefit fully from all the artist has included in his illustrations. Attention to all the details in each of the illustrations would lead the reader to a wealth of visual statements about the thoughts and feelings of the inspector and the dog as they traipse ever onward over flat lands, mountains, and waterways all of which are infested with fantastically ugly monsters. Furthermore, the visually literate reader of this book knows the setting in which the story takes place every bit as well, perhaps better, than does the myopic inspector! No doubt about it, Parnall's style of art, his use of detail, his talented use of lines and shading and space produced a masterful piece of graphic art, told a good story, skillfully created a mood of horror, developed unique and emotional characters, and depicted a setting that was real. The many facets of Parnall's style together create a vitally unique story-in-pictures.

The carefree pastel sketches that Ruth Carroll did in *The Chimp and the Clown* are beautifully compatible with the fun-filled adventures of these circus animals. Likewise, the quaint pen and ink sketches done by Mercer Mayer establish the naive but action-packed experiences of the little boy, his dog, and their new mutual friend, the frog. The adventures of this threesome are found in *A Boy, a Dog, and a Frog* and *Frog, Where Are You?* The intricate detail in Mitsumasa Anno's *Topsy Turvies: Pictures to Stretch the Imagination* reinforces the fact that this is not a book for the inexperienced student of visual literacy. And so on. Examples which might serve to demonstrate that the art work in large measure affects the "literary style" of a wordless picture book abound.

Literary Theme

The wordless picture books offer a rather unique and effective means by which one may help elementary school children to be able to recognize the theme of a literary selection. It is all well and good that they recognize the plot of a story and usually this is no problem if they can read the visuals at least on the most elementary level, namely, the literal level. But the reader must be a more competent reader of visuals, a more thoughtful reader of visuals if he is to move to the stage where he can identify the theme of the literary selection.

Not too many of the youngest readers would fail to recognize the theme presented by Edward Ardizzone in *The Wrong Side of the Bed.* There are few situations presented in this book that the reader would fail to identify with, for Ardizzone, in his readily recognizable pen sketches, has offered the reader a "think" in each and every illustration.

I suspect it would take a somewhat mature child, probably eight or nine years of age, to be fully cognizant that one-upmanship is the message of Kjell Ringi's *The Winner*. Illustrations depicting a small girl; mischievous, snoopy goblins determined to right social inequities; and a flying saucer full of spaghetti together tell a droll story in Fernando Krahn's book *A Flying Saucer Full of Spaghetti*. The plot in this story would be easily followed by the kindergarten-primary-school-aged child. The characters are portrayed distinctively enough for them to keep straight, but the theme is one that would not be easily identified and understood until the child was nine years old or so, at which point he would be likely to be more knowledgeable and perceptive about or even sympathetic with social inequities.

The Inspector created by George Mendoza and illustrated by Peter Parnall is a controversial book. Some readers of this macabre picture book may be able to recognize a theme in the story—don't become too bogged down with the little details in life, take the broader view if you want to get a true perspective of what is happening to you. Other readers will insist there is no message presented in *The Inspector*. There is much happening in each of the illustrations in this book. One will have to look very carefully to see what is happening to the inspector, his hound, and the grossly wild and improbable monsters. This is not a book for kindergarteners. It is a good book, I think, for the nine- to thirteen-year-old who is beginning to like detective stories or horror stories.

Conclusion and Summary

I am not so certain that what I have said about using wordless picture books to develop visual literacy skills has not been said before. To paraphrase Madeleine L'Engle, if I thought I were expected to say it better than anybody else I would have been more than a little disinclined to start! The important issue is that some more thoughts should be given about this aspect of visual literacy and I have tried to present some of these above. The wordless picture books are available in ever growing quantity and quality. They constitute an excellent type of literary material through which children might be taught to read, to become visually literate, and to study aspects of literature, especially fiction.

Children's Literature versus Wordless "Books"

Patrick Groff

A recent defense of wordless "books" for children makes clear its approval of this "interesting development."[1] Never in doubt here is Cianciolo's hopeful expectation such books will have a meritorious effect on the "juvenile trade book publishing arena," by permitting graphic artists to enjoy an even greater influence on the make-up of young children's books than has so far been the case.

To those who may have thought otherwise, Cianciolo argues that pictures especially drawn for children, and then bound up without words into hard covers, are not just emulations of the physical appearance of literature. They are "an excellent type of literary material," she insists, and when looked at by children will develop their "visual literacy."

The *literacy* to which Cianciolo refers is not to be confused with the ordinary meanings of this term, i.e., the ability to read and write, and to know literature. She borrows another definition taken from the comments of Debes at a recent National Conference on Visual Literacy. Debes (who works for the Eastman Kodak Company), said to have originated the concept of visual literacy in 1966,[2] explains that visual literacy is "a great amoeba-like entity with pseudopods reaching out in many directions. I see those pseudopods," he goes on, "as being labeled with the names of sources such as semantics, linguistics, etc. And I like the analogy because the amoeba feeds by reaching out with a pseudopod to a prospective meal, and then engulfing it. So," he continues, "in a sense, the pseudopods feed the main body and disappear into it."[3]

With this rationale for visual literacy set out, he contends it follows that semantically speaking, "there are many parallelisms between the visual communication and the verbal communication." ("Pictures do speak a language," Cianciolo agrees.) If you want a "verbal definition," Debes concludes, visual literary is a hierarchy of thirty-five separate "vision competencies." These abilities range upwards in complexity, he avers, from *No. 1:* "distinguish light from dark," through to *No. 16:* "group objects related by process commonly seen together," and finally to *No.'s 34* and *35* " 'read' a sequence of objects

SOURCE: Reprinted by permission of the American Library Association and the author from *Top of the News* 30 (April 1974):294–303.

and/or body language arranged to express, so others can understand it, a personal emotion"; and "compose an utterance as above." Cianciolo's defense for wordless books as essential material for children's study of literature is based, she notes, on these explanations of visual literacy (which are decodable to her satisfaction, at least).

Her argument for wordless books, actually a syllogism, runs like this:

a. Wordless books are "a sequence of illustrations arranged to transmit a fictional narrative," and thus to develop visual literacy.
b. A child with powers of visual literacy will be able to "recognize and evaluate" in these pictures "such basic components as plot development, characterization, theme, setting, and style," since the pictures "carry the completed load in the way of literary connotation."
c. Having experienced these literary conventions via wordless books (again, "an excellent type of literary material") the child is now prepared to successfully "distinguish between good and inferior stories," that is, to "study aspects of literature, especially fiction."

In short, Cianciolo would have us believe that the characteristics of visual (picture) "literature" and literature as it is generally thought of are so very similar that the child moves *naturally* from an understanding of the former to that of the latter. When the child becomes accomplished at noting "plot devices," "characterizations," etc., as depicted in pictures, she holds, he will also do this well with his literature.

But, as with any such faculty logic, the conclusion (c) of Cianciolo's syllogism is not supported by its two premises (a–b). That is to say, there is little doubt, as she attests, that pictures can be arranged so as to depict a kind of narrative "plot" or connected "story." Children also can be led to comprehend the interrelatedness of these pictures. It is quite another thing to assume, however, that sensing this plot in picture form is a literary experience. Or that this experience is what children need in order to understand the plots depicted in literature.

First of all, one can argue if Cianciolo's thesis held together that today's children, highly experienced with picture "plots" through their frequent and extensive viewing of television, would have developed keen sensibilities for plot and other conventions of literature. If wordless books are "literary," surely television pictures must be as well. This line of reasoning would conclude that modern children would inevitably become superior readers of literature.

Unfortunately, for Cianciolo's thesis at least, such a condition does not prevail. To the contrary, experienced teachers report it becomes increasingly difficult to involve children in the reading of books. (Not so unlikely a complaint, after all, when we learn from a recent survey, by Andreson and Company, New York, that today's average adult American reads books at his leisure all of five hours *per year*.) Even Debes, on whose theory Cianciolo admittedly rests her case for wordless books, would agree. "They [today's children] certainly are not interested much in reading," he observes.

So far, then, two faults in Cianciolo's argument are apparent. She has constructed only a semilogical argument for the wordless book for young children. And then, some facts of the matter do not bear her out. By why is it that some children highly attracted to the picture "plots" of television (therefore, who must understand their workings) find no such allurement in literary plots?

In the answer to this lies the *second* reason to question Cianciolo's notions about literature and wordless books. The relative amounts of mental effort it takes to read literature, as versus such energy used to view television or still pictures, is not the same. The latter takes little mental energy. Here the flow of stimuli is uninterrupted, self-initiated, smooth, and instantaneous. Television, especially, is dynamic, immediate, and vast. It permits the child's mind to get to a great number of images in an extremely short period of time.

One reason, therefore, why the viewing of television picture "plots" does not seem to have the desired carryover for children into the reading of literature plots, Cianciolo notwithstanding, would be that the child, because of cultural influences on his perception, is "prewired" to see plots in pictures—but not in writing. As an expert on perception explains, "it is perfectly possible that perceptual learning occurs in very early infancy, and resists further modification or relearning."[4] If so, children view television in gratifying ways because they are predisposed to do so. Because television represents pictorial realism, which we know generally appeals to children in pictures in books,[5] it must appear to the child as a more "natural," easier to enjoy, phenomenon than could writing. The representations on television are easy for the child to assimilate because he senses they are "normal." Writing, to the contrary, obviously appears "artificial."

Consequently, it takes a great jump in logic to assume that the lifelike, easygoing experiences the child has with television prepare him for the purposely ambiguous, difficult to attain plots of literature. In short, while Cianciolo believes pictures "speak a language," evidence from research in perception would suggest otherwise: "To speak of the information in the optic array does not imply that it consists of conventional symbols, or that pictures constitute a language. . . ."[6] For example, research on the effect of visual media on thought processes concludes "that the mechanism of internalizing language differs from that necessary for the internalization of visual codes."[7]

Actually, the single critical advantage of literature over pictures, when one compares the two in the above terms, is the fact "a pictorial system is inadequate to deal with many messages."[8] To be sure, one can spy passage after passage in children's literature that cannot be depicted in pictures. For example, from *The Cay*, by Taylor:

> "How old are you Timothy?" I asked.
>
> "Dat fact is also veree mysterious. Lil' more dan sixty, 'cause d'muscle in my legs b'speakin' to me, complain all d'time. But to be true, I do not know exact."

> I was amazed that any man shouldn't know his own age. I was almost certain now that Timothy had indeed come from Africa, but I didn't tell him that. I said, "I'm almost twelve."[9]

A scholar of the visual arts describes the peculiar power of language in this way: "The statue [or picture] being much more specific, restricts the range of pertinent connotations more severely. It is much less adaptable. One cannot take pictures or pieces of pictures and put them together to produce new statements as easily as one can combine words or ideographs. Pictorial montages show their seams, whereas the images produced by words fuse into unified wholes."[10] The reverse of this is to conclude that the primary function of pictures in books would be to provide experience that cannot be put into words. We must be careful, however, of "that nasty misleading cliche, that a picture is worth a thousand words." Indeed, "the point must be made that information presented through pictures probably has to be coded into words if it is to be readily retained."[11]

Nonetheless, despite its unusual powers to project our imaginations farther than is possible through the precise imitation of life that pictures offer, literature in comparison to television is clumsy, delayed in its message, and above all takes a good deal of mental effort.[12] And, to read verbal art (literature) takes an additional mental effort over that required by children to discuss what they have perceived in pictures.

So, in her argument to the effect that seeing and talking about pictures is a literary experience Cianciolo forgets about the essential differences between the rhetoric of literature and the rhetoric of conversation. The latter will not suffice as preparation of the child for the former since the orality that is involved here (speaking and listening at informal levels about pictures) does not involve the same "linguistic guessing game' " that is used in the reading of literature. As the above passage from *The Cay* illustrates, we now know writing is not simply speech written down. Otherwise we could all be novelists upon demand. The rhetoric of writing, and especially literature, can easily be shown to impose different mental demands on the child than does the rhetoric of orality. Literature has its own peculiar set of rules and contingencies, structures and devices that are explicitly different from those of ordinary language. Moreover, the writer of literature to gain distinction deliberately uses ever-unique forms of this special literature language. Critics of literature encourage him "to take the extraordinary step of developing accounts of the world quite different from the ways we see it." The advent of writing has "freed the brain [of man] from the tyranny of sensory perception,"[13] and most obviously in this respect the brain of the writer. It is only by ignoring these differences between the mental demands of orality and literature that Cianciolo's argument for wordless publications as "excellent literary material" can make any sense.

Moreover, we have learned much in the past decade of the mental demands on a child to read literature. Today's experts in reading instruction are coming more and more to recognize that in order to learn to read literature successfully the child must initially have had an extensive experience in *listening* to literature. In this listening experience children develop "a feel for the peculiarities of literary language and a sense of what to expect from it. They can predict in literary language as they can in more common language," Goodman's research of this process shows. Since the efficient reading of literature is a linguistic guessing game, where "the reader sweeps ahead sampling from the graphic input [print], predicting structures, leaping to quick conclusions about the meaning and only slowing down or regressing when subsequent sampling fails to confirm what he expects to find," experience for the child in hearing literature is a prerequisite to learning to read it.[14] But whenever the use of wordless books cuts into the time in libraries, schools, and at home available for developing an understanding in the child as to how literary language works, the realization of his capacity to learn to read literature doubtless will be handicapped.

It seems obvious, too, from the difficulties some television-minded children have in learning to read, that sometimes the transition from the relatively effortless task involved in television to that of learning to read is mentally intolerable. This is one reason some advocates of visual literacy refer only "to the numerous techniques used by people to communicate in nonverbal ways." "We are speaking in terms of those [children] who cannot learn visually [through print], as well as those who will not," they emphasize.[15] Consequently, one wonders whether certain television children will ever be conditioned to learn to read literature. In any event, the harsh mental break from viewing pictures to reading print (for that is what it is) must eventually be made. It does little good to delay this crucible by providing the television child with more pictures via wordless books.

Yet, picture books for children increasingly are being purchased on the merits of their pictures rather than on the qualities of their written text. The publishers and artists cannot be blamed for this deteriorating state of affairs. For obvious reasons they cannot indulge in premonitions as to the consequences of their production of virtually wordless books. They would be ingrates not to be thankful for the extra work (the artists), and the reduced costs for the production (no respectable writer is needed).

They are seldom brought to such soul searching in any case, however, since ironically enough the superiority of today's visual art in picture books apparently has obscured for many critics of these books the inferior linguistic effects of these pieces. The visual ingenuity or freshness of the art in these books tend to cover up, all too often, tired or nonexistent plots, shallow characterizations, trite descriptions and conversations, and the uses of cliché in place of wit or invention.

Thus it is difficult to believe the notion the wordless book is just a modern form of the memorable illustrated book. It is, instead, a type like no other. It exemplifies the (discredited) theory that the book artist and the writer can equitably compete and thus contribute equally to young children's literature. This theory has been put to the test and has been found to be false in far too many cases, as a perusal of the current crop of picture books will attest. Picture books are becoming the tool of the graphic artist to such an extent that significant numbers of them no longer represent a potential literary experience for the young child.

Third, Cianciolo is wrong in her assumption that the imaginative or emotional responses required by literature are identical to those stimulated by wordless books. She describes how wordless books are useful in motivating children to dictate stories about what they feel these pictures entail. These dictations, in turn, are used to teach children to read literature, she maintains. It seems apparent, however, that the pictures in the wordless book will strongly condition the imaginative responses children can make to them. The dictations or "stories" from children based on these pictures will tend to be relatively uniform, impersonal, and limited in number.

One proof for this seems to me to lie in the results of a simple experiment one can conduct. For this, select two picture books you believe to have about the same quality of *written text.* Read one of these to young children showing the pictures as you read along. Now, have your listeners draw for you their favorite part of the story. Repeat this exercise at another time, only now do *not* show the pictures as you read the story. You will find the drawings the young children pass on to you after this second reading are significantly more individualistic, contain a greater number of separate parts of the story, and are more entertaining to look at, as evidenced by other children's responses.

From this, the undesirable consequences of wordless books seem evident (if not ominous), therefore. It can be seen that looking at wordless books in lieu of hearing stories of literary merit read aloud may close down a young child's imagination, and thus act to hinder his access to the real literary world—so much so that the development of his appreciation of unusual language as such, which in the long run is what literature is essentially all about, may be handicapped. We have reason to worry, therefore, that the television child, already highly visually minded when he first approaches print, will become impatient with the original sounds and meanings of literature (and as noted, with the effort it takes to get to them) and, subsequently, insensitive and unappreciative of its attraction. It appears to me inevitable that the wordless book, as it dilutes the opportunities available to exploit the child's abilities, or to develop his will, to respond in imaginative ways to word stories, will become a potential threat to the realization of this major objective of children's literature. Thus the appearance of wordless children's books, in the "ever growing" numbers that Cianciolo approves of, will work against the development of children's verbal imagination and, correspondingly, can delay their appreciation of linguistic art.

In the *fourth* place, the wordless book appears to be able to serve no particular or separate function that a picture *storybook* would not. In the latter book pictures have a critical role, but know how to keep their place alongside the written text. They do not overwhelm the text, casting it into the shadow of "oversize, overplentiful and often overpowering illustrations," as Lanes puts it.[16] The text of the good picture storybook remains a piece of distinguished linguistic art even without pictures. That is, the presence of lack of pictures does not necessarily signal its success, or demise.

As an example of this role, literature versus pictures, return for a moment to he passage from *The Cay* given above. Suppose an ingenious graphic artist was able, somehow, to depict in pictures the character of Timothy as this is revealed here through his choice of words and his dialect. And along with this the dawning realization of 11-year-old Phillip of what this black man will mean to his survival on their shipwrecked raft. How cumbersome, even torturous, a task this likely would be for the artist. How many pictures would it take him to show accurately the essential meanings found in these seven quoted sentences? How would he graft them together? And, after this gargantuan job is done, what has the artist produced? Obviously, an explicit pattern for the viewer to attend to, in contrast to the speculations, mental calculations, and even psychological self-examination the reader must take to these ideas in print.

How is the case different with wordless books for young children? In fact, do wordless books offer the young child something the language of literature should not, will not, or cannot? To argue that pictures make it easier for the young child to mentally visualize what is offered is a non sequitur, as has been demonstrated so far. If we are concerned with the problem of readying the child to be a successful, and therefore a contented, reader of literature, it begs the question, of course, to propose he be given ever-more experiences with wordless books. These are no stairway to the realization of literature, but rather a dead-end street to the allure of television.

To assume, as Cianciolo does, that much (how much?) of the time presently given to reading children's literature must now be transferred to viewing wordless books, so that something called "visual literacy" can be developed in children, is even less tenable. Especially so, I think, when one learns that the case for visual literacy is just now beginning to be made. (The standard references to literary criticism or psychological and linguistic research do not as yet give it a separate heading.) We are told the plan is being tested in "tightly designed" research with "several hundred even thousands of students."[17] Since the findings of such studies on visual literacy are not yet available, it seems reasonable to plead that its advocates first establish with this research the vital importance to children of formal instruction in visual literacy, and the functions that wordless books *actually* perform. Then we can decide if it is necessary for children's literature to be the first of our linguistic arts to be sacrificed for this purpose.

It is predictable, as well, that unless we continue to demand that words be a significant requirement of picture books the wordless book will flourish, of course. But what of the effect of this on children's literature? We have too much evidence at present that if we followed Cianciolo's advice the market would be flooded even more than it is with the "glossy, flossy, supersized numbers" that Kuskin so easily can mock as "empty-headed—because, for the most part the pictures adorn nothing."[18] If today's picture books have "gone in many cases as far as they can go in the direction away from storytelling,"[19] at the time we still reserve some rights to demand they contain words of literary quality, imagine the effect on this already crumbling picture book field of a wholesale devotion of librarians and teachers to wordless books. If many picture books are at present "alien territory for a purveyor of words of any weight,"[20] it is chilling to think on the future of children's literature when book purchasing is based on the notion that wordless books are "excellent literary material."

Finally, if librarians and teachers are to give in to the onslaughts of visual literacy, they should be aware of the pathway down which they are being led. This leads inevitably into the camp of those who frankly admit they are fed up with reading and books: "The increasing emphasis on visual literacy is in large part due to the dissatisfaction with traditional education which relies on the printed word."[21] The "time has come" to de-emphasize reading (qua children's literature?), agrees a like-minded New York state supervisor of elementary education: "The inordinate amount of time that schools spend in teaching reading as an *isolated communication phenomenon* to today's visually literate children cannot possibly be justified in terms of cost, effort and results."[22] (Emphasis added.) This means the reading of literature will not be encouraged unless it serves a secondary, nonliterary or service function? Can we doubt the allegiance of such writers to McLuhan's pronouncement that "The handwriting is on the celluloid walls of Hollywood; the Age of Writing has passed"?[23] If teachers and librarians are to condone, moreover approve of, the wordless book as a legitimate rival of children's literature, surely they too will become its prisoner.

If literature for young children is to prevail there seems little doubt, therefore, we must reject the evangelism of visual literacy. And, for that matter, the kind of false reasoning that leads some to believe, as it does Georgiou, that in most cases today "a child's initial approach to a picture book is primarily a literary one," or that if these pictures "capture his interest and arouse his curiosity, he will then become absorbed in the art of reading."[24] There is simply no respectable evidence from psychology to allow for any such wishful thinking. To the contrary, research on this matter indicates "pictures may well provide incentives for purchasing, but they may not provide incentives for learning. This is still a matter for speculation."[25]

We must stop fooling ourselves, then, that literature and graphic art are natural allies, and that graphic art will rush to the aid of literature at its beck and call, if the reverse is true. Rather, it appears more and more likely that visual experiences given by the wordless book consistently act to remove the child, or at least keep him at an unfortunate distance, from both written literature and the values of the oral tradition of storytelling.

Because of all this, those concerned with the relative emphasis being given to words as versus pictures in young children's books should take a stand against the beliefs in this matter as exemplified by Cianciolo. This does not mean we would deny there are gratifications a child can receive from pictures in his books that would otherwise be absent. That argument was settled in the seventeenth century when John Comenius demonstrated the added attraction for children, when illustrations were added to their printed texts. The illustrated book, whose pictures illuminated or expanded a literary text, has a venerable history, indeed a tradition we want to expand into the future.

We take for granted, therefore, that today's literature for young children will be books with pictures and never of words alone. Picture books can have several uses beyond that as literature. They can be a source of visual pleasure or divertissement, without doubt. Their pictures help children match up visual forms and words, and thus help build children's vocabularies. The level of art in many of these books is so high that they undoubtedly help develop a child's appreciation of graphic arts.

Admitting this, however, should not mislead us to wrongly accredit pictures as literature. Nor to give way to wishful thoughts that wordless books will motivate children to read and appreciate literature.

References

1. Patricia Jean Cianciolo, "Use Wordless Picture Books to Teach Reading, Visual Literacy and to Study Literature," *Top of the News* 29:226–35 (April 1973).
2. J. R. Purvis, "Visual Literacy: An Emerging Concept," *Educational Leadership* 50:714–16 (May 1973).
3. John L. Debes, "The Loom of Visual Literacy—An Overview," in Clarence M. Williams and John L. Debes, eds., *Proceedings of the First National Conference on Visual Literacy* (New York: Pittman, 1970), p.1–15.
4. Julian E. Hochberg, *Perception* (Englewood Cliffs, New Jersey: Prentice-Hall, 1964), p.67.
5. Ethel M. King, "Critical Appraisal of Research on Children's Reading Interests, Preferences, and Habits," *Canadian Educational and Research Digest* 7:312–26 (Dec. 1967).
6. James J. Gibson, "The Information Available in Pictures," *Viewpoints* 47:73–95 (May 1971).
7. Gavriel Salomon, "Can We Affect Cognitive Skills through Visual Media? An Hypothesis and Initial Findings." *AV Communication Review* 20:401–22 (Winter 1972).
8. Ronald W. Langacker, *Language and Its Structure* (New York: Harcourt, Brace and World, 1968), p.61.
9. Theodore Taylor, *The Cay* (New York: Avon Books, 1969), p.43.
10. Rudolf Arnheim. *Visual Thinking* (Berkeley: University of California, 1969), p.253.
11. Robert M. W. Travers and Victor Alvarado, "The Design of Pictures for Teaching Children in Elementary School," *AV Communication Review* 18:47–64 (Spring 1970).

12. William Anderson and Patrick Groff, *A New Look at Children's Literature* (Belmont, California: Wadsworth, 1972), chap. 6.
13. R. L. Gregory, *The Intelligent Eye* (New York: McGraw-Hill, 1970), p.150, 147.
14. Kenneth Goodman and Olive S. Niles, *Reading: Progress and Program* (Urbana, Illinois: National Council of Teachers of English, 1970), p.19.
15. Samuel B. Ross, "Visual Literacy—A New Concept?" *Audiovisual Instruction,* 17:12–15 (May 1972).
16. Selma Lanes, *Down the Rabbit Hole* (New York: Atheneum, 1971), chap. 4.
17. Purvis, "Visual Literacy," p.714–16.
18. Karla Kuskin, "Books for Children," *Saturday Review of Education* 55:59–61 (19 Aug. 1972).
19. Lanes, *Down the Rabbit Hole,* chap. 4.
20. Ibid.
21. Jack Tanzman, "The Meaning and Importance of Visual Literacy," *School Management* 16:41 (Dec. 1972).
22. William L. Flynn, "Visual Literacy—A Way of Perceiving, Whose Time Has Come." *Audiovisual Instruction* 17:41–42 (May 1972).
23. Marshall McLuhan, *Counterblast* (New York: Harcourt Brace Jovanovich, 1969), p.140.
24. Constantine Georgiou, *Children and Their Literature* (Englewood Cliffs, New Jersey: Prentice-Hall, 1969), p.63.
25. Travers and Alvarado, "The Design of Pictures," p.47–64.

6

Illustrations

The Visual Language of the Picture Book

Olga Richard

Object recognition is the easiest standard for judging illustrations. There are historical precedents for this utilitarian approach. For years, illustrators have used their art to define and describe objects for encyclopedias—wild flowers, fossils, birds, and the like.

The picture book illustrator has a quite different function. There is no point, for him, in trying to be purely representational. The meaning in his picture comes from the way he arranges colors, lines, shapes, and textures into a special synthesis—one that will please the senses and achieve an aesthetic experience for the reader. Object recognition is a criterion based on the commonplace. It is concerned with simple imitation. The arts are the very antithesis of commonplace standards of imitation, recognition, and the sense of familiarity derived from such considerations.

The critic must make a special effort, both intellectual and emotional, if he is to accept this viewpoint. He must see that the pictorial statements are intended to add to, rather than merely describe, the text. The illustrations have an entity of their own, a quality within the visual area which adds another dimension to the perception of the book. This dimension is one of visual interpretation and the expression of the intrinsic nature of the text.

There might appear to be an easier way to evaluate picture books. After all, it has been suggested, children are unknowing; they merely "read" the pictures anyway. Thus if the story is about a bear and his adventures in the woods, all that is required of illustrations is that the bear be a recognizable bear. This criterion is based on the false premise that children recognize the subject content of the picture as their sole preoccupation with the illustration. Actually, the child's eyes, more than the adult's, see the whole of the artist's statement. Untutored, unshackled, unaware of fashion or fad, the child's eyes take in more of what the page offers.

Illustrators work within the boundaries of the visual arts, and the ability of their art to communicate depends upon the sensory responses of the audience. In order to evaluate picture book illustrations, criteria must be found

SOURCE: *Wilson Library Bulletin*, December 1969, pp. 435–447. Reprinted with permission of the publisher.

therefore in the graphic arts. Any consideration of illustration as less than art suggests that illustration lacks meaning in the very area it utilizes for communication—the visual.

Picture books are often chosen on the basis of a purely personal reaction: "I like it" or "I don't like it." Such acceptance or rejection is often simply a matter of familiarity. There certainly is room for personal taste within the visual arts. But such tastes should always be augmented by consideration of the art elements which contribute to the picture's effectiveness. The experienced critic withholds immediate personal judgments until the work of art has been given an open examination by criteria which particularly relate to art.

Unless one makes such a commitment, one might reject a sensitive illustration only because it is not in color. On such a basis, the simplicity of a thin line drawing, such as Reiner Zimnik uses in *Jonah, the Fisherman*, would be rejected in favor of the full and stunning color of Hanne Axmann's *The Little Owl*. This is all right, provided one knows what miracles are performed by Zimnik's brilliant little line. Very often color illustrations are preferred to line illustrations merely because they give more immediate satisfaction. Knowing this, many publishers use color to cover and gild inferior pictorial concepts and make them more saleable. (This is, however, not the case with the beautiful Axmann book.)

Again, one might prefer simple, flat, clean-edged areas of color to heavily textured, animated surfaces. If so, the selector of a children's book may unconsciously prefer Paul Rand to Antonio Frasconi as illustrator. But he would need to establish this as a sincere commitment to personal aesthetics, not a rejection of a new and relatively unfamiliar style. If he hastily rejects an unfamiliar style, he is missing the chance to grow in his appreciation of art, and he is depriving the child as well.

To understand more about good illustrations, the critic should attempt to relate himself to the artist's intention. He can, by careful examination, determine which of the art elements the artist was emphasizing, whether color, line, texture, or shape. By rethinking the work of art in this way, the viewer will begin to understand the image he thinks he sees.

The Elements of Art

The elements of art* can be thought of as anything the artist uses as a means to an end; for example, color, shape, line, texture, and the arrangement of these components within a specified picture plane. These are the means by

*Categories of elements vary. Gyorgy Kepes, for example, uses color, value, texture, shape, direction, size, and interval as his meaningful units. The author has chosen color, line, shape, texture, and arrangement (composition) because of the child's response in understanding, interpreting, and using these elements.

which the artist conveys his aesthetic statement. Just as an artist may belong to one school of art more than another (for example, he may think of himself as a realist, impressionist, expressionist, etc.) so does an artist often emphasize one of the art elements more than another. This is not to say that color is better than line, or texture better than differentiated shapes. By choice, each artist emphasizes some elements more than others, and perhaps finds a greater usefulness in certain elements for the interpretation of certain texts.

Color

Many people respond to just nine colors—red, yellow, blue, green, orange, purple, black, brown, and white. Red-oranges and rich pinks are called "red"; blue-greens and yellow-greens are put into a "green" category, since there is a lack of sensitivity to the range of shades and mixtures possible.

On the other hand, a seven-year-old at The University Elementary School (UCLA) once made a painting of thirty-two different shades of blue and proudly asked for their identification as separate colors. He had discovered the vast range possible in his color-mixing experiment. Inability to differentiate between light, shade, intensity, and tints of colors (which amounts to an inability to *see*) is due to lack of training. Children who are provided with mixing trays in their art classes and encouraged to experiment with colors rarely lack sensitivity in this area.

The important thing for the picture book critic to know is not the details of color theory, but rather that the artist is deeply concerned with color relations—with choosing, mixing, blending, and juxtaposing until he gets the appropriate shades. When colors appear to clash and shock, the artist has probably created this vibrating effect intentionally.

The potential of color is rarely exploited to the fullest in ordinary picture book illustrations. Color is used solely as a coloring material much of the time, rather than as an inherent part of the arrangement. This limited use of color is in part due to a vague feeling among some educators that too much color stimulates children and tends to confuse perception. Consequently, color has often been treated in the manner of the child's coloring book, with an outline of black filled in with flat color. In other illustrations, the color is like a window-dressing, included to attract attention but not really critical to the illustration's quality. In fact, in some cases, the color is allowed to obscure sensitive line work.

Hanne Axmann, Abe Birnbaum, John Burningham, and Brian Wildsmith are some of the talented artist-illustrators who utilize the full potential of color in their pictures. *Brian Wildsmith's ABC* demonstrates a bold and inventive use of color. In other artists' colored illustrations, one can often imagine the color taken out and the picture remaining essentially the same. This is not possible with Wildsmith. If the color is removed from one of his animals, there is no animal; the entire form has been constructed with varying colors.

In *Green Eyes*, Abe Birnbaum eliminates perspective and minutiae by choice. Objects are generically stated with main features exaggerated: cows have big-eyed cowness, goats a horned, bony quality, dogs a fuzzy-haired dogness, and so on. But the enormous sensory pleasure in this book is also due to Birnbaum's raw, bright, bold use of watercolor.

Line

Book illustrations are more frequently developed as drawings with line. Since such drawings are cheaper to reproduce than a color illustration, printing costs are undoubtedly a major factor here. Also, black-on-white drawing is a traditional mode of graphic illustration.

The linear illustration is deceptive. Variations in line are not immediately evident because we are accustomed to think of line only as an outline of an object. But in the hands of a competent artist, line can be suggestive of color and can build shape and texture. A line can be wide, thin, broken, continuous, spontaneous, controlled, tight, feathery, jagged, meandering and so on. By its style, a line can suggest mood and feeling. It can suggest movement more easily than any other art element, and many lines used together can suggest volume or form.

There are many artists of merit illustrating with linear techniques. Hans Fischer's style ranges from single, simple line to a full, textural, and tonal treatment with many close lines. He can be sketchy, as in his version of *Puss-in-Boots*, or build mood with contrasting grays and blacks, achieved by cross-hatching, as in the night scenes in *The Birthday* and *Pitschi*.

One marvels over the varied way Joseph Low achieves the feeling of texture in the feathers and fur of his animals in *Adam's Book of Odd Creatures*. Close scrutiny of the lines reveals the secret of Low's style. How does he invest the creatures with such vitality? They are so animated, so alive. Is it because of the color? Look at the picture of the Quagga and imagine it without the color. No, it would still have its vital quality. The secret is in the line, in the many directions the line takes, and the many textures made possible through line variation.

In *Cinderella*, Marcia Brown uses a delicate, wavy, curled line to build the illusion of lacy, frilly, and fragile fabrics. In her first portrait of Cinderella she uses minimal line and color to create a mood of sentimental, otherworldly femininity.

Chris Jenkyns meticulously uses line to detail hundreds of visual images in *Andy Says Bonjour*. He develops characterizations through countless details of dress and mannerisms, and gives similar scrupulous treatment to architectural details such as facades, windows, porticos, and roofs. Textural details are diversified and treated so that street stipple or brick details do not interfere with, or overload, the main concept. What appears to be merely "sketchy," becomes, under careful examination, a line technique in which many lines are organized in varied directions to perform rather specific assignments; for example, vitality and humor in the tourists in front of Notre Dame Cathedral and in the fishing scene. Minimal line accentuates the portrait of the cat, Minow.

In *Baboushka and the Three Kings,* Nicolas Sidjakov sometimes structures his line to build a feeling of mass. Juliet Kepes' brush work in *Beasts from a Brush* is sensitive and elegantly rhythmic.

Wood cuts and linoleum blocks are, for the most part, linear in nature. All parts of the wood or linoleum which will not leave an impression on the paper are cut away and the remaining wood or linoleum is inked and printed. Color may be used in block printing, but the print's strength as a visual statement is due to the light and dark contrast achieved by the cut-away and remaining areas, as well as the uneven textural effect achieved in the printing process. Antonio Frasconi's illustrations are magnificent examples. In *The House that Jack Built,* he reduces his ideas to an essence of form and texture, as can be seen in the illustrations of the potent rat, the self-satisfied cat, the worried cow, the maid in motion, and so on.

Shape

Since Paul Cézanne's time, we have seen the cubists, and others, stress the shape of things in their compositions. Sculptors are concerned with the relationships of shapes, and in Alexander Calder's mobiles we see shapes hanging in space. As with color and line, the artist is highly aware of the single and combined shapes which he arranges in his picture. Celestino Piatti, in *The Happy Owls,* reduces owls, roosters, peacocks, and trees to the simplest shapes possible and then richly surfaces them. The vitality of the pictures is due primarily to Piatti's feeling for simple, blunt, strong shapes.

Variations in shape can be seen by comparing the clean-edged positiveness of *I Know a Lot of Things* by Paul Rand, with the torn-edged, more indecisive and whimsical shapes of *Little Blue and Little Yellow* by Leo Lionni. "Little Blue" would take on a totally different personality if he were as clean-edged and brittle as the shapes in Paul Rand's books.

In Remy Charlip's *The Dead Bird,* all the object-shapes are carefully dimensioned and colored to create a sad, quiet, and still feeling. Extremely simple objects are placed on large, unmoving areas of close-harmonied colors, and these objects (trees, children, a dead bird) are seen from radically different "camera" angles. Some of the views are close-ups, as in the double-page of four large children finding the small, still, bird-form. This view is then enlarged, as though the artist has used a telescopic lens in his perception.

Jean Charlot's forms seem chiseled out of stone, permanently placed, quiet, secure, and unmoving. In *A Child's Good Night Book,* Charlot's forms are often large, and executed with great simplicity, thereby giving the feeling of much space.

From the free-formed to the rigidly geometric, one will discover that shapes can suggest awkwardness, delicacy or grace, complexity or precision, speed or stillness, and so on.

Texture

Texture is the surface characteristic of materials, such as the texture of wood, stone, grass, feathers, hair, and so on. Involvement with texture is peculiar to some artists and may be completely neglected by others. It would seem that the artist who falls into the realist category would be the one most preoccupied with texture; his drawing communicates the quality of materials, such as animal hides and furs in Feodor Rojankovsky's *Animals in the Zoo*. But the representation of the surface characteristics is not always limited to realistic art.

In *Inch by Inch* by Leo Lionni, some of the surface treatment is based on the natural object while other surfaces are suggested from sources other than nature. For example, the robin's surface texture is quite frankly a textile design pattern which has been most successfully and ingeniously appropriated. In *Swimmy*, every page is an experiment in surface texturing: paint sponged, dripped, rolled, applied through doilies, and so on. Young children are familiar with these experimental techniques since "gadget painting" is part of their art curriculum. Lionni has engaged in some of these same gadget printing experiences, but with the controlled talent of a mature artist.

Marianne Richter's use of texture is an intrinsic element in her art style. In *The Little Hedgehog*, both her light and dark forms are ingeniously textured, and this greatly enhances the visual interest of her illustrations.

Composition

Composition is the manner in which elements of art are arranged in a picture. Composing a picture involves such considerations as balance, harmony, contrast, unity, proportion, symmetry, rhythm, movement. There are many overlapping relationships. Balance, for example, is concerned with proportions, harmony, unity, and symmetry. It would be difficult to establish exact rules for these qualities. The only thing that can be stated is that one senses a perfect synthesis in a work of merit, and one senses the neglect or absence of compositional elements in the mediocre work.

In the picture book, the single-page or double-page spread is the limited area or picture plane within which the artist composes his elements. The mood of his picture depends very largely on the sparseness or intricacy of his arrangement. Many small forms create a feeling of busyness. The feeling is altered by the shape of the forms, whether clean-edged and geometric, or free-form or haptic. But the quantity of space surrounding the shapes, and the quality of this space, is of importance to the synthesis of the picture.

An individual's response to elements of proportion, balance, harmony, and so on, is often rooted in tradition. For example, the Western world has, until recently, had little tolerance for the void or the asymmetric in design. The acceptance of negative space is of comparatively recent occurrence in our culture. In the Orient, space is used as part of the arrangement, and the oriental home, screen, picture, etc., all demonstrate the totally different sense of aesthetics connected with space.

Remy Charlip consistently concerns himself with space and arrangement in *A Day of Summer* and *A Day of Winter.* His placement of objects is unusually varied, and by unusual perspective approaches and contrasting size relationships, he achieves a mood of quiet peacefulness. Tomi Ungerer makes ingenious use of page space in *The Three Robbers.*

Other Components of Book Art

After the critic has examined each illustration separately and in relation to the overall mood of the text, he must give some attention to the book-making as a whole. He is concerned now with binding, endpapers, margins, blocking of type, page layout, type, and illustration spacing. Such considerations can enhance or diminish the meaning of the visual art within a book. For example, a heavy black-and-white pattern of type face can make a thin, sensitive illustration seem inconsequential, as well as cause a discontinuity in the aesthetics of the page. In a similar fashion, a slight, delicate type face can make the broad strokes of some illustrator's graphic art seem awkward and heavy.

Type arranged over the illustration usually does an injustice to the artwork and creates a haphazard effect on the page. It serves the practical purpose of keeping viewer and reader together (the child can follow the story with his eyes as he listens to his elders read it) but a line of type does not enhance the picture as a picture, unless it is conceived as part of the overall design.

There are no rigid rules to follow in producing a consistent feeling in a book. What is needed is a creative appraisal of the book-making task at hand. Tomi Ungerer uses white type on black background to balance effectively and boldly a strong opposing page in the book *Rufus.* William Wondriska, in *Which Way to the Zoo,* gives the impression of an artist's sketchbook. He has given us the spontaneity of on-the-spot sketches in thin and thick black line, on brown wrapping-type paper. In his book *The Tomato Patch,* he is interested in the pattern and decoration of medieval castles. The front endpapers show flat decorative spears and arrows which are treated as patterns of alternating black on gray and white on gray. The back endpapers repeat a red, contourless tomato shape. The two designs are interesting in their contrast. Both are strongly stated, but the spear and arrow design is more rhythmic in overall quality while the tomato design is boldly staccato.

The Artist's Personal View

The inherent value of the artwork is not a value indigenous to the subject matter, but a value assigned to the content by the compelling manner in which an artist has translated this subject matter into an aesthetic, visual reality. The transformation occurs by means of a visual language—an arrangement of symbols consisting of lines, colors, shapes, textures. But even when artists emphasize the same art elements, the manner in which this emphasis is made varies. Zimnik and Sokol both use line, yet the tiny, precious, jewel-like precision of Zimnik's line in *The Snow Party* is not the same as Bill Sokol's elegant, smooth, and fluid line in *Cats, Cats, Cats, Cats, Cats*. Nor are either one of them similar to Sidjakov. Sidjakov's line is graciously decorative. It is as controlled as Zimnik's, but for a different purpose. Sidjakov controls to decorate, to stripe, dot, or enhance in any way imaginable, while Zimnik controls for the purpose of accumulating mountains of detail to make a sweeping, gleeful statement.

Artists working with color also vary greatly. Taro Yashima's treatment of color in *Umbrella* is in terms of light and dark and is combined with an abrupt foreshortening technique. Ludwig Bemelmans uses color for background wash in his *Madeline* books. Marcia Brown's color in *Cinderella* adds to the softness of the textural quality.

André François in *Roland* is a decorator and so is Nicolas Sidjakov in *Baboushka and the Three Kings*. Yet the difference between the two books is evident. It is more than a difference in content. It is more than a difference in art element, for they both use line.

The value of the artwork is not then a value inherent in the art elements, anymore than in the content, but rather a value assigned to this element by the genius of the artist, by the way his own unique interpretation has been communicated. This uniqueness is a function of personality. As the range of personality differences is limitless, so are the possibilities for use of any of the art elements singly or in combination.

The mediocre artist repeats the same stereotypes in every book, regardless of the content or mood required. In repeating his formula in book after book, he indicates either an unawareness of the varied possibilities, or the fact that he considers it unimportant to become involved. In either case, whether unwilling or unable, the result is predictably inferior to that work which shows respect for the book-form, the art elements, and the viewer-audience.

Separating the works of the hack-illustrator from those of the committed artist requires a recognition of several points. First, one must recognize that illustrations belong to the realm of visual art and are appropriately judged by criteria coming from the fine arts. Then, the illustration is analyzed to determine which elements of art seem to carry the burden of the artist's statement—color, line, texture, shape, arrangement.

Once this preference has been identified, the art elements are examined for the specific way in which they have been used. If the artist's statement is made with line, for example, one examines this line for variety, expressiveness, simplicity, or other dynamic qualities.

The closer the scrutiny, the more rewarding the returns will be. One discovers that the illustration which seemed to be brightly colored is in reality only strong in light and dark contrasts. Or, what seemed to be an interest in color, is in reality black brush drawing on differently colored background papers. Or you discover that the sense of movement is achieved by all the lines pointing in the same direction, the focal point of which lies outside the picture space. The extent of discovery depends upon the degree of commitment to this kind of visual analysis. One begins to *see,* literally, what the artist is able to do.

It is a natural function of the artist to interpret. No two artists bring an identical set of emotions, attitudes, and experiences to bear on picture making. This personal attitude is the background from which the artist interprets. When one says that an artist really "has something to say," this usually refers to the quality of synthesis that is felt in his work, and creating this quality is a disciplined sensory activity. It is only by looking at the picture with similar discipline that the critics can receive the communication intended and share its pleasures with children. When this kind of reception becomes intuitive, one perceives and receives a new work of art much as one does a new friend—by recognizing the differences, noting them, and finding satisfaction in having acquired something new, novel, and stimulating.

A Selected List

Axmann, Hanne, illustrator. *The little owl*. Text by Reiner Zimnik. Atheneum, 1962.

Balet, Jan, author-illustrator. *Joanjo; a Portuguese tale*. Delacorte, 1967.

Bemelmans, Ludwig, author-illustrator. *Madeline*. Viking, 1939.

______. *Madeline's rescue*. Viking, 1953.

______. *Madeline & the bad hat*. Viking, 1957.

______. *Madeline & the gypsies*. Viking, 1959.

______. *Madeline in London*. Viking, 1961.

Birnbaum, Abe, author-illustrator. *Green eyes*. Capitol, 1953.

Brown, Marcia, illustrator. *Cinderella*. Text by Charles Perrault. Scribner's, 1954.

Burningham, John, author-illustrator. *ABC*. Bobbs, 1967.

______. *Harquin*. Bobbs, 1968.

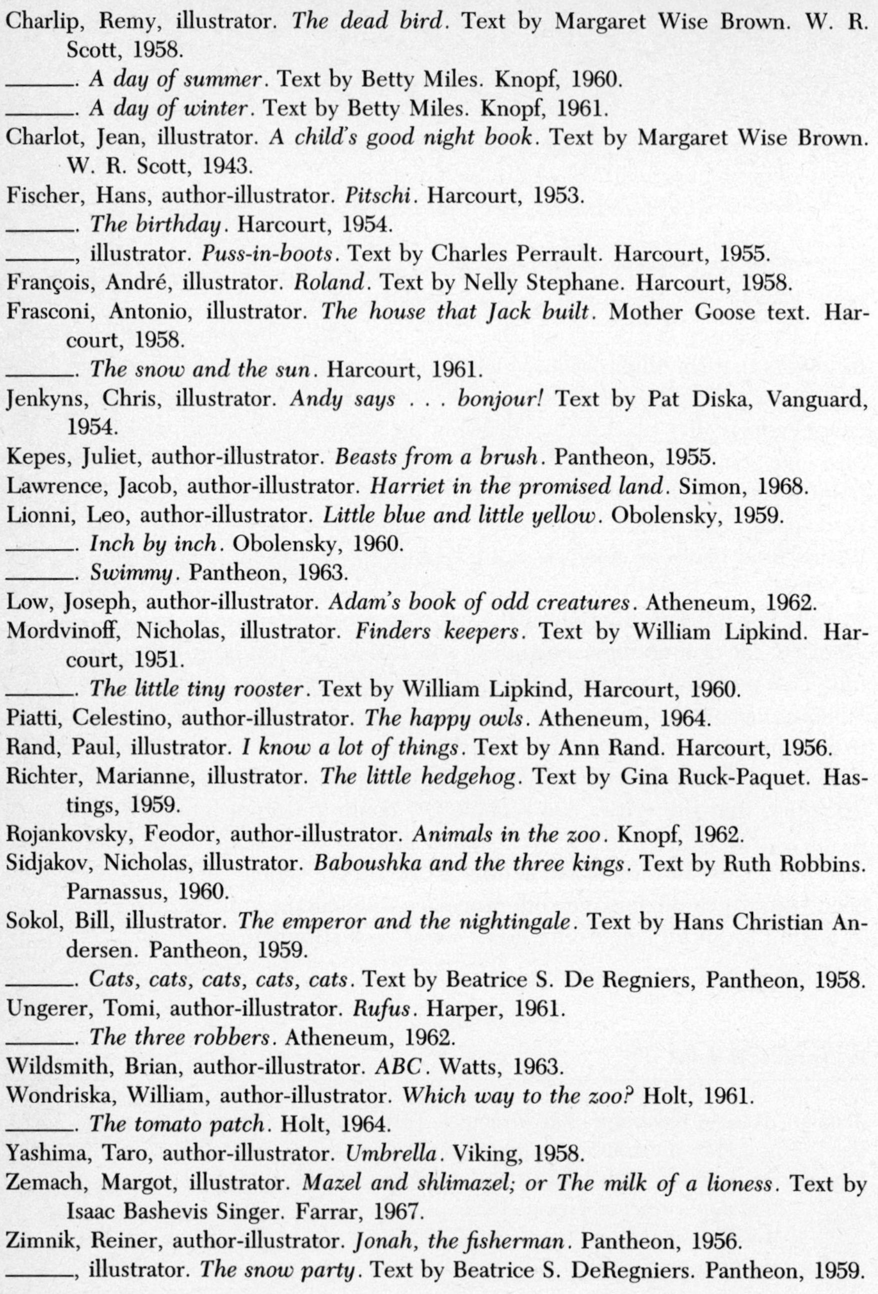

Charlip, Remy, illustrator. *The dead bird*. Text by Margaret Wise Brown. W. R. Scott, 1958.

———. *A day of summer*. Text by Betty Miles. Knopf, 1960.

———. *A day of winter*. Text by Betty Miles. Knopf, 1961.

Charlot, Jean, illustrator. *A child's good night book*. Text by Margaret Wise Brown. W. R. Scott, 1943.

Fischer, Hans, author-illustrator. *Pitschi*. Harcourt, 1953.

———. *The birthday*. Harcourt, 1954.

———, illustrator. *Puss-in-boots*. Text by Charles Perrault. Harcourt, 1955.

François, André, illustrator. *Roland*. Text by Nelly Stephane. Harcourt, 1958.

Frasconi, Antonio, illustrator. *The house that Jack built*. Mother Goose text. Harcourt, 1958.

———. *The snow and the sun*. Harcourt, 1961.

Jenkyns, Chris, illustrator. *Andy says . . . bonjour!* Text by Pat Diska, Vanguard, 1954.

Kepes, Juliet, author-illustrator. *Beasts from a brush*. Pantheon, 1955.

Lawrence, Jacob, author-illustrator. *Harriet in the promised land*. Simon, 1968.

Lionni, Leo, author-illustrator. *Little blue and little yellow*. Obolensky, 1959.

———. *Inch by inch*. Obolensky, 1960.

———. *Swimmy*. Pantheon, 1963.

Low, Joseph, author-illustrator. *Adam's book of odd creatures*. Atheneum, 1962.

Mordvinoff, Nicholas, illustrator. *Finders keepers*. Text by William Lipkind. Harcourt, 1951.

———. *The little tiny rooster*. Text by William Lipkind, Harcourt, 1960.

Piatti, Celestino, author-illustrator. *The happy owls*. Atheneum, 1964.

Rand, Paul, illustrator. *I know a lot of things*. Text by Ann Rand. Harcourt, 1956.

Richter, Marianne, illustrator. *The little hedgehog*. Text by Gina Ruck-Paquet. Hastings, 1959.

Rojankovsky, Feodor, author-illustrator. *Animals in the zoo*. Knopf, 1962.

Sidjakov, Nicholas, illustrator. *Baboushka and the three kings*. Text by Ruth Robbins. Parnassus, 1960.

Sokol, Bill, illustrator. *The emperor and the nightingale*. Text by Hans Christian Andersen. Pantheon, 1959.

———. *Cats, cats, cats, cats, cats*. Text by Beatrice S. De Regniers, Pantheon, 1958.

Ungerer, Tomi, author-illustrator. *Rufus*. Harper, 1961.

———. *The three robbers*. Atheneum, 1962.

Wildsmith, Brian, author-illustrator. *ABC*. Watts, 1963.

Wondriska, William, author-illustrator. *Which way to the zoo?* Holt, 1961.

———. *The tomato patch*. Holt, 1964.

Yashima, Taro, author-illustrator. *Umbrella*. Viking, 1958.

Zemach, Margot, illustrator. *Mazel and shlimazel; or The milk of a lioness*. Text by Isaac Bashevis Singer. Farrar, 1967.

Zimnik, Reiner, author-illustrator. *Jonah, the fisherman*. Pantheon, 1956.

———, illustrator. *The snow party*. Text by Beatrice S. DeRegniers. Pantheon, 1959.

Picture Play in Children's Books: A Celebration of Visual Awareness

Peggy Whalen-Levitt

Ordinarily when adults look at children's picture books, we display our tacit knowledge of picture book conventions. That Angus appears larger than the car behind him on one page of *Angus Lost,* we implicitly understand as a change in perspective. That a picture book character retains his or her identity, despite differences in size and shape across pages in sequence, we take on faith (with the exception of Treehorn, of course). Customarily, we know to "read" picture books from left to right, to acknowledge the decorative rather than the illustrative character of borders, and to expect a certain correspondence between pictures and words.

We could make a long list of picture book conventions and the expectations they elicit from beholders. However, as E. H. Gombrich writes in *Art and Illusion:* "I am not sure we are ever quite sufficiently surprised at our capacity to read images."[1] Perhaps we are not to be too stridently faulted for this. Our pleasure in entering the visual world of a picture book would certainly be diminished if we were forever called upon to bring into consciousness the tacit quality of our beholding. On the other hand, the process by which artists "make" and beholders "make meaning of" picture books is fascinating to explore.

The Process of Reading Images

There are two occasions where the "transparency" of this process is rendered naturally "apparent." The first is when the young child is mastering picture book conventions for the first time. Consider, for example, Carol White's response at age three to the picture of Angus and the car mentioned above: "But, that's only a little car."[2] Young children, in the act of acquiring a knowledge of such conventions as perspective and character identity, remind their adult companions of their own activities as skilled beholders. As children master each new convention, they turn the visual communication process inside out, as it were, and thereby provide adults with a glimpse of those activities so difficult to bring into consciousness once they are second nature

A second route away from "transparency" is taken by the picture book artist, who intentionally plays with convention and, therefore, with our expectations as beholders. When we read a picture book that compels us to break through the complacency of patterned responses, we are provided an opportunity to develop a more intimate awareness of our own expectations. We are also invited to acknowledge the conventional nature of looking at picture books and to contemplate new horizons for communications within the genre.

E. H. Gombrich has written that "though we may be intellectually aware of the fact that any given experience *must* be an illusion, we cannot, strictly speaking, watch ourselves having an illusion."[3] This article takes a look at several picture book artists who choose to live on the edge of illusion and, therefore, attempt to pull their beholders, however fleetingly, into the reflexive act of watching themselves having an illusion.

Visual Nonsense

Perhaps the most fundamental form of picture play is that which violates our visual common sense. As beholders we bring to the act of looking at pictures certain assumptions about "natural" appearances derived from our perceptions of the "real" world. When the "natural" is inverted or contradicted in some way, visual nonsense, absurdity, or irony results.

Edward Lear is a master of the form. In "Flora Nonsensica" *(Teapots and Quails)*, diagrammatic drawings of "The Clothes-Brush Tree," "The Kite Tree," "The Biscuit Tree," and "The Fork Tree" are accompanied by mock-scientific descriptions which heighten the incongruity of image and context. Through the use of the botanical dictionary format, Lear not only plays with our expectations of "treeness," he plays on our habits of reading scientific diagrams as well.

Mark Alan Stamaty's illustrations for Frank Asch's *Yellow Yellow* take visual nonsense even further. Here we encounter a visual carnival of the absurd. Cars travel on skates and tanks double as shoes in an inversion of customary functions; a train, puffing smoke, circles the train-track belt around a man's waist, bringing into relation images which in our reality are seldom related; feet face backwards, a basketball serves as a head, and a shoemaker is dwarfed by the size of the shoe upon which he works, in an unending series of images which exploits changes in habitual relations, functions, and dimensions.

Nonsense turns to irony when the visually incongrous is set in an otherwise naturalistic context. This is the effect of Jörg Müller's illustrations for Jörg Steiner's *The Bear Who Wanted to Be a Bear*. Müller depicts a world which, down to the Diners Club insignia above the motel clerk's desk, conforms to a contemporary Western natural order of things. Into this world is placed a plausibly bearish bear, who is nonetheless taken to be a man by the human characters in the story. The transformation of this "natural" bear into an "anthropomorphic" bear or a "bestial" human forces the beholder into a dual perspective. Bearish human or humanoid bear? The conflict between these two realms of reality is nowhere more ironically depicted than in the illustration where the bear, called to the modern office of the factory president, does a double-take of the bear rug on the floor.

"Impossible Pictures

If Lear, Stamaty, and Müller introduce us to "impossible" worlds, Mitsumasa Anno presents us with the world of "impossible" pictures as well. Lest we take for granted our mastery of the conventions of "correct" perspective, Anno plays games with the illusion of space. In this he follows directly in the footsteps of M. C. Escher. Elements of Escher's "Waterfall," "Ascending and Descending," "Mobius Strip I," "Relativity," "Another World," and "Above and Below" are readily recognizable in *Anno's Alphabet*, *Upside-Downers*, and especially in *Topsy-Turvies*.

Douglas R. Hofstadter offers this description of how the viewer understands Escher's "Relativity":

> Those staircases are "islands of certainty" upon which we base our interpretation of the overall picture. Having once identified them we try to extend our understanding, by seeking to establish the relationship which they bear to one another. At that stage we encounter trouble. But if we attempted to backtrack—that is, to question the "islands of certainty"—we would also encounter trouble, of another sort. There's no way of backtracking and "undeciding" that they are staircases.[4]

Anno's illustration of men climbing stairs is a world of "up the down staircase." Each staircase becomes, for the beholder, an "island of certainty"; it is only when we try to relate one staircase to the other, and to the landings which join them, that the contradictions of the arrangement become apparent. Figures walk up a staircase to a landing leading to a staircase which takes them up another flight, but back to the level they started from. Anno's figures, caught in this paradox, show signs of desperation, except for the artist at the lower left, who may just draw his way out of the situation he was drawn into.

By presenting us with visual paradoxes of this sort, Anno, like Escher, enables us to extend and explore the process by which we conventionally make meaning of space in pictures. Ordinarily, we quickly, even automatically, establish relationships between "islands of certainty" in pictures, provided they coincide with our conceptions of space and our expectations about perspective. When these conceptions and expectations are flagrantly violated, we come to know them better. We also take a fascinating journey into unimaginable, and yet imaginable, realms.

The Power of Suggestion

In the Western tradition of illusion, the beholder is called upon to infer three dimensional forms from flat surfaces, to imagine an unseen side of a figure, and to supplement the information given. Completion of the incomplete is a fundamental operation of looking at pictures.

This appeal to the visual imagination may be resisted by very young children, accustomed as they are to moving actively in the real world, exploring each new object from every possible angle. Indeed, a toddler may literally pick at an image on a page in a futile attempt to "see" inside or behind it, or, accepting symbol as symbol, to notice and wonder about what has been sacrificed to the art of illusion. Supplying what is not depicted soon becomes an implicit operation in a young child's repertoire, an accomplishment well documented by Maureen Crago in "Incompletely Shown Objects in Children's Books: One Child's Response."[5] Here, within the careful record of a parent's diary, we observe a young child in the process of learning to meet the artist halfway.

There are, of course, picture book artists who take pleasure in extending the beholder's half of the bargain. By limiting the amount of visual information given, they engage the viewer's imagination. In Tana Hoban's *Look Again*, for example, the viewer is invited to guess whole from part and to rediscover part in whole, as the book shifts from the concealed perspective of a peephole to the full page photograph behind. Richard Egielski likewise plays with the limits of suggestion in Arthur Yorinks' *Sid and Sol*. Having once introduced the giant Sol. Egielski delights in showing us only part of the whole. From a pair of feet, an ear, an eye, three fingers, or even his breath alone, we are to infer his whole galumphish self.

In *Yellow Yellow*, Mark Alan Stamaty oversteps the limits of incompletness. Accompanying a text that reads "One day . . . I found . . . a yellow . . ."is a nearly totally yellow page. Obviously it is a yellow part of a yellow something, but the beholder is inevitably stumped by Stamaty's highly curtailed hint. Turning the page introduces further visual information and resolves the beholder's dilemma.

The ultimate play with incompletion is, of course, the total blank. Confronted by nothing, the beholder must assume the artist's role, becoming co-creator rather than re-creator of the book. Thus, in *Fungus the Bogeyman*, Raymond Briggs "deletes" a picture with the following directive to the reader: "The Publishers wish to state that this picture has been deleted in the interests of good taste and public decency." Likewise, Henry Holiday in his illustrations for *The Hunting of the Snark* obliges Lewis Carroll's text by including a picture of an ocean chart that is, by all reckoning, "a perfect and absolute blank!" The effect is to heighten our awareness of the "book as book" and the "picture as picture."

Vantage Point

As we move through time and space, at any given moment we assume a vantage point from which we see the world. Part of the pleasure we derive from lookout towers, amusement parks, or airplane flights is the opportunity they afford us to move out of everyday points of view and literally see the world from different angles. When we look at pictures, on the other hand, we must assume the viewpoint assigned to us by the artist, who chooses the angle from which we are to behold any given scene, arrested in time and space. And generally, in the service of narrative, we are presented with a sequence of such scenes and invited to infer the time and space that has elapsed between them.

Occasionally, however, an artist chooses to make time stand still and move the beholder through space alone. Consider, for example, Charles Keeping's opening illustrations for *Through the Window*. The moment in time involves a young boy, Jacob, in the act of looking out the window. First, Keeping positions the beholder behind Jacob looking out—we are inside his front room, anticipating the world view that lies beyond the lace curtains. Then, across the page, Keeping shifts the beholder to a head-on point of view. We are outside Jacob's window looking in at him.

Philippe Dumas, in Kay Fender's *Odette*, and Peter Parnall, in Cora Annett's *When the Porcupine Moved In*, experiment with similar changes in perspective. The effect of these multiple vantage points on the same action is to shift the beholder's attention from "what" is pictured to "how" it is pictured. Instead of asking "What happens next?" we are invited to dwell on a single action, to explore various views of it, to heighten our awareness.

The artist's choice to view a scene from front or behind, sideways, up or down, makes different demands on the beholder. This is perhaps nowhere better demonstrated than in *The Long Slide* by Mr. and Mrs. Smith, which depicts the climb of Barley, Jacko, and Teddy up a ladder, into the sky, and their long slide down. But this is less a book about their adventures than it is a book about point of view itself. The beholder is called upon to view their actions from numerous angles. It is not what is happening, but rather how we see what is happening that holds our attention.

Breaking Ground

Our subjective experience when we look at pictures is that we see the whole picture at once. But research on perception makes it clear that we actually see only small portions of a picture in detail at a time; that we make multiple fixations when we look at pictures. The beholding process is therefore both active and selective. Our experience of a picture is something we create within ourselves.

What we focus on has to do with our own intentions as well as with the composition of the picture at hand. More often than not in children's books, we explore a picture on the basis of a distinction between figure and ground. There are picture book artists, however, who seem to delight in playing with this tendency to focus attention on discrete figures at the expense of a neglected ground.

One of the most obvious forms of this brand of picture play is camouflage. In camouflage, what we take as ground and unconsciously label as unimportant is shown, upon closer examination, to conceal familiar shapes and figures. Thus, when we first glance at Nancy Ekholm Burkert's illustration of Snow-White running through the great forest in *Snow-White and the Seven Dwarfs*, we are most likely to focus on the figure of Snow-White, as well as on the foregrounded wild beasts who spring past her. A more thorough reading of the picture is well rewarded. Hidden in the shapes and shadows of rocks and trees are other creatures of the forest. The beholder is lured into an exploration of the entire surface of this double-page spread in a search for further embedded figures. What was at first dismissed as ground is ultimately pored over and intimately known.

Frank Asch's *In the Eye of the Teddy* creates yet another play on the figure/ground distinction. This time the beholder is caught in an inversion. Through six pictures in sequence, we are brought into ever closer range of a teddy bear until nothing but the black, blackness of his eyes fills the sixth double-page spread. Still, we are imagining the eyeness of it all, since the eye, as figure, has been firmly established. But this is slippery business and with the turn of a page the blackness has become ground for a visual fantasy. As fantasy figures float into, through, and out of this black abyss, we are confronted with blackness once again. This time, somewhat wiser, the beholder asks, "Figure or ground?" Asch concludes with ever more distant views of a small boy's eyes. Through these two blank, black spreads, Asch conflates figure and ground and puts his beholders more closely in touch with what they focus on and what they ignore as they look at pictures.

Visual Allusion and Parody

Painting, unlike music and literature, is a non-notational art form. It cannot, like music (through notes) or literature (through letters), be rendered into numerous editions of the same work, one as authentic as the next.

As if to play with the non-notational quality of visual art, there are picture book artists who incorporate not a reproduction but an imitation of an existing artistic work into their own illustrations. Thus Etienne Delessert includes an image of one of Sendak's Wild Things in his fantasy parkscape for Ionesco's *Story Number 1*. But this displaced Wild Thing, a very accurate copy of the original from Sendak's first double-page spread depicting the wild rumpus, is taken less as a forgery than as an allusion. If literature can benefit from the reference of one text to another, why not visual art?

This same type of visual allusion is elaborately explored in *Anno's Journey*. Here, within the fabric of town and country scenes, are embedded imitations of Gustave Courbet's "The Grain Sifters," "The Stonebreakers," and "The Meeting"; Georges Seurat's "The Bathers" and "Sunday Afternoon on the Island of La Grande Jatte"; Jean-François Millet's "The Gleaners" and "L'Angélus"; and is that one of Renoir's nudes, her back turned to the beholder? These references to French paintings are accomplished through similarities of figure form, and composition to the originals. And they serve Anno on both the semantic and the stylistic level. Semantically, of course, they provide him with the content of French life; with the people and activities characteristic of the country he is exploring. But stylistically, it is eminently suitable to Anno's own *oeuvre* that he has chosen the work of the Impressionists.

Visual intertextuality can also be carried beyond the purposes of allusion into the realm of parody. In visual parody the beholder looks for variations between the original and the imitation, for the twists and differences that separate the two works. Fernando Krahn's *The Great Ape* includes enough of the features of the film "King Kong" to capture the spirit of the original, but it is the ways in which Krahn deviates from the familiar sequence of events that bring the beholder special pleasure. In Krahn's version, "the great ape" saves the young heroine from a near tragic fall; is lured back to the crew's ship by a giant banana; is left behind on his island; and, in recompense, is sent a photograph of his newfound and sorely missed friend standing, where else, but in front of the Empire State Building.

A Celebration of Visual Awareness

With their plays on visual common sense, perspective, incompletion, point of view, figure/ground, and the very nature of visual art itself, artists explore the inner workings of the visual communication process. By heightening our awareness of the procedures by which pictures are made and interpreted, they bring our tacit knowledge to the fore. Their illusions are never seamless, never complete. Thus they continually catch us in the act of having an illusion; make us conscious of the challenges and feats of our own re-creative actions.

Picture play in children's books creates challenges for the beholder on the road to transformation. It makes of the beholder a fellow traveller "in the creative adventure of the artist."[6] This, undoubtedly, is a key to the pleasure we derive from these books. They fully engage our visual imagination and offer us an opportunity to celebrate our awareness of the fascinating process by which artists "make," and beholders "make meaning of," pictures.

References

1. H. E. Gombrich, *Art and Illusion* (Princeton, N.J.: Princeton Univ. Press, 1969), p.39.
2. Dorothy White, *Books Before Five* (New York: Oxford Univ. Press, 1954), p.32.
3. Gombrich, *op. cit.*, p.5–6.
4. Douglas R. Hofstadter, *Godel, Escher, Bach: An Eternal Golden Braid* (New York: Basic Books, 1979), p.97–98.
5. Maureen Crago, "Incompletely Shown Objects in Children's Books: One Child's Response," in *Children's Literature in Education*, 10:3 (1979), p.151–57.
6. Gombrich, *op. cit.*, p.278.

Illustrators, Books and Children: An Illustrator's Viewpoint

Celia Berridge

In recent years, there has been a revival of the debate among literary critics and children's book reviewers on the central issue of how to define and evaluate children's literature. The argument has produced some splendid controversy (see *Signal* No's. 14,[1] 15[2] and 16[3]; and *Children's Literature in Education* 14[4] for example). One crucial strand in the debate has been the relevance or otherwise to the reviewer of children's possible responses. This article is not the place for an account of the historical background, but certainly the argument has rumbled on intermittently ever since Arthur Ransome declared in 1937, "You write not for children but for yourself."

The controversy provoked by this artist-centred approach has encompassed the genre of children's picture books, and some illustrators have become frequent targets for criticism, especially from educationists. Brian Alderson also has concerned himself with "the irrelevance of children to the children's book reviewer"—see his article of that title[5] and his famous catalogue for the 1973 National Book League exhibition, *Looking at Picture Books*.[6] I want to look at this debate from an illustrator's point of view.

It is rare for an individual writer or illustrator to reply to criticism. Charles Keeping[7, 8] is an interesting exception. His discussion of his own work is very different from that of, for example, Trevor Stubley.[9] The difference stems partly from the fact that Stubley illustrates other people's texts exclusively, whereas Keeping writes his own picture books, as well as illustrating those of other writers. When an illustrator writes his or her own words, the mental approach to the task of illustrating is subtly different: one assumes the author's stance of addressing oneself to an audience, as well as being involved in the construction of the book, trimming the plot to fit into 32 pages, and so on. The illustrator has total control over the creation of the book, and total responsibility too.

To consider the role of the picture book illustrator in relation to children, I'd like to sidetrack for a moment, turn to educational psychology, and consider by way of analogy Arthur Applebee's model for relationships be-

SOURCE: *Children's Literature in Education*, Spring 1980, pp. 21–30. Reprinted with permission of Agathon Press, Inc.

tween writer and reader.[10] In his doctoral thesis, drawing upon the theory of spectator role in children's developing knowledge of the conventions of stories which James Britton had outlined, Applebee suggested a three-part model consisting of: the author or speaker; the discourse or story itself; and the audience or responder. This gives us three relationships: author-discourse; author-responder and responder-discourse. Each of the three elements generates its own conventions or "systems of constructs"; hence, evaluations depend on whose perspective is adopted. This last point is significant. Traditionally, literary criticism has consisted mainly of values, ideologies, and concepts thought to pertain solely to the book itself—or discourse—as if it existed in isolation. In fact the reviewer or critic is in the position of the third relationship: responder-discourse.

I think Applebee's model can be adapted to study the position of the illustrator. When he/she is illuminating someone else's words, the illustrator feels wholly absorbed in the first relationship—in this case, illustrator-discourse. The task is to find images for the words, and the most appropriate medium and technique to realise these images. But if the illustrator is making the whole of a book, words and all, he or she is in an equivalent position to an author engaged in the first and second relationships simultaneously. An author may well be writing *for* himself, but presumably he's not talking *to* himself. The end product is intended to be read by someone else eventually, and this is so for illustrators too. It means that an illustrator *must* be accommodating his/her graphic execution to the child viewer in some way, whether consciously or not. Why else should there be a distinctly different style of illustration in children's books? Compare the graphic styles in comics for teenagers with those in comics for five-year-olds; the adaptions *by the artists* are clearly visible.

"An artist, like a writer,is, of course, always entitled to say that he does the work he has it in him to do, and what becomes of it afterwards is not his business," wrote John Rowe Townsend.[11] But he went on to say that it is not possible, nevertheless, for anyone whose work appears on a children's list to work without "a special sense of audience." Yet many picture book illustrators hotly dispute that they do this.

It is at art school that many would-be illustrators first absorb the professional values and attitudes that will colour their subsequent working life. Graphic design courses are an uneasy mixture of Fine Arts values—personal freedom of expression, self-exploration, etc.—supposedly independent aesthetic standards of assessing work, and design objectives of "problem-solving," meeting the client's needs, and fulfilling the brief. Probably the degree of emphasis on Fine Arts values or graphic design practicalities varies from college to college at any given time. But the art student enters a college world in which complex and often contradictory attitudes seem to be held by the teachers, but where, nevertheless, there seems always to be an underlying, unspoken tacit agreement about ways and standards of evaluating artwork.

The student's visual discrimination and taste become more sophisticated, even idiosyncratic; his/her standards of execution become increasingly perfectionist, although some of his ideas acquired at this time may be subsequently modified by experience. And when, as an illustrator, he/she becomes increasingly absorbed into the world of the professionals, there grows the inevitable gap between those who are highly involved inside an expertise and the ordinary public outside. Graphic design students are now trained to be competent in many areas of design, the assumption being that they may find work in anything from record covers to book jackets, TV graphics to book layout or typography, label and package design to toy design. (I wonder how many reviewers realize that a book illustrator may be doing other quite different kinds of work—Nicola Bayley and Alan Baker do advertisements, for instance.)

Illustrating is a craft; it is applied art, and that means, among other things, accepting the restraints imposed by the discipline of doing a picture for someone else, not just for yourself. That "someone else" may be an art editor acutely aware of what is likely to prove popular out there in the bookstores. That is not to say that illustrators are expected by the publisher to show their drawings to children as they work! The professional people involved in the business make informed guesses, based on experience, about what is the best, most appropriate presentation of a story. Short of testing every book at proof stage on a representative sample of not less than one thousand children (half boys, half girls; one-third inner city, one-third suburban, one-third rural; using teams of trained interviewers and calculating the results statistically, eliminating any possibility of bias), there is no accurate way to predict whether an individual book is going to prove popular with children or adults. Publishers make guesses; publishing is a gamble. So when a reviewer knocks a book for its probable lack of appeal to children—". . . is unlikely to interest those inner-city kids it's intended for . . ."—or makes *any* kind of assumption about children's responses to the pictures—". . . stirring stuff, Matilda thinks—children likewise, who aren't bothered by the sub-Scarry illustrations and forced ideas . . ."[12]—two thoughts spring to my mind: first, how does the reviewer know? and second, how is the illustrator supposed to know?

Consider the picture-book illustrator's working world. . . . Of all these interested parties, the only ones the illustrator will definitely meet are the publisher's children's book editor and art editor and occasionally another illustrator. But until the National Book League recently compiled a list of authors and artists willing to give talks about their work, very few illustrators ever met parents, teachers, librarians, or academics. They worked in happy oblivion.

And what about children? Brian Wildsmith claims never to show his work to his own family. Raymond Briggs summed up the attitude of many illustrators in a recent interview: "I'm not really aware of liking or disliking kids, but in general I do not choose to be with them. This does not affect my work. I write and I draw and then the publisher tells me that it is suitable for children of various ages."[13]

So to a large extent, the illustrator is locked in an isolated dialogue with the words and form of the book. And yet I believe that there is always some consideration of the audience, this ghostly circle of children for whom either the illustrator makes subtle accommodations in style, or towards whose supposed taste the illustrator's style naturally leans.

The business of deciding for what age a book is suitable is less clear than it might seem. For example, Alan Garner's *Red Shift*[14]—although it is written in words and sentences simple enough to be read by my seven-year-old daughter when I showed it to her—has a plot and structure far too complex for her to grasp yet and deals with emotions which will not be part of her experience for some time. I think that one can only guess a book's lower age limit, both in terms of content and technical accessibility. Like adults, children need in their reading some books which are safe, undemanding, and very easy; a lot of books which are just about on their current level of development; and constant encounters with books just that little bit too hard for them, so that mentally they have to stretch out towards them.

Naturally this applies to picture books, and publishers try to build up their children's lists so as to cater to these simultaneous needs. But an illustrator who likes to be innovative and to explore new forms within the picture-book convention is in danger of being accused of using picture books to explore his/her own artistic development. The defence argument (Keeping again!) is that picture books form part of a child's early art experience as well as book experience, and that being fresh, open-minded, and naturally experimental, children are less likely than adults to have rigid expectations of what should be in a book. Moreover, artists know more about their area than the general public and play a part in developing public taste. It is not an illustrator's job to take note of uninformed criticism, yet, paradoxically, the mass of critics (and purchasers) are amateur, untrained nonartists. So do we give them what they want, or do we stretch them a little?

Here is Jean Renoir discussing his father's disappointment when the public failed to appreciate his work, for Renoir père had had great faith in the good taste and natural discernment of ordinary people:

> Ultimately it is the public which, after a long period of assimilation, renders the final verdict. . . . This tardiness in making people accept the evolution of art, literature, music and even thought, frightened Renoir. . . . This evolution is slowed down by mass media, for example the press, which must provide its readers with material which does not startle them. The artist is obliged, in consequence, to take refuge in an ivory tower among a little band of admirers. Renoir frankly disapproved. "It quickly degenerates into a mutual-admiration society, and you're done for." My father hoped his works would last long enough to be judged by the public at the propitious moment. His hopes have certainly been fulfilled.[15]

Lucky Renoir. Poor illustrator—whose art is strictly for immediate consumption! In today's market, the illustrated picture book is hardly an appropriate arena for artistic pioneers. On the whole, the illustrator produces what both he/she and the publisher think will be popular and sell. The illustrator knows the job is a craft—but the purist critic/reviewer tends to judge the end-product by supposed Fine Arts values, ignoring the functional aspects. So, given the fact that critics are divided anyway on the issue of relevance, how much should an illustrator consider it while working?

So long as the debate remains theoretical, it continues revolving in the same old grooves. One way of moving forward would be to consider the known facts of children's needs and picture preferences—i.e., research carried out so far. Mentioning the relevance of "depth psychology" applied to children's reading. C. S. Hannabuss writes, ". . . there's a need to take psychology into account. You can't leave it out, for instance, in assessing a young child's experience of picture books."[16]

The trouble is, you can't easily use it either. I don't mean the solid background of Piaget, Bruner, the Gibsons and so on. I mean the papers on research into "children's preferences in illustration" and the like. There is often a lack of clarity in thinking among researchers about the purpose of the research; this leads them to draw inferences from the findings that are not applicable in another context. There is often also a carelessness in distinguishing different functions for various kinds of illustrations, so that incompatible pictures are lumped together in the experimental method. You cannot compare unlike with unlike, and you cannot generalise from slipshod findings.

From Rudisill in 1952[17] to Hutt in 1976[18] and Smerdon in 1977[19] the same fault persists: that of generalising from data obtained in an artificial testing situation because of the need to restrict the variables in the interest of scientific objectivity. The funniest example I can think of is Child, Hansen, and Hornbeck,[20] who studied age and sex differences in children's colour preferences by showing children bits of coloured paper, then generalised from their findings to recommend, for example, that children's textbooks should have red covers. Many researchers pick stimulus material to represent different graphic styles from widely differing sources, ignoring its precise intended function. For example, Hutt chose three kinds of illustration: a cartoon or representational illustration; some "abstract designs" from a Sunday colour magazine intended for adults; and some "realistic pictures," whatever that means. All these were "assessed as roughly comparable." Bloomer[21] acknowledged the different purposes of his stimulus material, then proceeded to ignore this factor.

Not counting reading research during the last year I have read over forty papers on children's responses to pictures in various kinds of tests. The only ones I could envisage an illustrator finding helpful have been the least "scientific," such as Rump and Southgate's study of children looking at pictures in an exhibition,[22] and the Crago's current study of their daughter and her picture books,[23] a similar exercise to the still unsurpassed account by

Dorothy Neal White, *Books Before Five.*[24] There is also an excellent study by Sharon White of children's responses to illustrations depicting characters of various races.[25] What makes these studies useful is that they treat the stimulus material in its real-life context, and the subjects of the experiments—the children—are similarly in their natural settings. We need many more such studies where the research is less esoteric and more applicable to other situations; less concerned with artificial constraints in the name of scientific rigour and more concerned with finding out what children think and feel in normal circumstances. "When you are working in the field, not the laboratory, your obligation is to be as rigorous as the situation will permit" wrote Lionel Elvin.[26]

We need some good research into pictures for children in "transactional modes" to use Harding's phrase—that is, we do need to know more about the effectiveness of illustrations in functional contexts such as reading primers, textbooks, instructional leaflets, and so on, so that they may be better designed in the future. But I wonder whether a so-called objective enquiry is the right approach to discovering those elements in a picture book which affect a child's response. Until some research or study has been documented sensibly, neither critics nor educationists nor psychologists can pronounce on children's picture preferences, in or out of picture books.

Much of the above-mentioned research was carried out with the aim of discovering principles underlying the effectiveness of graphics in learning materials. Even so, it's impossible to extrapolate from all the various findings a prescription for illustrators to follow in either information books or fiction, and I detect a strong urge on the part of the researchers to prescribe. You simply can't get every book in the country and produce a correct formula: "Who can say what is the right book for the right child? That, thank God, is the child's own adventure."[27] Which brings me back to illustrators and children, because for there to be freedom of choice, there must also be availability.

One of the undercurrents in the relevance debate has been the issue raised by the Children's Rights Group: that many children's books are racist, sexist, or anti-working class by default—that by simply not depicting the despised group, the author reveals his/her bias. Publishers have begun actively seeking stories which are less middle-class largely in response to the economic power of schools and libraries, their main customers. So far, though, illustrators have not been much involved in this. Caldecott and Greenaway in the last century drew children from a largely mythical era some fifty years before their own time, and illustrators have tended to do the same ever since. What a sentimental, escapist bunch we are! Each year, out of well over 250 new picture books, fewer than 20 will be illustrated with recognisably realistic contemporary settings. City settings are even rarer than rural ones. Why has "Mother Goose comes to Cable Street" taken two hundred years to appear?[28]

I suspect it has something to do with artists' heightened perception and greater sensitivity towards visual ugliness, plus conventions about books absorbed as children, mixed with notions about beauty acquired at art school. Artists aren't the only people who find cities ugly places in which to live. There is a wave of romanticism about "the country" everywhere just now. Personally I've always liked cities and town centres. One of my favourite childhood memories is of wet pavements reflecting the lights from shop windows late on a winter afternoon, and this is the kind of visual memory I like to use in my own picture books. I believe that young children are very observant; if they live in towns, they notice all sorts of funny things about buildings and vehicles and those slices of vistas you get looking down a narrow street with tall buildings on either side. Rows of shopfronts, crowded markets, busy docksides and disused ones, crumbling old houses all have their own beauty; and so do modern children dressed in chainstore clothes, doing all the daft things children do. There is no need to idealise it: let's just make the choice available, so that those children who live in towns and want to see their kind of life mirrored in a book can do so. If illustrators would only be a little more consciously aware of their child audience, we wouldn't have quite such a gross imbalance in book content. This is one aspect of the relevance debate about which artists should take notice.

In summary, the question of the relevance of children's responses to the evaluation of books must be faced and sorted out by examining the criteria of criticism and by considering the available evidence from both marketing and academic research.

The evidence of research must be carefully scrutinised: findings must be considered in the light of the research method and their appropriateness in a wider context. Shortcomings must be acknowledged, and better research approaches adopted. Experimental research may prove to be more suitable for non-fiction and learning materials than fiction.

Studies of children's responses to fiction must not attempt to straitjacket it in a mistaken pursuit of scientific objectivity. Let's consider the possibility that we can have "communication without necessarily explicit understanding."[29]

Illustrators must stop pretending that they make no concessions towards their child audience and stop being ashamed of it, as though it were some kind of awful weakness that debased one's status as an artist. Whether one sees oneself as an *artist* or as a *craftsman* is probably what causes the confusion.

There should be much more contact between all the various interested parties, with less prejudice all round. Let psychologists visit art schools, critics meet artists, illustrators go into primary schools, publishers meet parents, etc. After all, books are for everybody's children—aren't they?

Notes

1. J. R. Townsend, "Standards of Criticism," *Signal,* 14 (1974), 91–105.
2. Peter Hunt, "Criticism and Children's Literature, *Signal,* 15 (1974), 117–130.
3. Bob Leeson, "To the Toyland Frontier," *Signal,* 16 (1975), 18–25.

4. N. Tucker, "Looking at Pictures," *Children's Literature in Education,* No. 14 (1974), 37–51.
5. Brian Alderson, "The Irrelevance of Children to the Children's Book Reviewer," *Children's Book News,* 4, No. 1 (1965), 10–11.
6. Brian Alderson, *Looking at Picture Books* (London: National Book League, 1973).
7. Charles Keeping, "Illustration in Children's Books," *Children's Literature in Education,* No. 1 (1970), 41–54.
8. "Charles Keeping—Illustrator," *School Bookshop News,* 8 (1977), 16–18.
9. Trevor Stubley, "Illustrating Children's Books," *Growing Point,* 15 (1976), 2996–3002.
10. Arthur Applebee, "The Spectator Role: Theoretical and Developmental Studies of Ideas About, and Responses to Literature, with Special Reference to Four Age Levels," Ph.D. Thesis, London University, 1974.
11. J. R. Townsend, *Written for Children,* 2nd ed. (London: Kestrel, 1974).
12. Geraldine Carter, "From Sad to Zany," *Guardian,* 29 September 1978, p. 9.
13. Linda Christmas, "Coming Clean with the Snowman," *Guardian,* 7 September 1978, p. 9.
14. Alan Garner, *Red Shift* (London: Collins, 1973).
15. Jean Renoir, *Renoir, My Father* (London: Collins, 1962).
16. C. S. Hannabuss, "Review of *The Cool Web,*" *Signal,* 23 (1977), 88–90.
17. M. Rudisill, "Children's Preferences of Colour Versus Other Qualities in Illustrations," *Elementary School Journal,* 52 (1952), 444–451.
18. C. Hutt, B. Forrest, and J. Newton, "Visual Preferences of Children," *Journal of Child Psychology and Psychiatry,* 17 (1976), 63–68.
19. G. Smerdon, "Children's Preferences in Illustration," *Children's Literature in Education* No. 20 (1977), 17–31.
20. I. Child, J. Hansen, and F. Hornbeck, "Age and Sex Differences in Children's Colour Preferences," *Child Development* 39 (1968), 21–27.
21. Richard Bloomer, "Children's Preferences and Responses as Related to Styles and Themes of Illustration," *Elementary School Journal* 60 (1960), 334–340.
22. E. Rump and V. Southgate, "Variables Affecting Aesthetic Appreciation in Relation to Age," *British Journal of Educational Psychology,* 37 (1967), 58–72.
23. M. Crago and H. Crago, *One Child and Her Books,* (in press).
24. Dorothy Neal White, *Books Before Five* (Auckland: New Zealand Council for Educational Research, 1954).
25. Sharon White, "A Study of the Relationship Between Racial Illustrations Accompanying Stories in Basal Readers and Children's Preferences for These Stories," Ed. Diss. SUNY at Buffalo, 1972.
26. Lionel Elvin, *The Place of Commonsense in Educational Thought* (London: Unwin, 1977).
27. Mrs. Miller, *Horn Book* Editorial, quoted by P. Heins in V. Haviland, *Children and Literature: Views and Reviews* (London: Bodley Head, 1973), p. 406.
28. R. Stones and A. Mann, *Mother Goose Comes to Cable Street* (London: Kestrel, 1978).
29. Frank Eyre, *British Children's Books in the Twentieth Century* (London: Longmans, 1971), p. 146.

Picture Books for Children Who Are Masters of Few Words

Barbara Lucas

"One picture is worth 10,000 words," declares an ancient Chinese proverb. Not everyone agrees. There are picture book authors who say, "It was my idea. Where would the artist be without my words?" There are reviewers who write reviews of picture books without even mentioning the pictures. Still it is the picture that matters to children who are masters of few words. It is through the pictures that they first discover a relationship between their rudimentary worlds and the printed page. It is through the pictures that one lures backward readers to the words in-between. And it is with the help of pictures—in a book—that childrens' librarians may hope to make false prophets of McLuhan fans.

But Why Do They Cost So Much?

Pictures can create a lot of controversy: moral outrage is forever rampant and even the work of Caldecott winners has been X-rated. But the more common complaint gets down to the root of all evil—the price.

"It's lovely. But why does it cost so much?" asks the budget-weary librarian.

"This book has color only on every other page," a reviewer announces coldly.

"*Some* color," another adds tersely.

"The pictures are in brilliant full color—a winner!"

If, in reviews, color is thought of in terms of gold content, it is thought of in the same way in a printer's bill. Color costs rise six to eight percent every year. It is not just a matter of one color in a book costing this much and two colors costing twice that much and so on; it is also a matter of how the color is printed—*simple* or *process*.

Simple color printing is the less expensive of the two but requires more energy from the artist who must make his own color plates, called separa-

SOURCE: *School Library Journal,* May 15, 1973, pp. 1641–1645. © R. R. Bowker Co./A Xerox Corporation.

tions. These color separations are painted with an opaque ink on some transparent material. This is laid over the key or base plate (usually black line) which is drawn on very heavy paper or board. The transparencies are called overlays. These mechanics are difficult and tedious to perform and the outcome not always precisely predictable and satisfactory. Understandably then, this process is not popular among artists. It is much simpler and safer to paint the pictures and let the camera do the work. This is called color process printing. Color process is far more complex printing, and the expense is about 60 percent more than simple color printing. It is a meticulous matter of reproducing full color pictures (or paintings) with the camera making the color separations, instead of the artist. And camera work means costly work.

If the result of either of these two operations is not satisfactory, handwork on the negatives may be necessary, and specialists ("dot etchers") who are skilled in this process charge up to $20 an hour.

Color process work can be done abroad at much less cost. But because U.S. book manufacturers are so zealously protected (unlike the manufacturers of other daily necessities, i.e., shoes and clothing), our copyright laws require both U.S. citizens and foreigners residing here to either manufacture and publish first in the U.S. or else lose U.S. copyright protection. Publishers may, of course, have only the process color separations done abroad and do the actual printing at home. But this is still an expensive operation.

Many U.S. publishers find that translating and importing picture books (or sheets to be bound here) from Europe, Scandinavia, or Japan is one way that brilliant full-color books can be included on their lists. But occasionally, like some wines, the accompanying stories do not travel well, and it is not always a matter of translation but cultural collision.

Royalties for Typeface?

Color is the major but not the only cost factor in a publisher's budget for a picture book. Quality paper is becoming increasingly scarce in a tree-ravaged world. And paper, a most relevant factor in good color reproduction—its opacity (ink show-through), its texture (absorbtion of inks), and its shade (influence on ink colors)—can seriously enhance or hamper the final result.

A lesser cost factor is type. Yet even some kinds of jacket type can cost one dollar a letter. Moreover, some photo type is copyrighted and collects royalties when used!

The Time of the Artist

When the words of a manuscript have had their last tasting and testing and polishing, a crucial time has come—the time of the artist, or the choosing of one. This time may be the length of a moment's inspiration or weeks and months of fruitless seeking. Confronting the editor and the art director is an awesome overabundance of talent—some new and exciting but inexperienced; some so greatly acclaimed and sought after that a publisher may have to wait two years for their services.

Some artists' work is slow to change and thereby rather predictable. An editor then knows fairly well how that art will match the text to be illustrated. Other artists develop from one stage to another so quickly that their current work is nothing akin to what they produced even a year ago. This is exhilarating, unless the editor had hoped to have such an artist do a companion piece (using the same characters) to a successful book done in the now obsolete style!

But no matter how great the talent, the most important aspect to be considered is the artist's *interpretation* of a story. The styles can be unique and refreshing, but the book can be a failure if the interpretation is pedestrian. An editor, of course, should be helpful in preventing unimaginative and literal renditions.

A well-designed picture book can be compared to a well-produced film. The viewer's interest and attention is total because all the mechanical and creative elements are total in their integration. There is a distinct and pleasant rhythm created by the arrangement of the word and the image. The settings are not so extravagant that they dwarf or lessen the impact or meaning in the dialog or dramatic action. Nothing competes or attempts to call attention to itself alone. This is not to say that in its integration each element becomes negated or loses its identity. On the contrary, as each element is introduced, an exciting new dimension is added which produces the final, stunning, creative whole. This, at least, is what the director, actors, cameraman, and crew—editor, author, artist, and printer—should strive to accomplish.

Sometimes an editor can assist an artist by simply asking him to change his "camera angle." To establish locations or settings in the story, to heighten the drama of events, to introduce characters or emphasize meaningful objects, the artist, like the cameraman, should employ the use of panoramic, long, medium, and close-up views. The artist should consider himself a ubiquitous eye, selecting what he considers the most auspicious images and giving the reader the best possible view of all the action. Occasionally, of course, he should remind himself—in order not to let the picture's perspective become too sophisticated—that he is drawing pictures for eyes daily accustomed to a level of three to four and one-half feet above floor board!

The editor must also serve (as in the film world) as a continuity or script girl as well. If a girl has a red dress on and is carrying a lunch box on the way to school on one page, then she must have on a red dress and carry a lunchbox when she leaves the school on the same day. If she hasn't, an editor may expect letters from young readers pointing out the error.

In choosing the "cast" for a picture book, the artist sometimes finds that animals make better players than people. Animals are loved by children and they represent no race, creed, or political affiliations. In *James the Jaguar*, a little boy has three older sisters who dictate his every move until one birthday he receives a jaguar suit from his uncle. Predictably the jaguar suit gives him the confidence he needs to assert himself. The artist for this book first drew the characters as cats. But, beguiling as they were, it was later decided that a jaguar suit for a kitten might just be too much of a good thing. In this case a real little boy feeling transformed into a wild animal seemed far stronger and more attractive for reader identification.

Thus, as each individual word is the writer's raw material to be put into the widest, most imaginative and variable meaning, so is each picture or scene the artist's. All of these elements come into focus through their position in each completed phrase, sentence, or pictorial sequence to produce the total creative product. Ultimately, every creator must pay respect to the greatest art of all—the art of *selection*.

Remediation and Reinforcement: Books for Children with Visual Perceptual Impairments

Mary M. Banbury

Learning Disabilities

In 1968, Congress, upon recommendation of the National Advisory Committee on Handicapped Children, accepted the term *learning disability* to describe a specific category of handicapped children. It was agreed that the term incorporated conditions that previously had been described by such

SOURCE: Reprinted by permission of the American Library Association from *Top of the News* 37 (Fall 1980):41–46.

terms as *minimal brain damage, minimal brain dysfunction, minimal cerebral dysfunction, dyslexia, dysgraphia, dyscalculia, perceptually handicapped, neurologically handicapped, educationally handicapped, attention disorders, psychoneurological disorders,* and *language disorders.* There was no agreement, however, as to the exact prevalence of learning-disabled children, the exact cause of the problem, or the exact definition of the term.

There are experts in the field of learning disabilities who estimate that there are at least two million learning-disabled children in American schools: other authorities suggest that the number may reach as high as eight million. Percentage estimates range from 1 to 30 percent of the population. Not surprisingly, prevalence figures vary depending upon which definition and criteria for selection are used.

There are specialists in the field of learning disabilities who attribute the cause of the condition to prenatal or perinatal problems: others attribute the cause to such diverse factors as heredity, high fever, head injuries, malnutrition, pollution, or food additives. Etiological theories vary depending upon the perspective of the specialty group.

There are professionals in the field who define this exceptionality as a maturational or developmental imbalance, a neurological or organic impairment, a discrepancy between expected potential and actual performance; other professionals define the disability by exclusion, by stating that it is a condition not caused by mental retardation, emotional disturbance, environmental disadvantage, or sensory impairment. The definitions vary depending upon the point of view of the professional.

Although the experts do not concur on prevalence, the specialists do not agree on causes, and the professionals do not absolutely accept one definition, there *are* several generalizations that, for educational purposes, can be made:

1. There are a significant number of learning-disabled children in the schools.
2. Educators should focus on the symptoms and the learning characteristics of children rather than on causes.
3. Learning-disabled children, who are intellectually capable of learning and who have had the opportunity to learn, do not perform in expected ways or achieve at expected levels.

Learning disabilities vary from child to child according to the severity of the condition and the type of disorder that is exhibited. A learning disability could mildly, moderately, or severely affect one, several, or many of the following areas of learning: large or small motor coordination, spatial orientation, receptive language (listening), inner language (thinking), expressive language (speaking), visual or auditory perception, or behavior. These disorders are most noticeably manifested in the academic areas of reading, writing, spelling, and arithmetic.

Role and Responsibilities of Librarians

Many disciplines have contributed to the study of the diagnosis, prevention, remediation, teaching, and accommodation of the learning-disabled child. Much has been said and written on the roles and responsibilities of individuals in the fields of medicine, optometry, audiology, psychology, speech and language, and education. Little, however, has been said or written about the role and responsibilities of librarians.

Librarians possess special skills needed in the multidisciplinary response to children with learning disabilities; they are vital agents in the delivery of services to these youngsters. Their expertise includes a comprehensive knowledge of reading materials according to subject matter, reading level, and skill development; a thorough understanding of the developmental and sequential process of reading; and an insight into the child as a reader. Librarians can select or assist in the selection of books that will interest the learning-disabled child, that will match the appropriate ability level, and that will remediate, sustain, or develop specific reading skills.

Visual Impairments

The following analysis of books and guidelines for selection of appropriate remedial and developmental materials focuses on children who have limited strengths or mild impairments in the area of visual perception. Other areas will need other books and other guidelines. If children are dependent on the visual channel, then it is important that their skills in this area be highly developed since they will be compensating for deficiencies or lack of input in other areas. If children are impaired in the visual channel, then it is important that they be helped in overcoming deficiencies in the various components of visual perception.

Visual perception is an umbrella term. This general area encompasses the following abilities:

1. *Visual discrimination:* the ability to distinguish similarities and differences among objects, pictures, or symbols.
2. *Visual figure-ground:* the ability to attend to the salient features of an object, picture, or symbol while disregarding the extraneous visual background.
3. *Visual form constancy:* the ability to identify an object, picture, or symbol although it alters in size, color, or position in space.
4. *Visual memory:* the ability to recall objects, pictures, or symbols that have been visually presented.

5. *Visual sequential memory:* the ability to recall the correct succession in which objects, pictures, or symbols have been visually presented.
6. *Visual closure:* the ability to recognize an object, picture, or symbol when a partial or incomplete visual stimulus is presented.

Since there is a high degree of interrelation and overlapping among these components of visual perception, it is not possible to select one particular book to remediate or reinforce one particular skill; it is possible to suggest books that, moving along a continuum from the very obvious to the subtle, provide special assistance for visual difficulties and enhance visual strengths. These books, then, can be used sequentially and prescriptively.

Useful Books

One of the simplest and most enticing books is *Snail, Where Are You?* Tomi Ungerer, the author, used the figure of the snail as the chief component in a series of pictures. The identical shape appears in each illustration, but its function changes. The lines of the snail, varying in size, color, and position, are concealed in such forms as a pig's tail, a ram's horns, an owl's eyes, a harp, a party favor, and an umbrella handle. The signature, found in enough forms to maintain interest, is always there. Since the pages are uncluttered and there are few distracting elements, the child will succeed in the search for the elusive snail.

In Ungerer's next book, *One, Two, Where's My Shoe?*, detection of the figure is fractionally more difficult since the shoe changes shape as well as size, color, position, and function. Category is the only constant concept. Concealed pumps, boots, loafers, and slippers are incorporated in such unlikely objects as the face of a dog, the hull of a ship, the gown of a magician, the head of a snake. Clues are everywhere, however, as color and distortion are frequently used to set the shoe off from the rest of the figure. Uncluttered pages assure a challenging yet successful experience.

Two delightful books that can be read to preschoolers contain illustrations that require children to use imagination and experience to visualize internal detail and to recognize partial figures. The first, *It Looked like Spilt Milk*, by Charles E. Shaw, presents simple white figures on a dark blue background. As the text is read, children are actively engaged in guessing the actual identity of the object while visualizing the internal detail of suggested shapes. The second book, Janet and Allan Ahlberg's *Each Peach Pear Plum*, is an I Spy story that challenges children to locate the partially hidden figures of such characters as Mother Hubbard, Cinderella, Jack and Jill, and Robin Hood. The book allows the teacher or librarian to be as directive as the child requires in screening our background stimuli and locating and recognizing partially presented figures.

Tana Hoban's *Circles, Triangles, and Squares* and Bruce McMillan's *The Alphabet Symphony* use photographs to move children into the real world to search for shapes and letters in the environment and in architectural and instrumental designs. Hoban's photographic message is that shapes are everywhere. They can be found in bicycles, bubbles, bridges, trains, trucks, typewriters, houses, hoops, and hats. Regardless of dimension, viewing angle, or situation, the shape is constant. McMillan's camera eye sees letters in the music world. The bass clarinet is in the shape of a *J*; the *E* is embedded in the French horn; the first strand of strings and conductor form a *G;* the crossing of two flutes constitutes an *X*. To assure success in identifying the letters hidden in the symphony, McMillan isolates each one by reproducing it in white outline under each photograph. This serves to clarify perception and to reinforce recognition.

Through the vivid illustrations of José Aruego and Ariane Dewey's *We Hide, You Seek,* children learn that colors, textures, and patterns camouflage animals not only for the enjoyment of the reader but also for the survival of the animal. Fine drawings on the inside and outside covers depict animals who inhabit the bush, desert, swamp, plains, and river or forest areas of East Africa. These animals are engaged in a game of hide-and-seek with a rhino. Children join the game as they seek out animals that blend into the environment and assume such guises as trees, leaves, rocks, rushes, or roots. On one page the animals are hidden; on the next page they stampede out of their hiding places. Children go back and forth from page to page and cover to cover as they detect, compare, contrast, identify, and categorize the animals.

There is a natural movement from the drawings of *We Hide, You Seek* to the photographs of *Hidden Animals* by Millicent E. Selsam. The game of hide-and-seek, however, is no longer fun for the animals; it is essential. This book (a Science I Can Read book) stresses the fact that the animals' very lives depend upon their ability to be inconspicuous. Although both story and pictures are simple, children are challenged mentally and visually. The text examines the relationship between predator and prey, explains how natural camouflage evolved, and gives the reader clues as to how the animals merge with their surroundings. The task of separating the figure from the background is more meaningful because of this information and easier because of the clues.

The following three books are designed to reinforce, enhance, and challenge the visual abilities of children. Backgrounds are more complex, figures are less obvious, number of stimuli is increased, and degree of abstraction is heightened.

In *Where Is It? A Hide-and-Seek Puzzle Book* by Demi, children are required to locate the exact duplicate of each object in the black square. Locating that one object among a myriad of similar ones is a challenge. If children are not ready for this task, it is an exercise in frustration rather than a test of discrimination. The puzzles vary in complexity, shifting the invariant properties of the designated object while changing the number of figures from which the object is to be singled out. The search requires skill in visual discrimination, figure-ground, and form constancy.

One Dragon's Dream by Peter Pavey requires children to count from one to ten, thus enumerating all the animals and objects in the dragon's dream. However, when the dragon dreams that "two turkeys teased him" or that a "team of ten turtles towed him home to bed," children not only must count two turkeys or ten turtles, they also must count all the sets of twos and tens that appear on the pages. Since only one set is labeled for each number, children must discover what the other sets are as well as where they are located. This is a demanding task because the pictures are both complex and complicated. Drawings cover the whole pages; every section is rich in stimuli. Not only are figures rotated and partially obscured, but also the only property that remains constant is that of category. Children search for sets of such categories as writing utensils, brushes, dogs, insects, and flowers. The items vary in size, color, position, function, shape, and location. Children need to be able to associate visually similar items as well as to discover, discriminate, and provide closure.

Anno's Alphabet: An Adventure in Imagination by Mitsumasa Anno challenges children's perception and perspective. "Flaws" in the paintings of the three-dimensional wooden letters are barely perceptible; however, they are there. Upon careful inspection children will notice that the letters are twisted in the manner of a Möbius strip, or are half-completed, their other half seen through a strategically placed mirror or hinged in unworkable ways. Each letter provides the initial sound for the picture on the following page. Components are subtly transformed, and children sense the visual presentation is not possible. Careful scrutiny and an understanding of visual possibilities lead children to such observations as: a brand of wood cannot be heated to red hot because it would turn to ash; a tube of paint does not grow out of the artist's palate; pen nibs do not have pencil points; a scale cannot rest in its own balancing pan. The border surrounding each letter and picture is a pen and ink sketch containing many embedded figures whose names begin with the sounds of each letter. The children will be able to detect the figures, but they will need the glossary to label such flowers, animals, and creatures as *acanthus, knapweed, yew, iguana, quail, vole, dwarf, elf,* and *mermaid.* Intellectually and visually subtle, Anno's book is an adventure and a challenge.

John S. Goodall's book, *The Story of an English Village,* and Jörg Müller's portfolio of pictures, *The Changing City,* require a sense of persistence of images. The first depicts the same view of a medieval English village at intervals of approximately one hundred years; the second shows the same section of a contemporary European city at intervals of approximately three years. Both are beautiful and compelling statements concerning the mutability of the physical and social world. Both are vivid illustrations of spatial and temporal differences, and detailed portraits of progress and decay as well. Caught up in this panorama of life, children visually recall, compare, and contrast images, lifestyles, and social patterns. They perceive the obvious and subtle ways in which architecture, transportation, fashions, and occupations are altered, modified, and revised. These books engage children visually, cognitively, and emotionally.

Conclusion

There are many more challenging and interesting books that remediate and reinforce the visual perceptual skills of all children and, in particular, learning-disabled children. Librarians should select and suggest books that require children to compare and contrast visually, to distinguish and separate the stimuli from the visual background, to identify the visual constant regardless of changing properties, to recall sequentially visual images, and to recognize partial visual stimuli. Librarians should select and suggest books at the children's ability and interest level, utilizing the books to develop cognitive as well as perceptual abilities.

A learning disability is not always an immutable condition. It can be circumvented by working with intact channels, or it can be remediated by working with specific components. Learning-disabled children require the services of many individuals, and librarians play an integral part in the delivery of those services.

Bibliography

Ahlberg, Janet, and Ahlberg, Allan. *Each Peach Pear Plum*. New York; Viking, 1978.

Anno, Mitsumasa. *Anno's Alphabet: An Adventure in Imagination*. New York: Crowell, 1974.

Aruego, José, and Dewey, Ariane. *We Hide, You Seek*. New York: Greenwillow Books, 1979.

Demi. *Where Is It? A Hide-and-Seek Puzzle Book*. New York: Doubleday, 1980.

Goodall, John S. *The Story of an English Village*. New York: Atheneum, 1978.

Hoban, Tana. *Circles, Triangles, and Squares*. New York: Macmillan, 1974.

McMillan, Bruce. *The Alphabet Symphony*. New York: Greenwillow Books, 1977.

Müller, Jörg. *The Changing City*. New York: Atheneum, 1978.

Pavey, Peter. *One Dragon's Dream*. Scarsdale, N.Y.: Bradbury, 1978.

Selsam, Millicent E. *Hidden Animals*. New York: Harper, 1969.

Shaw, Charles E. *It Looked like Spilt Milk*. New York: Harper, 1947.

Ungerer, Tomi. *One, Two, Where's My Shoe?* New York: Harper, 1964.

———. *Snail, Where Are You?* New York: Harper, 1962.

7

Informational Books

The Art of Nonfiction

Betty Bacon

Whether it is natural history or human history or the abstractions of mathematics, good nonfiction for younger readers requires every bit as much craftsmanship as any imaginary narrative. Yet novels like *The Hobbit* or *Harriet the Spy* or *Island of the Blue Dolphins* have many enthusiasts—and deservedly so—while the suggestion that Kroeber's *Ishi, Last of His Tribe* or Meltzer's *Freedom Comes to Mississippi* are equally evocative and brilliant arouses doubt and skepticism.

The lists of prizewinning books for young people in the English-speaking countries reflect this attitude. In the United States, the prestigious Newbery Medal has been awarded for nonfiction books six times in the 58 years of its existence. Similarly, the Carnegie Medal in England has been awarded for nonfiction books five times in 42 years. The Australian and Canadian Books of the Year have a slightly larger percentage of nonfiction, but there is still a very heavy proportion of fiction. Most of the award-winning nonfiction is either history or biography, a type of material that lends itself to a chronological narrative in space and time, just like fiction. Of the major prizes in the United States, only the National Book Award has ever been awarded for a different kind of nonfiction. In 1978, the award went to Judith and Herbert Kohl for *The View from the Oak*. This is a beautifully structured volume of nature study in the grand tradition of the great naturalists from Humboldt and Darwin to Marston Bates.

Strangely enough, this situation is almost directly opposite from that in adult literature, where three times as many Pulitzer prizes are given each year to nonfiction as to novels. A look at the best-seller lists (or at any public library's circulation figures) shows nonfiction right up there at the top. While critics of adult literature complain bitterly of the disintegration of the modern novel, Carl Sagan's brilliantly written popularization of science, *The Dragons of Eden*, receives high critical acclaim, is reprinted in paperback, and becomes a best seller. But how many people have even heard of Henry B. Kane's *Four Seasons in the Woods?* This exquisite book combines a lyric, yet factual text with drawings and photographs. Together they give the reader a

SOURCE: *Children's Literature in Education*, (Spring 1981), pp. 3–14. Reprinted with permission of Agathon Press, Inc.

profound emotional experience, as well as delicately precise observation of the passing of the seasons.

Perhaps one of the problems is that juvenile nonfiction has a history of dreary utilitarianism to overcome. It was not until the early 1930s that a very few serious writers began the often thankless task of raising nonfiction for children to the statute of an art. One of the first bold pioneers in the field was M. Ilin (pseudonym of Illya Iakovlevich Marshak). This Russian writer had an easy-going style and a kind of bouncy enthusiasm that be brought to bear on a variety of subjects from the technology of the book (*Black on White,* 1932) to the development of early man (*How Man Became a Giant,* 1942). His work was lively and readable and often funny, and he proved conclusively that science and technology could be exciting in themselves without the assistance of heavy-handed, phony conversation.

Other writers appeared who really cared about their subject matter and wanted to pass on their knowledge and feeling to children. Henry Kane's poetic appreciation of the natural world, which set a new standard in the 1930s, was followed in the 1940s by Herman Schneider, who played a provocative game with size in *How Big is Big?* and brought astronomy down to earth in *You Among the Stars.* At this period, too, the prolific Herbert Zim began his long series of solid, no-nonsense books. The passage of the years has not dimmed the popularity of his *Dinosaurs* or *Snakes.*

Continuing to meet these high standards, writers like Millicent Selsam, Rose Wyler, and Laurence Pringle bring to their books on botany, geology, and ecology a high degree of skill and sophistication backed by solid scholarship. Even writers for adults sometimes shape their knowledge into books for children. Surely, Lancelot Hogben is every bit as brilliant in *The Wonderful World of Mathematics* as he is in *Mathematics for the Million.* And Colin Turnbull shows the same humanity and imagination in *The Peoples of Africa* that he demonstrates so beautifully in *The Forest People.*

The craft of writing nonfiction for children is not to be passed over lightly. It involves not only all the skills required for any good writing, but a number of special competencies as well. It is worth taking an analytical look at these to see how nonfiction for children has developed into a form that offers a variety of literary, emotional, and learning experiences to the reader. Simplicity without oversimplification, the choice of the revealing example, the relationship of content and structure, the ramifications of style and language, the many uses of illustrations—all these and more have their particular functions in the creation of the factual children's book.

In a poem about poetry, Archibald MacLeish once wrote:

For all the history of grief
An empty doorway and a maple leaf.

But it is not only in poetry that the evocative is the most informative statement. Indeed, a piece of nonfiction for children is the tip of the iceberg. The visible peak—the words on the printed page—rests on a vast underwater foundation of knowledge of the subject and understanding of its various complexities. How else can the writer make the unerring choice of the example that is going to reveal a whole subject in a kind of intuitive flash? It is the hidden erudition that makes the difference.

Jay Williams is master of such evocative detail in *Life in the Middle Ages*. To give some idea of the reality behind the pageantry at the medieval tournaments, he writes:

> A noble lady offered the prize of a swan-shaped diamond brooch to the man who was adjudged most worthy of all. By unanimous consent William the Marshal was chosen. But when the Count of Flanders went to give him the prize, William could not be found. At last, they located him in a smithy; he was kneeling with his head on the anvil, and the smith, with metal snips and pincers was cutting his helmet from his head. It had been so badly battered in the combats of the day that he could not otherwise get it off.

An entire way of life is suggested in the details of a short paragraph in Mary Elting's *The Hopi Way:*

> The clouds in my name, the uncle said, were the best of all clouds. Not the gray winter kind. Not the puffy little white ones, soft as sheep's wool, that frame the edge of the sky every day. Mine were the great rain clouds that rise tall above the earth. Rain coaxes living things to grow in the desert. And so rain clouds bring blessings to Hopiland. With such a name a boy might also bring happiness to his people some day.

In both these examples the authors have avoided the glib generalization. Of all the skills required in writing for children, concrete simplicity is the most difficult. "All living creatures are interdependent," writes an author. True, no doubt, but so what? Equally unrevealing is the too-detailed description, replete with technical jargon, of–say–the food chain in the Sargasso Sea. It's the carefully chosen example that brings the subject to life.

The old days of rote-learning still cast their shadow on the craft of nonfiction. As George Gaylord Simpson remarks in the biology text, *Life:* "Are you being a scientist when you count the sand grains on Coney Island Beach? No. It is true that you are gathering facts, but you are probably crazy." What, then, makes the detail significant? For children particularly, a factual book must communicate a sense of motion, and not random motion either, but motion with a direction, a pattern, and a rational basis that can be explained and understood. This is essential, whether the book deals with the history of child labor or the life of Queen Victoria or the clouds in the sky. Selsam says that a good science book for children links "many observable facts into fundamental concepts." This is equally true of books in the social sciences, in history, in mathematics, and in viewing the real lives of real people.

In *Red Power on the Rio Grande: The Native American Revolution of 1680*, Franklin Folsom begins with the 55-mile marathon (in the true sense of the word) of Catua and Omtua. These two Pueblo teenagers were the Paul

Reveres of the Pueblo Revolt, and their epic run is told in high style. But they were caught, and Folsom sets this scene in the plaza at Santa Fe:

> Terror seized Catua and Omtua, and they tried to break away. But the guards had them well bound. Standing quietly, because they had to, Catua and Omtua looked into the stricken faces of their friends. In the dark eyes of the Indians, they saw no sign of anything the future might hold, except death.

But the book is not an adventure story only, albeit a true one. Folsom goes on to explain the long history of the Pueblo peoples, and what the coming of the Spaniards meant to their way of life. The personal adventure and tragedy which so quickly involve the reader are firmly set in the social movements within which they took place. The one supplements the other, so that we are not only caught up in the events of the time, but are given a key to understanding the whys and wherefores. Neither a recital of past happenings nor an explanation of causes can by itself give the young reader a sense of the dynamics of history. The two taken together, as Folsom does, combine to provide a rich meaning to the happenings the book describes.

Mathematics is demystified by Robert Froman in *Angles Are Easy as Pie.* He takes one simple concept—the nature of angles—and develops it with examples and experiments until the reader has a very clear idea of what angles are, their variety, and their occurrence in the world around us. At the end, youngsters (and their elders as well) are ready to take a longer leap into geometry.

By this unification of the particular and the general, of the principle and the example, young readers gain their first insights into inductive and deductive logic. The interplay between theory and fact also gives structure and order to many books. It is a fallacy of fiction-centered critics that works of nonfiction do not "tell a story," do not have a real beginning, middle, and end; that they do not have a climax, and certainly do not have suspense.

Proof to the contrary is found in every good book of children's nonfiction. A case in point is *Death is Natural,* by Laurence Pringle. Working its way from the atoms of which all things are composed to the living individual and then to the species, it provides a solidly scientific base for understanding what death means in the natural world. The material is developed with inexorable logic in a sequence that rises to a climax in a final discourse on the influence of the human species on the rest of the world.

The nonfiction "narrative" can be structured in terms of either time or space. In *Four Seasons in the Woods,* Kane shapes his book around the passage of time and sees the forest as the setting for seasonal changes. In *See Through the Forest,* Selsam starts at the sun-drenched treetops and works her way down to the deeply shaded soil. Similarly, particular and general can be combined in a variety of ways. Edith Thacher Hurd looks at a single whale family in *The Mother Whale,* whereas Herbert Zim examines the whole group in *The Great Whales,* and Gladys Conklin deals with the seasonal migration in *Journey of the Gray Whales.* The permutations are infinite. But the point is that each of these writers is building the material into the cohesive whole that is the book, and the young reader is enmeshed in the structure.

That the writing in nonfiction for children is little more than dry textbook instruction is another widely held and deeply wrong belief. Good writing is good writing, whatever the field. The use and choice of words, the rhythm of sentences, the progress of paragraphs, the variety of language structures are as important in nonfiction for children as they are in fiction. Tolkien has no monopoly on style; nor do nonfiction writers for adults, from Barbara Tuchman to Joseph Wood Krutch to Norbert Wiener. The subtleties of style are equally consequential in writing nonfiction for children, with the additional problem of the use of technical terminology.

The primary quality of the text must be clarity. Without that, the book fails in its main purpose of informing its young readers. Beyond lucidity, it can be lyric or funny, purely factual or highly imaginative. Once a technical term is defined, it becomes the child's property and can be used with ease, for the technical term is usually the exact one. In her books on botany, such as *The Maple Tree,* Selsam is especially adept at integrating scientific terminology into a straightforward text.

In *The Color of Man,* Robert Cohen takes a subject with a high emotional charge and writes about it with a directness that has made the book a standard since its publication over ten years ago:

> Whatever their color [says Cohen] the first human beings had some things that no other animals had. They did not have the fangs and claws and speed of a lion, but they did have highly developed brains that helped them to catch food and defend themselves even better. They had soft, skillful hands that could sharpen sticks into spears, chip flints into knives and axes, build traps, and do many other things that no other animal could do. Their brains also told them how to work together.

And so with these simple words on complex concepts, we are off to a running start.

Dealing with some of the same kind of material for slightly older readers, S. Carl Hirsch in *The Riddle of Racism* adopts a more emotional tone:

> Strange and terrible events occur in wartime. In the hate-filled passions of the moment, ordinarily sane men perform violent deeds. Responsible leaders do things they later regret. What part does underlying racism play in some of these actions? . . . America has never wanted to face up to those kinds of questions.

The rhythms of the prose can reflect the rhythms of the subject matter. We would naturally expect highly rhythmic use of language in *Dancing Masks of Africa,* and Christine Price does not disappoint us:

> Stiff-legged prancers,
> bell-ringing dancers,
> swinging and swaying

and sitting on air!
When they are weary,
they rest on the rooftops!
All of the people
go running to see them,
and only the witches
are trembling with fear.

There is no rule that says that nonfiction can't be funny. Starting with *The Cloud Book,* Tomie de Paola sets out to prove that we can laugh *with* (not at) science. A factual account of different kinds of clouds ends up with funny sayings about clouds and a ridiculous story, all illustrated in his own inimitable style. In *The Quicksand Book,* he really hits his stride with a mad tall tale in dialogue that somehow manages to tell us all the important scientific facts about quicksand. We can't help laughing as he gets more and more absurd in his imaginative playing around with a ridiculous yet revealing situation. No didacticism laid on here.

In these books, style becomes an essential ingredient of the author's approach to the subject matter. The best nonfiction for children is neither didactic in tone, nor dry and dusty in language and pattern. Such books are a literary experience rather than a school assignment.

Even more, perhaps, than in fiction for younger readers, illustration is often a basic element of the nonfiction experience. Here one needs a cautious approach, for the shelves of bookstores and libraries are filled with lavishly colored volumes in tastes ranging from exquisite to garish. But do the books as a whole live up to the promise of the bright ornamentation of their pages?

Illustrations in nonfiction books have a variety of functions. They can give information that could not be presented otherwise. They can combine with the text to present a kind of audiovisual whole. They can decorate the printed page. And they can create an emotional tone that words alone could not achieve. Styles, of course, are as varied as the styles of painting in a major art museum. They range from the most traditional to the most modern, from the abstraction of graphs to the concrete portrayal of photographs, from the most literal to the most wildly imaginative, from subtly exact drawings to slap-happy cartoons. But the one quality they must have is clarity. The fuzzy, muddled painting, however decorative, has no place in a book designed to promote knowledge and understanding. Purpose comes first, then esthetic pleasure. That the two are so often combined in the best nonfiction for children is a tribute to the serious artists who have found in this medium an outlet for highly sophisticated talents. The qualities I have suggested here apply equally to photographs, drawings, woodcuts, and paintings.

Very few creators of children's nonfiction have as many talents as the late Henry B. Kane, who could write, draw, and take superb photographs. And what artist in any medium has conveyed the sense of the desert as Peter Parnall does in Byrd Baylor's *The Desert is Theirs?* The page becomes the place, and we end up knowing and feeling far more about the Southwest than we ever dreamed we could find in so few lines.

In some cases, the illustrations *are* the book. To introduce modern art in *Going for a Walk with the Line,* Elizabeth and Douglas McAgy take paintings apart, turn them sideways, tear them in pieces, or put them in provocative juxtaposition with each other. Explanations are minimal. It's the shock to the eye that reveals new meanings to the reader (old, as well as young!).

Aliki's amiable cartoons for Jane Srivastava's *Averages* are so cheerful that they immediately make mathematical concepts seem ordinary and even funny. They also illustrate ideas in rather unconventional graph form. Adding to her equally cheerful explanatory text, Srivastava puts balloon words into the mouths of Aliki's cartoon children. It's all very pleasant and *very* informative. This pattern is used more and more with books that explain difficult concepts to young readers, whether it is the nature of trees or the metric system or the U.S. Bill of Rights. It can be—and indeed is—misused to become mere comic-bookery, but in an imaginative partnership of artist and writer it is both agreeable and illuminating.

Partnership is the key word here. For above all, pictures and text must match each other in information, format, and mood. Perfection in its marriage of picture and text is *Frontier Living,* written and illustrated by Edwin Tunis. This account of the material culture of the American frontier as it moved westward from the Appalachian foothills to the gold fields of California gives a human touch to its wealth of factual material. However emphatic the technology, there are always people. Their wry comments in the words are matched by their wry expressions in the pictures. Tunis loves technical details. Whether it is showing how the gears worked in a sawmill, how a beaver trap was set, or how a dugout soddy was constructed. Tunis draws with a fine line and absolute exactness. It is a tribute to his book designer's eye that he not only makes a stewpot, skillet, and gridiron agreeable to look at, but also sets them on the page in harmony with the total design of type and picture. Neither pictures nor words stand alone; together they make the reading of a Tunis book an eye/mind experience that endows the subject with a kind of tangible life.

Illustrations of factual books for older readers fall into a special category. In some cases, they are not necessary at all. Certainly *The Riddle of Racism* does not suffer from the lack of them. Sometimes a group of pictures gathered together in the center of the book, like Shizuye Takashima's water colors in *A Child in Prison Camp,* are enough to answer the reader's curiosity about "what things looked like." *Red Power on the Rio Grande* uses abstract themes from Pueblo art as chapter headings—an attractive if not entirely necessary addition to the visual page. So the use made of illustration in *To Be a Slave* is unusual. In this book, Julius Lester, the author, brings together first-hand accounts by slaves of what their life was like. He introduces each account with his own sharply written comment setting the individual testimony in a larger historical context. Tom Feelings intensifies the book's emotional impact with dark, brooding lithographs that depict both the misery and the strength of the slaves.

Despite the skills and sophistication of the best children's nonfiction, the utilitarian bias persists. Why, the critics asks, do people write nonfiction? Because they want to teach something useful to the young. Because they can't write fiction and have to do with second best. Or even because they want to jump on a popular bandwagon, such as ecology or sex education or the misuses of nuclear power.

Yet many writers and artists turn their considerable talents to the creation of nonfiction for young readers for a far more compelling reason. Barbara Brenner's *A Snake Lover's Diary* is only one example of the situation in which an author's delight in a subject cannot be contained and overflows into a work of nonfiction for children.

In his grand peroration at the close of his book *Never to Forget*, Milton Meltzer makes a deeply felt statement not only about history but about the meaning of his own life:

> To remember it (the Holocaust) is to think of what being human means. The Holocaust was a measure of man's dimensions. One can think of the power of evil it demonstrated—and of those people who treated others as less than human, as bacteria. Or of the power of good—and of those people who held out a hand to others. By nature, man is neither good nor evil. He has both possibilities. And the freedom to realize the one or the other.

Sometimes writers have something to say that demands as urgently to be said as ever a poem knocked against a poet's brain, and nonfiction for young readers is the way it comes out.

General References

Fisher, Margery *Matters of Fact: Aspects of Non-Fiction for Children* New York: T. Y. Crowell, 1972; Leicester: Brockhampton, 1967.

Hogben, Lancelot *Mathematics for the Million*, 4th ed. New York: Norton, 1968; London: Allen and Unwin, 1967.

MacLeish, Archibald "Ars Poetica" In *The Collected Poems of Archibald MacLeish* Boston: Houghton Mifflin, 1962.

Sagan, Carl *The Dragons of Eden* New York: Random House, 1977; Ballantine, 1978; London: Hodder and Stoughton, 1978.

Selsam, Millicent E. "Writing About Science for Children" In *A Critical Approach to Children's Literature* (Ed. by Sara Fenwick) Chicago: University of Chicago Press, 1967.

Simpson, George Gaylord, and William Beck *Life: An Introduction to Biology* New York: Harcourt Brace Jovanovich, 1969.

Turnbull, Colin M. *The Forest People* New York: Simon & Schuster, 1961, 1968; London: Jonathan Cape, 1974.

Children's Nonfiction Works Referred To

Baylor, Byrd *The Desert Is Theirs* (Illus. by Peter Parnall) New York: Scribner, 1975.

Brenner, Barbara *A Snake-Lover's Diary* (Illus. with photographs) Reading, Mass. and London: Addison-Wesley, 1970.

Cohen, Robert *The Color of Man* (Photographs by Ken Heyman) New York: Random House, 1968.

Conklin, Gladys *Journey of the Gray Whales* (Illus. by Leonard E. Fisher) New York: Holiday House, 1974.

De Paola, Tomie *The Cloud Book* (Illus. by the author) New York: Holiday House, 1975; Scholastic, 1977.

De Paola, Tomie *The Quicksand Book* (Illus. by the author) New York: Holiday House, 1977.

Elting, Mary *The Hopi Way* (Illus. by Louis Mofsie) New York: M. Evans, 1969.

Folsom, Franklin *Red Power on the Rio Grande: The Native American Revolution of 1680* Chicago: Follett, 1973.

Froman, Robert *Angles Are Easy as Pie* (Illus. by Byron Barton) New York: T. Y. Crowell, 1976.

Hirsch, S. Carl *The Riddle of Racism* New York: Viking, 1972.

Hogben, Lancelot *The Wonderful World of Mathematics* (Art by André, Charles Keeping, and Kenneth Symonds; maps by Marjorie Saynor) Garden City, N.Y.: Garden City Books, 1955.

Hurd, Edith Thacher *The Mother Whale* (Illus. by Clement Hurd) Boston: Little, Brown, 1973.

Ilin, M. *Black on White: The Story of Books* (Trans. Beatrice Kinkead) Illus. by N. Lapshin) Philadelphia: Lippincott, 1932; London: Routledge, 1932.

Ilin, M. and E. Segal *How Man Became a Giant* (Trans. Beatrice Kinkead) (Illus. by A. Komarov and E. A. Furman) Philadelphia: Lippincott, 1942; London: Routledge, 1942.

Kane, Henry B. *Four Seasons in the Woods* (Illus. by author) New York: Knopf, 1968.

Kohl, Judith and Herbert *The View from the Oak: The Private Worlds of Other Creatures* (Illus. by Roger Bayless) San Francisco: Sierra Club, 1977.

Lester, Julius *To Be a Slave* (Illus. by Tom Feelings) New York: Dial, 1968; London: Longmans Young Books, 1970.

Kroeber, Theodora *Ishi, Last of His Tribe* (Illus. by Ruth Robbins) Emeryville, Calif: Parnassus, 1964; New York: Bantam, 1973; London: Harmondsworth; Puffin, 1976.

McAgy, Elizabeth and Douglas *Going for a Walk with a Line: A Step into the World of Modern Art* New York: Doubleday, 1959.

Meltzer, Milton *Freedom Comes to Mississippi: The Story of Reconstruction* Chicago: Follett, 1970.

Meltzer, Milton *Never to Forget: The Jews of the Holocaust* New York: Harper & Row, 1976; Dell, 1977.

Price, Christine *Dancing Masks* (Illus. by the author) Scribner, 1975.

Pringle, Laurence P. *Death Is Natural* Four Winds Press, 1977.

Schneider, Herman and Nina *How Big Is Big? From Stars to Atoms* (Illus. by A. F. Arnold. W. R. Scott, 1946) (2nd ed. illus. by Symeon Shimin) Reading, Mass.: Addison-Wesley, 1950.

Schneider, Herman and Nina *You Among the Stars* (Illus. by Symeon Shimin) New York: W. R. Scott, 1951.

Selsam, Millicent E. *The Maple Tree* (Photographs by Jerome Wexler) New York: Morrow, 1968.

Selsam, Millicent E. *See Through the Forest* (Illus. by Winifred Lubell) New York: Harper & Row, 1956.

Srivastava, Jane J. *Averages* (Illus. by Aliki Brandenburg) New York: T. Y. Crowell, 1975.

Takashima, Shizuye *A Child in Prison Camp* (Illus. by the author) Plattsburgh, N.Y.: Tundra Books, 1971; New York: Morrow, 1974.

Tunis, Edwin *Frontier Living* (Illus. by the author) New York: T. Y. Crowell, 1976.

Turnbull, Colin M. *The Peoples of Africa* (Illus. by Richard M. Powers) New York: World Publishing Co., 1962; Leicester: Brockhampton, 1963.

Williams, Jay *Life in the Middle Ages* (Artwork by Haig and Regina Shekerjian) New York: Random House, 1966; London: Nelson, 1967.

Wyler, Rose, and Gerald Ames *Secrets in Stones* Four Winds, 1970; London: Evans Bros., 1973.

Zim, Herbert S. *Dinosaurs* (Illus. by James G. Irving) New York: Morrow, 1954; London: World's Work, 1963.

Zim, Herbert S. *The Great Whales* (Illus. by James G. Irving) New York: Morrow, 1951; London: World's Work, 1964.

Zim, Herbert S. *Snakes* (Illus. by James G. Irving) New York: Morrow, 1949.

Writing the Literature of Fact

Jo Carr

Teacher. Scholar, Promoter. Artist. Reporter. Catalyst. Philosopher. A fine nonfiction writer is really all of these but is teacher and artist, most of all.

First, consider the nonfiction writer as teacher. After this, as artist. A writer who is a teacher must be able to explain something so clearly that the reader, or student, can understand. So the nonfiction writer—as teacher—

SOURCE: Jo Carr, comp., *Beyond Fact: Nonfiction for Children and Young People*, pp. 3–12;

must be able to command techniques of clarification—understandable language, tightly structured organization, analogy, illustration, metaphor, scholarly documentation—while respecting the intelligence of the reader and stimulating curiosity. In addition, the nonfiction writer must structure information to support or explore a perceived idea or principle, thereby giving significance to what could be in the hands of an inept expert merely a range of footnoted facts.

These techniques for clarifying complex subjects, for collecting facts and illuminating them, are basic. They are so important that a separate article on science writing in this book is devoted to them. Although the observations in that article have been confined, of course, to science writing, they actually apply to history and biography as well. Historians and biographers also must interpret facts according to their perceptions, formulating either deductively or inductively principles that clarify the subject.

But what about the author whose writing transcends clarification, one who reaches "beyond fact" to write what John McPhee has called "the literature of fact"? What qualities do we look for in a book that is so powerful we never forget it?

Perhaps the qualities we look for are the same as those we find in a great teacher. Most of us have been lucky enough to know at least one such teacher, and we never forget that person. Although Miss Lyon or Mr. Brown, or whoever it was, may have initially riveted our attention through breadth of knowledge and lucidity, eventually the appeal becomes more potent. We discover ourselves mesmerized by a dynamic personality or a far-reaching mind, or both. Persuasive charisma and vast knowledge combine so effectively that we end up thinking or feeling in a completely new way. We remember these teachers because their teaching changed us significantly. They gave us, not just information, but knowledge, or at least access to knowledge.

The effect of an outstanding nonfiction book is like that. Truly inspired and masterfully written, it can lead us, by way of facts and beyond facts, to awakened understanding.

What does a teacher actually do to achieve this? What does a writer actually do? These are difficult questions. What they do and how they do it are probably as various as the people who teach and write well. Still, even while acknowledging this, we can perhaps suggest some ways in which they are alike. There are at least two characteristics common to fine nonfiction writers that can be measured by their effect on the reader: first, like the best teachers, they make us think deeply. And second, like the best teachers, they make us feel deeply. The stimulation of thinking is obviously vital. A good nonfiction book, as it marshals facts, should create a challenge. It should encourage a child to think—to relate one fact to another and test a familiar idea against a new idea—until at last he or she is able to weave a pattern of increased understanding. What begins as idle curiosity should end as independent thinking.

When we recognize what other ideas children are absorbing, or not absorbing, during their school years, independent thinking seems precious indeed. With the publication of Frances FitzGerald's analysis of American history textbooks, *America Revised* (Atlantic-Little), we must acknowledge that textbook publishers, by trying to appeal to everyone and offend nobody, have too often reduced ideas to homogenized pulp. Unlike discovery texts in science, history textbooks are written "not to explore but to instruct—to tell children what their elders want them to know about their country. This information is not necessarily what anyone considers the truth of things. Like time capsules, the texts contain the truths selected for posterity."

Who is doing the selecting? Now we come to the scary part. Textbook publishers, who in turn have been instructed by school boards responsible for text adoption, are basically deciding how we should think about our country. Through the power of their blue pencils, editors have become "the arbiters of American values, and publishing companies the Ministries of Truth for children."

Some trade books, of course, are guilty of even worse oversimplification than textbooks. Some handle facts so irresponsibly as to convey untruths and sensationalism. But the best trade books are always challenging and thought-provoking. It is by way of these books that we are able to offer children an open marketplace for ideas of all kinds. Children, as well as adults, should be free to confront each side of the debate on nuclear power, to read the British version of the American Revolution, to consider the pros as well as the cons of communism. What we really want to do is to start the wheels of the mind turning by means of books. In other words, we want to teach children how to think, not what to think. This idea has been pursued further in the article "The Problem with Problem Books."

Teaching children how to think involves exposing them to a great deal of information, many ideas, and different interpretations of those ideas on a level that they can understand. This means that writers not only have to be informed, they must actually be authoritative at the outset.

Let us look at two examples of such sound scholarship.

Linda Grant De Pauw has written a thought-provoking book called *Founding Mothers* (Houghton, 1975) that is concerned with women at the time of the American Revolution. Her scholarship is impressive; her coverage of the subject so authoritative and written with such imaginative insight that the reader is almost compelled to seek more information about this time in our history.

The reader is similarly motivated after reading *The Visionary Girls* (Little, 1973) by Marion Starkey. In this instance the documentation required to produce an adult book strengthens this simpler book for young people and the story of the Salem witch trials emerges as the drama that it actually was.

There are, of course, volumes and volumes of comparable scholarship on nonfiction shelves, waiting to offer children real intellectual stimulation. Such books, combining scholarship with the imagination of the creative artist, endorse the truth of the statement attributed to Rabelais, "a child is not a vase to be filled, but a fire to be lit."

Thinking, then, is important. Intellectual content is basic. Yet strangely enough, so is feeling. Emotion too can be well expressed through the imaginative use of fact. In writing what we call "literature of fact"—as opposed to writing "plain fact"—the author probably proceeds from intellectual mastery of the subject to conviction and enthusiasm, in all likehood a natural development after reading widely and thinking deeply about that subject. This kind of keen enthusiasm, passion if you will, is then transformed through imagination until the reader's passion is awakened in response. The author must care deeply about the subject, or the reader won't care at all.

Passion, then, can be an energizing force in writing. Elaine Moss, a British authority on children's books, says that it is crucial. Asked once what she thought of a book that had been given one of the *Times Educational Supplement* (TES) nonfiction awards, she said that she thought it wasn't a book at all; it was television in print. She then went on to lament what she called "journalism" in children's nonfiction, a kind of superficial treatment of a subject, usually visually seductive, that is churned out by a group of editors. The result: a child going flip-flip-flip with the pages, much as he or she goes flip-flip-flip from one simplified idea to another on a mass-produced televison program. Unfortunately many works of nonfiction in this country bear the same mark of institutional writing that Elaine Moss has noted in England. Barbara Tuchman, eloquently castigating books that are written without personal enthusiasm, says that an author's passion is essential if there is to be, as there must be in all good writing, "a pulse beat on the printed page," the beating of the pulse on the page that keeps the book alive long after its author has turned to dust.

All the contributors to this collection confirm Barbara Tuchman's belief in the importance of individual enthusiasm, the value of the writer's "personal voice" that has been described by Milton Meltzer as a "quality of vision." Zena Sutherland underlines it. Margery Fisher considers it basic. Olivia Coolidge makes it a reality with biography. Their views become especially significant when we consider the current proliferation of publishing conglomerates, bookstore conglomerates, book distribution conglomerates. It is no wonder we are dismayed when a conglomerate of writers threatens to replace the individual author!

For an example of conglomerate writing, consider the "special award for an outstanding series of books on engineering and technology" given by the New York Academy of Sciences to Viking Press in 1978. These books, which explore the intricate workings of machines and airports and space technology and television production, are absolutely fascinating. They are, in fact, perfect examples of books that clarify complex subjects in an entertaining way. Without any question there is an important place for books like these. But we do need to ask ourselves the same question to which Elaine Moss responded in considering the TES award. Can such books be considered literature? Here is an example of the writing in *Jet Journey* (Viking), one of the books in the series, the work of two authors and nine contributors:

> Aircraft accidents are rare. Air travel is one of the safest forms of transportation in terms of numbers of people hurt for distance traveled. In 1977, figures show .387 accidents (.061 fatal accidents) per 100,000 landings.

The New York Academy of Sciences in its award is recognizing legitimate and important strengths in these books; but the quality of literary distinction that we are seeking obviously is lacking. The limitation of institutional writing like this will be further accentuated later when we contrast the selection quoted above with examples of vivid writing from *Ishi, Last of His Tribe* and two other well-written books.

Naturally not all kinds of facts lend themselves to imaginative interpretation. It would be hard to produce an almanac, for instance, that could be described as anything but "institutional." On the other hand, many so-called "reference" books contain facts so imaginatively assembled that we sense the enthusiasm of the editor behind tremendous scholarly effort. *The Encyclopedia of American Facts and Dates* (Crowell, 1966) by Gordon Carruth comes to mind, as do the "Everyday Life in . . ." books by the Quennells (Putnam). Edwin Tunis, an outstanding historian and illustrator, has also given ample evidence of his own personal commitment to his work as artist and writer. His books, although primarily reference books, are fine examples of facts magically transformed in a way that Paul Murray Kendall has beautifully described:

> At best, fact is harsh, recalcitrant matter, as tangible as the hunk of rusty iron one trips over and yet as shapeless as a paper hat in the rain. Fact is a cold stone, an inarticulate thing, dumb until something happens to it. . . . Fact must be rubbed up in the mind, placed in magnetic juxtaposition with other facts, until it begins to glow, to give off that radiance we call meaning.

It is someone writing with passion and enthusiasm who is most likely to produce books that will give off this kind of "radiance."

Intellectual content and passionate enthusiasm then, might be considered essential characteristics of the nonfiction writer whose books are as memorable as the seminars of our most memorable teachers. But these qualities are not enough. A book qualifying as "literature of fact" must be written by someone who is not only a teacher but also an artist. Gifted writers work with facts as sculptors work with clay—or artists with paint, composers with melody, poets with words—to give meaningful form to their perception of things.

The next question is "how?", and the answer is fairly crucial in determining when nonfiction writing qualifies as "literature." How do writers capture the reader's interest and hold it? How do scholars make a subject that could be dry as dust so intriguing that the reader can't bear to put down the book? The author's wisdom and enthusiasm, crucial as they are, obviously do not weave this kind of spell. A spell is woven only when the writing is equal to the task of communicating that wisdom and enthusiasm, only, in other words, when the author's style is good enough.

We might look at style as Rae Goodell does in her book *The Visible Scientists* (Little, 1977). She uses the term "Pied Pipers" to describe certain outspoken scientists whose dynamic writing has captured the imagination of the public. Perhaps "Pied Piper" is a term we might also use to describe our most gifted nonfiction writers. They play a tune, and the melody is so lively that we must follow. The tune they play is their way of writing, their genius with words.

The tune is nothing if not elusive, heaven knows, and "how" questions are nothing if not daunting. One way to analyze the "how" of the writer's magic, the notes in the piper's tune, might be to look carefully at the result. Perhaps if we examine examples from the work of "literary" nonfiction authors we can determine what they have in common, what range of writing techniques succeed in giving moving expression to personal vision.

Let us start with this excerpt from *Four Women in a Violent Time* (Crown) by Deborah Crawford:

> Penelope was left on the beach with her husband, whom others had pronounced all but dead. The night came on; crouched beside Kent she slept fitfully. She must have known by then that she was going to have to face the New World as a widow.
>
> But there are times when one's fears, great as they are, may be rendered pale by the onrush of reality. For in the morning came events more terrible than this pretty, sheltered young bride from Holland could possibly have imagined. In the morning the wild men came.
>
> She saw little—three or four men with feathers sticking up from shaved and coppery heads; then their arms were swinging down upon her with knives and with something she was to learn later was a tomahawk.
>
> One blow of this weapon and the dying young man was dispatched. Penelope was deftly scalped; a knife slashed into her shoulder, and another stroke drove into and across her abdomen.
>
> Then they left her for dead.

The foregoing isn't "just like a story." It is a story, and a good one. There is nothing like this kind of suspense—to say nothing of real drama—to keep the pages turning.

Here is a selection from a book by another author:

> Suddenly the storm was over, and the sun broke through. When we forced open the front door against the hailstones that had piled up on the porch, we beheld an unbelievable sight. What had been just a few minutes earlier a spring day with green grass, trees in full foliage, and lettuce and radishes growing in the gardens, was now the most beautiful winter scene imaginable! The trees, completely stripped, stood naked against the sky as in January.

> White, glistening hailstones covered the ground like new-fallen snow. . . . After a quick survey of the damage, grandmother Gordon, who had prayed aloud during the storm, quietly gathered hailstones from the back porch and made herself a cup of ice water.

This selection from *A Nickel's Worth of Skim Milk: A Boy's View of the Great Depression* by Robert J. Hastings also tells a story.

Narrative, then, offers scope for the author's imaginative insight. When, in addition, the narrative features a person, especially one with whom we can strongly identify, then we are truly hooked. What must it have been like to be scalped? What was the old grandmother thinking when she looked at the havoc outside? Had her prayers been answered or not? We automatically react this way to stories about people, it seems, and even more forcibly when the people are "real."

Even writers for adults depend on narrative. If John McPhee, in *Encounters with the Archdruid*, had tried to present his ideas in straight exposition, we would have been overwhelmed in our efforts to understand them—not just overwhelmed, bored! Instead, there we are, sharing a hazardous voyage down the Colorado with David Brower, then director of the Sierra Club, and a rancher named Floyd Dominy, a worthy opponent on environmental issues. With McPhee as referee, the two battle it out. David Brower: "Emotionally, people are able to look only two generations back and two generations forward. . . ." Floyd Dominy: "Nonsense, nonsense, complete nonsense." In such dramatic scenes as this McPhee habitually uses people as vehicles for abstract ideas, with stories about them carrying the reader from one idea to the next. If storytelling works this well for John McPhee—considered by almost everyone today as the top writer of adult nonfiction—no wonder it succeeds for Deborah Crawford and Robert J. Hastings and for all the other writers of children's nonfiction who use it so imaginatively.

This is not to say that the use of narrative is always justified. We need to beware of the writer who starts a book with the story of an archeologist who, after bravely enduring months of scorching desert heat, cries "Eureka!" as he finally unearths a valuable artifact, this moment of drama being followed by two hundred pages of boring exposition about the life-style of the ancient people who had produced that rare object. Or the type of science writer who introduces information about turtles by telling a story about a mother turtle with her three babies and the exciting adventures they had on the way to the water's edge. The artificial grafting of story to information with the transparent intent of capturing the reader's attention is so obviously manipulative that children are quite right to feel insulted by it.

Narrative is only one of the piper's tunes. What is the appeal in the following selection from *Ishi, Last of His Tribe*?

> When Ishi came down the ladder pole, the warmth rose to meet him: warmth from the fire and reflected warmth from the low bark-covered walls. There were many smells in Mother's house in winter—the bite of smoke, the sharp

> spice of burning pine and baywood; hot resin; green and drying grass and bark; meat broth; still-warm bread; and the different smells from the baskets which sat in a neat circle on the upper house level: dried salmon and deer meat and bulbs and fruit; pelts and rugs and blankets. And there were the smells of tobacco and medicines and herbs which hung in bunches along the walls.

And in this one from *Museum People: Collectors and Keepers at the Smithsonian* (Prentice) by Peggy Thomason?

> I liked the noisy excitement of [the Smithsonian], even just stepping around the edges the way I did, when the totem poles and heavy machinery and cannon were set in place. . . . But then I like the quiet excitement, too, in other parts of the buildings—the absorption and sense of purpose—where people were stitching sails or stirring rice paste or sketching pollen under a microscope, and where curators were writing in cubicles piled ceiling-high with books, maps, specimens, and stacks of print-outs from the computer.

And what about this selection by Francis Ross Carpenter from *The Old China Trade: Americans in Canton, 1784–1843*? (Coward)

> What a sight! Long before seeing the warehouses and long before catching sight of the shops, the temples, the beggars, the mansions, he would see the waterfront. No waterfront in the world was like it. The harbor was choked with boats. Some were family affairs with as many as three generations on board, the youngest tied perhaps to a ring on the inside to keep him or her from falling overboard. They laughed a lot among themselves as they artfully shoveled rice in with their chopsticks and shared their tea. Frequently it was just such a boat with just such a family that carried the cargoes down to Whampoa, where the American vessels lay, the water slapping at their empty hulls as they awaited a cargo. . . . To add to all that excitement, joss paper was lighted and thrown flaming into the river for a sacrifice to the gods of wind and waves. If a vessel were leaving, it might be given a send-off with baskets of exploding firecrackers from other ships. And everywhere there was shouting and there was the din of gongs, summoning up good spirits to protect the men at sea. Nowhere else had there ever been such a waterfront.

What do these passages have in common? Compare them to the passage from *Jet Journey*, quoted earlier, and the power of vivid description is obvious. Unlike the writing in *Jet Journey*, these are replete with fascinating detail, graphic images, and sensual appeal. The selection from *Ishi* is all smells, almost as redolent as Wilbur's barn. That of the Smithsonian is sights: totem poles, microscopes, cubicles "piled ceiling-high. . . ." And the scene at the Canton waterfront is both sounds—shouting, the din of gongs, exploding firecrackers—and sights—boats, temples, flaming joss paper.

What is more, you are there in every scene. You can imagine just what it must have been like. And you identify with the people being described: You are climbing down the ladder pole with Ishi; you are one of those Americans on the empty vessels, absorbing the sights and sounds of that incredible harbor, as their cargo is being loaded; you are alongside the author, peering into the museum's cubicles and moving about its exhibits. The writer's vision becomes your vision, the storyteller's story your story. This must have been what Paul Murray Kendall meant when he said that "fact must be rubbed up in the mind . . . until it begins to glow, to give off that radiance we call meaning."

Now try reading aloud Hal Borland's description of October in *The Golden Circle: A Book of Months* (Crowell):

> October is a time of far and misty horizons that beckon, a time of crow-caw and jay-jeer, before the slash of sleet or the gentle fall of snow. It is frost creeping down from the hills in moccasin-quiet feet to dust the valleys with glitter, of wind skittering down the road in a scuffling of leaves, of owl hoot and fox bark in the moonlight.

The author's sentences, rhythmic and rich in imagery, achieve a kind of grace that is extended by the magnificent illustrations of Anne Ophelia Dowden. In writing like this, our Pied Pipers seem to spin words with such beauty that their style becomes almost poetry. For a more comprehensive discussion of poetic power in nonfiction, read Zena Sutherland's article, "Science as Literature," included in this compilation.

Some excellent literature of fact is distinguished by qualities that are unrelated to language. Look, for instance, at *Peter Pitseolak's Escape from Death* (Delacorte, 1978) by Peter Pitseolak. The text of this autobiographical account of an Eskimo's ordeal on floating ice is appropriately simple, but it is the primitive pictures that embody the excitement and drama of survival.

Read also *A Northern Nativity* (Tundra, 1976) by William Kurelek. Notice how the rich paintings project the message of the nativity as it might have been received during the Depression years of the 1930s in the remote areas of Canada. Let the mood of the book capture your imagination, as the idea for it must have captured the imagination of the author-artist.

The foregoing two examples demonstrate beauty of artwork in combination with beauty of language, yet another manifestation of good literature. With so many talented artists illustrating and writing children's books, it is hardly surprising that they have brilliantly applied their pens and brushes to the pages of nonfiction books.

So far, then, we have discussed imaginative storytelling, masterful description, eloquent style, and graphic excellence. Now for the last selection:

> Most nations don't have to be made. They are there already. They have always been there. No one had to *make* France or England or Denmark. You might say that history made them. They don't have any "fathers" or any "birthday."
>
> The United States is different. Remember how Lincoln put it in the Gettysburg Address: "Our fathers brought forth on this continent a new nation."
>
> This is just what they did, too: They brought it forth; they almost invented it. What had been thirteen Colonies became thirteen States, and what had been thirteen States became the United States of America.

> Of course, it wasn't all that easy. After all, how does one go about *making* a nation? It isn't like making a cake, you know, or a table. Just follow the directions, and presto! there it is. No one had ever *made* a nation before. There were no directions.

These are the words of Henry Steele Commager, speaking about the origins of *The Great Constitution* (Bobbs-Merrill, 1961). He hit upon a single concept with which to give his book dramatic focus. Who had ever before thought of comparing the "making" of a nation to the making of a cake or a table? What an extraordinary thought! But how right it is! Once one has thought about our founding fathers in this way, one understands in a flash something significant about our country. Pages and pages of straight facts could never do it so well.

The technique of applying this kind of pivotal concept, what might be considered an extended analogy, is one that many writers use to unify their ideas. It was used by Linda De Pauw to discuss the "hidden heroines" in the Revolution; by William Kurelek in his refrain about the Holy Family, "If it happened there, why not here? If it happened then, why not now?"; by Gerald Johnson to compare the United States to a person growing to maturity in his trilogy *A History for Peter* (Morrow, 1959, 1960); by Marion Downer to link the maturing of a culture to the development of design in her book *The Story of Design* (Lothrop, 1963).

Storytelling skill, descriptive power, vivid prose, graphic excellence, and sharply defined focus—these are only some of the writing techniques that distinguish gifted nonfiction writing. You can probably discover many more the next time you reread your favorite book on the discovery of the Dead Sea Scrolls, the history of the Bayeaux Tapestry, or whatever.

In the final analysis, however, these techniques are only superficially significant. They are clues only. A writer is outstanding for reasons far more complicated than can be neatly summarized in a discussion like this. Perhaps we should look at nonfiction writing in this way: good nonfiction writers, like all teachers who know their subject well, distill from their knowledge a significant view of the world. But it is how the author communicates this insight that is crucial. In literature of fact the teacher's insight is vividly illuminated by the writer's art.

Characteristics of Good Science Materials for Young Readers

Illa Podendorf

Perhaps the first and most important question to ask oneself when beginning to write a book for children is: Why have I chosen this subject? Is it because children are particularly interested in it? Is it because there is a need for a book about this particular content? Does it offer an unusual opportunity to present accurate understandings of science as a method or as a way to make discoveries?

If the answer to at least one of these questions is positive there is good reason to proceed to develop the manuscript in the best possible way. If, however, the answers to all of the questions are negative the would-be author needs to reconsider the reasons for wishing to write the book. Maybe the subject is chosen because the writer is particularly interested in the subject and writing about it is an attempt to fill a personal need. In this case another body of content for the book should be explored unless the author is confident the book can be developed in a way that would satisfy the requirements of a good science book and create an interest on the part of the young reader and, just perhaps, demonstrate that there is a need for such a book. It should be remembered that a good science book provides opportunities for children to feel the excitement of discovery and the dignity of performance in an acceptable scientific manner.

Having satisfied oneself that the book meets the needs of a good science book and that it should be added to the literature, a more detailed selection of content is in order. The selected content should lend itself to an orderly and logical sequence. It should also be selected with consideration for the possibility of presentation with complete accuracy. If there is danger of incompleteness or overgeneralization in a way that would lead to error in the understanding of any part of the content, that particular part should be omitted.

The following demonstrates how a statement may appear to be accurate but actually lead to inaccurate inferences or understandings. Plants use carbon dioxide and give off oxygen whereas animals use oxygen and give off carbon dioxide. As stated this is accurate, but it is a dangerous statement to

SOURCE: Reprinted with permission from *Library Trends* 22 (April 1974): 425–431;

make because one possible but inaccurate inference is that plants in no way need oxygen and that animals in no way need carbon dioxide.

It is true that to write about science, authors need to know science. The above example illustrates that the author needs to know science to write about it, and it also illustrates that the author needs to consider the basic processes of science as he prepares his manuscripts. Some high school teachers have found it necessary to teach and reteach the needs of plants and animals for the gases of the air because of such errors as the one described. It may be wiser to decide against including this particular content unless it can be presented so that the reader can read it without danger of false inferences.

There are other ways in which material can be oversimplified. Statements such as, "All mammals give birth to their young" is for the most part correct, but there is one and maybe more exceptions. Thus the word *all* makes the statement incorrect. Adding the world *almost* in front of the world *all* is a safer way to present the idea and would make it read, "Almost all mammals give birth to their young." Other examples of more accurate phrasing are "Robins usually fly south in the winter from the place where Jane lives," or "Jane almost never sees robins at her feeding station in winter." Phrases such as almost all, nearly always, and usually are often more accurate than the more exact words such as all, always, and never.

Children need to become familiar with the idea that the natural environment is an orderly one and that there are definite patterns, but that there are also constant and newly found exceptions to almost all of the rules and/or laws which make up the patterns.

There is currently much discussion about science being more than a treatment of facts. Many of the new elementary science programs go beyond the content as such and deal with methods of science in terms of process development; some of them are weighted heavily on the side of process development. This is also true of junior and senior high school science curricula. This development has implications for the would-be author of science books for children of all ages.

Using any of the five senses is a basic way of obtaining information. Observing with all of the five senses is one, if not the most, basic process of science. It is not uncommon to make reference to observing, but it is uncommon to pay attention to particular observation skills such as looking, listening, touching, smelling, and tasting. All reference to observed activities or facts should be actual observations made by one or more of the senses and not inferred ones. Observations identify characteristics that are directly perceived through one or more of the five senses, whereas inferences involve an interpretation of the observations.

Consider the following: "The little raccoon went into the woods where he was safe from his enemies." The first part of the sentence can be easily observed in a picture, but whether or not the little raccoon was safe from his enemies is an inference. The sentence might better have been written as follows: "The little raccoon went off into the woods where he is most likely safe from his enemies." If the author wishes to stress the use of the process names, the sentence could have been written thus: "The little raccoon was seen to go off into the woods where it can be inferred it will be safe from its enemies." This author, however, is not recommending that process names be used on all possible occasions. This practice could easily result in very dull reading.

Another process needing careful consideration as authors prepare manuscripts is classifying—a way of imposing an order on a collection of things or objects. Many trade books and textbooks make reference to classification facts which have been handed down from scientists over a period of many years. For example: vertebrates are divided into five groups—mammals have fur, birds have feathers, fish have fins, reptiles have scales and lungs, and amphibians live part of their life in water and part on land. It is easy to leave the reader with the idea that vertebrate animals can only be classified in this way. Actually children are able to find many ways to classify animals and in so doing get a much better idea of classifying as a process.

There is no harm, however, in helping children to learn how scientists have classified vertebrate animals. Neither is there harm in presenting children with the system of classifying rocks in a way scientists have done it—igneous, sedimentary and metamorphic groups. It is wrong to give them the idea that this is the only way that rocks may be classified. Given proper activities children find other ways to classify them, i.e., characteristics such as color, hardness, or by texture. Classifying as a process can best be illustrated if more than one way to classify is presented. Presenting classification in this way has the advantages that children may get the idea that there is no one right way to classify and that their own ideas are valuable and useful; thus participation in individual thought and activity is encouraged.

Measurement is another process that plays an important part in science investigations and should be given a much more important place in science trade books than it often is. Experience in the use of the metric system, selection of units of measure, use of fractions to help interpret sizes and scale drawings are all important and should be incorporated in the manuscripts any time they add to the clarity of the presentation. Most science programs are putting particular emphasis on the use of the metric system since it has become more and more generally accepted in this country. It has been found that small children are able to use the system either as their only system of measurement or in addition to the British-American system with no apparent difficulty. In view of this it is entirely appropriate in the preparation of trade books to express measurement in the metric units only or in addition to the British-American units.

There are skills in the area of communication which are especially important in science. Graphing, illustrating, recording, and reporting are some of them. An author should make use of all opportunities in preparing a manuscript to use any of these and/or other communicating skills in an appropriate way.

Words are a medium of exchange in communicating. They should be carefully selected, especially as they relate to a technical vocabulary which is sometimes necessary in science. At an early age children are able to read and interpret graphs and can present their own ideas and findings in graphic form. A trade book which provides such experiences is a valuable addition to their literature. Any opportunity to help children get experience in interpreting data and making predictions from recorded data should not be overlooked. Such experiences often result in activities in which children can become actively involved. The temptation to present a dictionary definition should be avoided, even though there may be nothing wrong with the definition except that it will not fit into the text and thus not provide an accurate meaning. It is much more productive to develop an operational definition of the new words as they become useful.

Many basic processes such as those described or indicated are included in experimentation. Any time an author has included descriptions of experiments already done or can propose experiments to be done, interest is heightened for most young readers. Children get a lot of pleasure and excitement from what they believe to be "a real science experiment." Because of this the word has often been used in less than appropriate ways, and care should be exercised in the use of the word "experiment."

An experiment should be more than an interesting activity. To be acceptable, an experiment should have a question to be answered, done with techniques or procedures clearly understood, and have a testable conclusion. Other characteristics of an experiment, such as control of variables and making predictions, may not be evident in all experiments, but they should be clearly pointed up if it is possible without detracting from the interest. Children should be left with the feeling that the activity or the experiment is something they want very much to do for themselves.

This author does not imply that experimentation should be given a lesser place in the development of manuscripts for children's books, but that it should be given greater and more accurate scientific development. Vocabulary which deals with the scientific method should be used accurately and as often as it adds to the skill of carrying on scientific investigation without detracting from the reader's interest.

Mention has been made of the use of terms and vocabulary related to scientific method. There are other specialized or so-called "big words" which may prove difficult for the young reader. This author has followed the practice of using the needed vocabulary if it and it alone carries the message. If the word can be used more than once and in a context that makes the meaning clear for the young child, then it is the view of this author that it should be used. It follows, of course, that the number of such words in any one section of a book should be kept at a minimum. If the so-called "big words" are necessary but are feared to be troublesome, then the art of illustrating may add meaning and provide help for the reader.

Vocabulary should also be considered carefully for the older, even high school, readers. Older readers can handle more difficult vocabulary, including sophisticated scientific terms and constructions, and take great pride in so doing. However, they are able to read and participate more actively if they find the reading intriguing, challenging, and, at the same time, not difficult.

A criticism often made of material written for children is that it is anthropomorphic. Any material that treats animals as though they have human characteristics can be said to be anthropomorphic. There is at this time considerable research going on in an effort to determine how and why animals behave as they do. Some of their behaviors are remarkably human-like, but in no way should they be explained with phrases as though they were human behavior. "Little butterflies love flying about in the sunshine," and "The geese came swimming down the pond in a straight row. They like to play follow the leader," are examples of anthropomorphism.

When purpose is ascribed to anything in the natural environment the materials are said to be teleological. "The leaves of the plant curl up in the hot sun to prevent loss of water" and "Squirrels bury acorns in the ground so they will have food in winter" are well-known examples of teleological material. Many of the earlier science books which were very popular with children can be criticized because anthropomorphic and teleological phrases were common in them. It is an easy trap to fall into in an effort to make the material interesting and exciting. Aside from being anthropomorphic or teleological, such material, however interesting to children, may lead to wrong ideas and overly simplified ways of thinking.

Pictures, photographs, drawings, or diagrams add much to any material developed for children. These should be as carefully selected, prepared, or considered as the written word. They should be simple writhout being inaccurate if at all possible. They should be fitted carefully to the script, and as far as possible do what the written word cannot do. The location of the pictures, illustrations, or diagrams is also important. It should be easy for the reader to find the picture and then refocus on the text without loss of time or delay in thought development.

Any pictures that present several ideas may be confusing to the reader. They may be attractive and add interest to the book at a glance, but on closer examination prove to be less functional and may even provide distraction in trying to fit text to the diagram. The question: "Is this bit of art worth the space it occupies?" should be answered in the positive for each diagram, photograph, or illustration proposed for the manuscript. Nonverbal representations are useful in prepared directions for activities. Symbols, arrows, and outline drawings of pieces of equipment can be substituted for words. This adds to the interest of a page and at the same time may reduce the vocabulary load.

A real plus in evaluation for any book for children is the knowledge that it will continue to be functional for them after they have "put the book down." After they have finished reading the book they may spend considerable time thinking about what they have read, asking questions based upon what they have read, duplicating some of the activities or experiments described, or developing related activities or experiments in a creative way.

More and more trade books are coming on the market, and it is becoming less difficult to acquire a collection of enrichment reading materials to accompany a science curriculum suitably. To produce such materials has been a special challenge to authors. This challenge is still very much in evidence and many authors are making a sincere effort to meet the challenge in a way it has not been met before.

There is another special challenge for teachers—to find new and better ways of interesting young readers in quality reading materials beyond the textbook. Many science curricula for young children are not accompanied by a so-called textbook. Curricula for older children may be accompanied by a recommended book but may also depend heavily upon enrichment reading materials. Teachers then need to find, select, and decide more specifically upon the reading references as well as to guide the students in their free reading choices. Many teachers find a need to change their teaching techniques or methods and to be less dependent upon the course outline as prescribed through the textbook, if there is one. They need to become more involved with the trade books and other enrichment reading materials. Teachers and librarians need to work together to interest children in a quality reading program to accompany their subject matter areas of which science is a very important one.

This article does not intend to convey the idea that all science books for children should be factual and curriculum-oriented. Quite the contrary, it is the intention of the author to support a great variety of books being published and a part of the available literature. All books should be described, and the identity of the contents should be portrayed as honestly as possible, which would be helpful to librarians, teachers and children as they make their selections for free reading or for course work. If there is fiction included it should be so indicated. Children should not be expected to separate fact from fiction as they read, especially in new and unfamiliar areas. With the concerted effort of authors and the guidance of librarians, teachers and parents, children should have available a wide range of scientific literature and be able to make appropriate selections in line with their personal needs and interests.

An Evaluation of Biography

Denise M. Wilms

In theory, biography has much to offer children, but in practice its potential is too often undermined by unskilled execution. Moreover, the persistent weaknesses that mark these faulty life stories are perpetuated by the uncritical acceptance of teachers, librarians, and others who continue to put them into the hands of children.

This disregard for quality stems partly from pressure to look at biographies in functional terms—from being caught up in filling a need, whether it's for one child or a whole class with an assignment on Abraham Lincoln—when it's easy to forget about literary or artistic values. More seriously, though, the neglect stems from not knowing just what biography is about. I think there has to be more concern with substance in biography; there has to be more attention paid to its crafting and to its full value as a rich, entertaining, educational tool.

A review of what biography is supposed to do will help give some context to what I'm saying. Ideally, a biographer's aim is to bring a person to life in a way that is true to the reality of that person's life. Facts alone aren't enough; an encyclopedia can give the dry, bare-bones facts; and what is fact anyway? Did Margaret Fuller marry her impoverished Italian Count Ossoli or didn't she? One recent biography said she did; another says there's confusion and leaves the matter open.

Then there is the matter of context. No person operates independently of time, or society, or the world at large. A sound biography relates the subject to his or her time. John Anthony Scott does this well in *Woman Against Slavery,* the life of Harriet Beecher Stowe.

He writes:

> Harriet's work was extraordinary not only because it was a new and pioneer type of novel but because it was written by a woman. Until 1852 few American women had broken the barriers of convention that forbade women to write about anything so real and brutal as slavery. Angelina and Sarah Grimke had written about slavery and had agitated against it. Lydia Maria Child had edited an antislavery newspaper and published her own antislavery tracts. But

SOURCE: Reprinted by permission of the American Library Association from *Booklist:*75 (September 15, 1978): 218–220;

> the most popular women writers wrote polite or conventional novels in which discussion of the topic of slavery was taboo. . . . For a woman to depart so boldly from custom took both courage and conviction. It is part of Harriet's supreme achievement that she dared to give a bold and scorching expression to her feelings as a woman and a mother when she saw innocent and often defenseless human beings ground up or torn to pieces by the workings of slavery.

His last emotion-laden sentence gets its credibility from earlier portions in which Scott describes Harriet's experiences in Cincinnati, Ohio, where she came to know the stories of many escaped slaves.

Another consideration is the writer's own attitude, interest, and enthusiasm for his or her subject. You have to sense an author's pleasure in the subject, whether that involvement is highly visible, or subtle, or somewhere in between. Think of the humorous overtones in Jean Fritz's biographies, and then think of Virginia Hamilton's portrait of Paul Robeson. These are two very different books, but each one projects an authorial sympathy that pulls strongly at the reader's interest.

When biography is working, it sparks your interest—even if you thought you had none in the first place. It's a human encounter; it's literary people-watching, and that's what makes it many people's favorite reading. When it comes to this basic fascination, children are no different from adults.

In a working biography you watch the person grow, learn, achieve, or even fail; you might identify with the person, or be inspired, or you might not. But in each case there's a vital human connection; a life experience in all its richness has been transmitted. And because what you're dealing with is real, there's a special weight to it. This immediacy is at the heart of biography's potential as a teaching tool—it's a perfect accompaniment to the humanities and the sciences because it gives the chance to reflect on events from one individual viewpoint, to step off the beaten track and into fresh territory.

Biographies for children too often get bogged down by questionable notions of what is suitable for children to know and how it should be told. In this aversion to dealing head on with a subject, biography can be faulted for lagging behind the main body of children's literature. Look at fiction: We've watched, over the last ten to fifteen years, one breakthrough after another in what was thought to be suitable reading for children. Topics that were once taboo are now acceptable, as contemporary realism so pointedly shows. Nonfiction, too, has grown. Think of your science collections, your history collections. You find books on logic, on nuclear physics, on lasers, on the intricacies of ecology, on the histories of women and minorities. There are books on death, divorce, drugs. The enduring ones among these books are well written, straightforward, honest, and definitely informative. They show that in the hands of a skillful, sensitive writer, almost any subject can be responsibly explained. These books were written under the assumption that children are capable of understanding and appreciating the world around them. Why, then, does biography so often veer away from dealing more fully with the subject at hand?

Why, for example, is biography often looked on as the *story* of a life, rather than the *history* of a life, which in fact it is. Why is fictionalization so acceptable? Why are character and personality sidestepped in favor of a recitation of events and accomplishments? Why do we have biographies that leave out the negative or unfortunate aspects of a life? In short, where is the depth, the dimension, the richness?

At this point it's interesting to take a quick look at how biography developed. For one thing, it hasn't been around all that long; scholars say biography as we know it first appeared around 1640. Before that were so called lives of saints or kings, which set in motion the role of biography to set an example and/or glorify the subject. Unfavorable things were not considered proper form—the whole point was to show how special and different the subject was from ordinary humans. Invention was freely used to help the image along. There's a wonderful example of this in James Clifford's *Biography as an Art.* He tells of Agnellus, a ninth-century bishop of Ravenna, who was writing a series of lives of his predecesors. Agnellus had been unable to find any detailed information on some of them, either from oral tradition or any authentic source, and writes, "In order that there might not be a break in the series, I have composed the life myself, with the help of God and the prayers of brethren."

Then in the eighteenth century came Boswell's life of Dr. Samuel Johnson, which scholars mark as the beginning of modern biography. Boswell was interested in completeness; he said:

> Indeed I cannot conceive of a more perfect mode of writing any man's life, than not only relating all the most important events of it in their order, but interweaving what he privately wrote, and said, and thought; by which mankind are enabled as it were to see him live, and to live over each scene with him, as he actually advanced through the several stages of his life. Had his other friends been as diligent and ardent as I was, he might have been almost entirely preserved. As it is, I will venture to say that he will be seen in this work more completely than any man who has ever yet lived.

Boswell's Life of Johnson set an enduring standard that didn't change measurably until the twentieth century and is still considered one of the masterworks of English-language biography.

These broad developments in adult biography offer an interesting backdrop for looking at juvenile biography, for in some ways biography for young people has gone through similar stages. As with much of early children's literature, there was the wish to teach and set example: Lives of saints and cautionary stories are on record; Parson Weems gave us the image of honest George Washington, who couldn't lie about chopping down the cherry tree. In modern children's biography that pure intent is considerably diluted but it still crops up: In the D'Aulaires' *George Washington* you can read that

George sat quietly around the fireplace in the living room with his brothers and sisters listening to Bible stories, that George "learned to be good and honest and never tell a lie."

To be fair, though, children's biography has come a long way from the old days. With the '60s and '70s in particular there was a burst of life stories that paralleled information breakthroughs in other areas. Names like Malcolm X, Fanny Kemble, and Sojourner Truth reflected the new awareness of history, of women, of radical social movements, of information that had never seen the light in children's books. These books set precedents for looking at people from all walks of life and gave juvenile biography some necessary breadth. Now we need to deepen the genre.

Of course no one will argue that the mammoth works by dedicated scholars of biography need be replicated in children's literature. But the ideals they aimed for can't be forgotten: We must expect them, but it seems too often we don't. Compromises like fictionalization, lack of documentation, or a failure to examine personality and character or lend an appropriate examining eye need to be questioned. I think librarians need to pause and think about these things and ask whether "compromise biographies" are, in fact, useful and serve the purpose of a good reading experience. Does a strictly linear account of events that happened to or because of the person really constitute a biography? Is a biography that allows only one dimension of a person to show through really an educational reading experience? Where are the boundaries between artful simplicity and the overgeneralization that is distortion? Was it justifiable for the D'Aulaires not to include Lincoln's assassination in their account of his life or for Patricia Miles Martin not to identify the Emancipation Proclamation in her biography of Lincoln? And what about the truth of absolute statements like this one in May McNeer's generally strong biography of George Washington: "No one could ride a horse or hunt as well as George Washington." Or, to take an extreme, this enthusiastic endorsement in F. M. Milverstead's *Henry Aaron:* "He is the sum total of the best part of 200 years of American history."

And fictionalizing; is it really necessary? Take this passage from a biography of Elizabeth Fry by Spencer Johnson:

> Once upon a time there was a girl named Elizabeth who lived in a great house in England. . . . She should have been very happy, but she wasn't.
>
> "I like being kind to people," she said, "because it makes people happy."
>
> "I wish I could go out and be kind to those people who no one else thinks about."
>
> There were days when Elizabeth was sad. It was on one of these days that a butterfly came flitting into her garden.
>
> "Why are you so sad, pretty lady?" asked the butterfly. Elizabeth was surprised to meet a talking butterfly, but she was a very kind person and didn't

> want to be rude. So she pretended that it was quite usual to chat with butterflies.
>
> "I am sad because I am not being kind enough to people," said Elizabeth.

What child can happily relate to such a didactic pitch?

Much more common is the problem a child would face had he or she to do some comparing—as indeed some classroom assignments require. Here is how fictionalization might raise questions for the thinking reader: Take the case of a child who has to do a report on Mary McLeod Bethune and needs several sources. Here are two passages that might be found. One, Eloise Greenfield's *Mary McLeod Bethune* reads:

> The sun had just come up when Mary McLeod left the house with her mother and father and brothers and sisters to go to the fields. Every morning, the whole family had to get up very early to work on the farm. *But they didn't mind* [italics mine].

The other, in Beth P. Wilson's *Giants for Justice:*

> The family was constantly hoeing to keep the crab grass away from the young, tender plants. Mary Jane always sang as she worked. Sometimes she would stop to pray right in the field. "Please, God," she would say. "Help me get away from this crabgrass."

In fact each of the books from which I pulled these lines do a reasonably good job of introducing Mary McLeod Bethune to children; but the background details don't match, and so a reader might wonder what the facts of Mary's characterization really are. This third passage from Ruby Radford's *Mary McLeod Bethune* offers the most balance; listen to its simple, reasonable tone:

> The whole family worked on the farm. Even the smallest children helped plant cotton and grow vegetables and rice. It was hard work but the McLeods were thankful for their freedom.

No implied heroics here, or victimization; just a clean statement of what is known to be true.

Another situation that often comes with fictionalization is switching back and forth between story and straight narative. What is the logic of using an artificial novellike opening that's followed or interwoven with straight narrative? If you expect the reader to cope with facts, why not present them straight away? It's devious not to; and it doesn't have to be boring. What is a reader to make of the jolting and misleading stylistic switches like this one in Lillie Patterson's recent biography of Benjamin Banneker. Opening, it reads like a novel:

> "Tell me that story again. Please!"
>
> "What story, Benjamin?"
>
> "You know the one I mean. Tell me about how you came across the big ocean on a ship. Tell me how you came to this place."

Then, a page and a half later, there is smooth, straightforward narrative. In explaining indentured servitude the author writes:

> Hundreds of such prisoners were coming to the colonies during the seventeenth century. This was a way of bringing much-needed workers to the newly settled lands. Any businessman or landowner could sign a contract, called an indenture, to pay for prisoner's passage. In return, the prisoner worked free for this "master" for a number of years, usually seven.

Fictionalization seems too often an easy way out in suggesting color and character. The rationale is that you want to spark the child's interest, and imagined scenes are an effective way to do this. But biography is, in fact, the history of a life, and histories deal in fact, not fiction. A writer must decide if he or she is writing biography or historical fiction. For many figures, especially contemporary ones, there is sufficient material for the writer to merge the interesting *and* the factual.

When a writer feels invention is a necessity, perhaps the answer lies in the term biographical fiction—which is not to be confused with biography. Alex Haley, in discussing *Roots,* coined the term "faction"—a responsible merger of fact and fiction. Both these terms might rightfully fall under the umbrella of historical fiction. But referring as they do to real-life people and families, they are naturally associated with biography.

Biographical fiction offers a way to merge careful research with novel perspective or a strong sense of story that doesn't compromise the standards of biography. In juvenile literature the star practitioner in this area is Ferdinand Monjo, who also takes the time in his books to point out where the line between fact and fiction lies.

But biographical fiction is not biography, in the way that historical fiction is not history. Each has its rightful place and follows its own set of rules; and each one informs and entertains accordingly.

Clearly, writing biography is complicated business; Boswell said: "Biography occasions a degree of trouble far beyond that of any other species of literary composition." It demands both art and scholarship; neither can be compromised with good results. The best children's biographies we have show us the task isn't impossible. They set the standard for judging other works. So, what is a reviewer faced with? Very simply, compromise. Many of the examples I touched on came from books that *Booklist* reviewed. In fact there aren't many biographies around that successfully combine everything you'd hope would be in a biography. Some are stronger than others. Most are useful in some way, particularly when they cover a subject who is little written about. It's vital though, to pause, and take stock, to remind ourselves what's good and why, and demand more of it. If we don't, who will?

What Do We Do about Bad Biographies?

Jo Carr

According to Philip Guedalla, biography is "a region that is bounded on the north by history, on the south by fiction, on the east by obituary, and on the west by tedium."

If this is true, then in the region of children's biography we must add more points to our compass. On the northwest, hagiography: George with his little hatchet and Honest Abe gazing into the coals. On the northest, didacticism: Helen Keller obscured by "mists of adulation." On the southwest, oversimplification: Einstein and his theory of relativity reduced to the third-grade reading level. On the southeast, propaganda: Crispus Attucks, a black hero of convenience. And, from all directions, sentimentality, unwarranted fictionalization, lack of solid documentation, and distortion of history.

Are these views of children's biography too deprecatory? Not according to most of those who have written articles on this subject, including the writers in this collection. As Margery Fisher puts it: "It is in the sadly drab shelves of so-called biographical material for the middle years that a change is long overdue. Between the ages of eight and twelve, how much energy, curiosity, and good will is going to waste!"

What can we do about bad biographies? First, we can cultivate nimble dexterity to skirt the dreadful biographies already on the shelves. Then, we can cultivate equally nimble wits to keep such books off the shelves in the future.

Before we engage in any of this, however, we must decide what we expect biography to do for children. Patrick Groff, in two articles he has written on the subject, demolishes biography-as-inspiration-to-the-young. For one thing, as he points out, biography rarely works that way. And, most unforgivably and all too often, books of that sort are boring. Nobody likes to be preached at, children no more than the rest of us.

In only one particular might we modify what Groff has said about biography as personal inspiration to the young. Although there is certainly no defense for presenting public figures as "human saints," there is a place for "identification" as a child reads about a kindred spirit. Any child who stores

SOURCE: Jo Carr, comp., *Beyond Fact: Nonfiction for Children and Young People*, pp. 119–128.

dead birds in the refrigerator, for instance, might delight in reading Barbara Brenner's biography of Audubon, but this is an instance of one "odd-ball" of ten joyfully discovering another odd-ball of forty. Identification, yes; emulation, no.

There is no question that identification can be a real attraction to reading biography. Realizing that someone else has faced the same problems, a child may identify instantly with the hardships of the hero. As an example, Elizabeth Segel has ably demonstrated in her analysis of two biographies of Beatrix Potter that pain can result from social injustices over which we have no control. A child similarly victimized might be grateful to Margaret Lane's biography for the honest treatment of rigid social pressure—much the same now as then—instead of being falsely reassured that "nothing is impossible."

The power of biography to encourage the identification of one kindred spirit with another does appeal to children, but no less so than does the vivid dramatization of history. Good biographies, like all good history, reveal exactly what it was like to have lived long ago—"in olden times." It is only when biographies are irresponsibly written and history distorted that we face a problem of considerable significance. All too many biography collections for children fail to measure up to decent professional standards. In deciding what to do about these unfortunate books, since in most cases we are unable to replace them without inordinate expense, we might devise, in desperation, a fresh approach to the problem. Perhaps librarians who can manage to look at weak collections as a challenge might consider the suggestions that follow.

Encourage children to read more autobiography and less biography. In discovering the past, either for school work or for pleasure, a child reading an autobiography will be walking around in the skin of someone who lived in another place at another time. For example:

Johanna Reiss compels the reader to come with her when she enters *The Upstairs Room* (Crowell, 1972), where she and her sister spent two years in hiding during World War II.

Hiroko Nakamoto, in her autobiography called *My Japan, 1930–1951* (McGraw-Hill, 1970), shares with the reader her anguish after the bombing of Hiroshima.

Eloise Greenfield, her mother, and her grandmother all remember, in *Childtimes* (Crowell, 1979), what it was like when they were children. It is almost as if they were reminiscing together on the front porch, "Did I ever tell you about the time . . . ?" Since we all want to give children an enriching exposure to minorities, what a privilege to share these memories, to feel the love and solidarity that carries from one generation to another. The truth about this fine black family is ten times more inspiring than the fabricated idealization of Crispus Attucks, about whom we actually know next to nothing.

Margery Fisher maintains that the use of authentic social detail is the biographer's most important tool. In these three autobiographies, *The Upstairs*

Room, My Japan, and *Childtimes,* social detail, by the very nature of the first-person account, makes past life as real as today to the reader.

Promote books that focus on a short, but significant, period in someone's life. Often a chronological account, from childhood to death, must omit social details that children love. At least this is true if the book is not to be as long as *War and Peace.*

In illustrating and writing *The Boy Who Loved Music* (Viking, 1979), for instance, David and Joe lasker have revealed intriguing bathing rituals in the Austrian castle of Esterhaza, along with the musical protest of Haydn in his "Farewell" Symphony of 1772. This is a short book, covering only a few weeks in Haydn's life. In a cradle-to-the grave biography, such delightful detail would have been out of the question.

There are now quite a few of these sharply focused, miniature excursions into biography: Lindbergh flying solo across the Atlantic, Benjamin West learning from the Indians how to mix colors for his paints, Robert E. Lee struggling against defeat at Gettysburg in *Three Days* by Paxton Davis (Atheneum, 1980).

Avoid watered-down, talking-down biographies for younger children. In simplifying the life of a public figure, biographers are often forced to leave out facts that are essential for a balanced portrait. The result is distortion by omission, which is just as unfortunate as distortion by commission. It should come as no surprise, for instance, that history will inevitably be distorted when a biographer labors to give third-graders some understanding of FDR's efforts to pull the United States out of the Depression or to explain Jefferson's wisdom in drafting the Declaration of Independence. Should a child of that age even be expected to understand such complex ideas and issues?

But even the less complicated exploits of Benjamin Franklin can be distorted in oversimplified accounts. One author rattles off Ben's accomplishments, including the famous stove, without any explanation of how they worked or why they were important. Even Franklin's "Rules of Behavior" have been drastically abridged. Still another author covers sixty years of his life in six pages! Ben Franklin himself would turn over in his grave if he, or his ghost, could read these books.

Unfortunately there is really only one way to determine how flagrantly omissions have distorted a biographical portrait. This is to read many accounts of the same life, including an adult biography, as Margery Fisher has done so effectively in *Matters of Fact.* This exercise is so revealing that third- and fourth-grade teachers who presently assign biographies should be persuaded to try it.

Apart from distorting history, writers of simplified biographies frequently "talk down" to children in sentences that sound like the most boring of all easy readers: "Let's start libraries and hospitals. Let's clear the streets and put up lights. Let's work together to fight fires. . . ." Such choppy writing, combined with the adulatory tone that characterizes biographies for beginning readers, does an injustice to the person who is the subject of the book. For that matter, it also does an injustice to the reader.

The point is that there is no necessity for young children to read biography at all. Why not let them wait until they have enough historical background to understand the true significance of past events and the men who inspired them?

Seek out biographical material in subject areas. This may be the most productive way to resist misbegotten biographies. Admittedly, discovering these books may be a slippery process, since books are classified quite differently in various libraries. (*The Upstairs Room,* for instance, can be found in the 940s in some libraries, in fiction in others, and in biography in still others.) But the accuracy of these biographies, concerned as they are more with the person's working life than with childhood "stories" about curing a pet dog or buying a bun in Philadelphia, justifies extra effort. Besides, hunting for them can be intriguing, as children might agree if they were set loose on a biographical treasure hunt.

Consider the following examples:

Michael Collins, in *Flying to the Moon and Other Strange Places,* describes his extraordinary journey through space:

> The feeling was less like flying than like being alone in a boat on the ocean at night. Stars above, pure black below. At dawn, light filled my windows so quickly that my eyes hurt. Almost immediately, the stars disappeared and the moon reappeared. I knew from my clock that the earth was about to reappear, and right on schedule it popped into view, rising like a blue and white jewel over the desolate lunar horizon.

His book is classified in the 629s.

Polly Brocks and Nancy Walworth in their fine histories of Rome, the Middle Ages, and the Renaissance, have also placed public figures as the dramatic center of events. In *The World Awakes* (Lippincott, 1962), for instance, we find Lorenzo de Medici and Leonardo da Vinci "awakening" the Renaissance world of Italy. The classification number is 940.21.

William Kurelek, in *A Prairie Boy's Winter,* tells a great deal about himself as he describes life in Manitoba when he was a boy. In addition, he gives us a book of outstanding graphic beauty. The classification number is 917.1.

Lennart Rudstrom also has created three books of graphic distinction by presenting the artwork of Carl Larsson in *A Home,* and *A Farm,* and *A Family* (Putnam, 1974, 1976, 1980). These books are classified and shelved, logically enough, in 759.85, but, despite some unevenly written text, they are enriching as biographies in addition to being "art" books.

As a matter of fact, we can reap some special benefits by engaging in this kind of biographical treasure hunt. Many nonfiction books, not purporting to be biographies at all, may inadvertently give us a valuable glimpse into the lives of extraordinary "ordinary" people. Marilyn Jurich, commenting on the lamentable quality of biographies for children, pleads for more biographies of not-so-famous people who have led interesting lives in one way or another. Fortunately we can find some of these people at home in the various areas of nonfiction. *As I Saw It: Women Who Lived the American Adventure* (Dial, 1978), by Cheryl Hoople, is a notable example; so are *Museum People* (Prentice-Hall, 1977), by Peggy Thomson and *Plane Talk: Aviators and Astronauts' Own Stories* (Houghton, 1980), edited by Carl Oliver. And certainly many of us have been moved by the searing accounts of the slaves in Julius Lester's *To Be a Slave* (Dial, 1968). Anyone exploring the nonfiction shelves might be surprised at how many ordinary people, just as interesting as these, are waiting to be discovered.

Yet another bonus to be derived from reading biography from the nonfiction shelves is the privilege of experiencing the unfolding of events, just as they happened, recorded in the journals and diaries and eyewitness accounts of people who "were there." Eric Sloane, after finding a diary of a farm boy named Noah Blake from the year 1805, has illustrated, in scrupulous detail, the events described in words. The book, called *Diary of an Early American Boy* (Crowell, 1974), can be found shelved with the 630s in many libraries. This classification, perhaps logical but nevertheless absurd, effectively removes the book from circulation.

George Sanderlin has allowed Francis Drake and his shipmates to tell in their own words the story of their journeys. This account, in a book called *The Sea Dragon* (Harper, 1969), is one of several eyewitness histories compiled by Sanderlin. Other historians have done the same: Joseph Martin, Phillip Viereck, Cheryl Hoople, Henry S. Commager and Richard B. Morris, Robert Meredith and E. Brooks Smith, to name a few. John Anthony Scott once edited the "Living History Library," now unfortunately defunct, to which Milton Meltzer was a contributor. Honest books like these can be a most refreshing antidote to the sickly fictionalization that characterizes story biographies.

Do not lean on biography. Once we have reminded ourselves that the purpose of biography is not to edify children, we can find other, less troublesome, ways to discover the past. For one, we can move most directly to biographical fiction, of course, as Denise Wilms has pointed out in her article on biography. Happily oblivious to the scholarly restrictions shackling a biographer, we can share a cloud with Eleanor of Aquitaine as she waits in heaven for Henry to arrive from "down below" . . . or "kibbitz" a chess game between Ben Franklin and a French lady in her bath!

But if, as we have determined, our goal is simply to explain and enliven history, we can joyfully promote, not just biographical fiction, but all historical fiction. Here the writer intent upon satisfying the child's natural desire for a good story need not twist historical fact as so often occurs when a biographer puts imaginary dialogue into the mouths of real people. Fortunately, historical fiction needs no promotion. It has always been deservedly popular with children and adults alike.

What about straight history? Here we run into difficulties. As selections on history writing in this collection have suggested, we in the schools have been guilty of not-so-benign neglect. C. Walter Hodges, Gerald Johnson, Alfred Duggan, and all the other fine writers of history, deserve to be read more than they are. Without any question a lively history book can be a stimulating and honest alternative to undocumented biography.

These, then, have been some suggestions for working around problems already sitting on biography shelves.

What about buying better biographies in the future? Is it possible to find biographies that are both well documented and still a pleasure to read? Before deciding, we need to examine fairly critically, not only the reviewing of children's biographies, but also the intellectual climate surrounding their writing and publishing.

Trade publishers seem to be emulating textbook publishers of history, discussed elsewhere in this work, by working backwards, and inside out, as they manufacture new biographies. They have been quick to recognize the need for biographies about blacks, about women, about the Founding Fathers on the occasion of the Bicentennial, about sports figures appealing to reluctant readers, about. . . . Since the bandwagon is rolling, we can hardly blame the publishers for jumping on board. They are in business to make money, after all.

Patrick Groff in his article "Biography: The Bad or the Bountiful?" documents the extent to which biographers have responded to the lure of the market. He describes a practice that many of us have long suspected—the "borrowing" of material from an adult biography to construct one for children. Armed with scissors and rubber cement, almost anybody, according to Groff, can produce a juvenile version of an adult biography. His evidence reveals that some have already done so.

Reputable biographers, of course, would be aghast at this practice of "cutting and pasting" what is supposed to be original work. Original work is the result of a far different, and more arduous, process. The best biographers start, not with concern for what will or will not sell, but with a compelling interest in a particular public figure. Jane Yolen, in her book on writing nonfiction, describes this fascination as a "tap on the shoulder." She says she wrote the biography *Friend* because she was convinced that she had been tapped on the shoulder by the fiery mystic George Fox, just as Elizabeth Gray Vining had felt the same compulsion when she wrote the biography of William Penn. From this "summons" comes a serious commitment to the subject. Biographers then read all they can find by and about William Penn, or George Fox, or whoever has captured their imagination to begin with.

There must be, of course, a limit to the amount of original research that can reasonably be expected, and Olivia Coolidge considers these limitations in her article, "My Struggle with Facts."

In addition to dogged and sometimes tedious research, the biographer often walks in the footsteps of the person whose life is being recorded, visiting houses and schools and anywhere else where traces of that person might remain. Mary Haverstock, for instance, went herself to all the places that George Catlin had traveled on his painting trips to record the lives of Indians in the West. In addition, the biographer usually interviews anyone who might be able to supply unpublished information.

Once the facts have been assembled, the writer of biography must face what may be the most difficult task of all: to organize the material and select from it those details that will create an accurate and illuminating portrait. Naturally the portrait that emerges will reflect the biographer's perception of why that public figure is great. Any writer presuming to interpret someone's life must be particularly sensitive to the choices that person has made at crucial periods, choices that inevitably resulted in a decisive change of direction. By shaping the material to make it reveal the background behind these choices, the biographer has, in essence, explained why and how a human being eventually becomes important. In fact, the biographer has gambled on what might ultimately be the judgment of history.

Biographies crafted with this combination of hard work and imagination should be the ones, and the only ones, that we buy for our libraries. But how do we identify honest and inspired books among all the made-to-order stuff that floods the market? Unfortunately discriminating selection is not always as simple as it should be.

Reviews are the obvious selection tools, but reviewers have failed in the past to be sufficiently hard-boiled in their evaluation of biography. Either ignorance or compromise has seemed to dictate the same uncritical standards in reviewing as it has in publishing. As a consequence, it is instructive to contrast the reviewing of science books with the reviewing of biography; to recognize the impact of specialized reviewing, not only in what is bought for libraries, but also in what publishers think they can get away with. As has been pointed out in the article on science writing, children's book editors have become sensitive to the reviews of professional scientists in *Appraisal* and *Science Books and Films*. This is not surprising. How can any editor afford to risk having a science book disembowelled by a hawkeyed, predatory scientist?

Perhaps we need hawkeyed, predatory historians. Perhaps we need more reviews of biographies like the recent review of a history book about the making of the Constitution. Garry Wills, a historian who has won an award for an adult book on Jefferson and the Declaration of Independence, reviewed a children's history for the *Washington Post Book World* and censured it unmercifully. Two reviews of the same book in library journals, written of course by nonhistorians, picked up neither the "warmed-over scholarship" nor the abundance of errors pointed out by the historian. The book may not actually be as weak as Garry Wills maintains, but his professional judgment obviously adds valuable perspective in considering this book for purchase. The *New York Times* often uses specialists in the adult field to review children's books—Tom Wicker reviewing the book by Paxton Davis on Robert E. Lee, for instance—but unfortunately there are very few books reviewed in the *Times* during the course of the year.

So what would happen, one wonders not altogether facetiously, if Barbara Tuchman or Leon Edel were to review children's biographies? What would Catherine Drinker Bowen have said had she read *Abigail Adams: Girl of Colonial Days* (Bobbs-Merrill, 1962), a "life-story" for children in grades two to four? But this kind of speculation is nonproductive. Until historians give us the benefit of their knowledge, we must depend on standard review sources. What we need from these is more painstaking reviewing, more time and thought spent before arriving at a judgment. And we need more literary criticism of biography, especially criticism as analytical as that of Elizabeth Segel's evaluation of the biographies of Beatrix Potter in this collection. At the very least, we have a right to expect that a reviewer will check the facts in a juvenile biography against those in a reputable adult source, as well as to compare that book to other children's biographies. Unfortunately evidence suggests that not all reviewers do this. It can be especially revealing, as well as discouraging, to read a review of a particular biography after you have read three or four different versions of that same person's life.

Following is an example of one inaccuracy, among many unnoticed by the reviewer, in a biography of Benjamin Banneker. The biographer gives highly romantic significance to the fact that Banneker never married because the girl he loved killed herself. The adult biography, with impressive documentation, states simply that he was a bachelor all his life and that there is no evidence of a love interest at all. Not only does the biographer of this book for children invent scenes on the basis of what must be flimsy evidence—and of course there is no bibliography or list of sources to check the evidence—he also omits other facts and significant events. Yet a review in one of the most reputable library journals said of this biography that it was "well-researched" and admirable in every way.

Quite apart from the distressing fact that children may be swallowing misinformation in the biographies written for them, this kind of inadequate reviewing inevitably sends a message to publishers that accuracy is not important. Editors do respond to demands that are made on them. If reviewers would dig in their heels, they would probably stimulate the publication of good biographies, just as science reviewers have successfully set a higher standard of expectation in science books.

The first step toward a higher standard in biographies could be taken fairly easily. Surely it would not be too difficult for publishers to include a list of sources at the end of every biography, even those written for younger children. Then reviewers and librarians, as well as readers, would be able to tell how reliable the information is. In the case of contradictory evidence surrounding some details in a person's life, a common dilemma for biographers, perhaps the author could explain in a short note why one source was chosen instead of another. This sort of information can be intriguing, even for children. It may give them a fascinating glimpse of the challenge to the writer who had to decide what to include, which facts to choose in order to create the most accurate portrait. And some may even understand that truth is elusive and subject to interpretation. Being able to handle the mutability of truth, in fact, could be the first step toward a healthy, active skepticism. But, quite apart from any salutary effects on children, honest bibliographic information would be a godsend to reviewers. With a complete knowledge of scholarly sources, reviewers would be able to appraise a biography realistically and fairly. And those who buy the books and those who read them would all benefit.

Under the present circumstances, however, librarians have no choice but to read, critically, as many reviews as possible in order to determine which reviewers and which journals are most reliable, or, rather, least unreliable. In deciding whether to buy a particular biography they should probably be guided by the most negative comments. If, for instance, a review suggests that a book about Socrates might be stimulating reading for eight-year-olds, or if the words "fictionalized" or "story-biography" appear even parenthetically, or if no mention is made of the qualifications of the author or sources of information, then why not reject the book? Librarians do have the power of the purse, after all. Only by exercising that power can they, and reviewers, convince publishers that good books mean good business.

Denise Wilms in her article on biography says that we should "take stock" and demand the best. Yes, we should take stock, thoroughly and realistically, but at the same time we should recognize hopeful signs when we see them. Although it is true that most of the current biographies would appall Barbara Tuchman, enough fine books are also appearing to brighten the prospects for the future. For instance:

Selected illustrators have been drawing and painting their autobiographies. Erik Blegvard and Margot Zemach, as a start, have given us a taste of pleasures in store as other illustrators continue to interpret their lives with paint and brush.

Some biographies focus on scientists and their work in the laboratory and in the field. Although these simply written accounts give the reader little feeling for what the scientists were like as people, the importance and excitement of their discoveries come through without distortion.

Some new collective biographies, much neglected in school libraries, portray individuals—musicians, civil rights leaders, reformers, spies, whoever—in accounts so short that there is no need for unwarranted fictionalization. An abbreviated biography might also appeal to a child who would be discouraged by one hundred or two hundred pages of solid print in a longer book.

Another refreshing approach to biography is a play called *Escape to Freedom* (Viking, 1978) written by Ossie Davis about Frederick Douglas. Why hasn't this been done more often, one wonders?

Above all, there is Jean Fritz. Her lively biographical writing has blown like a fresh breeze across the children's book world. She sticks to the facts, but she ignites them with such a spark that they illuminate ordinary events. She especially loves to include little-known but authentic details to enhance the day-to-day life of the past: Paul Revere writing in his Day Book, "This is my book for me to ________" and never finishing the sentence because he was, as always, in too much of a hurry; John Hancock practicing his signature over and over again to make it as imposing as possible; Patrick Henry imitating a mockingbird imitating a jay. An example of her writing revealing her light, sure touch follows. It is taken from *Where Was Patrick Henry on the 29th of May?*

> Patrick Henry stood up and pushed his glasses back on his head which was what he did when he was ready to use his fighting words. . . .
>
> "I know not what course others may take but as for me . . ." Patrick dropped his arms, threw back his body and strained against his imaginary chains until the tendons of his neck stood out like whipcords and the chains seemed to break. Then he raised his right hand in which he held an ivory letter opener. "As for me," he cried, "give me liberty or give me death!" And he plunged the letter opener in such a way it looked as if he were plunging it into his heart.
>
> The crowd went wild with excitement. One man, leaning over the balcony, was so aroused that he forgot where he was and spit tobacco juice into the audience below. Another man jumped down from the window ledge and declared that when he died, he wanted to be buried on the very spot that Patrick Henry had delivered those words. (And so he was, 25 years later.)

As the foregoing selection vividly illustrates, fabricated dialogue and inaccurate fictionalization are not at all necessary for a lively interpretation of history.

So, all in all, the future for children's biography looks less hopeless than we might have feared. In terms of Philip Geudalla's dreary geography with which we began this exploration, Jean Fritz has changed the face of the map. Other writers are doing the same. In the future, boundaries of the new biography could be quite different from those described by Guedalla: to the north, scholarship; to the south, humor; to the west, well-documented detail; and to the east, pleasure.

8

Contemporary Realistic Fiction

Toward Pluralism: Resources for Avoiding Stereotypes and Bias in Children's Literature

Arthur N. Applebee

When children meet their literature, they are also likely to encounter bias and stereotyping in the portrayal of men, women, the old, the young, Native Americans, Chicanos, blacks, whites . . . of virtually any group that can be singled out and distinguished from any other. When the elderly are always depicted as passive and unproductive, when women always work diligently in the home, when blacks always live in the inner city ghetto, then the books being read are biased and narrow.

Awareness of such stereotypes has escalated since the early 1960s. Then, in the context of the Civil Rights struggle, educators discovered that many of the materials they were using presented a distorted portrait of black Americans—or simply failed to mention them at all. In the years that have followed, similar distortions have been found in the portrayal of women, of other racial and ethnic minorities, of the aged, and of the handicapped.

The items which follow, drawn from materials recently made available through the ERIC system, illustrate the biases that have been discovered and provide guidance for teachers who want to avoid them.

Racism

Blacks

Studies such as Broderick's [ED 082 233] extensive analysis of the image of the black have documented the stereotypes of black people in traditional children's literature, from the happy slave to the missionary for the race. Broderick commented, however, that the problem in most books is not outright racism (though there are a few examples of that), but a mixture of condescension and unrealistic "do-gooder" books that fail to recognize racism as a social-

SOURCE: *Language Arts*, April 1979, pp. 451–455.

political-economic problem. Her objections to the "do-gooders" are evident in her description of the changes necessary:

> First . . . is that a single white person cannot be shown to change a power structure. . . . Second, it is time to stop making the white individual the all-understanding benefactor of a single black. And third, books about blacks must depict the blacks in control of their own lives and fighting their own battles. The battles being fought must be those that are being fought—not one black against one white bigot, but the black community fighting the structure of white society, whether the fight concerns the right to go to a school of one's choice, or the right to eat at a lunch counter, or the right to work at a job of one's preference. (p. 180)

Stereotypes can be subtle, reflected as much in what is *not* depicted as in content which is objectionable in itself. A lesson sequence developed by Francione H. Lewis [ED 129 457] for the Far West Laboratory for Educational Research and Development provides extensive materials to give adults working with young children a better understanding of the black perspective. In addition to background material about black culture and history, the units include criteria for evaluating books and illustrations. Readers are shown how to apply these criteria to sample texts and how to interpret the results of their analyses. To avoid narrow stereotypes, the lessons stress the need to depict black people in a variety of contexts. Criteria for evaluating illustrations, for example, include attention to occupational and household responsibilities, housing and community settings, family situations, and skin tones (favoring a range from light to dark rather than a universal "brown").

Chicanos

Though stereotypes of black Americans have been studied and discussed most fully, other ethnic minorities are also inadequately depicted in many children's books. In a parallel set of materials from the Far West Laboratory, Oscar Uribe, Jr. and Joseph Martinez [ED 129 458] have prepared a lesson sequence for adults who will be working with young children of Mexican American heritage. In addition to criteria for detecting culturally negative biases and factual errors, the lessons underline the importance of understanding the history, culture, and language of the Chicano. Pictures and text from selections often recommended for use with the Chicano child are used for practice in applying the evaluative criteria; self-assessment activities involve the revision of sample paragraphs to conform with the guidelines given.

Asian Americans

A year-long study of books about Asian Americans, sponsored by the Council on Interracial Books for Children [ED 123 315], found an almost intolerable situation. Not only were there only sixty-six children's books about Asian Americans during the thirty-year period studied, but "the major conclusion was that, with one or perhaps two exceptions, the sixty-six books are racist, sexist, and elitist, and that the image of Asian Americans they present is grossly misleading." This image is of "foreigners who all look alike and choose to live together in quaint communities in the midst of large cities that cling to 'outworn,' alien customs." Many of the problems found by the committee echo those surrounding the image of blacks in children's literature—characters and settings are one-dimensional, and of limited variety, with stereotyping of occupations, personalities, home situations, and physical features. The books also suffer from what Broderick [ED 082 233] called "do-gooder" plots, depicting Asian Americans as a "model" minority and individual Asian Americans as flawless paragons who display outstanding abilities and talents in order to win approval and esteem from white Americans. Criteria for analyzing books on Asian Americans are included in the report, as are resources for counteracting prevailing myths and stereotypes.

Native Americans

Native Americans suffer from stereotypes born of the Western novel and its reflections in popular films and television serials. These stereotypes extend even to books that purport to be about the American Indian, as James A. Popp [ED 125 821] discovered when he started to use such books with a class of Indian children at Acomita Day School in Albuquerque, New Mexico. Analyzing forty-nine children's books about the American Indian, he found that seven of the books had an overall negative attitude toward Indians; that nine had at least some derogatory language; that twenty reflected narrow stereotypes in the text; and that twenty-seven reflected stereotyping in the illustrations. The stereotypes were fairly predictable, ranging from such characterizations as "Indians—red savages, noble, perhaps, but savages all the same . . ." to illustrations of "Eskimos standing near igloos in heavy, bright colored clothes, always looking happy, with a dog sled, polar bears, and seals nearby."

To help counteract such stereotypes, June Kahl [ED 128 795] compiled a bibliography of books selected for the authenticity of their content and the avoidance of stereotypes in their portrayal of Indians. More generally, Mary DeWitt Billings et al. [ED 137 177] highlight a variety of racial and ethnic minorities in their annotations of multiethnic books published during 1975 and 1976.

Sexism

Just as the Civil Rights movement discovered pervasive racism, the Women's movement found sex-role stereotyping in all aspects of American culture, children's books included. Nilsen et al. [ED 136 260] provide a thorough review of the movement and extensive documentation of sexism in areas as diverse as the language of law, the language of marriage, and the language of children's books and elementary teaching materials. Again, the bias took two forms: an underrepresentation of women in many materials, and the limitation of those women who do appear to a restricted range of roles, settings, and personality types. Summarizing earlier analyses of children's books, Nilsen notes that in one study which included reading texts from fourteen major publishers, five boys were pictured for every two girls, and "clever" boys appeared four times as often as "clever girls." In "nearly all stories, females played a supportive, appreciative role while males were showing their strength, bravery, and leadership skills" (p. 163).

In response to such concerns, many bibliographies and resource lists of sex-fair materials have been compiled. The Women's Action Alliance [ED 150 989] has annotated nonsexist picture books and children's stories, as well as instructional aids, reading texts, toys, and other materials. Judith Adell and Hilary Dole Klein [ED 122 267], limiting themselves to 141 books that portray boys and girls as people with the same kinds of strengths and weaknesses, provide more extensive annotations for the titles in their collection. Nancy Motomatsu [ED 127 408], writing in response to a request from the Task Force on Women and Girls in Education, has compiled a resource list of textbooks and other instructional media presenting a positive image of both sexes. The list is based on the recommendations of various groups, and concerned professional organizations. Motomatsu [ED 154 053] later updated and expanded her listing.

As a result, programs and materials do seem to be changing. In a study of 657 children's books published in 1975 and 1976, Ruth M. Noyce [ED 137 802] found that, in marked contrast with earlier studies, males and females were treated similarly. In her sample, 50.8 percent of the books had a hero and 49.2 percent had a heroine. Perhaps more importantly, when each major character was summed up with the single most appropriate adjective, males and females had very similar portraits. Nearly identical proportions were considered athletic, capable, and even clever; few negative characteristics were assigned to either sex.

The "New" Minorities

Racism and sexism in children's books have been widely documented, and the materials necessary to develop programs free of these sorts of bias have gradually become available. As Joan F. Jaffe [ED 149 379] has pointed out, however, there are many other groups who lack representation in children's books and school materials; these include the aging, the handicapped, and families with nontraditional lifestyles (e.g., those with a single parent, adopted children, or a divorce). Noting that schools should treat these minorities realistically and sympathetically, Jaffe describes books for children and adolescents that feature characters who are blind, mentally retarded, old, or from nontraditional family backgrounds.

Jaffe's concern with the aged echoes a frequently cited report by Edward F. Anselo, published as part of a special issue of the *Bulletin* of the Council on Interracial Books for Children [ED 131 144]. Reporting on an analysis of 549 children's books. Anselo noted that even when he included animal, magical, and "other" characters with humans, older persons were present in only sixteen percent of the books studied; only three percent had an older person as a principal character. Finding that three-fourths of the older characters had no real function or purpose in the books in which they appeared, Anselo commented that the major problem in the depiction of older characters was that they were boring. More materials are needed that show older persons adopting a full range of behaviors, good to bad, active to passive, strong to weak. Other articles in the *Bulletin* provide statistics on the aged in America, describe consciousness-raising activities, and list other resources that can be used in countering ageism in children's books.

Whether the concern is with racism, sexism, or the "new" minorities, the teacher's primary weapon is sensitivity to the issues involved. Few authors suggest removing titles from classroom or library. Rather they seek to insure that the program as a whole provides a realistic and unbiased portrait of our pluralistic culture. No one book is likely to include older characters who are both good and bad, active and passive, strong and weak; neither is any one book likely to depict women pilots, business executives, carpenters, and homemakers. But with careful selection of materials, teachers can make the program as a whole more balanced, and less biased, than it has been in the past.

The ERIC system, by making resources such as those cited here available to teachers throughout the country, is one way in which the effort involved in book selection can be shared. References to other materials on these and related topics can be found in the monthly issues of *Resources in Education*, under such terms as "Children's Literature," "Children's Books," and "Stereotypes."

References

Adell, Judith, and Klein, Hilary Dole. *A Guide to Non-Sexist Children's Books*. Chicago: Academy Press Ltd., 1976 [ED 122 267; not available from EDRS; available from Academy Press Ltd., 176 W. Street, Chicago, Illinois 60603. $3.95 cloth, 133p.]

Billings, Mary DeWitt, and others. "American Potpourri: Multi-ethnic Books for Children and Young Adults." Washington, D.C.: U.S. Office of Education, 1977 [ED 137 177; EDRS Price: MF $0.83 HC $1.67 plus postage, 13p.]

Broderick, Dorothy M. *Image of the Black in Children's Fiction*. New York: R. R. Bowker Co., 1973. [ED 082 233; not available from EDRS; available from R. R.

Bowker Co., 1180 Avenue of the Americas, New York, N.Y. 10036. $12.50, 210p.]

Council on Interracial Books for Children. *Ageism in Children's Books*. (Bulletin, v7 n6.) New York: Council on Interracial Books for Children, 1976. [ED 131 144; EDRS Price: MF $0.83 HC not available from EDRS; available from Council on Interracial Books for Children, 1841 Broadway, New York, N.Y. 10023, $2.00, 25p.]

______. *Asian Americans in Children's Books*. (Bulletin, v7 n2–3). New York: Council on Interracial Books for Children, 1976. [ED 123 315; EDRS Price: MF $0.83 HC not available from EDRS; available from Council on Interracial Books for Children, 1841 Broadway, New York, N.Y. 10023, 40p.]

Jaffee, Joan F. "The Hidden Minorities: Sex and Race Are Not Enough." Paper presented at the 67th Annual Meeting of the National Council of Teachers of English, New York, November 24–26, 1977. [ED 149 379: EDRS Price: MF $0.83 HC $1.67 plus postage. 24p.]

Kahl, June. "Non-Stereotyped Indian Literature: A Bibliography." Prepared in August 1976. [ED 128 795: EDRS Price: MF $0.83 HC $1.67 plus postage, 9p.]

Lewis, Francione N. *Selecting Children's Books with a Black Perspective (Preschool–Third Grade)*. San Francisco: Far West Laboratory for Educational Research and Development, 1975. [ED 129 457: EDRS Price: MF $0.83 HC $11.37 plus postage; also available from Far West Laboratory for Educational Research and Development, 1855 Folsom Street, San Francisco, California 94103, $7.95, 222p.]

Motomatsu, Nancy R. "A Selected Bibliography of Bias-Free Materials: Grades K–12." Olympia, Washington: Office of the State Superintendent of Public Instruction, 1976. [ED 127 408: EDRS Price: MF $0.83 HC $1.67 plus postage, 23p.]

______. "A Selected Bibliography of Sex-Fair Materials." Olympia, Washington: Olympia School District, 1977. [ED 154 053; EDRS Price: MF $0.83 HC $3.50 plus postage, 54p.]

Nilsen, Alleen Pace, and others. *Sexism and Language*. Urbana, Illinois: National Council of Teachers of English, 1977. [ED 136 260; EDRS Price: MF $0.83 HC $11.37 plus postage: also available from National Council of Teachers of English, 1111 Kenyon Road, Urbana, Illinois 61801—Stock No. 43733; members $5.50, nonmembers $5.95, 206p.]

Noyce, Ruth M. "Equality of the Sexes in New Children's Fiction." Report prepared at the University of Kansas, 1976. [ED 137 802; EDRS Price: MF $0.83 HC $.67 plus postage, 7p.]

Popp, James A. "An Examination of Children's Books on the American Indian." *Bureau of Indian Affairs Education Research Bulletin* v3 n1, p10–23, 1975. [ED 125 821; EDRS Price: MF $0.83 HC $1.67 plus postage, 18p.]

Uribe, Oscar, Jr., and Martinez, Joseph S. *Analysing Children's Books from a Chicano Perspective*. San Francisco: Far West Laboratory for Educational Research and Development, 1975. [ED 129 458; EDRS Price: MF $0.83 HC $6.01 plus postage; also available from Far West Laboratory for Educational Research and Development, 1855 Folsom Street, San Francisco, California 94103, $4.95, 105p.]

Women's Action Alliance. "Bibliography of Non-Sexist Materials: Annotated Bibliography of Non-Sexist Picture Books." New York: Women's Action Alliance, Inc., 1976. [ED 150 989; EDRS Price: MF $0.83 HC $1.67 plus postage, 23p.]

The Aged in Young Children's Literature

Phyllis Winet Barnum

> A peasant makes his old father eat out of a small wooden trough, apart from the rest of the family; one day he finds his son fitting little boards together. "It's for you when you are old," says the child. Straight away the grandfather is given back his place at the family table. (Beauvoir 1972, p. 6)

Literature has always had an important role in shaping children's behavior and in introducing them to the norms, roles, and values of society. Today, literature's potential influence on the attitudes of children toward old people may be more important than in earlier eras, because American children are more isolated from old people in real life than they have been in previous periods (Bronfenbrenner 1970).

There is strong negative feeling toward old age and the elderly in United States society. Researchers have found that even third graders have a more positive view of younger adults than of the elderly (Hickey and Kalish 1967), and people of all ages have negative feelings even for the phrase "old age" (Kogan and Wallach 1961). Children's literature may be able to counteract some of these negative attitudes, or at least not contribute to them.

In a recent study of one hundred randomly selected books, Barnum (1977) found that the aged are discriminated against in young children's literature. They appear less frequently than they should, in view of their proportion in the United States population, and are depicted as disadvantaged in many socioeconomic and behavioral characteristics.

It is not known, however, how the aged are represented in books in which they form a major part, or in books which deal specifically with the elderly. Also, the possible results on the young child have not been considered. This article examines those questions in books for children of preschool age through third grade.

Most of the books for young children display stereotyped roles for the female and male aged. The title character in *Mandy's Grandmother* (1975) by Skorpen, for example, wants her granddaughter to wear a frilly dress, and screams when she sees a frog. When two grandparents are shown, the grandmother is always the one found in the kitchen. In Low's *Grandmas and*

SOURCE: *Language Arts* 54 (January 1977): Copyright © 1977 by the National Council of Teachers of English. Reprinted by permission of the publisher and the author.

Grandpas (1962), for example, the grandmother cooks and keeps house, and the grandfather works outside. It is common, as in *Nana Upstairs and Nana Downstairs* (1974) by DePaola that the grandmother never even leaves the house. In contrast, the boy's grandfather takes him on an excursion to the store. Many a grandmother's life revolves around food, like the Italian grandmother of *Watch Out for the Chicken Feet in Your Soup* (1974) by DePaola, who urges the children to eat more.

The physical appearance of old people is depicted in diverse ways. The grandmother of *City in the Winter* (1970) by Schick is urban, lower class, and looks very nurturant. She wears white socks with open-toed bedroom slippers, and is plump, with a sagging bosom. In contrast, the grandmother of Buckley's *Grandmother and I* (1974) is dressed-up in a white collar and dress of subdued hue. Both she and the grandparents in Low's *Grandmas and Grandpas* (1962) are middle class. The witches of *Strega Nona* (1975) by DePaola and *Old Black Witch* (1966) by Devlin are caricatures of old people, since they are gnome-like, with large noses. One finds some minority old people: black grandmothers in *I Love Gram* (1971) by Sonneborn, *Black Is Brown Is Tan* (1973) by Adoff, and *Mary Jo's Grandmother* (1970) by Udry. There is a Mexican grandmother in *Grandma's Gun* (1968) by Martinson and a *Vietnamese* old woman in Coutant's *First Snow* (1974).

Old people in young children's literature are almost unfailingly pleasant. The grandmother of *Grandmother Dear* (1966) by Finfer, for one, endures all sorts of exhausting activities without complaining. In the twenty illustrations in which they appear in Low's *Grandmas and Grandpas* (1962), the grandparents are smiling in seventeen illustrations. The effect is a lack of humanness, since old people do not demonstrate a range of realistic emotions. One notable exception to this pervasive gaiety is the depressed grandfather in *Grandpa's Long Red Underwear* (1972) by Schoettle.

Most young children's books also elaborate on the pleasant activities grandparents and grandchildren engage in together. The grandfather and grandson in *Grandpa and Me* (1962) by Gauch spend their vacation alone together on the beach. During a blizzardy day the grandmother in *City in the Winter* (Schnick 1970) makes hot chocolate and soup, and plans activities for her grandson. The black city child in Sonneborn's *I Love Gram* (1971) thinks about how her grandmother picks her up at school and entertains her while her mother is at work. Although almost all books dealing with grandparents include a section with this theme, children in literature rarely spend such a pleasant time with aged who are not related.

Apart from the social life with their grandchildren, however, old people almost never engage in social activities outside the home. They do not become involved in politics, belong to clubs, attend concerts or lectures. They are typically shown at home or visiting grandchildren, occasionally at work, or in a brief excursion with a grandchild to the park or a store. One rare and delightful exception is the fictitious grandmother in *Kevin's Grandma* (1975) by Williams. A little boy tells his friend Kevin about his grandmother's interests: she belongs to a music club, a garden club, and a bridge club. Not to be outdone, Kevin invents some social activities for his grandma. He says that she belongs to a karate club, a scuba-diver's club, and a mountain-climbing club.

Many of the grandparents in children's literature are wise or able. In fact, some know more than the child's own parents. Albert's grandmother in *Albert's Toothache* (1974) by Williams knows just how to find out what ails him and how to make his toothache better. She is contrasted with Albert's impatient parents, who insist that turtles do not have teeth. Similarly, the grandmother in *William's Doll* (1972) by Zolotow knows that he should have the doll he wants with the china blue eyes, and that having a doll will not make him a sissy.

> He needs it . . . to hug and to cuddle and to take to the park so that when he's a father like you, he'll know how to take care of his baby . . . (pp. 30–31)

The old black witch in Delvin's (1966) book, while not wise, is competent. With a spell she turns two robbers into two big toads. Similarly, the title character of *Strega Nona* (1975) by DePaola knows so many potions that the townspeople come to her for help.

In many other books, however, the aged are passive or incompetent. In all of the seven illustrations in which the grandmother appears in Buckley's *Grandmother and I* (1966) she is either sitting in her rocker or leading the grandchild to the rocking chair. The grandmother of *Cranberry Thanksgiving* (1971) by Devlin foolishly judges people's character by their appearance and cleanliness, although her young granddaughter knows better. Granny Guntry in Parish's *Granny, the Baby, and the Big Gray Thing* (1972) cannot distinguish a wolf from a dog, and brings the wolf into her home. With good intentions but bad results, Granny carries home an Indian baby she finds in the forest that is really not lost. The Indians become so disgruntled by her foolish mistakes that they decide that they may have to shoot her yet. Even though the old woman in *Mary Jo's Grandmother* (1970) by Udry is warned by her children not to live alone in the country, she persists. When she sprains her ankle, her grandchild has to go out into the snow to summon help.

Some old people have a different sense of reality than younger adults. Senility causes the greatgrandmother in *Nana Upstairs and Nana Downstairs* (1974) by DePaola to enjoy the presence of a leprechaun on her dresser who does not exist. She tells Tommy:

> Watch out for the fresh one with the red hat with the feather in it. He plays with matches. (p. 10)

The old man in *Matt's Grandfather* (1972) by Lundgren does not recognize his son and grandson when they come to visit because of his senility. Matt's grandfather also has a differing sense of time than other people—a feeling of timelessness.

> For me, for happy people, there is no such thing as time. (p. 11)

In this sample of young children's literature in which the elderly play a major part, there are some positive features in the way old people are depicted. One finds old people with varying physical features; minority and non-minority, caricatured and more realistically depicted. Children who read these books are reminded of the pleasant activities they enjoy with their grandparents. Some of the old people are especially wise or competent. A different, though enjoyable, sense of reality is shown to be a by-product of old age for some people.

There are distressingly negative aspects of the treatment of the elderly in young children's literature, however. Old age is not depicted as the fruitful and enjoyable period of life it can be, because old people are seldom shown as engaged in social activities. Also, because male and female aged are presented in stereotyped sex roles, and so often lacking in a range of human emotions, they seem to be two-dimensional characters. Similarly unappealing is the fact that many old people are passive or incompetent. Encouragement is not given for casual socializing with old people, because children in literature do not engage in pleasant activities with aged people to whom they are not related.

The young child learns from these books unfortunate lessons about old people: that they are not active or interesting, that old age is a period of restricted social activity, and that unless they are relatives, one does not associate with them. The result then is that these negative characteristics help produce or reinforce society's negative stereotypes about old age.

References

Adoff, Arnold. *Black Is Brown Is Tan*. New York: Harper and Row, 1973.

Barnum, Phyllis W. "Discriminating Against the Aged in Young Children's Literature." *The Elementary School Journal* (1977): in press.

Beauvoir, Simone de. *The Coming of Age*. New York: G.P. Putnam's Sons, 1972.

Bronfenbrenner, Urie. *Two Worlds of Childhood: U.S. and U.S.S.R.* New York: Russell Sage Foundation, 1970.

Buckley, Helen E. *Grandmother and I*. New York: Lothrop, Lee and Shepard Co., 1966.

Coutant, Helen. *First Snow*. New York: Alfred A. Knopf, 1974.

DePaola, Tomie. *Nana Upstairs and Nana Downstairs*. New York: G.P. Putnam's Sons, 1974.

______. *Strega Nona*. Englewood Cliffs, New Jersey: Prentice-Hall, 1975.

______. *Watch Out for the Chicken Feet in Your Soup*. Englewood Cliffs, New Jersey: Prentice-Hall, 1974.

Devlin, Wende, and Devlin, Harry. *Cranberry Thanksgiving*. New York: Parents' Magazine Press, 1971.

______. *Old Black Witch*. New York: Parents' Magazine Press, 1966.

Finfer, Celentha, Wasserberg, Esther, and Weinberg, Florence. *Grandmother Dear*. Chicago: Follett Publishing Co., 1966.

Gauch, Patricia L. *Grandpa and Me*. New York: Coward, McCann and Geoghegan. Inc., 1972.
Hickey, T., and Kalish, R.A. "The Attitudes of Young People and Children Toward Adults and the Elderly." *Psychological Abstracts* 41 (1967): 1686.
Kogan, Nathan, and Wallach, Michael A. "Age Changes In Values and Attitudes." *Journal of Gerontology* 16 (1961): 272–280.
Low, Alice. *Grandmas and Grandpas*. New York: Random House, 1962.
Lundgren, Max. *Matt's Grandfather*. New York: G.P. Putnam's Sons, 1972.
Martinson, Patricia, M. *Grandma's Gun*. San Carlos, Cal.: Golden Gate Junior Books, 1968.
Parish, Peggy. *Granny, the Baby and the Big Gray Thing*. New York: The Macmillan Co., 1972.
Schick, Eleanor. *City in the Winter*. London: The Macmillan Co., 1970.
Schoettle, Lynn. *Grandpa's Long Red Underwear*. New York: Lothrop, Lee and Shepard Co., 1972.
Skorpen, Liesel Moak. *Mandy's Grandmother*. New York: The Dial Press, 1975.
Sonneborn, Ruth A. *I Love Gram*. New York: The Viking Press, 1971.
Udry, Janice M. *Mary Jo's Grandmother*. Chicago: Albert Whitman and Co., 1970.
Williams, Barbara. *Albert's Toothache*. New York: E. P. Dutton and Co., 1974.
______. *Kevin's Grandma*. New York: E. P. Dutton and Co., Inc., 1975.
Zolotow, Charlotte. *William's Doll*. New York: Harper and Row, 1972.

Guidelines for Equal Treatment of the Sexes

McGraw-Hill Book Company

Introduction

The word *sexism* was coined, by analogy to *racism,* to denote discrimination based on gender. In its original sense, *sexism* referred to prejudice against the female sex. In a broader sense, the term now indicates any arbitrary stereotyping of males and females on the basis of their gender.

We are endeavoring through these guidelines to eliminate sexist assumptions from McGraw-Hill Book Company publications and to encourage a greater freedom for all individuals to pursue their interests and realize their potentials. Specifically, these guidelines are designed to make McGraw-Hill staff members and McGraw-Hill authors aware of the ways in which males and females have been stereotyped in publications; to show the role language has played in reinforcing inequality; and to indicate positive approaches toward providing fair, accurate, and balanced treatment of both sexes in our publications.

One approach is to recruit more women as authors and contributors in all fields. The writings and viewpoints of women should be represented in quotations and references whenever possible. Anthologies should include a larger proportion of selections by and about women in fields where suitable materials are available but women are currently underrepresented.

Women as well as men have been leaders and heroes, explorers and pioneers, and have made notable contributions to science, medicine, law, business, politics, civics, economics, literature, the arts, sports, and other areas of endeavor. Books dealing with subjects like these, as well as general histories, should acknowledge the achievements of women. The fact that women's rights, opportunities, and accomplishments have been limited by the social customs and conditions of their time should be openly discussed whenever relevant to the topic at hand.

We realize that the language of literature cannot be prescribed. The recommendations in these guidelines, thus, are intended primarily for use in teaching materials, reference works, and nonfiction works in general.

Nonsexist Treatment of Women and Men

Men and women should be treated primarily as people, and not primarily as members of opposite sexes. Their shared humanity and common attributes should be stressed—not their gender difference. Neither sex should be stereotyped or arbitrarily assigned to a leading or secondary role.

1. a. Though many women will continue to choose traditional occupations such as homemaker or secretary, women should not be type-cast in these roles but shown in a wide variety of professions and trades: as doctors and dentists, not always as nurses; as principals and professors, not always as teachers; as lawyers and judges, not always as social workers; as bank presidents, not always as tellers; as members of Congress, not always as members of the League of Women Voters.
   b. Similarly, men should not be shown as constantly subject to the "masculine mystique" in their interests, attitudes, or careers. They should not be made to feel that their self-worth depends entirely upon their income level or the status level of their jobs. They should not be con-

ditioned to believe that a man ought to earn more than a woman or that he ought to be the sole support of a family.

c. An attempt should be made to break job stereotypes for both women and men. No job should be considered sex-typed, and it should never be implied that certain jobs are incompatible with a woman's "femininity" or a man's "masculinity." Thus, women as well as men should be shown as accountants, engineers, pilots, plumbers, bridge-builders, computer operators, TV repairers, and astronauts, while men as well as women should be shown as nurses, grade-school teachers, secretaries, typists, librarians, file clerks, switchboard operators, and baby sitters.

   Women with a profession should be shown at all professional levels, including the top levels. Women should be portrayed in positions of authority over men and over other women, and there should be no implication that a man loses face or that a woman faces difficulty if the employer or supervisor is a woman. All work should be treated as honorable and worthy of respect; no job or job choices should be downgraded. Instead, women and men should be offered more options than were available to them when work was stereotyped by sex.

d. Books designed for children at the pre-school, elementary, and secondary levels should show married women who work outside the home and should treat them favorably. Teaching materials should not assume or imply that most women are wives who are also full-time mothers, but should instead emphasize the fact that women have choices about their marital status, just as men do: that some women choose to stay permanently single and some are in no hurry to marry; that some women marry but do not have children, while others marry, have children, and continue to work outside the home. Thus, a text might say that some married people have children and some do not, and that sometimes *one or both parents* work outside the home. Instructional materials should never imply that all women have a "mother instinct" or that the emotional life of a family suffers because a woman works. Instead they might state that when both parents work outside the home there is usually either greater sharing of the child-rearing activities or reliance on day-care centers, nursery schools, or other help.

   According to Labor Department statistics for 1972, over 42 per cent of all mothers with children under 18 worked outside the home, and about a third of these working mothers had children under 6. Publications ought to reflect this reality.

   Both men and women should be shown engaged in home maintenance activities, ranging from cooking and housecleaning to washing the car and making household repairs. Sometimes the man should be shown preparing the meals, doing the laundry, or diapering the baby, while the woman builds bookcases or takes out the trash.

e. Girls should be shown as having, and exercising, the same options as boys in their play and career choices. In school materials, girls should be encouraged to show an interest in mathematics, mechanical skills, and active sports, for example, while boys should never be made to feel ashamed of an interest in poetry, art, or music, or an aptitude for cooking, sewing, or child care. Course materials should be addressed to students of both sexes. For example, home economics courses should apply to boys as well as girls, and shop to girls as well as boys. Both males and females should be shown in textbook illustrations depicting career choices.

When as a practical matter it is known that a book will be used primarily by women for the life of the edition (say, the next five years), it is pointless to pretend that the readership is divided equally between males and females. In such cases it may be more beneficial to address the book fully to women and exploit every opportunity (1) to point out to them a broader set of options than they might otherwise have considered, and (2) to encourage them to aspire to a more active, assertive, and policymaking role than they might otherwise have thought of.

f. Women and girls should be portrayed as active participants in the same proportion as men and boys in stories, examples, problems, illustrations, discussion questions, test items, and exercises, regardless of subject matter. Women should not be stereotyped in examples by being spoken of only in connection with cooking, sewing, shopping, and similar activities.

2. a. Members of both sexes should be represented as whole human beings with *human* strengths and weaknesses, not masculine or feminine ones. Women and girls should be shown as having the same abilities, interets, and ambitions as men and boys. Characteristics that have been traditionally praised in males—such as boldness, initiative, and assertiveness—should also be praised in females. Characteristics that have been praised in females—such as gentleness, compassion, and sensitivity—should also be praised in males.

b. Like men and boys, women and girls should be portrayed as independent, active, strong, courageous, competent, decisive, persistent, serious-minded, and successful. They should appear as logical thinkers, problem-solvers, and decision makers. They should be shown as interested in their work, pursuing a variety of career goals, and both deserving of and receiving public recognition for their accomplishments.

c. Sometimes men should be shown as quiet and passive, or fearful and indecisive, or illogical and immature. Similarly, women should sometimes be shown as tough, aggressive, and insensitive. Stereotypes of the logical, objective male and the emotional, subjective female are to be avoided. In descriptions, the smarter, braver, or more successful person should be a woman or girl as often as a man or boy. In illustrations, the taller, heavier, stronger, or more active person should not always be male, especially when children are portrayed.

3. Women and men should be treated with the same respect, dignity, and seriousness. Neither should be trivialized or stereotyped, either in text or in illustrations. Women should not be described by physical attributes when men are being described by mental attributes or professional position. Instead, both sexes should be dealt with in the same terms. References to a man's or a woman's appearance, charm, or intuition should be avoided when irrelevant.

no

Henry Harris is a shrewd lawyer and his wife Ann is a striking brunette.

yes

The Harrises are an attractive couple. Henry is a handsome blond and Ann is a striking brunette.

OR

The Harrises are highly respected in their fields. Ann is an accomplished musician and Henry is a shrewd lawyer. The Harrises are an interesting couple. Henry is a shrewd lawyer and Ann is very active in community (*or* church *or* civic) affairs.

a. In descriptions of women, a patronizing or girl-watching tone should be avoided, as should sexual innuendoes, jokes, and puns. Examples of practices to be avoided: focusing on physical appearance (a buxom blonde); using special female-gender word forms (poetess, aviatrix, usherette); treating women as sex objects or portraying the typical woman as weak, helpless, or hysterical; making women figures of fun or objects of scorn and treating their issues as humorous or unimportant.
   Examples of stereotypes to be avoided: scatterbrained female, fragile flower, goddess on a pedestal, catty gossip, henpecking shrew, apron-wearing mother, frustrated spinster, ladylike little girl. Jokes at women's expense-such as the woman driver or nagging mother-in-law cliches—are to be avoided.

no

the fair sex; the weaker sex

yes

women

no

the distaff side

yes

the female side or *line*

no

the girls or *the ladies* (when adult females are meant)

yes

the women

no

girl, as in: I'll have my *girl* check that.

yes

I'll have my *secretary* (or my *assistant*) check that. (Or use the person's name.)

no

lady used as a modifier, as in *lady* lawyer

yes

lawyer (A woman may be identified simply through the choice of pronouns, as in: *The lawyer made her summation to the jury*. Try to avoid gender modifiers altogether. When you *must* modify, use *woman* or *female,* as in: *a course on women writers,* or *the airline's first female pilot*.)

no

the little woman; the better half; the ball and chain

yes

wife

no

female-gender word forms, such as *authoress, poetess, Jewess*

yes

author, poet, Jew

no

female-gender or diminutive word forms, such as *suffragette, usherette, aviatrix*

yes

suffragist, usher, aviator (or *pilot*)

no

libber (a put-down)

yes

feminist; liberationist

no

sweet young thing

yes

young woman; girl

no

co-ed (as a noun)

yes

student
(*Note:* Logically, *co-ed* should refer to any student at a co-educational college or university. Since it does not, it is a sexist term.)

no

housewife

yes

homemaker for a person who works at home, or rephrase with a more precise or more inclusive term.

no

career girl or *career woman*

yes

name the woman's profession: *attorney Ellen Smith; Marie Sanchez, a journalist* or editor or business executive or doctor or lawyer or agent

no

cleaning woman, cleaning lady, or *maid*

yes

housekeeper; house or *office cleaner*

no

The sound of the drilling disturbed the housewives in the neighborhood.

yes

The sound of the drilling disturbed everyone within earshot (or everyone in the neighborhood).

no

Housewives are feeling the pinch of higher prices.

yes

Consumers (customers or shoppers) are feeling the pinch of higher prices.

b. In descriptions of men, especially men in the home, references to general ineptness should be avoided. Men should not be characterized as dependent on women for meals, or clumsy in household maintenance, or as foolish in self-care.

To be avoided: characterizations that stress men's dependence on women for advice on what to wear and what to eat, inability of men to care for themselves in times of illness, and men as objects of fun (the henpecked husband).

c. Women should be treated as part of the rule, not as the exception. Generic terms, such as *doctor* and *nurse,* should be assumed to include both men and women, and modified titles such as "woman doctor" or "male nurse," should be avoided. Work should never be stereotyped as "woman's work" or as "a man-sized job." Writers should avoid showing a "gee-whiz" attitude toward women who perform competently; ("Though a woman, she ran the business as well as any man" or "Though a woman, she ran the business efficiently.")

d. Women should be spoken of as participants in the action, not as possessions of the men. Terms such as *pioneer, farmer,* and *settler* should not be used as though they applied only to adult males.

no

Pioneers moved West, taking their wives and children with them.

yes

Pioneer families moved West.

Pioneer men and women (or pioneer couples) moved West, taking their children with them.

e. Women should not be portrayed as needing male permission in order to act or to exercise rights (except, of course, for historical or factual accuracy).

no

Jim Weiss allows his wife to work part-time.

yes

Judy Weiss works part-time.

4. Women should be recognized for their own achievements. Intelligent, daring, and innovative women, both in history and in fiction, should be provided as role-models for girls, and leaders in the fight for women's rights should be honored and respected, not mocked or ignored.
5. In references to humanity at large, language should operate to include women and girls. Terms that tend to exclude females should be avoided whenever possible.

a. The word *man* has long been used not only to denote a person of male gender, but also generically to denote humanity at large. To many people today, however, the word *man* has become so closely associated with the first meaning (a male human being) that they consider it no longer broad enough to be applied to any person or to human beings as a whole. In deference to this position, alternative expressions should be used in place of *man* (or derivative constructions used generically to signify humanity at large) whenever such substitutions can be made without producing an awkward or artificial construction. In cases where *man*-words must be used, special efforts should be made to ensure that pictures and other devices make explicit that such references include women.

Here are some possible substitutions for *man*-words:

no

mankind

yes

humanity, human beings, human race, people

no

primitive man

yes

primitive people or peoples; primitive human beings; primitive men and women

no

man's achievements

yes

human achievements

no

If a man drove 50 miles at 60 mph . . .

yes

If a person (or driver) drove 50 miles at 60 mph . . .

no

the best man for the job

yes

the best person (or candidate) for the job

no

manmade

yes

artificial; synthetic, manufactured; constructed; of human origin

no

manpower

yes

human power; human energy; workers; workforce

no

grow to manhood

yes

grow to adulthood; grow to manhood or womanhood

b. The English language lacks a generic singular pronoun signifying *he* or *she*, and therefore it has been customary and grammatically sanctioned to use masculine pronouns in expressions such as "one . . . *he*," "anyone . . . *he*," and "each child opens *his* book." Nevertheless, avoid when possible the pronouns *he*, *him*, and *his* in reference to the hypothetical person or humanity in general.

Various alternatives may be considered:

(1) Reword to eliminate unnecessary gender pronouns.

no

The average American drinks his coffee black

yes

The average American drinks black coffee.

(2) Recast into the plural.

yes

Most Americans drink their coffee black.

(3) Replace the masculine pronoun with *one*, *you*, *he or she*, *her or his*, as appropriate. (Use *he or she* and its variations sparingly to avoid clumsy prose.)

(4) Alternate male and female expressions and examples.

no

I've often heard supervisors say, "He's not the right man for the job," or "He lacks the qualifications for success."

yes

I've often heard supervisors say, "She's not the right person for the job," or "He lacks the qualifications for success."

(5) To avoid severe problems of repetition or inept wording, it may sometimes be best to use the generic *he* freely, but to add, in the preface and as often as necessary in the text, emphatic statements to the effect that the masculine pronouns are being used for succinctness and are intended to refer to both females and males.

These guidelines can only suggest a few solutions to difficult problems of rewording. The proper solution in any given passage must depend on the context and on the author's intention. For example, it would be wrong to pluralize in contexts stressing a one-to-one relationship, as between teacher and child. In such cases, the expression *he or she* or either *he* or *she* as appropriate will be acceptable.

c. Occupational terms ending in *man* should be replaced whenever possible by terms that can include members of either sex unless they refer to a particular person.

no

congressman

yes

member of Congress; representative (but Congress*man* Koch and Congress*woman* Holzman)

no

businessman

yes

business executive; business manager

no

fireman

yes

fire fighter

no

mailman

yes

mail carrier; letter carrier

no

salesman

yes

sales representative; sales-person; sales clerk

no

insurance man

yes

insurance agent

no

statesman

yes

leader; public servant

no

chairman

yes

the person presiding at (or chairing) a meeting; the presiding officer; the chair, head; leader; coordinator; moderator

no

cameraman

yes

camera operator

no

foreman

yes

supervisor

d. Language that assumes all readers are male should be avoided.

no

you and your wife
when you shave in the morning

yes

you and your spouse
when you brush your teeth (or wash up) in the morning

6. The language used to designate and describe females and males should treat the sexes equally.

a. Parallel language should be used for women and men.

no

the men and the ladies

yes

the men and the women
the ladies and the gentlemen
the girls and the boys

no

man and wife

yes

husband and wife

Note that *lady* and *gentleman, wife* and *husband,* and *mother* and *father* are role words. *Ladies* should be used for women only when men are being referred to as *gentlemen.* Similarly, women should be called *wives* and *mothers* only when men are referred to as *husbands* and *fathers*. Like a male shopper, a woman in a grocery store should be called a *customer,* not a *housewife.*

b. Women should be identified by their own names (e.g., Indira Gandhi). They should not be referred to in terms of their roles as wife, mother, sister, or daughter unless it is in these roles that they are significant in context. Nor should they be identified in terms of their marital relationships (Mrs. Gandhi) unless this brief form is stylistically more convenient (than, say, Prime Minister Gandhi) or is paired up with similar references to men.

(1) A woman should be referred to by name in the same way that a man is. Both should be called by their full names, by first or last name only, or by title.

no

Bobby Riggs and Billie Jean

yes

Bobby Riggs and Billie Jean King

no

Billie Jean and Riggs

yes

Billie Jean and Bobby

no

Mrs. King and Riggs

yes

King and Riggs
Ms. King (because she prefers Ms.) and Mr. Riggs

no

Mrs. Meir and Moshe Dayan

yes

Golda Meir and Moshe Dayan or Mrs. Meir and Dr. Dayan

(2) Unnecessary reference to or emphasis on a woman's marital status should be avoided. Whether married or not, a woman may be referred to by the name by which she chooses to be known, whether her name is her original name or her married name.

c. Whenever possible, a term should be used that includes both sexes. Unnecessary references to gender should be avoided.

no

college boys and co-eds

yes

students

d. Insofar as possible, job titles should be nonsexist. Different nomenclature should not be used for the same job depending on whether it is held by a male or by a female. (See also paragraph 5c for additional examples of words ending in *man*.)

no

steward or purser or stewardess

yes

flight attendant

no

policeman and policewoman

yes

police officer

no

maid and houseboy

yes

house or office cleaner, servant

e. Different pronouns should not be linked with certain work or occupations on the assumption that the worker is always (or usually) female or male. Instead either pluralize or use *he or she* and *she or he.*

no

the consumer or shopper . . . she

yes

consumers or shoppers . . . they

no

the secretary . . . she

yes

secretaries . . . they

no

the breadwinner . . . his earnings

yes

the breadwinner . . . his or her earnings *or* breadwinners . . . their earnings.

f. Males should not always be first in order of mention. Instead, alternate the order, sometimes using: *women and men, gentlemen and ladies, she or he, her or his.*

Little Girls and Picture Books: Problem and Solution

Kathy Byrne de Filippo

I have a vested interest in literature for little girls because I used to be one myself and because I have the privilege of being the mother of Betsy, who is six, and of Sharon, who is three. I also must admit that I relish the role of being champion of the underdog and, in the field of literature for young children, that's what little girls undeniably are.

SOURCE: *Reading Teacher,* April 1976, pp. 671–674. Reprinted with permission of the International Reading Association.

I read a number of articles on the subject by what I assumed to be feminist fanatics. I was all set to temper their enthusiasm with my more moderate rationality, but I found this to be unnecessary. I had underestimated their fairness. The research of Weitzman and others (1972), Stewig and Higgs (1973), and Nilsen (1971), points unmistakably to the unfair deal that little girls and women have gotten in the past in children's literature. However, I found none of them suggesting that we burn all the great books about little boys or change all the names from Joe to Joanne. Rather, I found the realistic suggestion that we start balancing those library shelves with books which bring the image of little girls up to date.

Weitzman, Eifler, Hokada, and Ross (1972) found by examining the Caldecott winners and runners-up for the past five years that only two of the eighteen stories were about girls. As a matter of fact, in one-third of the sample there were no women at all. They found 261 pictures of males as compared to twenty-three females. The activities of the girls were mostly passive, immobile, and took place indoors. Not one woman in the Caldecott sample had a job or profession (this is a country where 40 percent of the women work). Motherhood, they found, was portrayed in an "unrealistic" way.

> She is almost always confined to the house, although she is usually too well dressed for housework. Her duties are not portrayed as difficult or challenging . . . she is shown as a housebound servant who cares for her husband and children. (p. 1141)

Alleen Pace Nilsen did a similar study using, however, all the Caldecott winners and runners-up for the past twenty years. There were eighty books in all. She found 386 females illustrated as compared to 579 males. All of the books had at least one male character (human or animal) but females were omitted altogether from six books and in one-fourth of the sample only token females were found.

Nilsen sounded another distressing note when she pointed out that there has been a steady decrease of illustrated books written for or about girls (at least up to the time of her study in 1970). From 1956 to 1960 the percentage of girls pictured in the survey books was 41 percent, whereas the percentage from 1966 to 1970 had shrunk to 26 percent. She writes:

> There was not a single book in the survey that I would not want my daughter to read. On the other hand, I would be very distressed if these books were the only books available to her. If a girl is continually faced with books where the boy does all the explaining while the girl does all the listening, where the boy does all the traveling while the girl does all the waving, where the boy does all the complaining while the girl does all the smiling, and worst of all, where the boy does all the everything and the girl isn't even visible, then I think it reasonable to predict that the girl might have problems in finding her own identity. (p. 920)

Stewig and Higgs did their study on 154 picture books selected randomly from the library shelves in a university education department. The publication dates ranged from 1903 to 1971. They found in the books they studied that women played a "subordinate, home-related role." Only 65 percent of their sample included women in any role at all, and 83 percent of the time it was in a homemaking role. As Stewig and Higgs state:

> the inescapable conclusion to be drawn from this set of books is that women are not depicted in the rich variety of professional roles in which they are engaged today. (p. 241)

All of these studies show clearly that women, who comprise 51 percent of the population in this country, make a very paltry and unrealistic showing in the literature available for young children. The point now is what to do about it.

First, I think there must be an awareness of the problem by those in a position to do something about it. Publishers, writers, and illustrators, those who influence what is being produced today, can work toward presenting a more varied picture of females, one which is a more accurate reflection of women today.

Secondly, the purchasers of children's books can have an influence on what is being produced by carefully selecting those books which are fair to both sexes. This economic message will surely be heard by publishers.

Finally, while we wait for these long-term solutions to take effect, librarians, teachers, and parents must make a special effort to compensate for the imbalance on the library shelves of today. They should take the trouble to search for those books which contribute to a nonstereotyped image for little girls and which serve to balance the existing male dominance. I have done just that. The resulting book list is for Betsy and Sharon.

Like the studies I have quoted, I have restricted my list to picture books. Readers of picture books are at an important stage in their sex-role education. Their perception of sex roles and how they as individuals might fit into them is being formed. It is crucial at this stage to present a fair and balanced picture to them.

At my local library I was able to find very few of the books which are on the Non-sexist Children's Bibliography which I obtained from the National Organization of Women. Hopefully, this would indicate that more are available elsewhere.

The principal criteria I used in my selection process were: 1) the book must be a good piece of children's literature in its own right; 2) the book must be fair in its treatment of both sexes; and 3) the book must help to balance in some way the male dominance existing in picture books.

Books can do this in many different ways. I think it's important that we don't fall into stereotyping at the other extreme. Not all of the books on my list depict the "liberated" female image. Rather, they present a varied picture.

Additionally, I am not suggesting that these be the only books that little girls read. However, I think that many of them should be included in the reading material offered to a little girl to insure a balanced view.

One observation I would like to make, having completed my search, is that unfortunately there are far more books about girls available than there are *good* books about girls. Not too many of them come up to the caliber of *Where the Wild Things Are,* but many are still worth reading.

Perhaps we should set as the ultimate goal the day when we just enjoy the books with our children, when they are equally about girls and boys, so that we don't even notice which. However, we are not there yet and the existing problem must be dealt with. Betsy and Sharon and all the little girls like them deserve all the encouragement they can get to be all they can be.

Books for Girls

Anderson, C. W. *Pony for Three*. Macmillan. 1959. Equal presentation of both sexes.

Babbitt, Natalie. *Phoebe's Revolt*. Ariel Book, 1968. Active role.

Bemelmans, Lud. *Madeline and the Bad Hat*. Viking, 1956. Active role.

Burton, Virginia. *Katy and the Big Snow*. Houghton Mifflin, 1943. A children's classic. Female main character.

Burton, Virginia. *The Little House*. Houghton Mifflin, 1942. Excellent book. Female main character.

Carroll, Lewis. *Alice in Wonderland*. Golden Press, 1951. Active role.

Chorao, Kay. *A Magic Eye for Ida*. Seabury Press, 1973. Fun book. Nonstereotyped female.

Coombs, Patricia. *Dorrie and the Goblin*. Lothrop, Lee & Shepard, 1972. Active role.

Duvoisin, Roger. *Jasmine*. Alfred A. Knopf, 1973. Individuality stressed. Female leadership.

Estes, Eleanor. *The Hundred Dresses*. Harcourt, Brace & World, 1944. Good literature. Female main characters.

Ets, Marie Hall. *Play with Me*. Viking, 1955. Fine book. Female main character.

Fenner, Carol. *Tigers in the Cellar*. Harcourt, Brace & World, 1963. Nonstereotyped female.

Fisher, Aileen. *In the Middle of the Night*. Crowell, 1965. Beautiful book. Female main character.

Fisher, Aileen. *Up, Up the Mountain*. Crowell, 1968. Equal presentation of both sexes.

Flora, James. *Leopold, the See-Through Crumbpicker*. Harcourt, Brace & World, 1961. Active role.

Gaeddert, LouAnn. *Noisy Nancy Norris*. Doubleday, 1965. Strong female character.

Handforth, Tom. Mei Li. Doubleday, 1938. Active female role.

Hoban, Russell. *Bedtime for Frances*. Harper & Row, 1960. Lovely children's book. Female main character.

Hurd, Edith. *The Mother Beaver*. Little, Brown, 1971. Strong female model.

Kaufman, Joe. *Busy People and How They Do Their Work*. Golden Press, 1973. Nonstereotyped career portraits.

Kant, Jack. *Fly Away Home*. David McKay, 1969. Charming book. Female main character.

Kindred, Wendy. *Lucky Wilma*. Dial Press, 1973. Interesting book. Female main character.

Klein, Norma. *Girls Can Be Anything*. E. P. Dutton, 1973. Nonstereotyped career goals.

Lawrence, Jacob. *Harriet and the Promised Land*. Simon & Schuster, 1968. Strong female role model.

Lobel, Arnold. *Martha, the Movie Mouse*. Harper & Row, 1966. Active female role.

Massie, Diane. *Dazzle*. Parents' Magazine Press, 1969. Nonstereotyped image promoted.

Matsuno, Masako. *Chie and the Sports Day*. World, 1965. Nonstereotyped behavior.

McCloskey, Robert *Time of Wonder*. Viking, 1957. Beautiful book. Equal presentation.

Milhous, Katherine. *The Egg Tree*. Scribner's, 1950. Beautiful book. Important female role.

Ness, Evaline. *Sam, Bangs, and Moonshine*. Holt, Rinehart and Winston, 1966. Good story. Female main character.

Preston, Edna. *Pop Corn and Ma Goodness*. Viking, 1969. Nonstereotyped portrayal of adults.

Reavin, Sam. *Hurry for Captain Jane*. Parents' Magazine Press, 1971. Active female role.

Scarry, Richard. *Cars and Trucks and Things That Go*. Golden Press, 1974. Active female roles portrayed.

Scott, Natalie. *Firebrand: Push Your Hair Out of Your Eyes*. Carol Rhoda Books, 1968. Nonstereotyped image.

Udry, Janice. *Mary Ann's Mud Day*. Martha Alexander, 1967. Nonstereotyped behavior.

Udry, Janice. *What Mary Joe Shared*. Albert Whitman, 1966. Well-drawn female main character.

Udry, Janice. *The Sunflower Garden*. Harvey House, 1969. Active female role.

Waber, Bernard. *You Look Ridiculous Said the Rhinoceros to the Hippopotamus*. Houghton Mifflin, 1966. Charming book. Nonstereotyped female main character.

Wells, Rosemary, *Benjamin and Tulip*. Dial Press, 1973. Nonstereotyped behavior. Charming book.

Williams, Jay. *The Practical Princess*. Parents' Magazine Press, 1969. Nonstereotyped female portrayal.

Yashima, Taro. *Umbrella*. Viking, 1966. Beautiful book. Female main character.

Yolen, Jane. *The Emperor and the Kite*. World, 1967. Active female role.

References

Gersoni-Staun, Diane. "Feminist Criticism: An Overview." *Library Journal*, vol. 99 (January 15, 1974), pp. 182–84.

Jones, Bartlett C. "A New Cache of Liberated Children's Literature—in Some Old Standbys!" *Wilson Library Bulletin*, vol. 49 (September 1974), pp. 52–56.

Lanes, Seima. "On Feminism and Children's Books." *Library Journal*, vol. 99 (January 15, 1974), pp. 183–85.

Nilsen, Alleen Pace. "Women in Children's Literature." *College English* (May 1971), pp. 918–25.

Stewig, John and Margaret Higgs. "Girls Grow Up to Be Mommies: A Study of Sexism in Children's Literature." *Library Journal*, vol. 98 (January 15, 1973), pp. 236–41.

Weitzman, Lenore J. and others. "Sex-Role Socialization in Picture Books for Preschool Children." *American Journal of Sociology*, vol. 77 (May 1972), pp. 1125–49.

Children's Perceptions of Death: A Look at the Appropriateness of Selected Picture Books

Robert G. Delisle
Abigail S. Woods McNamee

Children's Exposure to Death

Thinking that children cannot avoid exposure to death, and having experienced with children the death of a grandfather, a dog, a goldfish, and a family of bunnies (not to mention an assortment of insects), the writers recognized the need to support children and to prepare them for exposure to this natural life event. This need is even greater when one examines the death experience as presented by media.

In recent years, the Charlie Brown Thanksgiving special has been run and rerun on television. It is a program planned, one might assume, with children in mind. The repeated flirtations with death are rather startling in that the characters always manage to escape unscathed. Snoopy is smashed in a folding Ping-Pong table—an event one would expect to be serious, if not terminal—but he reappears hardly dazed. As if such an experience is not enough, Snoopy—instantly recovered from the smashing—again finds himself smashed, this time in a folding deck chair. Woodstock, a canary on the same program, is smashed and struck, flattened, to a rolling basketball. Again, no injury, fatal or otherwise. A seven-year-old commented on the program: "Snoopy never gets hurt." "Why?" she was asked. Her response: "He's smart." How easy it is for children to reach such a conclusion and, perhaps, to ask the next question: "Why wasn't Grandpop so smart?"

Children experience death, too, through media originally planned for adults. Many children have viewed the original or television version of the record-breaking *Jaws, The Towering Inferno, Earthquake,* and *The Hindenberg*. Many children who have not actually seen such films experience them vicariously, detail by detail, through frequent retelling in the neighborhood. The experience of death in these films, perhaps because of the size and immediacy of wide-screen media, seems very real to children, who play and

SOURCE: *Death Education*, 5 (1981), pp. 1–13, with permission of Hemisphere Publishing Corporation, Washington, D.C.

replay the scenes with Barbie dolls and Ken or GI Joe guys (or whatever props are available).

Little need be said about children's exposure to death via the television series, whether planned for adult or child. Death may seem less spectacular on the smaller television screen, but it is death omnipresent, death often violent. Consider a history of "Hawaii Five-O," "Kojak," "Baretta," the two bionic people shows, "The Incredible Hulk," or "Dracula." The Hulk and the bionic man and woman are fascinating because of their ability to defy death again and again by supernatural means, as do Wonderwoman, Batman, and Spiderman. Radio programming, too, deals with death. Frequently repeated were a rock song with the refrain "I'm never gonna die" and another with the refrain "killing me softly with his song." How often children have heard one of these songs, or others with similar lines, as they ride along in the car, probably interpreting the words literally as they listened.

These examples are not intended to indicate that children do not regularly experience death as a natural life event in actuality and vicariously through media; they do. Herein lies the writers' concern: In addition to experiencing death as a natural life event, children experience it—often as an irresistible barrage, through media—as a supernatural event. Through such exposure, children form or reinforce conceptions or misconceptions. Although it is hardly possible in American society today to shield children totally from misconception, it is possible to facilitate exposure to materials that present death in a manner appropriate to children's current levels of perception and encourage subsequent levels of perception.

Children's Perception of Death

To facilitate the exposure of children to appropriate materials, it is necessary to understand the perceptions children have of death. There are apparent age-typical perceptions of death (Anthony, 1940, 1971; Ilg & Ames, 1955; Nagy, 1948) that may be directly related to a child's intellectual development (Koocher, 1973) (Table 1). It is crucial that adults who are working with children know and understand the stages through which children pass as they perceive death.

Nagy (1948) identifies three stages of development of children's perceptions of death. Between the ages of three and five, children tend to deny death as a regular and final process. Death is a departure, or a further existence under changed circumstances. Death is temporary. Between five and nine, children tend to personify death, to consider it a person. They know that death exists but try to keep it distant from themselves. People die only when the "deathman" carries them off, which does occur eventually. At about nine or ten, children perceive death as a process that takes place in all of us, the perceptible result being the dissolution of bodily life. They perceive death as inevitable. Their perception of death becomes more realistic.

Anthony (1940, 1971) also identifies three stages of development of children's perceptions of death. Between the ages of three and five, children are either ignorant of the meaning of the word *dead* or interested in the word although their concept is limited or erroneous. Between six and eight, there is no evidence of children not understanding the word *dead*. Children are, in fact, preoccupied with death ritual and define *dead* by reference only to humanity, probably including reference to phenomena not biologically or logically essential to the definition. At about 9 or 10, children understand the word *dead* and the event and define it in reference to biologic essentials.

Ilg and Ames (1955) add to our understanding of children's perceptions of death. They indicate that by four years of age the child's perception of death is still extremely limited and many be connected only in a rudimentary way with sorrow and sadness. Five-year-olds may recognize that death is the "end" for others but never for self; they probably think that death means that something is immobile. Increasingly, the concept of death becomes more detailed, more accurate, more factual. A five-year-old may be concerned that his or her mother will die; a six-year-old becomes even more concerned, evidencing new emotional awareness. A five-year-old can be calm and matter-of-fact about death; a six-year-old is often violent and emotional in threatening death ("I'll kill you") and in worrying about it ("Mommy, are you going to die?"). Six-year-olds may not realize, however, that they will die, even though they begin to connect death with old age and think that older people die first. Ilg and Ames consider that death for a six-year-old may still seem reversible, with only a beginning suspicion that it is not.

At seven years, children have a reasonably clear notion of death, but a notion that allows them to avoid it by concentrating on details such as the coffin, the graveyard, the burial service. In fact, their fascination with details may seem morbid to an adult. Seven-year-olds also are interested in the causes of death yet continue to resist the idea that they may die.

Eight-year-olds seem less morbid than seven-year-olds and often express an interest in what happens after death. According to Ilg and Ames, an eight-year-old understands more about death but is not much concerned or interested in it. Many can accept, without much emotion, the idea that everyone will die, even them. Ilg and Ames add that by 9 and 10 years of age children are ready to face death "quite squarely." They don't concentrate on the funeral or after. Many are quite scientific. Death means that there is no pulse, no temperature, no breathing. They are ready for as full an explanation of death as adults will give them

Koocher (1973) indicates that children's conceptions of death are related to their level of cognitive development and that they conceptualize death more realistically as their cognitive development advances through the preoperational, concrete operational, and formal operational stages described by Piaget. Children at the preoperational level of cognitive development tend to

TABLE 1 Age-typical Perceptions of Death

Age	*Nagy (1948)*	*Anthony (1940, 1971)*	*Ilg and Ames (1955)*	*Koocher (1973)*
3	Deny death as regular and final	Ignorant of meaning of word *dead;* may be interested in word *dead;* limited or erroneous concept of *dead*	Limited perception, little sorrow	Egocentric conceptualization; fantasy reasoning; magical thinking; symbolism closely tied to own experience
4	Death = departure or temporary change		Little sadness	
5	Death personified		Calmness evident; end for others, never for self; reversible; death = old age	
6	Death kept distant from	No evidence that children do not understand word *dead;* preoccupied with death ritual; define *dead* by reference to humanity but include nonessential information	Becomes emotional	
7			Interest in details; seems morbid; suspects he/she will die	Specific, concrete conceptualization; specific means of inflicting death; specific weapons, poison, assaultive acts
8			Less morbid; less emotional	
9	Death for all is inevitable; a realistic view of death	Understand word *dead* and the event; define it by reference to biologic essentials	Faces death squarely; scientific	
10			Interested in death	Abstract, generalized conceptualization; death a natural phenomenon and a physical deterioration

conceptualize death in an egocentric manner involving fantasy reasoning, magical thinking, and/or realistic causes of death marked by egocentric reasoning and symbolism closely tied to their experience. Children at the concrete operational level of cognitive development tend to conceptualize death specifically or concretely, including specific means of inflicting it, with or without intention, and with specific weapons, poison, or assaultive acts. Children at the formal operational level of cognitive development tend to conceptualize death in an abstract or generalized manner involving rather abstract clusters of more specific possibilities, perhaps stating or implying that death is a natural phenomenon and a physical deterioration. Children at this level name classes of potential causes of death, sometimes listing general causes, with specific examples of each.

Elkind (1977) also describes children's perceptions of death as occurring within the broader context of intellectual development. Children at the preoperational stage of development (usually ages three to six) tend to see the world in anthropomorphic terms: Physical objects are alive and have feelings, intentions, and purposes. In addition, past and future are barely grasped; they cannot conceive of the distant future or of the absence of life. At best, they conceive of death as a kind of change of stage, being hungry or asleep, but continuing with life.

Children entering the concrete operational stage (at about six or seven years) begin to understand time and have a pragmatic orientation toward the world. They conceptualize death as the end of one life but the beginning of another and as something that does not happen to everyone. Which people are to die and which are to live is not always clearly thought out. The concrete operational child evidences a number of contradictory ideas about death. Sometimes it is irreversible; sometimes it is the fate of a particular group. Toward the end of this period, children suddenly realize they will die.

Children entering the formal operational stage (at about 11 or 12) comprehend notions of historical time, can grasp metaphor and simile, and arrive at a scientific view of the world reflected in their conceptualization of death. Death is defined in biologic and medical terminology. They know that they and their loved ones will die, but probably far in the future. They can look at death from different points of view, such as the religious and the dramatic.

There seems to be agreement among these researchers that children's perceptions of death are developmental, passing from an early, immature level to a later, more mature level. Nagy, Anthony, and Ilg and Ames link children's perceptions closely to age; Elkind and Koocher group children's perceptions not on age alone but by the level of cognitive functioning.

As one considers children's developmental perceptions of death, it is important to ask what an adult's role might be in interacting with a child around death:

Through didactic teaching to hustle a child's limited (or seemingly incorrect) perception on to a higher level of understanding?

To leave a child with his or her perception in the confidence that he or she will move on when ready?

Or perhaps compromise by facilitating the development of a child's understanding of death by selecting materials that present death in a manner appropriate to his or her current level of perception and encourage subsequent levels of perception?

This compromise is what the writers advocate. Such a position implies trust in a child's development without leaving the child totally on her or his own. The most available materials for presenting death to children are picture books. They are easily obtained from neighborhood and school libraries and are repeatedly used by children at home and at school. They also offer a wide choice of death treatment, some more appropriate than others. The authors have selected six picture books from bibliographies on children and death and evaluated them for their appropriateness in dealing with the concept of death.

Death as Portrayed in Children's Picture Books

Across the Meadow (Shecter, 1973) Age range: 6–8

Alfred is an old cat who seems to be dying, though the word is never used. He decides that it is "time for a vacation" and travels across the meadow to an old, abandoned car, "a good place for a vacation," where he might stay "for a long time." Back at Alfred's house, a little kitten drinks milk out of Alfred's dish.

On their own, children between six and eight years would probably not be able to deal with the metaphorical use of language in referring to Alfred's death, nor would they be able to deal with the author's attempts to present the concept of the continuation of life through his use of the kitten as a symbol of life. The young reader would probably conclude that Alfred was, in fact, going on a vacation and that the kitten was just drinking out of Alfred's dish. If an adult pointed out that the vacation was a metaphor and that the kitten was symbolic of life, children between six and eight would probably be confused. As Elkind indicates, "Children do not understand metaphor because they are very literal in their interpretation of language" (1971, p. 176). When death is alluded to as "vacation," children might wonder, "Does someone who goes on vacation never come back . . . or die?" When Alfred goes to each of his friends to say good-bye, children might wonder, "Does saying good-bye mean you'll never come back . . . or die?" When Alfred goes to an abandoned car for his "vacation," children might wonder, "Do cats vacation in old cars?" When the kitten is seen drinking from Alfred's dish, children might worry that if one goes on vacation one's things are not protected back home. *Across the Meadow*, recommended for children between the ages of six and eight, attempts to present death as a metaphor; such treatment is inappropriate for the intended age range.

First Snow (Coutant, 1974) Age range: 6–8

A second book that makes use of metaphor is *First Snow*. Lien is a six-year-old Vietnamese girl who lives in the United States. When she discovers that her grandmother is dying, she asks of several people, "What is dying?" Only her grandmother answers, "Go out into the garden and hold your hand up to heaven and be patient. You will have an answer to your question. You will discover for yourself what dying means." Lien goes out during the snowfall, catches a snowflake in her hand, watches it turn into a drop of water, and then sees it roll to the ground. As she searches for the drop of water, she discovers a new plant coming through the snow. She looks at her grandmother peering through the window and says that she understands what dying is.

What the author wishes the reader to understand is that six-year-old Lien has seen that dying is like the snowflake. Just as the snowflake turns to water, which, in turn, feeds seedlings, which turn into trees, so life leads to death; but in death one discovers new life. The reader is asked to believe that Lien understands this metaphor. The author, however, has apparently neglected what is known about the ability of children to deal with this level of thinking. It is improbable that either Lien or the child reader between six and eight years would be able to understand the metaphor. What is intended as a book for young children is more appropriately a book for adolescents and adults.

Annie and the Old One (Miles, 1971) Age range: 7–9

Annie and the Old One is still another book written for young children that makes use of metaphor. Annie, a nine-year-old Navajo girl, learns that her grandmother is dying. She overhears her grandmother say that as soon as she finishes the weaving it will be time. Annie thinks that death cannot be allowed to happen to this person whom she loves, and she tries to prevent death by unraveling her grandmother's weaving. Only when Annie's grandmother explains, "You have tried to hold back time; this cannot be done," does Annie understand and accept.

The metaphor of the rug is used to explain life and death. Just as life has a start and a finish, so does the weaving of the rug. With its completion comes the end, but the start of another is allowed for. Although the age range of the children for whom this book is intended is slightly higher than that of the previously discussed picture books, it is improbable that children of this age would be any better able to understand the metaphor. This book, too, is more appropriate for adolescents and adults.

The Tenth Good Thing about Barney (Viorst, 1971) Age range: 5–11

The last of the books evaluated that makes use of metaphor is *The Tenth Good Thing about Barney.* Barney, a cat, has just died; and as part of a grieving process, his young master is asked to remember 10 good things about Barney. He thinks of 9 good things at first, then the 10th is suggested by his parent: that Barney will help the plants grow.

> He'll change until he's part of the ground in the garden.
>
> He'll help grow the flowers, and he'll help grow that tree and some grass.

Later, Barney's master repeats:

> Barney is in the ground and he's helping grow flowers.

The younger children for whom this book is intended cannot perform the abstract thinking required to understand how Barney can help plants grow. They would probably perceive the cat as alive but unseen: perhaps watering the flowers during the night, perhaps pushing the flowers up from below. It is only as children near 11, the upper limit of the intended age range, that they might be able to understand the metaphor and Barney's role as fertilizer. As Elkind indicates, it is at about 11 or 12 that children can grasp metaphor and simile and arrive at a scientific view of the world that is reflected in their conceptualization of death (1977, p. 28).

My Grandson Lew (Zolotow, 1974) Age range: 6–8

Lew is a six-year-old who remembers his grandfather in great detail even though his grandfather died when Lew was only two. Lew says that he remembers that "he had a beard and it scratched when he kissed me." He also remembers his grandfather's blue eyes and the "eye hugs" he would give Lew when he came into Lew's bedroom at night.

This book conveys the idea that a six-year-old can remember in detail incidents that occurred when he was two. There is some question as to whether this would, in fact, be possible. Aside from this, however, the manner in which Lew's remembrances are presented creates the probability of additional confusion and uncertainty. It would be impossible for the young reader to determine whether Lew is remembering an experience from four years before or currently experiencing his grandfather's presence. The use of flashback as a literary technique in a picture book intended for the six-to-eight age range is not appropriate because of their limited perceptions of space and time. It is not until the age of 11 or 12 that children acquire more abstract conceptions of space and time (Elkind, 1977, p. 28). It is probable that children between six and eight years of age would become confused, thinking either that dead people can return to give one "eye hugs" in the night or that Lew's grandfather is still alive.

The Dead Bird (Brown, 1965) Age range: 5–7

In *The Dead Bird*, a group of children find a recently dead bird. They notice what death is like as they touch and look at the bird. They plan and carry out a funeral for it, then continue to visit the bird's grave "until they forget." The final illustration portrays the children playing ball, the grave in the distance.

This picture book is appropriate for children between ages of five and seven. It is totally concrete and deals with the bird's death in a practical yet caring way. The children examine the bird as young children would do: He is, at first, "warm . . . there is no heartbeat . . . he grew stiff and cold." They feel "sad," a word and feeling that children within this age range would recognize. Later, they cry. They plan a funeral, which is described in detail, and place a stone on the grave, which says, in definite terminology, "Here lies a bird that is dead." Such a funeral would make sense to children within the five-to-seven age range; they would make a similar funeral for an animal they had known. The book's conclusion would also make sense: The group visits the grave until they forget. Young children know about forgetting; they do it; they see it in adult's behavior. They know what it is to go on to a new activity. As Elkind indicates, they have a "pragmatic orientation" toward the world (1977, p. 27). A book with a pragmatic orientation toward death is appropriate.

Conclusion

It is unavoidable that children will experience death through media, literature, and real-life experience. They need the help of adults as they work to understand what they experience. To be useful to a child as he or she attempts to understand death, the adult must consider how a child tends to perceive death at different developmental levels and must recognize which picture books present a concept of death appropriate to the child's current level of perception and encouraging of subsequent levels of perception.

References

Anthony, S. *The Discovery of Death in Childhood and After*. London: Allen Lan, Penguin, 1971.

Elkind, D. *A Sympathetic Understanding of the Child: Birth to Sixteen*. Boston: Allyn & Bacon, 1971.

Elkind, D. Life and death: Concepts and feelings in children. *Day Care and Early Education*, January-February 1977, pp. 27–39.

Ilg, F., & Ames, L. B. *Child Behavior from Birth to Ten*. New York: Harper, 1955.

Koocher, G. P. Childhood, death, and cognitive development. *Developmental Psychology*, 1973, 9(3), 369–375.

Nagy, M. H. The child's theories concerning death. *Journal of Genetic Psychology*, September 1948, *73*, 3–27.

Children's Books

Brown, M. W. *The Death Bird*. Reading, Mass.: Addison-Wesley, 1965.

Coutant, H. *First Snow*. New York: Harper, 1974.

Miles, M. *Annie and the Old One*. Boston: Little, Brown, 1971.

Shecter, B. *Across the Meadow*. New York: Doubleday, 1973.

Viorst, J. *The Tenth Good Thing About Barney*. New York: Atheneum, 1971.

Zolotow, C. *My Grandson Lew*. New York: Harper, 1974.

Children's Literature and Early Childhood Separation Experiences

Joan Fassler

Numerous reports concerning children's fears list separation fears (fear of being separated from one's parents for various reasons) as one of the strongest fears of early childhood (Berger 1971; Goodenough 1963). Separation fears and anxieties are universal experiences for young children. Nursery school teachers are quite familiar with the emotional reactions three- and four-year-old children experience as they attempt to cope with separation from their parents, each according to his or her own style or stage of development (Furman 1966; Gross 1970; Kessler et al. 1969). Today it is often suggested that the initial separation of parent and child, for school purposes, should be achieved in a gradual manner with both mother and child spending some time together in the school setting, and with children being given ample opportunities to become accustomed to a new school situation by means of gradually increasing time periods (Speers et al. 1971).

For very young children, separation from a parent, even a brief and well-planned separation, is seldom a simple matter. Anna Freud (1965) has noted that children must first develop some form of object constancy before they can realize that a mother's departure does not mean total loss. With further development, the need for adjustment to separation from one's parents does not suddenly stop; it continues as an ongoing process, a normal and often-repeated experience in a child's life (Pine 1971). As part of this ongoing process, it has been suggested that successful adjustment to one type of separation experience (such as staying for brief periods of time with a well-known and trusted babysitter) at one stage of development may help a child develop the inner resources needed to cope with future separation experiences (such as attending nursery or primary school).

It is also possible that reading and discussing carefully selected stories with young children might offer some help in this area of early child development. Previous reports have indicated that the presentation of stories, followed by opportunities for story discussion, can affect the behavior and attitudes of young children (Kimmel 1970; Meathenia 1971; Webster 1961).

SOURCE: Reprinted by permission from *Young Children* 29 (July 1974): 311–323.

Similar effects regarding separation experiences may also be possible. For example, some children might gain comfort from seeing that other children, even storybook children (or animals), often feel just as they do about new situations involving separations from their parents, and that their own actions and feelings regarding such separations are not shameful and can be mastered gradually. Other children may be reassured to discover that most storybook children do eventually overcome their hesitancies and do move on to more independent behavior. Reassuring also might be the fact that in the selected stories, parents and children are always reunited once again after brief periods of planned and unplanned separations. In addition, some children may feel particularly proud to discover that they have already accomplished the very separation-type task that a storybook character is still struggling to master. Most importantly, such stories may offer children and adults excellent opportunities to share some honest feelings and to air some inner concerns regarding a variety of early separation experiences in a potentially helpful and growth-producing manner.

The stories listed below have been selected because of the manner in which they seem to relate to several common separation-type experiences of early childhood. They are particularly suitable for the three- to five-year age range. Materials concerning separation for purposes involving either hospitalization, death, or divorce in the family have not been included in this listing as such materials appear to merit individual attention in their own right. Also, stories concerning bedtime situations (one type of early separation experience) have not been considered within the scope of the present article. Accordingly, the stories described in this paper, and the discussions precipitated by these stories, might be most helpful for those children and parents who are presently making an initial adjustment to an early school experience. Additionally, the stories listed here might be helpful for children who will be facing a first school experience in the near future, for the use of such materials in a thoughtful and sensitive manner may help certain children to build or maintain a kind of inner strength that could be of considerable value in coping with and benefiting from separation experiences yet to come.

Reassuring Stories to Help Contradict Fears of Abandonment

The Runaway Bunny by Margaret Brown

An imaginative hide-and-seek game that can be warmly reassuring to young children. Wherever the bunny hides, his mother finds him.

The Bundle Book by Ruth Krauss

After some playful puzzlement, a mother finally discovers that the strange "bundle" on her bed is simply a blanket, hiding exactly what she wants and needs most of all—her own little girl.

The Way Mothers Are by Miriam Schlein

A mother cat loves her very own kitten, not because he is good or clever or because he draws nice pictures. She loves him simply because he is her own kitten (child), and clearly she intends to go right on loving him for that very reason. Especially reassuring here is the fact that this mother's love is not offered or withdrawn because of good or "naughty" behavior on the kitten's part; it is, instead, a dependable, consistent emotion.

Separation-Type Stories that Might Relate Well to Early School Experiences

I'd Rather Stay with You by Charlotte Steiner

The baby kangaroo in this story does not want to leave his mother's pouch. "I'd rather stay with you," is his constant response to each invitation for more independent activity. Finally, with the aid of his encouraging mother and the lure of a bright red balloon, he does manage to step out of the protective pouch. Later, he makes a tentative try at kindergarten, and, apparently, enjoys school after all.

Of special significance here is the portrayal of a patient and understanding mother who does not abruptly push her child out of the pouch before he is ready to handle such an experience. At the same time, when the little kangaroo finally does appear ready for greater independence, his mother does not attempt to hold him back because of any of her own personal insecurities. Young children can easily identify with the baby kangaroo in this story, while mothers of preschool children might do well to take note of some of Mrs. Kangaroo's repetitive, encouraging, and confident behavior.

A Drink for Little Red Diker by Jane Thayer

Diker, a little red antelope, wishes that he were big enough and brave enough to go places by himself. After several timid and unsuccessful trials, he finally walks all the way through the forest to the lake, where he manages to get a drink of cool, refreshing water. However, in this story, the little antelope must first convince his own mother that he is indeed big enough to do things on his own. Although he is apparently quite ready to engage in some independent activities, his mother seems to be somewhat reluctant to let him try.

Some children entering nursery school, kindergarten, or first grade may have a similar problem—a parent who is not quite ready to let a child grow up. Professional literature frequently notes that separation problems are often parent problems. Perhaps some of the children of such parents will come to view Little Red Diker's eventual success as a kind of whispered encouragement toward the establishment of their own increasing readiness for more and more independent activities.

Umbrella by Taro Yashima

Enthusiasm for a gift received on her third birthday, a brand new umbrella and a pair of bright red rain boots, encourages Momo to take a very independent step. She walks all the way to nursery school, and all the way back home, without holding either her mother's or her father's hand.

Will I have a Friend? by Miriam Cohen

In *Will I Have a Friend?* a little boy named Jim, a newcomer to the neighborhood, is reluctant to be separated from his father on his first day at a new school. This story realistically shows some of Jim's anxieties and his initial feeling of loneliness at the new school. Many child readers will understand exactly how Jim feels, and they will, in all likelihood, be happy to discover that Jim does manage to find a potential friend among his new classmates. By the end of the first day, Jim apparently feels more comfortable and more relaxed about school. Later that same day, the quiet confidence in Jim expressed by his father serves to reinforce Jim's positive feelings about the new school.

Although written in a sensitive manner and enjoyed by teachers and children alike, this story might have been considerably more helpful in regard to early separation experiences if it had portrayed, or at least suggested, the gradual nature of Jim's adjustment to the new school. Analogously, child readers (or story listeners) might benefit from discussing this point and from considering the fact that it often takes a longer period of time than Jim's story seems to suggest for a young child to adjust to a new school situation.

The Two Friends by Grete Mannheim

In story and photographs, this book also portrays a young child's first day at school and offers a brief glimpse of the second day as well. Here, too, there are some realistic feelings expressed. Jenny admits that she is a bit afraid of so many strange children. She feels scared and lonely at first. Then, as in the previous story, finding a potential friend helps Jenny feel somewhat better about the whole situation.

Once again, the gradual nature of a young child's adjustment to school plays no part in this otherwise sensitive story. Some of the problems and anxieties that might be involved when a child first enters school are honestly and sensitively portrayed here. Unfortunately, such concerns appear to be resolved much too rapidly. In using this book with young children, it might therefore be valuable to follow the story with an opportunity for some frank discussion about the length of time that may, in reality, often be needed to help a young child feel comfortable in a new school setting.

Cathy's First School by Betty Katzoff

Sensitive photographs help tell the story of Cathy and her classmates. Most of the experiences portrayed in this story are happy ones, but one boy does momentarily burst into tears. Cathy, too, clearly expresses some temporarily hurt feelings. Since the story takes place on Cathy's sixth birthday, it ends with a classroom birthday celebration, complete with a variety of hand-made presents.

The portrayal of Cathy's first school in this story is both a happy and a realistic one. Cathy's experiences might help young children discuss some of their own school experiences. At the same time, children who have not yet attended school might be motivated by Cathy's story to role play what they think their own future school experiences will be like.

I Am Here: Yo Estoy Aquí by Rose Blue

Luz, a little Puerto Rican girl, attends kindergarten for the first time. Adjusting to a new country, a new school, and a new language is indeed difficult. Of special interest here is the suggestion of a warm and supportive relationship that is soon established between Luz and a thoughtful assistant teacher or teacher's aide who speaks Spanish. It is this relationship that helps Luz feel more comfortable at school and more confident about her own role in the classroom.

This story raises two important points regarding early school experiences. One is the scarcity of bilingual adults in those classrooms where their presence could be of much potential value. The positive benefits that young Luz derives from finding a Spanish-speaking adult in her new class emphasize that considerably more classrooms and more children would benefit greatly from such assistance. Bilingual parents from local school communities could fill an important need here. In this regard, the story of Luz could serve as a valuable catalyst for the encouragement of greater participation in school activities by parents and other volunteers with such bilingual skills. Perhaps, then, more children who speak a foreign language and who cannot yet understand much English will find, just as Luz did, a special kind of support and reassurance waiting for them in their new American classrooms.

Secondly, this story is an excellent one to help remind children, and parents as well, that there is likely to be a warm, pleasant, and likeable adult in the classroom who will try to ease early parent-child separations. This is particularly important because very few stories portraying an initial school experience emphasize an adult-child relationship. Emphasis is usually placed on materials and on relationships with peers. Teachers, however, and their assistants as well, are very important in regard to separation experiences in early childhood. The adults in a nursery school or kindergarten are, in fact, often viewed as temporary parents. They are, accordingly, turned to again and again for "emotional refueling." Unfortunately, very little of this "refueling" finds its way into stories for young children, particularly those stories portraying a child's initial school experience. Therefore, *I Am Here: Yo Estoy Aquì* does offer something unique by at least acknowledging that warm and supportive relationships between children and adults can often play an important role in a young child's early school adjustment.

Separation from Parents for Reasons Not Related to School Activities

Be Good Harry by Mary Chalmers

Harry, a very small cat, reluctantly stays with Mrs. Brewster, a well-known and trusted babysitter. Harry's mother tells him that she will return in one hour. Although Harry misses his mother and is rather unhappy at first, he finally responds to the warmth and friendliness of the babysitter. Most reassuring of all is the fact that Harry's mother does indeed return soon.

This story might help some very young children grasp the idea that mothers *do* return and that being left with a babysitter does not, in any way, represent the irrevocable loss of one's own mother. Young children, however, are not yet ready to fully understand time concepts such as "one hour."

Therefore, in reading this story, the adult might suggest that Harry's mother is leaving for just a short time and that she does return in a little while, just as she had promised, instead of emphasizing the more difficult concept of a one-hour time interval.

Ira Sleeps Over by Bernard Waber

Ira has planned to sleep at a friend's house. At bedtime, on this first night away from home, he has much difficulty getting settled comfortably. Finally, when he is reunited with a favorite toy, a small brown teddy bear, Ira feels better and soon falls asleep.

It might be reassuring for some young readers to see that other children, even storybook children, also have a few qualms about sleeping away from home. Additionally, it may be reassuring to note that other children, too, may especially need a favorite toy and are not at all ridiculed by their storybook peers for acknowledging this need.

First Night Away from Home by Myra B. Brown

Stevie is planning to sleep at his friend's house. As he announces this proposed visit to a number of his peers, a variety of separation experiences are discussed; e.g., staying at a grandparent's house, staying at a hotel, staying overnight at a hospital, etc. As in the previous story, Stevie gets settled in his friend's house only to discover that he is highly restless and lonely at bedtime in the strange surroundings. Not until his mother rings the bell and brings his favorite stuffed animal does Stevie feel comfortable and secure enough to fall asleep.

This story might encourage children to talk about some of their own experiences involving trips away from home. A consideration of some of the realistic feelings, both good and bad, provoked by Stevie's trip might be helpful to some children who are, themselves, ready to embark on overnight adventures.

Separation from a Well-Liked and Trusted Individual (Friend, Teacher, Therapist, etc.)

Little Bear's Friend by Else H. Minarek

During one summer vacation, Little Bear and Emily become very good friends. Then summer is over, and it is time for Emily to say goodbye. Little Bear is very sad.

Some honest feelings surrounding a necessary separation from a loved and trusted friend are sensitively portrayed in this story. A real-life child who must also face a separation from a good friend or perhaps a separation from a well-loved teacher or a change from one therapist to another may find special meaning in this story. In this sense, Little Bear's experience might provoke some helpful discussion about separation experiences in general. At the same time, Little Bear's story may be useful in a consideration of a particular separation experience that is either presently taking place or soon to occur in a young reader's life.

The New Teacher by Miriam Cohen

The separation in this story is a separation between a group of young children and a much-loved teacher. The first graders are most unhappy with this necessary change and staunchly reluctant to accept the expected newcomer. After imagining what the new teacher will be like, the children finally do meet her. The story ends on a rather hopeful note with an indication that a good relationship will probably be established, after a reasonable passage of time, between the first graders and the new teacher.

This story might have special meaning for young children who must deal with a similar personnel change, perhaps encouraging some helpful discussion of the feelings and fears involved.

Amos & Boris by William Steig

Amos, a mouse, and Boris, a whale, become the closest possible friends. As these two travel together, an unusually strong bond is established between them. "They told each other about their lives; their ambitions. They shared their deepest secrets." When circumstances eventually force them to separate, Amos and Boris do not forget each other, for the close relationship built between them leaves a lasting effect on each of them.

Young children, who are themselves about to face a required separation from someone important in their own lives, such as a close friend, a well-loved teacher, or perhaps a therapist, may find some personal significance in this story. As they become involved in the separations faced by Amos and Boris, such children may also begin to view their own separations in a new and somewhat clearer light. Additionally, they might benefit considerably from an opportunity to discuss selected separation experiences from the storybook world or from their own lives with an understanding and perceptive adult. A consideration of the story, *Amos & Boris*, might spark such discussion.

As indicated previously, the books discussed above have been selected because their use might be helpful in regard to early separation experiences, and because individuals working with young children might find it beneficial to know that such books are available. The list itself is certainly not an exhaustive one. Other publications relating to the same topic may also be helpful and, of course, new and possibly valuable material concerning separation experiences may appear from time to time in future juvenile book publications.

In a consideration of this topic, however, it does seem important to note that there are in existence today a number of books for young children portraying early separation experiences that cannot be considered potentially helpful from a child development point of view. Typical of such stories are those portraying an initial school experience in an unrealistic and nonchildlike manner, such as *The Little School at Cottonwood Corners* (Schick 1965). In this story, a little girl who is too young to attend school obtains a visitor's pass and spends an entire day, apparently on her own initiative, wandering from classroom to classroom in an unfamiliar school setting. The school itself is presented as an ideal place with ideal children and ideal teachers. No one ever frowns. The child's day is indeed delightful, the only problem being that the story is in no way reminiscent of real experiences with real children. Moreover, some children exposed to this book occasionally become disturbed by the stylized drawings and by the fact that none of the children in *The Little School at Cottonwood Corners* have noses; each child simply has two eyes and a mouth!

Other stories concerning separation experiences that are not particularly helpful, from a child-development point of view, portray such experiences in a seemingly flippant and rather casual manner. They seem to suggest that a child can be tricked into easily and cheerfully accepting separation from his or her parents by a series of clever maneuvers on the part of the surrounding adults. Such stories, typified by the publication *Amy Loves Goodbyes* (Gordon 1966), appear to encourage a denial and distortion of many of the true feelings that are involved in parent-child separation experiences, particularly those concerning a very young child, and therefore do not relate well to realistic experiences with real children.

In addition to the variety of stories described above, it may also be worthwhile to note that there are still some important themes concerning early separation experiences that have, to date, received little, if any, treatment in the juvenile literature available on this topic. For example, a sensitive story emphasizing the development of a *trusting* and *ongoing* relationship between a particular child and his or her teacher would be a welcome addition to the present list of stories portraying initial school experiences. Particularly lacking are stories suggesting the ongoing nature of a teacher-child relationship. As noted previously, there seems to be a great deal of emphasis in stories concerning introductory school situations on a child's experience with other children and with exciting materials, and very little portrayal of a young child's relationship with a warm and supportive kindergarten or nursery school teacher. It is, however, the teacher who can be most helpful in regard to early school-related separation anxieties. Perhaps, therefore, the teacher-role should receive greater emphasis in future stories concerning this theme.

Another theme that has not received sufficient treatment in the juvenile book field concerns the classroom participation of parents whose children are first starting school. At the present time, many nursery schools recommend that a parent remain at school, for gradually decreasing time periods, in order to help a young child become better accustomed to the new setting. When participating in such a plan, parents may remain in the classroom for varying time intervals during the first few days or weeks of the school term.

When inviting parents to initially remain in the classroom, nursery school teachers are likely to rely upon various criteria, in addition to their own intuitive reactions, in order to select the time that seems most appropriate for the actual separation of a particular parent and his or her child. They will, for example, notice if a child has made an attachment to a teacher and if he or she is able to turn to that teacher for assistance. They will notice if a child is beginning to feel comfortable in the classroom and if he or she is interested in the classroom activities. They will consider how often the child looks for or appears to need the parent and how the child relates to other children. They will, in all likelihood, prefer not to have a young nursery school child left too abruptly in a strange classroom nor will they want to become involved in an undue prolongation of a parent's participation in classroom procedures.

In any event, the presence of parents in selected classrooms at the beginning of a nursery school year is not an unusual phenomenon. It is, however, unfortunate that few, if any, children's books portray such a gradual separation procedure. In the storybook world, children entering nursery school seldom appear to need the reassuring presence of a parent nearby. It might, however, be helpful to have a perceptive story available centering around this very procedure in which a child *gradually*, over a period of time, gains the necessary confidence in himself, in the school situation, and in his or her own mastery skills, so that he can eventually manage quite well without the presence of his own parent in the classroom. The creation of such a story might be a worthwhile and realistic addition to those publications already existing on the entrance-into-nursery-school theme.

In conclusion, it must be emphasized that the story materials listed in this article are not, of course, a panacea. Children will take what they can from these stories, and from the discussions that such stories are likely to initiate, or what they most need or are most able to absorb in relation to their present developmental stages. Hopefully, however, a consideration of some of the materials described here will offer children and interested adults an opportunity to share some enjoyable reading experiences, as well as a further opportunity to achieve some degree of emotional growth from the particular stories selected, or, more importantly, from the adult-child interactions that such stories are likely to promote.

Juvenile Bibliography

Blue, Rose. *I Am Here: Yo Estoy Aquí.* Pictures by Moneta Barnett. New York: Franklin Watts, 1971.

Brown, Margaret W. *The Runaway Bunny.* Illustrated by Clement Hurd. New York: Harper & Row, 1942.

Brown, Myra B. *First Night Away From Home.* Illustrated by Dorothy Marino. New York: Franklin Watts, 1960.

Chalmers, Mary. *Be Good Harry.* New York: Harper & Row, 1967.

Cohen, Miriam. *The New Teacher.* Pictures by Lillian Hoban. New York: Macmillan Co., 1972.

Cohen, Miriam. *Will I Have A Friend?* Illustrated by Lillian Hoban. New York: Collier, 1967.

Gordon, Selma. *Amy Loves Goodbyes.* Illustrated by June Goldsborough. New York: Platt & Munk Co., 1966.

Katzoff, Betty. *Cathy's First School.* Photographs by Sy Katzoff. New York: Alfred A. Knopf, 1964.

Krauss, Ruth. *The Bundle Book.* Illustrated by Helen Stone. New York: Harper & Row, 1951.

Mannheim, Grete. *The Two friends.* New York: Alfred A. Knopf, 1968.

Minarek, Else H. *Little Bear's Friend.* Illustrated by Maurice Sendak. New York: Harper & Row, 1960.

Schick, Eleanor. *The Little School At Cottonwood Corners.* New York: Harper & Row, 1965.

Schlein, Miriam. *The Way Mothers Are.* Illustrated by Joe Lasker. Chicago: Albert Whitman & Co. 1963.

Steig, William. *Amos & Boris.* New York: Farrar, Straus & Giroux, 1971.

Steiner, Charlotte. *I'd Rather Stay With You.* New York: Seabury Press, Inc. 1965.

Thayer, Jane. *A Drink For Little Red Diker.* Illustrated by W. T. Mars. New York: William Morrow and Co., 1963.

Waber, Bernard. *Ira Sleeps Over.* Boston: Houghton Mifflin Co., 1972.

Yashima, Taro. *Umbrella.* New York: The Viking Press, 1958.

References

Berger, Allan S. "Anxiety in Young Children." *Young Children* 27 (1971): 5–11.

Freud, Anna. *Normality and Pathology in Childhood: Assessments of Development.* New York: International Universities Press, 1965.

Furman, Robert A. "Experiences in Nursery School Consultations." *Young Children* 22 (1966): 84–95.

Goodenough, Evelyn W. "Fear and Anxiety in Young Children." *Early Childhood Education: Eight Articles*. Edited by E. G. Pitcher. Medford, Mass.: Eliot-Pearson School Alumni Association, Tufts University, 1963, p. 3–11.

Gross, Dorothy W. "On Separation and School Entrance." *Childhood Education* 46 (1970): 250–253.

Kessler, Jane W., et al. "Separation Reactions in Young Mildly Retarded Children." *Children* 16 (1969): 2–7.

Kimmel, Eric A. "Can Children's Books Change Children's Values?" *Educational Leadership* 28 (1970): 209–211, 213–214.

Meathenia, Peggy Sue. "An Experience with Fear in the Lives of Children." *Childhood Education* 48 (1971): 75–79.

Pine, F. "On the Separation Process: Universal Trends and Individual Differences." *Separation-Individuation: Essays in Honor of Margaret S. Mahler*. Edited by John B. McDevitt and Calvin F. Settlage. New York: International Universities Press, 1971, pp. 113–130.

Speers, R. W., et al. "Recapitulation of Separation-Individuation Process When the Normal Three-Year-Old Enters Nursery School." *Separation-Individuation: Essays in Honor of Maragret S. Mahler*. Edited by John B. McDevitt and Calvin F. Settlage. New York: International Universities Press, 1971, pp. 297–321.

Webster, Jane. "Using Books to Reduce the Fears of First-Grade Children." *The Reading Teacher* 14 (1961): 159–162.

9

Folktales

Folktales for Children

Gertrude B. Herman

Folklore as a source of English language literature for children is time-honored, antedating John Newbery's early exploitation of these materials "ready for the taking," as the publishing of children's books became economically viable in the mid-eighteenth century. Folklore has significance in children's experience, and therefore in the materials collection intended for children's use.

For the purposes of this paper, the term *folklore* is confined to the traditional narrative in written form, whether drawn from oral or written sources, including folktales, myths, and traditional literature. Because the distinction among forms of the traditional oral narrative tends to be blurred in versions of folklore intended for children, such distinction will not be made. The word *folktale* will be used in a generic sense, without differentiation among myth, legend, epic literature, fable, and other categories used by folklorists. Such folklore forms as games, songs, rhymes, riddles, superstitions, customs, etc., will not be included. Nonprint media will not be considered, nor will the art of storytelling or other methods of presenting folklore to children.

Folktales in Children's Experience

Librarians have long been convinced of the positive function of folklore in the reading and listening experiences of children, despite the recurring dissent of a changing array of theorists. The Puritans, willing to fill children's heads with fantasies about hell-fire, denounced fairies, giants, and magical kingdoms. Mrs. Trimmer and Mrs. Sherwood banished the fairytale as contributing to unclear thinking and moral backsliding. Cruikshank, for all of his delightful illustration and retelling of traditional stories, was unable to resist using them as a vehicle for his temperance propaganda, much to the disgust

SOURCE: *Drexel Library Bulletin*, October 1976, pp. 42–53. Reprinted with permission of Drexel Library Quarterly and the author.

of Charles Dickens. In Cruikshank's version of Cinderella, the fairy godmother, discussing plans for the wedding, dissuades the king from his proposed "fountains of wine" by pointing out that such an example would lead his subjects into "vice, wretchedness, and crime." The writers of Sunday School Tracts, committed to the virtues of an industrial and imperialistic white Christian society, foreswore the evils of the supernatural and unredemptive elements in popular lore.

The new age of enlightenment, the twentieth century, found fresh reasons for rejecting the old stories. Said some educators, as the era of child study dawned: Children must be firmly grounded in the here and now; automobiles, skyscrapers, and how-milk-is-supplied-to-the-city provide more solid fare for the young than do fantasies about beanstalks and wolves in grandmother's nightgown. These latter do not contribute to the development of scientific thinking, and the ethical values are questionable as well.[1] Terrors and night-wakings are likely to plague the little reader of fairy tales, and an unhealthy retreat from reality is also encouraged thereby, said some psychologists.[2] The sexuality of folklore was analyzed by Freudian interpreters, thus pointing to hitherto unsuspected cause for alarm.[3]

Today new objections to folktales are voiced. On the liberal front, fairy tales are being cleaned up or discarded according to the precepts of feminist criticism or by those concerned with outworn social attitudes expressed in some stories.[4] On the right, there is the attack on folklore as dealing in untruths, immorality, and irreligion. In one article, Jack is accused of disobeying his mother, showing disrespect for authority in the person of the giant, stealing the giant's possessions, and vandalizing the beanstalk by cutting it down. Furthermore, says this moralist, the giant introduces ideas of cannibalism with his "Fee, Fie, fo, fum."[5]

Confronted with all of these serious and earnest objections, children's librarians may ask themselves whether their own commitment to the folktale is well-founded or whether it is simply an inherited enthusiasm light-headedly passed on from one generation of professional to another. Are there any intellectual foundations supporting such convictions? If so, some criteria for the selection and use of these materials may be established.

If one examines the anxieties about the effects of folktales upon children, there may be discerned several assumptions common to all of them: (1) that folktales are ordinary constructs of everyday life, subject to everyday moral judgments; (2) that the meanings of folktales are literal ones to be analyzed at a literal and didactic level; (3) that perceived content in reading or listening will have perceived and direct effect upon behavior. And underlying all of these assumptions is a fearfulness about exposing children to a breadth of experience beyond that officially approved of by the adult. An analysis of each of these assumptions brings into question its validity.

Assumption 1: The folktale is an ordinary construct of everyday life. The folktale cannot be defined as a realistic story, nor is it intended to be that. The formulaic introduction to the folktale at once alerts the listener or reader to its never-never land setting: "Once there was and was not"; "Once upon a time"; "Il était une fois"; "A story, a story; let it come, let it go." In all languages and cultures, openings such as these announce that one has moved into imaginary experience, where ordinary rules are suspended by a "willing suspension of disbelief." And so at the end, the experience is closed off by another formula: "And they lived happily ever after." "That's the way it was and that's the way it is, to this good day." "Off with the rat's tail!" The world of the fairy tale is an enclosed world, a world that never was, a world with a prescribed entrance and exit. At a very early age children learn the nature of this special world. They hear the formulas and know at once where they are, and it is not at the corner of First and Main. Things happen and are allowed to happen which do not happen and which may not be allowable in ordinary life. Knowing themselves in a world of make-believe, the conventions of that world are accepted by children. Three is a magic number; youngest children are recognized for their genuine selves and thus become kings, queens, heroes or heroines; giants are indeed fearful, but they are easily outwitted and quickly done away with; quests are dangerous but necessary, usually resulting in triumphant homecomings. Children know the difference between this simple and logical world and the complex one of reality. They do not mistake Jack's beans for the beans planted in their own gardens. They do not expect rowboats to fly by land and air. To delight in such magical and imaginative experience is not to forsake the world of natural laws and societal restraints. But such delight can provide an expansion of ordinary boundaries, a form of imaginative play which appears to be universally indulged in, and which may be necessary for creative leaps of the imagination into new concepts of reality.[6]

Assumption 2: The meanings of folktales are literal ones to be accepted or rejected at a literal and didactic level. On the contrary, because they exist in a world of make-believe, folktales must be accepted as a collection of extended images which present human experience in symbolic forms. Story has always been associated with pleasure. It is also associated with religion, with myth and ritual, with medicine and healing, with the hunt and with planting and reaping. It has incorporated into it elements of magic, of belief and ritual, of poetry and of dance. It is used to educate the young, to show them the way in which they are to go. Considerations of the function of folklore may proceed from aesthetic, historical, cultural, literary, or psychological modes of thought, but not from personal expediency.

Studied as literature, the folktale provides archetypal themes and motifs which may be used as a basis for literary criticism.[7] Analyzed by the anthropologist, the folktale is seen as an artifact of society, a clue to its patterns of behavior and thought.[8] Structuralists study myth and folktale to discern beneath the forms similarities which may lead to valid hypotheses about the operation of the human mind.[9] Studied by the psychologist, the folktale is seen as a symbolic language, related to that of dreams and common to all people, representing in its imagery the universal search of the individual personality for resolution of conflict.[10]

Children may be introduced to folklore simply as pleasurable experience. Folklore may also serve as an introduction to literary forms and genres, as well as to the symbolic and artistic use of language.[11] Folklore may serve as an introduction to other cultures, fostering an inquiring turn of mind and an increased sensitivity to the human condition.[12] Or one may find in folklore a psychological value, a source of that emotional catharsis which is one of the functions of vicarious experience.[13]

From whatever discipline one approaches the study of folklore, a commonality seems to emerge. Springing from the vast variety of individual and societal experiences, the folktale flowers out of the human need for the organization of experience. To attempt to set restraints upon or to control the forms of this creative energy seems not only undesirable but impossible. The meaning of myth lies in its origins, and in the power of those forces which require man to be a creator of myth. Bred out of the unconscious and the property of all the people, folklore resists any intellectual control of its content by individual, group, or government.[14]

Assumption 3: Perceived content in reading or listening will have perceived and direct effect upon behavior. Very little is known, really, about the effects of reading upon behavior. Nonetheless, as persons who care about children and what they read, children's librarians are implicitly committed to the belief that reading does have an effective power in the determined effort of children to "become," upon the power of the word to inform and inspire. But that power is often subtle and indirect, unrevealed to the literal-minded. If one accepts that folktales are symbolic representations of reality, then one must search for the reality for which the symbol stands, for art reveals itself in symbol. In a fairy tale, the form of the hero or heroine is unimportant; he or she may be animal or human or inanimate object, god or goddess, peasant or noble, wise man or simpleton. It does not matter whether the protagonist is male or female, whether he achieves his goals by magical, spiritual, or personal power. The essential is that the goal of becoming heroic is present. Thus the meaning of the story lies not in its overt forms, the described events of the tale, but in its symbolic representation of the struggle to become, which is precisely the first task of childhood. No relevance could be more apparent. Within each child is the need to grow, of discovering the means to liberate the creative energy of his growing self into creative acts, of inheriting the kingdom, whether that kingdom be on earth or in heaven. The hero or heroine must be separated from the role of child as he or she departs on whatever his or her quest may be. The successful completion of the quest assures the recognition of one's truest nature.

I would submit that no folktale sets forth, as a model, violence, fearfulness, inhumanity to man or beast, or dereliction in human love and responsibility. Evil exists in the folktale, but not as a model, not in a form to lead children to the love of evil. The function of all literature is to illuminate experience in its totality, not to set up vitiated models according to prescription. The fearfulness which lies beneath the desire to control the content of imaginative literature for children seems to me to lie in a fearfulness concerning the very nature of human experience, by denying the existence of the variability and sometimes threatening aspects of human life. But the knowledge of good and evil will not be denied.

The function of folklore has been defined as establishing sanctions for society, as a method of providing a framework within which the individual may learn ways of dealing with experience. As such, it may hold up models supportive of the authority of society, and others antithetical to it. It may criticize society by demonstrating how a clever or worthy person who sets himself in opposition to the established order may cleanse it by confounding the obtuse, the pompous, or the unworthy. Folklore has also a function of amusing and delighting, of satisfying the need for playful manipulation of the human condition. All of these functions, and others not discussed here, seem to be functions useful in the lives of children. One may not wish to introduce children to all the varieties of folktale at the same point in their development. Some tasks are more open to interpretation via folktale at one age than another. This is a matter for wise choices, and there is room for differences of opinion.

In its deepest sense, folklore is never immoral, for it deals with the order of things, delineating with psychological and cultural accuracy the search for personal and societal harmony. Folklore presents us with rich images and symbolic representations of cultures, times, and people among whom we may not have lived, but whom we can recognize. Underneath the images may be discerned the universal preoccupations of man, the desire to live honorably within one's society, in harmony with nature and one's fellow beings. Children, as well as adults, may be helped to deeper and more imaginative levels of understanding by sharing in the pleasures and wisdom of the folktale.[15]

Building the Collection of Folktales for Children

In building the collection of folktales for children, one is presented with a richness of materials confusing in its variety and extent. There are some principles useful to keep in mind. The scope of the collection should be considered. First, it is suggested that this be as broad as possible, including all the genres of traditional narrative: myth, epic, saga, hero tale, fable, medieval romance, beast stories, as well as fairy tales. Although most of this literature was never intended for children, much of it has been rewritten in forms which children can appreciate, and through which they may be introduced to literature. Stories drawn not only from the classic and Christian traditions, but from the Buddhist, Moslem, Judaic, and other religious traditions should be included. The cultural breadth of the collection should also be considered. Western European traditional literature has always been well represented in children's literature, and new editions and selections of it are constantly published. The post-war years have, in addition, seen a rich infusion of published folklore from non-Western societies. It is now possible to introduce children to the imagery and traditional literature of Asian, of African and Polynesian, and of Latin American societies. The ethnic diversity of American culture has also been increasingly represented in folklore for children, so that we have good collections of black folklore, Appalachian folklore, native American legends, Eskimo myths, regional tales. As far as possible, all collections for children should include as wide and diverse a range of materials as is available.

What criteria may be established for selection of individual titles in the folklore area? It is important to understand that, in spite of our constant reference to "the oral tradition," most of what is published for children as folklore is not drawn directly from oral sources, but is based upon literary sources.[16] Classical myth is drawn from written Greek or Latin originals. *Beowulf*, whatever the theories of its oral origins, exists for us in a single extant manuscript, from which all versions of the story are drawn. Most of the standard repertoire of European folktales depend upon written (and often translated) sources, such as Grimm, Perrault, Afanasiev, Asbjørnsen and Moe, Jacobs, Burton, etc. Asian sources include the *Ramayama*, the *Mahabharata*, and other Sanskritic literature, translated. African stories are often taken from versions set down by European missionaries or colonial officers such as Rattray, Calloway, or Bleek. The field recordings of anthropologists and folklorists as published in journals or monographs provide another mine of material.

In examining a new book of folklore for children one asks, therefore, what sources has the author used? In the relatively infrequent instances where the version at hand has indeed been recorded directly from an oral presentation, the author is usually explicit about the where, when, and who. In all cases of the use of materials written by others, acknowledgment of such sources ought to be made. It is worth noting that publishers of juvenile folklore have recently become much more explicit in meeting this criterion than used to be true. Such qualifiers as "retold by," "compiled by," or "edited by" are found in title pages, and more explicit notes are often to be found in colophon or explanatory materials.

Once the source of the stories has been established, one may evaluate the style.[17] The style of a rewritten story should approach known models. Folkloristic devices such as formulas, repeated phrases, or interpolated verse are usual. As one reads the literary models for European folktales, one becomes aware of distinctive styles: the dry humor of the Norwegian stories;

the sophistication of the French *contes de fées;* the peasant imagery of Grimm. These are definable, and should be preserved in versions drawn from these sources. African folklore draws more directly from the oral. Often it uses song as a connecting device. It is rich in ideophones, those representations of sound so provocative in effect.

The stock of animal characters or imaginary creatures will vary from culture to culture, as will formulaic openings and closings. A style which is too prosaic or one which is overelaborated may betray an unfamiliarity with the dramatic nature of oral literature. The elements which contribute to the lively and direct experience of oral performance should be approximated in the literary version: conversation rather than narration, emphasis on events rather than description. It is this dramatic simplicity which makes the folktale so compelling and popular. Mountains of descriptive verbiage change the very nature of the popular tale.

In selecting folklore for children one must also consider its appeal to children. Terse dramatic events following each other in rapid and fairly predictable order are the essence of the folktale. Characters tend to play archetypal roles rather than to be individualized in the manner of realistic fiction. Elements of magic and the whole pantheon of fabulous beasts and personages enter in.

Another consideration in evaluating folklore for children is the difficulty of the reading level. A number of levels of difficulty should be available, corresponding to the ages at which children most seem to enjoy the stories. The "Favorite Fairy Tales" series edited by Virginia Haviland and published by Little, Brown and Company are good examples of stories at the third or fourth grade reading level of the children who will choose them as voluntary reading. Dorothy Hosford's retelling of the Norse myths is admirably suited to the fourth grader who seems ripe for these tales. Recent versions of single Greek myths and old English stories by Ian Serrailler are excellent for the fifth grader. On the other hand, the old "color" series of fairy tales edited by Andrew Lang, with their small print and dense, dark pages do not have much appeal to modern children, accustomed to open-space pages and larger print. These old Lang books, parenthetically, include a few examples of racial or ethnic stereotypes which have been wisely eliminated in currently edited selections from Lang.

Some editions of folktales will not be on a reading level easily accessible to elementary school children, but are nonetheless useful in the collection as storytelling or read-aloud material for the adult. Padraic Colum's versions of the myths are examples, as are the collections published in the Myth and Legends Series by Henry Z. Walck. Various editions and versions of folktales make for interest and variety in the collection.

Illustrations are another consideration. Do they add to the cultural or aesthetic impact of the story? If an anthology is selected on a cultural or national basis, strength is added by illustrations drawn from the artistic traditions of that culture. Courlander's anthologies of folktales are good examples of such sensitivity to the supportive function of design and illustration, as are some of the recent African collections.

Heavy reliance upon folktales as the text of picture books has been a strong trend in recent years. The folktale supplies a source of inspiration for the artist, as well as relieving him of dependence upon his own or someone else's literary skills. An entire picture gallery could be devoted to "The House That Jack Built," Aesop's Fables, or Grimm's fairy tales in single editions. Selection here is based upon aesthetic judgments more than upon text. A cautionary word, however, reminds the adult that these stories are often not suitable, because of length and complexity, for the three- to five-year-old preschoolers of the picture book audience.

Conclusions

In recapitulation, the evidence seems to be that folklore is here to stay as a source of literature for children. Despite the negative opinions of various interest groups, evidence from scholarly disciplines shows a growing appreciation of the functions of folklore in human societies. That children should participate in this creative activity and the rich literature drawn from it seems wise and good. Criteria for the selection of such materials should include considerations of scope, cultural breadth, authenticity, style, reading level, and design. Drawing upon the excellence of the many materials now available, the folklore collection can provide a range of meaningful reading and listening experiences for the elementary school child.

Notes

1. Lucy Sprague Mitchell, *Here and Now Storybook: Two- Through Seven-Year-Olds*, new ed. rev. & enl. (New York: E. P. Dutton, 1921, 1948), pp. 23–36.
2. H. E. Wheeler, "The Psychological Case Against the Fairy Tale," *Elementary School Journal* 29 (June 1929):754–755. *Psychological Abstracts* of the same period includes abstracts of such psychological studies as H. Lobl, "Die Entmutigung duch das Märchen (Discouragement Engendered by Fairy Tales)," 1930, and S. Lorand, "Fairy Tales and Neurosis," 1935, citing negative effects of fairy tales in children's experience.
3. Ernest Jones, "Psychoanalysis and Folklore," in *The Study of Folklore*, by Alan Dundes (Englewood Cliffs, N.J.: Prentice-Hall, 1965), pp. 88–102. A psychoanalytical analysis of "Jack and the Beanstalk," by William H. Desmonde, is included in the same volume, pp. 107–109.
4. Betty Miles, "Atalanta and the Race," MS. 1 (March, 1973): pp. 75–78. Robert Moore, "From Rags to Witches: Stereotypes. Distortions and Anti-Humanism in Fairy Tales," *Interracial Books for Children Bulletin* 6, 1975, pp. 1–3.

5. Gary Alexander and Terry Warren, "What Should Your Children Read." *The Plain Truth,* April 1971, pp. 15–16, 37–39.
6. Erik H. Erikson in his *Childhood and Society,* 2nd ed. (New York: W. W. Norton, 1963) and Jean Piaget in *Play, Dreams and Imitation in Childhood* (New York: W. W. Norton, 1962) discuss the function of play and fantasy in children's development. See also Ruth E. Hartley and Robert M. Goldenson. *The Complete Book of Children's Play,* rev. ed. (New York: Apollo Editions, 1970), which includes books as play equipment at each age level beginning with the first year of life, suggesting that fairy tales be chosen with discretion in years before five. See also Susanna Millar, *The Psychology of Play* (Baltimore, Md.: Penguin Books, 1968).
7. Northrop Frye, *Anatomy of Criticism* (New York: Atheneum, 1966).
8. William R. Bascom, "Folklore and Anthropology," in Dundes, pp. 25–33.
9. Sanche de Gramont, "There Are No Superior Societies," *New York Times Magazine* 28 (January 1968): 28ff. A readable introduction to the thought of Claude Lévi-Strauss, "the father of structuralism."
10. Erich Fromm, *The Forgotten Language: An Introduction to the Understanding of Dreams, Fairy Tales, and Myths* (New York: Rinehart, 1951). Interprets the theories of both Freud and Jung.
11. Northrop Frye, "Elementary Teaching and Elemental Scholarship," *PMLA* 79 (May 1964): 11–19; *A Curriculum for English* (Lincoln, Neb.: University of Nebraska Press, 1966).
12. Jerome S. Bruner, *The Growth of Mind,* Occasional Paper No. 8 (Cambridge, Mass.: The Social Studies Curriculum Program, Educational Services, Inc., 1966); Alan Dundes, "Folklore as a Mirror of Culture," *Elementary English* XLVI (April 1969): 471–482.
13. Bruno Bettelheim, *The Uses of Enchantment: The Meaning and Importance of Fairy Tales* (New York: Alfred A. Knopf, 1976); Marcia Brown, "The Hero Within," *Elementary Enlgish* XLIV (March 1967): 201–207. Ursula K. LeGuin, "The Child and the Shadow," *The Quarterly Journal of the Library of Congress* 32 (April 1975): 139–148.
14. For an account of governmental intervention, see Kornei Chukovsky, *From Two to Five* (Berkeley: University of California Press, 1966), pp. 114–139. "The Battle for the Fairy Tale."
15. C. S. Lewis. *Surprised by Joy: The Shape of My Early Life* (New York: Harcourt, Brace, 1955); J. R. R. Tolkien. *Tree and Leaf* (Boston: Houghton Mifflin, 1965). Literary testimony to the mystique of the fairy tale by two of England's most celebrated writers of fantasy.
16. See, for example, Iona Opie and Peter Opie, *The Classic Fairy Tales* (London: Oxford University Press, 1974). ". . . the texts of twenty-four of the best-known fairy tales as they were first printed in English, or in the earliest surviving or prepotent text. . . ."
17. Elizabeth Cook. *The Ordinary and the Fabulous: An Introduction to Myths, Legends and Fairy Tales for Teachers and Storytellers* (Cambridge: Cambridge University Press, 1969). A study in style which compares texts of selected retold versions for children with original texts.

Comparison of Folk Tale Variants

Elinor P. Ross

Many variants of folk tales may be found in literature. These variants exist for many reasons. First of all, folk tales were passed down orally from generation to generation, and differences crept in as they were told again and again. Then, when the stories were transcribed, the writers incorporated their own points of view and adapted the stories for their audiences. Through translations, modifications, and simplifications, folk tales acquired many forms while retaining their basic story lines.

Elementary students may be unaware of the many existing forms of folk tales, and children in the intermediate grades can easily become absorbed in a fascinating study of variants. Children could be encouraged to collect all of the books on fairy tales they can find—those from school and public libraries, from home, and from the homes of grandparents. After providing an overview of the tales and an introduction to variants, the teacher could divide the class into three or four groups with each group investigating the variants of one folk tale in depth. Along with developing an appreciation for folklore, the children will also have the opportunity to become aware of expressive language and to sharpen critical reading skills by making comparisons.

There are several activities related to folk tale variants that children can pursue. They may compare different versions with regard to specific events that occur within the stories, character development, settings, style of writing, and the ways the stories end. They might check the circumstances surrounding the collection of the tales, the countries of their origin, and the approximate dates they were first published. In making their comparisons, the students should be able to identify the underlying motifs that remain the same despite modification of the stories.

Many of the popular tales originated in France, Germany, or England. Charles Perrault published a set of eight French fairy tales which are still popular. In Germany, Jacob and Wilhelm Grimm collected stories from country folk over a period of twelve years. Somewhat later Joseph Jacobs began compiling English folk tales. The purposes and cultures of these writers influ-

SOURCE: *Language Arts* 56 (April 1979): 422–426.

enced their styles, and, as the folk tales spread from one country to another, the stories changed.

Perrault's fairy tales were sophisticated stories of the rich with castles and fine clothes. They have the "consciously elegant style of the literary tale" (Huck 1976, p. 188). Perrault was a member of the French Academy, and his audience was the court society of Louis XIV. He wrote with charm and wit, and used magic only when it appeared natural and reasonable.

The Brothers-Grimm were philologists who studied the language and grammar of the stories they collected (Huck 1976). As such, they were careful to preserve the style and content of these tales. The stories came from the poor; they told of hardships and were heavy with cruel and malicious deeds. Intended for adult audiences, the German folk tales in their original forms were not suitable for young children.

Unlike the Brothers Grimm, England's Joseph Jacobs wanted to write stories that children would enjoy. He wrote as a nurse would speak when telling fairy tales to children. He occasionally omitted an episode which he felt was inappropriate for children, and he altered the language to make the tales more comprehensible. All of his modifications were carefully recorded at the back of his books so that folklore purists could take note of the changes.

Contemporary writers and storytellers continue to modify these tales for today's readers. Some new versions of folk tales remain true to the style of the old, retaining the cadences, phrasings, and unusual words which contribute to the rich literary quality of these tales. In an effort to simplify the stories, however, some writers omit the fanciful language and destroy their fairy-like nature.

Lang's "Beauty and the Beast" (1964) is filled with bright images. When Beauty agrees to marry the Beast, the scene is described in the following manner.

> As she spoke a blaze of light sprang up before the windows of the palace; fireworks crackled and guns banged, and across the avenue of orange trees, in letters all made of fireflies, was written: Long live the prince and his bride. (p. 126)

In a recent simplified version this event is reduced to "As she spoke a miracle happened" (Grimm 1975, p. 12).

The language of folk tales is quaint and picturesque, unlike the straightforward prose of most of today's fiction. In their study of folk tale variants, children could seek out unusual words and expressions from early versions that may or may not be retained in later versions. For instance, in Steel's "The Old Woman and Her Pig" (1918), uncommon words such as *stile, quench, crooked, sixpence, shan't,* and *yonder* are used. In a recent edition (Old Woman . . . 1973) all of these words are retained except *yonder*. In Grimms' "Aschenputtel" (1886), a variant of "Cinderella," the heroine is dressed in "an old gray *kirtle*," and in Lang's "Cinderella" (1964) the stepsisters send for the best *tirewoman* (lady's maid) to help them prepare for the ball. Both *kirtle* and *tirewoman* are lost in recent versions. In "The Story of the Three Little Pigs" the following familiar expressions are repeated in nearly every version: "Not by the hair of my chinny-chin-chin" and "I'll huff and I'll puff and I'll blow your house in."

The illustrations in folk tales are also worth studying. Many new editions have appeared with illustrations that differ from stereotypes created years ago. Walt Disney popularized "Snow White" with his cartoon drawings of seven dwarfs and a pretty little maiden. In contrast to Disney's style, Nancy Burkert recently illustrated an edition of *Snow White* (Grimm 1972) in which she used her own fourteen-year-old daughter as a model for Snow White. Her meticulous drawings of dwarfs are the result of intensive research into the proportions of actual dwarfs. Cinderella, as illustrated by Pablo Ramírez (Perrault 1965), is an Oriental girl rather than a blond Anglo Saxon. After soaking up the atmosphere of the German fairy tale country, Maurice Sendak authentically illustrated an edition of Grimms' tales entitled *The Juniper Tree and Other Tales from Grimm* (Grimm 1973).

In recent years teachers, parents, librarians, and psychologists have become concerned about the horror, cruelty, and gory details found in some of the original versions of folk tales. Flaumenhaft (1969) denounced many of the popular tales; he called their heroes/heroines cannibalistic, villainous, or sadistic, and the tales themselves violators of ethical and educational codes. In response to criticisms such as these, many of the newer versions have been rewritten so that acts of cruelty are minimized and stories end happily.

Three folk tales with numerous variants are "Cinderella," "Little Red Riding Hood," and "The Three Bears." These will be discussed to provide a basis for classroom study. Other tales with interesting variants that children might choose to investigate are "Rumpelstiltskin," "The Elves and the Shoemaker," "Lazy Jack," "The Story of the Three Little Pigs," and "The Lad Who Went to the North Wind."

Cinderella stories are found all over the world, with more than five hundred European versions and at least one hundred non-European variants on record (Nelson 1972). Variations of the Cinderella motif occur in real life, as in the case of the Swedish maid who married a Rockefeller. In some variants, the main character is a hero instead of a heroine, but the same motif of the humble and kind triumphing over the proud and haughty remains.

There are many sources of Cinderella tales which can provide a basis for a comparison of variants. Nelson's anthology (1972) includes thirteen tales which are part of the Cinderella cycle, and Bingham and Scholt (1974) wrote synopses of twelve Cinderella tales from various countries. One of the oldest versions (Grimm 1886) highlights the cruelty of the stepmother and stepsisters toward Aschenputtel, and shows how the stepsisters are punished by self-inflicted wounds and blindness. On the other hand, the Irish Cinderella, "Tattercoats" (Nelson 1972), is light and amusing with a prince who loves Cinderella even when she is dirty and tattered. The version found in Lang (1964) is probably the most familiar of all, with a fairy godmother and a forgiving Cinderella.

Some interesting comparisons for children to make include the following: What is Cinderella's relationship to the other family members? How does Cinderella receive her magic gifts? What obstacles interfere with Cinderella's attendance at the ball? How many nights did Cinderella go to the ball? What must the prince do in order to win Cinderella? What happens to the stepsisters at the conclusion of the story?

"Little Red Riding Hood" is believed by some scholars (Arbuthnot 1972) to be an allegory of sunset and sunrise. The wolf represents night and devours Little Red Riding Hood who, in her red cape, represents the setting sun. In the Grimm version the hunter cuts open the wolf and releases Little Red Riding Hood (the sun) from her imprisonment in the wolf (the night).

Few stories have more variants than "Little Red Riding Hood." Originally Perrault wrote this fairy tale so that the heroine is eaten by the wolf and not restored to life (Lang 1964), but Grimms' story (1886) shows a hunter slitting open the wolf and rescuing Grandma and Little Red Riding Hood. Mavrogenes and Cummins (1976) analyzed variations in the language of twenty-seven versions of "Little Red Riding Hood" and reprinted an 1856 edition in which Little Red Riding Hood is saved from the wolf because of her kindness to a wasp, little tom-tit, and an aged crone. In some newer versions the story is modified so that Grandma runs out the back door, Little Red Riding Hood escapes the clutches of the wolf, and the wolf is chased from the hut and never seen again. One recent edition of *Little Red Riding Hood,* written in a humorous version by Beatrice Schenck de Regniers (1972), is based on the old versions by the Brothers Grimm.

In comparing variants, children might see answers to the following questions: What does Little Red Riding Hood take with her to Grandma's house? Is there only one wolf in the story? What happens to the wolf at the end of the story? Are Grandma and Little Red Riding Hood rescued and, if so, how? What morals can be drawn from different versions?

"The Story of the Three Bears" is not actually a folk tale because its origin can be traced to a single author, Robert Southey. The protagonist varies in different versions, however, so interesting comparisons can be made, and it is reasonable to include this story in a study of variants. In an early form entitled "Scrapefoot" (Told Under . . . 1966) the bears are visited by a fox instead of Goldilocks. In a later version (Jacobs n.d.) a naughty old woman walks into the bears' house, eats the porridge, and uses their chairs and beds. In another version (Steel 1818) the old woman becomes Goldilocks, who still has the characteristics of a rude woman. Contemporary versions often show Goldilocks as a sweet, innocent child who mistakenly wanders into a cottage and later becomes friendly with Baby Bear.

Nelson (1972) observed that a common motif in folk tales is a confrontation with a monster. As more recent versions of "The Story of the Three Bears" evolve, it is difficult to determine who represents the monster. In earlier versions the impudent old woman who invaded the bears' home appeared to be the monster, but in today's versions the bears seem to pose a threat to a naive child.

Children may consider the following questions: Who wanders into the house of the three bears? What words or phrases are used to describe the visitor? What sentences are repeated in nearly all versions? What happens to the visitor at the end of the story?

Similar questions may be used to guide children in their comparisons of other stories. These questions should be used only to get them started in noting differences. As they work, they will quickly find other variations in language, characterization, description, objects, and events. At the same time, they will be acquiring an intimacy with tales of wonder and enchantment that are part of their cultural legacy.

References

Arbuthonot, May Hill and Sutherland, Zena, *Children and Books*, 4th ed. Glenview, IL: Scott, Foresman and Company, 1972.

Bingham, Jane and Scholt, Grayce. "The Great Glass Slipper Search: Using Folktales with Older Children." *Elementary English* 51 (October 1974); 990–98.

DeRegniers, Beatrice Schenk. *Red Riding Hood*. New York: Atheneum, 1972.

Flaumenhaft, A. S. "Children's 'Sick' Stories." *Educational Forum* 33 (May 1969): 473–477.

Grimm Brothers. *Beauty and the Beast*. Los Angeles, CA: Gallery Books, 1975.

______. *Grimms' Fairy Tales*, translated by E. V. Lucas, Lucy Crane and Marian Edwardes. New York: Grosset and Dunlap, 1945.

______. *Household Stories*, translated by Lucy Crane. New York: Dover Publications, Inc., 1963 (1886).

______. *The Juniper Tree and Other Tales from Grimm*, translated by Lore Segal and Maurice Sendak. New York, N.Y.: Farrar, Straus, 1973.

______. *Snow-White and the Seven Dwarfs*, translated by Randall Jarrell. New York, N.Y.: Farrar, Straus, 1972.

Hannabus, C. Stuart. "The Moral of the Story." *The Times Educational Supplement* 3080 (June 7, 1974): 51.

Huck, Charlotte S. *Children's Literature in the Elementary School*, 3rd ed. New York: Holt, Rinehart and Winston, 1976.

Jacobs, Joseph. *English Folk and Fairy Tales*, 3rd rev. ed. New York: G. P. Putnam's Sons, n.d.

Johnson, Edna et al. *Anthology of Children's Literature*, 5th ed. Boston: Houghton Mifflin Company, 1977.

Lang, Andrew. *Blue Fairy Book*. New York: David McKay Company, Inc., 1964.

Lonsdale, Bernard J. and Mackintosh, Helen K. *Children's Experience Literature*. New York: Random House, 1973.

Mavrogenes, Nancy A. and Cummins, Joan S. "What Ever Happened to Little Red Riding Hood? A Study of a Nursery Tale and Its Language." ERIC ED 132576. Arlington, VA: ERIC Document Reproduction Service, 1976.

Nelson, Mary Ann. *A Comparative Anthology of Children's Literature*. New York: Holt, Rinehart and Winston, Inc., 1972.

The Old Woman and Her Pig, retold by Vera Southgate. Loughborough, England: Ladybird Books Ltd., 1973.

Perrault, Charles. *Cinderella*. Los Angeles: Gallery Books, 1973.

______. *Cinderella,* adapted for Walt Disney. New York: Golden Press, 1950.

______. *Cinderella,* retold by Doris R. Miller. Cleveland: The World Publishing Company, 1965.

Steel, Flora Annie. *English Fairy Tales*. New York: The Macmillan Company, 1962 (1918).

Sutherland, Zena, Ed. *The Arbuthnot Anthology of Children's Literature,* 4th ed. Glenview, IL: Scott, Foresman and Company, 1976.

The Three Bears. Racine, WI: Western Publishing Company, Inc., 1960.

The Three Little Pigs. Racine, WI: Whitman Publishing Company, 1936.

Told Under the Green Umbrella, selected by the Association for Childhood Education International. New York: The Macmillan Company, 1966.

What Ever Happened To Little Red Riding Hood? A Study of a Nursery Tale

Nancy A. Mavrogenes
Joan S. Cummins

Little Red Riding Hood was my first love. I felt that if I could have married Little Red Riding Hood, I should have known perfect bliss.

CHARLES DICKENS

The story of Red Riding Hood was first published in Paris in 1697 by Charles Perrault in his *Histoires ou contes du temps passé; avec moralités*. Within the last twenty-five years, however, an original manuscript containing five of Perrault's tales (including "Little Red Riding Hood") has come to light, dated 1695. This was a deluxe dedication copy intended for Mademoiselle Elisabeth Charlotte d'Orléans, niece of Louis XIV, and is now in the Pierpont Morgan Library in New York City. Before the end of 1697 Perrault's now famous

SOURCE: *The Horn Book Magazine,* June 1979, pp. 344–349. © by The Horn Book, Inc.

tales—"Little Red Riding Hood," "Sleeping Beauty," "Blue Beard," "Puss in Boots," and "Cinderella," among others—had been reprinted in Holland and France.

The existence of the story before Perrault's collection is unclear. Some scholars have attempted to find its origin in primitive mythology as early man's attempt to explain natural phenomena. Thus Red Riding Hood becomes dawn (or sometimes the sun) swallowed by and delivered from night represented by the wolf; or she is described as spring crowned with flowers, who cannot remain in the belly of the wolf (or winter). Furthermore, the story is linked to ancient legends like those of Cronus disgorging his devoured children in Greek mythology or Jonah swallowed by the whale in the Old Testament.

Other scholars have attempted to find evidence of the folk origin of the story in Perrault's language. The word *chaperon,* for instance, in the French title "Le Petit Chaperon rouge" is defined in seventeenth-century dictionaries as a type of hat worn in the Middle Ages. Also, the name Mother Goose has been connected with early folklore and even history. This familiar term was made famous by Perrault in his 1697 edition, the frontispiece of which showed three children and an old woman in front of the fire with a plaque on the wall reading "Contes de ma mère l'Oye." It has been suggested that in medieval French villages an old woman kept track of the geese and, as a stock teller of tales, could be called "ma mère l'Oye." The name Mother Goose in French has also been traced back to the mother of Charlemagne—Bertha, "Queen Goosefoot"—or to Bertha, called Bertha Goosefoot, wife of Robert II, king of France in the eleventh century. Finally, comparative folklorists, by matching Perrault's story with folk versions coming after him, can find elements which he removed as being in bad taste: for instance, the girl invited to eat her grandmother's flesh or her question about the hairy body of the wolf.

Such theories, however, have by no means been proved. In fact, it is clear that the story of Red Riding Hood has never circulated widely where folk tales are learned orally; practically all versions are based upon Perrault's tale or on that of the Brothers Grimm. Indeed, there are scholars who go so far as to believe that Perrault invented the story. It is also clear that fairy tales were fashionable in the court of Louis XIV twenty years before Perrault's publication. A letter by Madame de Sévigné to her daughter written in 1676 mentions the fairy tales "that they amuse the ladies with at Versailles." This was the Age of Reason, the neoclassical age, when bucolics and eclogues on classical models and thus stories of peasants were in fashion. There would be two aspects of the tale: the literal one for children and the symbolic for adults, wherein the wolf in bed seduces the girl. At least Perrault has a "moralité" at the end of his story warning young ladies about gentle wolves, a rational effort by Perrault, it has been suggested, to excuse adult enjoyment of puerile matter.

Since Perrault's publication of his tales, they have been translated into

English, German, Russian, Swedish, Chinese, and Japanese and have become thoroughly familiar to children everywhere. The first translation of Perrault into English was made by Robert Samber in 1729; it appeared in London, and before the end of the eighteenth century the translation had been reprinted many times in England. The first American editions, Samber's translation, were issued by Peter Edes in Haverhill, Massachusetts, in 1794, and by J. Rivington in New York in 1795.

The Brothers Grimm collected a peasant version of "Little Red Riding Hood," which was based on Perrault and included some German traditions, and printed it as "Rotkäppchen" in their collection of 1812. Their ending, which presumably came from German folklore, is different from Perrault's: Red Riding Hood alone or with her grandmother is rescued, either before or after being swallowed by the wolf.

During the nineteenth century individual tales by Perrault or by the Grimms were produced as chapbooks, or cheap books, costing only a penny in England or a few cents in America; it was through these editions that the stories became so popular. The 1856 version of "Little Red Riding Hood" described below cost six cents plain or twelve cents colored. The period was one of rapid growth in the children's book trade in both England and America; the first Hans Christian Andersen tales were published in English in 1846, and the first of Edward Lear's nonsense books appeared in 1841. "Little Red Riding Hood" was published in England in the *Home Treasury* series in 1843 by Felix Summerly; the series was designed to combat the unimaginativeness of the Peter Parley books, so popular in both England and America.

By this time there were many variances in the tale. For instance, Red Riding Hood would carry in her basket custard, butter, cakes, eggs, dainties, bread, cookies, meat, wine, or any combinations of these. And the endings were numerous. The wolf drowns in hot sausage water; he is slit open and filled with stones; he is burned in the throat by Red Riding Hood's cap; he tears the entrails and brains out of the girl and her grandmother; or after he is killed Red Riding Hood, her mother, her grandmother, and some wood nymphs all join in singing the "Marseillaise."

An 1856 version of the tale, published by McLoughlin Brothers in New York City as part of "Aunt Mary's series,"* features some unusual differences:

> While she was thus occupied [in sorting out the strawberries and flowers she had been picking], a wasp came buzzing along, and delighted at finding so many flowers without the trouble of searching for them, he began to drink up their honey very voraciously. Little Red Riding Hood knew well the difference of a wasp and a bee—how lazy the one, and how industrious the other, yet, as they are all God's creatures, she wouldn't kill it, and only said: "Take as much honey as you like, poor wasp, only do not sting me." The wasp buzzed louder, as if to thank her for her kindness, and, when he had sipped his fill, flew away. Presently, a little tom-tit, who had been hopping about on a bough opposite, darted down on the basket, and pecked at one of the strawberries.

*The copy is owned by Mr. Joseph R. Burton of Geneva, Illinois.

> "Eat as much as you like, pretty tom-tit," said Little Red Riding Hood; "there will be still plenty left for grandam and for me." The tom-tit replied, "Tweat—tweat," in his own eloquent language; and after gobbling up at least three strawberries, flew away, and was soon out of sight. Little Red Riding Hood now bethought her it was time to go on; so putting her wreath into her basket, she tripped along demurely enough, till she came to a brook, where she saw an aged crone, almost bent double, seeking for something along the bank. "What are you looking for Goody?" said the little girl. "For water-cresses, my pretty maid," mumbled the poor old woman; "and a sorry trade it is, that does not earn me half bread enough to eat." Little Red Riding Hood thought it very hard the poor old creature should work and be hungry too, so she drew from her pocket a large piece of bread, which her mother had given her to eat by the way, and said, "Sit down, Goody, and eat this, and I will gather your water-cresses for you." The old woman willingly accepted the offer, and sat down on a knoll, while Little Red Riding Hood set to work in good earnest, and had presently filled her basket with water-cresses. When her task was finished, the old crone rose up briskly, and patting the little maid's head, said, in quite a different voice: "Thank you, my pretty Little Red Riding Hood, and now, if you happen to meet the green huntsman as you go along, pray give him my respects, and tell him there is game in the wind." Little Red Riding Hood promised to do so, and walked on, but presently she looked back to see how the old woman was getting along, but, look as sharp as she might, she could see no trace of her, nor of her water-cresses. She seemed to have vanished clean out of sight. "It is very odd," thought Little Red Riding Hood, to herself, "for surely I can walk faster than she." Then she kept looking about her, and prying into all the bushes, to seek for the green huntsman, whom she had never heard of before, and wondered why the old woman had given her such a message. At last, just as she was passing by a pool of stagnant water, so green that you would have taken it for grass, and have walked into it, as Little Red Riding Hood, who had never seen it before, though she had gone that same way often enough, had nearly done, she perceived a huntsman clad in green from top to toe, standing on the bank, apparently watching the flight of some birds that were wheeling above his head. "Good Morning, Master Huntsman," said Little Red Riding Hood; "the old water-cress woman sends her service to you, and says there is game in the wind." The huntsman nodded assent, and bent his ear to the ground to listen, and then drew out an arrow tipped with a green feather, and strung his bow, without taking any further notice of Little Red Riding Hood, who trudged onwards, wondering what it all meant.

At the end of the story the girl is saved by the huntsman, and the old crone has turned into a beautiful young fairy who will always protect Red Riding Hood because of her "goodness of heart" in being so kind to the wasp, the tom-tit, and the watercress woman. The only indication of the origin of this version has been found in F. H. Lee's *Folk Tales of All Nations* (Coward), wherein the wasp, a little bird, and an old dame looking for cresses appear in the section "France." The fairy element and moral are not included in this version, however. It may be of additional interest to note that both the wasp and watercress are conception symbols—that is, in some folk literature they cause conception when eaten.

Another interesting feature of the McLoughlin story is the quality of its language. The vocabulary is sophisticated—"infantine," "voraciously," "demurely"—and the sentences are complex. For example,

> "The better to eat you up," exclaimed the wolf, who was just about to make a spring at the poor little girl, when a wasp, who had followed her into the cottage, stung the wolf in his nostril, and made him sneeze aloud, which gave the signal to a tom-tit perched on a branch near the open casement, who called out "Tweat—tweat," which warned the green huntsman, who accordingly let fly his arrow, that struck the wolf right through the ear and killed him on the spot.

Not only is this a very long sentence—eighty-eight words—but it is a sentence in which idea is piled upon idea, requiring of the reader or the listener a highly developed sense of language. Furthermore, another kind of literary sophistication is exhibited by the way the whole story is put together; there are subplots, interior monologue, multiple morals, and imagery.

In more recent times the wide interest in "Little Red Riding Hood" can be seen in a variety of places. A Freudian interpretation of the tale sees the girl's adventures as the oedipal stage in the development of the child, the huntsman being the strong father figure. Bruno Bettelheim, in his 1976 book on the significance of fairy tales for children, explains that " 'Little Red Cap' takes up some crucial problems the school-age girl has to solve if oedipal attachments linger on in the unconscious, which may drive her to expose herself dangerously to the possibility of seduction." The psychoanalyst Erich Fromm goes even further: "The wolf is really displaying pregnancy-envy when he fills his belly (womb) with the girl and her grandmother, and is punished when Little Red Riding Hood stows stones, the symbol of sterility, in his insides. This is presented as a tale of women who hate men and sex."

On a less exalted plane a modern version of the tale shown on television by the Public Broadcasting System was entitled "Little Black Riding Hood," and her basket contained soul food; she wore a red pants suit, and at the end everyone was saved, including the wolf, who was taken to the city zoo where he would be assured of three meals a day. Finally, even more recently, we find Soviet leader Leonid I. Brezhnev referring to the story in a toast to President Tito on a state visit to Yugoslavia in 1976. Alluding to statements made during the American election campaign, which cast shadows on Soviet-Yugoslav relations, Mr. Brezhnev said, " 'Authors of such fairy tales try to present Yugoslavia as a helpless Little Red Ridinghood, whom the terrible and bloodthirsty wolf—the aggressive Soviet Union—is preparing to dismember and devour.' "

Surely the sturdy folk tale has had a long and active life.

The Uses of Bettelheim's *The Uses of Enchantment*

Anthony Arthur

Late last winter Dr. Bruno Bettelheim spoke to a large and appreciative audience at the CATE (California Association of Teachers of English) convention in Los Angeles about his new book, *the Uses of Enchantment: The Meaning and Importance of Fairy Tales* (New York: A. Knopf, Inc., 1976). After his speech I asked Dr. Bettelheim if he might be able to join in the table talk I would be leading on his book that afternoon. No, he said, he would like to come, but he had already made arrangements to take his grandson to Disneyland.

The participants in the table talk were sorry to hear that Bettelheim would not be available, but delighted with the reason; it was totally consistent with the image of a man who had himself integrated the demands of his personal life with his professional concerns—especially the need for fantasy. That feeling itself was consistent with the impression conveyed by his talk and by his book, which is a wise, learned, and humane argument for the fairy tale.

There are so few critical books of real merit about children's literature that those of us who deal with the subject on any level must rejoice that a man of Bettelheim's staure has devoted his considerable talents to it. Despite some reservations that I have about both the premises and the conclusions of *The Uses of Enchantment*, it is without question a valuable and stimulating book. Because it deals with the "uses" of enchantment, I think it is appropriate to discuss Bettelheim's book in two ways: first, what are its uses for teachers, both of children's literature and of children, and second, how effective is his method of psychoanalytical criticism in terms of giving us a better understanding of fairy tales as literature?

Before considering these questions, we should be clear as to what Bettelheim considers the "uses of enchantment" to be for children. Literature must, he says, "enrich a child's life; it must stimulate his imagination; help him to develop his intellect and to clarify his emotions; be attuned to his anxieties and aspirations; give full recognition to his difficulties, while at the same time suggesting solutions to the problems which perturb him. In short, it must at one and the same time relate to all aspects of his personality"

SOURCE: *Language Arts* 55 (April 1978): 455–459, 533.

(p. 5). Fairy tales, he says, deal with basic problems of existence; i.e., the death of parents, desertion, the desire for eternal life. They teach that "a struggle against severe difficulties in life is unavoidable—but that if one does not shy away, but steadfastly meets unexpected and often unjust hardships, one masters all obstacles and at the end emerges victorious" (p. 8).

Specific examples of this process are frequent and unequivocal in Bettelheim's reading of fairy tales: we read, abstracted in the breathless prose of the dust-jacket, "how the Wicked Stepmother releases the child's terrors when his or her own loving mother is suddenly, out of frustration or fatigue, transformed into a frightening stranger; how the advent of the Fairy Godmother reassures children that their own 'lost' loving parent will reappear and protect them; how the triumph of the Youngest Son or Daughter (or the youth labeled dumb) promises that one can hope to match the intelligence and success of an older sibling or, more deeply, of the giant and clever race of adults among whom the child feels powerless and inadequate," and so on.

None of this is formally apprehended by children, Bettelheim notes, nor should it be. "A child who is made aware of what the figures in fairy tales stand for in his own psychology will be robbed of a much-needed outlet, and devastated by having to realize the desires, anxieties, and vengeful feelings that are ravaging him" (p. 57).

To sum up Bettelheim's position, fairy tales provide a world for children that reflects their impressions of what life should be like; they provide necessary assurance that the world has meaning and purpose, and that children can succeed despite their own limitations and in spite of imposed hardships.

Fairy tales, then, are not only useful but essential for children, in Bettelheim's view. What are the uses of his book for teachers? There are several, both personal and professional in nature. Personally, I suppose, every teacher in the elementary schools will find his observations on the appeals of fairy tales intriguing. For example, speaking of "Little Red Riding Hood." Bettelheim says that it is believable for a child that a kindly grandmother who sometimes punishes him could become a wolf; it is common for parents to be split, in the child's eyes, between "benevolent and threatening aspects," and beneficial for the child to vent aggression on a substitute parent—the wolf—without "feeling guilt" (p. 68).

Personal benefits, especially for teachers in the elementary schools, shade quickly into professional benefits. In a general sense, *The Uses of Enchantment* provides teachers not only with a humanistic overview of fairy tales but with arguments for their inclusion in the school curriculum and answers, if they are still needed, to parents who object to them as irrelevant timewasters. More specifically, there are several ways in which I have found Bettelheim's approach useful.

The first is that he provides confirmation of many observations which come under the heading of common-sense, observations which any attentive reader of children's literature will make. The transformation motif, for example, noted above in "Little Red Riding Hood," is one that my students have frequently commented on. Equally common is the fear of isolation, which Bettelheim discusses: "There is no greater threat in life than that we will be deserted . . . ; and the younger we are, the more excruciating is our anxiety when we feel deserted, for the younger child actually perishes . . . Therefore, the ultimate consolation is that we shall never be deserted" (p. 145).

These are, as I noted, common-sense observations. For those who are teachers of literature, and not psychologists, and are wary of psychological generalizations even when making them, they are pleasant confirmations of our intuition. But Bettelheim also provided insights perhaps not so readily available. Two examples, out of many, are his comments on the punishment of evil and the effects of dream deprivation.

Concerning the first point, the punishment of evil, I have generally contented myself with noting Chesterton's comment, popularized by C. S. Lewis, that children, being naturally good, love justice, while adults, who are wicked, prefer mercy—particularly in discussing the sanitized versions of "Cinderella." Bettelheim takes us one step closer to the truth, I think, when he says that it is not that children are naturally good, but that they need to see punishment inflicted that fits the crime. If those who inflict injury are not punished, Bettelheim says, "the child thinks that nobody is serious about protecting him; the more severely those bad ones are dealt with, the more secure the child feels" (p. 191).

Again, when Bettelheim discusses the effects on patients deprived of the opportunity to dream and explains that they are prone to emotional disturbance (p. 83), I find support for the illustration I often use of John Stuart Mill and the sad results of his education, so rigorously deprived of imaginative literature.

A third benefit for teachers to be derived from Bettelheim's approach is that he provides very close readings of a number of familiar tales. One example should suffice. "The Three Languages" is about a boy who learns in turn the languages of dogs, birds, and frogs, and is rejected by his disgusted father for not gaining a useful education. Bettelheim begins by noting that there is a mutual rejection involved: the father places no value in what the son learns, and the son must forfeit his father's esteem in order to learn what he could not learn at home. The creatures he encounters represent the elements: dog and earth, birds and air, frogs and water. Reading more deeply, the dogs represent instinctual freedoms—the freedom to "bite," to excrete in an uncontrolled way, and to indulge sexual needs without restraint; however, they also represent loyalty and friendship, and can be tamed. They are, Bettelheim says, equivalent to the ego. The birds are "the superego, with its investment in high goals and ideals, its soaring flights of fancy and imagined perfections." The frogs, associated with the original element from which all life came, water, represents the id in an unformed but changeable aspect. Bettelheim's psychological point in discussing this story turns around the idea of personality integration, and he argues, more persuasively than my schematic outline can indicate, that one must learn the "languages" of all three aspects before such integration is achieved (pp. 97–102).

The fourth benefit of Bettelheim's book is his comparisons of different versions of the same tales, especially "Cinderella," and between fairy tales and other genres such as fables and myths. An excellent brief example of the latter is his discussion of "The Three Little Pigs" and "The Ant and the Grasshopper." Bettelheim values "The Three Little Pigs" as a "pleasant" warning for children that "we must not be lazy and take things easy, for if we do, we may perish. Intelligent planning and foresight combined with hard labor will make us victorious over even our most ferocious enemy—the wolf!" The pigs' houses, Bettelheim says, are "symbolic of man's progress in history: from a lean-to shack to a wooden house, finally to a house of solid brick. Internally, the pigs' actions show progress from the id-dominated personality to the superego-influenced but essentially ego-controlled personality." The fable of "The Ant and the Grasshopper" has the same moral, Bettelheim says, but has "no hidden meaning." There is nothing left "to our imagination." More important, there is no hope left for the child who identifies with the grasshopper. Whereas the child who identifies with the younger pigs has the older pig triumphant, only "doom" awaits the grasshopper "beholden to the pleasure principle." It is an either-or situation, in which "having made a choice once settles things forever" (p. 43).

There are, then, a number of uses for the reader of Bettelheim's book. Naturally there are objections, or at least qualifications, to be considered. They have to do with aspects of culture, psychology, and morality.

Concerning the first point, Alison Lurie (*Harper's*, June 1976, pp. 94–96) has objected that Bettelheim's selection of tales is too culture-limited to be convincing—that Bettelheim's handful of stories are known because "they are the ones chosen from among . . . thousands . . . by Victorian editors to suit a rigid, paternalistic, bourgeois society not unlike Freud's Vienna." As Lurie has just finished noting that the stories depict fathers as weak because they "date from an early matriarchal society . . . and were handed on principally by women," we need not take her objection seriously. In any case, Bettelheim's extensive analysis of "Cinderella" alone as it appears in ancient Egypt, Rome, and China shows how, rather than being bound by cultural restrictions, he is trying to break free of them, to show that the emotions depicted by fairy tales are indeed universal and not limited by cultural conditions.

A more serious limitation than Lurie's cultural one is that Bettelheim's Freudian interpretations inevitably force the ordinary reader to stop at a certain point and say "enough!" It is a tribute to Bettelheim that the reader does not, in fact, backpedal ferociously out of the book, that he or she will go to the trouble of separating the useful from the doubtful. For example, consider the account of the glass slipper in Bettelheim:

> In the slipper ceremony, which signifies the betrothal of Cinderella and the prince, he selects her because in symbolic fashion she is the uncastrated woman who relieves him of his castration anxiety, which would interfere with a happy marital relationship. She selects him because he appreciates her in

> her "dirty" sexual aspects, lovingly accepts her vagina in the form of the slipper, and approves of her desire for a penis, symbolized by her tiny foot fitting within the slipper-vagina. That is why the prince brings the beautiful slipper to Cinderella and why she puts her tiny foot into it—only as she does so is she recognized as the right bride. But as she slips her foot into the slipper she asserts that she, too, will be active in their sexual relationship; she will do things, too. And she also gives the assurance that she is not and never was lacking in anything; she has everything that fits, as her foot snugly into the slipper.
>
> A reflection on a universally accepted part of the wedding ceremony may lend support to this idea. The bride stretches out one of her fingers for the groom to slip a ring onto it. Pushing one finger through a circle made out of the thumb and index finger of the other hand is a vulgar expression for intercourse. But in the ring ceremony something entirely different is symbolically expressed. The ring, a symbol for the vagina, is given by the groom to his bride; she offers him in return her outstretched finger, so that he may complete the ritual.

Only a True Believer, washed in the blood of Freud, will buy this, but it doesn't invalidate the excellent points made earlier about "Cinderella." It does, however, raise a question in terms of the usability of *The Uses of Enchantment.* How is one to use such information, other than to wake up an eight o'clock class?

A more serious objection to Bettelheim's Freudian position has to do with his initial premise that fairy tales must benefit the child in some way. Early on, Bettelheim admits that fairy tales are art, and admits that the process of art is a mystery. Apparently he is willing to evaluate the results of art in ways which discount those works not up to his psychological standards. This happens a number of times in his book; two examples are pertinent.

First, "Little Toot" is criticized by Bettelheim as harmful because it encourages children in the false belief that they can accomplish whatever they really desire. "I think I can" chug-chug is a third rate contrivance with no claim to art, so Bettelheim's objection to it on psychological grounds is unobjectionable. But Bettelheim also objects to Hans Christian Andersen, whose stories are works of art, in his discussion of the "youngest child as simpleton." Bettelheim notes that "it is helpful for the child to identify with the stupid or degraded child hero of the fairy tale, who he knows will eventually show his superiority . . ." (p. 104). "The Ugly Duckling," though a good story, is not helpful to the child, Bettelheim says, because it misdirects that child's fantasy. The point is that happiness is not to be achieved by changing into a being of a different nature. A "depressive world-view" that "one's fate is inexorable" underlies the story, Bettelheim says (p. 104).

The practical effect of this evaluation will be to make the parent or teacher who values Bettelheim's advice dispense with "Little Toot" and with "The Ugly Duckling" on the same ground: that they are not good for the child *psychologically.* Thus the moral imperative that children's literature has been struggling to replace with a more general principle of artistic evaluation rears its ugly head again. The inevitable result is withdrawal of the works, or censorship—though for the best of motives, of course.

The final point that has to be made is that Bettelheim sees fairy tales as both psychologically useful and as morally instructive. Children, he says, see that good characters are rewarded and evil characters are punished. Sensibly enough, they decide they will be good. Admittedly this is true of many stories, but at the same time they are clearly amoral as well—wishfulfillments celebrating the escape from poverty and weakness and the achievement of freedom, represented by wealth, physical beauty, and social position.

Bettelheim's analysis of "The Frog King" is worth noting in this regard. The princess, it will be recalled, consistently violates the bargain she has made with the frog, and the story concludes with her slamming the frog against the wall, whereupon he turns into a prince and they live happily ever after. As I read it, the story is a perfect example of a selfish, petulant child being rewarded for an act of malicious spite, and not "moral" in any sense. Bettelheim, however, provides an entertaining reading which turns around the argument that the story is a paradigm of emerging maturity. The key to his argument is contained in this passage:

> The steps toward intimacy with the other are clearly sketched: first the girl is all alone as she plays with her ball. The frog begins conversing with her when it asks what troubles her; it plays with her as it returns the ball. Then it comes to visit, sits by her, eats with her, joins her in her room and finally in her bed. The closer the frog comes to the girl physically, the more disgusted and anxious she gets, particularly about being touched by it. The awakening to sex is not free of disgust or of anxiety, even anger. Anxiety turns into anger and hatred as the princess hurls the frog against the wall. By thus asserting herself and taking risks in doing so—as opposed to her previous trying to weasel out and then simply obeying her father's commands—the princess transcends her anxiety, and hatred changes into love.
>
> In a way this story tells that to be able to love, a person first has to become able to feel; even if the feelings are negative, that is better than not feeling. In the beginning the princess is entirely self-centered; all her interest is in her ball. She has no feelings when she plans to go back on her promise to the frog, gives no thought as to what this may mean for it. The closer the frog comes to her physically and personally, the stronger her feelings become, but with this she becomes more a person. For a long stretch of development she obeys her father, but feels ever more strongly; then at the end she asserts her independence in going against his orders. As she thus becomes herself, so does the frog; it turns into a prince. (p. 271)

Though the argument is engagingly developed, it is not persuasive, for me at least, requiring as it does a reversal rather than an extension of what the story actually depicts.

In fact, most of the detailed analyses which take up the second half of the book suffer from this kind of reading. To range far afield for a moment, the problem presented by *The Uses of Enchantment* for the general reader as well as for the professional student of literature is like that found in Robertson's *Preface to Chaucer*, which argues that Chaucer must be read as a Catholic. The first part of Robertson's book is a valuable description of Chaucer's time and significance and of Robertson's premises. The development and application of those premises is unsatisfactory because the perspective is ultimately limited and the purpose persuasive in an extra-literary sense. The same is true of Bettelheim's book: *The Uses of Enchantment* is indeed useful in many ways. But not the least of these is in its demonstration that the meaning and importance of fairy tales resist, as all literature must, conclusive exploration by even the most gifted of reductionists.

The Brothers Grimm: Folktale Style and Romantic Theories

Christa Kamenetsky

The paradox involved in the *Kinder-und Hausmärchen* of the Brothers Grimm is that the folktales contained in this work have a strong appeal to children around the world, yet that they were neither collected nor written for children. Unlike Hans Christian Andersen, the Brothers Grimm considered children as an incidental reading audience only. "The book of folktales was not at all written for children," wrote Jakob Grimm, "but they like it very much, and I am glad they do."[1] Another paradox of the work lies in the nature of its style, the so-called *Buchmärchenstil* or folktale style, which has exercised a strong influence on writers of folktales and fantasies. In all its natural simplicity, it is far from being simplistic, and not at all a mere product of nature. All too often, we may have been tempted to confuse the original

SOURCE: *Elementary English*, March 1974, pp. 379–383.

[1]See Max Lüthi, Märchen, 2nd ed. (Stuttgart, 1962), p. 48

recordings of some tales with their actual appearance in print. Particularly in studies on the history of children's literature we may observe a tendency to praise the Grimms' contributions to folklore research at the expense of their literary achievements. Thus, we may read, for example: "The Grimms were determined that the language of the people should get into print exactly as it was, and it did."[2] Or: "They wrote the Märchen exactly as they were rehearsed to them, without any preparation or adornment, by the ordinary peasants who had handed them down orally from generation to generation."[3]

The Brothers Grimm were indeed loyal to the oral tradition, as far as their linguistic research project was concerned, which was their initial motivation in collecting the tales. Also, they deserve the highest praise for having been the first ones to show a deep respect for the unique characteristics of the German folktale. Wilhelm Grimm commented himself on this behalf: "In this sense, there exists in Germany not yet a single collection. Almost always one has used folktales as resource material only, as a mere basis for other tales that might be expanded or changed arbitrarily."[4] When the Brothers Grimm modified the original tales which they collected and recorded, they never proceeded arbitrarily. Also, they would not have other reasons in mind except to enhance the unique value of folk literature. Their work was a creative process, demanding the analytic attitude of a scientist and the perceptive mind of a poet. The language of their printed folktales resembles natural speech, although it is not identical with it. At one time, they were actually challenged on this account by a publisher who intended to take the liberty of reprinting the *Kinder- und Hausmärchen* with new illustrations. His argument ran that these folktales were common knowledge, written in "everyman's" language, and therefore, common property. The Brothers Grimm protested and pointed to the fact that they had done substantially more than collecting driftwood on public beaches. Fortunately, they won this case, although they encountered similar misunderstandings more than once.[5]

The great variety of sources which the Brothers Grimm used for their *Kinder- und Hausmärchen* in itself represents a touch stone of their literary accomplishments. Besides the "living sources," the folk whose tales they recorded initially, they also used the folktale collections of friends and acquaintances, including those of Brentano and Runge. Further, they adapted tales from the literature of earlier centuries by such writers as Sachs, Montani, Wickram, Frey, Kirchhoff, and Perrault. In most cases, the Brothers Grimm were conscious of their debts, acknowledging them generously in the form of notes later compiled by Bolte and Polivka.

In their effort to integrate the various folktales in their *Kinder- und*

[2]May Hill Arbuthnot, *Children and Books* (Chicago, 1957), p. 237.

[3]Harvey Darton, *Children's Books in England: Five Centuries of Social Life*, 2nd ed. (Cambridge, 1948), p. 220.

[4]Wilhelm Grimm, "Vorrede," *Kinder- und Hausmärchen*. Original version (manuscript found at Oelenberg), ed. by Joseph Lefftz (Heidelberg, 1927).

[5]Wilhelm Schoof, *Zur Entstehungsgeschichte der Grimmschen Märchen* (Hamburg, 1959), p. 133.

Hausmärchen, the Brothers Grimm actually had to "translate" them from more than twenty dialects into high German. In this process alone they were bound to take certain liberties, if only for the sake of clarity and smoothness in style. They weeded out needless repetitions, simplified the plot structure, substituted for indirect speech some lively conversations, added some action where the description became too involved, and even modified the titles of the tales. Wilhelm especially rewrote and changed the tales at various times, without, however, sacrificing his respect for the oral tradition. With the poet's sensitivity he developed a feeling for the oral style and used his skills as a storyteller to enhance the natural flow of speech. The style thus created leaned heavily upon that of their friend and collaborator, Phillip Otto Runge, who became particularly well known for his contribution of "The Fisherman and his Wife" and "The Almond Tree."

We may observe the growth of Grimms' folktale style by comparing some of the preserved original notes of the tales with the first printed version of 1812, the 1816 edition, and the 1856 edition. The most significant changes in style and content are apparent between the so-called *Urform* and the first edition, and between the 1812 and 1816 editions respectively. Even the addition or omission of certain tales betrays the Grimms' growing consciousness in creating greater unity of style throughout the *Kinder- und Hausmärchen.* From the 1816 edition, for example, they excluded various tales based too heavily upon the literary tradition, among them Hans Christian Andersen's "The Princess and the Pea," Madame d'Aulnoy's "Okerlo," and Charles Perrault's "Puss in Boots."[6] It was at this time when they began to make a clear distinction between folktale and fantasy. Neither Wilhelm nor Jakob held Perrault in a very high esteem, considering him merely lucky in having succeeded to popularize his own fantasies among the common folk. Wilhelm thought his style far too ornate and descriptive, and lacking altogether in childlike or naive qualities.[7]

The peculiarity of Grimms' folktale style lies in its intimate connection with certain Romantic theories that stimulated various other scholarly efforts of the Brothers Grimm, be it in the direction of mythology, linguistics, law, or ancient history. The German folklorist Max Lüthi well recognized the Romantic qualities of Grimms' folktale style when he underlined its vivid imagery, its closeness to nature, and its kinship to the world of dreams. In particular, he acknowledged the folktale's Romantic appeal to the adult yearning for an identification with the golden age of the innocent past, the "childhood" of the nation. At the same time, Lüthi, in a similar vein as Stith Thompson at a later date, dwelt to a considerable degree upon the aesthetic and formalistic aspects of the folktale style. He called the folktale "two-dimensional," not only because of its black-white portrayal of characters and types, but also because of its strong colors, simplicity and clarity of action,

[6] *Ibid.*, pp. 170–87.
[7] Wilhelm Grimm, "Vorrede."

closed episodes, and quick movements.[8] Stith Thompson primarily called attention to the "linear quality" of the tales, which he saw reflected by the sharp and clear outline of the main hero's actions, formulas in the text, repetitions of dialogues, and magic clue words. Interesting is his observation that the folktale favored a world of polarity and sharp contrasts by dwelling to a great extent upon hard objects, such as minerals, glass, and metals, for example.[9]

The Brothers Grimm were much less concerned with the formalistic and aesthetic elements of the folktale style than with its origin, its effect upon the listener, and ultimately, its effect upon the patriotic spirit of the German nation. As genuine students of Romanticism, they did not analyze and dissect the folktale style, but they absorbed its melody and rhythm, hoping to affect again the heart and soul of the nation. Wilhelm Grimm underlined particularly its capacity to appeal to human emotions by speaking the vivid language of God and nature. In his notes to some early collected folktales he wrote:

> It is the poetry of the simple naive life that we may find among the negroes in Africa or even among the Greeks—folktales are the harvest of forgotten places, cherished by the common folk and preserved by them. They possess the same purity as we see it reflected in the souls and eyes of children; they are simple, yet always fresh in their appeal. Like myths, they reflect an animated nature of a golden age; nature is humanized, alive. Sun, moon, and stars have dresses and give gifts; there are dwarfs working in the mountains, digging for metal; mermaids inhabit the waters; animals, stones, and plants can talk and are capable of human compassion . . . the very blood talks . . . This innocent and intimate relationship between the largest and the smallest creatures creates a beauty beyond comparison . . .[10]

With many other German Romantic writers the Brothers Grimm shared a deep concern for the sources of German folkdom. In their nation's cultural heritage they searched for a time when man had still lived in unity with God and nature. When they spoke about the child, they usually thought of it not so much in realistic terms as a potential reading audience, but rather as a symbol of innocence, purity, and naiveté, which correspond to their concept of the "childhood" of the nation. To them, the child and the man of the "golden age" shared a vision and a language that had found their reflection in myth and folktale. One of their main reasons for publishing the *Kinder- und Hausmärchen* was to keep alive this spirit of childhood, its warmth and creativity, its spontaneity, and refreshing simplicity.

Wilhelm believed that myths and folktales were alive with the creative spirit of nature. To him, nature was "humanized," that is, he thought that it spoke the language of the soul. Like the child and the ancestor of long ago, folktales reflected this animated view of nature. Animals, stones, and plants

[8]Lüthi, pp. 22–49. Also: Max Lüthi, *Volksmärchen und Volkssage: zwei Grundformen erzählender Dichtung* (Munich, 1961), p. 459.
[9]Stith Thompson, *The Folktale* (New York, 1946), pp. 449–61.
[10]Wilhelm Grimm, "Vorrede."

did not merely speak the language of a given culture, but a language that appealed to the heart of man. We may well recognize in this theory the philosophy of Schelling which inspired as well many other Romantic writers. Schelling maintained that there was no arbitrary division between man and nature, the animate and the inanimate world. Since all creatures and things equally shared in the spirit of God, all of them were also endowed with the same spirit that touches the soul. It only needed the power of the imagination to perceive this spirit in rock, flower, cloud, tree, or stone. The imagination alone was capable of transcending the sphere of reality and moving to a higher one.[11]

If, on the one hand, the Brothers Grimm supported the theory that folktales spoke the language of nature and the poetic imagination, on the other hand they defended the idea that German folktales belonged to the essential language-building powers within the era of German culture. It is this aspect of Grimms' folktales that Lüthi had in mind when he wrote: "Children who grow up in this language, who are familiar with it, and who get used to it, later may form a certain resistance to those factors that contribute to the decay of language."[12] Lüthi echoes here the belief of the Brothers Grimm in the "healing power" of the "old languages." This belief was based on the theory that a nation and its character were formed by the people who shared its language and folklore. To old languages they contributed the health, vigor, and wisdom of the "golden age," whereas in modern languages they perceived nothing but a lack of vision and a fading strength.

Like Herder, the Brothers Grimm believed in an identity of the ancient folk language and the ancient folk character. "The ancient language is physical, sensual, and innocent," wrote Jakob, "whereas the modern language works more toward abstract concepts."[13] This theory accounts for the Grimms' high respect for the language of the folktales, and for their stubborn resistance to the pressure of changing the style and contents of the *Kinder- und Hausmärchen* for other than literary reasons. Similarly as still in our time, some parents in their days objected to certain elements within this collection because of moralistic and didactic considerations. Achim von Arnim once suggested to Jakob to give in to this pressure by seeking a compromise solution. He might simply add a subtitle to the forthcoming second edition of the *Kinder- und Hausmärchen,* indicating quite plainly that the tales were not intended to be read by the children themselves but by adults, who alone were then responsible for the selection. Jakob strongly rejected this proposal. "To the pure everything is pure," he replied to Arnim, "and although there are many passages that some overly anxious parents might do without, this is,

[11]See: Oscar Walzel, German Romanticism (New York, 1965). Also: Alfred David and M. E. David, "A Literary Approach to the Brothers Grimm," *Journal of the Folklore Institute* 1 (1964) 172–88.

[12]Lüthi. *Volksmärchen und Volkssage,* p. 19.

[13]W. E. Peuckert, "Wilhelm und Jacob Grimm," *Die grossen Deutschen: Eine Biographie* III (Berlin, 1961) 128.

after all, a collection of folktales, endowed with all the riches of an enchanted world that corresponds in its spirit to the heart and mind of the child."[14] Significantly, the 1816 edition, although shorter than the first one and less objectionable to some people because of the omission of certain obscenities, still included such cruel tales as "The Almond Tree" and "The Jew in the Bush."

The Brothers Grimm thought that children, in their healthy judgment, would choose from the folktale collection what suited them, similarly as they did it when they read the Bible. According to the Grimms' theory of *Naturpoesie,* both folktales and the Bible had been created by the genius of the common folk, and their language had much in common. Like Herder, they saw in *Naturpoesie* not only what we today consider as "folklore," the peasant folk, but also the poetry of Homer, Shakespeare, and the Bible, for instance. According to their theory, history, myth, and epic had preceded the folktale, and thus the folktale was the latest and most precious remnant of the *Urzeit* (primeval times) in which spiritual things had still been expressed in a very vivid and concrete manner. Moreover, in the German folktale the Brothers Grimm perceived a document of the Nordic-Germanic past, a linguistic evidence of a forgotten national heritage. In folktales and Norse mythology alike, Wilhelm Grimm admired foremost the poetic language of the ancients. Jakob emphasized to a greater degree their value as source material for his linguistic and patriotic theories. Also Wilhelm, however, was fascinated by the historical and linguistic aspects of folklore, which may be perceived from his greater concern for accuracy in the recording of *Deutsche Sagen* (1816) and *Dänische Heldenlieder* (1811).

The Grimms' Romantic theory of language found its expression in the *Deutsche Grammatik,* a work on which both brothers worked with a painstaking effort between 1819 and 1837. Here they acknowledged the influence of the Danish linguist Rask, who had taught that a grammar should *describe,* but never *prescribe.* In language and folklore alike the Brothers Grimm perceived an organic growth, a natural development from the "roots" of native folkdom. It is this theory which we will discover also in their studies of law and mythology, *Deutsche Rechtsaltertümer* (1828) and *Deutsche Mythologie* (1835). Jakob well expressed the relationship between folklore and the ancient folkways when he wrote in an "Appeal to all Friends of German Poetry and History":

> On the high mountains and in the small villages where there are neither paths nor roads, and where the false Enlightenment has had no access and was unable to do its work, there still lies hidden in darkness a treasure: the customs of our forefathers, their sagas and their faith. We, the Undersigned, have experienced this truth quite often, yet we also know how difficult it is to lift the treasure. Needed for this task is not only a certain innocent naiveté, but also

[14]Schoof, pp. 225–26.

> an education enabling us to grasp this naiveté in the virtue that is unconscious of itself. Needed especially are a strict loyalty to the tradition and a mild friendliness . . .[15]

It was Jakob who saw to it that no major deviations were made from the oral tradition. Wilhelm, with his poetic inclinations, possibly was better equipped to grasp the naiveté of the folktale and to add to the style of the *Kinder- und Hausmärchen* a certain "mild friendliness." The Romantic theories of the Brothers Grimm give evidence of their consciousness in creating a folktale style that would be warm and vigorous enough to appeal to the soul of the nation.

[15]See Reinhold Steig, *Clemens Brentano und die Brüder Grimm* (Stuttgart, 1914), pp. 164–71.

10

Storytelling

Storytelling: Preparation and Presentation

Augusta Baker
Ellin Greene

Storytelling is an art and, like all arts, it requires training and experience. However, anyone who is willing to take the time to find the right story and learn it well, and who has a sincere desire to share enjoyment of the story, can be a successful storyteller. A good part of our daily conversation is composed of stories, incidents, and anecdotes, for we are all storytellers a few steps removed from professional storytellers. Our language is somewhat less formalized, but we are still sharing our experiences and emotions.

Storytelling is an individual art. Every storyteller develops different methods of learning stories. However, there seem to be two basic approaches: the *visual* and the *auditory*. In the visual approach, the storyteller sees the story in a series of pictures, much like the frames of a filmstrip. In learning the story of "The Woman Who Flummoxed the Fairies," for example, the storyteller might see the following pictures:

1. the woman baking cakes and pastries for a wedding or a christening
2. the fairies longing for a bit of her cake and plotting to steal her away to be their baker
3. the woman baking cakes in the castle kitchen for the great wedding
4. the fairies hiding in flower cups and under leaves along the woman's path home
5. the fairies flying out at the woman and drifting fern seed in her eyes to make her sleepy
6. the woman asleep on the fairy mound
7. the woman waking up in fairyland and pretending to be happy and willing to bake a cake for the fairies
8. the woman asking the fairies to fetch things from her kitchen so that she can bake a cake for them
9. the fairies fetching the eggs, sugar, flour, butter, bowl, wooden spoons, and egg whisk, till they are tired out

SOURCE: *School Library Journal,* March 1978, pp. 93–96.

10. the woman asking first for her cat, then for her dog, her babe, and finally her husband
11. the woman beating the cake batter, the baby screaming, the cat purring, the dog snoring, and the husband looking bewildered
12. complete bedlam—the woman giving the baby the spoon to bang with, the husband pinching the dog and treading on the tail of the cat
13. the fairies exhausted by the noise
14. the woman asking for an oven
15. the fairies letting her and her family go home after she promises to leave the cake by the fairy mound for the fairies
16. the woman and her family at home and content
17. the woman leaving the cake behind the fairy mound and finding the little brown bag of gold pieces the fairies left for her
18. the woman baking a cake every week for the fairies and receiving a bag of gold pieces in return
19. everyone living happily ever after.[1]

In the auditory approach, the storyteller is conscious of the sound of words and their arrangement. A break in the rhythm is a warning that the telling is off the track. Those who use this approach often record the story on tape before learning it. Playing back the tape in relaxed moments or while doing undemanding chores facilitates the learning process. A word of caution may be in order for the neophyte. It is best to be sure that you want to be a storyteller *before* you tape. The tape will bring out every imperfection of voice and timing. Do not be discouraged. If the story you have chosen to learn has been recorded by a professional storyteller, you may prefer to listen to it until you have gained confidence in yourself. There are many recordings of stories available.

The beginning storyteller who has a great deal of self-confidence may wish to videotape the story. The videotape captures facial mannerisms and gestures as well as imperfections of voice and timing. It is a harsh learning tool but a very helpful one, provided you do not let it rob you of the pleasure of sharing the story. Videotaping is probably more helpful to the experienced storyteller who wants to perfect style and technique.

Perhaps this is an appropriate place to mention mechanical devices, other than tape recorders, that storytellers may find helpful. Some storytellers claim that typing a story makes a carbon copy of it on the mind. Others find that outlining the story impresses it on the mind and serves as a quick refresher of memory when the story is told at a later date. This may be a formal outline or a freely written-out version.

Cue cards may be used. As you read, whenever you come across a story you enjoy and want to learn, make a 4-by-6-inch card with the following information: title, author, source, running time, characters, scenes, synopsis, and any rhymes or characteristic phrases you wish to memorize.

Choreographing, that is, marking the story to indicate voice inflections, pace, and timing, is another technique.

Learning a Story

Allow time each day over a period of at least two to three weeks to make a new story your own. Live with your story until the characters and the setting become as real to you as people and places you know. You must remember it well enough to tell it as if it were a personal reminiscence.

Read the story from beginning to end several times. Read it for pleasure first. Then read it over with concentration. Analyze the story to determine where the appeal lies, what the art form is, what word pictures you want your listeners to see, what mood you wish to create.

Read the story aloud and time it. Time it again when you begin to tell it. Some variation in time of reading and telling is to be expected, but if the telling takes much less time than the reading, it may indicate that parts have been omitted or that you are speaking too quickly. If it takes much longer, you may have added to the tale or you are speaking too slowly.

Learn the story as a whole rather than in fragments. Master the structure of the story. There are three parts to the story line: the *beginning,* which sets the stage and introduces the characters and conflict; the *body,* in which the conflict builds up to the climax; and the *resolution* of the conflict. Do not alter the essential story line. Note how the action starts, how it accelerates, how and where the transitions occur. Note sequences of names and events. Know absolutely what the successive steps are in the course of action. Test yourself by closing the book and making a list of these steps in proper order.

Master the style of the story. To retain the original flavor and vigor, memorize rhymes of characteristic phrases that recur throughout the story.

Study the sentence structure, phrases, unusual words and expressions. The beginning and ending are important. You may want to memorize them. "Crick crack," says the storyteller on the Caribbean island of Martinique, and the children reply, "Break my back." "Once there was and twice there wasn't, when genies played polo in the old Turkish bath, when the camel was a salesman and the flea a barber . . ." is one traditional way of beginning a Turkish tale. "So of course they lived, as why should they not, happily ever after," and "He was then married to the king's daughter, and the wedding lasted nine days, nine hours, nine minutes, nine half minutes and nine quarter minutes, and they lived happy and well from that day to this," are characteristic endings.

Make the story your own. Become familiar with the characters and the scenes. Build in your imagination the setting of your story. What are the main characters like? Are they clever, kind, greedy, timid, mischievous? How are they dressed? How do they speak—in vernacular, short sentences, pompously? Visualize the happenings. Reproduce these happenings as though you were seeing and experiencing them. Imagine sounds, tastes, scents, colors.

Timing is an essential part of storytelling. Each story has its own pace, for example, "Sleeping Beauty" is slow and stately, "The Gingerbread Man" is sprightly, "Robin Hood" is strong and firm. Good timing makes the difference between the neophyte and the accomplished storyteller. Herein lies the value of listening to recordings by notable storytellers.

A few suggestions about timing:

1. Pause before any change of idea, before any significant word.
2. Emphasize words that carry meaning.
3. In general, poetic and imaginative passages should be taken slowly; parts narrating action should be taken rapidly.
4. Build toward the climax. Change pace as you near it so that your listeners may know the pleasure of anticipation. Some climaxes are made more impressive by a gradual slowing down. Others are highlighted by speeding up the rate of telling. Knowing whether to slow down or speed up comes with experience and sensitivity.
5. Conversation should be taken at a speed that is appropriate for the character speaking. Beginning storytellers often are afraid of using pauses, but when they are handled well, pauses can add drama and meaning, and they do not suggest nervousness or hesitancy.
6. Remember that the pause and a dropped voice can be more effective than the shout.

Practice telling the story aloud—to yourself, your pet, your family and friends, to anyone who will listen! Any hesitation reveals weak areas in your knowledge of the story. Practice wherever and whenever you can—while waiting in the doctor's or dentist's office, while traveling on public transportation, while doing undemanding chores. Ignore the stares of strangers, friends, family! Practice, practice, practice. As a final aid, just before going to sleep at night, read the story as printed in the book, slowly and aloud.

Practice in front of a mirror to catch distracting mannerisms. Gestures should be natural to the story and to the storyteller. The art of storytelling should not be confused with the art of acting. The storyteller interprets and expresses the ideas, moods, and emotions of the author, but never identifies with any character. The storyteller is not an actor or actress but the medium through which the story is passed. There should be no studied gestures, no gimmicks, no tricks of changing voices to suit each character in the story. These only tend to be distracting.

Relate your tone of voice to what is going on in the story. The storyteller develops a sensitivity to words. Feel the appropriate emotion when you sound words so that the word "dull," for example, has a dullness about it. Train your ear to hear rhythmic phrases. For practice, try chanting the skipping-rope rhyme in "Elsie Piddock Skips in Her Sleep" in time with a jump rope.

The way you use your breath is important. Breathing from the upper chest or head will give you a lighter, weaker tone; breathing from the abdomen will give you rich, full tones, connoting strength and vigor. Instead of assuming different voices for different characters, suggest characters by the amount of breath used. For example, instead of using a high-pitched squeaky voice for the wee little bear in the story "The Three Bears," use a lighter breath. However, once you have differentiated the characters in any way you must be consistent throughout the story.

Take time to learn your stories. Allow at least six to eight hours of concentrated study to learn a folktale, and longer to learn a literary fairy tale. Marie Shedlock advised her students to learn no more than seven stories a year. She herself learned only three stories a year, but they were learned to perfection. Don't be afraid to repeat your stories. Children enjoy hearing them again and again. Tell them at library story hours, to school classes, during visits to youth organizations. A repertoire of 20 stories of different types will serve you well.

Presentation

A story hour can be held anywhere. Lack of a separate room is no excuse for not having a storytelling program. What is needed is a setting that is informal and an atmosphere that is relaxed and intimate. In the classroom, children may remain in their regular assigned seats, but an informal seating arrangement is preferred. A semicircle of listeners facing the storyteller seems to be the most effective arrangement. The storyteller can be heard and seen easily by all the children. Do not let the semicircle be too wide, or the storyteller's head will have to turn from side to side like a spectator's at a tennis match. If there are 32 children in the group, it is better to have four rows of eight chairs than two rows of sixteen chairs. Seat the children on chairs or on the floor so that no child is directly behind another. The children should face away from the sunlight or any windows where traffic or other distractions may divert their interest. The storyteller will sit or stand, depending on the size of the group and visibility. It may be more comfortable to sit when telling to a small group or to younger children, but standing gives better eye span and, therefore, better control. It also gives the storyteller freedom of movement. If the storyteller is comfortable and confident, the children will be too.

The storyteller establishes the mood of the story hour. Physical appearance, a pleasant expression, a smile, personal warmth, pleasure in the story all give a sense of enjoyment. Sometimes new storytellers wonder what to wear. Dress comfortably and simply. Children appreciate a bright scarf or attractive jewelry, but nothing should distract from the story. In a large hall, colorful clothing will focus attention on the storyteller. However, there is no need to wear a "costume." Beware of jangly bracelets, long beads, and other potential distractions.

Ask the children to put aside anything they are carrying (books, marbles, purses, dolls, and so on) on a separate table or under their chairs. If they have books in hand, they will surely peek into them during the storytelling. They really are not uninterested in your telling, but many children can focus on two things at once. This can deflate you as a storyteller, and it may distract other listeners.

If there is a separate story-hour room, check the heat and ventilation before the program begins. A room that is too warm and without sufficient air will make children drowsy.

If there is no separate story-hour room, a screen can be used to give a sense of privacy. Locate the storytelling area away from room traffic, circulation desk, and telephone.

On the "story-hour" table have the books from which you are telling, some fresh or dried flowers or leaves, and, if you like, the wishing candle and realia related to the stories.

Introduce the book from which the story is taken. This can be done naturally by picking up the book, either before or after the story, and saying, "This story is from. . . ." All children, whether or not they are readers, like to hear a good story well told. After they have heard it, book-loving children want to read it again for themselves. Even girls and boys who are not natural readers will turn to a book once it has been "opened" for them by the warmth and intimacy of a storyteller's voice and personality.

No explanations of the story are necessary. Occasionally the storyteller may wish to give a short introduction. Some books have natural introductions. They include Eleanor Farjeon's *The Little Bookroom* (Oxford Univ. Pr.), Howard Pyle's *The Wonder Clock* (Harper), and Harold Courlander's *Uncle Bouqui of Haiti* (Morrow). Introductions should be interesting and simple. You are not giving a lesson. You can develop your own short introduction, for example, "In Haiti there are two very important men. One is named Bouqui and he is a fat, good-natured fellow. The other is his best friend, Ti-Malice, a skinny little fellow who always tricks Bouqui. One time, Bouqui . . ." And then go straight into the story. The age of your listeners will determine the type and extent of your introduction. If you are telling a long story serially, prepare a short summary to refresh the children's memory and to introduce the story to newcomers. If you tell one incident from a long book, briefly introduce the characters and the situation in which they find themselves.

No definitions of "strange" words are necessary. Frequently, inexperienced storytellers feel that they must define all unfamiliar words in order for children to understand the story. They forget that the context of the story and the child's imagination are enough to supply definitions. If children do not understand a word they will ask, or if they look puzzled, and understanding the word is essential for meaning, the storyteller can substitute a synonym the next time the word is used in the story. For example, if the storyteller is telling "The Squire's Bride" and realizes that the children do not know what a bay mare is, the storyteller can substitute the word "horse" in the following sentence: "Some pulled at the head and the forelegs of the mare (horse) and others pushed from behind, and at last they got her up the stairs and into the room."

If the storyteller becomes bogged down in a vocabulary lesson the pleasure is diminished for the children, who should be allowed to relax and enjoy the story.

Before beginning, call up the essential emotions of the story as you first felt them. Breathe deeply and begin. No matter what the opening words of the story are, the tone should be intimate.

Look directly at your listeners. As you tell, let your gaze move from one to another so that each child feels involved in the telling of the story. Break direct eye contact only to look at an imaginary scene or object you want your listeners to see, or when you engage in dialogue between two or more characters during the telling.

Speak in a pleasant, low-pitched voice with enough volume to be heard easily by listeners in the last row. Speak clearly, distinctly, smoothly, and at a pace suitable for the story.

Gestures, if used at all, should be natural to the teller and to the action of the story. If gestures draw attention to themselves they are wrong. Exaggerated gestures usually indicate a futile attempt to draw attention away from inadequate preparation. Do not stand motionless as if you were a stick of wood, but do not dramatize the action of the story, for example, "marching up and down the road," "bowing," and so forth. The children may be fascinated with your movement, but they will not remember your story.

Use your hands naturally. Don't jam them in your pockets. Don't stand with arms crossed in a hostile posture. If you do not know what to do with your hands, hold them behind your back. "Keep your listeners in the *what* of the story, not in the how of the telling," advises an experienced storyteller.

Success

A small boy sat down between two adults at the village soda fountain. He had just been collected from his first library story hour, and a celebration was in order. The storyteller sat three stools away, unrecognizable in winter scarf and hood. The curious adults were trying in vain to pry some statement of reaction to the story hour from the boy, a most reluctant informer, until at last one of them complained with some asperity, "You could at least tell us how the teacher told the stories? Did she read them from a book? Did she tell them from memory?" "Oh, mother," he explained with a long sigh, "she just told them from herself."[2]

No storyteller ever received higher praise, for the ultimate goal is to tell a story so simply and directly that it appears to be told "from yourself." All the emphasis should be placed upon the story rather than upon the storyteller, who is, for the time being, simply a vehicle through which the beauty and wisdom and humor of the story comes to the listeners.

References

1. Leodhas, Sorche Nic. "The Woman Who Flummoxed the Fairies." *Heather and Broom: Tales of the Scottish Highlands*. Holt, 1960, p. 35–43.
2. Ross, Eulalie Steinmetz. Manuscript in the files of the Office of Children's Services, New York Public Library.

Storytellers in the Classroom

Stewart Marsden

The children hurry to their desks, stuffing books and notebooks under chairs, working nervous fidgets out of excited hands and feet. The room is finally quiet. When every eye is looking toward the front of the room, the Story Lady steps in.

She glances quickly at each child, her large brown eyes sparkling with mystery and humor. The children are ready. She is ready.

"Outside it was very dark, dark, dark. But I decided to take a walk down the street. All the street lights were off, and it was dark, dark, dark!"

Two children slide down in their seats, their eyes wide.

"As I walked I could hear a dog howling in the wind, out of sight in the dark, dark, dark. I continued to walk, and the night grew darker, darker, darker."

The Story Lady continues, and the classroom seems to darken. Nighttime swirls in the minds of the young listeners, and it is they who walk down the street to some unknown destination. They are in another world, a world filled with giants, unicorns and things that go "bump" in the night.

The Story Lady is Jackie Torrence of High Point, N.C., one of a dwin-

SOURCE: Reprinted from *Teacher*, November/December 1980, pp. 33–36.

dling number of people in a unique profession. Torrence is a storyteller with a repertoire of more than 500 stories.

Becoming a storyteller was not Torrence's childhood ambition.

"I wanted to be an actress as a child, but that ambition was ruled out by my aunt before I got a chance to become stagestruck." Her aunt could not keep her from becoming "storystruck," however. Torrence's career started in the early seventies at a branch library situated near the low-income area of a Southern town.

"It was a very troubled place. We had quite a few kids who were angry with the world, and I began thinking of ways we could help them work through their feelings."

Ghost Tales Bring Rapport

Her interest and her craft created a solid rapport with young people and they began frequenting the library. She had collected a number of ghost tales from various regions of North Carolina, as well as other states, and used the stories to hold her new friends captive.

"I could get them to listen to me for hours. My main interest was in the kids, and I was less thrilled with library paperwork."

As the demand for Torrence's storytelling increased, the main library capitalized on her growing popularity by organizing regularly scheduled story hours for children.

"We started our first story hour with 35 children. Within a few weeks we couldn't accommodate the growing number of eager listeners, including the children's parents!"

News of the storyteller and her fame spread through the town and nearby communities until she was flooded with requests to entertain all kinds of groups, young and old. During this period Torrence decided on storytelling as her profession.

An Ancient Art

One of only a few hundred storytellers in the United States, Torrence perpetuates a profession that is as old as humanity. Storytellers were once vital to the preservation of the history of early civilizations. Their stories were the records which were passed from generation to generation, with great care given to the accuracy of the events.

With the advent of alphabets and various writing implements, storytelling lost its special position in the community. No longer needed for remembering specifics, storytellers modified fact with supernatural and mystical elements. They developed stories not only for entertainment, but also for instruction in proper behavior. They told stories to explain natural phenomena, such as how the caterpillar becomes a butterfly, or why the spider weaves a web.

Technology pushed storytellers deep into the corners of modern civilizations and many centuries-old tales were lost as a result. The dwindling number of storytellers, along with the vast numbers of uncataloged stories that were in danger of being lost, became the concern of one former teacher in Tennessee.

While Torrence blossomed into a storyteller in North Carolina, Tennessean Jimmy Neil Smith grew interested in the art. In 1973, in order to encourage new interest in storytelling, he founded the National Association for the Preservation and Perpetuation of Storytelling (NAPPS). Through NAPPS, he organized the first National Storytelling Festival, held in Jonesborough, Tenn. The festival brought together storytellers from across the nation for a weekend of tale swappin'.

Storytellers from all over the country began joining the NAPPS movement, helping the organization develop a library of books, tapes and recordings concerning all aspects of storytelling. Most recently, NAPPS administered a pilot program that introduced storytelling as an educational tool to the Tennessee school system.

In-School Programs

The Tennessee In-School Storyteller Program provided artists like Torrence for six Tennessee city and county school systems for periods of one week. During the week, the storytellers conducted workshops for elementary and high school teachers, stressing the use of the story as a learning device. They then visited classrooms and told their stories. Students had the opportunity to visit the National Storytelling Center in Jonesborough to learn more about storytelling in the United States and other parts of the world. On Friday night a community story concert climaxed the event.

Torrence participated in the program and believes in its effectiveness.

"Our objectives were to stimulate student creativity through storytelling, to motivate young children to read and to equip and encourage teachers to use storytelling as a part of their regular curriculum. I have seen problem students make great strides in the classroom as a result of storytelling used effectively."

She stresses that the by-products of storytelling are as important as the story itself and the entertainment it produces.

"In storytelling, your relationship with the student is much different from that of the lecturer or instructor. It is less formal and more open. If the stories you use are personal experiences, then you open yourself to students to an even greater degree."

Many teachers who are involved in the In-School Program express a reluctance to use storytelling in their classrooms after a "real" storyteller has visited.

"They feel that they don't have either the talent or the time to become a good storyteller. My answer is that anybody can tell a story, provided some guidelines are understood and followed," comments Torrence.

Effective Storytelling

The following tips can help anyone tell a story effectively:

Know the story. Memorizing is not as important as a "feel" for the key elements.

Enunciate words correctly. Diction is as important to the storyteller as it is to the actor.

Regulate the pace of your story. Some stories move quickly from start to finish. Others need pauses.

Use simple props, such as handkerchiefs and sticks, to increase interest.

Keep the listening group small in number. (Eight to 10 persons is the optimum size range.)

"It does take time to develop yourself as an effective storyteller in the classroom," says Torrence. "I realize that teachers' free hours are few and precious, but there are bits of the day we all waste that can be used productively. The rewards I'm talking about are worth the extra effort."

The ghost story that follows is for your experimental use in the classroom. Keep the guidelines in mind as you tell the story to a group. Ask each student to draw pictures of the story when you finish, perhaps what they envision as the "thing in the box." Your students may have ghost stories they would like to tell or write as a result of this experience.

Dark, Dark, Dark

Outside it was very dark, dark, dark. But I decided to take a walk down the street. All the street lights were off, and it was dark, dark, dark!

As I walked I could hear a dog howling in the wind, out of sight in the dark, dark, dark. I continued to walk, and the night grew darker, darker, darker!

I walked a long, long distance from my home. Somewhere close by I heard a cat screeching, and I was scared! I looked around and suddenly realized that I didn't recognize anything around me! This was not my street! Why, this wasn't even my town!

What had happened to me? Where was I?

I looked up, and there on a steep and barren hill stood an old house. It was very dark, dark, dark! I climbed the walkway to the porch of the house and peered in through one of the dusty windows. It was dark, dark, dark. But something drew me inside.

I walked into the house. It was dark, dark, dark! With my arms outstretched I felt my way along a wall and down a hallway. It was dark, dark, dark! I was afraid, but something drew me down the hallway anyway!

At the end of the hallway I felt a heavy old door. I turned the knob of the door and pushed against it with my shoulder. The door groaned as it turned on its rusty hinges, and opened into a dark, dark, dark room.

I was drawn into the room. I moved very slowly. My arms were stretched out, searching the darkness for whatever was there. Then I touched something! It was rectangular and had hinges and a latch. It was a big wooden chest!

"Perhaps there's a treasure inside!" I thought. Then I shuddered. "Or perhaps there's Something Else!"

I opened the heavy chest slowly in the dark, dark, dark—not knowing what was inside. The lid creeked loudly on its old hinges. I reached into the chest and touched something! It was a little box.

I took the box in my hands and thought, "Perhaps there's a diamond necklace in here!" Then I shuddered, "Or perhaps there's Something Else!"

So I opened the little box, ever so slooooowly. And as I did . . . . SOMETHING JUMPED OUT!!! I ran out of that house and down the street to my house, and I have never been back again! (Story courtesy of Jackie Torrence.)

For more information about storytelling and the In-School Program, write to the National Storytelling Resource Center, Jonesborough, TN 37659.

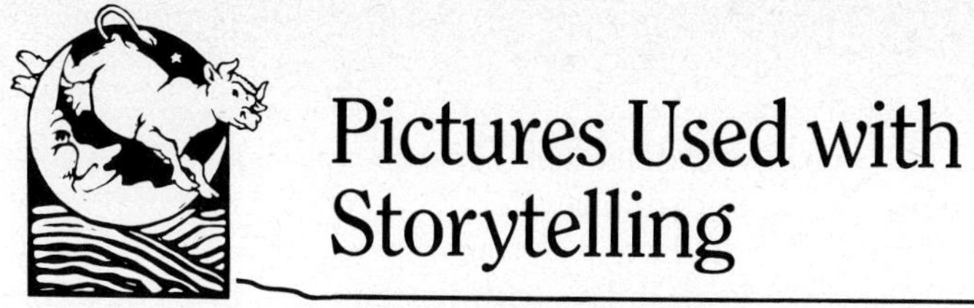

Pictures Used with Storytelling

Anne Pellowski

While the majority of storytelling among the folk was and is accomplished without objects (other than musical instruments), there were and are important exceptions. This is especially true in the use of pictures to enhance the story or to sustain the audience's interest for at least part of it. The reports of some early experiments in North American schools and libraries with "picture" storytelling are often filled with the naive belief that they were trying something totally new. This was perhaps justified in view of the paucity of folkloristic or ethnographic research at that time concerning street storytelling in Europe and Asia.

An article in *Publishers Weekly* in 1934, for example, describes the "new" technique of story hours with lantern slides devised by Julia Wagner and Ruth Koch after nine years of experimentation.[1] The method of projection may indeed have been new, but, in fact, Wagner and Koch were taking their places in a long line of picture storytellers, dating back to at least the Middle Ages.

Picture Scrolls & Sheets

In Europe the first evidence of narration accompanied by pictures appears to be in one of the *exultet* rolls, Christian picture scrolls produced in Italy during the 11th and 12th Centuries. Although the text was usually the same (part of the Easter vigil service), the various artists who illustrated the parchment rolls each selected different scenes to be emphasized and depicted. The roll illuminated in the 11th Century at the Abbey of Monte Casino, and now in the British Museum, has fourteen illustrations, each about a foot square. It begins with a figure of Christ, continues with two angels, and then shows a female figure personifying "Mother Church." Following this is a vivid por-

SOURCE: *The World of Storytelling*, by Anne Pellowski, with permission of the R. R. Bowker Company.

trayal of "Mother Earth," teeming with animal and vegetable life, and then scenes from episodes in the Old and New Testaments.

Surely this must have provided fuel to fire the imaginations of many in the congregation, who probably had limited exposure to sequential visual story materials of such beauty and drama. For those children standing or seated close to the pulpit, it must have been an experience at least faintly resembling the picture-story hour of today, with its sequence of pictures on page or filmstrip, accompanied by the voice of the reader/narrator. It should be obvious that this experience would be quite different from the passive, introspective study of statues, altarpieces, mosaics, frescoes, or windows on view in the church, in which case the story would be provided partly by the artist and partly by the viewer, much the way a book stimulates a story only partly conceived by the writer and then completed by the reader.

It is just possible that these *exultet* rolls were the inspiration for the religious *bänkelsänger* (German street singers) that Brednich[2] and Schmidt,[3] among others, believe to have been the forerunners of the secular *bänkelsänger*. Both of them have shown pictorial documentation for the 16th and 17th Centuries that includes examples of religious and secular picture canvases separated into squares or rectangles so as to create a story by depicting a series of actions. The terms sometimes used for this are tessellated or tessellation.

Some of the *bänkelsänger* were regular employees of the printing companies whose wares were being sold. Others, perhaps the majority, were itinerants who had obviously developed some talent in presenting the stories in song, bought up supplies from various printers,[4] made their own picture sheets (or possibly got a talented folk artist to do so), and then went on the road, stopping at towns on market days, when the crowds would be largest.

The technical term for these picture sheets is *schilder*.[5] In the paintings or etchings of the 17th through the 19th Centuries in which *bänkelsänger* are depicted, the *schilder* appear to be either wood-block prints, copper engravings, or oil on canvas. These *schilder* are now extremely rare. The inexpensive ballad sheets, called broadsides in English and *flugblätter* in German, were printed in the hundreds of thousands, but they, too, are difficult to find today. It is no wonder, then, that the *schilder*, made in very few copies or in unique examples, are to be found in very few museums or in the hands of a few private collectors. Examples of 19th-Century *schilder*, some printed and hand colored and others individually drawn and colored, are more common than those from previous centuries.

The picture sheets were large enough to be seen by a small crowd standing around and generally contained up to a dozen or so of the most dramatic scenes from the ballads or songs. A common size was roughly 1½ meters wide and 2 meters high.

Brednich points out that publishers were not the first to use large pictures and sticks or pointers for advertising their wares. Two examples among many that he cites are Hogarth's view of Southwark Fair and the church-fair scene of the Flemish *Imagerie Populaire,* both of which show the use of large picture sheets advertising various services or goods.[6] But it was in the *schilder* depicting story ballads that the specially displayed picture advertising sheet was most effective and long lasting.

That they had a powerful influence on the audience is attested to by many writers, among them Goethe. In his *Wilhelm Meister's Theatralische Sendung* he writes:

> The folk will be most strongly moved above all by that which is brought under their eyes. A daub of a painting or a childish woodcut will pull the attention of the unenlightened person much more than a detailed written description. And how many thousands are there who perceive only the fairy tale elements in the most splendid picture. The large pictures of the *bänkelsänger* impress themselves much deeper on the memory than their songs—although these also captivate the power of the imagaination.
>
> Book 2, Chapter 5[7]

Their impact lasted until well into the 20th Century, as the text and photographs of Janda and Nötzoldt's *Die Moritat vom Bänkelsang* so clearly demonstrate.[8] Visitors to the Munich *Oktoberfest* and to other similar yearly markets or festivals could still listen and watch as the singer pointed his stick from picture to picture and intoned the many verses of the ballads. But they were not able to compete with films, and later radio. With the spread of these two forms of mass media into all parts of Europe, the picture sheets of the *bänkelsänger* disappeared from public view.

Earliest Uses of Pictures

A very early mention of the public exhibition of pictures, combined with the recitation of a narrative, appears to be in a work called *Mahabhāsya* (c. 140 B.C.) by Patañjali. In it, he refers to dramatic representations of the Krishna legend in pictures, pantomime, and words, as performed by *śaubhikas,* or actors. There is quite a bit of disagreement among scholars about whether narration was involved. The Indian scholar Coomaraswamy believes that it probably was.[9] There are slightly later references to picture showmen, called *yamapattaka,* who showed scrolls on which there were series of pictures representing legends. Some Brahmanical teachers were known to use a portable frame on which they would have pictures drawn, showing what would happen if one did this good deed or that evil one. The later game of Snakes and Ladders probably developed from this.

These early forms of picture storytelling are the likely forerunners of modern Indian storytelling that employs pictorial devices. There is no readily accessible documentation to indicate how the practice was handed down from one era to the next. It is easier to find references to the ways in which this picture storytelling was carried by Buddhism to China and Java and other parts of East Asia than it is to find information on how such storytelling progressed in India.

It is known that picture storytelling made its way to Java also. A Chinese writer, Ying-yai Sheng-Ian, wrote in 1416:

> There is a sort of men who paint on paper men birds, animals, insects and so on; the paper is like a scroll and is fixed between two wooden rollers three feet high; at one side these rollers are level with the paper, whilst they protrude at the other side. The man squats down on the ground and places the picture before him, unrolling one part after the other and turning it towards the spectators, whilst in the native language and in a loud voice he gives an explanation of every part; the spectators sit around him and listen, laughing or crying according to what he tells them.[10]

This might have been the forerunner of the *wayang kulit*, the shadow-puppet play.

Picture Cloths in India

In India today there are narrators who use pictures, just as their ancient predecessors did. Unlike the *bänkelsänger*, the Indian bards have pictures on cloths that fold or roll up, rather than on paper or canvas sheets.

Among the types of storytelling cloths to be found today are the *kalamkari*, bard cloths of Madras and Andhra Pradesh; *pabuji kaa pat*, cloths from Rajasthan; Saurashtra temple cloths from Gujarat; and *badd* cloths used by the *dakkalwars* of Maharashtra.

The name *kalamkari* implies that the design is created by pen, but the process is really more complex than that. The Fergusons, who have observed the entire process in Andhra in South India, describe it thus:

> Essentially, the design is created by a master of the art who draws it on hand-spun-handloomed cotton cloth which has been bleached. Some of his design may be printed with clumsy-looking wooden printing blocks, and this is usually the case these days with the border designs. The details of the process are complex. Suffice it to say that the students of the master are responsible for filling his design with color. . . . But the heart of the *kalamkari* is the fresh design on each. . . . Thus, while to the untutored eye *kalamkaris* may seem to be alike, a few moments of study will show the individuality of each piece done by a single artist and his school. Different artists and schools create substantially different pieces. Yet all the themes and symbols are stylized and . . . the stories depicted are limited in number and quite familiar to all.[11]

The *pabuji kaa pat* are made by a completely different technique. *Pat* means scroll, and the *pabuji* are just that—large scrolls. They are generally about 1 meter high and from 2 to 4 meters in length. Traditional painters from Rajasthan, in the northwestern part of India, paint the pictures on canvas, using locally made colors, usually five. They paint episodes of the birth of the hero, his adventures, his marriage, his fight with the enemy, and his death, together with the death by self-immolation of his wife.[12]

The *mata ni pachedi* comes from Saurashtra, a region of the state of Gujarat in western India. Just the preparation of the cloth for printing takes days, for it is boiled twice, buried once, soaked and rinsed many times, and dried in the sun. When it is finally received by the printer, it is a pale yellow. The printer applies the design by hand, using carved wooden blocks and a thick black ink. The sons or apprentices then fill in with various compounds the areas that will be red or black. After boiling, rinsing, blueing, and bleaching in the sun, the cloth is ready to be used in the religious ceremony. There are two standard sizes for the *mata ni pachedi:* a 6-foot square cloth used for a ceiling over a small temple or area of worship; and a rectangular cloth 3½ or 4½ feet high and 6 feet long. The finished cloths are all red, black, and white.[13]

No sample of the *badd* cloths could be obtained, but from the brief written description available, they would appear to be similar to the *kalamkari.*[14]

Kamishibai Picture Cards

The *kamishibai* of Japan, a traditional storytelling art form descended from *kabuki* theater, also utilized pictures as a come-on, only in this case the articles being sold were candies or, in rare cases, books or medals showing popular heroes. The children who bought something were allowed to stay and listen to the story or stories and watch the pictures.[15]

The wooden holder for the *kamishibai* picture sheets was generally about 1 foot high and about 18 inches wide. On the top was a handle for carrying. The front had flaps that opened out like a triptych or miniature stage. These wooden frames were produced by carpenters who specialized in building temples or altars, and each player bought his own, sometimes after arranging for a special design or adaptation.[16]

The picture cards were usually printed in color and contained the highlights of scenes from the stories. Some sets of hand-painted pictures can be found, but most were printed and sold for the express use of the *kamishibai.* In 1937 there were some sixteen of these publishers in Tokyo, and most of them reinstated their wares after the war.[17]

There were usually from 6 to 20 cards in a set, and these fitted into a slot on the side of the wooden carrier (Plate 4). The teller could see the text relating to the picture being shown, because it was printed on the back of the card preceding it. In other words, when the first picture card, which was usually a title card, was pulled out from the front position and slid into the back position, the text shown on the back of it related to the second picture card.

Considering the impact that the *kamishibai* had on children's literature and the fact that the same publishers who produced the cards were also later producing children's books, it is no wonder that one of the most popular formats for children's picture books in Japan is the horizontal style reminiscent of the *kamishibai.*

Picture Books

The picture-book story hour in libraries probably began soon after the regular story hours, at least in a few libraries. Yet there is little evidence that it was scheduled regularly prior to the Second World War. Professional journals make no mention of a "Picture Book Story Hour" before 1949. There are a few articles on the preschool story hour in the 1940s, but they still refer essentially to orally narrated stories unaccompanied pictures. In one of them the librarian specifically mentioned that showing the pictures while telling or reading the story was attempted but proved unsatisfactory, and she concluded: "We have found it better to show the pictures after the story has been told."[18] This was probably an echo of the advice given in the most widely used storytelling manual of the time. *The Art of the Storyteller* by Marie Shedlock. In her first chapter, "The Difficulties of the Story," she states most clearly in Point 6:

> After long experience, and after considering the effect produced on children when pictures are shown to them during the narration, I have come to the conclusion that the appeal to the eye and the ear at the same time is of doubtful value, and has, generally speaking, a distracting effect. . . .[19]

However, internal reports in the New York Public Library indicated that in 1910 "there were 1,133 story hours including the extra story hours, *informal picture book hours* [author's italics], and story hour sessions held in connection with the playground association."[20] It was not until Eulalie Steinmetz became supervisor of storytelling (1945–1953) that the story-hour sessions were divided into two distinct types: 1) Story Hour for boys and girls third grade and above, and 2) Picture-Book Hour for those below the third grade.[21]

The earliest article describing actual picture books and how they were used in a story hour appears in *Library Journal* and was written by Florence Sanborn. In it she suggests the use of picture books as a "vehicle for the hesitant, new storyteller to gain confidence." Since she gives explicit instructions on how to hold the book, turn the pages, and so forth, it would appear that she was writing about a new approach to library storytelling. Nowhere in the article does she suggest, though, that an entire story hour could be made up of picture storybooks.[22]

Such a suggestion is made in a little pamphlet written by F. Marie Foster and published by the Division of Adult Education and Library Extension of the New York State Education Department, some time in the mid-1940s. Foster recommended a short "picture book program" of from 20 to 25 minutes in length, and actually described (in text and photos) the kind of physical location needed, the manner of holding the picture book, the arrangement of the chairs, and many other factors. One of the main reasons she cites for such a program is that it "gives the librarian a real opportunity to see children's reactions to the books so carefully selected" for the public library children's room.[23]

In another article in *Library Journal* some years later, Adeline Corrigan implies by her title, "The Next Step—the Picture Book Hour," that this was not a widely scheduled practice in the public library. She does refer to the fact that children have enjoyed stories through pictures for hundreds of years. But she states that it is because of the recent increase in large picture books, clearly visible and understandable when shown to a group, that one can now have a picture-book hour as a regular storytelling session for groups of children.[24]

Obviously the publishers were listening and reading. The number of picture storybooks with illustrations selected, not for family or individual reading, but for their ability to stand out and be seen when held up in front of a group began to increase dramatically. The lavishly illustrated picture book had become too expensive for most individual buyers. In the institutional buyer, the publisher had a much steadier market for well-produced picture books.

Librarians adopted this new type of story hour very quickly once they discovered it and saw the steady stream of books being published to suit the programs. Also, they became much more adept at reviewing and criticizing the new picture books, not necessarily from an artistic point of view, but rather from the point of view of the library picture-book storyteller. To work well and hold the attention of a group of children already visually stimulated by films and television, the stories had to be very strong, with no unnecessary text. The pictures needed to strike a balance between showing too much and too little, and the most successful artists were clever and careful in building up suspense and surprise, just as the texts did.

The more librarians used picture books successfully in the story hour, the more they realized how much easier this kind of program was, in relation to the long and difficult-to-learn tales they were expected to prepare for the regular story hour. The more the story hour came to be associated with picture books, the more the older children stayed away, believing such things were for "babies." By the mid-1960s, a familiar lament was voiced, exemplified by this statement by a children's librarian of the Toronto Public Library:

> Almost all the librarians I have talked to report the same thing. Some of the enthusiasm has gone and what is more of the older boys and girls have gone. Imperceptibly, week by week, their numbers dwindle until the librarian faces, on a Saturday morning, a sea of very young faces: little children who want *The Three Bears,* not the *Three Men of Power* and who thrill to the exploits of Mike Mulligan rather than Grettir the Strong.[25]

Beginning in the 1950s one can find in the professional reviews of children's picture books more and more frequent comments about the usefulness of the book in story hours, or, conversely, negative remarks about how difficult the pictures will be to see or how unnecessarily long the text is, making its use in the picture-book story hour limited. The reviewers were, for the most part, children's librarians who were reflecting their storytelling needs. It was not surprising, therefore, that in response to these reviews, an increasing number of trade picture books were published in the United States after World War II of the type suited to presentation in a group situation. They can almost invariably be differentiated from the European picture books of the same period, most of which have much greater detail in both text and illustration.

The picture-book hour (also called the preschool hour) is now an established routine in most public libraries in the United States, Canada, Great Britain, Australia, New Zealand, and the Scandinavian countries. Even continental European public libraries, slower in their development, now have this activity in many places. Well-developed public library systems in such places as Singapore and Japan also maintain the picture-book hour as a regular program.[26]

References

1. "Children Like Pictures: TheWagko Story Hour Stimulates the Child's Interest." *Publishers Weekly* 126 (August 25, 1934): 589.
2. Brednich, Rolf Wilhelm. "Zur Vorgeschichte des Bänkelsangs." Österreichisches Volksliedwerk. *Jahrbuch* (Wien) 21 (1972): 78–92.
3. Schmidt, Leopold. "Geistlicher Bänkelgesang." Österreichisches Volksliedwerk, *Jahrbuch* 12 (1963): 1–16.
4. Coupe, William A. *The German Illustrated Broadsheet in the Seventeenth Century,* Bibliotheca Bibliographica Aureliana, 17 (Baden-Baden: Heitz. 1966–1967), p. 13–17.
5. Janda, Elsbeth and Fritz Nötzoldt, *Die Moritat vom Bänkelsang: oder das Lied der Strasse* (München: Ehrenwirth Verlag, 1959), p. 9.
6. Brednich, "Zur Vorgeschichte des Bänkelsangs," p. 84.

7. Von Goethe, Johann Wolfgang. *Wilhelm Meister's Theatralische Sendung*, vol. 51 of his *Werke* (Weimar, 1911), p. 150.
8. Janda and Nötzoldt. *Die Moritat vom Bänkelsang*, p. 9ff.
9. Coomaraswamy, Ananda. "Picture Showmen," *Indian Historical Quarterly* 5, no. 2 (June 1929): 182.
10. Quoted in Coomaraswamy, "Picture Showmen," p. 186.
11. [Ferguson, Henry and Joan Ferguson]. "Textiles That Tell a Story" (Thompson, Conn.: InterCulture Associates, n.d.), unp.
12. Ibid.
13. Erikson, Joan. *Mata ni Puchedi: A Book on the Temple Cloth of the Mother Goddess* (Ahmedabad: National Institute of Design, 1968), p. 9ff.
14. Mande, Prabhaker B. "Dakkalwars and their Myths," *Folklore* (Calcutta) 14 (January 1973): 69–76.
15. Kito, Morio. *Nireke no Hibobito (The Nine Families)* (Tokyo: Shinchoshi), p. 231.
16. Kata Koji. *Machi no jijyoden (Autobiography of a Street-Person)* (Tokyo: Banseisha, 1977).
17. Ibid.
18. Huls, Ardis. "Pre-school Story Hour." *Wilson Library Bulletin* 16 (May 1942): 730.
19. Shedlock, Marie L. *The Art of the Storyteller* (New York: Dover, 1951), p. 13–14 (first pub. in 1915).
20. Fannin, Gwendolyn Marie. "A Resume of the History, Growth and Development of the Story Hour in the New York Public Library" (Master's thesis, Atlanta University, 1958), p. 10.
21. Ibid., p. 14.
22. Sanborn, Florence. "How to Use Picture-Story Books," *Library Journal* 74 (February 15, 1949): 272–274.
23. Foster, F. Marie. *A Round of Picture Book Programs* (Albany: New York State Education Dept., Division of Adult Education and Library Extension, c. 1944), unp.
24. Corrigan, Adeline. "The Next Step—the Picture Book Hour," *Library Journal* 81 (September 15, 1956): 2014–2016.
25. Kane, Alice. "The Changing Face of the Story Hour," *Ontario Library Review* 49 (August 1965): 141–142.
26. Based on personal observation.

11

Sharing Picture Books

Do Swans Really Eat Fudgesicles? The Picture Book and Child Drama

Robert Barton
David Booth

> The city had never before and has never since witnessed such a celebration as that which greeted the adventurers on their return from the battle with Humbaba. A holiday was declared. All work ceased. Feasts were laid out everywhere, and the people went up and down the streets carrying standards and bright banners. The young and the old gathered in the family house and sat crosslegged while the two heroes told the story repeating it again and again and answering all the questions that were asked. Singers immediately made up long songs about the adventure; dancers acted it out; and scribes laboriously engraved it on stone, or pressed the words and letters into tablets of wet clay. Runners carried the clay tablets from city to city . . . (From Bernarda Bryson, *Gilgamesh*)

The source of excitement and activity in the foregoing excerpt is the victorious return of the heroes from battle. In the classroom which will be described in the following article, the source of excitement and activity will be the picture book.

Ordinarily, there is a reluctance on the part of many teachers to use picture books with children other than the very young. For that reason, the children used in the samples to follow were all over the age of twelve. In addition this article concerns drama and its relationship to children's literature. Drama may be described as struggling, doing and discovering about ourselves and our world. Learning through drama rather than learning about drama is the point of the activity. Therefore in drama many sources can be tapped. We feel that the picture book provides an excellent source for engaging the imagination of the participants. At the same time appreciation of the literature is heightened as pictures and words are elaborated through movement and speaking activities. The playing out of thoughts, feelings and emotions add much to the child's understanding of the material. The work described is indicative of the many ways that we are using picture books in classrooms, with children of all ages. This work has been going on for the past five years and many teachers, librarians and children have been exposed

SOURCE: *Children's Literature in Education,* May 1973, pp. 13–24. Reprinted with permission of Agathon Press, Inc.

to it through workshop situations. Hopefully more and more use of picture books beyond the infant school will be realized.

> "According to Stanislavsky, you have to feel like an onion. Do you feel like an onion?"
>
> "Not in the least," said Harriet.
>
> "Oh, come on. What are they teaching you in school these days?" (Louise Fitzhugh, Harriet the Spy)

Item 1: *Cinderella*

Starting Point

> "Cinderella had never been to a ball but she knew just what it would be like." (Alan Suddon, *Cinderella*)

When one sees three boys dressed in women's cast-offs mincing and guffawing at the front of the class while fellow students hurl insults at this loose interpretation of *Cinderella,* one fears that old Cinderella is done for, and certainly child drama in its true sense is nowhere to be found, at least not in that particular classroom at that particular time. How exciting, then, to find Alan Suddon's interpretation of that generational folktale told anew in twenty-nine full-colour collages. He is head of the fine-art section of the Metropolitan Toronto Central Library. If he could create a wholly new text and yet remain faithful to tradition, if he could produce a witty and comic bilingual treat for today's child, could not the teacher of child drama create a similar feeling of art and fun with a drama lesson using as its source our girl, Cinderella?

What does the teacher want or hope to accomplish with this child drama? Certainly it has to do with involvement rather than voyeurism, with sensitivity rather than showing off, with self-awareness rather than type casting. Wouldn't it be interesting for everyone to sense relationships rather than to watch David do what he does all the time? Wouldn't it be interesting to work in groups of two or three or six with no fear of competition from other groups or from those demanding to be entertained? Can we explore mood and movement, body and space, emotion and others, talk and silence, gesture and effect, story and laugh, poem and moment? Can every single child have a chance to create a prince—not the same, but unique for him at this time and place? Will each boy have a chance to realize Cinderella's feelings and to talk about them without adopting the facile effete mannerisms of classroom cutups? Will there be sustained moments of tradition and responding? Will we achieve total group sensitivity, or will we simply talk to a friend, with no other aim except giving and receiving? Perhaps Alan Suddon's well-thumbed book that he had made originally for his own children for rainy afternoons and winter evenings holds the magic of child drama. The play is not the thing, but rather, playing and growing and realizing that each frail person is a part of the whole.

The Action: A Collage of Ideas

1. With a partner, how many fairy tales about stepmothers can you list in two minutes?
2. Come and tell me orally the jobs at your house that you would like to have an assitant to help with.
3. In threes, show me Cinderella and her stepsisters. I want to see a frozen picture and I want to know which one is Cinderella.
4. You are Cinderella's father. Why are you going away? Tell me aloud.
5. It is Saturday. Show me in groups of four the stepmother talking to her three daughters, giving them a list of jobs to do. What excuses will the stepdaughters give in order to have Cinderella do all of the work?
6. Show me the neighbour women on either side of Cinderella's house talking as they hang up their laundry about this odd family next door.
7. In pairs make a list of the four books that Cinderella would like to read, and four books that her sisters would like to read. Tell the pair next to you your suggestions.
8. Choose three things that Cinderella has to do. Number them 1, 2, and 3. Show me #1 #2 #3 . When I play the music show me the action as I call out the different numbers. . . .
9. In this town is the great clock at townhall. In tens create the clock for me and have it chime four o'clock.
10. In pairs, be the queen and the royal cook creating a menu for the ball.
11. Show me the court orchestra practising for the ball on instruments that no longer exist. Show me the instruments made of three parts in groups of three as I play the music.
12. And now the prince is practising his dancing in front of a mirror. Use A and B partners. A the mirror, B the prince. Listen to the music.
13. The stepmother has gone to a shop to buy a dress for the ball. Show me a sales person persuading her to buy a dress that really does not suit her.
14. In the cellar of the palace, the cooks are grumbling about working conditions. Show me the cooks talking aloud about their problems. Elect a leader to take these problems to the king and demand better conditions. Whom will you elect? The king will correct only one problem. Which one shall it be?
15. In groups of six, make a coach for Cinderella to ride in.
16. Show me the Fairy Godmother singing a gentle song to Cinderella.

17. Make a huge swinging bridge over which the coach must pass.
18. Could you turn your school gymnasium into a place where the ball could be held? What changes would you make?
19. Photograph for the town newspaper a picture of the royal family waiting for the ball to begin. How will you have them posed?
20. Everyone has a rhythm band instrument. In sixes create the sounds I would hear as the party begins with everyone behaving shyly, the noise gradually increasing as people talk and dance, the arrival of Cinderella, the chiming of the clock, the leaving of the glass slipper, the coach changing to a pumpkin, and the loneliness of the prince.
21. The Fairy Godmother keeps getting her spells confused. In pairs, show me the results of a confused spell as each person becomes something other than a coach! Let me hear the spell that made you this.
22. The six mice did not want to become horses. Tell the godmother your reasons.
23. Roll into a ball like a seed. As the tambourine rattles, grow into a pumpkin, a very special pumpkin. Feel very heavy.
24. Show me the glassblowers creating the glass slippers. The slippers are fragile, so take care.
25. Who has the most food piled on his plate from the buffet? Tell me what it is by the way you handle it.
26. Create an interesting dinner roll for the buffet table. Be the cook explaining your recipe; become the roll.
27. In groups of ten, form a coach. Become a pumpkin on the stroke of twelve.
28. Show me the king and queen trying to make the prince forget the girl who lost the slipper.
29. The slipper was either too big or too small for those who tried it on, although everyone pretended that it fit. Show me all of the people that tried it on and I will know if the slipper was too big or too small.
30. The stepmother is trying to apologize to Cinderella for not letting her go to the ball.
31. Create the wedding picture that occurs at the end of the story.
32. If the stepmother ran a circus what would Cinderella and her sisters do for jobs? Create a frozen picture.

Item 2: *The Golden Swans*

Starting Point

In teaching and exploring creative drama, why does the picture book present such an ingenious and all encompassing source?

The picture book, of course, is a little understood medium by teachers of pupils after they learn to read. So much can be discovered and rediscovered by young people as they explore language and picture by themselves. It is a unique medium because the words were written to be spoken, and the pictures not to illustrate but to broaden and complement. The settings for the story books are rare and already dramatic: the visuals seem to say "involve and perceive." It may be that the words speak to the artist, demanding to be visual. Perhaps this is what the drama teacher feels as well.

Should a teacher read and show the book to the class before the drama lesson, after, or dramatize while she reads it? Of course, this answer depends on many variables—the aim of the particular lesson, the children, the time, the place, the story, the visuals. The teacher benefits always, even when the book is simply there for a child to read.

The Golden Swans is a folk tale which has been told for generations in Thailand. It comes from Chaiyapum province, on the mountainous western edge of the Mekhong plateau in northeastern Thailand. Because the lake is hard to reach, few people have ever seen the statue by the lake. In Thailand, Buddhism and Hinduism overlap. In this story, Indra, a Hindu god, works within the framework of Buddhist doctrine. Even in the driest of years, when the forests of Green Mountain are dusty brown and all the ponds and lakes near it are murky, the water remains pure and clear. Kermit Krueger the author became interested in Thai culture in the two years he spent as a Peace Corps volunteer in northeastern Thailand. Ed Yong, the artist, has combined free flowing watercolour washes with bold collage to express the deeply spiritual and emotional content as well as the drama of this ancient legend.

What does *The Golden Swans* have to say to thirty fifteen-year-olds in an inner city school during a drama lessson? Perhaps the most interesting point was the students' moving like birds. There was no flapping of wings—no weak bird calls—no trying to outdo each other. No one looks at you in drama; you simply develop. Each boy and girl felt the swan movement in their spines. The individual feeling was striking, and always, the feeling of giant birds, of swans. Music helped, just as the visuals and the story helped. It seemed to be a focus of all feeling. It is amazing to see Floyd, a seventeen year old Canadian Indian with no front teeth, the obvious class leader, becomes a part of the whole class, even when he was the swan statue that was created. How does he feel that bird and show its flight while frozen? How does he attend a noon hour session, and as he glides to the lake, munch a fudgesicle from the corner store without losing a moment of concentration, a moment of feeling of the telling of the Golden Swans? How far away is Thailand, how close the people, the story?

Why do these young people participate freely? Why are they involved? The boys in this age group seem to move more freely and easily than the girls. Certainly this is reflected in their social lives and their activities in other drama sessions. Why?

The Action

The class works in a cul-de-sac outside their classroom. There are twenty-eight students ranging from twelve to seventeen years. The book has not yet been displayed or read. The teacher begins:

> Whenever there is a village, there are common activities. With your partner, establish seven such activities for any village, changing activities as I clap my hands.

The children work in partners, quickly and to the point, showing their past experience.

> We will be working in Thailand today. There are many swans found there. When the music begins, create from a small tight position the egg as it hatches, the swan as it begins to walk, to feel his wings, to float, to fly. As the music rises, the golden swans will gather in the sky and alight on the waters. Keep the feeling of the swans as you move.

It is amazing to see children of such varying sizes and shapes all creating this tale of the swans, each making a definite effort to understand his body and the way it moves.

> As villagers, talk amongst yourselves discussing where the swans come from or go to each day. Listen to several neighbours' comments. The wise man tells you that hundreds of years ago a city stood on Green Mountain. Create the outline of the city.
>
> A great fire burned the city down. Decide how and what you will be as the fire burns until the crescendo of the music, when everyone will evolve into one giant pulsating flame.
>
> John will he a hunter lost among the trees. Let there be twenty-seven different trees that grow more ominous as the music builds. When the hunter sees the lake, become the swans that glide down and float serenely on it.
>
> In pairs, one is the hunter and one is the swan. The hunter wants to capture a swan to examine it. He tosses a rope around her neck, ties it gently and securely, and the swan beats her great golden wings and struggles to free herself but can not escape. Her struggles cease and she is completely still and the hunter strokes her golden features. But the swan holds her breath until she dies. One person be the dead swan and the others realize what has happened and in horror fly away, leaving the hunter wondering what he has done.
>
> The villagers find the dead swan and are very angry. Read the dialogue on the overhead projector:
>
> *The swans did not hurt anyone*
>
> *We loved them and they brought joy to us all with their gentleness and beauty*
>
> *Now, because you were greedy, one swan is dead and the rest are gone*

Create the gentle sound of the grieving murmurs of the people and blend it into the sounds of the waves of the lake.

In pairs, A is the hunter, B is the priest. A keeps asking B for forgiveness and offering to atone for his deeds but the priest walks away.

Why do you think the swan held her breath and died? Tell me.

Read in pairs the overhead transparencies:

Hunter: Is there nothing I can do to make up for the harm I have done?

Priest: I do not think you can bring back the swans. But perhaps you can find a way to help the villagers remember the beauty that once was theirs to enjoy.

Create by yourself a way in which you, the hunter, could help the villagers be reminded of the swan's beauty every day. Show me your method.

With a partner, A be the hunter, B a block of marble. A carves the marble into the shape of the swan. How will the swan look?

Choose a hunter. Everyone else form one great block of stone. As the music begins, show each piece of the stone falling off as the hunter carves. In the centre of the block will be the swan. When the music finishes, the pieces of stone can become the sun rays at the back of the statue. Form a frozen picture.

The class now examines the book, listening to the story, looking at the beautiful watercolour collages. They are obviously captured by the size of the drawings and the colours. Their comments indicate the differences in interpretation that the artist held compared to theirs.

Item 3: *The Buried Moon*

Starting Point

Scarcely has the Lady Moon set foot upon the squishy mools and gurgling waters of the bog than she finds herself snagged in a life and death struggle with the Quicks, Bogles and other evil doers who dwell in the darkness of the Carland. This splendid tale from Joseph Jacobs' collection of English Fairy Tales is now available in picture book form. New York artist Susan Jeffers' haunting illustrations combined with the richly imaginative language of the text create a treasure of experiences for all age groups to talk about and play out. Often a story will speak strongly to the teacher keen on drama and suggest approaches that will enhance the children's appreciation of it. Thus it was that teacher and class described in "The Action" chose to experiment with "Soundscape" and "Sound Chronicle." In Canada there is a growing awareness of the work of Murray Schaffer, who has realized exciting accomplishments in the realm of sound exploration. In the workshop experiment outlined, Schaffer's methods are employed to investigate in a unique way some intense moments of the Lady Moon's adventure. Commencing with Soundscape, a collection of sounds heard in a given place, the children move to Sound Chronicle, the telling of the story without words. At the same time as these children explore sound, they are deeply engaged in concentration and sensory awareness, both necessary if progress in drama is to be made. Although most of the work described involves individual exploration, eventually an exercise is attempted which requires the concentration of the whole class. Always though the magic of the story is present. How much easier it is at first for children and teacher to be creative with something rather than attempting to create out of a vacuum!

The exploration of sound, related to movement, expression, and interpretation is an important activity in any drama program. Equally important is the central place which children's literature holds in such an endeavour.

The Action

The room is filled with the sound of humming. It is as if a great pipe organ was slowly being activated. The children sit with eyes closed, scattered about the room each concentrating on the sound of his own voice. Moments before, the children were asked to take a deep breath, find a comfortable pitch and sustain a soft humming sound. Now the teacher is encouraging the class to increase the volume, change the pitch, experiment with the tone and to vary the rate.

From the suggestions the children continue their experiments with sound, this time working with letters such as "z," words which are onomatopoeic—(pop), and colour words like "fuchsia." The cacophony continues. Each child works with his sound—there are some self-conscious giggles, occasionally an eye opens, peers about and closes quickly. A routine check has been made; everyone else has his eyes closed. By and large, most faces reflect deep concentration as the sound rises and falls about the room.

The room is hushed and still, the goal now is to be aware of silence. A sigh, a sneeze, a rattle of coins all get in the way. It's hard to find silence. Yet silence is as important as sound.

The children have been asked to think about the marshes in the story. Each child is making a mental inventory of the sounds he thinks might burst forth from Quicks, Bogles and other Evil Things. And once again the air is rent with high-pitched squeaks, elongated "oohs" and raspy "thrafkas." The teacher says:

> Think about the Lady Moon bright and shining and how she decided to step down into the swamp and see for herself the horrors mankind spoke about.

> Begin with silence . . . and as the Lady Moon approaches get ready to make the sound of one of the creatures you want to be. All is well until she slips, loses the struggle with the Snag and is eventually dragged underwater and buried. Keep your eyes closed and concentrate on all the sounds around you as well as your own. If you all listen hard you will know how the story is proceeding.

The children are concentrating very hard. All is quiet . . . and then a faint whispering is heard. Other baleful sounds accumulate. The volume increases, the diversity of sounds is exciting and now the thrashing death struggle of the moon is underway—for a moment the air is ripped by vocal thunder and then, as if by some unheard signal, the sound gradually dies away until only a clicking echo is heard, soft sighing, and then . . . silence.

The children are excited and talk all at once about the composition. Little wonder, for the concentration was superb, the group sensitivity electric!

The discussion continues—only part of the story has been told—could the entire story be done this way? Might words be included? Could rhythm instruments add to the effect?

The planning continues enthusiastically. Little groups huddle in nooks and crannies, under tables and in doorways. Each group has taken up a task as the class prepares to tell the story in sound. One group explores the sound possibilities of tambourines, shakers, drums, bells and triangles. Another clusters about a large sheet of paper printing out all the words they can think of that might be used as synonyms for moonlight. And yet another group is composing a poem to be chanted chorally about the moon's adventure.

There is talk of adding movement: someone else suggests that the room be darkened and flashlights used to add a visual "story in light" to accompany the sound. The possibilities of course are endless as the free flowing ideas brainstormed indicate.

Was Alastair Reid thinking of drama or of literature or of children or of life when he wrote these lines?

> something was ending
> something was beginning
>
> I read new lessons in the leaves
> I breathe with the wind in the flickering grass
> I tell my time by the teetering tortoise
> Slowly I open my ears and my eyes
> It was a new kind of seeing
> a new kind of knowing.
>
> Listen. I have birds in my head
> stars in my feet, clouds on my mind.
>
> What will we find at the end?
> Our selves again, but changed.

References

Bryson, Bernarda (1967) *Gilgamesh* New York: Holt, Rinehart and Winston
Fitzhugh, Louise (1964) *Harriet the Spy* New York: Harper and Row
Jacobs, Joseph (1969) *The Buried Moon* Scarsdale: Bradbury
Krueger, Kermit *The Golden Swans* New York: World Books
Suddon, Alan and Aubry, Claude (1969) *Cinderella* London: Dobson

We add here a list of other picture books used by the authors as sources for dramatization:

Bishop, Elizabeth (1968) *Ballad of the Burglar of Babylon* (illus Ann Grifalconi) New York: Farrar, Straus & Giroux
Wondriska, William (1966) *John John Twilliger* New York: Holt, Rinehart and Winston
Crossley Holland, Kevin (1966) *The Green Children* London and New York: Macmillan
Alexander, Lloyd *The King's Fountain* (illus Ezra Jack Keats) New York: Dutton Papas, William (1967) *No Mules* London and New York: Oxford University Press
Keeping, Charles (1970) *Through the Window* London: Oxford University Press; New York: Watts
Bolognese, Don (1967) *Once Upon a Mountain* Philadelphia: Lippincott
Coalson, Glo (1970) *Three Stone Woman* New York: Atheneum
DiNoto, Andrea (1967) *The Star Thief* New York: Macmillan
Lobel, Anita (1967) *Potatoes, Potatoes* London: World's Work; New York: Harper and Row
Mosel, Arlene (1968) *Tikki Tikki Tembo* London: Bodley Head; New York: Holt, Rinehart and Winston
Zemach, Harve (1969) *The Judge* London: Bodley Head; New York: Farrar, Straus & Giroux
Ungerer, Tomi (1967) *Zerelda's Ogre* London: Bodley Head; New York: Harper and Row
Bulla, Clyde Robert (1970) *Jonah and the Great Fish* New York: Crowell
Watts, Bernadette (1970) *Jorinda and Jorindel* London and New York: Oxford University Press

Twenty-Four Things to Do with a Book

Geoff Fox

During a summer workshop course, a group of teachers in British Columbia recently considered ways of encouraging the response of readers in their classes. Time was limited, and their ideas reflect a sustained "brainstorming" session rather than an attempt to produce a definitive list. More-idiosyncratic ideas which depended upon the peculiar skills of individual teachers have been omitted, as have highly specific illustrations relating to particular books. A dance drama version of Watership Down, for example, was not seen as a readily transferable classroom activity.

The suggestions below are for individual work, for work in pairs, groups, or with the whole class. The Canadian teachers were concerned to confirm a climate in which books were readily handled, shared and exchanged as a central and regular practice of the class.

Reading is normally a private activity: a transaction between reader and writer in which the experience and sensitivities of the reader fuse with the printed text. Reading in school classrooms is a more public matter. At its worst, fiction is used as a superfluous preface to other work: a novel about the relationship between a grandfather and his grandson becomes the stark demand on a worksheet, "What can we do to help old people?" A recent study carried out by student teachers at Exeter University involving conversations with one hundred children in twenty different schools revealed that only one out of every ten readers said that books "done in class" were amongst the five favorites titles.

If a teacher is concerned to foster the unique response of his pupils, he may well provide much time in which his children are "just reading"; ideally amongst an abundant and various supply of books. He may further provide space through exploratory writing and talk for a reader to define and examine his own response to a book. However, the sharing of a book in a public fashion—with a partner, in small groups, or as a class—can have its value. Some activities may lead to a closer reading and a deeper relishing of a book, a refinement of the individual's own response. The ideas which follow are drawn from the group's practical experience.

SOURCE: *Children's Literature in Education*, Autumn 1977, pp. 135–138. Reprinted with permission of Agathon Press, Inc.

For Individual Readers

1. Keep a "reading log"—possibly in a special notebook printed by a school's resources centre. The record might include: title, author, when and where the story takes place, notes on the main characters, the part which was most enjoyed, further reflections.
2. Write a description of one of the characters in the book "as if he or she were coming through the door now," or at a particular moment in the story. Do a drawing or painting that is consistent with the text to set alongside the writing.
3. Write a letter to a friend about a book which you especially liked. This activity is most successful (and educationally justifiable!) if there is a real recipient of the letter in another school. The scheme might best be run therefore by two teachers in different schools, perhaps as part of a wider exchange of letters, information, tapes, etc.
4. Write a letter to the author of a book (via the publisher) containing questions, criticism, expressions of enjoyment, etc. The general experience of this activity is that children's writers are not merely long-suffering, but welcome the contact with their rather elusive audiences.
5. Make a poster for the "film-of-the-book"; stars, what-the-critics-say, etc.
6. Redesign and make a cover (including front, spine, and back) for a new edition of the book. Include the title, author, publisher's blurb.

For Pairs, Small Groups or the Whole Class

7. Begin each lesson with a three-minute (maximum) reading, *prepared beforehand,* by a member of the class. Initially the extracts are chosen simply from a book the reader has enjoyed. Sometimes the class may talk about the reading, sometimes not. If the daily ritual is popular, and continues for several weeks, it may be useful to give the topics of the reading a focus; for example, the reading should be "exciting," "about an event in the past," "funny," "about someone you admire or envy," "about a family," "about someone alone."
8. Ask a local author to come to the class and talk about his books; ideally, at least some members of the class should have read some of them.
9. In a book where a journey is important (as is the case in many books for young readers), create one or several large wall maps on which the movements of the characters are plotted and perhaps illustrated by groups in the class.
10. Another journey idea is a long collage or painted background on which

the class places characters, pictures of episodes, etc., as the story develops.

11. For historical fiction or novels with complex relationships, family trees either in two dimensions or as mobiles can help understanding.
12. Set aside a corner of the room, or even transform the whole room, in order to recreate aspects of the book there. Have maps, collages, models, or writing about the book. In a neighbourhood school with younger children, it may be possible to aim for a "display day" straight after school for parents and siblings.
13. Draw or paint a series of pictures mounted on a long sheet of paper (e.g., wall paper) so that a "strip cartoon" of episodes can be put on a roller and displayed.
14. Have a taped "Book Programme" in which a group discusses one book or each member contributes a short review of different titles.
15. Retell a short extract from the story as a radio play onto tape recorders (include sound-effects, introductory music, etc.). Play it back to the rest of the class or to other (younger) classes.
16. Make the sound-track of a very short extract from a novel. Action-packed pieces are most fruitful and enjoyable for this work, which promotes very close reading of a text: for example, Grendel's arrival at Heorot as the warriors sleep off the previous evening's feast, and his ensuing murder of Hondsciow and struggle with Beowulf.
17. Assign groups to work either on the same book or on different books. The task is to promote the book to readers of their own age—the group is, as it were, hired as an advertising agency by the publishers. Their promotions can be written, spoken, or taped. The effectiveness of the groups is evaluated by another class to whom their efforts are offered. A rank order might be produced by the listening class's votes.
18. Tape a simulated "Phone-In" programme with "calls" either to characters in a book, asking about their motives, attitudes, actions, etc., or to the author. The teacher can judge how heavily he needs to become involved in this, depending on the abilities of his class and how accustomed they are to this sort of work.
19. Write a set of "opening-out" questions about a book (*not* mere factual checks) for the use of individuals and groups in younger classes.
20. Retell a fairly short extract from the story with puppets (short because it seems better to become immersed in a close and thorough reading rather than spreading energies too thinly).
21. The group is employed by a movie tycoon to "vet" possible sources for scripts. Would the book under consideration make a good film? Has it box office appeal, and for what kind of audience? Is the subject likely to be interesting *to look at*? Will the dialogue as it stands in the book sound like "real speech" or will it have to be rewritten? Do any stars immediately seem appropriate for any of the roles?
22. Select some events or one major incident from a book. Using these epi-

sodes, compose a page from a newspaper that could have been printed where the story takes place. Include appropriate headlines, news stories, interviews, pictures (drawn or photographed with a Polaroid camera using "staged " subjects), advertisements, etc.

23. Divide students into pairs—"A" is a librarian, "B" is a borrower who likes to know what a book is about before taking it home. Have "B" cross-question "A" about plot, characters, setting, and "the way it's written." This is a useful exercise to introduce books to potential readers or to deepen understanding of a book.
24. Conduct a *post mortem,* having members of a class discuss *in role as characters in the novel* the parts they have played. This activity fosters close examination of motivation. For example, a character who has been a "victim" in the plot now has the opportunity to challenge the actions of more powerful characters. Discussion should be consistent with the text.

Presenting Literature to Children

Terry D. Johnson

As long as Alice, Peter Rabbit, or Little Tim remain shut in on the bookshelf, literature will not happen. My own definition of literature is something that happens in the mind of a human being when that person reads or listens to a story. Adults who work with children serve as a vital link between the world of books and their intended audience. It is most important that these adults be conversant with ways to share books with children which, on one hand, increase the child's appreciation, but, on the other, do so without marring the enjoyment of the work. I am sure every reader can identify at least one book, poem, or play that was ruined by overenthusiastic or misguided "analysis."

The role of the parent and librarian is relatively easy. Parents should read to their young children and share opinions about books read by their

SOURCE: *Children's Literature in Education,* Spring 1979, pp. 35–43. Reprinted with permission of Agathon Press, Inc.

older children. Discussions should be low-key, voluntary, and free from pressure. Librarians need to indicate the options available to a child choosing a book and follow much the same process as parents with regard to what happens after the book is read.

Teachers work with relatively large groups of children. Unlike librarians, they often do not have time to discuss each book read with each child, as they also have the responsibility of teaching something about the material presented. Teaching arithmetic is pretty straightforward. You show children how to do a particular arithmetical process and then see if they can do it. Each example is neatly, objectively, and satisfyingly right or wrong. Because the same pressure to teach is operant when literature is introduced into the classroom, the same kind of thinking is sometimes applied. An author may have striven to convey the ambiguity of shifting motives as a given character struggles with an important decision. Such trifles may be given short shrift in the classroom. "Why did Alexander abandon the cat? Check A, B, C, or D."

In rejecting such travesties of education, some teachers have swung too far in the other direction. Stories are merely presented and no guidance is offered. While there is some benefit to be gained through the "exposure-only" approach, there remains the problem of merely presenting in class a story that many of the children could have acquired just as easily through the public library or the home. What particular benefit have such children derived from encountering that particular story in the company of that particular teacher? Teachers cannot justify their salaries on the basis of being mere purveyors of children's stories. Children are already well served in that regard via radio, television, librarians, and parents.

A third unsatisfactory option is the mindless association of stories and activities. This might well be called the Pin-the-Tail-on-Squirrel-Nutkin Syndrome. One young student-teacher enrolled in my children's literature class, when required to produce a classroom activity associated with a story of her choice, produced a large, pale facsimile of Squirrel Nutkin replete with detachable tail. The idea was, having listened to the story, children would, in turn, be blindfolded and attempt to reunite Squirrel Nutkin with his scissile tail. While such an activity may give limited amusement to children at a party, it does little to enhance one's appreciation of Beatrix Potter's story. Mary White (1976) makes the same point:

> Too often, the activities proposed for use with Children's literature lead to merely surface responses. Games and arts and crafts projects are frequently tangential to the literature but do not enable children to make any in-depth responses to books.

The key to selecting activities that will help children to develop greater appreciation of the stories they encounter under the guidance of a teacher lies in an understanding of what literature does that no other discipline does.

When asked why literature should be taught in schools teachers typically respond with answers such as, "To develop a love of literature, to increase reading ability, to gain knowledge, to develop aesthetic awareness, to become acquainted with one's cultural heritage, to discover more about oneself." Although such goals are worthwhile, they do not reach the heart of the literary experience. In the first place, literature is not the sole means of achieving them. One may be acculturated through travel, observation, and conversation. Self-awareness may be developed through various forms of psychotherapy, and so on. The first and second of the goals listed above are only incidental by-products of the literary experience; if one reads a great deal of literature one may well come to love it and, in the same process, become an adept reader.

Elizabeth Ann Parker offers one of the most succinct statements of the unique perceptions offered by fiction. She begins by contrasting fiction to informational writing.

> Informational writing presents the reader with facts, but does not interpret them. For example, take this description by Glen Blough:
>
> > The lower part of the rabbit's hind leg is long. The upper part is short. This makes the leg just right for running and jumping.
>
> Blough (1961) does not tell the reader how it *feels* to have legs just right for jumping. But Robert Lawson (1944), the author of *Rabbit Hill,* does.
>
> > His legs were like coiled springs of steel that released themselves of their own accord. He was hardly conscious of any effort, only of his hind feet pounding the ground, and each time they hit, those wonderful springs released and shot him through the air.

To put the matter even more briefly, a good writer of literature puts the reader inside the rabbit—or hobbit, or war orphan, or castaway, or delinquent. Other disciplines (e.g., science, history, geography, etc.) make the reader an observer of the phenomena discussed. Only fiction puts the reader within the situations presented. Observing that fiction offers unique perceptions of the world is not to suggest that such perceptions are superior. The views of the priest, poet, or politician may be of equal validity.

Appreciation of the uniqueness of fiction offers some guidance as to the ultimate role of the teacher in teaching literature. Fiction offers myriad opportunities to gain insight into the human condition. Because children are lacking in worldly experiences they tend to miss some of the more subtle effects intended by the author to communicate such insights. The teacher's role is to help children to develop a deeper insight into the stories that they encounter. Through repeated guidance with particular stories it is hoped that the principles underlying the guided experiences will be internalized, generalized, and applied to future reading experiences of the child's own choosing. The art of teaching involves developing such insight without making the process coercive or unpleasant, thereby creating a dislike of the work under discussion which eventually generalizes to all literature.

Insofar as each piece of literature is unique, the teaching opportunities provided by a given story are also unique. For this reason, lists of teaching tips should be approached with caution. There are no universally good ideas for teaching literature. For example, if the children have listened to *The Fisherman and His Wife* and have not seen an illustrated version it may be useful for them to review the desciptions of the increasing opulence of the wife's dwellings and interpret what they heard or read through drawing and painting. Visualization evoked by verbal descriptions will continue to be a useful asset to a reader in many other reading situations. But to have children draw scenes from *A Snowy Day* or *Charley, Charlotte and the Golden Canary* would produce little more than slavish imitations of the magnificent imaginings already present in these works.

Any planned activity associated with a piece of literature should result from considering three things in relationship to one another: the story, the nature of the children to whom the story is to be presented, and the manner of its presentation.

When considering the teaching opportunities by a particular story it is necessary to distinguish between a literature lesson and lessons in other subject areas that may be enriched by literature. Teachers should resist temptations such as the use of *Charlotte's Web* to engender an interest in spiders or *Treasure Island* to teach map-reading skills. Such gimmicks may enhance the study of science or geography but they will not result in greater appreciation of stories so used. In order for classroom activities to develop literary insights, it is necessary that they send the reader/listener back into the story either via memory or by rereading. For example plotting out the events depicted in *Joseph's Yard* on a time line requires the reader/viewer to look more closely at the illustrations, and reconsider how long it must have taken for the roses to grow, bloom, wither, and die. Engaging in such an activity will result in the appreciation that the events must have taken place over at least two years. In this way, the young child's perception of the story may be deepened.

Appreciation of literary structures can be developed through some activities, but a word of caution is in order. In suggesting that young children as early as the infant years can he helped to appreciate some literary structures, it is not being suggested that children can comprehend such ideas in their abstract form. It *is* being suggested that even very young children can identify the particular problem of a particular character in a particular story. High-level generalization of such abstract principles is not likely to occur until the mid-teens. But such levels of appreciation will occur more readily at that age if the child has had a wealth of repeated concrete experiences with such matters.

William Steig's *Sylvester and the Magic Pebble* (1969) offers a splendid opportunity for helping school-age children to appreciate plot. A class of seven-year-olds listened to a reading of *Sylvester* and viewed the illustrations as they did so. When the story was finished, the children were invited to halt a visual review of the story when the pictures showed Sylvester's problem. Right on cue they identified the encounter with the lion. They were then asked to identify "the part of the story that made you feel the happiest or best." Once again, they noted the reunion of Sylvester with his family. In passing, various individuals noted mood changes in the story. When the winter scene was reshown, one little girl said, "That was the worst part. I felt awful when you read that." The spontaneous reaction of the children (e.g., gasps, squeals of excitement, standing up, crowding closer) occurred during the review of the picture as Sylvester's reunion with his mother and father was approached. Their behaviour indicated that they were responding to the rising action. At no time were technical terms used, and yet those children were engaged in thinking about plot, mood, problem, rising action, and denouement.

The dramatization of a story is a flexible strategy but one that must be used judiciously. Acting out *Where the Wild Things Are* will very likely help children come very close to the psychological key to the story. Like Max, they may begin to experience the relief that comes with the reassurance that one's night fears are controllable. But acting out a cumulative rhyme such as *The House That Jack Built* and *Drummer Hoff* would serve little purpose. Such works call for activities that will bring out their rhythmical repetition and building tension. Choral speaking with new voices added as new characters enter would tend to enhance the major literary characteristics of these works.

The means of presenting the story can also influence the activities that make literary sense. An excellent way to get children involved in a story is to encourage them to predict what is going to happen next or how the story will eventually turn out. On the basis of knowing only the title, and/or having an opportunity to see one picture, the children are invited to speculate as to the nature of the story. At first hypotheses are wide-ranging and general. As more information regarding the story is acquired, some hypotheses are confirmed and others rejected. The technique is highly involving and creates a tremendous motivation for proceeding further into the story. It works best when the teacher reads aloud from a single copy of a story that is unfamiliar to all the listeners. Timing of intervention such as pregnant pauses and cliff-hanging chapter endings so often maximizes the tension that it is an indispensible skill in the reader's repertoire.

The children's predictions may range from the next word or phrase the author is going to use to speculation about the eventual resolution of the problem. Predictions may involve no more than a breathless guess as to the identity of the dark figure looming in the doorway (confirmed one-half second later by the continued reading of the text) or develop into fifteen-minute discussions at chapter breaks as to how certain situations will work out as new problems arise.

There is quite an art to asking anticipatory questions. A good example will include a review of the potentially relevant information gleaned from the story thus far plus a question that invites speculation in a productive direction. For example, if one is reading Joan Aiken's *Wolves of Willoughby Chase* (1963) aloud to the class and the point where Grimshaw is seen in the library with Miss Slighcarp has been reached, the following question might be posed: Grimshaw rescued Sylvia from the wolves. Now he's seen with the awful Miss Slighcarp. Whose side do you think he will be on? The pros and cons of Grimshaw's behavior up to this point should be reviewed and weighted. Children should be asked to support their predictions.

A less effective question would be, "Do you think Bonnie's father and mother will return to rescue them?" This question asks for blind guessing since there have been no clues provided to suggest that they might. Moreover, it is not an area of productive speculation as the story does not, in fact, turn out that way. Asking the listeners if they think Simon will help the girls escape from Miss Brisket's School is too informative. A better question at that point would be, "Do you think the girls will escape?" followed by a supplementary "How?" question.

As with all the other techniques presented, the long-term intent is that such attitudes and expectations with regard to narrative fiction will become internalized and applied, consciously or unconsciously, by the individual in his or her own private reading.

The way in which character is handled depends very much on the maturity of the children. With very young children, who tend to see things in black and white, one may wish to do little more than have them classify characters as "good" or "bad." Such an activity would require the use of a story where the characters are clearly definable in positive and negative terms. Fairy stories offer a wealth of opportunities for such categorization. Perhaps the next step toward greater maturity would be the indecision or divided opinion experienced when more fully developed characters are encountered.

In deciding how to draw special attention to particular words or phrases, teachers should bear in mind that language conveys meaning via a web of associations. Full understanding may be said to occur when every word or meaningful phrase is familiar to the listener/reader and the whole relates in some meaningful way to some aspect of a real or imagined world. However, most of us can manage on less than total comprehension. Unfamiliar words and phrases or familiar words and phrases used in unfamiliar ways represent holes in the web of language, but such losses do not always produce a complete loss of understanding of the complete work.

Indeed it is by noting the "shape" of the hole caused by such a loss that new words are learned. Readers unfamiliar with the word "temblor" will have little difficulty in understanding the sentence, "A temblor measuring 6.5 on the Richter Scale was recorded in Chile today." Moreover the reader will acquire some understanding of the new term as a result of understanding the sentence. Children are quite accustomed to hearing and being addressed in language that contains many unfamiliar terms.

Teaching the meanings of unfamiliar words is a matter that requires delicate handling. Some teachers have a tendency to pick out all the difficult words and explain their meanings so that they will be understood when encountered in the story. In many cases this is a mistake. The meaning of words is largely determined by the context in which they occur, as for example, in the sentences:

1. We will have to compromise if we wish to avoid further argument.
2. The judge found himself in a compromising position.

The word *compromise* takes on quite different meanings. In many cases, even the meaning and pronunciation of the word is affected by its context, e.g., refuse (rubbish or rejection), wind (bind up or moving air), lead (a metal or the act of showing the way).

In general it is better to leave the words alone and let the children encounter them within the meaningful flow of language. When an unknown word prevents them from understanding something in which they are interested, they will ask. Two reasons support this somewhat cavalier approach:

1. Struggling to understand a word encountered in the flow of meaningful language is the usual, normal, and natural way that children acquire new vocabulary.
2. IIt gives the children practice in doing what they must do when they encounter unfamiliar words in their private reading. No one will have "prepared the vocabulary" for them and there may not even be an adult to answer questions. The only resources they have are their own abilities and the context.

It is important to recognize that the child will not have a complete understanding of a word the first time it is encountered. When a child first meets the word "barque" it may be sufficient to appreciate that it is a boat. A later encounter may reveal that it is a sailing ship. Further refinements may involve the poetic or rhetorical uses in modern English. Recognition of this developmental sequence means that teachers must have the patience to accept the child's limited understanding and trust that, given a stimulating educational environment, the child will indeed reencounter and thus refine his or her meaning of the word. Furthermore, teachers should recognize the developmental process described as one in which they share. If the teacher continues to be a learner, he or she will also come across deeper, more subtle, or variant meanings of familiar words.

On some occasions authors will use language by one character that mystifies the protagonist. For example, Robert C. O'Brien in *Mrs. Frisby and the Rats of NIMH* (1971), has Dr. Schultz, a neurologist, say:

> The A Group is now three hundred per cent ahead of the control group in learning and getting smarter all the time. B Group is only twenty per cent ahead. It's the new DNA that's doing it. We have a real breakthrough, and since it is DNA we may well have a true mutation, a brand new species of rat.

There is much in this speech that many junior school children will not understand. But it is artistically important that the young listener/reader *not* fully understand the doctor. In order to get his reader to identify more closely with his protagonists, O'Brien tries to mystify his young reader as the rats themselves are mystified.

The only occasion when advanced preparation of vocabularly is required is when certain key words or phrases are present whose understanding is crucial to the understanding of the story. For example, the repeated spell of supplication in Freya Littledale's *The Fisherman and His Wife* (1969) needs to be understood before the full story is comprehensible:

> Flounder, flounder in the sea
> Prythee, hearken unto me.
> My wife, Ilsebil, must have her own will,
> And sends me to beg a boon of thee.

Similarly a simple explanation of the work of a miller may be necessary if young children are to understand the reason for the wolf's visit to the miller in the story of *The Wolf and the Seven Little Kids*.

Concluding with a summary we note that adults who come into contact with children are crucial to the child's joyful and productive entry into the world of literature. Teachers have a special responsibility since they must help the child appreciate literature more fully without damaging enjoyment of literature.

The development and selection of meaningful activities associated with literature must take into account the nature of the work, the maturity of the children and the manner in which the story is presented. Vocabulary should be prepared in advance only if a lack of understanding of certain words seriously disrupts appreciation of the story. Literature may be used to enrich other subjects but activities for the development of literary appreciation must send the child back into the work for reconsideration.

The argument presented here in some detail for vocabulary may be applied to phrases, sentences, paragraphs, chapters, stories, novels, and all other language structures. The child's breadth and depth of apprehension will increase with repeated encounters. Mere practice will go far to increase the child's growth in understanding, but full realization of each child's potential requires guidelines of sensitive, concerned, and informed teachers.

References

Aiken, Joan (1963) *The Wolves of Willoughby Chase* New York: Doubleday
Ardizzone, Edward (1955) *Little Tim and the Brave Sea Captain* New York: Walck
Blough, Glenn O. (1961) *Who Lives in This Meadow?* New York: Whittlesey House
Dodgson, Charles (1866) *Alice in Wonderland* New York: Macmillan
Emberley, Barbara (1967) *Drummer Hoff* Englewood Cliffs, N.J.: Prentice-Hall

Galdone, Paul (1961) *The House That Jack Built* New York: McGraw-Hill

Grimm Brothers (1973) *"The Fisherman and His Wife" Grimm's Fairy Tales* New York: Viking

Grimm Brothers (1968) *Grimm's Fairy Tales: The Wolf and the Seven Little Kids* Chicago, Ill.: Follett

Keats, Ezra Jack (1962) *A Snowy Day* New York: Viking

Keeping, Charles (1967) *Charley, Charlotte, and the Golden Canary* New York: Franklin Watts

Keeping. Charles (1969) *Joseph's Yard* London: Oxford University Press

Lawson, Robert (1944) *Rabbit Hill* New York: Viking

Littledale, Freya (1969) *The Fisherman and His Wife* New York: Scholastic Book Services

O'Brien, Robert C. (1971) *Mrs. Frisby and the Rats of NIMH* New York: Atheneum

Parker, Elizabeth Ann (1969) *Teaching the Reading of Fiction* New York: Teachers College Press

Potter, Beatrix (1902) *The Story of Peter Rabbit* London: Frederick Warne & Co.

Potter, Beatrix (1903) *The Tale of Squirrel Nutkin* London: Frederick Warne & Co.

Sendak, Maurice (1963) *Where the Wild Things Are* New York: Harper & Row

Steig, William (1969) *Sylvester and the Magic Pebble* New York: Windmill Books

Stevenson, R. L. (1911) *Treasure Island* New York: Charles Scribner's Sons

White, E. B. (1952) *Charlotte's Web* New York: Harper & Row

White, Mary Lou (1976) *Children's Literature: Criticism and Response* Columbus, Ohio: Charles E. Merrill

Books . . . Love 'Em and Use 'Em

Carol Hurst

We'll are agree, I think, that it's tougher than ever to get kids up those steps these days. There are so many learning and teaching demands made on children and teachers that we simply don't spend enough time just reveling in books, books, books. Most of us will loudly proclaim our commitment to

SOURCE: *Early Years*, November 1980, pp. 37–50, 106. Reprinted with permission of the publisher Allen Raymond, Inc., Darien, Ct. 06820.

books, but how often do we demonstrate this commitment in our teaching? How many books do we ourselves read just for pleasure? How often do we make the no holds barred effort to get children really interested in the world of books? An all-out effort *doesn't* mean marching your class to the library once a week to go through the mechanics of exchanging one unread book for another that will never be opened. Putting forth real effort means showing children, by your example, how vital books can be.

The sustained silent reading periods that are growing in popularity are a decided step in the right direction. In this way we are at least according trade books the dignity of a place and time in the school program. These silent reading periods also give children a chance to see you, as a teacher, *reading for pleasure,* something many children rarely see an adult do.

Reading stories aloud is another good way to lure children into the world of books. Any elementary teacher worth his or her salt has a carefully thought-out read-aloud program underway. No, grabbing an unknown book and struggling and stumbling through it for the duration of snack time does not suffice. A good read-aloud program exposes children to a wide variety of literature of increasing sophistication; a well-thought-out program allows good, moderate and poor readers a chance to experience the magic of a great story well read.

Opening Doors. But not even sustained silent reading and reading aloud are enough to give children the feeling of being in the midst of books. A few lucky children come to school with this attitude because of the prominent place books hold in their own homes. But in order to help *all* your students see books as the door-openers they are, we, as teachers, must use books as often as possible as keys to open a variety of doors. Think about it. If you introduced every subject in the curriculum for a week by reading from a trade book, wouldn't this point begin to sink in?

Just to give you a few ideas for getting more books in the curriculum we've used some of the newer books in developing a series of possible lessons. You'll come up with many more of your own ideas once you get started. As you look through the titles you'll probably find few you've ever heard of before. Where are the old favorites you ask? The old favorites are probably still on the library shelves just where you left them. Of course you can and should use the traditional favorites in some of the ways we suggest you use the brand new books. We're concerned with new books here because first, we like new ideas and challenges; second, if new books are not bought and used, they may go out of print and be lost before they're found.

Schools are the largest purchasers of trade books. Presently, publishers are making a large scale effort to give you what you want, so support them in their efforts to bring out some fine new products—we'll all be richer for it.

One of the new fall books we didn't include here but which is worth talking about is *Folktales of the Amur, Stories from the Russian Far East* by

Dmitri Nagishkin, illustrated by Gennady Pavlishin (Harry N. Abrams, Subs. Times Mirror Co., 110 E. 59th St., New York, N.Y. 10022). Price: $25.00. Yes, we know it's very expensive, but it's also very beautifully done. And wouldn't it be nice if children, raised in this age of consumable everything were given a chance to see something as exquisite as this book of folk tales? If you can manage to obtain this luxurious volume, I'll guarantee it will lead to plenty of good social studies, music and art activities.

Of course, you may find some of your old favorites in the form of paperbacks: the paperback publishers, bless them, are keeping many titles from going out of print.

We know school library budgets are being cut down to rock bottom and we know this is a terrible state of affairs. However, unless your library budget was eliminated altogether, your librarian *did* buy some new books for this fall. He or she may even have purchased some of the books we've listed here.

And speaking of purchases, we teachers are notorious for spending our own money in order to stock our classrooms. We're not suggesting you do this, it's just that we've seen too many other teachers also buying supplies with money out of their own pockets to deny that it happens and happens often. But if you *are* buying a choice something for your classroom, think of all the mileage a single picture book can give you. A book is a great deal more versatile than so many things I could name. And book clubs now make it easy for teachers and kids to acquire books inexpensively. Keep an eye out for titles you can use from that source.

In this portfolio, we've also included a selection of audio-visual materials and ways to use them. This media form has come a long way—filmstrips no longer consist of dull pictures explained by even duller captions. Many of today's filmstrips are lively and beautiful expansions of picture books. Records are first-rate, and sound films are a tremendous resource.

Keep the Magic In. Obviously, not all the books we selected will be suitable for your children's ages and interests. However, you'll be surprised how many ways a picture book can be stretched using a little ingenuity. For this reason, we've not assigned a grade level to any of the lesson plans.

You'll also want to exercise some judgment in working with the lesson plans themselves. We've taken each book in as many directions as possible but if you try to carry out each activity you'll be sure to wring the book dry of all its fun and magic. Don't do it. Pick and choose judiciously from among the activities using those that appeal to you and have some relevance to the goals of your curriculum directions.

We've categorized our book selections under fantasy, realism, folk tales, poetry and non-fiction. You may disagree with our categorization of some of the books—after all, one person's reality is another's fantasy. However, we wanted you to see that all types of books can be used throughout the curriculum.

Our major point is that trade books *belong* in your classroom. They shouldn't be relegated to sparetime periods, they are an integral, vital departure for a host of explorations in social studies, language arts, math, music, art and science. Remember, "From them, anything. From here, anywhere."

Fantasy

The Green Man
Gail Haley
Charles Scribner's Sons
597 Fifth Ave., New York, N.Y. 10017
1979

Summary: The author speculates on how the legendary character of the Green Man might have come about. In creating her own basis for the legend, Ms. Haley weaves the tale of Claude, a selfish nobleman who unwittingly, but temporarily, turns into the Green Man.
Pre-Reading—

1. History: Using a time line locate the Middle Ages for the children. Make references to other historical events and times with which they're already familiar.

2. Ask for the names of any characters commonly associated with the Middle Ages such as Robin Hood. King Arthur and characters from some fairy tales.

3. Show children pictures depicting life in that time period.

4. Show the children the title page of *The Green Man*. Ask them to determine the wealth and character of the people they see there. Discuss the many activities taking place on the page.

5. *Interpreting Pictures:* Look at the second two pages with the same care. Ask the children to find 11 trades or occupations and three games or amusements amid the goings on. What about those legs seen in the second story window? Look at the houses and try to decide of what materials they're made.

Reading: Read the story without showing any pictures except the ones I've described.
Post-Reading—

1. Ask the children who the Green Man was before, during, and at the end of the story.

2. Tell the children you would like them to look carefully at the pictures in the book when they have the time. Tell them a little about Gail Haley.

3. Display the following poster near the book on a table, or give each child a copy in the form of a check list—

Things to look for:

The sign above the door of the inn that tells its name in pictures.
The first glimpse of the Green Man.
A cross-bow.
The changes in Claude's face which show his changing feelings.

Look at the man dressed in blue on the page where Claude's Father's men are looking for him. Does he look familiar? Can you find at least one picture of each of the following animals:

white sheep	owl
goose	rabbit
squirrel	bird
badger	duck
rooster	goat
black sheep	hen
brown dog	hedgehog
striped cat	3 baby hedgehogs
boar	bees
mouse	white deer
brown deer	cow
horse	calf

The Knight and the Dragon
Tomie de Paola
G.P. Putnam's Sons
200 Madison Ave., New York, N.Y. 10016
1980

Summary: A young knight prepares to fight his first dragon. At the same time, a dragon is making his preparations to fight a knight. The battle ensues and has surprising results.

Pre-Reading—

1. With the children, make a list of knights and dragons found in storybooks. This should provide a good climate for incidental storytelling as children acquaint each other with the stories they know.

2. Vocabulary: Amass a collection of books on knights and knighthood and ask the children to find pictures of the following—

crossbow
lance
tournaments
armor
shield
castle

3. Vocabulary: Make lists of the qualities one usually expects to find in a knight and a dragon.

Reading: This book has few words. Most of the plot is advanced through pictures and this makes it a good partner book. Pair a reader or an upper-grade child with a non-reader and tell them to look carefully at each picture and talk about what's going on.

Post-Reading—

1. Some of the pictures from the book could be classified under the title "Preparation"; others might belong in a category called "Oops." Ask the children for nominations for each category.
2. The most heroic figure in this book is probably the lady. Where does she first appear? What is her occupation? Where do you think she is at the end of the story?
3. Ask the children to look at the last two-page spread in the book. Have them find all the fighting tools shown there and tell how they are being used.
4. Ask the children to write or make a drawing for a story called "The Dragon at School." These stories should be the further adventures of the dragon in the de Paola story.
5. Devise menus for the restaurant. Name all the dishes and design an appropriate cover. Give your finished menu to the school cafeteria manager for display on a portable bulletin board.
6. Have each child design a shield on which a coat of arms is displayed. Have the child include objects or items in his coat of arms that have some meaning in relation to his personality or background. Have the children explain their shields.

Follow-Up: Amass a good supply of books written and illustrated by Tomie de Paola. Ask the children to read as many of his books as possible and to describe some of the qualities consistent in de Paola's work.

Paddy's New Hat
John S. Goodall
Scribner Atheneum
597 Fifth Ave., New York, N.Y. 10017
1980

Summary: As in most of Goodall's Books, the plot of *Paddy's New Hat* is advanced with half- and full-page illustrations. The intricate plot of this wordless book involves an "accidental" policeman.

Pre-Reading—

1. Talk about books without words. Why would an author/illustrator create a book and not use any words? What skills does an illustrator need to create such a book? What skills does a reader need to "read" a wordless book?
2. Look at the cover of the book. What can we learn about Paddy from the cover? What do the costumes tell you?

Reading: Paddy's New Hat should be read in groups of two. Try to give children many opportunities for conversation.

Post-Reading—

1. Using the book and a tape recorder, several children record the story as they see it. Ask other children to listen to one of these versions as they read the book. Ask them to offer additions or corrections for the taped versions.

2. Collaborate with the children and write a text for the book.

3. Have the children make drawings of the different events in the book. Then have the children jumble the drawings and put them in the proper sequence.

4. Suggest that the children select musical accompaniment for the various scenes; then, using the drawings, narrate the story with a musical background.

5. Read other *Paddy* books and create a series of experience charts around them.

6. Find one word and only one word that best describes the action on a single page of the book.

Follow-Up: Ask the children to retell the story so completely that pictures will be unnecessary.

Leprechauns Never Lie
Lorna Balian
Abingdon Press
201 Eighth Ave., S. Nashville, Tn. 37202
1980

Summary: Granny and Ninny Nanny are starving in their leaky hut because Ninny Nanny is too lazy to work. A crafty leprechaun tricks Ninny Nanny into doing all the work while keeping his pot of gold from this greedy girl.

Pre-Reading—

1. Talk about accents and encourage the children to start being aware of various dialects they hear.

2. Review some of the popular stories and legends about the "little people" of the world.

3. Have the children locate Ireland on a world map.

Reading: Read Balian's tale using your best Irish brogue.

Post-Reading—

1. Make a list of characters from fact and fiction that have had a special talent for outwitting others, such as: Granny, leprechauns in general (and this one in particular), Br'er Rabbit, Burt Dow, the shipwrecked mariner from Kipling's *How the Whale Got His Throat,* characters from Aesop.

2. Make a list of the kinds of little people with their characteristics.

3. Display a large world map. Near the map, put up the chart from activity two. With pins and yarn, connect the names of the little people on the list to their geographical origins on the map.

Follow-Up: Obtain a large black kettle or pot. Spray-paint a quantity of poker chips with gold-colored paint. Have the children find and read as many stories and poems as possible about the little people. Children write the title of each story or poem on a poker chip, drop it in the pot and fill 'er up!

Fables
Arnold Lobel
Harper & Row Publishers
10 E. 53rd St, New York, N.Y. 10022
1980

Summary: This delightful collection of original fables pokes gentle fun at the genre and gives us some wonderful stories and characters.

Pre-Reading—

I wouldn't try to conduct a formal lesson using this book. Instead, I would discuss the fable genre briefly with the children, bringing up some of Aesop's and La Fontaine's fables. Children won't appreciate Lobel's satire until they're familiar with the original models. *Jack Kent's Fables of Aesop* and *More Fables of Aesop* (Parents Magazine Press, 212 W. 79th St., New York, N.Y. 10024) will be useful in setting the stage. Brian Wildsmith has also done beautiful renditions of several of the La Fontaine fables including *The Lion and the Rat* and *The Hare and the Tortoise* (Franklin Watts, Inc., Subs. of Grolier, Inc., 730 Fifth Ave., New York, N.Y. 10019). Read many of these fables aloud and show the accompanying pictures before using Lobel's *Fables*.

Reading: When reading Lobel's fables, I would use only two or three fables each day. I would show the pictures first and pause before reading each moral, giving the children time to guess what it might be.

Post-Reading—

1. Lobel wrote his book by first making a list of animals he liked and then creating a fable about each one. Have the class make a list of animals and discuss each animal's characteristics in both reality and folklore. Compose some fables about them.

2. Try writing a group-poem about one of Lobel's fables—

A crocodile liked things in rows
Organization's fine, as far as it
goes,
But, to make things too neat
Is to ask for defeat,
That isn't the way nature grows.

3. Have children compile a list of morals from as many sources as possible. Spend some class time developing a fable around one of the morals.

Turn the class loose on any of the morals that appeal to them and have them develop fables around these.

4. Assign one moral to each child in the class. Give children permission to shout out their moral whenever an appropriate situation comes up.

Folklore

Dragons and Other Fabulous Beasts
Richard Blythe
Illustrated by Fiona French and Joanna Troughton
Grosset & Dunlap
51 Madison Ave, New York, N.Y. 10010
1980

Summary: This is a collection of stories about dragons, birds, horses, unicorns, chimerae and other strange beasts of mythology.

Pre-Reading—

1. Vocabulary: Letter a sign like the one below and place it near the book on the reading table.

Find one of these and read its story.

bunyip	hippogriff
mermaid	sphinx
thunderbird	Minotaur
phoenix	kraken
unicorn	black swan
chimera	basilisk

anansi

Make a list of its characteristics.

2. Art and Writing: Invite the children to draw a fabulous creature and write a brief caption describing its characteristics.

3. Art: Mythical beasts appear often in children's book illustrations as well as in many paintings. Display a few of each.

Reading: Read one or two of the tales.

Post-Reading—

1. Research: Assign each child one of the real beasts in the book. Ask him to compare the real beast with a mythical beast using information from this book and from other reference sources.

2. Read Mercer Mayer's *Everyone Knows What a Dragon Looks Like* (Four Winds Press/Scholastic, Inc., 50 W. 44th St., New York, N.Y. 10036).

3. Music: Play the song "Puff the Magic Dragon."

4. Write a group-poem about one of the mythical beasts.

5. Read Maurice Sendak's *Where the Wild Things Are* (Harper & Row, 10 E. 53rd St., New York, N.Y. 10022). Compare Sendak's monsters with those in this dragon book.

6. Read Kenneth Graham's *The Reluctant Dragon* (Holiday House, 18 E. 53rd St., New York, N.Y. 10022). This dragon's characteristics are very different from those in Blythe's book.

Follow-Up: Make a huge classroom dragon. Each one of his scales should contain a book title and author, song, or painting and artist that the children have discovered concerning mythical beasts.

My dragon was made on an enormous sheet of white Kraft paper (about 15 feet long—yours can be as long as your classroom wall or the hall wall). The way we drew our dragon made it appear to be flying through the air with his feet tucked under his body. A child reading a book rested on his head. His scales were made of many large and small circles of different colors of tissue paper glued on with rubber cement. We wrote the various titles on the scales after the glue dried. You could use construction paper just as well.

The Greedy Shopkeeper
Irene Mirkovic
Harcourt Brace Jovanovich
757 Third Ave., New York, N.Y. 10017
1980

Summary: This is a Serbian version of a tale concerning a poor man who finds a rich man's purse. The wise judge settles the ensuing disagreement.

Pre-Reading—

1. Social Studies: Locate Yugoslavia on a map and explain how Serbia became part of Yugoslavia.

2. Ask the children to make suppositions about Serbia using a relief map.

3. Ask the children to attempt to glean other facts about Serbia while listening to you read, or as they read the book.

Reading: Read the story.

Post-Reading—

1. Write down the "facts" about Serbia the children found in the story.

2. Have some children check their suppositions in reference sources.

3. Share some of the tales of Solomon (found in the Bible) with the children. Compare them with this Serbian story.

4. Have the children search for other folk tales in which judges play a part.

5. With the children, make a simple chart listing the names of these folk tales, the countries in which they originated and whether or not the judge in the story used wisdom and justice.

Follow-Up—
Vocabulary: Give the children the following vocabulary list—

haggling	retraced
anxiety	dishonest rogue
threaded	cobblestone
overawed	preside
stern	verdict

Ask them to find these words in the story and determine their meanings from past experiences or by using context. Discuss answers—check dictionary for accuracy.

How the First Rainbow Was Made
Ruth Robbins
Parnassus Press/Houghton Mifflin
2 Park St., Boston, Ma. 02107
1980

Summary: This California Indian tale tells why a rainbow appears in the sky after a rain.
Pre-Reading—

1. Social Studies: Help the children locate Mt. Shasta on the map.
2. Social Studies: Use maps (the kind that show the distribution of major Indian tribes across the U.S.) or other reference sources to decide which tribe might have been responsible for this myth.
3. Social Studies: Help the children understand that a myth usually explains a natural phenomenon. Make a list of possible titles for myths concerning those natural events with which the children are familiar.
4. Science: Show a picture of a coyote; outline this animal's habits.

Reading: Read the story, sharing a few of the pictures.
Post-Reading—

1. Speculate why the Indians would use the coyote as the embodiment of wisdom.
2. Make a list of the other animals found in picture books and folk tales that are depicted as being wiser than the other animals: owls, elephants, foxes, etc.
3. Social Studies: Research other Indian legends. Make a chart showing the name of each myth, the tribe involved, the predominant animals, the qualities of each animal, name of supreme being.
4. Social Studies and Science: Look up other interpretations of rainbows and research the scientific explanation. Read the story of Iris found in Greek mythology.
5. Science: Find as many ways as possible to make rainbows—prisms, soap bubbles, water, oil, etc.

6. Read Carl Sandburg's poem "Bubbles."
Follow-Up: Have the children write or dictate their own rainbow myths and then illustrate them.

Sun Flight
Gerald McDermott
Four Winds Press/Scholastic, Inc.
50 W. 44th St., New York, N.Y. 10036
1980

Summary: This is the Greek myth of Deadalus and Icarus, told with beautiful simplicity and illustrated in McDermott's incomparable style.
Pre-Reading—

1. Social Studies: Using a map, show the children where Crete, Greece and the Aegean Sea are located.

2. Talk about some of the myths to which the chilren have already been exposed.

3. Talk about mazes and labyrinths. Show some examples of mazes from Rick Brightfield's *Amazing Mazes* (Harper & Row Books, 10 E. 53rd St., New York, N.Y. 10022).

4. Vocabulary: Introduce the children to any one of the following words with which they may be unfamiliar:

intricate	ascended
wrath	artisan
recesses	perish

Reading: First, read the text aloud up to the point at which Icarus heads for the sun. Now show the pictures up to and beyond that point; let the children comment on the pictures and what they depict.
Post-Reading—

1. Invite the children to examine one picture closely. Ask them to give a few words that describe Mr. McDermott's style of illustration. Can the children discover what medium was used?

2. View the filmstrip of McDermott's book *The Stone Cutter* (Weston Woods, Weston, Ct. 06883). The filmstrip shows how the author drew the illustrations for the book and then how the book was made into an animated film.

3. Read Ingri & Edgar Parin d'Aulaire's version of the same myth in *d'Aulaire's Greek Myths* (Doubleday & Co., 245 Park Ave., New York, N.Y. 10167). Compare this version with McDermott's. Many details of the myth are omitted in the McDermott version.

4. Read the wordless book *The Silver Pony* by Lynd Ward (Houghton

Mifflin, One Beacon Street, Boston, Ma. 02107) and see how it parallels the myth of Icarus.

Follow-Up: Find other books by Gerald McDermott, many of which are folk tales or myths.

The Three Little Pigs
Erik Blegvad
Scribner Atheneum
597 Fifth Ave., New York, N.Y. 10017
1980

Summary: This is the well-known nursery tale of the practical pig and his less fortunate brothers. The author illustrates the book charmingly, with precise detailed drawings.

Pre-Reading—

1. When you introduce this book, most of the children should tell you they've already heard the story. Ask the children who have already heard "The Three Little Pigs," to tell the story. Now have the entire group help form the story.
2. Write their story in experience chart form.
3. Ask them to listen while you read Erik Blegvad's version and see where and how it differs from theirs. Since the Blegvad version is a traditional one, only details will vary as children may have forgotten some parts or have some events out of sequence.

Reading: Read the story aloud.

Post-Reading—

1. Compare the children's story with the book version. Account for variations if possible.
2. Tell the children that this story is a folk tale and that it existed many years in oral form before it was recorded. This may account for the many versions of the tale.
3. If the children are non-readers, ask them to tell the tale into a tape recorder as they look at the pictures. This will give you an idea of their ability to use complete simple and compound sentences, their general sophistication of language and their ability to remember details.
4. Using the taped version you or the children like best, pantomine the story.
5. Write this refrain on the chalk board: *Little pig, little pig, let me come in. Not by the hair of your chinny chin chin.* Ask the children if they know chants from other folk tales such as *Rapunzel, Rapunzel, let down your golden hair, that I may climb the golden stair.* How about, *Nibble, nibble, like a mouse, who is nibbling at my house?* from Hansel and Gretel.
6. Create illustrations for each of the chants.

7. Make a flow chart of the action in *The Three Little Pigs*. Print the major events in larger letters to set them apart.

8. Compare the various versions of this folk tale to be found in picture books.

Follow-Up: Tell the story with puppets (use stick puppets or sock puppets).

Realism

The Ox-Cart Man
Donald Hall
Illustrated by Barbara Cooney
Viking Press 625 Madison Ave., New York, N.Y. 10022
1980

Summary: New England family of the early 1800s works all year to make goods to sell at the Portsmouth market.

Pre-Reading—

1. Social Studies: Talk about life on a modern farm, discussing the responsibilities of each member of the household.

2. Discuss the Caldecott Medal, the award given to the illustrator of the best picture book published in America in a given year.

3. Art: Look at some early American paintings. Discuss their characteristic stiffness, their distortions and their subject matter. Explain that Barbara Cooney attempted to capture some of these characteristics in her illustrations.

Reading: In this book the illustrations dominate the text so they must be viewed as the text is read. Use the book with small groups or use the opaque projector so the class as a whole can view the pictures.

Post-Reading—

1. Art: Talk about the illustrations. Ask the children why Barbara Cooney should be awarded a prize for her drawings. Have the children look up other picture books published in this country in 1979 for rivals for the prize. To which book would the children have awarded the medal?

2. Social Studies: Have the children make a list of the months of the year. Beside each month they write the kinds of chores done on this farm during that time. The book tells exactly when some of the chores were done. Children will need to make educated guesses about other chores.

3. Next year some of the chores on the farm will be different because of the kinds of materials the farmer purchased this year. Ask the children to determine what the items are and what the farmer might buy next year. Will he have more or less money to spend? What will the governing factors be?

4. Social Studies: Locate Portsmouth, New Hampshire, on a map. What do the illustrations tell about Portsmouth in the early nineteenth century?

5. Social Studies: Although this family does not seem to live luxuriously, they are not poor. Ask the children to look for clues as to their wealth.

6. Music: Such a family would probably enjoy music on those long winter evenings. What songs might they have sung? What instruments might they have played? Around the docks in Portsmouth, other music might have been heard. What would it have been?

7. Math: Decide on possible prices the farmer might have received for his goods or paid for his purchases. Would he have any cash left when he was through trading? If so, what would he have done with the money? If not, would the family's year's work have been worthwhile?

Follow-Up: Find books by other Caldecott winners. Give the children ample time to examine them. Ask for their nominations for a Super Caldecott Award. Such nominations should be backed up with well-documented arguments.

Emma Wendy Kesselman
Illustrated by Barbara Cooney
Doubleday & Co.
245 Park Ave., New York, N.Y. 10167
1980

Summary: Emma is a lonely grandmother who finds a new interest and love in painting.

Pre-Reading—

1. Discuss grandparents—their names, (first names, last names, nicknames), occupations, hobbies, likes, dislikes.

2. Ask each child to write a story telling all he knows about a grandparent or other person of an older generation.

3. Discuss children's stories and depth of knowledge or lack thereof.

Reading: Read *Emma,* sharing some of the pictures.

Post-Reading—

1. Vocabulary: Make a before-and-after list of adjectives describing Emma at the beginning and at the end of the book.

2. Art: This is a story of one artist and how she began to paint. Bring a variety of art prints to class. Ask small groups of children to choose one print they like and then find out who the artist is and how he or she began to paint or draw. Use their research to compose group stories for the classroom library.

3. Discuss Emma's loneliness. Talk about being alone as averse to being lonely. Have the children share their ways of averting loneliness.

4. Read parts of *How It Feels to Be Old* by Barbara Hazen and Trina Hyman (Unicorn/E. P. Dutton, 2 Park Ave., New York, N.Y. 10016). Discuss aging.

5. Hold a "Reach Out" day for which the children plan hobby-sharing or story-sharing sessions with some older members of the community. En-

courage the older people to describe for the children the way things used to be. Have them tell what they do now for pleasure or occupation. Tape as many reminiscences as possible.
Follow-Up: Have an artist-of-the-week display selected by a committee. Have the committee then research the artist-of-the-week's life's work and achievements and report to the class.

We Be Warm Till Springtime Comes
Lillie D. Chaffin
Illustrated by Lloyd Bloom
Macmillan Publishing
866 Third Ave., New York, N.Y. 10022
1980

Summary: A young Appalachian boy braves the winter cold and the hazards of an abandoned coal mine to get fuel for his family.
Pre-Reading—

1. Art: With the children, examine the picture of the shoes on the back cover of the book. What are some obvious statements about the picture? These are probably a child's shoes, badly worn; a chair which must be valuable or loved because it is protected from the shoes by paper or cloth; shoes must have importance in story, probably a poor household, etc. Notice how the eye is riveted to the pair of shoes because of the stark whiteness surrounding them. Talk about the curved lines dominating the picture. What effect does the lack of color have on the picture as a whole?
2. Social Studies: Show children the Appalachia area on a map. Tell them a little about this area.
3. Poetry: Read the poem "Poor" by Myra Cohn Livingston (from *The Way Things Are and Other Poems,* a Margaret K. McElderry Book published by Atheneum, 597 Fifth Ave., New York, N.Y. 10017). Discuss the evidence of poverty in both urban and rural areas.
4. Social Studies and Science: Bring a piece of coal to class and ask the children what they know about this substance. Tell them about using coal furnaces in homes and bring out some facts about coal mining.

Reading: Read the author's dedication. Ask your class what she might have meant by it. Read the book without showing the pictures.
Post-Reading—

1. How old do the children suppose the boy is in the story? What parts of the story support their ideas?
2. Show the children the pictures. Have them tell what's happening in each one. Point out the many curving lines.
3. Ask your class why they think Lloyd Bloom decided to use only black and white oil paints in illustrating the book.

4. Although the people in the story are poor and quite desperate, love is the predominant emotion in the tale. Ask the children to recall events or statements in the story showing feelings of love.

5. Music: Play or sing folk songs that originated in the Appalachian Mountains, such as "Jennie Jenkins" or "By'n By."

Follow-Up: Creative Writing: What do the children think will happen to the family when springtime finally comes?

Barnaby and the Horses
Lydia Pender
Illustrated by Inga Moore
Oxford University Press
200 Madison Ave., New York, N.Y. 10016
1980

Summary: This beautiful mood story illustrates that language is something to be savored. It seems that Barnaby has inadvertently allowed three horses to leave their paddock. The story tells of his oft-distracted search for the horses.

Pre-Reading—

1. Show the children the pictures carefully but don't allow them to read the story just yet.

2. Vocabulary: As children view the pictures, ask them for words that describe Inga Moore's drawings. Accept all answers, but search for such words or phrases as: detailed, real-looking, realistic, sometimes blurry, soft, etc.

3. Ask the children why some of the branches are blurred or indistinct in a few of the pictures.

4. Ask your class what they can tell about Barnaby from the pictures. Is he dreamy? nature-loving?

5. Art: Look at the first picture and note all the vertical lines. Ask children to point out the vertical lines in some of the other pictures. Notice how the vertical lines call attention to the non-vertical lines.

Reading: Read the story through slowly. Ask the children to picture in their heads what's happening while you read.

Post-Reading—1. Lydia Pender uses language so lavishly in this story we'd be foolish not to capitalize on it for a language arts lesson. Write these similes on the chalk board:

. . . willow leaves lay like split butter over the grass
. . . willow leaves fluttered yellow as butterflies
. . . clumps of leaves rustling like shaken paper
. . . the bird, flashing like a blue-green flame
. . . their wet backs glistened bright and brown and shiny as apples.

2. Tell the children that the author compared two dissimilar things in each of these phrases yet finds a similarity in each. Discuss how the two items

in each comparison are alike and different. Identify this kind of comparison as a simile.

3. Use Joan Hanson's books *Similes* and *More Similes* (Lerner Publications, 241 First Ave., N., Minneapolis, Mn. 55401) for extension activities.

4. Make a ditto sheet containing the following—

In the book, "Barnaby and the Horses," Lydia Pender uses many unusual words:

scrambled
rippled
thudded
tugged
glistened
trudged
gurgled
clambered
shook

Find three of these verbs in the story. Copy the sentences in which they are used. Under each of Lydia Pender's three sentences, write a sentence of your own containing the same verb. Try to include a simile in one of your sentences.

Non-Fiction

Pop's Secret
Maryann Townsend and Ronnie Stern
Addison-Wesley Publishing Co.
2725 Sand Hill Road, Menlo Park, Ca. 94025
1980

Summary: This is a touching photographic story of a boy and his grandfather. The story ends with the boy slowly adjusting to his grandfather's death.
Pre-Reading. Talk about death. How has it touched your children's lives? Give everyone a chance to talk.
Reading: Tape the text of the book; encourage the children to listen to it and look at the photographs either alone or in groups of two or three. Allow plenty of conversation.
Post-Reading—

1. Talk about the glimpses this book gives of life in the early 1900s. Use the books from the *Fabulous Century* series (Time-Life Books, 777 Duke St., Alexandria, Va. 22314), to add to the pictorial information given.

2. Encourage the children to bring in books, pictures and models of old planes and automobiles.

3. Make a time line showing the life of the old man in the book. Then place other lives on the time line and compare and contrast them with the old man's, for example, George Washington, Abraham Lincoln, a living adult with whom the children are familiar, lives of a few of the children themselves.

4. Bring in clothes of another time to show the children. If possible, let them try on the clothing.

5. Make a list of some of the things we have today that the people born in the first part of this century would not have had; be sure to list some "negatives" as well as "positives."

Follow-Up: Read the *Hundred Penny Box* by Sharon Mathis (Viking Press, 625 Madison Ave., New York, N.Y. 10022). Compare it with this book.

The Sixteen Hand Horse
Fred Gwynne
Windmill Books, Div. Simon & Schuster
1230 Avenue of the Americas, New York, N.Y. 10020
1980

Summary: This book, like Gwynne's previous *The King Who Rained* and *A Chocolate Moose for Dinner* (Windmill Books), plays with idioms, homonyms and mispronunciations.

Pre-Reading: Much vocabulary and concept work needs to be done before the children will get true enjoyment from the book's humor. They need to know about—

a. the measuring of a horse's height in hands
b. the canon of a church
c. the meaning of the homonyms peal and peel
d. a law suit
e. the meaning of plant (as in a factory)
f. the idea of palm reading
g. the meaning of the homonyms eerie and eary
h. being moved by something, meaning, being touched emotionally
i. the meaning of the homonyms tear and tier
j. the "spoon lure" used by fishermen
k. the engine block in a car
l. the similarity in sound of "rabid dog" and "rabbit dog"
m. the locks that allow ships to change water levels in a canal
n. white-Anglo-Saxon-Protestants being referred to as WASPS
o. the meaning of A.W.O.L.
p. fish roe
q. banking a fire
r. stakes in card-playing
s. flushing prey in hunting

Reading: Cover all of the above concepts you know will be comprehensible to your children. Now read the book and share the pictures as you go.

Post Reading—

1. Print some of the following phrases on sentence strips and ask the children to illustrate any one of them, showing the possible absurdity of the phrase.

"He can't carry a tune."
"It's a small world."
"He was bored stiff."
"I'm all in."
"I'm a big baseball fan."
"Mommy says that salesman is crooked."
"He stole second base."

2. Ask the children to find other statements, while watching television, reading or talking, which could have two meanings. Have them illustrate their phrases.

3. Read Gwynne's other books *The King Who Rained* and *A Chocolate Moose or Dinner*.

Follow-Up: Use the statements and illustrations the children brought in to make a book. Select the best statement and use it as the title. Present the book to your library.

People
Peter Spier
Doubleday & Co.
245 Park Ave., New York, N.Y. 10167
1980

Summary: This is an exploration of people: the way they look, dress, laugh and cry; their houses, ways of working, living, praying and dying. It's really a year's worth of social studies work, but we will only touch a few bases in this lesson plan. However, do try to extend this book's potential on your own—it's worth it.

Pre-Reading—

1. Amass as many world globes as possible. Ask the children to work in small groups, finding the names of as many countries as possible on the globes. Hold a competition: the team listing the most correctly spelled countries is the winner.

2. Ask the children to tell one thing they know about any country on the list.

3. Post two charts with the categoreis "Alike" and "Different." Have the children list ways in which people of various cultures are similar or different: their likes and dislikes, their different foods, type of education, etc.

4. Display pictures of people from around the world.

5. Post a large world map on the bulletin board attaching pieces of yarn to it with pins. Ask the children to find the place they live on the map and extend a piece of yarn from that point to the countries they researched as part of Activity #3.

6. Tell the children they are to keep a list of the countries mentioned in the book they are about to read.

7. Play the record "It's a Small World" (Wonderland Music Company, Div. Walt Disney Music Co., 350 S. Buena Vista St., Burbank, Ca. 91521). Ask the children what they think the song means.

Reading: Since the pictures in this book are full of fascinating detail, it is important the children experience the pictures simultaneously with the text. Share the book in small groups of children or use an opaque projector. It is also feasible to record the text on a prepared tape so the children can look at the book individually. The best way to experience the book would be a teacher/class discussion of pictures and text.

Post reading—

1. Make a master list containing all the countries the children have found in the book.

2. Look again at the page in the book that shows the many different kinds of clothing. Discuss which are uniforms, everyday clothing, or special occasion costumes.

3. Look at the pages of houses. Ask the children what each picture shows about the climate and the type of building materials available in that country. Check other sources to confirm or refute their findings.

4. After looking at the page listing all the different occupations, ask the children to name an advantage and disadvantage of each job.

5. Have the children bring in a phrase or sentence from a foreign language, along with its translation. Ask them to obtain the translation from sources other than books. Suggest that they try grandparents, other senior citizens, brothers and sisters studying foreign languages, etc.

6. Have each child choose a country on the map and find one fact about the people of that country. Put the fact and an accompanying picture at one end of a piece of yarn. Attach the other end to the appropriate country chosen.

7. Replay "It's a Small World" and have the children expand or amend their earlier statements about its meaning.

8. Make a Small World mural. Use Kraft paper the length of your longest wall (or even a hall wall). Have the children print the names of the countries they researched at various angles all along the top of the mural. Illustrate whatever elements of the country they found most fascinating such as costumes, clothing, toys, transportation, flowers, or even a scene combining all their favorite elements. When done, they can see the similarities and differences among nations.

The Freight Train Book
Jack Pierce
Carolrhoda Books, Div. Lerner Publications Co.
241 First Ave., North Minneapolis, Mn. 55401
1980

Summary: This book of captioned photographs gives information on freight trains and their components.

Pre-Reading

1. Leave the book on the library table with the suggestion that each child look through it to find out one thing they did not previously know about freight trains.
2. List their findings.
3. Talk about freight trains and why we need them.
4. Play some railroad folk songs: "A Railroad Man For Me" from *Laura Ingalls Wilder Songbook* (Harper & Row Publishers, 10 E. 53rd St., New York, N.Y. 10022).

"The Train is A'Coming" from *American Folk Songs for Children* (Doubleday & Co., 245 Park Ave., New York, N.Y. 10167).

"I've Been Working on the Railroad" from *The Fireside Book of Folk Songs* (Simon & Schuster, Inc., 1230 Avenue of the Americas, New York, N.Y. 10020).

5. Start a vocabulary list of words that crop up in your discussions.

Reading: Sit with small groups of children and examine the pictures and read the captions. Allow plenty of time for observation and discussion.

Post-Reading—

1. Write the following vocabulary on chart paper:

diesel	cargo
locomotive	tank car
throttle	top hatch
couplers	compartment
caboose	ramp
boxcar	hopper
welding	flatcar

2. Ask the children to use the book to define, orally, most of the words.
3. Read *Freight Train* by Donald Crews (Greenwillow Books, Div. William Morrow & Co., 105 Madison Ave., New York, N.Y. 10016). Compare information from this book with your existing information.
4. Read the poem "Clickety Clack" by David McCord (*One at a Time*, Little Brown & Co., 34 Beacon St., Boston, Ma. 02106).
5. Ask the children to find other train poems, stories and songs.
6. Install a set of electric trains in the classroom.

7. Have each child use 12″×18″ construction paper to make one car for a freight train. Fasten the cars in a string around the room, making one long freight train; label each identifiable part.

8. Make a list of the jobs connected with the railroad and what the people holding those jobs do each day.

9. Take a field trip to the local railroad station and freight yards.

My Friends Live in Many Places
Dorka Raynor
Albert Whitman & Co.
560 W. Lake St., Chicago, Il. 60606
1980

Summary: This is a series of photographs of children from all over the world.
Social Studies: Because of the nature of this book, the format I have used for the other book suggestions does not really apply here. I would suggest instead turning the children loose in groups of two or three and arming them with the book, some maps and a scavenger hunt list. Although a scavenger hunt sometimes encourages the children to look for minutiae, it should require careful observation and may result in some concept development.

Scavenger Hunt

Place the number of the correct photographs after each sentence—

1. Find nine photographs taken in France.
2. Find seven photographs showing pets.
3. Find 17 photographs in which a hat or some sort of headdress is being worn.
4. Find one photograph taken in South America.
5. Find two photographs taken in Africa.
6. Find four photographs in which children are barefoot.
7. Find six photographs of children playing.
8. Find ten photographs in which children seem to be showing that they love each other.
9. Find nine photographs in which someone seems unhappy.

After most of the children have completed the scavenger hunt, compare their findings.

Show each photograph on a large screen using an opaque projector. Ask for the children's observations on each one. Try to decide which children are wearing everyday clothes and which are wearing costumes.

Compare the understandings gained from this book with those gained from Peter Spier's *People,* mentioned elsewhere in this classification, and from the photographs in Edward Steichen's *Family of Man* (Simon & Schuster, Inc., 1230 Avenue of the Americas, New York, N.Y. 10020). You can also use pictures from National Geographic's monthly magazine *World* to develop some around-the-world posters.

The First Americans
Jane Werner
Pictures by Troy Howell
Pantheon, Div. Random House, Inc.
201 E. 50th St., New York, N.Y. 10022
1980

Summary: This controlled-vocabulary book surveys the Indians of the plains, woodlands, tundra, Pacific Northwest and desert.

Pre-Reading—

1. Ask each child to think of a statement about Indians that he or she believes to be true; ask the child to write that fact on a sentence strip, encouraging the children to be as specific as possible.
2. Display many pictures of Indians but do not include any captions. Ask the children to group the pictures of Indians into those categories to which they feel the pictures belong.
3. Make a list of those Indian tribe names that are most familiar to the children.

Reading: Since the book is meant to be read by a child with a second or third grade reading level, allow the children to read it themselves but offer help as needed. Give the children a copy of the following chart to complete as they read, using words from the book.

Post-Reading—

1. Put a star beside any sentence strip fact that the book substantiates. Divide the remaining strips among the children and have them research and substantiate each fact.
2. Go through the pictures again to see if any need regrouping.
3. Group the tribal names under the area divisions used in the book.
4. Make a large, brown Kraft paper buffalo on which the children write the ways the plains Indians used the buffalo.

	Houses	*Food*	*Clothing*	*Women's Jobs*	*Men's Jobs*
Plains					
Woodlands					
Tundra					
Pacific Northwest					
Desert					

5. Make a large outline of a birch bark canoe. Ask the children to write the ways in which the woodlands Indians used birch bark.

6. Make a totem pole outline. Ask the children to write about the ways the Northwest Indians used logs.

A First Poetry Book
Compiled by John Foster
Illustrated by Chris Orr, Martin White, and Joseph Wright
Oxford University Press
200 Madison Ave., New York, N.Y. 10016
1979

Summary: This collection includes English poems as well as some well-known American entries.

1. Read "The Rescue" by Ian Serraillier. Ask the children why the poet repeats so many of the lines. Give the children a copy of the poem and ask them to read the repeated lines in unison.

2. Read "What Is Red?" by Mary O'Neill. Ask the class to decide on a color for a group poem. Without trying to make a poem at first, ask the children for words and phrases that describe the sights, feeling and smells of the color they chose. Now organize the words and phrases into a poem. Give everyone a copy of both O'Neill's poem and the class poem.

3. Read "Alone in the Grange" by Gregory Harrison. Compare it to the book *Emma* by Wendy Kesselman (listed in our Realism section). Both depict a lonely person.

4. Read "Flying" by J. M. Westrup. Compare it to other moon poems such as "Windy Nights" by Robert Louis Stevenson, which appears in this collection, as well as with other moon poems like "The Moon and a Star" from the book of the same name, by Myra Cohn Livingston (Harcourt Brace Jovanovich, 757 Third Ave., New York, N.Y. 10017).

5. Ask the children to begin their own anthologies made up of poems they like.

Dogs and Dragons
Karla Kuskin
Harper & Row Publishers
10 E. 53rd St., New York, N.Y. 10022
1980

Summary: This is a delightful compilation of some of Karla Kuskin's poetry.

Because so many poems in this book are worth working with, we have changed the format of this lesson plan by listing some of the poems and suggesting one or two activities for each.

1. "Thistles" Read Ms. Kuskin's introduction to this one. Bring in a thistle if possible, or if not, bring in a picture of one. The first two lines of the poem are a tongue twister; write them on the board and let the children practice saying them quickly. Point out that many poems are full of such word play.

2. "Where Would You Be?" After you've read this to the children several times, ask them to move to it. The steady rhythm should come through.

3. "Spring" Try a choral reading with this one; have a different child speak with every repetition of the word "I'm" and have everyone join in on the last two lines.

4. "William's Toys" Have some children jump rope while others chant the poem.

5. "Counting" Assign the children to groups and have them illustrate each verse using tempera paints. Ask some of the children who print well to letter a stanza under each picture.

6. "It Is Grey Out" Talk about the feelings of colors. Use Myra Cohn Livingston's "Bad Day" (from *The Way Things Are: And Other Poems,* a Margaret K. McElderry Book published by Atheneum, 597 Fifth Ave., New York, N.Y. 10017) to contrast with this one.

7. "The Gold-Tinted Dragon" and "Let Me Tell You All About Me" Ask each child to imagine a dragon and describe it. Show them James E. Seidelman's book *Fourteenth Dragon* (Harlin Quist, Dist. by Dial/Delacorte Sales, 245 E. 47th St., New York, N.Y. 10017). Let the children draw their imaginary dragons.

8. "Square as a House" After the children have listened to the poem, ask them to draw themselves but in the form of something mentioned in the poem. Have them add some feature or piece of clothing that will show their identity.

9. "If You Stood" Find some other picture poems and share them. Ask the children to make word pictures in which each part of every object is made of words printed over and over again.

10. "Alexander Soames" Try a choral reading for this one. Have one child read Alexander's speech.

Follow-Up: Find more poems by Karla Kuskin. Allow the children to practice some of their favorites and then ask them to read them aloud to the class.

Paperbacks

It took me too many years to realize it, but children love paperbacks! Given a choice of two books, the deluxe hardbound edition and the paperback edition, with identical covers, placed side by side on a library table, most children will grab for the paperback. I've never yet been able to explain this phenomenon to my own satisfaction so I'll not try to explain it to you.

Nevertheless, paperbacks are good news in bad times. You can buy all the books listed in this section for less than $3.95 each, and although that's nothing to sneeze at, it represents a considerable savings over hardbound book equivalents.

True, paperbacks don't last as long as hardbound books but this situation can work for you—it will force you to locate new books and new ways to use them, sooner. The books described here are far from a comprehensive listing of paperbacks—they're merely a representative sample including some possible uses. Browse through a good bookstore or a stack of publisher's catalogs and you're bound to net a great catch of titles.

Non-Fiction

The King Who Rained
Fred Gwynne
Windmill Books, Div. Simon & Schuster
1230 Avenue of the Americas, New York, N.Y. 10020

Summary: This book illustrates, literally, some of our figurative speech as well as some mixed-up homonyms and homographs.
Things to Do—

See activities for *The Sixteen Hand Horse* in the Non-Fiction hardbound book category.

The All Around Pumpkin Book
Margery Cuyler
Illustrated by Corbett Jones
Holt, Rinehart and Winston
383 Madison Ave., New York, N.Y. 10017

Summary: As the title implies, this is a collection of pumpkin lore: how to grow, carve and cook a pumpkin, pumpkin jokes, riddles and pumpkin crafts.
Things to Do—

1. Math: Place a large number of dried pumpkin seeds in a glass jar. Ask children to estimate the total number in the jar. Offer a pumpkin prize to whoever comes up with the closest estimate.
2. Read the *Legend of Sleepy Hollow* by Washington Irving.
3. Art: Bring in as many pumpkins as you can and draw pumpkin faces on them using magic markers.
4. Cook some of the pumpkin recipes found in *The All Around Pumpkin Book.*

5. Language Arts: Ask children to amass pumpkin facts. Each fact should be stated as a complete sentence and placed on a sentence strip on the bulletin board. New facts should be evaluated against existing ones.

Merry Ever After
Joe Lasker
Puffin Books/Penguin Books
625 Madison Ave., New York, N.Y. 10022

Summary: This story is of two medieval weddings. Its illustrations are inspired by the paintings of the masters of that period and are full of fascinating details.

Things to Do—

1. Social Studies: Compare our formal weddings of today with these two medieval weddings. Several of the customs have survived. Discuss and list these and do research on the sources of other wedding customs.
2. Art: Display prints of as many of the paintings used in the book as possible. Display other prints depicting that time. Discuss them with the children.
3. Explore the meanings of some of these words from the text: betrothed, serfs, peasants, commoner, noble, herbs, masons, intertwined, dowry.
4. Table manners have changed since medieval times. Have the children bring in rules for behavior at meals and then have a classroom luncheon at which all rules are carefully observed.

Folk Tales

Big Anthony and the Magic Ring
Tomie de Paola
Voyager/Harcourt Brace Jovanovich
757 Third Ave., New York, N.Y. 10017

Summary: Although *Big Anthony and the Magic Ring* is not a true folk tale, it has many elements of one. Big Anthony tries to use Strega Nona's magic but fails.

Things to Do—

1. Find other chants from folk tales and compare them with Strega Nona's.
2. Determine why this is not a true folk tale.
3. Explore these Italian words from the story: Strega Nona, tarantella, ragazzo, caro, un momento, amore, mamma mia.
4. Find the place in the story where Strega Nona could have used magic, but did not. Compare this with a similar situation in de Paola's *Strega Nona.*

Snow White by the Brothers Grimm
Translated by Paul Heins
Illustrated by Trina Schart Hyman
Atlantic Monthly Press/Little Brown & Co.
34 Beacon St., Boston, Ma. 02106

Summary: This is the full, unaltered fairy tale from Grimm, unadulterated by the modernists. Here, the dwarfs are seven nameless men and the queen is an aging, evil beauty. Hyman's gothic illustrations add romance and intriguing beauty to this ageless tale.
Things to Do—

1. Compare this Snow White, visually and contextually, with other versions.
2. Discuss the cruel nature of this ending and the children's feelings about it as contrasted with other cruelties carried out against Snow White.
3. Write a sequel about the life of the dwarfs.
4. Find other fairy tales in which lengthy sleeps play a part.
5. Find other fairy tales illustrated by Trina Schart Hyman. Have children try and verbalize the characteristics of her style.

Poetry

Hailstones and Halibut Bones
Mary O'Neill
Illustrated by Leonard Weisgard
Zephyr/Doubleday & Co.
245 Park Ave., New York, N.Y., 10167

Summary: The sights, sounds and feelings of color are explored through lovely, imaginative verse.
Things to Do—

1. Art: Read one or two color poems. Let groups of four and five children make collages on large sheets of oaktag of a color of their choice. They should use as many kinds of paper and as many hues of the color as possible.
2. Let the same groups compile a list of objects and feelings that look or sound like their color. Print these across the collage or have the children create a poem using the words.
3. Let each group read O'Neill's poems about their color to the rest of the class. Make sure everyone has had plenty of rehearsal time first.

The Winter Bear
Ruth Craft and Erik Blegvad
Aladdin/Scribner Atheneum,
597 Fifth Ave., New York, N.Y. 10017

Summary: This story of three children on a winter's walk is told in rhyme. The book is charmingly understated and beautifully illustrated.
Things to Do—

1. Explore the meanings of these words from the text: jaunty, bryony vine, old man's beard, oddments.
2. Read other rhyming stories and compare and contrast them.
3. Set up a toy repair hospital stocked with thread, needles, glue, cloth, bits of wood and leather and paint. Encourage children to bring their damaged toys to school and repair them in the workshop.

Realism

Ira Sleeps Over
Bernard Waber
Sandpiper/Houghton Mifflin
2 Park St., Boston, Ma. 02107

Summary: Ira's looking forward to spending the night at his friend Reggie's house until his sister points out the fact that he's never before slept without his teddy bear.
Things to Do—

1. Math: Make a graph showing the various types of toys with which the children in the class sleep.
2. Math and Science: Have children bring in favorite toys and then classify them according to age, degree of softness, size, etc.
3. Writing: Make up ghost stories like Reggie's.

Zeek Silver Moon
Amy Ehrlich
Illustrated by Robert Andrew Parker
Pied Piper Publishing Co.
350 S. Central, Hamlin, Tx. 79520

Summary: This is a gentle, loving chronology of the first five years in a boy's life.
Things to Do—

1. Ask each child to find out about one event he or she could dictate into a tape recorder about each of his or her years.
2. Let the children listen to each other's tapes to find similarities to events from their own early years.
3. Invite children to bring in baby pictures to identify and compare.
4. Arm the children with tape recorders and send them out to interview school personnel about their earliest memories.

5. Have the children do the same with individuals from several generations. Compare and contrast the collected data.

Gilberto and the Wind
Marie Hall Ets
Viking Press
625 Madison Ave., New York, N.Y. 10022

Summary: A small boy plays with the wind and personifies it.
Things to Do—

1. Use this book on a windy day and then take the children outside to watch and feel the wind. Encourage them to make statements about the wind as if it were a person. Experiment with how kites, bubbles and umbrellas react in the wind. Discuss the results.
2. Come indoors and re-read the book. Make an experience chart of the children's experiences in the wind.
3. Science: Do some simple wind experiments.
4. Read several poems about the wind.
5. Read the chapter in *Owl At Home* by Arnold Lobel (Harper & Row Publishers, 10 E. 53rd St., New York, N.Y. 10022), in which Owl treats the wind as a guest in his home.

Fantasy

The Grouchy Ladybug
Eric Carle
Scholastic Inc.
50 W. 44th St., New York, N.Y. 10036

Summary: Carle's feisty ladybug is forever searching for someone big enough with which to fight. The tale contains much material for use in concept-building.
Things to Do—

1. Explore some of the following vocabulary words: aphid, yellow jacket, stag beetle, praying mantis, boa constrictor, hyena.
2. Math: Make 16 clocks, each showing a time listed in the story. Have the children put the clocks in order and decide how much time has passed between the introductions of the animals and from the beginning to the end of the story.

Use large sheets of oaktag to make each animal mentioned in the story. Cut out a face-sized hole or opening in each animal cutout. Ask a child to put on one of the animal cards without looking at it. The child should ask the class questions to determine his/her animal.

4. Use the animal cards to act out the story.

Ready for More?

We haven't neglected the very important audio-visual side to books. Here are ways to work and play with films, filmstrips, film loops, recordings, and tapes.

Gone are the days when using audio-visual aids in the classroom meant showing a dull filmstrip frame by frame while one child after another struggled through an oral reading of each caption. Now catalogs are full of exciting, superbly-executed films, records, film loops, tapes and 8 and 16 millimeter films. Used with imagination, good timing and adequate preparation on the part of teacher and learner, these audio-visual materials can greatly enrich the classroom. Used indiscriminately, these same materials can dehumanize, entertain or even deaden the educational experience.

The temptation is great to misuse or overuse these materials for sheer entertainment value. After all, we've all faced the two o'clock Friday afternoon doldrums when the discovery of an available audio-visual package seems like manna from heaven. Who cares what it's about or whether it's educationally defensible? The kids love it, don't they? Possibly, but do remember that many of these same children will sit mesmerized by the Saturday morning cartoon marathon with no measurable gain on anyone's part but the late-sleeping parent's.

Use audio-visual materials and enjoy them. But don't let them become a mere extension of Saturday morning cartoons. Inject the human element often; manipulate them as you do any teaching tool. Here are some suggestions.

1a. Provide your own soundtrack. This can be as simple as reading the accompanying text yourself. Creating your own soundtrack allows you to pace the material to suit your class' ability and makes explanation easier. Even if you use the soundtrack provided, remember you can stop it at the drop of a question.

1b. It's possible to take the soundtrack even further. Encyclopaedia Britannica Educational Corporation (425 N. Michigan Ave., Chicago, Il. 60611) produces a film called *Growing.* It is a beautiful, computer-designed film accompanied by a lovely soundtrack. The whole meaning and feeling of the film changes completely when the music is changed. Run the film and play your own ragtime piano, jazz or symphonic accompaniment.

2. & 3. It is also possible to play with some films visually. Try projecting the film *Growing* on surfaces other than a screen. The effect of the altered images (especially curved images) is exciting. It is also possible to alter the images this way: give the children hula-hoops covered with sheets; have them move into the path of the film projection, catching various images and moving them forward and backward; encourage the children to move to the music at the same time.

4. Draw your own ending. Use the filmstrip *The Judge* (Miller Brody/ Random House, 342 Madison Ave., New York, N.Y. 10022) and stop the action just before the "horrible thing" comes in. Let the children make their own slides and soundtrack and form a conclusion for the story.

5. Add dialogue. Some filmstrips are based on wordless books; McGraw-Hill has one called *The Inspector* (McGraw-Hill, 1221 Avenue of the Americas, New York, N.Y. 10020), based on the book by George Mendoza. Have the children write a monologue for the inspector as he tracks the ghoulish monster that's tracking *him.*

6. Find more films. The *Violin,* a film produced by Learning Corporation of America (1350 Avenue of the Americas, New York, N.Y. 10019), tells a wonderful story of two boys, an old man, and a violin. Have the children hunt for other books that explore the relationship between age and youth.

7. Write your own sequel. Weston Woods (Weston, Ct. 06883) has a new filmstrip called *Fourteen Rats and a Rat Catcher,* a wonderful story in which honky-tonk piano and baroque flute and harp play an important part. The story ends in a delightful compromise. But I think it would be fun to take it further. What happens when there are 24 rats? Have the children write and illustrate their own sequel. Can they set it to music?

8. Take charge of a filmstrip. The Walt Disney Educational Media (500 S. Buena Vista St., Burbank, Ca. 91521) Movie Script Series allows the children to take over the filmstrip script. The first filmstrip in the program has a soundtrack while the second filmstrip asks the children to assume the roles and responsibility for production. Try *The Mystery in Dracula's Castle* or other titles from this series.

9. Follow the pattern. In its "How to Study Series," Learning Tree Filmstrips (P.O. Box 3009, Englewood, Ca. 80155) uses an actor portraying Abraham Lincoln to instruct a group of children in various study skills. Ask your class to think of another historical figure and how he or she might instruct their group in a given skill.

10a. Make your own living filmstrip to acompany a soundtrack. Macmillan (866 Third Ave., New York, N.Y. 10022) publishes a filmstrip called *The Little Brute Family* based on the book by Lillian Hoban. Have the children pantomime this fable about the use and misuse of manners while the tape is played.

10b. Make your own slide filmstrip. Random House (201 E. 50th St., New York, N.Y. 10022) has done a delightful job with Leo Lionni's book *Swimmy.* In his fable about the advantages of cooperation, Lionni uses doilies, sponges and hands to print the underwater scenes of the story. Have the children use these and other materials to create their own version of *Swimmy.* If available, use a visual-maker or 35mm camera to make slides of their production. Project these slides in conjunction with the filmstrip illustrations.

11. Show filmstrips or films backwards. Besides giving us sometimes hilarious results, reversing the action obviates the need for the soundtrack. A film such as Weston Woods' *Harold and the Purple Crayon* becomes "Harold

and the Purple Eraser" when shown backwards. The children can then give reasons for erasing each object just as, in the forward version, a reason was given for each object's creation.

12. Start a research project. A series of tapes published by knowledge Tree Group (360 Park Ave. So., New York, N.Y. 10010) features folk songs and jump rope rhymes. Have children research one of these forms by interviewing various generations of family and friends. Compare the various versions with those on the tapes and those obtained by other class members.

13. Look at another point of view. Use the filmstrip, *Patterns of Homespun,* produced by the New York Times Company's Educational Enrichment Materials division (formerly Teaching Resources Films), 357 Adams St., Bedford Hills, N.Y. 10507. This filmstrip explores the daily chores and events that occur on an eighteenth century farm. These events are seen from the point of view of each member of the family and some of the townspeople. Have the children take the same approach with a Pilgrim household.

14. Note the sequence. Use the film or filmstrip version of Weston Woods' *Rosie Walk.* Have the children, individually, list as many events as they can remember. Collaborate to make one list. Write each event on a 12″×18″ piece of cardboard in the order recalled by the children. Replay the film and have children re-order their cards as necessary.

15. A living Mother Goose. Play the recording *Mother Goose* available from Melody House, 819 N.W. 92nd St., Oklahoma City, Ok. 73114. Have small groups of children follow the rhymes with one of the Mother Goose books. When each group is familiar with two or three rhymes, have them present the rhymes with motions to the rest of the class. Mother Goose will be alive and well in your classroom.

Now that we've given you the ways and means to extend audio-visual materials, use these selected titles in the same ways. Preceding each filmstrip (or film, or record; our suggested methods will still apply) you'll see a number. This number corresponds to the numbered methods we've outlined above for using audio-visual materials. We're asking you to use the materials below in just the same ways (with slight variations of course). As with our book selections, these are just *suggestions*—you can take any audio-visual material in any direction you see fit.

(9) *Basic Concepts in Social Studies* by Scholastic (50 W. 44th St., New York, N.Y. 10036) asks children to determine why we need laws. Children can also find facts to answer the questions, why we need money, why we need schools, etc.

(10a) Two puppet-tape sets from SVE (1345 Diversey Parkway, Chicago, Il. 60614), *Sylvester and the Magic Pebble* and *The Snowy Day,* are great stories for acting out.

(10b) Use the *Marine Life* set of posters published by Argus Communications (7440 Natchez Ave., Niles, Il. 60648) for inspiration; have children create their own posters.

(11) *How the Elephant Got His Trunk* (Learning Corporation of Ameria) can be played backwards for interesting results. It becomes "How the Elephant Lost His Trunk." Have children invent reasons for each event that occurs on the way back to the beginning.

(12) For the filmstrip *American Song Stories* (Coronet Educational Films, 65 East Southwater, Chicago, Il. 60601) find or invent additional verses for some of the tunes ("Arkansas Traveler," for example, has many versions and verses.) Compare the different forms of the songs you find.

(13) Explore different points of view with Learning Corporation of America's *Unicorn in the Garden*. The events in this film are seen differently by different people. Help your class see the events from different points of view.

(14) Using *The Princess Who Never Laughed* (Imperial International Learning, Box 548, Kankakee, Il. 60901) have your class try and remember the order in which the events occurred.

(14) If you want to try for a more complicated series of events, use *Life Story* (the story of evolution) published by Educational Enrichment Materials (formerly Teaching Resources Films), 357 Adams St., Bedford Hills, N.Y. 10507.

(15) Use Spoken Arts Company's record *Treasury of Nursery Rhymes*. Compare these rhymes with the ones on the *Mother Goose* recording available from Melody House. Are any of the words different? Can the children find some Mother Goose rhymes included on one record and not on the other?

Selecting Picture Storybooks for Young Children with Learning Disabilities

Jed P. Luchow

Picture storybooks are a valuable source of learning and pleasure with preschool and primary students. As a teacher of young learning disabled children, I became curious about which type of books had the greatest appeal to students. In spite of hyperactivity and distractibility in many of my students, certain picture books seemed to hold their interest and attention far better than others. I wondered if there were common characteristics in the more popular books which both teachers and parents might use in the selection of picture storybooks for young children with learning disabilities.

In order to explore these common characteristics, I began a survey. Using the *Directory of Facilities for the Learning Disabled,* I sent questionnaires to over 100 special class teachers. The questionnaire requested that they list picture storybooks both "enjoyed" and "not enjoyed" by the children. Enjoyment of a book was determined by student behavior such as repeated requests for a book, voluntary use of the book by individual students, and attention during storytime. Nonenjoyment was to be noted for books which were rarely or never selected by the children. From the 44 returned questionnaires, I compiled a list of those books which were mentioned 5 or more times in one of the categories. The list came to 30 "enjoyed" books and 9 "not enjoyed" books.

The next step was to compare these books with a set of specific literary characteristics to see which factors occurred frequently and which did not. The following list of items was used to help identify various aspects of content and illustrations of the books. These factors were derived from Leland B. Jacobs of Teachers College, Columbia University. Dr. Jacobs has been involved with the study of children's literature for many years.

Content Factors of Picture Storybooks

The following factors represent broad characteristics common in children's literature.

SOURCE: *Teaching Exceptional Children,* Summer 1972, pp. 160–165.

C-1. Plot centers about one main sequence of events.
C-2. Outcome of events can be easily anticipated.
C-3. There is no midstory shift from realism to romance to fantasy.
C-4. Much direct conversation is used.
C-5. Detail development is limited to its place in the story, as opposed to its importance in life.
C-6. Colorful, tongue tickling words and phrases that can be easily memorized are used (example: *Green Eggs and Ham*).
C-7. Stories are not melodramatic or theatrical; story climaxes are simple.
C-8. There is one main character or a group operating with oneness.
C-9. Either boy or girl hero is present.
C-10. Plot has brevity.
C-11. Everyday experiences are described.
C-12. Imaginative play is used.
C-13. Talking animals are present.

Illustration Factors of Picture Storybooks

The factors describing characteristics of illustrations are more subjective than the content factors. Therefore, any statements about the illustrations of the various books are brief and inconclusive.

I-1. There is complete harmony of print and picture.
I-2. No discrepancies appear between text and content of illustrations.
I-3. The art captures the mood and tone of the story.
I-4. Illustrations avoid pastoral passivity or decorativeness for its own sake.
I-5. Various media are included—photography, charcoal, watercolor, stone, lithographing, pen and ink drawings—but the medium is appropriate to the spirit of the story. For example, charcoal and pastoral colors *can* be appropriate if the story is light.
I-6. Amount of detail in illustrations is dependent on the demands of the text.
I-7. Illustrations may be black and white or color but are outlined with strong lines.
I-8. Picture is large, simple, and uncluttered.

The procedure for rating each of these factors in the 30 books chosen was uncomplicated. One point was recorded for each factor occurring in a particular book. Thus, if one factor were present in every book, it would receive a score of 30. Conversely, if one factor were present in none of the books, it would receive a score of 0. The range of actual scores was 0–28.

Characteristics of the Enjoyed Books

In respect to the 30 books on the "enjoyed" list, the most important positive factor was the underlying theme of "unity." In factors C-3, C-6, C-8, I-1, I-2, I-6, unity was expressed in the oneness of mood, plot, character, harmony between picture and story, or harmony between picture and detail. So often the problems of children with learning disabilities center around poor motor organization and poor organization of behavior. The children have trouble in sorting out details and structuring the world around them. Perhaps, they enjoy these stories which are organized with one main plot, one main character, and without elaborate illustrations because they organize a seemingly disorganized world in a rather pleasant way for this kind of child.

For example, *Are You My Mother?* is apparently enjoyed because it revolves around one character's pursuit of one goal until it is eventually found. *The Camel Who Took a Walk,* though lengthy, has a main character, repetition, and suspense. *Horton Hatches the Egg* with its theme of steadfastness also has one main character. *The Carrot Seed* is perhaps the best example of this unity and simplicity. Its ideas are—

Could It Happen?
Would It Happen?
It Happened!
The End.

A number of stories on the list have a slightly more complicated plot, but the oneness is still present, i.e., *Mike Mulligan and His Steam Shovel, The Story about Ping, Play with Me, The Story of Ferdinand,* and *The Little House.* In each case, although there are a number of minor incidents, the author never allows us to lose sight of the goal for one page, i.e., to dig a foundation in one day, to return to the safety of home, to get animals to play, to be allowed to roam free, and to return to the simple pleasures of the past, respectively. In all, the theme of each of these books is present on every page. The children know it, feel it, and sense it. Perhaps this is still another reason why these books are enjoyed.

Characteristics of Books Not Enjoyed

In evaluating the nine books which appeared on the list of books "not enjoyed," one factor seemed most significant—complexity. In each one of those books, either the plot was too complex, too long, had too many characters, or contained illustrations that were too cluttered. For example, in *Blueberries for Sal,* the switching between the bear episode and the people episode occurs too rapidly. With *In the Night Kitchen,* there is no story or character at all. *The Little Airplane* appears on this list because of the attempt to instruct rather than to tell a story.

Characteristics of the Illustrations

As far as illustrations are concerned, it seems that the children accept either those in color or black and white. It is important to add, however, that in all the illustrations of either variety, strong lines are prevalent. Strauss and Lehtinen (1947) observed that if a picture which the child is to color is outlined with heavy black crayon, the heavy line is a cue which enables the child to keep constant the relationship between the foreground of the picture and the background of the paper. Strauss also noted that color perspective and responsiveness to color remained intact in spite of the most severe disturbance to perceptual or general integration. Again, we see that illustrations must have some kind of organization, a primary need of these children.

Less Important Aspects of Picture Books

In examining those factors which do not seem to affect the popularity of picture storybooks among children with learning disabilities, we do not find such a unified causal theme as we did in the positve factors. It might be helpful, however, to note which factors in our survey appeared to be the least important factors in selecting appropriate books for a special classroom.

First, good picture storybooks for learning disabled children do not have to be centered around everyday experiences, imaginative play activities, or animal stories. Neither do they have to contain direct conversation or lengthy dialogue. This factor widens the horizon for selection since it negates the notion that concrete stories are more favorable for these children. These children enjoy the fancy of *Where the Wild Things Are* just the same as other preschoolers. They also seem to enjoy with equal enthusiasm other such fanciful stories as *The Cat in the Hat, Green Eggs and Ham,* and *And to Think That I Saw It on Mulberry Street.*

Brevity, another one of the factors which is not significant in the selection, might be misleading. Although the learning disabled child is often hyperactive and easily distracted, when given lengthy books like *Mike Mulligan and His Steam Shovel, The Story of Ferdinand,* or *The Camel Who Took a Walk* he may be found to be an unusually attentive listener.

Colorful, tongue tickling words are another less important aspect of a good picture storybook. In some cases, noting the confusion and perseveration of these children, one might especially want to avoid such phrases. Though the children may perseverate on lines like "Caps! Caps for sale. Fifty cents a cap!," these same lines can be used for language stimulation. Although books like *Hop on Pop* and *Fox in Socks* were not among those reported as "not enjoyed," I have found they add to the language confusion. The speech and sound patterns of the *Horton* books or *The Cat in the Hat* series are more rhythmical and, therefore, not confusing to the children.

Finally, as far as a hero, the children do not seem to have a preference for a special type—boy, girl, animal, or machine. The factor that is important is that there be only a main character or a group operating with oneness.

List of Enjoyed Picture Storybooks

Madeline, Ludwig Bemelmans (Viking Press, 1939).

Mike Mulligan and His Steam Shovel. Virginia Lee Burton (Houghton Mifflin Co., 1939).

The Little House, Virginia Lee Burton (Houghton Mifflin Co., 1942).

Are You My Mother?, P.D. Eastman (Random House, Inc., 1960).

Play with Me, Marie Hall Ets (The Viking Press, 1968).

Gilberto and the Wind, Marie Hall Ets (The Viking Press, 1963).

The Story about Ping, Marjorie Flack (The Viking Press, 1933).

Angus and the Ducks, Marjorie Flack (Doubleday and Co., 1939).

Millions of Cats, Wanda Gag (Coward-McCann, Inc., 1938).

Snowy Day, Ezra Jack Keats (The Viking Press, 1962).

Whistle for Willie, Ezra Jack Keats (The Viking Press, 1964).

The Man Who Didn't Wash His Dishes, Phyllis Krasilovsky (Doubleday and Co., 1950).

The Carrot Seed, Ruth Krauss (Harper and Row, 1945).

The Story of Ferdinand, Munro Leaf (The Viking Press, 1938).

The Little Train, Lois Lenski (Henry Z. Walck, 1940).

Polceman Small, Lois Lenski (Henry Z. Walck, 1962).

Little Blue and Little Yellow. Leo Lionni (Astor-Honor, Inc., 1959).

Make Way for Ducklings, Robert McCloskey (The Viking Press, 1941).

Bruno Munari's ABC, Bruno Munari (World, 1960).

The Little Engine That Could, Watty Piper (Platt and Munk Publishers, 1946).

Curious George, H. A. Rey (Houghton Mifflin, Co., 1941).

Mike's House, Julia Sauer (E. M. Hale and Co., Inc., 1954).

Where the Wild Things Are, Maurice Sendak (Harper and Row, 1963).

And to Think That I Saw It on Mulberry Street, Dr. Seuss (E. M. Hale and Co., Inc., 1937).

Horton Hatches the Egg, Dr. Seuss (Random House, 1940).
The Cat in The Hat, Dr. Seuss (Random House, Inc., 1957).
Green Eggs and Ham, Dr. Seuss (Random House, Inc., 1960).
Caps for Sale, Esphyr Slobodkina (William R. Scott, Inc., 1947).
The Camel Who Took A Walk, Jack Tworkov (E. P. Dutton and Co., 1951).
Harry the Dirty Dog, Gene Zion (Harper and Row, 1956).

List of Less Enjoyed Picture Storybooks

Mister Penny, Marie Hall Ets (The Viking Press, Inc., 1935).
Goggles, Ezra Jack Keats (Macmillan and Co., 1969).
The Little Airplane, Lois Lenski (Henry Z. Walck, 1938).
Blueberries for Sal, Robert McCloskey (The Viking Press, Inc., 1948).
One Morning In Maine, Robert McCloskey (The Viking Press, Inc., 1952).
Songs of the Swallows, Leo Polite (Charles Scribner's Sons, Inc., 1949).
In the Night Kitchen, Maurice Sendak (Harper and Row, 1970).
The Biggest Bear, Lynd Ward (Houghton Mifflin Co., 1952).
Hide and Seek Day, Gene Zion (Harper and Row, 1954).

References

Carlson, R. K. Ten Values of Children's Literature. Paper presented at International Reading Association Conference, Kansas City, Missouri, May, 1969.

Larrick, N. *A teacher's guide to children's books.* Columbus, Ohio: Charles E. Merrill Books, Inc., 1960.

McCutchen, C. C. Evauating young children's experiences with literature. In L. B. Jacobs (Ed.) *Using literature with young children.* New York: Teachers College Press, 1965.

Schatz, E. E. Evaluating picture books, *Elementary English,* 1967, 44, 870–4.

Strauss, A. A., & Lehtinen, L. E. *Psychopathology and education of the brain-injured child. New York: Grune and Stratton, 1947.*

Should Picture Books and Young Children Be Matched?

Patrick Groff

A widely accepted principle appears to guide the selection of picture books for young children—that is, if the number of favorable comments as to its usefulness is any measure of its importance. This conventional rule states that "in the selection of all illustrated books, we will be more successful if we keep in mind that they are for the use of the child and not the adult" (Warnock 1938). Georgiou repeats this notion about illustrations and children when he asserts that the "final judgment [of picture books] should be based on . . . above all, appeal to children" (1969, p. 64). Arbuthnot concurs that "the child himself must be the starting point if we are to meet his needs and improve his taste" for illustrations in picture books (1964, p. 23). It is rare, indeed, to see questions as are posed by Klemin: "Are illustrations directed toward children or adults? Does it matter?" (1966, p. 15).

Do We Know What Illustrations Children Like?

To answer the question the title of this discussion poses requires, first of all, that one determine to what extent we know what young children like or dislike about book illustrations as such. There would be no need for calculation as to whether the preferences these children have in illustrations are of any educational importance, of course, unless we actually know what these choices are. The opinions or judgments made so far about this matter seem to be of little help, however.

This is because, for one thing, they are contradictory. For example, from his review of most of the research on young children's preferences, Stewig contends that we do not know specifically what these preferences are: "There is no definite statement which can be made about the types of pic-

SOURCE: "Should Picture Books and Young Children Be Matched?" *Language Arts* 54 (April 1977): 411–416.

tures children prefer" (1972, p. 277). In opposition to this, Huck maintains that young children like all the various kinds of art used in picture book illustrations. She states, "a young child's taste in art is quite catholic, including realist, impressionistic, stylized, abstract and caricatured art" (1976, p. 122). Cianciolo echoes this belief. She agrees that "every child needs and enjoys variety" (1973, p. 4) of style in picture book illustrations, to include primitivism, expressionism, impressionism, pointillism, cubism, and even surrealism. Largely in assent with this is Rue, who observes that "many 'picture books' of literary and artistic excellence have no age limits" (1962, p. 319). Instead, she goes on, they have a "universality" in their art, something that transcends the differences in life experiences that children have had, and in the attitudes toward art they have developed. A third, contrary position is exemplified by Sebesta and Iverson. To them, the best picture books for young children are ones "that take few liberties with reality but enhance photographic literalism with art" (1975, p. 134).

Research on Children's Preferences for Illustrations

Some of the conclusions and opinions about young children's preferences for book illustrations are unacceptable for a second reason. This is because they do not conform to the research evidence on this subject that has been gathered for at least the last fifty years. By and large, this research does not support the conclusion that we do not know enough about what young children like about illustrations, as such, to make any definitive statements about this matter. Above all, it rejects the notion that these children like all kinds of illustrations equally well. We have enough research evidence at present, on the one hand, to make reasonably reliable generalizations about children's preferences for isolated book illustrations. These research findings, on the other hand, depict young children not as catholic, but parochial in their choices of illustrations.

It is found, for example that:

1. They prefer factual, realistic, and familiar-appearing illustrations to stylized, impressionistic, fanciful, whimsical, or ironic ones (Ayer 1940; Bencetic 1960; Bou and Lopez 1953; Clegg 1968; Freeman and Freeman 1933; French 1952; Katz 1944; Mellinger 1932; *Publishers Weekly* 1939; Rudisill 1952; Sloan 1972; Van der Mark 1929). The single exception to this conclusion seemingly is the finding by Amsden (1960) that fanciful drawings were preferred to modified realistic drawings by the preschool children she surveyed.

2. They like eventful illustrations which have objects or animals involved in action or which tell a story, better than they do stationary-appearing or inert ones (Ayer 1940; Bamberger 1922; Clegg 1968; Freeman and Free-

man 1933; Hildreth 1936; Lark-Horovitz 1937; Martin 1931; Morrison 1935; Whipple 1953).

3. They choose illustrations with many colors. Blue and red are especially favored colors (Bou and Lopez 1953; Miller 1936; Templeton 1975) over black and white ones (Ayer 1940; Bamberger 1922; Freeman and Freeman 1933; Hildreth 1936; Lark-Horovitz 1937; Mellinger 1932; Miller 1936; *Publishers Weekly* 1939; Rudisill 1952; Whipple 1953). Rich, dark, brightly saturated, generalized primary colors are voted for rather than pastel shades (Bou and Lopez 1953; Clegg 1968; Freeman and Freeman 1933; French 1952; Katz 1944; Van der Mark 1929). There appears only one finding (Amsden 1960) that young children prefer light tints to bright, saturated colors. Also in a distinct minority is Arbuthnot, who reports that nursery school children have "no conclusive preference for primary colors" (1964, p. 24).

4. They select humorous illustrations over those of a sobersided nature (Ayer 1940; Bamberger 1922; Martin 1931; *Publishers Weekly* 1939).

5. They opt for the artist's use of clear, definite or bold outlines for figures and objects rather than for faded, blurred, washed-out, or otherwise indistinct shapes (Ayer 1940; Freeman and Freeman 1933; French 1952; Martin 1931; Miller 1936; *Publishers Weekly* 1939; Van der Mark 1929).

Notwithstanding this, whether young children like a few, large, easily distinguishable central objects in book illustrations more than they do illustrations with many minute details, each of which is given more or less equal visual dominance, is an unsettled matter. Three researchers say this is so (Ayer 1940; Bamberger 1922; Whipple 1953). Opposed to this, Freeman and Freeman (1933) found nursery school children preferred small central figures to large ones. Martin (1931) also found her young subjects preferred illustrations with small figures and minute details. This contradiction in findings makes it impossible to say for sure if young children "gloat over small details in a picture," as Arbuthnot (1964, p. 24) claims they do.

Should Illustrations and Children Be Matched?

The research evidence reported here makes it apparent that certain kinds of illustrations indeed are favored by young children. Therefore, the findings suggest that a matching of these kinds of preferences to the picture books now available is altogether possible to do. The question that still remains is whether we actually want to cater to this extent to this type of like and dislike of young children. That is, to what degree should children's preferences for isolated illustrations become the dominant criterion used for the selection of picture books for schools and libraries?

As noted, many writers about children's picture books insist that children's preferences in illustrations must, in large measure, be the most influential factor in decisions as to what picture books are provided these youngsters. Nonetheless, the implementation of this ideal is fraught with several difficulties. Even though we know that children's selections in illustrations are "guided by the type of pictorial pattern they have explored or comprehended in their own art work" (French 1952, p. 95), to make this kind of art the only model for choosing children's picture books invites numerous problems.

First, it can be reasonably argued that experiences with picture book illustrations should be a way of improving children's "taste for art," a way of commencing a series of aesthetic "chain reactions that will continue into adulthood" (Viguers *et al.* 1958, p. 9). Young children's visual tastes do need to be elevated, for they are shown to have varying degrees of visual illiteracy when it comes to illustrations. For example, Miller has demonstrated that they see "relatively few of the items which make up a picture." In fact, he found that "most important items of a picture often escape the notice of children" (1938, p. 288). But by age nine, however, it has been demonstrated that children's appreciation of pictures can be radically improved. After picture appreciation lessons children of this age made significant changes in the number of their references to the techniques used by artists in pictures (Waymack and Hendrickson 1932). In other words, they became significantly more aware of the elements of art that these pictures expressed. Children younger than age nine doubtless could also be taught to have a greater appreciation of the art effects in the picture book illustrations provided them.

We should remember, as well, that the results of the surveys discussed above generally indicated only what the "average" child prefers in illustrations. Accordingly, would not the result of a successful match of preferences with picture books mean that a significant number of preferences of "non-average" children must remain unfulfilled or ignored? If this match is to be made, one must also ask, at what point in time, if ever, would "average" young children be exposed to illustrations that are not of the style and content they favor? Answers to these critical questions have not yet been offered by those who favor using children's preferences for illustrations as the guideline for picture book purchases or for use in classrooms.

Second, it seems that picture book illustrators are no longer content with being governed in their work by children's expressed preferences for illustrations. As early as 1932 Newton noted that "new and strange pictorial forms appear [in picture books] which threaten to upset our former ideas of finished and beautiful workmanship" (p. 89). Ward has more recently observed book illustrators' dissatisfactions with the "traditional approach," which he explains as a picture book artist's way of "trying to make pictures that the artist thinks children will like." As Ward (an illustrator himself) correctly reveals, these artists then moved beyond this simple attempt at the gratification of children's preferences to a second stage in their relationship with children. At this point an artist would rather arrogantly insist, "I will make the best pictures of which I am capable," regardless of children's preferences. At present, Ward points out, illustrators' views have changed further. Now they want to "make pictures not that children will like, but that will be close to those that a child himself might do." Present-day illustrations for children, therefore, often evoke "a childlike spontaneity of conception and a consciously unliteral rendering" (1958, pp. 14–35). This was no overnight decision on the artists' part, it is plain to see. Over thirty years ago Newton saw this "conscious imitation of their [children's] untrained handiwork" by picture book illustrators (1932, p. 94).

One cannot equate this recent attitude toward art by artists entirely with the pictures drawn by young children, however. The modern picture book artists do conform somewhat to the "established organizational patterns" French used in children's art work (1952, p. 91). That is, modern artists may use unaccented outlines, generalized color, flat two-dimensional figures, and a lack of implied depth in their pictures. On the other hand, as Stewig notes, the most-acclaimed picture book artists indulge in what he calls "a wider range in Realism Quotient" (1968, p. 223). A larger percent of their picture books employ unrealistic styles and details, and unnaturalistic colors than did those of the past. Young children do not either like or use these techniques, we can say for sure.

Third, one must be careful not to concede the control of the selection of picture books for schools and libraries to children's preferences for illustrations, for yet another reason. This is because of a fundamental weakness in the design of the surveys of these preferences. In all these surveys children were asked to choose or comment on illustrations or parts of illustrations *in isolation.* Never, for instance, was a picture book read to a child at the same time the child was questioned about its pictures. Would young children's preferences for picture book illustrations be different from those found in the surveys of the past if they reacted to a complete or total picture book experience, that is, simultaneously to both the words and pictures of the book? Sloan's (1972) findings suggest that this would probably be the case. She found that young children preferred photographs to pictures done with realistic or stylized art, when the photographs and these pictures were simply compared. But, after hearing an *information* selection about the picture in question the children's preferences were then divided between a photograph and a realistic art picture. And, after they had heard a *narrative* selection about photographs and pictures, these children preferred a stylized art picture. This suggests that the linguistic narrative of a picture book likely has a significant effect on how attractive its pictures are to young children. Further research on this relationship is sorely needed. We are left with an intimation, nonetheless, that this kind of investigation might significantly change the present conclusions as to what young children like about picture book illustrations.

Finally, we need not fear that providing young children picture book illustrations which require them, as Brown puts it, to "learn to enjoy pictures with our senses instead of demanding logical explanations" (1958, p. 9), will hinder these children's learning to read. On this point Cianciolo is right when she emphasizes that picture books should be utilized "as aesthetic works and not as educational tools" (1973a, p. 4). Unfortunately, Cianciolo seems to change her mind on this matter. On another occasion she has proclaimed that wordless picture books are excellent, educational tools—for developing children's readiness for reading literature (1973b). Since the overall frailty of this latter proposal is clearly apparent (Groff 1974), her original conclusion seems all the more tenable.

Moreover, there have been direct attempts to use pictures as tools for helping children learn to read. These efforts have been shown to be relatively futile. Concannon's able review of the research on this question comes to the recent judgment that "the limited research indicates findings that pictures serving as motivating factors actually do not contribute significantly to the child's ability to decode [recognize words or comprehend meanings]" (1975, p. 256).

Conclusions

It has been stated often that young children's preferences for illustrations should form the basis for judgments as to which kinds of picture books are provided for them in homes, schools, and libraries. A match between these children's preferences for illustrations and the present stock of picture books conceivably could be successfully accomplished. Some opinion to the contrary notwithstanding, at present we do know enough about what young children like and dislike about isolated illustrations to make this matching possible. Children are parochial in their preferences for illustrations, as well as eager to make these choices known. Nevertheless, this hardly answers the question of whether this correspondence between young children and picture books should actually be established.

It is argued here that there are four explanations why such an arduous and time-consuming sorting out of picture books should not be undertaken. For one thing, giving young children only the kind of picture books they like may hinder the development of their taste for visual art. This decision would also be unacceptable to many modern book illustrators. There is a serious flaw, as well, in the surveys of children's preferences for illustrations which may render their findings invalid. And, finally, it has been shown that the loss of favored illustrations in picture books will not likely have any significant effect on young children's learning to read. So, instead of attempting to make this match, teachers and librarians will better spend their time and efforts seeking out and providing young children with the outstanding picture books that are available as these are designated by the *Children's Catalog* and other well-designed bibliographies (Cianciolo 1973; Kingman *et al.* 1968; Klemin 1966; Mahoney *et al.* 1947; Viguers *et al.* 1958).

References

Amsden, Ruth H. "Children's Preferences in Picture Book Variables." *Journal of Educational Research* 53 (1960): 309–312.

Arbuthnot, May Hill. *Children and Books*. Chicago: Scott, Foresman, 1964.

Ayer, Jean. "Format and Reading Appreciation." *Elementary English Review* 17 (1940): 213–217.

Bamberger, Florence. *The Effect of the Physical Makeup of a Book Upon Children's Selections*. Baltimore: Johns Hopkins University, 1922.

Bencetic, Stephen T. "Picture Preferences of Elementary Children." *Dissertation Abstracts* 20 (1960): 3117.

Bou, Ismael R., and Lopez, David G. "Preferences in Colors and Illustrations of Elementary School Children of Puerto Rico." *Journal of Educational Psychology* 44 (1953): 490–496.

Brown, Marcia. "Distinction in Picture Books." In *Illustrators of Children's Books 1946–1956,* edited by Ruth Viguers, Marcia Dalphin, and Bertha M. Miller, Boston: Horn Book, 1958.

Cianciolo, Patricia Jean. *Picture Books for Children*. Chicago: American Library Association, 1973a.

———. "Use Wordless Picture Books to Teach Reading, Visual Literacy and to Study Literature." *Top of the News* 29 (1973b): 226–235.

Clegg, Luther B. "An Analysis of the Picture Illustration Preferences of Primary Grade Children." *Dissertation Abstracts* 29 (1968): 1672A-1673-A.

Concannon, S. Josephina. "Illustrations in Books for Children: Review of Research." *Reading Teacher* 29 (1975): 254–256.

Freeman, G. LaVerne, and Freeman, Ruth S. *The Child and His Picture Book*. Chicago: Northwestern University, 1933.

French, John E. "Children's Preferences for Pictures of Varied Complexity of Pictorial Pattern." *Elementary School Journal* 53 (1952): 90–95.

Georgiou, Constantine. *Children and Their Literature*. Englewood Cliffs, New Jersey: Prentice-Hall, 1969.

Groff, Patrick. "Children's Literature Versus Wordless 'Books.' " *Top of the News* 30 (1974): 294–303.

Hildreth, Gertrude H. "Color and Picture Choices of Young Children." *Journal of Genetic Psychology* 49 (1936): 427–435.

Huck, Charlotte S. *Children's Literature in the Elementary School*. New York: Holt, Rinehart and Winston, 1976.

Katz, Elias. *Children's Preferences for Traditional and Modern Paintings*. New York: Teachers College, Columbia University, 1944.

Kingman, Lee; Foster, Joanna; and Lontoft, Ruth G. *Illustrators of Children's Books 1957–1966*. Boston: Horn Book, 1968.

Klemin, Diana. *The Art of Art for Children's Books: A Contemporary Survey*. New York: Clarkson N. Potter, 1966.

Lark-Horovitz, Betty. "On Art Appreciation of Children: I. Preference of Picture Subjects in General." *Journal of Educational Research* 31 (1937): 118–137.

Mahoney, Bertha E.; Latimer, Louise P.; and Folmsee, Beulau. *Illustrators of Children's Books 1744–1945*. Boston: Horn Book, 1947.

Martin, Helen. *Children's Preferences in Book Illustrations*. Cleveland: *Western Reserve University*, 1931.

Mellinger, Bonnie E. *Children's Interests in Pictures*. New York: Teachers College, Columbia University, 1932.

Miller, William A. "The Picture Choices of Primary-Grade Children." *Elementary School Journal* 37 (1936): 273–282.

______. "What Children See in Pictures." *Elementary School Journal* 39 (1938): 280–288.

Morrison, Jeannette G. *Children's Preferences for Pictures*. Chicago: University of Chicago, 1935.

Newton, Lesley. "Modern Trends in Book Illustration for Children." *Elementary English Review* 9 (1932): 89–94.

Publishers Weekly Editors. "Children's Preferences in Book Illustrations." *Publishers Weekly* 136 (1939): 2321.

Rudisill, Mabel. "Children's Preferences for Color Versus Other Qualities of Illustrations." *Elementary School Journal* 52 (1952): 414–451.

Rue, Eloise. "An Appreciation of Some Modern Picture Books." *Elementary English* 39 (1962): 314–319.

Sebesta, Sam Leaton, and Iverson, William J. *Literature for Thursday's Child*. Chicago: Science Research Associates, 1975.

Sloan, Margaret A. "Picture Preferences of Elementary School Children and Teachers." *Dissertation Abstracts International* 32 (1972): 6018-A.

Stewig, John Warren. "Children's Preferences in Picture Book Illustration." *Educational Leadership* 30 (1972): 273–277.

______. "Trends in Caldecott Award Winners." *Elementary English* 45 (1968): 218–223.

Templeton, Grace W. "The Development of a Method of Determing Characteristics of Pictures Which Attract and Retain Visual Attention." *Dissertation Abstracts International* 36 (1975): 3376-A.

Van der Mark, Parthenia J. "An Experimental Study of What Types of Pictures Children Are Most Interested In and Why." Master's Thesis, Teachers College, Columbia University, 1929.

Viguers, Ruth H.; Dalphin, Marcia; and Miller, Bertha M. *Illustrators of Children's Books 1946–1957*. Boston: Horn Book, 1958.

Ward, Lynn. "The Book Artist: Ideas and Technique." In *Illustrators of Children's Books 1946–1956,* edited by Ruth Viguers, Marcia Dalphin, and Bertha M. Miller. Boston: Horn Book, 1958.

Warnock, Lucile. "Illustration of Children's Books." *Elementary English Review* 15 (1938): 161–165, 208.

Waymack, Eunice H., and Hendrickson, Gordon. "Children's Reactions as a Basis for Teaching Picture Appreciation." *Elementary School Journal* 33 (1932): 268–276.

Whipple, Gertrude. "Appraisal of the Interest Appeal of Illustrations." *Elementary School Journal* 53 (1953): 262–269.

Word Meaning and the Literary Experience in Early Childhood

Dorothy H. Cohen

We have long known that children who read build their vocabularies in the process. Many of us have tended to assume that the vocabulary growth is related to that oft repeated dictum of teacher or parent, "Look it up in the dictionary!" The truth as we remember it from our own childhood, however, is more likely that we preferred to take our chances on getting the meaning somehow from the book itself rather than break the continuity of a story by running off to the dictionary. In recent years, a study on the effectiveness of the dictionary revealed that children remember word meaning better when the teacher just tells them than when they are made to look up a word in the dictionary. We can say that research has at last caught up with children in this regard.

It continues to be true, however, that readers of books do have better vocabularies than non-readers, and this difference was found to be true in a study in which stories were read to a group of "disadvantaged" second grade children whose inadequate reading level did not permit such pleasures on their own. At first, as the teachers read to the children, they relied quite heavily on the illustrations and their own explanations to clarify meaning of unfamiliar words. But the time came when these seven-year-old, urban slum children were able to listen to books in which the sentence structure and length were somewhat more complicated than in the beginning picture books and the illustrations were somewhat fewer. They were listening to books in which the authors used words to clarify the meaning of other words, and the children's increased ability to hear and follow the flow of words, to imagine the imagery developed by words was then dependent on the author's skill in making unfamiliar words and concepts comprehensible within the context of the story.

The majority of words thought to need clarification (by the authors of the books or by this writer) turned out to be among those used least frequently by young children when rated on the frequency listings in Rinsland's *A Basic Vocabulary of Elementary Children* (1) and in Figurel's *The Vocabulary of Underprivileged Children*. (2) However, teachers of young children

SOURCE: *Elementary English*, November 1969, pp. 914–925.

know that even frequency of occurrence on a word list is not in itself evidence of comprehension. There is a difference between verbalizing and understanding, and this the sensitive author knows. Thus, in the primary grades, "dead" could be known as a word, but not understood in depth; "city" could be pronounced, but its intrinsic character missed because its geographic scope is too big; and the old-fashioned "steamshovel" could seem an overwhelmingly complex machine to a child. Changes from rural to urban living make words like "spring" (water) or "market" (supermarket conceals the original) far less familiar than they once were; and the complexity of urban living makes the meaning of many once commonplace words obscure, largely because phenomena are so often remote from their origins and sources. Yet words in children's literature continue to reflect the past as well as the present, the complex as well as the simple, and need to be explained.

The authors most successful in depicting meaning through words and without illustration seemed to be conscious of what is important to a child and what is likely to be confusing, building meaning out of words through the kind of imagery that makes sense to a young child.

In their explanations of functions, descriptions of objects, or clarification of concepts, such authors developed comprehension of unfamiliar words through a number of techniques involving sensory imagery, and did this without losing the quality of the story as a story. Clarification was built in, not added on as a preached lesson. This paper will deal with the several techniques revealed by an analysis for this purpose of the fifty books used in the research mentioned above, where vocabulary was increased by hearing stories. Although the intent of the authors was clearly storytelling, concern for the children's full appreciation of meaning led to ways of increasing understanding intrinsic to the tale itself.

Piling Up Examples to Illustrate Meaning

In the very much loved *Mike Mulligan and His Steamshovel* (3) the meaning and role of a steamshovel are clarified by tallying the many tasks in which powerful digging is called for and accomplished by Mary Anne.

> Mike Mulligan was very proud of Mary Anne.
> He always said that she could dig as much in a day
> as a hundred men could dig in a week
>
> It was Mike Mulligan and Mary Anne and some others

who dug the great canals
  for the big boats
    to sail through

It was Mike Mulligan and Mary Anne
  and some others
who lowered the hills
and straightened the curves
to make the long highways
for the automobiles.

It was Mike Mulligan
  and Mary Anne
  and some others
    who smoothed out the ground
      and filled in the holes
    to make the landing fields
      for the airplanes.

And it was Mike Mulligan
  and Mary Anne
  and some others
who dug the deep holes
  for the cellars
of the tall skyscrapers
  in the big cities.
When people used to stop
  and watch them,

Mike Mulligan and Mary Anne
    used to dig a little faster
  and a little better
Some days they would keep
  as many as thirty-seven trucks
busy taking away the dirt they had dug.

Phyllis McGinley (4) uses the same technique in this passage from *The Horse Who Lived Upstairs* when she develops the meaning of the word *adventure* as having to do with the not-so-usual in one's life. The application is in terms of the perspective of the horse Joey, a perspective that makes absolute sense to a child:

> And every day he [Joey] had many interesting adventures. Sometimes he met a policeman who gave him sugar.
>
> Sometimes ladies patted him on the nose and fed him carrots.
>
> He was introduced to the high-bred horses who drew the hansom cabs along the Plaza.
>
> He saw the children playing in the playgrounds and the parks.
>
> But it made no difference to Joey.

Yashima (5) brings impact to the word *forlorn* in the same way in *Crow Boy*.

> He was afraid of the children and could not make friends with them at all.
>
> He was left alone in the study time.
>
> He was left alone in the play time.
>
> He was always at the end of the line, at the foot of the class, a forlorn little tag-along.

Some authors scatter the many references or incidents that build up to a common meaning. Thus in *Down Down the Mountain*, the word *steep* becomes meaningful because Credle (6) uses the concept up and down in a variety of situations real to children yet germane to the mountain on which they appear, and *steep* is associated with the up and down.

> "You can't find shoes like that in these hills! Such shining shoes come from the town, away down, down at the foot of the mountain."
>
> "Plant some turnip seeds," said Granny, "and when they have grown into fine big turnips, you can take them all the way down to town and trade them for some shining, creaky, squeaky, shoes."
>
> The next day they climbed up the steep, steep mountain-side to see if the turnip seeds had come up.
>
> "It's no trouble to find the town," said Granny. "Just keep to the road and it will lead you down. Sometimes it's steep, just like the stair. Sometimes it's narrow—like a hair. It twists and turns and winds around, but at the end, you'll find the town."
>
> Down, down, down they went between the rows of tall blue mountains, down, down, down until they came to a little stream flowing over the rocks.
>
> And off they started on the long trip home. Up Up Up they wound, round and round and round the mountain . . . After a long, long climb they reached their own little cabin.

Description of a Function or Procedure in Detail

Sometimes meaning is achieved by careful analysis or description of the functional aspects of the meaning. The passage quoted from *Mike Mulligan and His Steamshovel* does this, and Margaret Wise Brown (7) tackled the meaning of *dead* in *The Dead Bird* in this way.

> The bird was dead when the children found it. But it had not been dead for long—it was still warm and its eyes were closed.

> The children felt with their fingers for the quick beat of the bird's heart in its breast. But there was no heart beating. That was how they knew it was dead. And even as they held it,it began to get cold, and the limp body grew stiff, so they couldn't bend its legs and the head didn't flop when they moved it. That was the way animals got when they had been dead for some time—cold dead and stone still with no heart beating.

On less serious topics, but in the same way, other authors develop function to clarify meaning. Marcia Brown (8) gives life to the word *carousel:*

> Suddenly, thin high music was coming up from Spring Street. . . .
>
> "It's a merry-go-round!" shouted Anthony and ran down the stairs into the street. A red wagon drawn by a black-and-white horse rolled down the street on red and gold wheels. The horse had a red harness with brass studs. He was proud. He almost danced to the music that came from the painted box behind the driver's seat. On the back of the wagon was a circular platform that turned round and round. Prancing horses, fierce lions and a white elephant raced dizzily by. Fat gold tassels dangled from the red and yellow canopy. They stuck straight out when the carousel whirled around. . . .
>
> "How much for a ride, Mister?"
>
> "Five cents—ten cents for a long one.". . . .
>
> Mr. Corelli closed the door, turned the crank, and the music began to play.

Clyde Bulla (9) defines a *spring* by describing its functional behavior.

> It was a spring of clear cold water. It came from the foot of the mountain, ran a little way, and disappeared among the rocks. They heard the spring running over the rocks, but they never stopped for a drink of the cold, fresh water.

Phyllis McGinley (4) explains *stall,* even though it is for a city horse, in a way that allows a child to understand it as a horse's own living quarters.

> So every night, when Joey came home, he stepped out from the shafts of the wagon, and into an elevator, and up he went to his stall on the fourth floor of the big brick building. It was a fine stall and Joey was very comfortable there. He had plenty of oats to eat and plenty of fresh straw to lie on. He even had a window to look out of.

The word *city* takes on universal meaning even within the special frame of reference given to it by Helen Garrett (10) in *Angelo the Naughty One:*

> On the steep side of a tall mountain in Mexico there was once a lovely little city. The houses were snowy white with red roofs, and the tall church towers were a soft rosy pink. Tiny stone streets ran here and there, and up and down, and around about the houses.

In the same book, the word *feast* comes to life in the following passage:

> After the wedding such a feast!

Such good food and such gay music! All the neighbors and all the friends came to the party. They ate and drank as much as they wished, and they sang and danced to the music.

Words like *contest* and *judging* are made meaningful by careful attention to significant detail in *Down Down the Mountain*. (6).

"Howdy, young ones," said the old man who was looking at the turnips. "Do you want to enter that turnip in the contest?"

"What contest?" asked Hank.

"Why there's a prize offered for the finest turnip at the fair," replied the old man.

"Mercy me!" said Hetty. "Let's try it."

"You bet your life!" said Hank.

So the old man wrote their names on a tag and tied it to the fat turnip. Then he laid it carefully among the other turnips. "You are just in the nick of time," he said, "for I was just a-getting ready to do the judging."

He began to examine the turnips. He weighed each one to see how heavy it was. He felt each one to see how firm it was. And when he had tried them all, he held one large turnip high above his head. "Folks!" he cried, "here's the finest turnip at the fair. It belongs to a little girl and a little boy!"

Hetty and Hank listened with all their ears.

"Come forward, young ones and receive the prize!"

Foreign sounding words describing foreign customs are made familiar by Munro Leaf (11) in *The Story of Ferdinand* as he explains *Banderilleros, Picadores,* and *Matador* for the benefit of the unknowing Ferdinand and the equally unknowing young reader.

First came the Banderilleros with long sharp pins with ribbons on them to stick in the bull and make him mad.

Next came the Picadores who rode skinny horses and they had long spears to stick in the bull and make him madder.

Then came the Matador, the proudest of all—he thought he was very handsome, and bowed to he ladies. He had a red cape and a sword and was supposed to stick the bull last of all.

The word *fierce* is given genuine character in a series of associative actions and feelings that together add up to what fierce means.

One day five men came . . . to pick the biggest, fastest, roughest bull to fight in the bull fights in Madrid. All the other bulls ran around snorting and butting, leaping and jumping so the men would think they were very very strong and fierce and pick them.

(Ferdinand, who was a gentle bull, sits on a bee and behaves in a way that is interpreted as fierce.)

> Ferdinand jumped up with a snort. He ran around puffing and snorting, butting and pawing the ground as if he were crazy. The five men saw him and they all shouted with joy. Here was the largest and fiercest bull of all. Just the one for the bull fights in Madrid!
>
> . . . . . everyone shouted and clapped because they thought he would fight fiercely and butt and snort and stick his horns around. He wouldn't fight and be fierce no matter what they did.

Building Up Mood and Anticipating Action or Feeling

In some instances, an author builds the mood of the story to the point where the suspense involved leads inevitably to an understanding of the words used, even if these are unlikely to be words used in daily speech. Such is the case with the word *coax* in Phyllis Krasilovsky's (12) *Scaredy Cat.*

> Scaredy Cat was afraid of everything.
>
> He was scared of footsteps.
>
> He was scared of the children who wanted to hold him.
>
> He was scared of the children's mother who wanted to feed him.
>
> He was scared of the children's father who had a big deep voice.
>
> He was scared of the daytime and hid under the couch all day long. Sometimes he hid under one of the beds. The children were always crawling on their hands and knees trying to coax him to come out.

Meaningful Context Clarifies Individual Words

Auntie Katushka comes from the old country in Margery Clark's (13) *Poppy Seed Cakes,* and among her presents are *poppy seeds* and a *feather bed,* neither likely to be too familiar to the current generation of American children.

> The five pounds of poppy seeds were to sprinkle on little cakes which Andrewshek's Auntie Katushka made every Saturday for Andrewshek.
>
> One Saturday morning Andrewshek's Auntie Katushka took some butter and some sugar and some flour and some milk and seven eggs and she rolled out

some nice little cakes. Then she sprinkled each cake with some of the poppy seeds which she had brought from the old country.

While the nice little cakes were baking, she spread out the fine feather bed on top of the big bed for Andrewshek to take his nap. Andrewshek did not like to take a nap. Andrewshek liked to bounce up and down and up and down on his fine feather bed.(Auntie Katushka leaves for market)

[But] Andreeshek kept bouncing up and down and up and down on the fine feather bed and paid no attention to the little cakes sprinkled with poppy seeds.

Just as Andrewshek was bouncing up in the air for the ninth time, he heard a queer noise that sounded like "Hs-s-s-sss," at the front door of his house.

"Oh, what a queer noise!" cried Andrewshek. He jumped down off the feather bed and opened the front door. There stood a great green goose as big as Andrewshek himself. The goose was very cross and was scolding as fast as he could. . .

"What do you want?" said Andrewshek. "What are you scolding about?"

"I want all the goose feathers from your fine feather bed," quacked the big green goose. "They are mine."

"They are not yours," said Andrewshek. "My Auntie Katushka brought them with her from the old country in a huge bag."
"They are mine," quacked the big green goose.

(In an effort to placate the goose, Andrewshek feeds him poppy seed cakes. The big green goose eats too many and explodes; his feathers fly all over the room. Auntie Katushka has returned in the meantime.)

"Well! Well!" said Andrewshek's Auntie Katushka as she gathered up the pieces of the big green goose. "We soon shall have two fine feather pillows for your fine feather bed."

In the same little volume are stories of the misadventures of Erminka, and the words *market* and *crate* are woven into the context of the story.
Notice the use of *market:*

"Well, Erminka," said Erminka's mother as she locked the kitchen door. "I am ready to go to market now. I think I will buy some gooseberries. . . ."

Erminka and her mother started for the market. They went down a hill and across the tracks and up two blocks until they came to a big red shed.

It was the market. Inside, the farmers and the farmers' wives were selling vegetables and fruit and chickens and flowers, and one farmer had five little white pigs for sale.

Erminka's mother saw many friends among the farmers' wives. "How do you do, Mrs. Smith," she would say. "Have you any sweet butter this morning?"

> "How do you do, Mrs. Gray? Have you any nice fresh buttermilk?"
>
> "Good morning, Mrs. Popolovski! Have you any nice little cabbages today?"

Notice *crate* in context:

> She [Erminka] saw a crate full of chickens. "You nice chickens!" she said. "Wouldn't you like to see my red topped boots?"
>
> "Yes, indeed," said the chickens.
>
> Erminka opened the door of the crate with the toe of the red topped boot.
>
> As soon as the crate was open, five white chickens flew past Erminka. The market was upset. Everyone stopped buying apples and selling eggs and ran after the chickens. The chickens flew wildly about the market in all directions. One chicken fluttered out of the front door of the market and down the street.
>
> Only a baby chicken was left in the crate. The market master and the farmers caught the chickens and put them back in the crate.
>
> "I did not mean to let the chickens run away, Mother," said Erminka. "But it looked so easy to open the door of the crate with the toe of my red topped boot."

Several other examples of this kind of clarification, within the context of the story itself, follow.

See how *lonesome* is used:

> *The Story of Ferdinand* (Leaf) (11)
>
> Ferdinand the Bull enjoys being by himself:
>
> Sometimes his mother, who was a cow, would worry about him. She was afraid he would be lonesome all by himself.
>
> "Why don't you run and play with the other little bulls and skip and butt your head?" she would say.
>
> But Ferdinand would shake his head. "I like it better here where I can sit just quietly and smell the flowers."
>
> His mother saw that he was not lonesome, and because she was an understanding mother, even though she was a cow, she just let him sit there and be happy.
>
> *team*
>
> *Two Is a Team* (14)
>
> They worked hard the rest of the day building a wagon. Paul let Ted help him put the box on. Ted let Paul help him put the wheels on. And together they made a fine strong wagon . . . Every day after school they delivered the groceries. Sometimes Paul steered the wagon and Ted delivered the groceries. Sometimes Ted steered and Paul delivered the groceries.

fleet

Curious George Rides a Bike (15)

So George decided to make some more boats. Finally he had used up all the papers and had made so many boats that he could not count them—a whole fleet. Watching his fleet sailing down the river George felt like an admiral.

drifted

Lee Fong and His Toy Junk (16)

Lee tied a long line to the stern of his junk and put the little boat into the water. As the junk drifted slowly out to sea, he tied small baited hooks, a few inches apart, on the line. When his line was let out all the way, Lee had tied on it more than fifty baited hooks.

The toy junk had sailed away so far by this time it could hardly be seen.

beckoned

Make Way for Ducklings (17)

Mrs. Mallard, the mother duck, attempts a crossing at a busy Boston intersection with her ducklings:

The cars kept speeding by and honking, and Mrs. Mallard and the ducklings kept right on quack-quack-quacking.

They made such a noise that Michael [the policeman] came running, waving his arms and blowing his whistle.

He planted himself in the center of the road, raised one hand to stop traffic, and then beckoned with the other, the way policemen do, for Mrs. Mallard to cross over.

dither

Make Way for Ducklings

"I like this place," said Mrs. Mallard as they climbed out on the bank and waddled along. "Why don't we build a nest and raise our ducklings right in this pond? There are no foxes, and no turtles, and the people feed us peanuts. What could be better?"

"Good," said Mr. Mallard, delighted that at last Mrs. Mallard had found a place that suited her. But—[illustration of a child on a bike riding by fast] "Look out!" squawked Mrs. Mallard, all of a dither. "You'll get run over!" And when she got her breath she added, "This is no place for babies, with all those horrid things rushing about. We'll have to look somewhere else."

In some stories, the context in which a word appears is repeated and gives emphasis to the meaning. For example, in *Blueberries for Sale,* (18) Little Bear comes with his mother to eat blueberries on the hill. His mother gives him advice.

store up

"Little Bear," she said, "eat lots of berries and grow big and fat. We must store up food for the long winter.

Little Bear and his mother went home down one side of Blueberry Hill, eating blueberries all the way, and full of food stored up for next winter.

In the popular *Five Chinese Brothers,* (19) the words *condemned* and *assembled* are clear to understand in the context of the action. *Execution* is made unmistakably real by the repetition of its meaning over several episodes. Each of the brothers has a different magic which they all use to divert punishment from the hapless brother who has lost a little boy by mistake.

When the First Chinese Brother returned to the village . . . he was arrested, put in prison, tried, and condemned to have his head cut off.

All the people were assembled to witness the execution. The executioner took his sword and struck a mighty blow.

[The second brother comes to be drowned, which is the second attempt to punish the guilty one.]

On the morning of the execution, he said. . . .

On the morning of the execution, the Third Chinese Brother [who was to be burned] said to the judge, . . .

On the morning of the execution, the Fourth Chinese Brother (who was to be smothered) said to the judge. . . .

[But] the judge stepped forward and said, "We have tried to get rid of you in every possible way and somehow it cannot be done."

disgrace

Angelo the Naughty One (10)

Angelo is a boy who hates baths and is always dirty. His sister's coming wedding forces the issue.)

Papa said he was a disgrace to the family and Mama was ashamed.

[Angelo runs away, is found and bathed by soldiers, and the soldier-groom says,] "Brother soldiers—after the wedding he (Angelo) will be younger brother to a soldier and I am sure he will be proud and happy to take baths so he won't disgrace the army."

[Later, his family, still unaware of his whereabouts, discuss Angelo.]

"He was afraid to take a bath," explained Mama.

"He is a disgrace to the family," Papa said.

"He shall not have any of the good food at the wedding party."

[Still later, on the church steps, all the children were lined up except the missing Angelo.]

Next was Angelo's place in the family, but he had run away and brought disgrace to them all. What a naughty, naughty boy!

Contrast and Comparison

brave, bold, and by contrast, *timid* are thus used in the story Timid Timothy, (20) although "timid" appears only in the title.

He [Timothy] looked like a big, brave,
bold kitten.
But he wasn't.
He was afraid of the rain on the roof.
He was afraid of footsteps on the stairs.
He was afraid of the little mice.
He was afraid of dogs.
So every one called him Fraidy Cat.
Except his mother.
One day his mother said, "Timothy, you must learn to be a big, brave, bold kitten. We shall go to the zoo."
"Why?" asked Timothy trembling.
"So I can teach you not to be afraid of other animals," said his mother.
[After many adventures, Timothy does frighten a dog.]
Timothy was very surprised.
"I scared a dog!" he said,
He stuck out his chest.
He waved his tail.
And he strutted along home to tell his mother.
"I am a big, brave, bold kitten," he told her.
"I scared a lion,
and a bear,
and an elephant
and a rabbit
and a DOG!
I'm not afraid of ANYTHING!"

discontented

The Horse Who Lived Upstairs (4)

There was once a horse named Joey
who was discontented.
He was discontented because
he didn't live in a red barn

> with a weathervane on top
> like this,
>
> And he didn't live in a green meadow where he could run about and kick up his heels like this. Instead, he lived upstairs in a big brick building in New York.
>
> . . . in New York, there isn't room for barns or meadows.
>
> So every night when Joey came home, he stepped . . . into an elevator and up he went to his stall on the fourth floor of the big brick building. It was a fine stall, and Joey was very comfortable in it. He had plenty of oats to eat and plenty of fresh straw to lie on.
>
> He even had a window to look out of.
>
> But still Joey was discontented.

disappeared

Angelo the Naughty One (10)

> He dashed across the yard, through the gate and disappeared.
>
> The brothers and sisters ran to the gate too.
>
> But all they saw was a herd of dainty goats tripping downhill to the market.
>
> And two sleepy donkeys climbing uphill under enormous loads of cornstalks.
>
> Only their little white noses and big ears showed.
>
> Angelo was gone!

(6) Sometimes the whole story capitalizes on the meaning of a word, often the word in the title. *Timid Timothy* (20) does this, and so does *Curious George* (15). The word *curious* is at the heart of the antics of the little monkey in Rey's series of stories, and the concept is developed and reinforced by repetition of the word in connection with George's numerous activities.

e.g.

> He wondered how they [seagulls] could fly. He was very curious. Finally, he *had* to try.
>
> George watched [the man telephone]. He was fascinated. George was curious. He wanted to telephone too.
>
> George watched [the balloon man]. He was curious again. He felt he *must* have a red balloon.
>
> . . . a big box was standing in the yard. George was curious.
>
> When he came to the last house he saw a little river in the distance. George was curious. He wanted to know what the river was like.
>
> George was curious: would the ostrich really eat anything? He wouldn't eat a bugle—or would he?
> [and so on through all the volumes]

Simile

(Scaredy Cat by Phyllis Krasilovsky) (12)

arched

And when he was scared, his back arched like half a circle and his tail stood straight up in the air like a black flag.

Linking Familiar Experiences to Give Meaning to the Unfamiliar Word *Quarrel*

Millions of Cats by Wanda Gag (21)

And they began to quarrel.

They bit and scratched and clawed each other and made such a great noise that the very old man and the very old woman ran into the house as fast as they could. They did not like such quarreling.

pond

They came to a pond.

"Mew mew! We are thirsty!" cried the
hundreds of cats
thousands of cats
millions and billions of cats.

"Well, here is a great deal of water," said the very old man. Each cat took a sip of water and the pond was gone.

lapped

Scaredy Cat by Phyllis Krasilovsky (12)
Scaredy Cat found a saucerful of milk that the children's mother had left for him on the kitchen floor. He lapped it up with his pink tongue. How good it tasted!

Explanation Woven Directly Into the Story, Sometimes Frankly, Othertimes Less So

junk

Lee Fong and His Toy Junk (16)

Now Chinese boats are called junks. Most of them have two bright eyes painted on their bow to help them see where they are going. Some of the junks are houseboats and some are sailing boats and some are fishing boats. Lee loved the fishing boats best. The more he watched them the more he wished he were a fisherman, with a line of his own, fishing off a big junk in the beautiful China Sea.

molt

Make Way for Ducklings. (Robert McCloskey) (17)

So they chose a cozy spot among the bushes near the water and settled down to build their nest. And only just in time, for now they were beginning to molt. All their old wing feathers started to drop out, and they would not be able to fly again until the news ones grew in.

middle

Middle Matilda (22)

She had four older sisters: Molly, Janie, Kate and Linda; and four younger brothers: Timothy, Andy, Joey, and Michael the baby. She came right in the middle. "Middle Matilda" Great-Aunt Matilda called her.

Many of the classifications and examples offered here tend to overlap, obviously, since it was not any author's intention, in writing for children, to follow specific procedures for clarifying meaning. It becomes clear, however, after examining many books, that the sensitivity to children which authors might reasonably be expected to have, differs with the interpretation given to childhood itself. Conceptions about childhood have altered sufficiently over the centuries so that once-children's books are today often acknowledged to be better understood by adults (e.g., *Alice in Wonderland*) and once-adult literature is enjoyed by children (e.g., *Mother Goose*). But in addition, the rapidly changing social scene has made anachronisms out of contemporary adults' childhood memories to an amazing event. Therefore, sensitivity to what children might be expected to know is dependent on the degree to which an author is aware of just how swiftly the childhood environment experienced by today's adult has been displaced, and in what ways. The fact is, of course, that much in childhood over centuries has remained universal, but it is likely that universality refers to feelings, somewhat less to relationships, and at least to forms of living or to specific words used to express experience. Authors may need to distinguish between the universal and the changing in their concepts of what children will understand and identify with.

Children who read books increase and enrich their vocabularies, and they undoubtedly do so because of the techniques for comprehension unconsciously employed by sensitive authors among other qualities of writing. For the children who are not yet readers themselves in the full sense of the word, stories read to them in which words illuminate other words carry significance for their growth in later reading comprehension. The more words carry meaning to them through their ears the more they will later be able to draw meaning out of the printed page themselves.

References

(1) Rinsland, Henry D., *A Basic Vocabulary of Elementary Schoolchildren,* New York: The Macmillan Company, 1945

(2) Figurel, J. Allen, *The Vocabulary of Underpriviledged Children,* The Graduate School, University of Pittsburgh, 1948

(3) From *Mike Mulligan and His Steam Shovel,* Story and pictures by Virginia Lee Burton. Copyright 1939 by Virginia Lee Demetrios. Reprinted by permission of Houghton Mifflin Company, Boston

(4) From *The Horse Who Lived Upstairs* by Phyllis McGinley. Copyright 1944, by Phyllis McGinley and Helen Stone. Reprinted with permission from the publishers, J. B. Lippincott Company, Philadelphia

(5) From *Crow Boy,* written and illustrated by Taro Yashima. Copyright 1955 by Mitsu and Taro Yashima. Reprinted by permission of the Viking Press, Inc. New York

(6) From *Down Down the Mountain* by Ellis Credle. Copyright renewed 1961 by the author. Reprinted with permission of the publishers, Thomas Nelson and Sons, Camden, N.J.

(7) From *The Dead Bird,* story by Margaret Wise Brown, illustrated by Remy Charlip. Copyright 1938 by Roberta B. Rauch and Remy Charlip. Reprinted by permission of the publisher, Young Scott Books, New York

(8) From *The Little Carousel* by Marcia Brown. Copyright 1946 by the author. Reprinted by permission of the publisher, Charles Scribner's Sons, New York

(9) From *The Poppy Seeds* by Clyde Robert Bulla. Copyright 1955 by Clyde Robert Bulla. Reprinted by permission of the publishers, Thomas Y. Crowell Company, New York

(10) From *Angelo the Naughty One* by Helen Garrett, illustrated by Leo Politi. Copyright 1944 by Helen Garrett and Leo Politi. Reprinted by permission of the Viking Press, Inc., New York

(11) From *The Story of Ferdinand* by Munro Leaf, illustrated by Robert Lawson. Copyright 1936 by Munro Leaf and Robert Lawson, copyright renewed 1964 by Munro Leaf and John W. Boyd. Reprinted by permission of the Viking Press, Inc., New York

(12) From *Scaredy Cat* by Phyllis Krasilovsky. Copyright 1959 by The Macmillan Company. Reprinted by permission of the publisher. The Macmillan Company, New York

(13) From *The Poppy Seed Cakes* by Margery Clark. Copyright 1924 by Doubleday and Company. Reprinted by permission of the publisher, Doubleday and Company, Inc., New York

(14) From *Two is a Team* by Jerrold Beim. Copyright 1945 by Lorraine and Jerrold Beim. Reprinted by permission of the publisher, Harcourt, Brace and World, Inc., New York

(15a) From *Curious George* by H. A. Rey. Copyright 1941 by H. A. Rey. Reprinted by permission of the publisher, Houghton Mifflin Company

(15b) From *Curious George Rides a Bike* by H. A. Rey. Copyright 1952 by H. A. Rey. Reprinted by permission of the publisher, Houghton Mifflin Company, Boston

(16) From *Lee Fong and His Toy Junk,* written and illustrated by William Carmichael.

Copyright 1955 by William P. Carmichael. Published by David McKay Company, New York. Reprinted by permission of the author

(17) From *Make Way for Ducklings,* written and illustrated by Robert McCloskey. Copyright 1941 by Robert McCloskey. Reprinted by permission of the Viking Press, Inc., New York

(18) From *Blueberries for Sale,* written and illustrated by Robert McCloskey, Copyright 1948 by Robert McCloskey. Reprinted by permission of the Viking Press, Inc., New York

(19) From *The Five Chinese Brothers* by Claire Huchet Bishop. Copyright 1938 and renewed 1965 by Coward-McCann, Inc. Reprinted by permission of Coward-McCann, Inc., New York

(20) From *Timid Timothy* by Gwencira Williams. Copyright 1944 by Gwencira Williams. Reprinted by permission of the publisher, Young Scott Books, New York

(21) From *Millions of Cats* by Wanda Gag. Copyright 1928 by Coward McCann, Inc., Reprinted by permission of the publisher, Coward-McCann, Inc., New York

(22) From *Middle Matilda* by Winifred Bromhall. Copyright 1962 by Winifred Bromhall. Reprinted by permission of the publisher, Alfred A. Knopf, Inc., New York

The Effect of Literature on Vocabulary and Reading Achievement

Dorothy H. Cohen

The existence of large-scale reading retardation that stems from weakness of motivation and lack of readiness, and seems unresponsive to different methods of teaching reading, led to the search for an approach to the problems of poor motivation and inadequate readiness that would stimulate children's desire to achieve competency in reading while strengthening their ability to do so. Literature read aloud was chosen as an appropriate solution to the problem because the children's weakness of motivation and readiness could be

SOURCE: *Elementary English* (February 1968), pp. 209–217.

attributed to two major factors (1) lack of experience with books as a source of pleasure, and (2) inadequacy of language as a consequence of limitations in variety of experience in a milieu that offers restricted language models. Recognition of the need of young children to be ego involved in their learning led to the selection of stories to be read to them which were conceptually comprehensible yet held possibilities for emotional reponse at their maturity level. It was expected that positive involvement of a conceptual and emotional nature with the variety of experience and vocabulary that literature offers would lead the children to a realization of the pleasure to be gained from books and an assimilation of much of the vocabulary. Specifically, the objectives of the research were:

1. To increase and strengthen the vocabulary of socially disadvantaged children at the second-grade level as a means of preparing them better for effective experiences in reading.
2. To offer socially disadvantaged children experience with books as a source of pleasure in order to stimulate and deepen their desire to read.
3. Through strengthening verbal readiness and heightening motivation to read, to increase the actual achievement in reading of children of culturally limited backgrounds who tend to fall behind in reading and therefore in academic achievement.

Procedure

Seven elementary schools in New York City, designated by the Board of Education as Special Service schools because of their academic retardation, low socio-economic population, and high percentage of ethnic and racial minorities, became the setting for this research.

Five hundred eighty second-grade children in 20 classes in 7 schools were tested at the beginning of the research. Of these, 285 yielded post-test data, 130 in the control group, 155 in the experimental group. All children fell into the accepted age for second grade in New York City, with boys and girls about equal in number. Holdovers were eliminated, and there were no known cases of mental retardation in the sample. Group testing for I.Q. was not permitted by the New York City Board of Education at the time of the research, but a broad range of learning response was assured by using homogeneously grouped classes at the top, middle, and bottom of the second grade. These placements were determined a priori by the teachers and school administrators according to levels of reading and reading readiness achieved by the children at the end of first grade.

The populations of all the schools included a range of 30-45 percent Puerto Rican children, 40-55 percent Negro children, and the rest white. The number of non-English speaking children proved to be negligible.

The experimental variable, story reading, was introduced and maintained by the teachers of the experimental classes, all of whom were regularly licensed teachers of the New York City Board of Education and who had been evaluated by their principals as of average competency. Each teacher had had at least one year of teaching experience before the research began. All classes were using a basal series approach to reading, and were following the prescribed curriculum for second grade in New York City Schools.

Experimental and control classes were established in separate schools to avoid contamination as a result of the realistic probability that teachers on the same grade level in a school were likely to share experiences, and the experimental variable of story reading was too easy to imitate.

Materials and Methods for the Special Program

Fifty books for the teachers to read to the children were placed in each experimental classroom, some on open shelves, others in the closet until read.* Book selection followed validation by four judges of the following criteria:

(a) Events, concepts, and relationships must be within the scope of young children's conceptual grasp. The stories shall deal with the universal in childhood experience regardless of class and ethnic variation. Stories shall be of the here-and-now, realistic type, but not primarily informational in intent, nor necessarily familiar in detail. Language, plot, character must enhance a story that is pleasurable and interesting to a young child of about seven. Since the children of this study were assumed to be linguistically unsophisticated and limited in general range of experience, books were geared to a somewhat younger level of maturity than might be selected for middle class seven year olds. This meant that while the basic plot would interest all seven year olds, degree of complexity and length of story were more suitable to younger children.

(b) The stories must allow for emotional identification with characters, aspirations, fears, mishaps or other feelings and adventures within the range of childhood experience, such as occur regardless of class, and to an extent regardless of cultural specificity.

(c) The stories shall be written in language which flows naturally and best conveys the precise idea or colorful image to the juvenile listener. Language shall not be confined to a single grammatical structure nor a fixed sentence length. Sentence length and complexity need to be intrinsically related to the theme and character of the story, but not of such length and complexity that a young child cannot follow the development of the thought from the beginning to the end of the sentence. There shall be no limitations on vocab-

*The list of books may be obtained from the author upon request.

ulary, either of type of word or number of syllables. All vocabulary likely to be unfamiliar to the children shall be so used in the story that meaning can be readily inferred from the context, illustrations, or explanation by the teacher. Language shall deal with the concrete and sensory, rather than with abstractions or difficult time-space relationships.

Three of the judges were asked to indicate by the number 1, 2 or 3 the level of difficulty of each book according to length, complexity of plot and language. The final 50 books given to the teachers were categorized in these sub-groups of difficulty, and each book so labelled for the teacher's information.

A Manual of Accompanying Activities and story-reading techniques was given to each experimental teacher. Discussion, dramatization, additional reading on the theme, illustrative material other than what is in the book, children's own illustrations, explanation by the teacher of words and references, follow-up activities appropriate to the story such as a trip, construction, letter-writing, crafts or whatever else lends itself to enhancement of comprehension, were among the suggestions offered to insure a variety of approaches to strengthening comprehension of the story and individual words.

Teachers were asked to read a story every day of the school year from the books given to them by the investigator. They were urged to read the stories with attention to phrasing, dramatic quality in the voice, pace, and knowledge of the story before reading. They were also asked to choose a suitable follow-up activity from the types suggested in the manual, and to introduce books in the order of increasing difficulty, as indicated by the number 1, 2, 3 next to each title. Once introduced, a book could be read as often as the teacher or the class desired.

Teachers in the control group proceeded as usual, with stories an occasional treat, if read at all, and not chosen according to the specific criteria indicated for the experimental group.

Administration and Scoring of Tests

1. Form B of the Metropolitan Reading Achievement Test, Upper Primary was administered in October and Form C in June of the school year. Separate scores for Word Knowledge, Word Discrimination, and Reading Comprehension were entered for each child.
2. A Free Association Vocabulary test, validated by Tinker, Hacker and Wesley as a measurement of specific vocabulary knowledge, was given to all children in October and again in June of the research year. Before the test

was given, each classroom was carefully prepared to avoid copying of words from blackboard, wall charts, books, *etc.* Coded, lined booklets with each child's name, school, and class on the cover were distributed to the children and identical instructions given to all classes for writing as many words as they could remember in 20 minutes, without regard to spelling.

Quantitative Count

Words were counted according to the following criteria:

1. Every legible word was counted without regard to its spelling, except proper names of people, made-up words, and words representing sounds. Names of places, days of the week or months, numerals and contractions were considered important word learnings at this age and for this population and were counted.
2. All forms of a verb were considered as separate words rather than as one root word. Tenses may be considered important word learnings at this age and for this population.
3. Inflections represent a maturing level of development in speech, so plurals formed by simple "s" (houses) as well as plurals formed by change of word (mice) were counted separately:
4. Comparative and superlative forms of adjectives and adverbs were counted separately.
5. All derived forms of a word were counted separately rather than as derived forms of one root word.
6. Any word appearing more than once on a given child's paper was counted only once in the total count of that paper.

In view of the discrepancies in handwriting and spelling of children so young, the count was checked by a jury of three college students both as to number of words and agreement on meaning of ambiguous words. The total number of different words for each child was recorded and used to make a master list of the number of different words for each class. Lists of the total number of different words for the experimental and control groups were compiled from the pre- and post-test results of the Free Association Vocabulary Test.

Qualitative Count

The pre- and post-experimental and control word lists were submitted to comparison with Rinsland's frequency ratings of words used by children in free composition. The more rarely the word was used, the higher was its quality rating. Rinsland's frequency ratings, listed in groups of half thousands, were converted into point values in a pre-determined formula according to the index symbol listed for the frequency grouping of the word in the column for second grade: If a word did not appear in the second-grade column it was given the converted value for the group frequency at the next higher grade in which it appeared. If the word appeared in several higher grades, the first appearance was counted. Frequency groupings below the first thousand were not given quality point value because the words are too commonly used to indicate a qualitative differentiation.

Converted quality points were totalled for each child and entered on the prepared space in the booklet and on the master sheets.

Five scores for each of 285 children, 155 experimental, 130 control, were submitted to statistical treatment. The five scores were *Word Knowledge, Word Discrimination,* and *Reading Comprehension* from the Metropolitan Reading Achievement Test, Upper Primary; and *Vocabulary, Numerical Count, and Vocabulary, Qualitative Count* from the Free Association Vocabulary Test. An analysis of covariance was made, using the pre-test scores as covariate.

Results

The following is a summary of the results obtained by an analysis of covariance.

1. The experimental group showed an increase in vocabulary over the control group, significant at .005.
2. The experimental group showed an increase in Word Knowledge (Metropolitan Reading Achievement Test) over the control group, significant at .005.
3. The experimental group showed an increase in Reading Comprehension (Metropolitan Reading Achievement Test) over the control group, significant at .01.
4. The experimental group showed a numerical superiority in quality of vocabulary over the control, with an F ratio of 3.45. Since an F of 3.84 is necessary for significance at the .05 level, significance at the .05 level was narrowly missed.
5. There was no significant difference in Word Discrimination (Metropolitan Reading Achievement Test).

Although the above results apply to the entire group, an examination of the achievement of the three lowest classes in the experimental and control groups is of special importance, inasmuch as these lowest classes have been the most difficult to affect academically.

Six Lowest Classes Considered Separately

1. The experimental group showed an increase in Word Knowledge (Metropolitan Reading Achievement Test) over the control group, significant at .05.
2. The experimental group showed an increase over the control group in quality of vocabulary as measured for frequency rating in the Rinsland Vocabulary List, significant at .05.
3. The experimental group showed an increase in Reading Comprehension (Metropolitan Reading Achievement Test) over the control group, significant at .005 and showing a reversal of a clear trend toward regression among the controls.

Conclusions and Implications

1. The importance of reading to children as a precursor to success in learning to read has been shown to be vital in the case of socially disadvantaged children who do not have experiences with books at home.
2. Ego-involvement and comprehension of concepts are important criteria in the selection of stories to read to disadvantaged children. The role of these factors in stimulating motivation to read while at the same time strengthening language power seems to be an indispensable one in the school learning of the slowest non-readers in the early primary grades.
3. Individual differences play a major role in learning style and aptitude at the same age and within the same socio-economic class. The data suggest that among children of the same age and low socio-economic class, language ability exists along a continuum at one end of which is inadequate comprehension of the spoken word and limited concentration in listening. The continuum proceeds through stages of oral usage of differing complexity and ends at ability to handle the symbols of reading and writing at differing levels of facility. While comprehension, oral language, and the use of written symbols may and do occur in the same child at the same time, the levels of competency vary considerably across the age group in an overlapping pattern of increasing skill.
4. Continued exposure in early childhood to stories read aloud apparently affects basic, beginning stages of the transition that must take place in growth from comprehension of oral language to the final use of symbols in reading. The effect seems related to the stage along the continuum at which the child is functioning at the time of exposure.
5. The slower the children are in academic progress, the more difficult it is for them to deal with words in isolation, unrelated to a totally meaningful

experience. Vocabulary thus appears to be learned best by young children in a context of emotional and intellectual meaning.

6. Socially disadvantaged children come to school with a paucity of the kinds of words more likely to be found in books than in daily speech at home. They need continuous clarification of the words they hear in story books, even when these are suited as a whole to their level of maturity.
7. Levels of competency in comprehension, oral language, and reading are interrelated, but facility in the last, *i.e.*, the use of symbols, seems to be dependent on facility in the first two, *i.e.*, oral language and comprehension. This would imply that comprehension of meaning is basic to growth in the language arts.
8. Continued and regular listening to story books chosen for their emotional appeal and ease of conceptualization seems to aid facility in listening, attention span, narrative sense, recall of stretches of verbalization, and the recognition of newly learned words as they appear in other contexts.
9. The relationship believed to exist between oral language and reading has been confirmed. At the same time, it has been shown that primary grade children retarded in reading strengthen their language power when language learning is incidentally associated with experiences of intellectual and emotional meaning for the age and stage of development of the child.

Reading, Imagination, and Television

Dorothy G. Singer

The potential for imaginative play and creativity may exist in all children. Why some people develop these gifts and why others do not intrigues the social scientist. Looking back at the lives and childhood experiences of great artists, writers, poets, and musicians offers us some clues and allows us to search for some common denominators that existed in their early childhoods and nurtured budding talents. Vladimir Nabokov's rich use of language and fantasy episodes, for example, may be traced to childhood experiences where

SOURCE: *School Library Journal*, December, 1979, pp. 31–34.

make-believe games and his exposure to books played important roles. Nabokov learned to read in Enlgish before he could read Russian. His earliest "friends" were "four simple souls in my grammar, Ben, Dan, Sam, and Ned," although the book focused on three-word sentences such as "Who is Ben?" and "Here is Dan." Nabokov's rich imagination endowed these characters with physical attributes and personality traits of the various people who worked on his estate. Nabokov also remembers the pleasant moments with his mother as she read to him in English each evening at bedtime. He recalls how he leafed through picture books before he learned how to read, and most important of all, he remembers the great discovery of some books stored in the attic of his country home. Eight-year-old Nabokov carried them down to his room by the "armloads," and his deep friendship with books was firmly established.

Not only Nabokov, but Tolstoy, Ibsen, Shaw, and Milne remembered the childhood games they played, the importance of books in their lives, and a key person—whether parent, relative or teacher—who prompted and encouraged their imagination and curiosity.

Today, the important member of the family may be the television set rather than the parent. Indeed, television occupies a large part of children's daily lives. Preschoolers spend about three hours per day watching television while elementary-school-aged children spend from four and a half to five hours per day (Lyle and Hoffman, 1972; Singer and Singer, 1979). George Gerbner (1979), Dean of the Annenberg School of Communications at the University of Pennsylvania, found that before a child enters school he or she will have spent more time in front of a TV set than is spent in his or her entire school career.

Television has been accused of interfering with a child's acquisition of language skills and reading, and of impeding his or her imagination. In actuality, there is a paucity of empirical evidence that can substantiate these claims. Although there are numerous articles dealing with television's effect on aggression, only more recently have researchers begun to critically examine the relationship between television, reading, and imagination.

Imagination and Vocabulary

Our work at the Yale Family Television Research and Consultation Center has focused on television and the development of imagination in preschoolers. We find, for example, that children who watch the least amount of television but who engage in make-believe play are the most imaginative children. They are also rated by research observers in the nursery schools as cooperative, persistent, and more joyful than those children who are heavy television viewers. These results have been found with two different samples of children—middle class and lower class. Each sample was studied over one year's time. We have found, too, that children who are light television viewers have more imaginary companions than children who are heavy television viewers.

The data on imaginary companions is quite interesting. For example, we found that television characters played an important role in a child's choice of an imaginary companion. Both boys and girls named their companions after television characters, but while the girls were willing to use male and female characters as "friends," the boys only used male characters.

We have also looked at the language structure of preschoolers in order to determine the relationship between television viewing and the acquisition of language. Milkovich and Miller (1975) found that elementary-school-aged children who were heavy TV viewers had a less-advanced syntactic structure than those children who were light television viewers. We found similar results with the preschoolers we studied. The light viewers in one sample of middle-class children used longer sentences, more adjectives and adverbs, and more future tense verbs than the children who were heavy television viewers. These children used nouns, pronouns, and present tense verbs. They tended to label objects, and use shorter, less complicated sentences. We found that the light television viewers were more imaginative than the heavy television viewers. The children who engaged in make-believe games were actually learning more mastery skills alone than were children who spent considerable time in front of television sets or who played only physical games such as climbing or swinging.

Our study shows (Singer and Singer, 1976) that make-believe play may have many benefits for a child such as developing a capacity for imagery, flexibility, and empathy. Pretend play helps a child to concentrate, to learn sequencing, to delay gratification, to develop a clearer distinction between reality and fantasy. We have found that make-believe play leads to vocabulary growth. Two studies by Corinne Hutt (1979) in England, and one by Sarah Smilansky (1975) in Israel have substantiated this. They have found that through the encouragement of make-believe play by teachers or parents, children made significant vocabulary gains. Just think of all the words a child needs to play a fairy princess—crown, wand, castle, moat, gate, dragon, witch, and more. If the child does not know the word, an adult can supply it. Active use of the words in play reinforces the meaning of the words for the child so that they become part of his or her long-range memory system.

One of our studies (Tower, Singer, Singer and Biggs, 1979) found that children who watched the slow-paced "Mr. Rogers" TV program, compared to those who watched the fast-paced "Sesame Street" program, increased significantly in their imaginative play. These children who were high in imagination also showed significant differences in their speech from those children low in imagination. A good deal of conversation during free play is egocentric, fulfilling the same functions as Vygotsky has termed "inner speech." When a child is thinking, verbalization helps to clarify ideas: the scenario in play becomes more vivid. Children who are watching considerable amounts of television do not have ample time to use language with their parents or peers. Among poor children who are the heaviest television viewers, there may also be a lack of opportunity for rehearsal of expressive language. Parents permit these children to watch a great deal of television and may not be interacting with them. Work by Cook et al. (1975) found that children who were encouraged to watch "Sesame Street," and then talked with their parents about the programs made the greater cognitive gains. He also determined that the gap between advantaged and disadvantaged children actually widened in terms of skill acquisition from this program. Thus, it is important for an adult to act as a mediator between program content and child if *learning* is to take place.

Visual and Verbal Processes

Although television is obviously a visual medium, there are relatively few systematic studies concerned with hemisphere functioning and television viewing. The right side of our brain seems more closely related to reprocessing in imagery of visually related material, while the left side of the brain appears to process verbal-lexical or arithmetic material. Human beings use both verbal and imagery coding systems. If children are to learn more effectively from television, they need the opportunity to rehearse the picture material, whether through their own verbalization of the content, or through parental mediation. This dual processing, visual and verbal, will help children store the material into their coding systems more effectively. Dual processing enables children to develop language and to apply these skills to reading.

Blumenthal (1977) believes that an efficient reader is an active thinker who, when reading, devotes "much greater effort to constructing internal representations on the basis of rapidly scanned cues." The reader is anticipating what comes next and scans the text for inferences to support his or her developing configurations. It makes one wonder if a person watching television forms images of the upcoming scene before it appears. We wonder, too, if persons with imagery skills store the television's picture in their memory systems more readily than those who do not have such well-developed imagery capacities.

Some researchers, Karl Pribram among them, have expressed concern that television viewing is enhancing a strong preference for or reliance upon global visual representations. The fear is that children will become impatient with the efforts needed to process auditory verbal materials such as teachers' directions or explanations. Males appear to be more differentiated in right and left brain functioning (Witelson, 1976), and this may account for the fact that more boys have reading difficulties in school than girls. Boys do watch more television than girls. (Singer, 1979) and are therefore exposed to more visually-oriented material in which the verbal component is presented very rapidly. We do know that imagery skills help a child in conservation tasks (Adams, 1978; Fink, 1976; and Golomb, 1976). For example, if a child can envision that the pennies spread out in one row actually equal the same number of pennies placed together in another row, or the tall glass of water equals the same amount of water in a short, wide glass, he or she has less trouble with transformations of quantity and volume. In light of such results, it may be that the use of imagery training as part of a school curriculum could enhance reading as well. Each time a child reads, he or she must picture the scene in his mind. Certainly as they grow and read more extensively, there are fewer pictures in their books, necessitating more effort on their part to provide the images.

TV Exposure and Reading

Reading requires an active stance on the part of the child. Compared with television, reading poses some challenges, and some decided advantages. When a child reads, he or she is in *control* and can reread a section, pace himself or herself and can stop, at any point, and elaborate the material through his or her auditory or visual imagery. There is time to look up a difficult word and still go back to the text without missing a part of the "action," as compared to television where material is presented so rapidly that if a sentence is missed it cannot be retrieved. And while television offers instant replay for sports alone, reading allows the child the opportunity to reread a treasured passage and return to the printed page of a favorite story again and again, weeks, months, and years later.

We ask then, what are the long-term effects of television viewing on reading acquisition? At the moment, we are following 340 children over a three-year period, attempting to assess their reading readiness, and later their reading levels in relation to the amounts of television viewed since nursery school days. We are now analyzing the data, and it is too soon to know the results. We do have data on older children (Zuckerman, Singer and Singer, 1979) who are not typical of children in the same age group or socioeconomic bracket so far as television viewing *time* is concerned. This sample watched about 15 hours per week, compared to the national norms of 30 to 40 hours per week. Their pattern of program choices, however, is similiar to the nation as a whole when Nielsen tables are examined. We found that those middle-class children who spent more time reading had higher IQ's and more highly educated fathers, and watched fewer fantasy-violent programs. One of our speculations is that fantasy-violent programs provide the same kinds of excitement as fairy tales, adventure books, comics, and other popular children's books, and may, therefore, satisfy similar needs for escapism and fantasy. These results are consistent with recent findings (Murray and Kippax,

1978) which indicated that watching television tended to replace reading comic books.

Research on reading in the 1950s and 1960s (Greenstein, 1954; Ridder, 1963) found no significant relationship between television viewing and grades. These studies, however, did not control for IQ, or socioeconomic status. When these variables are controlled, the relationships between television-viewing and school achievement were no longer significant (Furo, 1971; Thompson, 1964).

More recently Hornik (1978) found that there is a negative relationship between television exposure and the attainment of early reading and general school skills. This study, carried out in El Salvador, compared children whose families did or did not own television sets. It is difficult to generalize Hornik's results with studies made in the United States, since his study centered on the introduction of television into households, not the long-range impact on children. In the United States, it is virtually impossible to find children who have not had some television exposure. As a result, studies trying to explore the relationship between reading and television are confounded by numerous variables. For this reason, we are studying a preschool sample before and during the acquisition of reading.

It seems to me that we have to take a more realistic approach and stop blaming television for all our national ills. Since the visual impact of television is so exciting and attracts children, we must begin to think of ways to combine television interests and reading. Some attempts are already under way—the use of television program scripts in the classroom, guides to *Prime Time School Television* for children in the upper elementary grades, and various instructional programs that use television as auxiliary teachers. Although the instructional programs and guides to television are available, teachers have not taken full advantage of them. Indeed, perhaps parents will have to take a more active role in controlling the television viewing of their children and in directing them to books.

Television can be used to entice children to read if parents become aware of books that are related to television subject matter or if the story itself appears in a visual form. Certainly book sales of *I, Claudius; Roots; Nancy Drew; Little House on the Prairie;* and other television-produced novels increased their sales after the broadcasts. A campaign to "advertise" books will begin this fall on CBS.

It is up to parents to be sure that television is used with discretion and that other modes of information and entertainment—especially books—become a habitual part of a child's life.

Bibliography

Adams, J. S. "Pretense-play: A Study of Its Cognitive Implications." Paper presented at 49th annual meeting of Eastern Psychological Assoc., March 1978, Washington, D.C.

Blumenthal, A. L. *The Process of Cognition*. New Jersey: Prentice-Hall, 1977.

Cook, L. D.; Appleton, H.; Conner, R. F.; Shaffer, A.; Tomkin, G.; and Walker, S. J. *Sesame Street Revisited*. New York: Russell Sage Foundation, 1975.

Fink, R. "The Role of Imaginative Play in Cognitive Development." In *Piagetian Theory and the Helping Professions*. Edited by M. K. Paulsen, J. F. Magary, and G. I. Lubin. Los Angeles: University of Southern California Press, 1976.

Furo, L. *The Function of Television for Children and Adolescents*. Tokyo: Sophia University Press, 1971.

Gerbner, G. Personal communication, July 1979.

Golomb, C. "Pretense Play: A Cognitive Prospective." In *Symbolization and the Young Child*. Boston: Wheelock College, 1976.

Greenstein, J. "Effects of Television Upon Elementary School Grades." *Journal of Educational Research* 48 (1954): 161–76.

Hornik, R. "Television Access and the Slowing of Cognitive Growth." *American Educational Research Journal* 15(1978):1–15.

Hutt, C. "Towards a Taxonomy of Play." In *Play and Learning*. Edited by B. Sutton-Smith. New York: Gardner Press, 1979.

Hutt, C. "Play in the Under-Fives: Form, Development and Function." In *Modern Perspectives in the Psychiatry of Infancy*. Edited by J. G. Howells. New York: Bruner/Mazel, 1979.

Lyle, J., and Hoffman, H. R. "Children's Use of Television and Other Media." In *Television and Social Behavior,* edited by E. A. Rubinstein, G. A. Comstock, and J. P. Murray (Vol. 4, "Television in Day-to-Day Life: Patterns of Use"). Washington, D.C.: U.S. Government Printing Office, 1972.

Milkovich, M., and Miller, M. "Exploring the Relationship Between Television Viewing and Language Development." Report #3, *TV Advertising and Children Project,* College of Communications Arts, Michigan State University, 1975.

Murray, J P., and Kippax, S. "Children's Social Behavior in Three Towns with Differing Television Experience." *Journal of Communication* 28(1978):19–29.

Riddler, J. "Public Opinion and the Relationship of TV Viewing to Academic Achievement." *Journal of Educational Research* 57(1963):204–207.

Singer, J. L., and Singer, D. G. "Imaginative Play in Early Childhood: Some Experimental Approaches." In *Child Personality and Psychopathology*. Edited by A. Davids. New York: Wiley, 1976.

Singer, J. L., and Singer, D. G. "Television-Viewing and Imaginative Play in Preschoolers: A Developmental and Parent-Intervention Study." National Science Foundation and Spencer Foundation, New Haven, June 1979.

Smilansky, S. *The Effects of Sociodramatic Play on Disadvantaged Preschool Children,* New York: Wiley, 1968.

Thompson, C. "Children's Acceptance of Television Advertising and the Relation of Televiewing to School Achievement." *Journal of Educational Research* 58(1964):171–75.

Tower, R.; Singer, D. G.; Singer, J. L.; and Biggs, A. "Differential Effects of Television Programming on Preschoolers' Cognition, Imagination, and Social Play." *American Journal of Orthopsychiatry* 49(1979):265–81.

Witelson, S. F. "Sex and the Single Hemisphere: Specialization of the Right Hemisphere for Spatial Processing." *Science* 193(1976):425–27.

Zuckerman, D. M.; Singer, D. G.; and Singer, J. L. "Television Viewing and Children's Reading and Related Classroom Behavior." *Journal of Communication,* in press.

Encouraging Children's Creative Oral Responses through Nonnarrative Films

Jill P. May

Only a few years ago no one seriously considered the study of film a relevant part of the college, high school or elementary school literature program. Although adult critics were well aware that film had some real social implications and possible learning uses, it was not considered artistically equal to written literature. Within the past twenty years, this assumption has been increasingly challenged until film as a literary medium began to be vocally supported and established in the college English curriculum. U.S. English literature students were encouraged to consider film as an artistic endeavor dependent upon stylistic devices. Film as a literary pursuit was added to more and more college English programs. College graduates of such programs have begun introducing solid courses designed to study film as an art form at the high school level. Books such as *Film Study in the High School* (Culkin 1965) have been published and read. Articles which concentrate on film usage in the classroom have been published in professional education journals and have been widely accepted. Thus, adult film as a literary medium changed from the stepchild of print to become a legitimate scholarly subject for English classes. Children's film, however, is still largely ignored as a worthwhile literary medium.

In 1969 UNICEF's children's literature expert Anne Pellowski wrote:

> The distribution and use of children's films in this country are heavily influenced by the same professional groups and individuals who influence children's books, to a far greater degree than adult or general films are affected by those groups and individuals involved with adult or general books. . . . One gets the distinct impression that children are taken or sent to see films in theaters only when such lavish productions as *Mary Poppins* come along, or when the cause of some "good" children's film is promoted, as the case of *Run Wild, Run Free* and *My Side of the Mountain.* Children may or may not enjoy these films but they will certainly get a very one-sided view of what film experience can be . . .
>
> This makes it all the more important that the educational films shown in schools be of the best quality and wide variety. (p. 6)

SOURCE: *Language Arts* 56 (March, 1979): 244–250.

Many educators in the field of children's literature will not consider film as an acceptable literary genre. Some will accept book-purist productions such as those created by Weston Woods. While these productions have merits and are excellent visual adaptations of a story, they are seldom considered in terms of the artistic devices used in good filming. Instead the adult critics are usually evaluating the film in terms of the book's theme, plot, writing style, characterization and setting. The element rated highest by them is authenticity.

Audio visual productions have had a great impact on the young people of today. During their formative years, most children will watch television more hours than they spend in the elementary school classroom. Many will have less interest in pleasure reading than in watching poorly produced entertainment shows. Their minds, dulled by programs that do not build their knowledge by directly involving them through questioning or problem solving techniques, grow up lacking the intellectual framework which allows them to critically judge the values of popular visual entertainment. They seek and rely upon the instant analysis found within a newspaper column, a magazine article, or even a television spot. Thus, they become a captive audience for programs and for commercial films long before the productions are ready to be viewed. Their creative imaginations are stifled by pat programming.

If students are introduced to good educational programs which do demand input and thought, they will become more aware of film's techniques, values and limitations. Hopefully, the end result will be that future adults will see the unique possibilities of both print and visual presentations, and will become discriminating viewers who would rather turn off a mediocre television show and read a good book.

It is important to begin a program of film appreciation within the elementary schools. These are the years when youngsters are forming their reading and viewing habits. Language arts teachers have long been interested in developing an appreciation, and understanding of the written word, and are already aware of the need to nurture good reading habits. An awareness of film could create for the student an educated response to visual stories and could help develop a young cadre of objective media users. Like good literature programs, film could be used in several areas within the elementary curriculum. Thus, film would become less a discipline and more an art worth sharing, analyzing, and criticizing. An introduction to one film genre, the nonnarrated short, could broaden the critical skills of youngsters in both the areas of film criticism and of creative writing. In each case, the film's story, theme, and setting must be interpreted by the viewer.

Before the primary child can read there is a need to encourage oral expression and creativity. An appreciation of plot structure and of creative writing can be developed by using *Tchou Tchou* (Encyclopaedia Britannica)[1] and *Balthazar the Lion* (Wombat Productions, Inc.). A National Film Board

[1]The films mentioned may be requested for preview by the distributing company listed in parenthesis. Addresses of the companies appear at the close of this article.

of Canada production, *Tchou Tchou* is a brilliantly executed animated film that uses red, blue and yellow building blocks to create a fantasy story of two children—a girl and a boy—who tame a dragon by changing him into a train. Everything in this visual story—the boy, the girl, a splendid beetle, etc.—moves jauntily along to the musical beat of a carefully edited audio presentation. The movement is quick and has eye appeal. The plot and characters seem realistic to a young audience because of the skillful creation of detailed movement. The boy's legs move as he walks even though they are painted onto the blocks. The girl's eyes open and shut. Some sound effects are used, but there are no spoken lines in the entire production. This film's uses are unlimited. Students who can write could easily produce their own narration to go along with the story. Younger children could orally express their reactions to the main characters and could discuss the difference between imagined and real adventures. Blocks could be used to create imaginary creatures of their own. Finally, the film could be used to start a discussion on plot structure in a story, and on the difference between visual and written stories. *Balthazar the Lion* also uses commonplace objects in an animated film. This is the story of an overly hungry lion who eats the moon and finally learns his lesson. Because this film uses simple background music, children could be encouraged to use it as a model to create their own audio presentation to go with another story that has been a class favorite. The film could also be tied into the picture book *Mother, Mother I Feel Sick* (Charlip and Supree 1966), discussing with the children the possibility of removing swallowed objects through surgery.

New environments can be introduced, using nonnarrated films as the springboard for field trips or classroom visits by community workers. Two films which create distinct, positive images of two different locales are *Chick Chick Chick* (Churchill Films) and *Night People's Day* (Film Fair). *Chick Chick Chick* uses thirteen minutes of excellent close-up photography combined with a well produced audio that intertwines the sounds of the barnyard with a musical soundtrack to create the story of the birth of one baby chick and the adventures of another when it loses its mother. The presentation is fun and lighthearted; yet, it is also a realistic representation of barnyard inhabitants from the eye level of a small chick. Children unfamiliar with farm life would delight in the presentation. Farm children could be encouraged to engage in role playing and to consider what it would be like to be the barnyard pigs, cat or cows. *Night People's Day* has won many awards, including a CINE Golden Eagle and a Silver Medal at the Atlantic International Film Festival. Produced in 1971 by Bob Kurtz, the film is at once realistic and whimsical. The visuals show all kinds of real activity found in the "sleeping" city (street cleaners and bakers, post office workers, etc.) but the sound effects are created by people. Some of the people discuss their feelings toward night work, but the implications of night life in a big city are only visually explored. Thus, the young person is shown the workings of a city and is left to interpret the importance of this late night activity.

Nonnarrated film often allows the viewer to discover the film's theme without providing its message through one brief verbal encounter or statement. Like many good fiction books, the theme in this film genre is implied through the actions of the main characters, but the impact of the film is dependent upon the viewer. Young children who see either the film series by Short Film Prague concerning a little girl named Dorothy and her parrot (Phoenix Films, Inc.) or the series concerning the mole and his woodland friends produced by Czech animator Zdenek Miler (McGraw-Hill Films) will not only be exposed to good foreign animation, but will also be able to watch main characters who have an international appeal because of universal social norms. In both series the main characters learn basic behavior lessons. Dorothy is an upbeat young girl; her outgoing personality and quick temper create problems for her, but her overall positive attitude makes her an endearing young heroine. The entire series concentrates on good manners and on good health habits. Surprisingly, the social growth stressed in this heroine is typical of U.S. standards. The mole is a plucky main character whose antics will cause children to laugh. Throughout the series it is the mole's playful, kind hearted nature that brings both his problems and his solutions. Mole's curiosity embarks him on several lighthearted escapades, all of which come to a satisfactory conclusion. In each of the four films in this series, the mole learns something useful about his environment. Both series feature excellent animation and audio soundtracks. Even more important, the characters react realistically to events and grow through their experiences. The young person is indirectly introduced to an important theme concerning social behavior and/or kindness. Teachers working in the lower elementary grades could use the films to begin a discussion on social decorum or on the universal appeal of good stories which have an important message.

In her discussion of film Pellowski stated:

> It does not even disturb me that films based on books and books based on films rarely live up to the original. When a child flatly concedes that "it wasn't as good as the book" he is subconsciously recognizing that the author and film maker tried for the same effect, but the artistic vision of the original was more intense. . . . To me, this chance to see or read two versions gives validity to such efforts, even when they fail. (1969, p. 7)

The concept that two representations of the same plot (and in many cases the same theme) can be valuable as unique contributions and should each be studied for their individual values can be presented to young children in many ways. By sharing with children the same story in a nonverbal visual production and a written format, the teacher can begin to explore with youngsters the idea that literary preference depends upon the audience's own tastes. Two films which could be used with primary-aged students are *Whazzat?* (Encyclopaedia Britannica) and *Tom Cat's Meow* (Phoenix Films, Inc.). *Whazzat?* is a modern interpretation of the east Indian tale, *The Blind Men and the Elephant* (Quigley 1959). Using animated clay sculpture, the film is a lively, enjoyable production concerning the discovery of something new, and the need to combine the parts to understand the whole element. This colorful film presents the same plot and theme found in Quigley's book. Short Film Prague's presentation *Tom Cat's Meow* is an unnarrated film whose plot is similar to several well known oral folktales, including *Toads and Diamonds* and *Puss and Boots*. But, in this case, it is not identifiable as any one tale. Young children will enjoy the gay animation and sympathetic character portrayal. They could also be encouraged to discuss the similarities between this and the oral presentations, if oral literature is used with the film, and to determine the rationale for their literary preferences.

The many benefits of using nonnarrated film continue in the upper elementary grades and throughout middle school. Some materials, such as *Arabesque* (Pyramid Films) and *Fire!* (Encyclopaedia Britannica) have definite subject uses, and can thus be included within the normal curriculum structure. *Arabesque* is an enjoyable visual assault of computer art that is immediately spellbinding. A nonnarrated film with no real theme (other than that computers can be artistic), the presentation will capture the imagination of children with its constant flow of shapes and use of Arab music. In addition to using this film as a quick introduction to math concepts, *Arabesque* could be used as an introduction to art design, and to the elements of line and shape in artistic endeavors. *Fire!* is a film Polski animated short that is a fine example of filming techniques which rely upon visual impact supplemented by a nonverbal audio presentation. Developed around the scene of a forest blaze, *Fire!* vividly demonstrates how animals suffer and forests are ruined when flames eat up a countryside. The film uses oil paintings to show the sensations a forest community faces, and would be an excellent production to use when discussing how an effective representation of emotional trauma can influence the reading or viewing audience. Youngsters could also be encouraged to discuss the artistic techniques used to display realistic emotions in both verbal and nonverbal communication.

Other equally fine productions portray a vauable positive image of the environment. *Thoroughbred* (Pyramid), *A Mountain Day* (Arthur Barr Productions, Inc.) and *Solo* (Pyramid) all poetically depict man's recreational use of nature. *Thoroughbred* deals with the racing horse. Using a combination of casual banjo strumming, joyous humming by a male singer, and classical music, the audience is shown a race horse's life from birth to the track. The film creates a feeling of kinship between the horse and the viewer. In the end, the audience is left to decide for itself whether this is the story of a champion, since the action concentrates on the development of a fine colt into a well trained, high spirited horse. The use of closeup photography, panning, and fade-out techniques create an illusion of time lapse. Students watching the production could discuss horses, racing styles, and the training of any athlete, animal or human. They could also be encouraged to criticize the filming techniques used. Winner of the CINE Golden Eagle, *A Mountain Day* visually demonstrates the beauty of mountain foliage and flowers through the use of closeups, double exposure, and slow motion shots. Once again horses are used to express both freedom and restraint as the camera follows three young people riding horseback and portrays their daydreams. A tribute to nature, this production is worth sharing with young people when discussing mountainous regions, ecology, or outdoor activities. It could also be used to begin a study on the difference between the real and the imagined world, or the use of filming techniques to evoke a mood by producers. *Solo* is one of the finest productions available concerning nature and man's desire to conquer his surroundings. Although the actual nonverbal story was shot on several climbing expeditions, careful editing has created a solid, easily followed, highly believable picture of one young man's painstaking climb to the peaks of a tall mountain and exhilarating descent to the valley below. This film won several awards. It has many possibilities for classroom use. The main character shows courage and determination throughout the film. He also aptly demonstrates his self-reliance in his knowledge of a lonely sport. The film's theme of respect for nature is strongly exemplified when the climber finds a frog in the rock crevice, pockets it, and carefully returns it to the valley's stream at the film's end. Since the film has the same elements found in good fictional stories, the plot and theme might be compared to James Ramsey Ullman's fiction book *Banner in the Sky* (1954). Further, the difference in character growth between the book hero and film hero could be explored.

Other fiction genres can be introduced through film. For instance, by using the humorous films *DeFacto* (Encyclopaedia Britannica) and *Self Service* (Connecticut Films) satire can be presented. Produced by Filmbulgaria, *DeFacto* is a humorous film with an ironic ending. In the beginning scenes of this animated short, a building is built and dedicated. But as the celebration music is played, the building crumbles. The film then depicts each man responsible for some part of the building's creation—the architect, the bricklayer, the carpenter, the painter—proving himself innocent to the crowd. When someone finally suggests the musicians are the guilty ones, the crowd goes wild. As their drums are being broken, the crowd wildly cheers, and the remaining building also falls down. The film has many discussion possibilities, including mob reaction to events, proving oneself innocent, and foreign animation. *Self Service* is a lively animated production that subtly exposes society's progressive economic movements. The main characters are a group of mosquitoes who have a "healthy" capitalistic attitude toward man's potential as a natural resource. In this nonnarrated film the mosquito portrays the hypocritical and opportunistic attitudes of man.

There are artistic nonnarrated films that inspire the viewer with their beauty. Several of the finest are foreign. Two examples are *Flower Storm* (ACI Media) and *Wise Masters of Wind and Water* (Perspective Films). In *Flower Storm,* the music, creative visuals and theme have been successfully combined to relate the story of two neighboring kingdoms and their wars over trivial kingly squabbles. Because it is the children in the film who end the first war when they replace the cannon balls with flower and bird balls, the story is an appealing visual fairy tale to use with all ages. The vivid colors used in the illustrations are eyecatching; the drama is maintained by the musical score. The film's subject uses are unlimited, as are its artistic values. *Wise Masters of Wind and Water* is an award-winning Hungarian film which uses film shots of man's use of water and wind power to help him in his work. Shot in several rural areas, the film vividly captures Hungarian people and their working conditions. Although the film has several subject uses, its greatest asset is its use of good film photography and editing.

Humor, satire, drama, beauty are all waiting for youthful audiences in short nonnarrated films. The successful teacher will see the film and determine its classroom use according to a specific group of students. Each film will offer not only a good chance to integrate media into subject areas, but also to introduce different production techniques to youngsters. Once taught to critique films, they should be encouraged to apply the same principles to other visual productions. Furthermore, young students can develop good visual taste, and will become more aware of the disadvantages in poor programming if film is discussed in the elementary classroom. Like all art, film as a creative form deserves to be studied.

Film Distributors

ACI Media, Inc.
35 West 45th Street
New York, NY 10036

Arthur Barr Productions, Inc.
3490 E. Foothill Blvd.
P.O. Box 5667
Pasadena, CA 91107

Churchill Films
622 N. Robertson Blvd.
Los Angeles, CA 90069

Encyclopaedia Britannica
425 N. Michigan Avenue
Chicago, IL 60611

Film Fair Communications
10900 Ventura Blvd.
Studio City, CA 92675

McGraw-Hill Films
1221 Avenue of the Americas
New York, NY 10020

Perspective Films
369 W. Erie Street
Chicago, IL 60610

Phoenix Films, Inc.
470 Park Ave. S.
New York, NY 10016

Pyramid Films
Box 1048
Santa Monica, CA 90406

Wombat Productions, Inc.
77 Tarrytown Road
White Plains, NY 10607

References

Charlip, Remy and Supree, Burton. *Mother, Mother I Feel Sick, Send for the Doctor Quick Quick Quick*. New York: Parents, 1966.

Culkin, Rev. John. *Film Study in the High School*. New York: Fordham University, 1965.

Pellowski, Ann "Children's Cinema: International Dilemma or Delight." *Film Library Quarterly* (Fall 1969): 5–11.

Quigley, Lillian. *The Blind Men and the Elephant: An Old Tale from the Land of India*. New York: Scribner's, 1959.

Ullman, James Ramsey. *Banner in the Sky*. Philadelphia: Lippincott, 1954.

The Picture Book Projected

Morton Schindel

Though I work largely in the audiovisual field, I have long been convinced that no medium speaks more directly and intimately to a child than a book. My conviction dates back to the years when I read to my own children. At first, my own imagination, like that of most adults, had long since atrophied, and my reading was a fairly mechanical process of sounding the words and glancing at the illustrations.

But my children, like children everywhere, literally felt what the author was saying. For them the characters jumped live off the pages; there was no doubt in their minds that here's where the action was. Their eyes were glued to each picture as they listened. "Tell it right, Daddy," I'd be admonished if I changed a word or missed a sentence in a book they knew. Cathy, then a preschooler, invariably made me wait as she counted the eight eggs that Mrs. Mallard sat on in *Make Way for Ducklings*, just to be sure, each time we read the book, that all the eggs were still there. The Halloween after we read *Jenny's Birthday Book*, my Jeanie chose to dress up as a shy little black cat.

Gradually, I, too, was stirred by my own children's pleasure, and through books we came to know more of one another. Expressing the thoughts and feelings of authors and illustrators helped us say things to each other that we never could have articulated on our own.

I was amazed, too, at the children's involvement as they handled the books, turned the pages, and pored endlessly over their favorite parts. In choosing stories I was always responsive to their requests, for they knew, inevitably, which books they wanted read night after night, and which they had had enough of the first time around.

From our reading together, I slowly became aware of the structure that underlies many story books and helps to sustain their interest. Many develop like a three-act play: they build up, taper off, and then repeat this ever heightening pattern to a climax. (*The Little Red Lighthouse*, *The Story About*

SOURCE: *School Library Journal*, February 15, 1968, pp. 836–837.

Ping, and *Little Toot* came easily to mind.) Though written as prose, the words of many picture books read like poetry which one effortlessly commits to memory after only a hearing or two. There is a fascination for children in the sound and flow of words, the cadences of books like *Time of Wonder or Millions of Cats*, the alliteration of names like Mike Mulligan and Norman the Doorman.

As I look back, I realize that while reading to my children I was discovering something that youngsters seem to know intuitively: the special qualities that make books a unique medium of communication—especially picture books.

The book is an intimate, direct conversation between an author and the person who reads or hears his words. It never hurries anyone. It makes no demands until it is picked up and read. You can choose to browse through the front, the back or the middle. And when it is well designed, the book is a pleasure to touch and invites handling.

Above all, the book is intended for an audience in close proximity, and for a situation in which time is not a factor. Often the picture book is for a single pair of eyes, or a reader closely half-circled by at most six or eight children.

But precisely because of its format and intimacy, the book's "message" is for only a few at one time. I became acutely aware of this some years ago when attending a public library story hour. About 30 youngsters were assembled on a carpet in front of the librarian, who was telling *The Tale of Peter Rabbit*. She obviously enjoyed the story and told it well, but like most teacher and librarians who are not storytelling specialists, she would first read a page of text, then hold the book toward the children so that they could see the picture. The children became restless, first as they were deprived of the sight of the picture while the librarian read, then as the flow of words stopped while she held the book high so that those in the back row could see.

As we talked later, the librarian seemed almost apologetic about the success of her story hours. "A year ago, only 10 or 12 showed up regularly," she explained. "Now the community has grown so that there are usually 30 or more." But she was obviously finding it hard to keep the attention of a much larger group.

Her experience is not unique. Yet many teachers and librarians, faced with this dilemma, blame themselves and feel that they, personally, have limitations as storytellers. They are not at fault—except perhaps in the failure to recognize the limitations of the picture book.

For the book is not a "group" or "distance" medium. Its words were never intended to be orated to a vast audience, and its illustrations were created for children to examine at leisure, down to the minutest detail. Even if a storyteller knows the book by heart and can show the pictures without first having to unwrap himself and turn the book around, only a few children in a larger group will see well enough to really appreciate a picture.

Iconographic Filming

It was when some perceptive librarians pointed this out to me that I began to produce sound films. Wanting them to be as faithful to the book as possible, I developed what is known as the *iconographic technique*. Unlike animation, where hundreds of pictures are drawn to impart motion to an illustration, it is only the camera that moves in iconographic photography. Hovering over the enlarged projection of the page much as the child would examine it, concentrating always on the picture as it was originally drawn, the camera probes for the essence of each idea that went into the total composition of each picture. By varying light intensity and perspective, by emphasizing one detail and then another, by moving in a deliberate direction at a controlled speed, the camera is made to release the mood and action that the illustrator captured in the pages of his book.

When the pictures are completed, a recorded sound track comprised of the telling of the story, an original musical score, and sound effects is placed in careful juxtaposition to the pictures. In making the recording to accompany the filmed illustrations, I tried to emulate the approaches and impact of superior storytellers I had heard while learning my craft. But I soon discovered that a richer concentration of elements was required to compensate for the fact that the sounds *my* audience heard would emanate from an impersonal loudspeaker, rather than the lips of a live human being.

In recording a story, the director must explore the text for the nuances of mood and action that the author so carefully framed his words to express. Once these are understood, pace, intonation, and characterization flow almost intuitively as new techniques, superimposed on the storytellers' performance, revitalize the words. To evoke the emotional harmony of an intimate story-hour experience, we introduce background music and subtle, muted sound effects to heighten the mood and action. At each step, care is taken not to intrude upon, but only give expression to, the communication in the book.

A Static But Flexible Medium

These films opened books up to many parents who had never seen them before, to professionals in workshops or classes, and to television audiences. Teachers and librarians were intrigued by the way the enlarged, projected illustrations could involve large groups of children. But many, being skilled storytellers themselves, rightfully wanted to remain part of the act, not just part of the audience. They began to ask me about the feasibility of turning off the sound track and telling the story live while the pictures were being projected. Some of them had tried it but were frustrated by the inexorable pace of the film. A medium had to be improvised to put the storyteller in control of the medium, rather than the other way around! Ten years later it has become obvious that filmstrips were the solution. But the concept of the "filmstrip" had first to be broadened. For in those days the pictures in a filmstrip were always horizontal on the screen, while the text was almost a condensed caption, superimposed in two or three lines below each frame.

The format created special problems for anyone who wanted to transpose a literary work to the screen with fidelity. The vertical illustrations in a book like *Andy and the Lion,* for example, could not, I felt, be distorted to accommodate themselves to the horizontal proportions of the screen, and paring the text to fit the medium was unthinkable for me. Hence the innovation which today is commonplace to most librarians, and accepted for a "filmstrip": pictures photographed on the frames just as they appear in the book, but with the text now deleted; and the complete text printed in a separate booklet, which is keyed to the filmstrip by a tiny reproduction of the picture alongside the words which it accompanies. In this way, the right words are always with the right picture, with almost no possibility of confusion. Although the screen projection is much larger, this type of filmstrip is still a direct reproduction of the pictures in a book, so that filmstrips come closer to retaining the author's intent than any medium except the book itself. They can be stopped or started at will, and frames, like pages, can be skipped or turned forward and backward. In a darkened room the filmstrip rivets the child's attention even more than the pages of a book, and it has the advantage of reaching far more children listening to a story than could comfortably be assembled around the book itself. Of course, communication through a filmstrip does lose some of the close feeling that comes only from direct contact with the book or its reader. But the enlarged pictures, in turn, take on even more life than their originals.

Breaking the Sound Barrier

So part of the gap was bridged: larger groups could get into the pictures. But those who were farthest away from the storyteller still couldn't always *hear;* even if they could, the attempt to project the mood of a story to children way back in the classroom or library distorted the normally intimate storytelling situation.

Now the question came: "Can't you provide us with the sound tracks from the *film*? We could use them in conjunction with the filmstrips in our classrooms and libraries." So we took the recordings already made and reproduced them as phonograph records, two stories on a side of a 12-inch LP, simply because that was the number that fit the best. At first, people ordered these records to accompany the filmstrips they had already acquired or for listening libraries. In time, the natural affinity of the recorded sound to the filmstrip and its text booklet became apparent as the number of requests mounted for these elements in combination. It was from this phenomenon that sound filmstrip sets derived, not needed, perhaps, by the expert storyteller, but useful for many teachers and librarians, and for children, whether they could read or not, to use alone in the library. The multimedia cycle was complete.

None of these media duplicate the child's private pleasure in holding his own book, yet they can also transmit with integrity and fidelity what the author and illustrator have to say. The medium you choose—reading a book, showing a film or filmstrip, having children listen to records or tape, or combining the various media—should depend on the number of children you are trying to reach at any one time, the surroundings they will be in, and the talent, materials, and equipment available to you.

Each of these techniques has its own traditions, peculiarities, advantages—and disadvantages. Each must be considered with an eye to the circumstances under which it will be used. The choice is easy when you understand the factors involved and the unique qualities of each resource you can use. Through electronic and mechanical means, given materials artfully prepared, you have at our disposal many ways to share with the rising tide of eager children more of the thoughts and feelings that you, yourself, have discovered between the covers of good books.

Walt Disney's Interpretation of Children's Literature

Jill P. May

Walt Disney's great entertainment films based upon children's literature have gained him more recognition than any of his other endeavors. His use of substantial literary classics has been praised by some, loathed by others, but remembered by all. The films which first made him a household name—*Snow White, Cinderella, Pinocchio,* and *Bambi*—are the very films most sharply criticized by scholars in children's literature. All four, typical Disney productions, are animated feature films first designed to entertain an American audience which would include children and adults. None was designed to reflect the literary elements of theme, characterization, and writing style found in the original books. What Walt Disney wanted when he bought the rights to a children's classic was the basic setting and plot.

Disney's position in the field of the entertainment film based upon children's literature is unique in many ways. He produced the most film adaptations of children's classics. Since all of these feature-length films were first designed to be shown in movie theaters and were not planned around educational or literary objectives, they represented a calculated look at children's stories. Disney sought the memorable drama, the action and the villainy long remembered by the reader after finishing the original of a well known book. He planned his film versions around satisfying emotional experiences that would remain with the viewer. Disney never produced films that demanded much intellectually of the audience. Seldom did he reflect the book's theme or original characters with accuracy. And while his settings depended upon the author, the scene rarely maintained its original cultural and geographic heritage. It was this manipulation of children's stories that has continuously raised the ire of professionals in the field of children's literature. Perhaps the best protest within the ranks of children's librarians and educators is that of former librarian and teacher Frances Clarke Sayers, who said:

> I find almost everything objectionable. . . . There is a curious distortion . . . in Disney's folklore. He does strange things. He sweetens a folk tale. Everything becomes very lovable. In Cinderella for example, the birds are too sweet, and a great deal of attention is paid to the relationship of Cinderella to

SOURCE: *Language Arts* 58 (April 1981): 463–472.

> the birds and the mice. You realize this technique gives animation a chance to operate, but it destroys the proportion and purpose of the story, the conflict and its resolution. Folk tales are so marvelous in structure and symbolism that this distortion of the elements is particularly bad. (1965, p. 603)

Disney never formally responded to criticism leveled from the ranks of educators and librarians. Perhaps this is because he knew he had captured the hearts of his intended audience and he didn't intend to become involved in an intellectual argument that might point out some of the weaknesses of his productions. Since most of the sharp criticism was published in professional journals there is a possibility that he never read it. In any event, the criticism never reached the ears of his intended audience, middle Americans who reveled in these new feature-length "family films" based upon a well known title in children's literature which they probably had never read. That audience's continued support of Disney has never diminished.

In 1977 eighty-one Purdue University junior and senior elementary education students were polled concerning their favorite film experience within the category of "family fare." All were told they could name any type of film, whether it be educational, animated, or musical. Forty-eight named a Disney full-length film as their favorite, twenty students said they had no favorite movie suitable for children, and the remaining thirteen voted for either an adult musical or a live-action adaptation of a children's book. Thirty-two of the forty-eight students who voted for Disney voted for an animated feature based on children's literature; three voted for any production by Disney. The survey was repeated the next semester, and the results were similar. Students voted for a Disney film four to one,and preferred animated films three to one.

Disney advocates come from both sexes. Young men often confess that as children they went to and enjoyed his animated fantasies. Most admit that they want their children exposed to Disney renditions of the classics. Young women can recall scenes of terror and scenes of romance from the early animation. When asked, they can describe each heroine in minute detail. Yet, they rarely remember the conversations of these characters. All the lovely young Disney ladies floated by in a series of electric adventures. Many young people of both sexes say that they still enjoy watching a full-length film by Disney more than reading the story in book form.

One of Disney's greatest achievements in the realm of film was to replace the reader's desire to pursue a book's theme through the viewing pleasure of light-hearted American entertainment. Instead of recreating the book, he created an entirely different medium and used a familiar title to give a comfortable feeling of recognition to the audience. When criticizing this Disney trait Sayers said:

> Disney takes a great masterpiece and telescopes it. He reduces it to ridiculous lengths, and in order to do this he has to make everything very obvious. It all happens very quickly and is expressed in very ordinary language. There is nothing to make the child think or feel or imagine. (1965, p. 604)

Perhaps to adult critics versed in children's literature Disney lacked scholarship. But to the average American youngster his films reflected real entertainment and the stuff that dreams are made of. It is doubtful that Walt Disney sought more. Hollister wrote about Disney:

> The Disney library contains all the durable children's stories ever told. It also contains five hundred joke books and bound files of the notable humorous publications. It contains a battery of steel filing cabinets which hold a million and a half typed and classified jokes, each legally ascribed to the source from which it was set down. There are 124 classifications of such jokes, and each has from five to twenty sub-classifications . . . Along one wall is a steel file of sixteen solid cabinets of cartoon jokes. (1940, p. 697)

Disney looked for a laugh and wrote into classical literature humorous characters designed to steal the hearts of their audiences with their human foibles (though they were usually depicted as personified animals) and their slapstick humor. Disney changed literature from the classical to the mainstream folk. He could not maintain the tempo of highbrow literature in animation and so he envisioned a grass roots story based upon classical elements. Disney's studio library reflected his own taste. Nowhere in the critical writings concerning his productions, both pro and con, is he discussed as an intellectual person whose reading stimulated his films. He abandoned formal schooling before completing high school and, although he received numerous honorary degrees for his achievements, he never sought a degree from a university. It is questionable that such a degree would have been within the arts had he sought one. His interest was not in scholarship but in the entertainment and the attitudes of the typical American.

It is interesting that Disney seldom used U.S. books as background for his feature-length films. Later productions, including *Robin Hood, Mary Poppins,* and *Winnie-the-Pooh,* are based upon European classical literature. All the animated films most remembered by college students were based upon European literature. Yet Disney's versions were strangely Americanized and his packaging was very American.

Disney used total merchandising techniques for the family fare. He created a film production which led the reader not to the classic, but to the Disney adaptation. Children introduced to Disney's films felt most comfortable with the Disney books. When commenting upon Disney's ability to create a new story only identified in the Disney version, *Newsweek* once wrote:

> Walt Disney's career may be founded on elfin fantasy and hybrid corn, but it thrives on the hardest sell in Hollywood: The "total merchandising" concept. "Once a decision is made to make a picture, the marketing starts," says soft-spoken Roy Disney, Walt's brother and financial mentor. "All the moves are geared to publicizing the final product, and making money while you do it." (1962, p. 50)

Usually the sheet music, records, children's toys and Disney book versions of any classic were available before the film was released. Disney was thus assured that the audience would be familiar with the main characters long before the film could be shown. Children raised on Disney merchandise were ready for the film, a film which would become an American classic.

In a critical article concerning Disney, Sneed wrote:

> It would be going fanatically far to blame Disney and his hulking studio for everything soft and sleazy in our culture. Yet one can trace his influence back and forth through movies, comic strips, even decor. . . . [F]or a long time, the Disney-like inanities ruled the roost and dictated what cartoons were supposed to be like—brainless and smooth and manic. (1967, pp. 26–27)

Disney's popularity does not rest with his literary knowledge. He was not impressed with a book's intricate development of a universal theme. He was simply concerned with finding a good story that could be simplified and Americanized for his audience. In fact, Disney never sought to promote literature in the book format. He was intent upon selling American audiences a new kind of entertainment medium: the feature-length film which reflected middle American values. In order to obtain his goal he used European stories (thereby indirectly suggesting that American social values and prejudices were universal), but he changed the story to contain a simple, rosy plot that depended upon fast action, music, and emotional reactions. In his versions, the conflict would be simplified into no more than five pages of dialogue, original upbeat songs, and the cute antics of minor characters. Thus, he could create a highly successful animated film that would appeal to the masses without directly offending the minorities which he depicted in stereotyped caricatures.

As a film producer Walt Disney was a genius. He was one of the first to make a sound film (*Steamboat Willey,* 1928), the fist to create a full-length animated film (*Snow White,* 1937), and the first to use stereophonic sound (*Fantasia,* 1939). But his ethnic understanding and literary values were strongly lacking. He used black voices for monkeys and apes *(The Jungle Book),* depicted Italians as aggressive, mindless people who spoke in broken English and were strongly influenced by their emotions *(The Lady and the Tramp* and *Pinocchio),* and implied that higher education was inhabited by an intellectually inferior group of people who could not handle their day-to-day existence *(The Absent-Minded Professor).* In his book, *The Disney Version,* Schickel commented:

> Perhaps if he had had a little less technological imagination—and a great deal less business acumen—to distract him, he might have found a way to be faithful not to the letter of his material, but be faithful instead to its true spirit, its animating spirit. Unfortunately, he lacked the tools, intellectual and artistic, he needed for this task. He could make something his own, all right, but that process nearly always robbed the work at hand of its soul if you will. In its place he put jokes and songs and fright effects, but he always seemed to diminish what he touched. He always came as a conqueror . . . hoping to do good but equipped only with know-how instead of sympathy and respect for alien traditions. (1968, p. 227)

Disney used children's literature as a means to subtly support his own image of middle America's strengths and of U.S. societal weaknesses. He made stories that reflected his own ideology, an ideology that was based upon innate prejudices and practical experiences. Born into a lower middle class family, Walt learned the importance of hard work at an early age, but he was never truly introduced to the merits of good literature. He understood the midwestern use of an indirect social slur, of the ethnic joke, but he was never schooled in the need for diversity within society. Disney believed in and supported the concept of the white Anglo-Saxon Protestant American society that thrived because of its work ethic and its honest principles. His productions reinforced mainstream values. His skillful use of humor and music made his films lighthearted and therefore acceptable to minorities. His use of personified animals and of outlandish behavior in many of the main characters within any one film kept the typical audience laughing. Furthermore, his use of a quick pace and of several scenes so engrossed the audience that they had little time to consciously catch the social slur or the ethnic slight found within the script. Yet, a close look at the animated productions most remembered by American audiences reveals those American qualities Disney promoted—and criticized—through his films.

Snow White

Snow White was Disney's first real attempt to reproduce classical children's literature. Actually, Disney chose to begin with a story whose roots were in oral adult folklore. The tale as first collected by the German brothers Grimm was intended for adult entertainment long before the printed page was invented. As such, it contained the morals of the common folk, and it stressed two main themes found in most early folklore: that the good humble person shall be rewarded and that the wicked shall be punished. The original tale is much more graphically violent than early children's literature. The characters are actively involved in a drama, but they are discussed with such lack of development that their emotional appeal is low. They can be offensive and frightening or beautiful and kind, but they are never more than shadows of human bings. This is the episodic adventure of a young princess faced with a beautiful arrogant woman who is obsessed by jealousy of the young stepdaughter's beauty and youth. It contains all the stylistic devices of oral literature. The princess hides with seven nameless dwarfs, the queen directy tries to kill the princess three times, the father is ineffective, the princess is rewarded for her goodness by being saved and marrying a prince, and the wicked queen is punished with death. The themes gain impact not from the characterizations, but from the culminating action. It is a brutally satisfying story that stresses early social justice over human emotions. In the original story, Snow White is a young girl whose survival depends upon her innocence and her youthful beauty. She is neither clever nor independent. But she is trusting and obedient, two characteristics that both hinder her and help her. Once the hunter has gone, the original story relates:

> Now the poor child was completely alone in the great forest. She was frightened and did not know what to do. She began to run, and stumbled into sharp stones and into thorns. Wild animals sprang past her, but did her no harm. She ran as long as her legs could carry her until just before evening she saw a little house and went inside to rest. In the house, everything was small, but neat and clean. (Grimm 1974, unpaged)

Disney pictured an Americanized story of a princess who more closely resembles a winner of the Miss America contest. His princess is sweet, has a talent (singing), works hard, and wants more than anything to marry and settle down. She is the earth mother whose love of animals and general kind-hearted nature fills the queen with rage. The queen is not torn by her own oncoming old age and loss of beauty, but is shown to be a mean crature who can't stand Snow White because of her cheerfulness. Disney is so intent upon building a melodramatic scene that he changes the entire family relationship. The original story never tells the listeners anything about Snow White's father once he remarries. Disney changed this and pictured the father as a sympathetic American industrialist when he wrote:

> The queen paid small attention to the King himself. So he kept on working harder and harder at being a King, and he worked so hard he died. (*Good Housekeeping* 1937, p. 35)

But the scene stealers in Disney's version are the seven dwarfs who are no longer clean, sensible fellows who protect a sweet innocent child, but are children themselves in desperate need of a mother. And Snow White is very much a confident young woman capable of handling these unruly little men. Instead of answering "Oh yes, with all my heart!" to their demands that she cook and clean if she is to remain, Disney's princess surveys the mess and like any good, clean housewife exclaims:

> "Seven children must live here . . . And from the looks of things, seven very neglected children. Why, I never saw so much dust! And my, how untidy! . . . Tsk! Tsk! Tsk!" said Snow White. "You'd think their mother—" She stopped, and a tear came into her eye "Oh, maybe they have no mother!" . . . Suddenly she brightened. "I know! I'll clean the house and surprise them. Maybe then they will let me stay. Perhaps I'm just what these children need!" (*Good Housekeeping* 1937, p. 222)

Disney understood his medium, and knew that he had to change the original so that it would last almost two hours instead of the short twenty minutes it originally took to tell. So he beefed up the story with cute scenes that included animals, dwarfs, and music. He also realized that the original story's finale was too severe for the screen. In the original the tale ends:

> Snow White was happy to go wih him. Their wedding was arranged with great splendor and magnificence and, among others, Snow White's evil stepmother was invited to the festivities. After she dressed herself in beautiful clothes, she stood before her mirror and said,
>
> Mirror, mirror on the wall
> Who is most beautiful in
> the land?
>
> The mirror answered,
>
> Lady Queen, you are the
> most beautiful here,
> But the young Queen is a
> thousand times more
> beautiful than you. . . .
>
> [S]he could not rest; she had to see the young Queen. As soon as she arrived, she recognized Snow White and stood there—full of anguish and terror—and could not move. But iron slippers had already been placed on a coal fire and were brought in with tongs and placed before her. She had to step into the red hot shoes and dance until she fell down dead. (Grimm 1974, unpaged)

American audiences would not be entertained by such a brutal scene. The philosophy of "an eye for an eye" is not an acceptable one to mainstream Americans. So, Disney's queen is sent to her death through an accident during a rain storm. At this point the movie loses its melodramatic qualities and becomes the U.S. story of boy meets girl, boy wins girl, boy marries girl, and they live happily ever after.

Cinderella

Disney used this same formula when creating his second fairy tale fantasy, *Cinderella.* This time he used one of Charles Perrault's tales taken from the French court. A much more elegant tale, it lacked the violence found in Grimm. In fact, this tale was so nonviolent that Disney felt obligated to change the story so that the villains could truly be despised, and the heroine could be considered even more beautiful and charming than any others in the story. Concerning the two stepsisters the original tale explains:

> It happened that the King's son gave a ball, and he invited all persons of high degree. The two young ladies were invited amongst others, for they cut a considerable figure in the country. (Perrault 1961, p. 60)

Disney's stepsisters could never have cut a fine figure anywhere. They are purposely grotesque to heighten the drama. They are lazy, nasty creatures whose main purpose in life seems to be to argue among themselves.

While they are not as frightening as the wicked queen in *Snow White,* they are equally repulsive. The cuteness and charm found within Disney's story is depicted through Cinderella's little mice friends who talk to her. Yet these very characters solidify Disney's use of humorous portrayals concerning physical or mental handicaps. Disney's subtle use of the social slur is so mild it seems at first glance to be but a wholesome comic picture of human deficiencies. But at second glance Disney's poke at the retarded (Dumbo in *Snow White*) and the fat person with a speech impediment (Gus in *Cinderella*) is very American. In these characterizations he has used the ploys so popular to U.S. audiences who had earlier viewed the slapstick humor of the overdramatized silent films. The handicaps of both characters are used to create comic relief in order to keep these tales from becoming too somber. Both princesses survey their handicapped friends' antics much like one would the activities of a frisky puppy who has not been trained to control his natural instincts: they are cute, but they need paternalistic guidance if they are to exist in society.

Pinocchio

There are few youngsters today who are familiar with the original *Pinocchio* or *Bambi.* These two books are now a part of American popular culture as designed by Disney. When commenting about Disney's *Pinocchio* Sayers said:

> [T]here's an illustration of Pinocchio smoking the pipe and Lampwick playing at billiards. The description of Lampwick is supposed to be childlike, and these are the games that they play: billiards and smoking pipes. . . . I think the truth is that Walt Disney has never addressed himself to children once in his life—never. This material is made to reach an adult audience. (1965, p. 607)

Mrs. Sayers' perception of Disney's audience is right. The films created for family audiences were designed to entertain adults and children alike while not offending parents. Although Pinocchio is an excellent children's classic concerning a wooden puppet's gradual growth into a sympathetic youngster, many of the scenes in the original books might offend. The Italian author Carlo Lorenzini created his story in the late 1800s; its lively prose depicts a wild cast of characters tied together in an absurd drama. Disney chose to change the story and to focus the drama on a naughty but never malicious puppet and his conscience, Jiminy Cricket. Just after Pinocchio is given life by the Blue Fairy in Disney's version Jiminy Cricket says "Remember what she told you—always let your conscience be your guide!" to which Pinocchio replies (with due respect) "Yes, sir, I will!" (*Good Housekeeping* 1939, p. 68). In the original story, Pinocchio's first encounter with the cricket ends after the puppet becomes angry at this wise old philosopher's advice to study and be good. Finally he exclaims:

> "Careful, ugly Cricket! If you make me angry, you'll be sorry!"
>
> "Poor Pinocchio, I am sorry for you."
>
> "Why?"
>
> "Because you are a Marionette and, what is much worse, you have a wooden head."
>
> At these last words, Pinocchio jumped up in a fury, took a hammer from the bench, and threw it with all his strength at the talking Cricket. Perhaps he did not think he would strike it. But sad to relate, my dear children, he did hit the cricket, straight on its head. With a last weak "Cri-cri-cri-" the poor cricket fell from the wall, dead! (Collodi 1939, pp. 16–17)

Throughout the book Pinocchio's behavior does not improve until after he is thrown into the sea with a stone around his neck. He is at once one of the most obnoxious and entertaining heroes within children's literature. He would be a totally unsympathetic character if it were not for Lorenzini's crisp writing style which abounds with quick scenes and wit.

Disney could never have recaptured Lorenzini's style with his, and he probably knew it from the start. Without the clever narrative the activity within the book becomes unbelievable. Furthermore, nothing in the original plot is really cute or lovable. American parents have never wholeheartedly accepted fresh kids; as the active, doing hero in an animated film, the original Pinocchio would have provoked them to fury. Realizing this, Disney refocused the plot line, changed the personalities and responsibilities of the main characters, and reorganized the theme to be one of needing to live clean and not to smoke or gamble in order to grow up and get ahead. Disney's Pinocchio is a sweet personality who strives to be good. His cricket is not smashed, but is listened to and made a hero. This fare would be much more acceptable to U.S. families. Lorenzini's subtheme of attending school to learn and to become someone is played down. Disney's episodic story pleased the popular press and the American family. Ferguson in his review for *The New Republic* wrote:

> If little has been said of the story, it may be because all these excitements make up for very little story at all: it's a string of adventures in very adventuresome places, and surely the last part with the charging bull whale is as fast action as your digestion will allow. . . . We get around the problem of no old word for a new thing by saying, It's a Disney. (1940, p. 346)

Bambi

The most interesting thing about *Bambi* was Disney's miscalculation of the average person when he created the film. Felix Salten's book is bounding with gentle, realistic conversations among the animals. While the film contains memorable characters, the gentle nature of the book is traded for the humorous. Thus, Salten's Hare is changed from a quiet, knowledgeable forest elder to Thumper, a noisy, lovable rabbit who steals every scene when he appears. One reviewer wrote:

> Newcomer Thumper carries most of Bambi's comedy. Just a normal growing bunny, he won't eat his greens, and adds sly innuendoes to the maxims his mother makes him recite. As court jester to Bambi, who is prince and must maintain a reasonable reserve, he is very funny. (*Time* 1942, p. 78)

Disney recreated Salten's characters and changed the setting from the German Black Forest to Maine, but he left Salten's anti-hunting message intact. Bambi's real enemy is shown to be man, the hunter, the invader of the forest. When Raymond J. Brown, editor of *Outdoor Life*, protested that *Bambi* should be appended with a foreword acknowledging the sportman's contribution to wildlife, Disney failed to respond. As a result, the editor branded the film "the worst insult ever offered to American sportsmen and conservationists" (*Newsweek* 1942, p. 70). Disney never directly responded concerning his film's message; perhaps it did not affect him directly. Nevertheless, he never again presented such a strong theme concerning ecology in his major films. Instead, he maintained his strong technological skills in family film, both animated and live action. Sayers said:

> What I am eager for people to do is to realize that in his own medium Walt Disney has made a great contribution to the humor of the world. What I object to is his treatment of traditional literature. . . . In the early days and in certain other films, Disney is a master in his own field. I just would like to have him stay in that field and not attempt to impose his particular gifts on the literature and the arts of children. (1965, pp. 610–611)

What Sayers is discussing is the impact Disney has had upon written literature. Yet, what she and all other critics who complain of Disney's restructuring of children's classics fail to acknowledge is that Walt Disney perceived American society from a very different viewpoint. Disney began creating his middle American films during a period of decline in reading. By the time he was recognized as a leader in children's productions school language arts programs had refocused their goals from interest in the literary qualities in literature to reading skills as reflected in the "Dick and Jane" primers. Society was attuned to middle class values; it was less interested in classics than in reading skills. Furhtermore, no other major film producer had turned to children's literature in the field of entertainment. Disney's feature-length animated films were singular for their production, distribution, and popularity. In his book *The Disney Films* Marten commented:

> It is wrong for critics to chide Disney for not living up to his potential, for it was his potential as *they* saw it. Disney was satisfied with his films because they lived up to his visions of them, and when released to theatres, his judgement was echoed by countless millions who delighted in what he gave them. (1973, p. 15)

Despite what adult literary critics may think about Disney and his values, he was shrewd enough to understand modern U.S. families and their visual and literary interest. He created episodic films based on the plots of classical literature, and replaced the intellectual theme with a satisfying emotional experience. His films have dominated in the field of family film entertainment because of their technical excellence and their optimistic message. When evaluating Disney, Bright wrote:

> I think the man's unique success can be understood only by reference to his personal non-uniqueness. Of all the activists of public diversion, Uncle Walt was the most precisely in the American midstream—in task and morality, attitudes and opinions, prides and prejudices. (1967, p. 303)

Disney is a part of children's literature that must be recognized. His technology, his use of children's classics, his popularity and his lasting effect upon American culture are significant. He was capable not only of establishing trends in the area of family entertainment, but of misusing classical literature to his (and perhaps U.S. cultural) preferences. Though Walt Disney is dead, his spirit lives on in the hearts of many Americans. Their reading and viewing attitudes have often been shaped by his splendid animation and his use of stereotypic characters. Disney did more about the reading interests of children during the last half of the twentieth century than any other person. What American has not seen at least one Disney film of a particular classic and remembered it vividly henceforth?

References

Bright, John. "Disney's Fantasy Empire." *The Nation* (March 6, 1967): 299–303.

Collodi, Carlo. *The Adventures of Pinocchio*, translated from the Italian by Carol Della Chiesa. New York: The Macmillan Company, 1939.

Ferguson, Otis. "It's a Disney: Pinocchio." *The New Republic* (March 11, 1940): 346.

Good Housekeeping. "The Story of Walt Disney's New Feature-Length Motion Picture *Pinocchio*." *Good Housekeeping* (October 1939): 39–41, 67–84 (November 1939): 39–41.

Good Housekeeping. "Walt Disney's *Snow White and The Seven Dwarfs:* Adapted from Grimm's Fairy Tales." *Good Housekeeping* (November 1937): 35–38, 221–226 (December 1937): 35–38.

Grimm Brothers. *Snow White*, translated from the German by Paul Heins. New York: Little, Brown and Company, 1974.

Hollister, Paul. "Walt Disney: Genius at Work." *The Atlantic Monthly*. (December 1940): 689–701.

Martin, Leonard. *The Disney Films*. New York: Crown Publishers, Inc., 1973.

Newsweek. "*Bambi's* Debut." *Newsweek* (August 27, 1942): 70–71.

Newsweek. "The Wild World of Disney." *Newsweek* (December 31, 1962): 48–51.

Perrault, Charles. *Perrault's Complete Fairy Tales,* translated from the French by A. E. Johnson et al. New York: Dodd, Mead and Company, 1961.

Sayers, Frances Clarke. "Walt Disney Accused." *The Horn Book Magazine* (December 1965): 602–611.

Schickel, Richard. *The Disney Version*. New York: Simon and Schuster, 1968.

Sneed, Wilfred. "Films." *Esquire* (November 1967): 26–27.

Time. "The New Pictures." *Time* (August 24, 1942): 78–79.

Film Productions of Children's Books: Weston Woods Studios and Disney

Jill P. May

In 1965 children's literature expert and former librarian Frances Clark Sayers sharply criticized Walt Disney's movie productions of the classics, and said, "I find genuine feeling ignored, the imagination of children bludgeoned with mediocrity, and much of it overcast with vulgarity."[1] In 1967 when Morton Schindel, President of Weston Woods Studios, discussed his beginning interest in reproducing quality children's literature on the screen, he wrote that his early ideas were considered blasphemy to some children's educators. Schindel remarked: "I got the same reaction I could have expected from telling them a dirty joke. It was all right to promote books; but filmstrips and records were commercial! . . . Books are every bit as 'commercial' as adapta-

SOURCE: *Catholic Library World,* December, 1980, pp. 210–214.

tions of them. . . . Each medium has unique qualities that give it superiority over others—depending upon the message to be transmitted and the characteristics of the audience for which the message is intended: Where the people are, who they are, their background, abilities, interests."[2]

While librarians and educators have continued to attack Disney's productions as inferior adaptations of well written classical children's literature, they cmpletely embrace the productions of Morton Schindel. American school age children, on the other hand, readily recognize Disney characters and enthusiastically recall Disney productions. But they have little or no knowledge concerning Weston Woods' productions. Both men have developed a lucrative business based on the selling of children's books, and both have applied American marketing practices. Their real differences lie in overall objectives and techniques.

During an interview in 1953, Disney explained his films, saying: "If there is a secret to what I do—and where maybe my competitors make their mistake—I guess it's that I never make the pictures too childish, and so they do not become strictly children's films. I always try to get a little satire about human foibles, like when I kidded academic pomposity in *The Absent-Minded Professor*."[3]

In a Weston Woods promotion piece Morton Schindel wrote: *It is our role at Weston Woods to create audiovisual adaptations that are faithful reflections of the books themselves. We seek the best books from all over the world and adapt them in such a way as to preserve the integrity of the original. By so doing, we help children discover the riches that are trapped between the covers of books and motivate them to want to read for themselves.*[4]

Walt Disney used literature to support his own ideology and his own image of middle America. Morton Schindel has used filming techniques to promote children's literature. Disney was less interested in the overall literary values of a presentation than in its entertainment value; Schindel is less interested in a production's monetary value than in its artistic contribution to children's literature. In order to best understand their ultimate ideological differences, it is essential to review their early backgrounds.

A Comparison of Backgrounds

Walt Disney was born in Chicago in 1901. His father was never successful in either business or hard labor. Walt watched his father try several avenues of employment, including farming and newspaper route promotions, but he never saw his father succeed in business. His father was a strict man who drove all the family in his belief of the lower middle class work ethic. Walt Disney's greatest influence on his early life was his older brother Roy. It was

Roy's confidence and positive attitude that inspired Walt Disney. And it was Roy's *savoir-faire* that inspired him in his adult ventures. Disney was from a poor, but proud Americanized family. His Midwestern tradition taught him to be shrewd in business affairs, but it never truly introduced him to the merits of good literature.

Morton Schindel was born in New Jersey in 1918. His father was a relatively successful businessman who had worked hard and earned a good position within The Bamberger retail business. Schindel's father's success in the business world inspired him as a youngster. His family's desire for his own success frightened Schindel as a young man; Schindel believes it may have triggered his early tuberculosis problems. Schindel's greatest influence on his business ideology was Louis Bamberger, an honest successful bachelor who believed in the U.S. and devoted his wealth to the growth of its people.

Disney and Schindel used their production talents to work with the U.S. government. Although the experience was beneficial to both men, their assignments differed in both location and ultimate values received. Disney's early animated films were lauded for their animation techniques, but they were expensive to make By 1940 Disney was forced to go public. By the summer of 1941 his artists were on strike. Walt Disney Productions was in financial trouble, and Disney needed a way out. He saw little public interest in full length animated films. The U.S. Treasury offered to pay Disney to make war films at little more than cost, and Disney agreed to create those films in his studios with his staff. When the war ended Disney was still in debt, and the studio's days of concentrating on a single technique—film animation—were over. From that time on Disney began to diversify. The entire experience kept Walt Disney Productions alive during the war, but it did not heighten his success.[5] Morton Schindel's interest in film had grown from an interest to an avocation while he was first institutionalized with tuberculosis. The doctors urged Schindel to become an artist, to devote himself to a talent which could be done without closely adhering to a daily time schedule. He was advised against a career in the business world. By the mid 1940s Schindel had determined to work in the field of film production. He returned to college and completed an M.A. degree in educational visual arts at Columbia. Because the program was new, Schindel developed much of his film skills on his own. He rented films from the Museum of Modern Art and read all he could find on film production. By 1948 he was producing and selling educational films. He determined to leave the city and to set up a self paced work schedule in the country. By 1950 Morton Schindel had moved to Weston Woods' present location. In 1951 he was offered the U.S. State Department position of directing educational film programs in Turkey. For the years 1951–1953 Schindel lived in Turkey, directing the film program and producing films on location as a part of the Marshall Program. Although the position was not a lucrative one, Schindel has always counted the experience as a valuable one: "I learned a lot about transmitters that I've continued to apply in my Children's Caravans. Now I've developed a traveling bus that can run all its equipment on its own generator."[6] Schindel's experience extended his practical knowledge and thus expanded his ultimate creative scope.

Disney's Philosophy and Goals

Disney was a poor boy whose major ambition was to make money. He left formal schooling before completing high school. Not one of his biographers describes him as a reader. Nowhere in the vast amounts written about the Disney success is there mention of a concern for children's literature. All authors pay tribute to early animation techniques and his daring, but little is said concerning his intellectual concern towards visually conveying a book's theme, writing style, or real setting. When discussing his films, reviewers comment upon the changes made in the filmed version. Whether or not they defend his right to delete characters and scenes in order to add Disney innovations, they are all aware that Disney never quite liked a story the way it was written, and that he always played the part of literary editor to the materials he used. Many critics point out that most children who have seen a Disney film are more likely to read one of his simple printed versions of it than to read the original version. When commenting on Disney's business shrewdness, *Newsweek* once wrote: "Walt Disney's career may be founded on elfin fantasy and hybrid corn, but it thrives on the hardest sell in Hollywood: the 'total merchandising' concept. . . . 'Once a decision is made to make a picture, the marketing starts,' says soft-spoken Roy Disney, Walt's brother and financial mentor. 'All of the moves are geared to publicizing the final product, and making money while you do it.' "[7]

Total merchandising in the realm of children's literature includes introducing sheet music, records, television and newspaper ads, children's toys, and Disney book versions before the film is released. By the time any of Disney's large scale animated productions has hit the theaters, children are familiar with all the main characters. And they're sure to recognize the story as it has been concocted in the Disney Studios. Furthermore, the Disney renditions will sell long after the film has left town. In 1976 alone Disney consumer products brought $378 million in gross income compared to $119 million in gross income from films and television.[8]

Disney's effect upon the literary judgements of this and future generations of young adults is easily quantified by college age students. During the past two years in the undergraduate children's literature course at Purdue University students have consistently named one of the Disney films as their favorite childhood experience in theater going, and have rallied in defense of his changes in classics. When asked to explain their interest in Disney products one student commented, "I prefer the Walt Disney versions. This is probably because I'm one of the typical people who Walt Disney writes for. I don't appreciate fine pictures and original accounts." Another student wrote, "I like his happy endings. They make me feel good."

Disney films are not preferred by one sex over another. They are liked and supported strongly by young men. Most admit that they saw and enjoyed "Snow White" when they were youngsters. Almost all have watched the Disney weekly television show based on his fantasies, live action stories, and "documentary" productions. Many confess that they still enjoy watching it.

In fact, Disney's greatest monetary strategy seems to be to replace the child's ability to pause in reflection on a book's theme by eliminating the author's theme as created by that person's unique stylistic characteristics and by replacing it with glitter. His ability to create a shiny new package from an old classic has been imitated in U.S. marketing many times in recent years (i.e., the all American hamburger in sterile packaging available everywhere) but no one has so successfully used the gimic of selling instant literature "classics" as Disney. For little money and few words a child can gain knowledge of a well known title. Parents who never venture inside a public library to borrow free books for their children readily pay for the privilege to own a Disney classic. The Disney line of"Little Golden Books" sells 24 million copies yearly. The hardback book *Walt Disney's Story Land*, which costs over $5.00, sells 100,000 copies yearly.[9] One of Disney's strong supporters wrote: "I think the man's unique success can be understood only by reference to his personal non-uniqueness. Of all the activists of public diversion, Uncle Walt was the one most precisely in the American midstream—in task and morality, attitudes and opinions, prides and prejudices."[10]

Disney never promoted literature; he sold millions of Americans on the idea of the great animated entertainment film. Later, he just sold Americans on middle American values in various disguises. He made everything seem rosy and simple. He simplified all real conflicts into no more than five pages of dialogue, and added lots of cute songs and scenes with frolicking creatures. In the realm of film production he was an innovator. He was one of the first to make a sound film (*Steamboat Willy*, 1928), the first to make an animated feature film (*Snow White*, 1937), and the first to use stereophonic sound (*Fantasia*, 1939). But in the realm of literacy and ethnic understanding, he was totally lacking. Black voices were used for monkeys and apes *(The Jungle Book)*, Italians were always depicted as aggressive souls who spoke in broken English and wrung their hands *(The Lady and the Tramp* and *Pinocchio)*; all story lines were changed to depict a simple love story and a happily-ever-after theme. His literary creations are vast and mindless. They entertain by playing on middle American social virtues and vices. Their conflict relies upon physical problems rather than intellectual problems.

Librarians are well aware of Disney's popularity, but they have always choked on his successes. The most famous criticism of Walt Disney is Frances

Clarke Sayers' "Walt Disney Accused." In her comments Ms. Sayers said: "I feel that anybody who addresses himself to children has a responsibility, and that responsibility is to make available to children the very best that has ever been produced and to sustain the distinction of what has been produced."[11]

Schindel's Philosophy and Goals

Morton Schindel explained in a recent interview that Weston Woods was an antidote to the Disney Productions. His early interest in the possibilities of educational visual aids and their uses with children led him to create an entirely different medium than Disney.[12]

While the differences between Schindel's goals and Disney's are obvious, it is worthwhile to briefly mention them. Morton Schindel had been physically driven from the center ring of business at an early age. Raised by intelligent parents in an upper middle class family, he had been impressed with the idea that success could not be measured in money alone. Once he was faced with his physical limitations, Schindel began to look for a field where he could achieve success based on intellectual goals as well as monetary goals. Disney never professed any real interest in cultivating further bookish knowledge; Schindel has never stopped reading. Disney counted his wealthy empire his greatest asset; Schindel considers his reputation as an authority on good literary audiovisual production techniques among educators and librarians his greatest achievement.

Schindel's far sighted production philosophy was based on the concept that by giving a worthwhile medium to children it would improve their literature and artistic tastes, so he made available excellent book materials in the film medium. His products were not designed to sell through merchandising gimmicks, but through the use of scholastic authenticity. He never expected his films to compete with the book. Instead they were designed to encourage the reading habit.

Schindel's first films were designed for television use. He devised a close up panning technique which depended on a simple device he developed and used. His process, termed iconographic filming, created active motion pictures of the picture book illustrations. Schindel depended upon the artist's sense of movement as reflected in the original illustrations and his own effective use of smooth camera movement. Once he finished his films, he tried to find a firm interested in releasing them. Much to his chagrin, the films were considered too slow moving by television people, and too entertaining by educational visual arts people. Since he could not find a market in already established businesses, Schindel determined to create his own company which would produce and release films.

There was no doubt in his mind who would most appreciate his productions: librarians had helped him find something worth filming and they had expressed enthusiasm for his ideas. Once Schindel had created Weston Woods in 1955, he began work on a brochure discussing his first films. Since that first mailing in 1956 to some 60 public libraries, Weston Woods has grown to be a worldwide distributor of authentic productions in children's literature.

Schindel has remained a leader in the field of quality educational visual arts products. Weston Woods was the first company to contract with both children's book publishers and the book author/illustrators for reproduction rights on a royalty participation basis. His company today produces live action, iconographic, and animated films. Weston Woods was the first company to produce uncaptioned filmstrips, and to create sound filmstrips of children's books. While Schindel does not see the formation of an archival collection on good contemporary children's artists and authors as a major goal for Weston Woods his company has the most significant collection of audiovisual interviews with current authors and artists. Schindel's explanation of these is simple: "It's part of the Weston Woods image. We're interested in educators, and they're interested in the people who make children's books. We've produced materials designed for university literature courses and library school courses not only to inform, but to show Weston Woods' real concern for the artistic talents in children's literature."[13]

An Evaluation

In the field of education Schindel is considered the ultimate early authority in film media based on book presentations. Weston Woods is not a household name. Morton Schindel is not even listed in the current edition of *Who's Who in America.* Yet his contribution to literature is significant. He has set trends in the field of educational audiovisual materials that are currently being practiced by many other major companies. He has always credited the author/illustrator of the book equally to Weston Woods. He has always kept a low profile, and has cultivated a profile of concerned leadership. His company has a reliable image, and is a name touted in library schools throughout the U.S. Schindel has been positively discussed in several professional education and library magazines. He has never been negatively reviewed in professional journals. His scholastic image remains sterling. One author who had praised his work in the area of film stated: "Weston Woods is a business. It sells or rents films, filmstrips, and books, all of which are dedicated to the purpose of bringing creative experiences to children. But, Weston Woods is not like an ordinary business. Even in his business affairs, Morton Schindel brings a touch of magic and artistry to his dealings."[14]

Both Walt Disney and Morton Schindel have succeeded in their theoretical and monetary goals. Their basic differences lie in audience acceptance, and in their influence upon future production trends. Disney's greatest contributions to American popular culture lie in his use of total merchandising techniques to promote cute, stereotyped characters, his use of familiar children's literature titles, and his misuse of those books' plots, themes, and characterization in order to create a product which, though it seems familiar, is only available in a Disney rendition. Disney's appeal is emotional. His most endearing scenes often involve the antics of wild animals. He is the patriarch of effective merchandising methods which play upon the emotions of immature audiences. Yet, he is best known and loved by the general populace for these very reasons. His marketing techniques will be emulated by many because they reap profits from adults as well as children.

Morton Schindel's greatest contributions to the American populace have been his authenticity in reproducing children's books into films, his educational goals, and his creation of a literary archival collection. Schindel's purpose is to introduce intelligent, knowledgeable adults to children's materials. Although only some of his films and filmstrips have a strong emotional appeal, they all capture the unique qualities of the author's style and theme and of the artist's techniques. The techniques developed by Weston Woods have greatly influenced the realm of educational media.

Disney never looked upon his audience as simply children, nor did he believe that he produced children's films. In one interview he looked back at his plaques "For the Best Children's Picture" and commented: "They persist in giving me that blasted award every year. I don't make children's pictures. Why do they do it?"[15]

Schindel's main goal has consistently been to produce good educational materials to use with children. He has never stopped being an educator or trying to create worthwhile entertaining materials. Schindel once wrote: "If we keep our eyes open and our imaginations free, we can choose whatever means will work best for us and for the new generation we are entrusted to educate. We can examine impartially all the media in selecting the ideas we want to transmit . . .With a realistic view of the role and value of books, we can comfortably begin an exciting romance with the "newcomers" in town—the new media—to derive ever greater satisfaction from professional endeavors."[16]

References

[1]"Walt Disney Accused," *The Horn Book Magazine*. December 1965, p. 603.

[2]"Confessions of a Book Fiend," *Library Journal*. February 15, 1967.

[3]Bill Davidson. "The Fantastic Walt Disney," *The Saturday Evening Post*, October 31, 1953, p. 74.

[4]"A Multimedia Invitation to the World of Children's Literature," Weston Woods Publicity Release.

[5]John McDonald. "Now the Bankers Come to Disney," *Fortune* May, 1966, pp. 223–224.

[6]Interview with Morton Schindel at Weston Woods, November 26, 1977.

[7]"The Wide World of Walt Disney," *Newsweek*, December 31, 1962, p. 50.

[8]Peter Brown, "Mickey Mouse the Yule Star?" *Gannett News Service*, Wednesday, September 28, 1977 (Lafayette, Indiana *Journal and Courier*).

[9]Lila Freilicher. "Disney Books Continue to Reap Profits—And More Are on the Way," *Publisher's Weekly*, September 29, 1975, p. 37.

[10]John Bright. "Disney's Fantasy Empire," *The Nation*, May 6, 1967. p. 303.

[11]*The Horn Book Magazine*, December 1965, p. 608.

[12]Interview with Morton Schindel, November 26, 1977.

[13]*Ibid*.

[14]"Morton Schindel: A Magician and His Film," *The Reading New-report*, March 1968.

[15]Bill Davidson. "The Fantastic Walt Disney," *The Saturday Evening Post*, October 31, 1953, p. 74.

[16]"Confessions of a Book Fiend," *School Library Journal*, February, 1967.

Creating Preschool Resource Centers

Eileen M. Earhart

Rural families with young children often find that the resources available to them are quite limited. Few child development centers or nursery schools exist, and in many areas the only preschool services available are Head Start and programs for handicapped children.

This was the situation in a large rural area in Michigan in 1973, when I began to investigate ways to create community resources for preschool children and their families. My goal was to provide resources—particularly

Source: Children Today, March/April 1980, pp. 16–18.

books, games and toys—which would enhance children's intellectual and motor development and foster parent-child interaction.

I thought that the toy-lending library approach developed by the Far West Laboratory and used in numerous locations, the "Toys That Teach" project in Silver Spring, Maryland and the Children's Center at the University of South Carolina in Columbia, for example, illustrated effective ways of reaching children and families in rural Michigan. However, since my objective was to make a broad selection of materials available to any parent and child in the community who wished to borrow them, there would be no limitations placed on who could participate and no training would be required before participation.

In January 1974 the Preschool Resource Center project began with a grant from the Agricultural Experiment Station at Michigan State University. Selecting locations for centers which would be central and available to all community members was the first step. Members of the Human Development Commission, an agency serving 14 counties in rural Michigan, canvassed elementary schools, libraries and community centers to determine the availability of space and staff members' interest in participating in the project. Based on the information collected, one library in each of three counties was chosen. During the past year, three additional libraries in other rural communities have developed preschool resource centers.

Resource Center Materials

The materials placed in the libraries included toys, games and books appropriate for children aged three months to five years. The Human Development Commission provided funds for the materials in the original three libraries and, later, the project supplemented these funds to make sure that complete, comparable sets of materials were available in two libraries. The resource centers in these libraries were also used for special research projects conducted by graduate students in the Department of Family and Child Sciences at Michigan State. Because less space was available in the third library, a smaller set of materials was provided.

Approximately 150 toys and games and 30 books were selected for these libraries. "Starter sets of 30 toys have been placed in the libraries which have begun programs during the past year. Service organizations, women's clubs, individuals and library boards have made contributions to supplement the starter sets. In one community, memorial contributions are frequently made to the local library and some of these contributions have been designated for the purchase of additional toys and books for preschool children.

The selection of materials was based on recommendations of child development specialists from the university. The criteria used were durability of the materials, the likelihood that they would supplement games and toys already in the home, the probability that they could be used to promote parent-child interaction, and the contribution they could make toward a child's intellectual and motor development. The materials ordered from commercial toy manufacturers were those not readily available to or already being utilized by parents in the communities.

The books selected, which were particularly appropriate for 2- and 3-year-olds, had very few words and clear, uncluttered illustrations. In several, photographs were used to help tell the story.

Since many of the toys and games were unaccompanied by guidelines suggesting ways to use them—or, when directions were included, the procedures outlined were often very limited—project staff members developed suggestion sheets to accompany each toy or game. Care was taken to use simple language and easily understood directions so that parents could carry out the suggestions without additional interpretation. Each sheet explains the skills and/or information that a child learns by playing with the toy or game, notes the age range for which it is most appropriate and provides some specific ideas for parents to use with their child.

For example, the suggestion sheet which accompanies the "Duck Hand Puppet," particularly suitable for children aged three to five, notes that "playing with puppets helps children use their imaginations and encourages them to talk." The first suggested activity explains: "Show your child this duck puppet and let him or her examine and explore it. Say to your child, 'What animal do you think this looks like?' Talk about how you can tell it's a duck—the shape of its head, the bill. Talk about the sounds it makes and its colors."

Next, parents work the puppet for the child and then help the child put his or her ideas and feelings into words through the puppet.

Using the Centers

The first three preschool resource centers began lending materials in May 1974. The Human Development Commission publicized the new additions to the libraries in each of the communities and prepared and distributed a brochure on the resource centers through community organizations. Local newspapers also carried reports and photographs.

Each librarian devised a system for storing and checking out the materials. In several libraries a special room was devoted to the resource center books and toys. In others, one section of the library was used for the materials. The least successful location was in the basement of one library. Low bookshelves, small tables and chairs and pillows were set up in the areas to encourage children to explore the materials.

Some materials, such as balls, arrived without containers. Clear plastic boxes were purchased to store odd-shaped materials and those without containers, and sturdy plastic bags have been used to hold toys with several pieces when the original box was no longer usable. We found that toys displayed on shelves without boxes or in clear boxes attracted children's interest more readily than toys stored in cardboard containers.

The checking out of items has been handled in different ways. Some libraries lend materials for 2-week periods, others for a month. In some resource centers, the librarian writes down the name of the toy, the name of the borrower and the date it was checked out. Others have prepared cards filed alphabetically for each item and attached the cards to the boxes, when possible.

One librarian, who decided to keep some of the materials in the library instead of lending them, placed several toys in the playpen and displayed others on tables to entice shy children to investigate the new area in the library.

Community Involvement

Several community projets have been undertaken since the resource centers opened. In one county, the Jaycee Auxiliary purchased a doll house, built by a man in the community, as a permanent addition for the library. In another, the librarian's husband built a play house for children to use in the library.

The librarians agree that the preschool resource centers have attracted many young families who had not previously used the library's services. One estimates that 75 to 100 new families have come to borrow resource center materials. Almost always, she says, the parents and children soon become interested in other books and begin checking them out, too.

Activities for Parents

Interest in extending the preschool resource center materials led to a workshop sponsored by several community groups and held at one of the libraries. The workshop, conducted as a research project with the assistance of graduate students, was well attended and many finished products resulted, among them, soft cloth balls, memory and board matching games, sock puppets and lacing boards, all made from scraps of fabric and other inexpensive materials.

A booklet prepared for the participants listed materials needed, gave instructions for making the toys, offered suggestions for using them and explained how children learn by playing with them.[1] Some participants made play materials for their own children or grandchildren while others prepared games and toys for use in summer church school sessions.

In many of the libraries story hours for preschoolers are conducted over 6-week periods several times during the year. While the children meet in a separate room to hear stories, the librarian often arranges special activities for the parents. One series of parent activities, planned and presented by a graduate student, focused on how play contributes to a child's growth and development. An evaluation of the sessions found that mothers who participated made significant gains in their knowledge of play.[2] The librarian also noted that the mothers who participated checked out many more materials to use with their children than mothers who were not involved in the program.

Since other librarians expressed interest in conducting similar activities, the original series has been modified and used with several parent groups. A series of six slide-tapes, focusing on the importance of play in a child's development, has been developed for dissemination to community groups through the University's Cooperative Extension Service and Instructional Media Center.[3]

In one recent session, parents were especially interested in discussing the relationship of television viewing to play behavior. They were concerned that their children were substituting television viewing for active play, were dramatizing undesirable episodes and had difficulty distinguishing between fantasy and reality in television programming. The session enabled them to share their concerns and discuss approaches which might be used to resolve problems.

In another research project conducted by a graduate student, 32 mothers and fathers, all of whom had borrowed materials from the resource center, participated in a study to determine the extent of marital agreement concerning attitudes and knowledge of play. The amount of money spent on toys and games by these families varied greatly, ranging from $30 to $200 per year, with an average of $96. The study revealed an interesting relationship between the amount of money spent on play materials and marital agreement concerning attitudes toward play: as the amount of money spent on home play materials increased, the likelihood that the parents would agree on their attitudes toward play decreased.[4]

Problems Encountered

The packaging of materials has continued to be a problem. Many boxes were quickly torn and needed to be replaced, and some toys do not fit easily into the plastic boxes or bags. At one center, cloth drawstring bags are used to carry the toys to and from the library. The bags were made by one of the library board members, a senior citizen, as a special contribution to the preschool resource center.

Some toys have not withstood the tests of time and usage. A xylophone came apart; wooden puzzle pieces were broken in some fragile places; connector parts for a tractor and wagon broke off very soon after arrival; the covers on some hard-cover books did not hold up with use. How to treat baby toys is still a question to be resolved—librarians are concerned about the problems of germ transmittal when infant toys are used in several households. Many of the toys for babies are used infrequently.

When toys are returned with missing parts, families are not charged a fine. If a missing part (a puzzle piece, for example) is needed to enable the child to gain satisfaction from playing with the toy, the toy is not put back on the shelf. Several librarians have reported that missing pieces frequently show up later and many are returned to the library.

Frequency of Use

Complete records were kept in the library at Pigeon, Michigan, and data were gathered from these to determine how many toys were checked out each month.

December has been the lowest month for distribution and May the highest, and more toys were checked out during the first 12-month period than the second. The lower number of toys checked out during the summer months of the second year contributes significantly to the difference. Since the library originally opened in May, much publicity continued through the first summer. Even though the average distribution during the second year was lower, the demand for toys was still relatively high, and the librarian was pleased with the continued community response beyond the initial publicity.

The popularity of the toys during the same 2-year period was determined by a frequency of distribution count. Three toys—a duck puppet, picture dominoes and bristle blocks—were checked out more than 50 times. The most popular toy was the duck puppet, which had been borrowed 75 times. Other puppets—a chicken, a dog and a frog—were each checked out 48 times. Eighty-two of the toys had been checked out 10 times or more, and 20 toys, 30 times or more. In addition to the puppets, other items in the "top 20" included transportation toys such as a crane, moon car and train; games and toys requiring motor dexterity. Such as the pounding board and sewing cards; construction toys such as bristle blocks and ring-a-majigs; and other toys (cooking sets and farm models, for example) which support dramatic play.

Maintenance and Replacement

The library boards have supported the costs of maintaining and replacing materials in the preschool resource centers. Other community organizations have contributed money and materials to supplement the original items and their support and involvement have contributed significantly to the success of the project.

Summary

The results of the Preschool Resource Centers project lead us to believe that two elements are necessary if such centers are to be successful. First, there must be adequate space for storing materials and for children to explore the contents of the boxes and containers. Child-sized tables and chairs encourage exploration.

Secondly, the librarian must be enthusiastic and willing to have children make noise in the library. The librarians who have promoted the Preschool Resource Centers have made significant contributions to the young children and families in their communities.

Notes

[1]Eileen M. Earhart, *Toys and Games to Make and Play With Your Child,* Bulletin #E1034, Cooperative Extension Service, Michigan State University, 1977.

[2]Alice P. Whiren, *The Effect of Parent Education on Knowledge About and Attitudes Toward Children's Play,* unpublished dissertation, Michigan State University, 1976.

[3]The slide-tapes, entitled "Developing Through Play," may be obtained from the Instructional Media Center/MD, Michigan State University, East Lansing, Michigan 48824.

[4]Joan H. Smith, *Marital Agreement on Conceptions of Parenthood and Knowledge of Play as Predictors of Attitudes Toward Play,* unpublished dissertation, Michigan State University, 1976.

Beyond Illustration: Information about Art in Children's Picture Books

Ruth Straus Gainer

There are ordinary children's books, and there are works of art for children. John Gardner notes this distinction in a recent book review and cites the drawings of Chris Van Allsburg as having "a beautiful simplicity of design, balance, texture and a subtle intelligence beyond the call of illustration."[1] While the striking graphic qualities of children's books are widely recognized, little attention has been paid to the invitations these qualities offer for influencing children's perceptions about art. Still less consideration has been given to the possibility of directing children to picture books for potential solutions to their self-defined problems in art.

Although we usually represent children as "original," "creative," always "fresh" in their observations, and ever "spontaneous and direct" in producing art gleefully, the facts of the classroom are often quite different. Drawing is difficult. It requires skills which are acquired gradually. It is accompanied by many problems which even naiveté cannot escape. Chief among these are (1) translating private, mental images into public, concrete designs, and (2) rendering three dimensions in two. Social human beings of all ages make comparisons between their intentions and practices, their own work and that of others, their observations of the real world and their attempts at facsimiles. Perhaps because children today are less naive, more pressured to produce competitively, and more bombarded by sophisticated graphic designs, they register frustration in drawing much more prevalently than heretofore. The refrains, "I muffed up," "I messed up," "I goofed," "Mine stinks," "Do it for me," "I can't draw horses" (or faces, or people, or trucks), "I'm no good in art," "I just can't" are all too familiar to every teacher. If the crumpled papers are retrieved from the trash can, they are often pathetically blank. Still more evident than these despairing lamentations are the endlessly repeated clichés of rainbows, hearts, Snoopies, and scalloped daisies, all indicating the same avoidance of challenge, the same tensions associated with lack of self-confidence. Building confidence is the art teacher's, as well as the classroom teacher's, most pressing problem.

Our problem is made difficult by the overwhelming explosion of sophis-

SOURCE: *Art Education*, March 1982, pp. 16–19. Reprinted by permission of the Journal of the National Art Education Association, 1916 Association Drive, Reston, Virginia 22091.

ticated graphics in advertising and packaging, television, films, and magazines. But these media are here to stay and cannot be avoided. They should be confronted studiously. Children through their art must grapple with new sets of problems in new eras. This interaction is basic to the very nature of art. How have we as art teachers changed our methods to deal with this age of "high-powered" graphic communication? Traditional methods for coping with frustration have included:

(a) gentle encouragement ("Of course you can, just *try*!")
(b) referral to the picture file, and/or
(c) demonstration of a teacher-made "sample."

The first approach attempts to deny the struggle of the art process. It is distrusted by students who protest defeatedly or scoffingly. The second method usually provides photographs which help some but are habitually seen as the real things themselves and not as artistic solutions to problems of changing actuality into something else. The third approach generally yields thirty plus replicas of the teacher's model.

For years Kenneth Marantz has been alerting art teachers to new and beautiful children's picture books.[2] However, few art rooms exhibit these books. But when the books are used systematically in the art program, many possibilities occur for connecting the child's world with the best in current graphic design. This approach can provide a "support system" for combatting the frustration so frequently expressed by children drawing. The method is a simple one. When children express problems, they are advised to get outside opinions, to consult specialists in the field. This is done by directing them to "look it up" in books. The teacher explains: "I understand that you are having difficult problems. It is very hard to draw a beautiful horse, especially since we don't have one here in school. Besides, showing the roundness of form, the motion of galloping, the texture of fur is not easy for anyone under any circumstances. Other people have faced these challenges, too. Perhaps we can learn from them. Let's look at some of the ways they have worked out solutions. You don't have to choose their ways, but you may get some ideas for figuring out your own way." The teacher then suggests three or four picture books that include different representations of the problematic subject. The variety is important because students should see that there is more than one way to deal with a specific problem. Students are asked to make interpretations about their observations and how they may fit their immediate dilemmas. The teacher points out: "Look at the way Anno's line curves here and thickens there to suggest the horse's bulk.[3] These lines suggest the force of rapid motion while these short, repeated lines make a pattern which gives texture. If you like Anno's horse, why don't you try some of these kinds of lines in your horse?"

The child's problem is thus made much easier. Instead of having to define vague images, the issue now becomes: "How can I adapt this material in hand to my own work?" Until now, the children may have been giving only cursory glances to illustrations, looking merely for story clues. Specific discussion can train students to focus on many other dimensions, especially when it is tied to a personal search. Lest readers raise the copying controversy here, consider the method used by adult artists when they are stymied. Turning to the works of master artsts for study and even copying has long been recognized as a legitimate means of mastering technique. In this case, the child is not urged to copy an entire work but to adapt a relevant part of it to fit specific needs. It is understood that the child's drawing is part of a learning process and is not intended for immortality or for sale. Similarly, the teaching of writing often involves reading classics and adapting their various styles to one's own efforts.[4] Composition in music proceeds this way too, as does training in dance. It is necessary to experiment with a variety of previously developed ideas before developing a unique statement. That unique expression is often a synthesis of multiple influences. This is axiomatic teaching practice. Otherwise we would forever be reinventing the wheel.

In art, careful observation should include works of art as well as nature. Original masterworks are usually inaccessible. Reproductions of them are often crticized as inadequate because they vary so greatly in size, color, and texture from the originals. Book illustrations, however, may be considered originals because their creators intended them for the form in which they appear. Thus the approach described here establishes habits of going to books for information and for scrutinizing illustrations carefully. It does not detract from an appeciation of the whole book but creates personally meaningful bonds with books which cause students to return to them pleasurably again and again. Furthermore, the habit of going to books for information about art brings many rewards. Frustrated children who formerly made cranky demands or disruptions now have a plan of action and a definite strategy for working toward a goal. In comparing treatments of similar themes in different sources, they are becoming literate verbally and visually. Most important, they are learning that there are many points of view about similar things; yet each view may be interesting in a different way.

My students have been impressed that representations of ideas don't have to mirror reality. Some favorite illustrations, such as those by Antonio Frasconi,[5] are powerful abstractions. Student work in response to Frasconi becomes more daring in its divergence from minutiae in favor of bold simplification. Of course, students are not compelled to try Frasconi's methods, but turn to him by choice when their own efforts are thwarted by feelings of inadequacy. The specific options offered to students, their own observations of different, individual, yet valid treatments of subjects, and their increasing awareness that realism is not necessarily the preferred option all contribute to building self-confidence. Also important is the fact that students are searching out and choosing their own solutions in a self-reliant fashion. And instead of considering graphic design subliminally while choosing cereal or passing billboards, consideration of higher quality work becomes conscious and deliberate.

When I recently made a purchase at a children's book shop, an onlooker grumbled rather snobbishly, "Those illustrations were made more for adults than for children." Whatever did she mean, I wondered? For whom did Gustave Doré illustrate *Don Quixote,* or Rockwell Kent *Canterbury Tales*? Is their work inappropriate for children? The illustrations in my new book are beautiful.[6] Certainly children should see them, learn to think about their aesthetic qualities, possibly learn from them and make them part of their lives, if they choose. In so doing they may become more discriminating in their aesthetic choices in many realms and at many ages. My own eagerness to share the unusual color combinations and expert draftsmanship of my acquisition with my students was matched by their enthusiasm to read the book and to draw trees and/or strawberries in new ways.

Feldman has stated: "What youngsters desire from books is experience."[7] In his discussion of linguistic dividends from the act of aesthetic perception, he draws many parallels between verbal and visual literacy and compares visual conventions "like perspective, outline, modeling by light and dark and determination of importance by placement" to parts of speech. These conventions are the very areas that pose problems for children trying to use art as a language that will shape their ideas. When children use picture books as models of usage for their own art work, their grammar and syntax in structuring visual forms may improve greatly. This is essentially a conversational method of instruction where the dialogue is between the child's artistic efforts and aesthetic observations.

A short list of books which have been rich sources of information in our art studio at Whetstone Elementary School follows:

Anno, M. *Anno's Journey,* Philomel, 1978.
Balet, J. *The Fence,* N.Y.: Delacorte, 1969.
Bang, M. *The Grey Lady and the Strawberry Snatcher,* N.Y.: Four Winds, 1980.
Baylor, B. *When Clay Sings,* N.Y.: Scribner's, 1972.
Beisner, M. and Laurie, A. *Fabulous Beasts,* N.Y.
Bohdal, S. *Tom Cat,* N.Y.: Benn, Doubleday, 1977.
Bryan, A. *The Dancing Granny,* N.Y.: Atheneum, 1977.
Craft, R. *Pieter Brueghel's The Fair,* Pa.: Lippincott, 1975.
Feelings, T. and E. Greenfield, *Daydreamers,* N.Y.: Dial Press, 1981.
Fern, E. *Pepito's Story,* N.Y.: Ariel, 1960.
Frasconi, A. *The Elephant and His Secret,* N.Y.: Atheneum, 1974. Based on a fable of G. Mistral, trans. by Doris Dana.
Hogrogian, N. *The Contest,* N.Y.: Greenwillow, 1976.
Isadora, R. *Ben's Trumpet,* N.Y.: Greenwillow, 1979.
Kesselman, W. *Emma,* N.Y.: Doubleday, 1980.
Lasker, J. *Merry Ever After,* N.Y.: Viking, 1976.
Lawrence, Jacob, *Harriet and the Promised Land,* N.Y.: Simon & Schuster, 1968.

Lionni, L. *Frederick*, N.Y.: Pantheon, 1966.
Manniche, L. *The Prince Who Knew His Fate*, N.Y.: Metropolitan Museum of Art/Philomel, 1981.
McDermott, B. B., *The Crystal Apple*, N.Y.: Viking, 1974.
Otsuka, Y. and S. Akaba, *Suho and the White Horse*, N.Y.: Viking, 1981.
Piatti, C. *The Happy Owls*, N.Y.: Atheneum, 1964.
Price, C. *Dancing Masks of Africa*, N.Y.: Scribner's, 1975.
Rose, A. and Janosch. *How Does a Czar Eat Potatoes?* N.Y.: Lothrop, Lee, Shepard, 1973.
SanSouci, R. *Song of Sedna*, N.Y.: Doubleday, 1981.
Schick, E. *One Summer Night*, N.Y.: Greenwillow, 1977.
Seeger, P. and C. *The Foolish Frog*, illus. by Miloslav Jagr, N.Y.: Macmillan, 1973.
Sendak, M. *Where the Wild Things Are*, N.Y.: Harper & Row, 1963.
Tanobe, M. *Quebec, Je T'Aime, I Love You*, Plattsburgh, N.Y.: Tundra, 1976.
Testa, F. and Burgess, A. *The Land Where the Ice Cream Grows*, N.Y.: Doubleday, 1979.
Velthuijs, M. *The Painter and the Bird*, Reading, Mass.: Addison-Wesley, 1975.
Yaroslava, *I Like You*, N.Y.: Scribner's, 1976.
Yolen, J. and E. Young, *The Girl Who Loved the Wind*, N.Y.: Thos. Crowell, 1972.

References

[1]John Gardner, "Fun and Games and Dark Imaginings," *The New York Times*, book review, April 26, 1981, p. 49.
[2]Kenneth Marantz, "Books for Children," (regular column), *Art Teacher*, National Art Education Association, Fall, 1980.
[3]Mitsumasa Anno, *Anno's Journey*, Philomel, 1978.
[4]Kenneth Koch, *Rose, Where Did you Get That Red?*, N.Y.: Random House, 1973.
[5]Antonio Frasconi, trans. by D. Dana and based on a fable by Gabriela Mistral, *The Elephant and His Secret*, N.Y.: Atheneum, 1974.
[6]Molly Bang, *The Grey Lady and the Strawberry Snatcher*, N.Y.: Four Winds, 1980.
[7]Edmund B. Feldman, "Art Is for Reading: Pictures Make a Difference," *Teachers College Record*, Vol. 82, No. 4, summer 1981.

Controlled Vocabulary Books

What the Cat in the Hat Begat

David C. Davis

A railroad express baggage clerk received a shipment of two guinea pigs which subsequently were not called for by the addressee—the pigs multiplied in the waiting days; and as a result children have the delightful story by Ellis Butler, *Pigs Is Pigs.* As in the case of the multiplying pigs and the similar habits of rabbits, it would seem that anything that multiplies guarantees square roots of laughter!

In today's trade books for the very young, the cats have caught the habits of rabbits and the book world is fast becoming populated with those millions of mewing mongrels that Wanda Gag so delightfully invented. If today's cat stories could catch the magical ingredient possessed by *Millions of Cats,* there would be no need for concern. Yet, magic and literary value are the least of the worries of the authors who are producing more *hats, cats, balls of string, bears, purple crayons,* and *green pigs* than could ever hope to be collected on primary classes' library shelves.

Easy to read or controlled vocabulary trade books for the primary child have been multiplying since 1958 with such speed that the professional worker can neither evaluate nor afford to purchase them. It would appear as though Dr. Seuss's *Cat in the Hat* has begot a family which has matriculated at the famous humorist's own *Fumigated Academy of Psychologically Researched Re-researched and Re-re-researched Data and Agenda.* The existence of this mythical institution—admittedly his own creation—was announced in an address before the University of Wisconsin Book Conference, November, 1958, by the beloved Dr. Seuss.

However, before we are overrun with cats, fish and purple crayons and their imitative counterparts, it is best to define the use of the term *trade books* and consider the implications such publications have for the textbook field. In the publishing world a *trade book* is one which is written and printed to be sold in book stores and in general public market places. Trade books are usually thought to be author inspired, publisher selected and edited with loving care.

In contrast to the trade books are the textbooks which are written to be sold in a special market. Generally a textbook is a systematic unfolding of a subject area or study field. Textbooks are expected to be school inspired,

SOURCE: *Elementary English,* November 1962, pp. 677–679, 746.

publisher selected, and edited with merciless care. Few textbook authors are inspired to produce these systematicaly filled-in outlines, but nevertheless enjoy the pleasure of seeing their texts followed in classrooms across a nation.

Now, the most recent problem is, how does one tell the *difference* between a trade book and a textbook, especially in the three instructional programs of reading, science, and social studies?

For some time since the invasion of the primary grades by the "here and now" theme, there has been an increasing class consumption of trade and textbooks. The year 1921 heralded the advent of the simple factual child experience book. Lois Lenski, Margaret Wise Brown, Irma Webber, Inez Hogan, Ruth Krauss, H. A. Rey, Charlotte Steiner, and Francoise quickly followed the formula set by the pacesetter, writer Lucy Sprague Mitchell. These early writers were the trail blazers who controlled the length of the sentence, stressed the repetition of words and phrases, and in general, blended picture writing with a minimum of alphabetical texts for the beginner reader. It was not, therefore, Dr. Seuss who truly invented the *trade-text* book. No, this Pagliacci of the sand lot can be rightly called the best humorist since Edward Lear but the rumored credit for begetting all the cats stems only from the sight of the giant kneeling to join the fumigated college at which others have already matriculated.

The early "here and now" themesters had the greatest effect upon the basal readers. Textbook writers concluded that the simple, everyday experiences which Davy, Kiki, or Muffin had would make realistic meaningful material for instruction in reading, so they borrowed the ideas of everyday life episodes, repeated phrases, blended pictures with words, and controlled vocabulary. The result was the graded readers from pre-preprimers through the readers number eight that we have today.

This change in story content for basal texts has undergone several evolutionary changes. Prior to the Civil War the reading texts used in America were moralistic and highly didactic. Post Civil War books began a slight trend towards stories of the simple love of nature, care of pets and general principles concerning the joy of living in the present. Models such as Sanders NYS Union Readers Series, McGuffey graded readers and Heath's Classic Readers tended to include selections and excerpts of the world's best literature. This trend of selected literature finally broke down at the primary level with the following of the here and now theme of the 1920's. It was this assumed utilitarian criterion for selecting materials which gave reading texts an antiseptic flavor and laid grounds for this present trade-texting development.

Now that both the text and trade publishers are producing these unendowed reading aids and beginners beginning books the time has come for a thorough evaluation. The classroom teacher, the administrator, the parent, the librarian, and the conscientious book publisher should take stock, should peer around the corner to see if some dangers might not be lurking there.

There are many reasons prompting such investigation. First, budgetwise no one family or school can afford even a selected supply of the ever-increasing number of reading aids, and it is impossible for library organizations or graduate schools to carefully evaluate by proxy and recommend which are the best trade titles to purchase. But, perhaps most frightening of all, the trade book by moving into the trade-text field, is taking on the characteristics of the textbook. For example, these trade-text books may even now be accompanied by a teacher's manual on how best to use them. The inspiration that sparked the author to write the trade book is now classified, dissected, and enriched!

A trade book—no matter where it is bought, read, or shelved—must be *author inspired*, and any normal author will soon find that there is very little that can be said effectively in two, four or five hundred words. Controlled vocabulary and length will drive inspiration to desperation. Inspired authors will abandon this trade-texting—leaving the field clear for the authors who have already abandoned the inspiration! A trade book is designed to meet literary and story standards, some, doubtless, higher than others, yet, the standards imposed by the trade-text have no relationship to those literary standards. It is not entirely unfeasible to imagine a whole generation of American children being affected by this lack of standards in trade books. If they become attuned to the literary level of a controlled vocabulary and the repetitious simple ideas that can be communicated by it, how can we ever hope that they will seek those trade books which scorn the limited word list and resulting thought patterns? A diet of the mediocre and less than mediocre can scarcely be expected to whet the appetite for the superlative. How is it that we can talk out of both sides of our mouths at one time? How can we be committed to the idealistic objectives of a reading program that encourages the individual to choose for himself a varied and challenging pattern of reading which will formulate habits to last his lifetime, when, on the other hand, we confuse his efforts by supplying for his use, with the blessing of the school, books that are so lacking in literary and story characteristics?

In 1958, Dr. Seuss, the pied piper who has called the tune for this trade-texting, spoke to a group of intensely interested teachers, librarians, parents, and students in this manner. "I wanted to write a book which a six-year-old child could read, and I discovered that no publisher would publish it unless I followed the fumigated rules, so I sat down and followed the fumigated rules and it is like making apple struddle without struddles. At the end of a year and a half I managed to put together a little sixty-page volume entitled, *A Cat in the Hat*. Now I am doing a worse thing than that. I am now forcing other writers to do the same thing, working with fumigated word lists."

It is sad when an outstanding author must make such statements. It is sad to watch the parade that has followed, the parade that includes other well-known authors and a poetry critic. It is appalling to think of a child's world with *Roundabout Turn*, *And to Think I Saw It on Mulberry Street*, *Let's Go to the Seashore*, *Johnny Crow*, *Babar*, *Benjamin Bunny*, *Ask Mr. Bear*, *Goops and How to Be Them*, and *Sing-Song*. Yet, they, too, might have never been born had the flair for controlled vocabularies and controlled concepts presented such lucrative prospects to their creators as we are witnessing today.

The time is now when a concerted effort should be made to discover if we *really* need these accumulating easy to read trade-texts. Budgets, authenticity, oversimplification—especially in the science and social studies areas—and the glaring lack of vocabulary overlapping between publishers (which, to the thoughtful observer defeats the much advertised point of a *controlled* vocabulary), in adition to the obvious lack of literary characteristics should be faced before the profession turns to supposed reading material composed of books presenting a text which describes nothing that cannot be pictured! Picture writing and alphabetical code systems are two different forms of communication. We need not begin reading instruction with alternate systems.

Educators are becoming more aware of these trade books and the relationship to textbooks with the trend in method research to individualize reading instruction. Rutgers University's published study by Martha Condit, 1959, dealt with one aspect of the problems facing us. Condit's investigation concerned itself with selection of trade books for first-grade and second-grade children with normal interests and no special problems. Out of the 759 titles submitted for evaluation only 151 were selected on the basis of the child and his interests, vocabulary, and format. Approximately five percent of the 151 titles were judged readable by first-graders, but of these, 63 books were intended for superior readers. The conclusions drawn from this evaluation study were unrelated to the findings. Summarization showed a poor batting average for interesting reading material yet the authors of the investigation hinted for more trade-text writing.

The investigation concerning the selection of trade books is only one angle of the problem. Controlled or lack of controlled vocabulary is even more discouraging. If one took randomly from five different publishers a beginners trade book or easy to read story and counted the number of words common to all the books the concept of controlled vocabulary would disappear. There will be less than four percent of the words common to all the books and the total word count of these five randomly selected books will total close to five hundred words. Here is the breakdown of this random selection of trade-text books and the word count.

> Five easy to read books selected from five different publishers produced a total word count of 496 words.
>
> 17 words were common to all five books.
>
> 328 words appeared in only one of the five books.
>
> 25 words were common to four books.
>
> 41 words were common to three books.
>
> 85 words were common to two books.

A Cat in the Hat has begat something more than a flourishing publishing venture. It has made the profession aware of how easily dead-end paths can be trodden. There are new roads to travel concerning reading, new roads for textbooks and tradebooks, but we must step off where we have been and where we are going at this present time before these new paths are traveled. Graduate students, professional persons and the publishers themselves should recognize the value of introspection. Cats are said to have nine lives and with the fertility of these present trade-text-cats, bears, rabbits and sundry we fall heir to a problem equal to the Asiatic overpopulation.

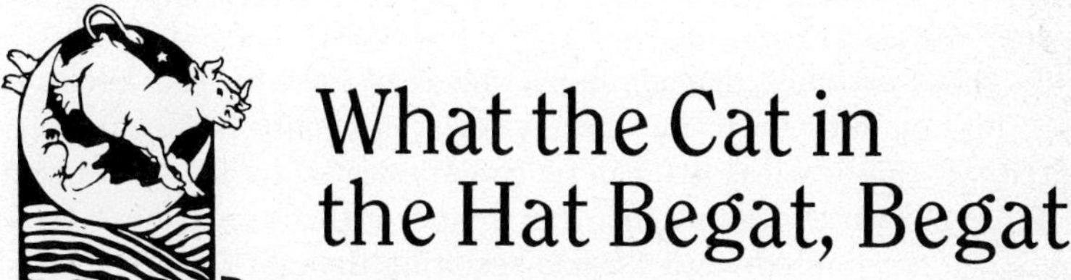

What the Cat in the Hat Begat, Begat

Robert E. Newman

The burgeoning easy-to-read collections in primary classrooms seem to be viewed with much more alarm than favor by David Davis in the November, 1962, *Elementary English.** I hold the opposite point of view and in this article contest the logic and assumptions that Davis presents.

I must admit, however, that I do agree to some extent with Davis' concern. My agreement arises from the propensity of American school people to suffer from a malady that we might call "the bandwagon effect"; that is, anything that is good in some school situations and for some educational purposes, and to some extent seems suddenly to become fashionable and adopted in wholesale fashion by school systems with virtually no sharply critical evaluation, and with much attendant publicity. When complete publishers' catalog listings of easy-to-read books or any other teaching material are purchased *en masse* and used uncritically the children are cheated. But here is the point that we must consider in relation to these easy-to-read books: does this con-

SOURCE: *Elementary English,* November 1963, pp. 751–752. Copyright © 1963 by the National Council of Teachers of English. Reprinted by permission of the publisher and the author.

demn the material or necessarily suggest that such material or teaching practice which utilizes this material is unsuitable for widespread but carefully selective use?

Now to Davis' points:

First, he maintains that "any normal author will soon find that there is very little that can be said effectively in two, four, or five hundred words. Controlled vocabulary and length will drive inspiration to desperation." But, we should ask, what about poetry? Take the beautiful Haiku form in which a sensitive author can express far more in about a dozen simple words than some authors do in a dozen chapters. Also, what about the pictures in the easy-to-read books? Sid Hoff cartoons for the *New Yorker*. Does the simple sentence under his cartoon need several pages of rhetoric to make his sometimes subtle and sharp points? When Hoff puts a few words in his easy-to-read books do children need verbiage to *feel* his stories—to feel the delightful phantasy of a dinosaur who came to be a playmate for a day. The *Little Bear* stories by Minarik and illustrated by Sendak again demonstrate this. After some children read these books they retell the story in a way that suggests that their deep feelings are aroused—by a very few words.

Second, Davis assumes that children who read easy-to-read books in quantity will "become attuned to the literary level of a controlled vocabulary and the repetitious simple ideas that can be communicated by it." He further maintains: "How can we ever hope that they [children] will seek those trade books which scorn the limited word list and resulting thought patterns?"

All I can say is that they do seek the better books. I've watched and helped children grow from a beginning literary diet which includes the most appealing of the easy-to-read books. What prevents a child who builds up his ability to read by widespread practice on books such as P. D. Eastman's *Are You My Mother?* to want to read books like *Mr. Popper's Penguins*, and then, *Charlotte's Web?* From my experience, children see most good easy-to-read books as "larks." They're for fun. And that is one of the prime values of this type of reading material. Favorite easy-to-read books can build an enthusiasm for books and reading. For the last two years I directed a reading clinic where college students in children's literature classes attempted to make books and reading vital to groups of children from primary grades who could read at the beginning level but who couldn't care less about doing so in their spare time. One of the most effective tools that we had at our disposal was multiple copies of about twenty easy-to-read titles. These children would take home three or four books and come back with relaxed chuckles and approving smiles as they discussed many of their books. They also learned quickly, by the way, to discriminate and compare the contrived and pedantic stories with such favorites as *Cerf's Riddles* and Dr. Seuss' *Green Eggs and Ham*.

In addition, the best of the easy-to-read books give us our long awaited opportunity to teach reading *from the beginning* as inter-communication of ideas and feelings—not simply as exercises to gain teacher approval if the child can do them well. And add to this advantage the chance that these books give us in the primary grades to offer children books in which they can *practice* reading. With these books many more children can *read* for at least a half hour each day after the first few months in the first grade. This supplementary reading can help build reading vocabulary quickly. Children can learn to read by involved personal *reading* as well as by teacher-directed reading experiences.

But, argues Davis, these easy-to-read books really do not have the claimed controlled basic vocabulary that is *duplicated* in each book. This is true but this doesn't seem to bother the reading of children who are captivated by the illustrations and the clever story lines—the FUN that it is to read many of these books. Perhaps here the children are showing us that the thing that really builds reading vocabulary in normal chldren is not pedantic repetition of the same few words in book after book, as much as it is *personally involved* reading of vocabulary that children use frequently in their everyday speech and experience. I agree with Davis that many modern basal readers have an "antiseptic" flavor and perhaps here the children are giving us a clue to how we can improve them.

But even if Davis' degree of alarm is not justified, there is still cause for moderate concern. The problem is not overwhelming in magnitude, but schools do need help in answering these two questions: which easy-to-read books are worth bringing to school and how might they be used most effectively as important teaching tools? I feel that these readily answerable questions are the extent of the problem. The books don't merit blanket condemnation, but we do need to help teachers to know which books are most appealing to children and we need to train teachers in the most effective use of these books. Perhaps this kind of assistance could be offered in a periodical which biannually reviewed for teachers all of the new easy-to-read and high-interest but low-vocabulary level books. Such a publication should specify those books that children have found most captivating, and it might also carry a few articles discussing how teachers have used the books most effectively. With help of this sort, teachers could introduce more children to the best of these books in such a way that the young readers could experience continually what fun it was to read—from the beginning.

I Can Read! Predictable Books as Resources for Reading and Writing Instruction

Lynn K. Rhodes

Many children begin first grade expecting that the magic moment of learning to read has arrived. That expectation often dies, however, as readiness worksheets, phonics exercises, and sight word drills are used for weeks and sometimes months in preparing the children to read.

In other first grade classrooms, that magic moment arrives almost immediately. Why? Because some teachers believe that first graders can read some kinds of books right away since they have enough knowledge of language and the world to deal with them. These teachers believe that first graders' expectations can be met, creating an enthusiasm in children that helps make written language instruction a joy for the rest of the year.

This article includes a bibliography of books, referred to as "predictable books," that can be used with beginning readers (and with remedial readers). The characteristics of predictable books are discussed as well as ways to use the books with children for reading and writing instruction.

Characteristics of Predictable Books

One first grade class read *The Bus Ride* (Scott, Foresman Reading Systems, Level 2, Book A, 1971) the first day of school. It is a predictable book because children can quickly begin to predict what the author is going to say and how he is going to say it. By the time the teacher has read a few pages aloud, most children in the room can chant the text right along with the teacher. Here are some excerpts from the text.

> A girl got on the bus.
> Then the bus went fast.

SOURCE: *Reading Teacher,* February 1981, pp. 511–517. Reprinted with permission of author and the International Reading Association.

A boy got on the bus.
Then the bus went fast.

A fox got on the bus.
Then the bus went fast.

Seven other characters get on the bus including a hippopotamus, a rhinoceros, and finally, a bee. When the bee enters the bus, the story suddenly changes it pattern:

A bee got on the bus.
Then!

The rabbit got off the bus.
The horse got off the bus.
The fish got off the bus. . . .

After all the characters get off the bus, the story ends, "Then they all ran fast!"

The Bus Ride exemplifies several characteristics of predictable books. Most noticeable is the *repetitive pattern* the author uses, a pattern that children use after only a few pages. Passengers riding a bus, the various animals and the bee as something to avoid are *familiar concepts* to most first graders. The third characteristic which makes this book predictable is the *good match between the text and its illustrations;* each character getting on or off the bus is pictured with the appropriate sentence.

The same characteristics are also apparent in John Langstaff's *Oh, A-Hunting We Will Go* (1974). Two verses follow:

Oh, a-hunting we will go,
A-hunting we will go;
We'll catch a mouse
And put him in a house,
And then we'll let him go!

Oh, a-hunting we will go,
A-hunting we will go;
We'll catch a pig
And put him in a wig
And then we'll let him go!

In all 12 verses, Langstaff varies only the last word in lines three and four of each verse. Those two words in each verse are made predictable not only by the good match between Langstaff's text and illustrations but also by *rhyme.* Also contributing to the overall predictability of the book is the *rhythm of the language,* particularly if the verses are sung.

Instead of repetitive patterns, sometimes authors use *cumulative patterns* in their books. In Tolstoy's *The Great Big Enormous Turnip* (1968), an old man attempts to pull a turnip out of the ground. When he does not succeed, he calls his wife to help. When they don't succeed, the granddaughter is called upon to help; finally, the following characters are involved:

> The mouse pulled the cat.
> The cat pulled the dog.
> The dog pulled the granddaughter.
> The granddaughter pulled the old
> woman.
> The old woman pulled the old man.
> The old man pulled the turnip.

Yet another characteristic of predictable books is the *familiarity of the story or story line* to the child. Children often come to school knowing folktales and songs. They can predict what the wolf says when they read *The Three Little Pigs* (Galdone, 1970) or what *The Three Billy Goats Gruff* (Brown, 1957) say as they elude the troll. They will also be able to use their considerable intuitive knowledge about the structure of folktales and other types of stories. For the same reason, songs like *I Know an Old Lady* (Bonne and Mills, 1961) and *This Old Man* (Adams, 1974) are read easily by any child who knows the songs.

Familiar sequences are often characteristic of predictable books. Eric Carle uses two familiar sequences, the days of the week and numbers, in *The Very Hungry Caterpillar* (1969).

> On Monday he ate through one apple. But he was still hungry.
>
> On Tuesday he ate through two pears, but he was still hungry.

These characteristics make predictable books very different from typical first grade instructional materials. The language flows naturally, and the vocabulary and content reflect what children know about their world and their language. Children can use this knowledge to develop word recognition strategies while reading, rather than before reading. Predictable books encourage from the beginning reading for understanding.

As Resources for Reading Instruction

To demonstrate how predictable books can be used for reading instruction, let's review what happened with *The Bus Ride* in the classroom mentioned above. As the story of how the children interacted with the book unfolds, the teacher's rationale for the procedures will also be examined.

> The first time the class encountered *The Bus Ride* was before lunch the first full day of school. The teacher gathered the class together to read the book and told them to feel free to read along with her when they felt ready. With no further introduction, she began to read *The Bus Ride* aloud, holding the

> book so the children could see the illustrations. After the second page, some children had begun to read along and by the fifth page, all were reading. When they reached the page where the bee got on the bus, some children faltered while others repeated the established pattern, "Then the bus went fast." The teacher asked the children to listen for a moment while she read the section about the bee and then to read along again when they felt ready. She read the transition page ("The bee got on the bus. Then!") and began the new pattern ("The _____ got off the bus") with the children quickly joining in again. The teacher read the end of the story ("Then they all ran fast!") and several of the children commented that they would run fast too.

Up to this point in the lesson, the teacher's instructional procedures had two major purposes. First, the teacher wanted the children to enjoy and become familiar with the content and organization of the book. She accomplished this in a way natural to most of the children—she read the book to them. The focus was on meaning, on sharing and understanding the story. The children's involvement in the book and their comments at the end were clues that they enjoyed and comprehended the book.

The teacher's second purpose was to encourage the children to use their knowledge of the world and language in responding to the book. She perceives her job as creating an environment in which the children can use successfully what they know about language as they encounter and deal with unfamiliar aspects of language. Her long range goal is to encourage the children's development from successful readers of highly predictable materials to successful readers of a wide range of materials.

> Expecting and getting an enthusiastic response, the teacher asked the children if they wanted to read *The Bus Ride* again. As the book was read the second time, the teacher read no louder than the children and frequently pointed to the sentence being read. Although she raised her voice at the transition point and at the end of the story, she noted that many of the children dealt with those points well. She also noted that some of the children appeared confused by the difference between a rhinoceros and a hippopotamus. When the story ended, she turned to the illustrations of these animals and asked the children to describe the differences that could be observed in the illustrations and in habitats like the zoo. Following that discussion, she wrote the names of the two animals on the board and asked which word was "rhinoceros" and which was "hippopotamus." Several children knew and explained that they figured it out from the first letter. With the children's input, the teacher listed the names of children in the class that began with *r* under "rhinoceros" and followed the same procedure for "hippopotamus."

In this segment of the lesson, the teacher used her knowledge that children like to reread enjoyable stories. Multiple readings encourage the students' familiarity with and control over the content and organization of the story, resulting in a greater dependence on the children's own knowledge and less dependence on teacher support. In pointing to the sentences in the book during this second reading, the teacher showed the children the placement of the text in relation to the illustrations and emphasized the importance of the print in the book.

By the end of the second reading, the teacher felt that the children had enough control over the story as a whole to deal with some of its parts. Because of this and the difficulties she noticed among some children, she helped the children to develop stronger concepts about two characters in the story and also led them to an awareness of the availability of graphophonic information and the consistency of sound/letter relationships.

> Later the same day, the children came back from recess to find multiple copies of *The Bus Ride* on a table. After the teacher asked the children to think of various ways to read the book, they settled down to read—some reading the whole book alone, others reading every other page in pairs, etc. The teacher read the book again with some children who requested it, and then walked around the room listening to children read, noting which children were using only illustrations to guide their reading and which were attempting to deal with the print. The teacher also listened to or entered into several conversations that confirmed or broadened her observations. Some children, for example, wanted to know if the book could be taken home and read. Others wanted to demonstrate that they knew the difference between a hippopotamus and a rhinoceros. And one little boy named Frank wanted to show her that his name started the same way as "fox," another story character.

Once again, the teacher provided an environment for another reading (and for most of the children, several readings) of *The Bus Ride*. This encouraged them to consolidate their previous experiences in reading the book and gave them experience in handling the book and deciding how to read the book. Although she acceded to a request from a small group to read the book with them again, the teacher made time for them to read the book alone after she finished. The teacher expected that the children would feel confident enough at the end of this experience to want to read the book to others *outside* the class, and her expectations were fulfilled when children asked to take the book home.

During this segment of the lesson, the teacher also wanted to gather more information about individual children's abilities. As she observed the children, she began to formulate ideas about such things as which children needed more experience hearing stories, the extent to which children were already dealing with the graphophonic system, and the level of enthusiasm for reading books. She believes that her observations of children in natural reading situations are extremely valuable as data for future instructional decisions.

As Resources for Writing Instruction

An effective way to develop written language in children is to encourage them to write. Beginning writers can compose in forms ranging from a word written on a drawing to an entire story. Although children can and should compose from the beginning without the aid of predictable books, they should also learn that other authors' writings can be used as resources for their own compositions.

One 5 year old's favorite book for some time was a predictable book entitled *Brown Bear, Brown Bear* (Martin, 1970). An excerpt from the book reads:

> Brown bear,
> brown bear,
> what do you see?
> I see a redbird
> looking at me.
>
> Redbird,
> redbird,
> what do you see?
> I see a yellow duck
> looking at me.

The 5 year old, Kara, decided one day to draw a rainbow and label each of the colors in it. She found one color name at a time in *Brown Bear* to copy. To copy "purple," for example, she located the purple cat in the illustrations, said "purple" out loud several times to determine what letter it began with, found the "p" word in the text next to the illustration, and copied "purple" letter for letter. The child's system worked beautifully except when she copied "redbird" for "red" because it was all one word.

As children use predictable books again and again, they learn where to locate the words and phrases they need. They learn, for example, that they can find the days of the week in *The Very Hungry Caterpillar* (Carle), and *One Monday Morning* (Shulevitz, 1967); that they can find body parts of animals in *Here Is a Cat!* (Rokoff, no date); that they can find animal names in any number of books.

Children should use predictable books for reasons other than finding words and phrases; they can invent whole stories on the basis of an author's pattern.

It looked Like Spilt Milk (Shaw, 1947) is a picture book that has a cloud resembling a common object on each page. Two sample pages from the book read:

> Sometimes it looked
> like an Ice Cream Cone.
> But it wasn't an Ice Cream Cone.
> Sometimes it looked
> like a Flower.
> But it wasn't a Flower.

Children who read this story can form clouds by folding in half pieces of blue construction paper that have blobs of white paint on them. Then they can write accompanying verses, based on Shaw's verses, to describe what common object the cloud resembles. In one afternoon, a first grade class made their own *It Looked Like Split Milk* book with each child in the class contributing one cloud and one verse.

Another group of children, a remedial reading class in this case, read *Fire! Fire! Said Mrs. McGuire* (Martin, 1970), which is excerpted below:

"Fire! Fire!" said Mrs. McGuire.
"Where? Where?" said Mrs. Bear.
"Down town!" said Mrs. Brown.
"What floor?" said Mrs. Moore.

Several of the children wrote their own versions, using the book as a resource for their writing.

"Flood, Flood!" said Mr. Hud.
"Where? Where?" said Mrs. Mare.
"In the valley!" said Mr. Palley.
"Get out of town!" said Mr. Clown.
"Find the boat!" said Mrs. Hoat.

Dianna

"Snow! Snow!" said Mrs. Low.
"Where? Where?" said Mr. Glare.
"Up there!" said Mrs. Pear.
"In the sky!" said Mr. Li.
"Get the shovel!" said Mrs. Lovel.
"Scoop it up!" said Mr. Lup.

Lisa

As children find that they can use other authors' patterns to generate and shape their own ideas, they often become rather prolific writers. They may borrow a considerable amount from other authors at first, but their writing tends to deviate more from the authors' ideas as they gain control over print and take greater risks.

Children learn a myriad of things that contribute to growth in reading and writing when predictable books are used as writing resources. A great deal is learned intuitively about story structure as children use authors' patterns to structure their own stories. The conventions of written language can also be discovered; Dianna and Lisa used *Fire! Fire! said Mrs. McGuire* as a model for punctuating the dialogue they created for their own characters. And a considerable amount can be learned about the graphophonic system. An activity like Kara's is sometimes the first situation in which some children will give purposeful attention to the print of the text. In another example, Dianna and Lisa and their classmates discovered that words could rhyme even if the endings had different spelling patterns, a discovery that came about as they began to write their own versions of *Fire! Fire!*

In summary, using predictable books as writing resources fosters success and growth in written language. As children manipulate written language patterns and conventions, they become aware of and gain control over the patterns and conventions used by other authors. Such learning leads naturally and meaningfully to reading and writing growth.

A Bibliography of Predictable Books

A bibliography of some predictable children's literature appears with this article; commercially published predictable stories can also be found in the early levels of Scott, Foresman's Reading Systems (1971) and Reading Unlimited (1976) as well as in Bill Martin's Sounds of Language series (Holt, Rinehart and Winston, 1970) and his Instant Readers (Holt, Rinehart and Winston, 1970).

The books below are suggested as instructional resources for teachers who want to provide first graders or remedial readers with the language cues they use in oral language. The books will encourage children to use the experiences and language competencies and strategies they bring to school as they continue to develop and enjoy written language.

A Bibliography of Predictable Books

Adams, Pam. *This Old Man*. New York, N.Y.: Grossett and Dunlap, 1974.

Alain. *One, Two, Three, Going to Sea*. New York, N.Y.: Scholastic, 1964.

Aliki. *Go Tell Aunt Rhody*. New York, N.Y.: Macmillan, 1974.

Aliki. *Hush Little Baby*. Englewood Cliffs, N.J.: Prentice-Hall, 1968.

Aliki. *My Five Senses*. New York, N.Y.: Thomas Y. Crowell, 1962.

Asch, Frank. *Monkey Face*. New York, N.Y.: Parents' Magazine Press, 1977.

Balian, Lorna. *The Animal*. Nashville, Tenn.: Abingdon Press, 1972.

Balian, Lorna. *Where in the World Is Henry?* Scarsdale, N.Y.: Bradbury Press, 1972

Barohas, Sarah E. *I Was Walking Down the Road*. New York, N.Y.: Scholastic, 1975.

Baum, Arline, and Joseph Baum. *One Bright Monday Morning*. New York, N.Y.: Random House, 1962.

Becker, John. *Seven Little Rabbits*. New York, N.Y.: Scholastic, 1973.

Beckman, Kaj. *Lisa Cannot Sleep*. New York, N.Y.: Franklin Watts, 1969.

Bellah, Melanie. *A First Book of Sounds*. Racine, Wis.: Golden Press, 1963.

Bonne, Rose, and Alan Mills. *I Know an Old Lady*. New York, N.Y.: Rand McNally, 1961.

Brand, Oscar. *When I First Came to This Land*. New York, N.Y.: Putnam's Sons, 1974.

Brandenberg, Franz. *I Once Knew a Man*. New York, N.Y.: Macmillan, 1970.

Brown, Marcia. *The Three Billy Goats Gruff*. New York, N.Y.: Harcourt Brace Jovanovich, 1957.

Brown, Margaret Wise. *Four Fur Feet*. New York, N.Y.: William R. Scott, 1961.
Brown, Margaret Wise. *Goodnight Moon*. New York, N.Y.: Harper and Row, 1947.
Brown, Margaret Wise. *Home for a Bunny*. Racine, Wis.: Golden Press, 1956.
Brown, Margaret Wise. *Where Have You Been?* New York, N.Y.: Scholastic, 1952.
The Bus Ride, illustrated by Justin Wager. New York, N.Y.: Scott, Foresman, 1971.
Carle, Eric. *The Grouchy Ladybug*. New York, N.Y.: Thomas Y. Crowell, 1977.
Carle, Eric. *The Mixed Up Chameleon*. New York, N.Y.: Thomas Y. Crowell, 1975.
Carle, Eric. *The Very Hungry Caterpillar*. Cleveland, Ohio: Collins World, 1969.
Charlip, Remy. *Fortunately*. New York, N.Y.: Parents' Magazine Press, 1964.
Charlip, Remy. *What Good Luck! What Bad Luck!* New York, N.Y.: Scholastic, 1969.
Cook, Bernadine. *The Little Fish that Got Away*, Reading, Mass.: Addison-Wesley, 1976.
de Regniers, Beatrice Schenk. *Catch a Little Fox*, New York, N.Y.: Seabury Press, 1970.
de Regniers, Beatrice Schenk. *The Day Everbody Cried*. New York, N.Y.: The Viking Press, 1967.
de Regniers, Beatrice Schenk. *How Joe the Bear and Sam the Mouse Got Together*. New York, N.Y.: Parents' Magazine Press, 1965.
de Regniers, Beatrice Schenk. *The Little Book*. New York, N.Y.: Henry Z. Walck, 1961.
de Regniers, Beatrice Schenk. *May I Bring a Friend?* New York, N.Y.: Atheneum, 1972.
de Regniers, Beatrice Schenk. *Willy O'Dwyer Jumped in the Fire*, New York, N.Y.: Atheneum, 1968.
Domanska, Janina. *If All the Seas Were One Sea*. New York, N.Y.: Macmillan, 1971.
Cuff, Maggie. *Jonny and His Drum*. New York, N.Y.: Henry Z. Walck, 1972.
Duff, Maggie. *Rum Pum Pum*. New York, N.Y.: Macmillan, 1978.
Emberley, Barbara. *Simon's Song*. Englewood Cliffs, N.J.: Prentice-Hall, 1969.
Emberly, Ed. *Klippity Klop*. Boston, Mass.: Little, Brown, 1974.
Ets, Marie Hall. *Elephant in a Well*. New York, N.Y.: The Viking Press. 1972.
Ets, Marie Hall. *Play with Me*. New York, N.Y.: The Viking Press, 1955.
Flack, Marjorie. *Ask Mr. Bear*. New York, N.Y.: Macmillan, 1932.
Galdone, Paul. *Henry Penny*. New York, N.Y.: Scholastic, 1968.
Galdone, Paul. *The Little Red Hen*. New York, N.Y.: Scholastic, 1973.
Galdone, Paul. *The Three Bears*. New York, N.Y.: Scholastic, 1972.
Galdone, Paul. *The Three Billy Goats Gruff*. New York, N.Y.: Seabury Press, 1973.
Galdone, Paul. *The Three Little Pigs*. New York, N.Y.: Seabury Press, 1970.
Ginsburg, Mirra. *The Chick and the Duckling*. New York, N.Y.: Macmillan, 1972.
Greenberg, Polly. *Oh Lord, I Wish I Was a Buzzard*. New York, N.Y.: Macmillan, 1958.
Hoffman, Hilde. *The Green Grass Grows All Around*. New York, N.Y.: Macmillan, 1968.
Hutchins, Pat. *Good-Night Owl*. New York, N.Y.: Macmillan, 1972.
Hutchins, Pat. *Rosie's Walk*. New York, N.Y.: Macmillan, 1968.
Hutchins, Pat. *Titch*. New York, N.Y.: Collier Books, 1971.
Keats, Ezra Jack. *Over in the Meadow*. New York, N.Y.: Scholastic, 1971.
Kent, Jack. *The Fat Cat*. New York, N.Y.: Scholastic, 1971.
Klein, Lenore. *Brave Daniel*. New York, N.Y.: Scholastic, 1958.
Kraus, Robert. *Whose Mouse Are You?* New York, N.Y.: Collier Books, 1970.

Langstaff, John. *Frog Went-A-Courtin'*. New York, N.Y.: Harcourt Brace Jovanovich, 1955.

Langstaff, John. *Gather My Gold Together: Four Songs for Four Seasons*. Garden City, N.Y.: Doubleday, 1971.

Langstaff, John. *Oh, A-Hunting We Will Go*. New York, N.Y.: Atheneum, 1974.

Langstaff, John. *Over in the Meadow*. New York, N.Y.: Harcourt Brace Jovanovich, 1957.

Laurence, Ester. *We're Off to Catch a Dragon*. Nashville, Tenn.: Abingdon Press, 1969.

Lexau, Joan. *Crocodile and Hen*. New York, N.Y.: Harper and Row, 1969.

Lobel, Anita. *King Rooster, Queen Hen*. New York, N.Y.: Greenwillow, 1975.

Lobel, Arnold. *A Treeful of Pigs*. New York, N.Y.: Greenwillow, 1979.

Mack, Stan. *10 Bears in My Bed*. New York, N.Y.: Pantheon, 1974.

Martin Bill. *Brown Bear, Brown Bear*. New York, N.Y.: Holt, Rinehart and Winston, 1970.

Martin, Bill. *Fire! Fire! Said Mrs. McGuire*. New York, N.Y.: Holt, Rinehart and Winston, 1970.

Mayer, Mercer. *If I Had . . .* New York, N.Y.: Dial Press, 1968.

Mayer, Mercer. *Just for You*. New York, N.Y.: Golden Press, 1975.

McGovern, Ann. *Too Much Noise*. New York, N.Y.: Scholastic, 1967.

Memling, Carl. *Ten Little Animals*. Racine, Wis.: Golden Press, 1981.

Moffett, Martha. *A Flower Pot is Not a Hat*. New York,: N.Y.: E. P. Dutton, 1972.

Peppe, Rodney. *The House that Jack Built*. New York, N.Y.: Delacorte, 1970.

Polushkin, Maria. *Mother, Mother, I Want Another*. New York, N.Y.: Crown Publishers, 1978.

Preston, Edna Mitchell. *Where Did My Mother Go?* New York, N.Y.: Four Winds Press, 1978.

Quackenbush, Robert. *She'll Be Comin' Round the Mountain*. Philadelphia, Pa.: J. B. Lippincott, 1973.

Quackenbush, Robert. *Skip to My Lou*. Philadelphia, Pa.: J. B. Lippincott, 1975.

Rokoff, Sandra. *Hero is a Cat,* Singapore: Hallmark Children's Editions, no date.

Scheer, Julian, and Marvin Bileck. *Rain Makes Applesauce*. New York, N.Y.: Holiday House, 1964.

Scheer, Julian, and Marvin Bileck. *Upside Down Day*. New York, N.Y.: Holiday House, 1968.

Sendak, Maurice. *Where the Wild Things Are*. New York, N.Y.: Scholastic, 1963.

Shaw, Charles B. *It Looked Like Spilt Milk*. New York, N.Y.: Harper & Row. 1947.

Shulevitz, Uri. *One Monday Morning*. New York, N.Y.: Scribner's, 1967.

Skaar, Grace. *What Do the Animals Say?* New York, N.Y.: Scholastic, 1972.

Sonneborn, Ruth A. *Someone is Eating the Sun*. New York, N.Y.: Random House, 1974.

Spier, Peter. *The Fox Went Out on a Chilly Night*. Garden City, N.Y.: Doubleday, 1961.

Stover, JoAnn. *If Everybody Did*. New York, N.Y.: David McKay, 1980.

Tolstoy, Alexei. *The Great Big Enormous Turnip*. New York, N.Y.: Franklin Watts, 1968.

Welber, Robert. *Goodbye, Hello*. New York, N.Y.: Pantheon, 1974.

Wildsmith, Brian, *The Twelve Days of Christmas*. New York, N.Y., Franklin Watts, 1972.

Wolkstein, Diane. *The Visit*. New York, N.Y.: Alfred A. Knopf, 1977.
Wondriska, William. *All the Animals Were Angry*. New York, N.Y.: Holt, Rinehart and Winston, 1970.
Zaid, Barry. *Chicken Little*. New York, N.Y.: Random House, no date.
Zemach, Harve. *The Judge*. New York, N.Y.: Farrar, Straus and Giroux, 1969.
Zemach, Margot. *Hush, Little Baby*. New York, N.Y.: E. P. Dutton, 1976.
Zemach, Margot. *The Teeny Tiny Woman*. New York, N.Y.: Scholastic, 1965.
Zolotow, Charlotte. *Do You Know What I'll Do?* New York, N.Y.: Harper and Row, 1958.